"The Man Who Took the Rap"

TITLES IN THE SERIES

THE HISTORY OF MILITARY AVIATION

Paul J. Springer, editor

This series is designed to explore previously ignored facets of the history of airpower. It includes a wide variety of disciplinary approaches, scholarly perspectives, and argumentative styles. Its fundamental goal is to analyze the past, present, and potential future utility of airpower and to enhance our understanding of the changing roles played by aerial assets in the formulation and execution of national military strategies. It encompasses the incredibly diverse roles played by airpower, which include but are not limited to efforts to achieve air superiority; strategic attack; intelligence, surveillance, and reconnaissance missions; airlift operations; close-air support; and more. Of course, airpower does not exist in a vacuum. There are myriad terrestrial support operations required to make airpower functional, and examinations of these missions is also a goal of this series.

In less than a century, airpower developed from flights measured in minutes to the ability to circumnavigate the globe without landing. Airpower has become the military tool of choice for rapid responses to enemy activity, the primary deterrent to aggression by peer competitors, and a key enabler to military missions on the land and sea. This series provides an opportunity to examine many of the key issues associated with its usage in the past and present, and to influence its development for the future.

"THE MAN WHO TOOK THE RAP"

Sir Robert Brooke-Popham and the Fall of Singapore

PETER DYE

NAVAL INSTITUTE PRESS
Annapolis, Maryland

Naval Institute Press
291 Wood Road
Annapolis, MD 21402

Library of Congress Cataloging-in-Publication Data is available.
978-1-68247-358-0 (hardcover)
978-1-68247-359-7 (eBook)

♾ Print editions meet the requirements of ANSI/NISO z39.48-1992
(Permanence of Paper).
Printed in the United States of America.

All photos courtesy of Philip Brooke-Popham.
Maps created by J-P Stanway, jupper@co.uk.

26 25 24 23 22 21 20 19 18   9 8 7 6 5 4 3 2 1
First printing

TO SQUADRON LEADER
"DICKIE" DYE
1924~2017

If you can meet with Triumph and Disaster
And treat those two imposters just the same;

—Rudyard Kipling, "If—," Rewards and Fairies

CONTENTS

MAPS

FOREWORD

When, some three years ago, I opened an interesting-looking letter and found it was from a retired air vice-marshal wishing to write a biography of my father, I thought that my long-held intention might be achieved at last. Ever since his death in 1953, my mother had tried to find an old friend of my father who was willing and able to take on the task but without success. After she died in 1983, I felt it my duty to get the job done.

Up in the attic there were boxes of letters, photographs, and albums dating back to the reign of Queen Victoria, waiting for scrutiny. Air Vice-Marshal Dr. Peter Dye was the ideal man for the task. He had experience in searching through archives, having written a book on the Royal Flying Corps' supply organization during the First World War, which had first raised his interest in my father, so the material in my attic posed no problems.

My own memories of my father are rather few and far between as I was only twenty-five when he died and I was away at sea for much of the time from the age of eighteen, before which I was at boarding school. I have learned a lot more about him thanks to this biography. Even now, with the book written, I keep finding clues to his character, including a 1902 copy of Rudyard Kipling's *Barrack Room Ballads*, signed by my father before he had added Popham to his name. His life was based on the same beliefs and values that inspired Kipling. It seems appropriate, therefore, to draw on one of Kipling's most inspirational poems for an epigraph to this biography.

This work is a carefully researched account of my father's life and offers a vivid and powerful picture of English attitudes at the end of the nineteenth and the first half of the twentieth centuries, the climax of the British Empire. My father was an aide-de-camp to three kings, a brave early aviator, a hard-working administrator in the armed forces, and a devout Christian. I commend this book to all who study great men.

—Francis Philip Brooke-Popham
Bagborough House, November 2017

ACKNOWLEDGMENTS

This book could never have been written without the support and encouragement of Philip and Diana Brooke-Popham. They have been courteous and generous in equal measure, willingly sharing their papers, putting me in touch with other family members, uncovering further documents, and answering my many questions. I am also grateful to the Trustees of the Liddell Hart Centre for Military Archives for permission to quote from their holdings and to the Archive Services staff who have been consistently helpful and, in the process, fully justified Opal Brooke-Popham's decision to entrust her husband's papers to their care nearly fifty years ago. The remainder of the Brooke-Popham family papers (including Opal's extensive private correspondence and papers covering Kenya and the wartime Waifs and Strays children's home at Cottisford) will shortly be joining them.

I would like to acknowledge all those friends and colleagues who have kindly read and commented on my draft work, notably Jeff Jefford, a selfless and dedicated volunteer editor. I must also thank J-P Stanway for his outstanding work in producing the supporting maps. Finally, I am grateful to my own family who have been patient and understanding about the time, effort, and frequent absences required to bring this book to a conclusion.

Acronyms and Abbreviations

AASF	Advanced Air Striking Force
ABC	American-British Conference
ABCD	American, British, Chinese, and Dutch
ABDACOM	American-British-Dutch-Australian Command
ADA	Anglo-Dutch-Australian
ADB	Australian-Dutch-British
ADC	aide-de-camp
ADGB	Air Defence Great Britain
ADRC	Air Defence Research Committee
AFC	Air Force Cross
AHB	Air Historical Branch
AIF	Australian Imperial Forces
AMT	Air Member for Training
AOC	Air Officer Commanding
AOCinC	Air Officer Commander-in-Chief
ARC	Aeronautical Research Committee
ATC	Air Training Corps
AVG	American Volunteer Group
AVM	Air Vice-Marshal
BCATP	British Commonwealth Air Training Plan
BE2	Blériot Experimental 2
BEF	British Expeditionary Force
BPFP	Brooke-Popham Family Papers
CAS	Chief of the Air Staff

CB	Commander of the Order of the Bath
CBS	Columbia Broadcasting System
CFS	Central Flying School
CIA	Central Intelligence Agency
CID	Committee for Imperial Defence
CIGS	Chief of the Imperial General Staff
CinC	Commander-in-Chief
CMG	Companion of the Order of St. Michael and St. George
COS	Chiefs of Staff
COSC	Chiefs of Staff Committee
DAA & QMG	Deputy Assistant Adjutant and Quartermaster General
DA & QMG	Deputy Adjutant and Quartermaster General
DFC	Distinguished Flying Cross
DGSR	Directorate-General of Supply and Research
DMA	Director of Military Aeronautics
DRC	Defence Requirements Committee
DSO	Distinguished Service Order
EAWL	East African Women's League
FEB	Far Eastern Bureau
FECB	Far East Combined Bureau
FEPOW	Far East prisoner of war
FY	fiscal year
GCHQ	Government Communications Headquarters
GCVO	Knight Grand Cross of the Victorian Order
GHQ	General Headquarters
GOC	General Officer Commanding
GSO1	General Staff Officer 1st Class
HMG	His Majesty's Government
HMS	His Majesty's Ship
HMSO	His Majesty's Stationery Office
HQ	headquarters
IDC	Imperial Defence College
IWM	Imperial War Museum
JATS	Joint Air Training Scheme
JIC	Joint Intelligence Committee
JPS	Joint Planning Sub-Committee
KCB	Knight Commander Order of Bath

KDF	Kenya Defence Force
KWEO	Kenya Women's Emergency Organisation
LHCMA	Liddell Hart Centre for Military Archives
MBC	Malayan Broadcasting Corporation
MBE	Member of the British Empire
MC	Military Cross
MCS	Malayan Civil Service
MEW	Ministry of Economic Warfare
MI5	Military Intelligence 5
MOI	Ministry of Information
MP	Member of Parliament
NAAFI	Navy Army Air Force Institute
NEI	Netherlands East Indies
No.	number
NPL	National Physical Laboratory
OBE	Officer of the British Empire
OH	Old Haileyburian
OM	Orient Mission
OM/P	Orient Mission Propaganda
OSS	Office of Strategic Services
Oxf & Bucks LI	The Oxfordshire and Buckinghamshire Light Infantry
PA	personal assistant
PLENAPS	Plan for the Employment of Naval and Air Forces of the Associated Powers in the Eastern Theatre in the Event of War with Japan
POW	prisoner of war
RAAF	Royal Australian Air Force
RAE	Royal Aircraft Establishment
RAF	Royal Air Force
RAFM	Royal Air Force Museum
RCAF	Royal Canadian Air Force
RDF	radio direction finding
RFC	Royal Flying Corps
RN	Royal Navy
RNAS	Royal Naval Air Service
RSU	Repair and Salvage Unit
RUSI	Royal United Services Institute

SAAF	South African Air Force
SD	secret document
SIS	Secret Intelligence Service
SOE	Special Operations Executive
SPRO	Services Public Relations Office
SS	steam ship
S&T	supply and transport
TNA	The National Archives, UK
UK	United Kingdom
USS	United States Ship
VC	Victoria Cross
VHF	very high frequency

INTRODUCTION
TRIUMPH AND DISASTER
1878–1953

The Japanese conquest of Malaya, accomplished in just under seventy days between December 1941 and February 1942, marked the beginning of the end for the British Empire.[1] The loss of Singapore, the "impregnable fortress," has been described as "an event comparable to the sack of Rome by Alaric the Goth."[2] Although its Far Eastern territories were recovered in 1945, Britain's prestige would never recover. Defeat was more than symbolic; it strengthened the arguments for independence, emboldened nationalists, and encouraged the belief that there was an alternative to colonial rule.[3] The result has been an outpouring of books, papers, and articles seeking to explain the disaster, allocate blame, and identify the wider implications.[4] The unconditional surrender of Singapore's garrison on 15 February 1942, and the capture of 120,000 officers and men, precipitated a sequence of events that disrupted and ultimately swept away the European hold over Southeast Asia.[5] While there is a touch of dramatic license to this picture, and an implication that great changes require great events, the Japanese occupation of large swathes of the Far East—including Borneo, Burma, Hong Kong, Indochina, Java, Malaya, New Guinea, the Philippines, Sarawak, Singapore, Sumatra, and Timor—signaled the end of the existing colonial order.[6] This played out in various ways during the immediate postwar years, not all of them peacefully. For anti-British revolutionaries such as Chandra Bose, Singapore, once a bulwark, was now "the graveyard of the mighty British Empire."[7] Even those who aspired to a less violent transition to self-rule believed that defeat in Malaya sounded the end of British rule.[8] *The Economist*, reflecting on Ian Morrison's graphic dispatch for the *Times*,[9] sent from Batavia immediately after the fall of Singapore, was moved to comment, "'Soft' troops, unenter-prising commanders, outwitted strategists, an incompetent administration, an apathetic native population—these are not the signs of a gallant army betrayed only by bad luck; they sound uncomfortably like the dissolution of an empire."[10]

The man blamed at the time for what Churchill described as "the worst disaster and largest capitulation in British history" was Air Chief Marshal Sir Robert Brooke-Popham, Commander-in-Chief Far East (CinC Far East) from November 1940 to December 1941, responsible for the defense of Borneo, Burma, Hong Kong, Malaya, and Singapore.[11] Brooke-Popham was violently condemned by the Australian and British press, as well as attacked in Parliament as a "nincompoop" who deserved to have been removed from command.[12] History has offered more muted criticism, partly because of a developing narrative that has found other culprits, including Churchill him-self, as prime minister and minister of defense; General Arthur Percival, General Officer Commanding (GOC) Malaya; Duff Cooper, British min-ister in residence; Shenton Thomas, governor of the Straits Settlements; Admiral Tom Phillips, CinC Eastern Fleet; and General Gordon Bennett, GOC Australian Imperial Forces (AIF). The passage of time has also enabled the contributory factors to be better understood, including the influence of policy decisions dating back to the early 1920s and the near-impossible task of balancing Britain's finite resources with its colonial obligations and war-time priorities.

Unfortunately, such nuanced and sympathetic perspectives were for the future. The contemporary view was less forgiving and included an anony-mous couplet, a parody on Wordsworth's Fall of the Venetian Republic:

> Once did we hold the glorious East in fee
> Then came Sir R. Brooke-Popham K.C.B.[13]

Criticism came from every direction. A Welsh Labour member of parliament (MP) called for a "purge of pansies" belonging to the colonial and diplomatic service ("hyphenated, be-monocled, school-tie wallahs"), while the newly homeless "White Rajah of Sarawak," Sir Charles Brooke (a distant rela-tive), demanded the sacking of "Singapore brass-hats, old-school-tie, la-di-da incompetents and others responsible for the fantastic Malaya position."[14] The most scathing postwar assessment has come from Norman Dixon, who saw the debacle as a story of military incompetence driven by the psychologically damaged Brooke-Popham, whom he accused of "stupidity, arrogance and dishonesty."[15] Failure was the result of threatened egos that produced "disastrous hesitancy and indecision."[16] Other historians have been less strident and more measured in their search for explanations, but Brooke-Popham is still seen as a ditherer who led Britain's "B Team" to inevitable defeat.[17] In fact, the passing years have not been particularly kind to any of the actors involved in the Greek tragedy that was the fall of Singapore. "Many victims, few heroes; simply people caught in a situation created by Britain's past that they were powerless to alter."[18]

Other than his official dispatch (completed in 1942, although publication was deferred until 1948), Brooke-Popham did not provide an account of his time as CinC Far East, nor did he respond to the widespread public criticism of his conduct.[19] By comparison, Percival wrote a personal memoir (following publication of his official dispatch), and maintained a vigorous defense of his actions through lectures, letters, and lobbying, until his death in 1966.[20] Churchill, Cooper, and Bennett each published their own accounts, while third parties have set out the case for Cooper, Percival, Phillips, and Thomas.[21] Even the official historian, Major-General S. Woodburn Kirby, was driven to offer a separate, independent interpretation of the campaign.[22] Brooke-Popham was alone among the leading figures to have refrained from discussing the events surrounding the fall of Singapore, adhering to the principle that "a defeated general should not speak of the battle."[23] There is no evidence that he was aware of the saying, popular in Japanese military circles, but he might well have acknowledged the irony.[24] To his mind, he was a defeated general and the Japanese his victors.[25]

Brooke-Popham's dignified silence lasted until his death in 1953. His official papers have been in the public domain since 1966 when they were donated to the Liddell Hart Centre for Military Archives (LHCMA) and have been widely referenced by historians. Unfortunately, this has not stimulated any substantial commentary on his career other than a series of pen-pictures, drawing on selected correspondence, that are occasionally sympathetic, but generally of the "Colonel Blimp" variety—witness the claim that while in Singapore he was "nothing more than a buffer—the unkind might say an old buffer."[26] For reasons that are unclear there has been no biography or in-depth study of a man who reached the highest ranks of the Royal Air Force (RAF), took the first steps in the development of British airpower doctrine, created the first "modern" logistic system, laid down the basis for RAF Fighter Command's victory in the Battle of Britain, and served as a highly successful colonial governor before being recalled in 1939 to set up the flying training schemes in Canada and South Africa that did so much to sustain Allied airpower.[27]

The successes and triumphs of Brooke-Popham's early career have been entirely overshadowed by the disaster that was Singapore, even though he used his twelve months as CinC Far East to considerable effect, instigating closer collaboration with the Australians, Dutch, and Americans, improving local defenses, and working with figures such as Brigadier General Claire Chennault, General Douglas MacArthur, and Admiral Thomas Hart, as well as Generalissimo Chiang Kai-shek, to deter a potential Japanese attack. Notwithstanding his energetic leadership, the lack of resources and low priority afforded by Britain to reinforcing the Far East, allied to German military success and the loss of top-secret intelligence detailing Britain's military weakness, encouraged the Japanese in the belief that their "favourable opportunity" had arrived and the time was right to replace the European powers in Southeast Asia and, if necessary, to wage war on the United States.[28]

In preparing this narrative considerable use has been made of the Brooke-Popham Family Papers (BPFP), comprising Robert Brooke-Popham's private notebooks, documents, diaries, photographs, and personal letters, including those written by Lady Brooke-Popham.[29] I am grateful to Philip Brooke-Popham for providing full access to these and other materials belonging to his parents. The notebooks are not diaries as such, but a brief record of meetings, issues, and actions. They include his time at the Imperial Defence College, the Air Ministry (in 1940 and 1943), and Singapore—as well as his journey back to the UK in early 1942 (concluding with summary points for the official dispatch). Dates are few and the entries are often cryptic, but the six volumes covering 1940 and 1941 offer a unique window on the working regime of CinC Far East and the issues that were foremost in his mind during the months prior to Japan's attack. When added to his private letters and material available in public archives, or published since the end of the war, it is now possible to provide a comprehensive picture of "a man who took the rap."[30]

1

EARLY LIFE AND
MILITARY SERVICE
1878–1909

Henry Robert Moore Brooke was born on 18 September 1878 at Wetheringsett Manor, Suffolk, the only son of Henry and Dulcibella Brooke. "Bob," to avoid confusion with his father, was the couple's second child. His sister "Polly" (Dulcibella Mary) was five years older and was to become an important influence during his early years.[1] The Brooke family had been closely linked with the East India Company and the Far East since the eighteenth century, occupying senior positions in the army, judiciary, and civil service. James Brooke, the original "White Rajah" of Sarawak, was a relative. Bob's great-grandfather, Henry Brooke, had served as governor of Fort George at Madras where his son Robert Brooke (Bob's grandfather) was born in 1771. Bob's father, Henry Brooke (born in Bath in 1837) served as an ensign with the 42nd Highlanders (Black Watch) in India for three years, arriving shortly after the end of the Indian Mutiny.[2] Henry Brooke had resigned his commission in December 1862 to marry the twenty-three-year-old Dulcibella Latica Moore of Wetheringsett Manor, Suffolk.[3] The marriage appears to have been a happy one, although Dulcibella suffered from "delicate health." The Victorians had a range of terms employed to describe those of nervous disposition, including neurasthenia and dysautonomia. At this distance, it is impossible to determine the exact nature of her disability or the cause, but when Henry Brooke died suddenly in November 1892, shortly before his fifty-fifth birthday, Bob's sister, Polly, became head of the family—rather than their mother, who was unable to travel from Eastbourne to attend the funeral.[4]

The Brooke family could be best described as landed gentry. Henry Brooke was recorded as being of independent means in the 1891 census. Wetheringsett Manor, built by Dulcibella's father the Reverend Robert Moore in 1843, was a large household with eight staff—including a butler, cook, housemaids, and a footman. In 1881, the estate comprised 170 acres with six laborers and a boy (apprentice). Henry Brooke was respected and liked in the local community. On his arrival at Wetheringsett he had "settled down to the responsibilities attaching to the life of a country squire which from first to last, he discharged in a manner worthy of all imitation."[5] The loss of his father weighed heavily on the fourteen-year-old Bob, as did his mother's increasing incapacity. As a result, Polly became a key figure in his life and he regularly turned to her for advice and reassurance. They remained extremely close, using childhood nicknames, "Tote" (Bob) and "Nan" (Polly), in their private correspondence for more than fifty years.

Brooke entered Haileybury College in the third term of 1891 (after local schooling at Lowestoft). Haileybury, previously the East India College, had been founded in 1862 for the education of young men destined for the empire. He was one of seventy-eight students who entered the school that summer, all aged between thirteen and fifteen years.[6] A surviving report from 1893 indicates that he was an average scholar, but weak in mathematics. His academic performance improved over the next two years, although there is also a glimmer of a rebellious character emerging. "He has once more shown his tendency to disobedience when it does not suit him to obey. All the same, he has greatly improved in every way."[7] In his last year at Haileybury, Brooke became a member of the Haileybury Volunteer Company, attached to the Bedfordshire Regiment. Whether this was the cause for (or result of) a conscious career choice, it can be safely assumed that he was set on joining the army. This was neither unusual nor unexpected; eighteen of his class became officers in British or Indian Army regiments.[8] A analysis conducted by the school in 1900 of 2,300 surviving Old Haileyburians (OHs) revealed that the largest single group (more than five hundred) had joined the Army (compared to fourteen who had joined the Royal Navy), while nearly four hundred OHs were living or working overseas—mainly in the colonies or India. Brooke had intended to enter the Royal Military Academy Woolwich (for those seeking commissions in the Royal Artillery or Royal Engineers) through the exam administered by the Civil Service Commissioners. To his enduring regret (he had set his heart on joining the Royal Engineers) he failed the 1895 examination and, in particular, the mathematics element (plane trigonometry and total mathematics).[9] Brooke remained at Haileybury until he could sit the 1896 examination for the Royal Military College Sandhurst.[10] On this occasion he was successful, scoring 8,303 marks for mathematics in the final examination (compared to 6,294 marks the previous year), suggesting that the extra year had been employed to good effect.[11] In qualifying near the top of the list, Brooke was also in a position to join the infantry rather than the cavalry (where competition for commissions was less fierce).[12] The director general of military education, Major General C. W. Wilson, summoned Brooke to present himself at a medical board in London on 12 January 1897. This was evidently successful, because he was enrolled as a gentleman cadet at Sandhurst the same month. Sandhurst was organized on a three-term basis (junior, intermediate, and senior) and the course of study lasted eighteen months. The syllabus included military law and administration, tactics, and topography, alongside drill, gymnastics, and practical exercises, such as the construction of field fortifications. A contemporary account has described the instruction at Sandhurst as archaic, military law a jest, and the atmosphere "Crimean."[13] One of the manuals studied in detail was Philips' *Text-Book on Fortifications*, illustrated by pictures of gabions and other field works that had to be hand-copied into exercise books.[14] The cadets were then expected to recreate these same fortifications in the College's grounds. A contemporary photograph survives showing a very young-looking Cadet Brooke with the remainder of his class in working dress, and tools at the ready, on top of a newly completed revetment.

In many of these early photographs Brooke is not looking at the camera but slightly to one side, suggesting an innate shyness. An unwillingness to make eye contact with the camera lens is not of itself significant, but a contemporary caricature offers additional clues about Brooke's character and personality:

> Temper variable, inclined to be irritable and not well under control at times. Very slow to forgive an injury. Self-willed and opinionated. Not at all susceptible to outside influence, but in a way impressionable. Capable of a good deal of feeling, although very undemonstrative. Kind hearted, but given to rash judgements. Thoughtful for

the comfort of others, but selfish and *very* impatient. Brain power good and active, ditto memory. Sense of humour only moderately seen. Very self-conscious. Power of observation very highly developed. *Extremely persevering*! Conceited and obstinate, plenty of pluck. On the whole, an affectation of indifference to everything and everyone, excepting Napoleon. Not a bad character on the whole and which will improve with age.[15]

It is tempting to see the sixty-two-year-old air chief marshal in the nineteen-year-old officer cadet. As we will discover, there are aspects of this picture that emerge time and again throughout his career. His concern for the comfort of others was an enduring characteristic, as were his intellect and determination. The youthful admiration for Napoleon was lifelong—even to the extent of quoting the great man about love to his future wife. While it would be unwise to suggest that this anonymous caricature is anything other than a pale imitation of the real man, it does offer a glimpse of the individual behind the public face.

In his June 1897 progress report, Brooke was placed forty-first on the order of merit list, but this had risen to twenty-fifth by December 1897. His final position was high enough to gain a commission as a second lieutenant in the Second Battalion, Oxfordshire Light Infantry—gazetted on 6 May 1898.[16] The Second Battalion (Fifty-Second Regiment) was based on the North-West Frontier, having served continuously overseas since 1884. Pending embarkation for India on the next trooping season, Brooke was instructed to join the First Battalion (Forty-Third Regiment) garrisoned in Ireland (Curragh Camp), effective 8 June 1898.[17] Brooke remained at the Curragh Camp for the next three months before leaving for India on 8 September, accompanying a draft of one hundred rank and file commanded by Lieutenant C. Chichester.[18] He just missed the arrival of another newly commissioned subaltern, Second Lieutenant J. F. C. Fuller, destined to become one of the foremost military thinkers of the twentieth century.[19] "Boney" Fuller, who had been in the term behind Brooke at Sandhurst, was appointed to the First Battalion on 3 August 1898, but did not arrive at the Curragh until 12 September.[20] Surprisingly for members of the same regiment and of the same age, Fuller and Brooke do not appear to have been close. There were some similarities—they read widely, had inquiring minds, and were not strong academically. On the other hand, Fuller lost his faith early while Brooke,

who was a staunch Anglo-Catholic, retained strong religious beliefs throughout his life. Brooke was also a passionate horseman and enthusiastic follower
of field sports, particularly hunting and riding—activities that had little or
no appeal to Fuller.[21] Nevertheless, it remains unclear why Fuller, military
innovator and advocate of mechanization, and Brooke-Popham, pioneer
aviator and airpower strategist, did not forge a more intimate professional
relationship.[22]

The sea voyage to India normally took between four and six weeks.
Brooke reached Deolali (the main depot in India for the arrival and departure of British Army troops one hundred miles northeast of Bombay) in late
November 1898 and by the end of the year was with the Second Battalion,
commanded by Lieutenant-Colonel F. H. Plowden, at Landi Kotal (some
three hundred miles from the regimental depot at Ferozepur), where the
battalion had been based since the end of the 1897–98 Punjab campaign.[23]
Brooke's time in India was not exceptional. He was assigned to C Company,
under Captain E. D. White and Lieutenant K. R. Hamilton.[24] As a junior
officer, he participated in the active life enjoyed by young subalterns posted
overseas. He played cricket (albeit not very well) for his company, rode regularly, and was an enthusiastic polo player as well as a good shot and accomplished hunter.[25] Promoted to lieutenant on 24 November 1899, Brooke took
his wider regimental duties seriously, playing in intercompany matches, organizing athletic meetings, and overseeing the battalion's Waterloo Sports Day
at Deesa (the British Army's cantonment in northeast Gujarat), some 450
miles north of Bombay.[26] The battalion's officers numbered fewer than thirty
(excluding medical staff) and the garrison formed a close-knit community.
Brooke made several lifelong friends, notably his fellow subaltern Lieutenant
(later Colonel) Cyril Frith, who was appointed the regiment's adjutant in
1908.[27] For the next three years Brooke was engaged in routine garrison duties,
escorting troop details to and from Deolali, and attending training courses.
As far as active service was concerned, he had arrived during a relatively quiet
period for the North-West Frontier, although he did participate in the Dalhousie Hill maneuvers (October–November 1900).[28] This peacetime exercise
was designed to rehearse the relief of Dalhousie, notionally under siege by a
hostile force.

On 10 January 1901, Brooke left for Deesa with an advance party to take
over garrison duties from a detachment of the Norfolk Regiment. Later in the
summer he took six weeks' leave in the Chamba region. It was during this trip

that he contracted dengue fever. On his return, he was initially hospitalized at Deesa and then transferred to the station hospital at Colaba to facilitate his recovery. His health did not improve and a medical board, convened at Bombay on 18 November 1901, concluded that he was suffering from debility resulting from dengue fever exacerbated by malaria, the disease being entirely due to the effect of climate.[29] The board further recommended that Lieutenant Brooke "be granted leave to proceed to England for six months by the next troopship, unfit for duty with troops on the voyage." Brooke left Bombay on 23 November on board the military transport ship *Assaye*, reaching Southampton via Gibraltar in late December 1901.[30] Several sources state that he left India to serve in the Second Boer War, but this is a case of mistaken identity, Lieutenant H. R. M. Brooke of the Second Battalion being confused with Lieutenant R. R. M. Brooke of the First Battalion (who did serve in South Africa).[31] A notice in the *London Gazette* stating that "Lieutenant H. R. M. Brooke" had been seconded for service in South Africa was later corrected to read "Lieutenant R. R. M. Brooke."[32] In fact, Brooke's illness meant that he could never have served in South Africa.[33] Brooke's three years in India exposed him to the reality of garrison service and the role of the military in policing the empire. It cemented his affection for the regiment as an institution and created deep and enduring friendships. India provided the foundation for his military career. Although not involved in active operations, he had proved a successful and energetic officer with the qualities required for advancement. The experience had also left him with sympathy for the tribes of the North-West Frontier, even though he might have to fight them in the future.[34] This willingness to acknowledge the rights of those under British rule would characterize his time in Iraq, Africa, and the Far East. A loyal and dedicated servant of the empire, Brooke nevertheless possessed an open mind and an instinctive empathy toward the demos—whether at home or overseas.

During his recuperation, Brooke was assigned to the regimental depot at Cowley, where he successfully sat his captaincy exam.[35] At the end of the year, possibly on a doctor's advice, he took the opportunity to travel through Europe with Polly, visiting Moscow as well as Warsaw and Switzerland before returning to Cowley early in 1903. The next twelve months were to be significant for several reasons. His second cousin once removed, Susan Bisset, died at Bagborough House, Somerset, in May; the Second Battalion returned from India in October; and Polly married George Pooley (a surgeon who had been attached to the Royal Army Medical Corps during the Boer War) in November.[36] Of these events, it was the last that had the deepest impact. His sister's marriage cut the last of his ties to Suffolk (Wetheringsett was sold as part of the marriage settlement), while her subsequent move to Uganda deprived him of her guidance and advice. Polly was extremely proud of her brother and his achievements. Indeed, when he visited her rooms in Hampstead, shortly before her death, he wrote to his wife that, "curiously, on the mantelpiece, there were four photographs of me and one of you, but none of any of her children anywhere."[37] Polly found the personal criticism of her brother, following the loss of Singapore, a heavy burden. It may well have contributed to her depression and suicide from an overdose of sleeping pills in June 1942.[38] On Brooke's part, Polly had been an important presence in his life. She was the mother that he never had. "The picture I chiefly have of her now is 44 years ago when I was driving to the station to catch my train to join up with the 43rd, when I was first commissioned, and she rode with me part of the way and then turned off to go to luncheon somewhere."[39]

A less important, but more visible, change was the adoption of the name Brooke-Popham. Susan Bisset (née Popham), who had extensive property in Somerset (including Bagborough House and estate), had been widowed in 1884 with no surviving children. Brooke was the oldest male heir (via his mother), but his inheritance required he adopt the surname of Popham. This involved a royal warrant—a lengthy process that was not completed until 1904.[40] Thereafter, Henry Robert Moore Brooke was formally known as Henry Robert Moore Brooke-Popham. To his colleagues (and his many friends) he would always be known as "Brookham," to his immediate family as "Bob," and for the remainder of this book, simply as "Brooke-Popham."

Although the Second Battalion was in England (at Chatham), permitting a resumption of his regimental career, Brooke-Popham remained for the time being at Cowley. He was an enthusiastic horseman and his work at the depot allowed him to ride regularly, whether to hounds, point-to-point, or polo. He had a deep love of horses and respect for good horsemen. "I suppose some people have no sort of sympathy with a horse and never realize how he's feeling; never think of getting off his back when nothing's happening and trot him home full out up to his stable door."[41] His passion for riding did not diminish over the years, despite falls and injuries. It was later said that, although he had a shrewd judgment of men at his own level, he was "perhaps a little prejudiced in favour of a good horseman among his junior officers."[42]

Brooke-Popham found time to visit Egypt early in the new year, travelling the length of the Nile and gaining a lifelong interest in the Middle East, particularly its ancient history and architecture. On his return, he attended a mounted infantry course at Longmore, from July to September 1904, shortly before being appointed captain adjutant to the Oxford Militia—one of the regiment's two militia battalions (the other being the Royal Buckinghamshire Militia).[43] Among his first duties in this role was to provide a guard of honor for the king and queen of Portugal (the king was honorary colonel of the regiment) on their arrival at Paddington Station on 17 November 1904. He finally returned to the Second Battalion in February 1905, to command G Company at Chatham, moving with them to Tidworth in 1906.[44] A report describes him as "a hard working, capable and zealous company commander. Rides well and is a good horsemaster. A good disciplinarian and takes great interest with the welfare of men and horses. A quick and decided leader in field work and in service would prove a resolute and forward commander."[45] Brooke-Popham's enthusiasm for riding may have won the approval of the battalion's new commanding officer, Lieutenant-Colonel (later Major-General Sir) Robert Fanshawe, who had instigated a rigorous training program, designed to prepare the battalion—"softened" after the leisurely life of an Indian cantonment—for a future European war. Exercises, long marches, musketry practice, drill, and autumn maneuvers were introduced, alongside games, athletics, and inter-regimental contests. Fanshawe also encouraged young officers to hunt whenever their duties permitted, as he considered "a long day in the saddle finding one's way across country much better training for war than that offered by a winter's day in barracks."[46]

One of Brooke-Popham's new subalterns was a promising young officer, Lieutenant Felton Vesey "Tony" Holt, who was full of ideas and energy. The two became firm friends and, having learned to fly in 1912, Holt followed Brooke-Popham into the Royal Flying Corps (RFC), winning the Distinguished Service Order (DSO) while commanding No. 16 Squadron.[47] It was at Tidworth that Brooke-Popham first turned his hand to writing about military affairs. His essay on the organization of armies, based on a system of voluntary enlistment, won the Southern Command Winter Essay Prize (1906–1907), and received favorable comments from the chief of the General Staff.[48] Brooke-Popham was still with G Company in 1908 when the two militia battalions were replaced by a single (Special Reserve) battalion and the regiment was restyled as "The Oxfordshire and Buckinghamshire Light

Infantry" (Oxf & Bucks LI). As an ambitious young officer, with a sound reputation and obvious potential, Brooke-Popham was now set on gaining admission to the Staff College at Camberley. He had taken the first step a year earlier by passing his examination for promotion to major. Only ten officers from his regiment had attended Staff College since 1858, when it was created as part of the reforms following the Crimean War. A place at Camberley was highly sought after and was the stepping-stone to a successful career in the Victorian army. Selection was by a combination of nomination and competitive exam (comprising papers in history, strategy, tactics, organization, engineering, algebra, and languages).[49] Brooke-Popham's work diary shows that he prepared with determination, seeking special tuition in mathematics—his weakest subject—and spending more than 1,100 hours on studying and practice papers between October 1908 and July 1909. The exam (held over a ten-day period and comprising eighteen three-hour exams) was held at the beginning of August 1909 and, when the results were announced by the director of staff duties (Major-General Douglas Haig) on 29 September, Brooke-Popham had the highest aggregate score of all the entrants.[50] Major (later General) Charles ("Tim") Harington at the War Office, who oversaw the Staff College examination, wrote personally to congratulate him, noting that "this is the third year running that the Infantry had defeated all the other arms!"[51] A flurry of congratulatory telegrams followed from family and friends, applauding his achievement and the opportunities that lay ahead. Attending Staff College was undoubtedly the turning point in Brooke-Popham's career. It marked him as an officer destined for the highest ranks. It also set in motion a series of events that, thirty years later, took him to Singapore and the outbreak of the Pacific War.

2

ARMY STAFF COLLEGE
AND AIR BATTALION
1910–1912

Apart from a brief period in 1912, immediately prior to joining the RFC, Brooke-Popham's arrival at Camberley marked the end of his regimental service.[1] The Staff College had grown in importance since the Second Boer War through the efforts of "modernizers" such as Sir Henry Wilson, commandant from 1907 to 1910, who were determined to create a coherent system of training and education for the Army.[2] Wilson believed that it was vital to produce a corps of officers "imbued with uniform methods of work."[3] His aim was to create general staff or superior commanders capable in administration, but with the soldierly and field qualities of physical superiority, imagination, sound judgment of men and affairs, and constant reading and reflection on the campaigns of the great masters. Wilson was an inspiring and notably successful commandant. He encouraged his students to think expansively but also stressed practical exercises, such as staff tours and battlefield visits.[4] Brooke-Popham arrived at Camberley on 22 January 1910, during the last year of Wilson's tenure.[5] The latter's successor, Major-General W. R. Robertson, maintained the emphasis on developing capable staff officers able to think independently, but increased the number of practical exercises.[6] Despite Camberley's growing reputation, there were continuing concerns about the quality of its graduates. Criticism of the staff officers involved in the 1910 Army maneuvers and the effectiveness of their training at Camberley was robustly rebutted, but there remained a sense that there was a great deal of ground to catch up if Britain was to match the professionalism of the French and German armies.[7]

Staff College lasted two years (split into Junior and Senior Divisions), the year comprising three terms, each of ten to eleven weeks' duration (late January to mid-April, mid-May to the end of July and early October to the end of December).[8] This pattern offered plenty of time for travel and sport, as well as broader professional development. The opportunity to read extensively and debate contemporary defense issues with his peers had a profound impact on Brooke-Popham. Camberley's influence, both personal and professional, would be felt throughout his career—as he later reflected: "The most striking feature of the Army Staff College is the feeling of a happy family pervading the whole place. Friendships formed there last throughout one's service life and are the greatest value in war and I can truthfully say that going on a visit to Camberley is to most ex-students like returning to one's home."[9]

Brooke-Popham's surviving notebooks, including copious notes on past campaigns, grand strategy, and the administration of modern armies, suggest that he thrived at Staff College, finding the course both stimulating and inspiring. He formed strong friendships with the other students, notably Captain (later Major-General) Richard Pope-Hennessy, a fellow member of the Oxf & Bucks LI, who had been selected through nomination. Brooke-Popham acted as his best man in July 1910 and proudly claimed to have organized the engagement.[10] The two infantry officers prepared several lectures together, including one on the regeneration of the Prussian Army after its crushing defeat by Napoleon at the Battle of Jena in 1806.[11]

It is not clear when Brooke-Popham's interest turned to flying. According to family tradition, the catalyst was a lecture when he was challenged by a fellow student about the future role of aircraft in warfare. It is possible that the trigger was the General Staff Officers' conference in January 1911 (held at Camberley before the students returned from their Christmas break) reviewing the 1910 maneuvers—the first occasion on which airplanes and dirigibles had been employed in England for military work.[12] However, if Brooke-Popham wanted to fly an aircraft, in the military or simply for enjoyment, he had first to gain his pilot's brevet. This was administered by the Royal Aero Club and required the candidate to make two distance flights of at least five kilometers each (following a figure-of-eight course), landing each time within fifty meters of a predetermined mark and, on a third flight, to achieve a height of fifty meters. In passing this examination the pilot was regarded as having demonstrated effective control of an airplane and could participate in all aerial contests and displays organized by the Club and its overseas affiliates. Although flying was steadily gaining in popularity, it remained an expensive and dangerous sport—seven British pilots died in 1911, two under instruction. In 1910, there were six flying schools operating in England (they had trained just eighteen pilots between them, although this had increased to thirteen schools and 109 new pilots by the end of 1911).[13]

Toward the end of the summer term Brooke-Popham travelled to Brooklands where the Bristol School—the leading school during this period—offered flying training up to brevet standard at a cost of forty pounds (with contractual provision for crashes or injury). He flew solo in a Bristol Boxkite (a pusher biplane) on 6 July 1911, reaching a height of several hundred feet "in good style." He appears to have been a fast learner: on his third outing (8 July) he demonstrated "extraordinary left and right hand turns over the top of the sheds and sewage farm."[14] All of these flights involved an early start (around 4 a.m.) to take advantage of the calm conditions. Once the wind was over ten miles per hour, controlling the Boxkite became increasingly difficult—as did making any headway. By Saturday morning (15 July 1911) Brooke-Popham was able to take his certificate flights (at 170 and 250 feet respectively) in front of the official representatives of the Royal Aero Club. He was formally granted his Aviator's Certificate No. 108 three days later (on 18 July 1911).

There are conflicting views on Brooke-Popham's abilities in the air. It has been claimed that he was not a natural pilot,[15] although his instructor, Howard Pixton, recorded that "he flew very well."[16] Other contemporary accounts also provide a positive picture ("skillful and persistent" according to one commentator).[17] Philip Joubert de la Ferté, in describing a successful forced landing near Farnborough in 1913, stressed that Brooke-Popham was a very good pilot—as well as a well-behaved passenger.[18] Brooke-Popham's own letters reveal that he found flying an enjoyable and relaxing experience, bordering on the spiritual: "Just down from an hour's relaxation in the air. Such a glorious day for flying. I went up to about 9,000 ft above all the cloud, with wonderful clear blue sky above and away right towards the sun a great mass of broken cloud all lit up by the sun. And the broken bits all showed a dark grey and had a sort of filmy mist over them—as if to say, 'Herein are dark secrets, let no man enter.'"[19]

Having obtained his brevet, and with two months before his final term commenced, Brooke-Popham was attached for the summer to the recently

formed Air Battalion.[20] The War Office's interest in aviation was more positive than is sometimes claimed, dating back to before the Boer War, but it was
also as cautious as it was longstanding. Despite the rapid expansion of military aviation in France and Germany, following the Wright Brothers' public
flying displays in 1908–9 at Rheims and Berlin respectively, the British government had pursued a measured, evidence-based approach under the direction of Secretary of State for War Richard Haldane. It was not until April
1911 that the Air Battalion was created (by reorganizing the existing Royal
Engineers' Balloon School) with the purpose of training officers and men
in the handling of all forms of aircraft and providing a small body of expert
airmen from which air units for war could be formed.[21] The battalion was
organized into two companies: No. 1 (Airship) Company, also responsible for
balloons and kites; and No. 2 (Aeroplane) Company. Under Sir Alexander
Bannerman's leadership, the Air Battalion existed for less than a year, but it
provided the foundation for the Royal Flying Corps (RFC) and supplied
many of its most influential officers.[22]

The Air Battalion was to have participated in the September 1911 cavalry division and army maneuvers to be held in Cambridgeshire, but these
were subsequently cancelled because of the tense international situation.[23]
Nevertheless, it was decided to deploy No. 2 Company's aircraft to Hardwick,
near Cambridge, from their flying base at Larkhill.[24] Although eight Bristol
Boxkite aircraft had been ordered for the Air Battalion's use (the first British
contract for a quantity of aircraft for military purposes), only four had been
delivered by early August. These joined the battalion's existing Farman and
Paulhan pusher biplanes, alongside the privately purchased Blériot XII
monoplane belonging to Lieutenant R. A. Cammell.[25] It was therefore a mixed
bag of machines that set off for Cambridge. Brooke-Popham, in company
with Captain Charles Burke, flew in the Farman with the aim of making
Oxford, but only managed as far as Wantage owing to a headwind.[26] The
pair reached Oxford the next day where they were joined by three other aircraft, "the whole air force of the British Empire."[27] Unfortunately, a series
of accidents caused by a combination of unreliability and poor weather
meant that only Lieutenant Basil Barrington-Kennett (Bristol Boxkite) and
Lieutenant Cammell (Blériot) actually reached Cambridge, while the Bristol
Boxkites flown by Lieutenants Connor and Reynolds were both written off.[28]
Returning to Camberley, and undeterred by his aerial adventures, Brooke-
Popham started work on a conceptual model for military aviation. He was

heavily involved in writing and lecturing on this subject for the next thirty years. Early in November 1911, he was invited to speak on military aviation to both divisions. This talk was subsequently published in *The Army Review*,[29] and received a warm welcome by the editor of *Flight* (Stanley Spooner), a longstanding critic of the government's aviation policy:

> Although the prevailing attitude of the Government towards aviation in the past has been in the main one of apathy—or at least apparent apathy—an attitude which we are glad to say seems to be passing in favour of one much more in consonance with what we believe to be the need of the moment, it by no means follows that the same want of interest has been manifested by the officers of the Army and Navy to whom we shall have to look in the future to supply us with the *personnel* of our aerial forces.[30]

Spooner went on to applaud Brooke-Popham's analysis, which he described as of "the greatest possible interest to all who have given more than a little thought to the subject." Several important roles were identified, including battlefield reconnaissance and aerial bombing; however, it was the prediction that a struggle for the command of the air would be an essential feature in any future great war that produced the greatest excitement. "One side is sure to start with an advantage in the numbers or quality of its machines, or in the ability and *moral* [sic] of its pilots, and it is inconceivable that the latter will rest content with a mere exchange of information, and not make determined attempts to prevent the enemy doing any aerial reconnaissance whatever."[31] Field Marshal Frederick Lord Roberts, who had retired as commander in chief of the British Army in 1904 but remained an influential figure in military affairs, was greatly impressed by the lecture and drew on it for a letter he wrote to the *Times* in December 1911 about Britain's lack of military preparedness.[32] He questioned Brooke-Popham on the size of Germany's aviation budget and the number of aircraft possessed by the British Army. Roberts' interest was in stark contrast to the chief of the Imperial General Staff, Sir William Nicholson, who had told the students at Camberley in 1909 that "he could conceive of no conditions under which aeroplanes could be of any value in war."[33] Even members of the Air Battalion were skeptical about the military utility of airplanes (as compared to airships). According to Brooke-Popham this included the commandant (Sir

Alexander Bannerman), who ridiculed the idea of anyone doing observation of troops from an airplane "as he'd be squeezing sap out of the struts or any other part of the machine he could hold on to,"[34] as well as the Air Battalion's adjutant (Captain P. W. L. Broke-Smith).[35]

Many of the points raised in Brooke-Popham's lecture to the Staff College were repeated in a paper presented just two weeks later at the Royal United Services Institute (RUSI) by his friend Charles Burke. In a lecture titled, "The Aeroplane as an Aid to the Solution of Existing Strategical Problems," Burke discussed the future role of military airplanes and the possibility of fighting in the air.[36] Brooke-Popham was in the audience and added that success in the battle for air supremacy at the beginning of a campaign depended on the number of airplanes employed and their quality—as well as the quality of their pilots.[37] However, his comment that air fighting with firearms might take place was vehemently rejected by Captain John Fulton, also of the Air Battalion, who wrote to *Flight* to disassociate himself from such suggestions.[38] Fulton, together with Captain Bertram Dickson, was a leading pioneer of British military aviation, but his interests lay largely in the practical and engineering aspects of powered flight.[39] Dickson, unlike Fulton, found time to lecture and write. In evidence to the Committee for Imperial Defence (CID), submitted in early 1912, he also predicted that there would be a struggle for air supremacy in any future war.[40]

It would be misleading to claim that Brooke-Popham was alone in advocating military aviation, any more than the Air Battalion was united about the potential of the airplane. On the other hand, Brooke-Popham and Burke were more clear-sighted than many of their peers. They took up flying because they realized the importance it was going to play in warfare. According to Brooke-Popham, Burke had an instinctive understanding of aviation—even if he was neither a skilled pilot nor a great thinker.[41] This may seem harsh criticism, particularly coming from a close friend, but it was a view shared by Sefton Brancker, who also knew Burke.[42] Burke later became famous for his "Maxims" on flying, although it was Brooke-Popham who collated them after the former's death, leaving some uncertainty about their precise authorship.[43]

Staff College offered Brooke-Popham both time and encouragement to look beyond the immediate technical challenges of powered flight and to consider the long-term impact of airplanes on military operations. Just as importantly, publication in *The Army Review* gave his arguments considerable weight and a degree of official approval.[44] The article even generated interest among the military aviators at Rheims, where it was translated into French.[45] Combat in the air between opposing airmen may seem (with the benefit of hindsight) to have been an inevitable development, but the concept was not so obvious at the time. Brooke-Popham was the first in the British Army to predict that airplanes would fulfil an important role in future conflict and that this would lead inevitably to fighting in the air. It was a profound insight and its importance cannot be exaggerated.[46]

Some of the contemporary surge in public interest about military airplanes can be traced to the War Office's plans for a competition to select a new military airplane.[47] This seems partly to have been a response to a French government competition held at Rheims in October 1911. The specifications for the War Office competition (to be held in the summer of 1912 on Salisbury Plain under the auspices of the RFC) generated a great deal of debate and heated letters in the national press.[48] These developments reflected a deeper change in the government's attitude to aviation. Conscious of the progress being made in France and Germany, and stung by criticism inside and outside Parliament, it instigated a review of military aviation. The CID, chaired by Haldane, was asked by the prime minister to "consider the future development of aerial navigation and the measures that might be taken to secure to this country an efficient aerial service."[49] The detailed work was undertaken by a technical subcommittee under the leadership of Colonel J. E. B. "Jack" Seely, supported by a small informal group comprising Brigadier-General David Henderson (director, Military Training), Major Duncan MacInnes (Directorate of Military Training), and Captain Frederick Sykes (Directorate of Military Operations). The committee's report was ready by February 1912. It proposed the creation of a single organization, the RFC, incorporating the existing military and naval services. The RFC was to be divided into a Central Flying School (CFS) on Salisbury Plain and separate Army and Naval Wings.[50] The Army Aircraft Factory at Farnborough would become the Royal Aircraft Factory. The CID agreed to these recommendations and the RFC was constituted by royal warrant on 13 April 1912. The Air Battalion was formally absorbed by the RFC a month later, on 13 May 1912.[51] Frederick Sykes was appointed as the officer commanding RFC, in the rank of major, with Basil Barrington-Kennett as his adjutant. At the same time, the CFS was formed at Upavon with Captain Godfrey Paine (Royal Navy) in command. The speed with which the new aeronautical organization was created reflected the sense of urgency felt across Whitehall and the belief that military aviation would have a significant role in any future war. Brooke-Popham's decision to pursue a career in military aviation was therefore both timely and prescient.

Having completed his staff course at the end of 1911, Brooke-Popham travelled to Rheims in early January to observe French Air Service operations.[52] On his return, he was posted to the Air Battalion, effective 29 March 1912, to command No. 2 (Aeroplane) Company, in succession to Captain Fulton—with detachments at Larkhill on Salisbury Plain and Farnborough.[53] This was an extraordinary and life-changing choice for a Staff College graduate. Pope-Hennessy wrote to his friend begging him to change his mind and "not to ruin his career in order to join a branch that would only lead to a dead-end."[54] Instead of enjoying an important and highly regarded staff appointment, Brooke-Popham found himself in a somewhat isolated coterie: "We were regarded with suspicion as men whose necks were cheap and with annoyance as making the air hideous with noise when all respectable people should still be asleep."[55]

In these early months, with military aviation in its infancy, a wide range of aircraft types (including Avro, Bristol, Deperdussin, Dunne, Martin Handasyde, and Nieuport) were employed rather than a single design. Machines were allocated to individual pilots. Brooke-Popham was given Bristol Boxkite No. F7 and flew this for the next few months.[56] Because of the wind and low engine power, flights were generally conducted in the early morning or early evening. He used these opportunities to carry passengers, either fellow officers or mechanics, on a range of aircraft. Among his visitors was Barrington-Kennett, whose death in 1915 (after leaving the RFC to rejoin the Grenadier Guards) greatly shocked Brooke-Popham.[57] Other lifelong friends from these pioneering months included Charles Burke, Charles Longcroft (Brooke-Popham was godfather to both the Burke and Longcroft families), Edward Ellington, and Robert Pigot.[58] All would play important parts in the development of British military aviation.

3

ROYAL FLYING CORPS
1912–1914

With the formation of the RFC, the Air Battalion's two companies were reorganized into squadrons (based on the French Air Service's escadrille). No. 1 (Airship) Company became No. 1 Squadron, while the Farnborough and Larkhill detachments of No. 2 (Aeroplane) Company became Nos. 2 and 3 Squadrons respectively.[1] This process has been the cause of some small controversy down the years because No. 2 Squadron and No. 3 Squadron both lay claim to being the senior airplane squadron in the RAF. The two units have an identical lineage, although it was undoubtedly Brooke-Popham's No. 3 Squadron that did much, if not all, of the RFC's early flying on airplanes.[2] The squadron's initial establishment was modest, comprising six pilots and some eight aircraft. Further officers joined over the next few months, together with additional aircraft. Numerous accounts describe Brooke-Popham's time with No. 3 Squadron as a happy and productive period. According to W. J. Smyrk, an engine fitter who joined the unit at Larkhill in September 1912, Brooke-Popham was a very popular boss. After someone had borrowed one of the small adjustable ("King Dick") spanners used on his motorcar, Brooke-Popham went around all the flight sheds asking people whether they had seen his "King Willie."[3] Another recruit was Private James McCudden, later Major James McCudden, VC, who arrived at Larkhill in June 1913 as an engine mechanic. He also remembered the squadron as a happy place, with a family atmosphere and a "magnificent set of officers."[4]

Under Brooke-Popham's leadership a concerted effort was made to cooperate with other arms, notably the artillery. A variety of methods was employed for signaling the fall of shot, but eventually they settled on colored Very lights (pyrotechnic flares). At that stage, airplanes were quite incapable of carrying the weight of wireless apparatus. His conclusion, "that in war, airplanes will be of the greatest value to artillery in the observation of fire at concealed targets,"[5] anticipated the pivotal role that the RFC was to play in directing artillery fire on the Western Front.[6] At this stage, there were few aviators or gunners in the British Army who had the determination or the resources to develop the necessary capabilities. The RFC's efforts were largely directed at improving its reconnaissance capabilities. Brooke-Popham did a considerable amount of flying during the year, accumulating a little more than sixty hours in the air and covering 596 miles cross-country.[7] These may not seem impressive figures, but they represented nearly one hundred flights in machines that could only be flown in calm conditions, were difficult to control, and equipped with unreliable engines. It was around this time that he wrote in his logbook: "On a calm day, especially if you have had a rocking previously, lean back in your seat and think how you are enjoying yourself or try to recognise someone on the ground and wave to them."[8]

At the beginning of August, the War Office's military aircraft trials took place on Salisbury Plain. This was Brooke-Popham's first opportunity to fly in Geoffrey de Havilland's new design, the Blériot Experimental 2 (BE2), produced by the Royal Aircraft Factory. In its developed form the BE2 provided the foundation for the RFC's air operations on the Western Front until the end of 1916 and remained in use (through successive modifications) until the end of the war. The aircraft was ineligible for the trials as Mervyn O'Gorman (the head of the Factory) was on the adjudication panel. At the end of the competition, de Havilland returned to Farnborough on the BE2 with Brooke-Popham as passenger. On 5 July 1912, No. 3 Squadron had suffered its first fatalities when Captain Eustace Loraine and Staff Sergeant Richard "Bertie" Wilson, the squadron's senior technical noncommissioned officer, crashed while flying a two-seat Nieuport monoplane.[9] When Brooke-Popham reached the scene Wilson was dead and Loraine dying. He gave evidence at the coroner's inquest, held that same evening at Bulford Camp Hospital, where it was concluded that the crash was the result of the pilot overbanking in a turn and stalling through loss of flying speed.[10] The jury returned a verdict of "accidental death." Brooke-Popham chose not to reveal everything that he knew. "There was a girl most unrespectable, once fallen very low, but who loved him and her name was the last word to pass his lips. But I never told his people this for they were scandalised when her wreath was given an honourable place."[11] He was less restrained about the lack of medical facilities available to the RFC and was vociferous in arguing for the provision of motor ambulances on airfields to help recover casualties.[12] Later that month, on 23 July 1912, Brooke-Popham (with Sergeant Frank Ridd of No. 3 Squadron, who had recently qualified as a pilot) flew a newly delivered Avro Type 500 to Hungerford to take tea with the Portal family, whom he had first met through hunting.[13] While at Eddington House he took the opportunity to offer a flight to the Portal's eldest son, the nineteen-year-old Charles "Peter" Portal, who would join the RFC in 1915 and command the RAF in World War II.[14] It was an encounter that both recalled with affection.

The loss of Loraine and Wilson was a heavy blow, but worse was to come as further fatal crashes occurred in the next two months. Captain P. Hamilton and Lieutenant A. Wyness-Stuart were killed on 6 September near Hitchin, while flying a Deperdussin monoplane, and four days later Lieutenant E. Hotchkiss and Lieutenant C. A. Bettington crashed while flying a Bristol Coanda monoplane at Wolvercote, Oxford.[15] Both aircraft were travelling to Cambridge to participate in the 1912 army maneuvers, where Hamilton was hoping to "put up some sort of a show for Sykes' sake."[16] The loss of two monoplanes and the deaths of four airmen in a matter of a few days led the War Office to impose an immediate ban on the use of monoplanes. As a result, No. 3 Squadron's participation was more limited than planned (they had hoped to employ an entire flight of monoplanes).[17] Even so, the 1912 maneuvers were particularly successful in demonstrating the value of aircraft to the two opposing commanders and, in particular, to Lieutenant-General James Grierson, who was able to defeat Lieutenant-General Douglas Haig, partly because of the information they provided.[18] Brooke-Popham, with No. 3 Squadron, played a vital role in persuading Grierson to use his airplanes to provide information on the enemy's troops. "He was perfectly delighted and the whole of the rest of the manoeuvres relied almost entirely on information received from us."[19] A distinguished visitor to the maneuvers was General Ferdinand Foch, later the Allies' supreme commander, who showed a great interest in Brooke-Popham's efforts. Following the maneuvers, Brooke-Popham was appointed a member of the departmental committee established to investigate the three fatal monoplane accidents.[20] The committee's work was completed in December, although the findings were not made public until February 1913. Their final report was an important milestone in aviation safety, not only because it exonerated the monoplane as a type (subject to certain modifications) but also because it introduced arrangements for the regular independent inspection of all aircraft types, in construction and in service, and for the formal investigation of aircraft accidents and the publication of the findings—a robust and effective regulatory system that remains in place to this day. "It did great service in the general fathering of aeronautical design and the establishment of proper standards for safety."[21]

There was little flying during the autumn. The squadron had returned to Larkhill but the lack of winter accommodation and poor weather limited what could be achieved. Toward the end of the year domestic accommodation was found at Netheravon, where work started on the construction of permanent aircraft sheds. Brooke-Popham used this opportunity to return to Camberley and deliver a further lecture, this time about military aircraft.[22] His talk built on the issues raised in his previous paper—with the benefit of a year's practical experience. Once again, he argued that fighting in the air would inevitably follow the use of aircraft in wartime as each side strove to achieve ascendancy. Among those in his audience were Captain (later Air Chief Marshal Sir) Geoffrey Salmond, Lieutenant (later Air Chief Marshal Lord) Hugh Dowding and Captain (later Air Commodore) Lionel Charlton—all yet to learn to fly but destined to do so once they had graduated from Camberley.[23] It was not until the spring of 1913 that flying at Larkhill was resumed on a regular basis. At the beginning of May, Brooke-Popham led the entire squadron from Salisbury Plain to Farnborough, flying as a single unit—an unprecedented procedure. The nine aircraft left at five-minute intervals and only one pilot failed to arrive, forced down by engine trouble. The aircraft, together with those of No. 2 Squadron, were reviewed by the king and queen on Friday, 9 May 1913. The subsequent flying demonstration involved seventeen machines, the largest display of British military aviation to that date. "The machines manoeuvred together like a swarm of gigantic gnats dancing in a sunbeam."[24] Two weeks later, nine aircraft from No. 3 Squadron performed the RFC's first "fly past"—in front of General Sir Horace Smith-Dorrien, GOC Southern Command—during a review of more than 10,000 regular and territorial forces on Perham Down, Salisbury Plain.[25] The squadron provided the final element of the parade, with Brooke-Popham directing operations from the ground. Because of a crosswind, the machines had to crab their way past the reviewing officer, although one of the pilots was still able to dip the nose of his aircraft in salute while sounding a klaxon—much to the entertainment of those watching. The image of Smith-Dorrien, with plumed hat, astride his charger and surrounded by his headquarters staff, saluting the passing machines, has come to symbolize the end of an era and (for those blessed with hindsight) the triumph of the airplane over the horse.[26]

No. 3 Squadron worked closely with the CFS at Upavon, their nearest neighbor. Indeed, CFS provided some of the aircraft and pilots for Smith-Dorrien's review. This would prove an important relationship in Brooke-Popham's career since the chief instructor at CFS was Major Hugh "Boom" Trenchard, who became the deputy commandant from August 1913. Trenchard, an officer of the Scots Fusiliers, had learned to fly in July 1912 at the encouragement of Eustace Loraine, whom he had known in West Africa.[27] Trenchard and Brooke-Popham worked closely together over the next twenty years. The two of them, together with Philip Game, can claim to have laid the foundations for the RAF. "Boom rightly goes down in history as the great pioneer of our Service. Philip Game and yourself, it seems to me, had a very great share in bringing about what happened but not a sufficient share in the glory—not that you wanted that."[28]

Brooke-Popham's promotion to brevet major (substantive) was confirmed in June 1913.[29] During the same month the squadron detached a flight to Lydd, under the command of Captain (later Air Marshal Sir) John "Josh" Higgins, to work with heavy artillery. This subsequently became the nucleus of No. 5 Squadron, formed at Farnborough in July 1913. The RFC would successfully use this "divide and grow" technique to create additional squadrons until mid-1916, when the rate of expansion (and hence the level of dilution) became too much for the operational squadrons to absorb. As a result, Brooke-Popham and Burke, as the RFC's first squadron commanders, had a disproportionate impact on the ethos and culture of the RFC and, in due course, the RAF. The squadron had by now resumed the trials it had initiated the previous summer, working with artillery units on Salisbury Plain as well conducting armament experiments, including bomb dropping.[30] The first night flights by the RFC also took place at this time. In the autumn, Lieutenant Philip "Erb" Herbert, who had joined the squadron in the summer, conducted experiments at Hythe to select the most suitable type of machine gun for fitting to aircraft. It was not long since Brooke-Popham had become the first member of the RFC to fire a weapon from an aircraft. At that time, there was no understanding as to whether this was feasible (because of the recoil) or whether a weapon could be aimed accurately: "I can remember going out one morning in a Henri Farman with Major Higgins to try what the effect would be of firing a rifle from an aeroplane in the air. In fear and trembling I pulled the trigger, with Major Higgins all alert in case the machine got out of control. Our relief was great when we found no untoward result."[31]

The increasing importance of military aviation was reflected in organizational changes within the War Office. It had become clear that the specialist needs of the RFC could not be met by the existing arrangements that allocated responsibility for the supply, organization, and training functions to different departments—in line with previous practice. The Military Aeronautics Directorate was accordingly created in September 1913 to handle selection, training, supply, and administration aspects of the new corps.[32] David Henderson, previously director Military Training, was appointed director of Military Aeronautics (DMA) with a dedicated staff, including Captain Edward Ellington, who had been appointed to the Aviation Branch in October 1912, and the recently arrived Captain Sefton Brancker—both Staff College graduates and qualified pilots.[33] According to Charlton, the arrival of staff-qualified officers generated a degree of resentment among the young RFC officers who had been the pioneers of aviation.[34] If this was the case, it was the price paid for transforming an experimental battalion into a warfighting corps. The 1913 army maneuvers took place in Buckinghamshire and Northamptonshire in September. The two Army commanders were Major-General Douglas Haig and Major-General Henry Rawlinson. No. 3 Squadron was attached to the southern army with a heterogeneous collection of aircraft. Brancker, who was responsible for press liaison, recorded that the maneuvers were an unqualified success for the RFC and "gave Seely the power to demand and obtain a million pounds for military aviation in the financial year 1914–15."[35] A number of practical lessons emerged, including the ability to observe activity from what was considered a great height (more than six thousand feet) and the importance of adequate ground transport.[36] The squadron returned to camp at Netheravon after the maneuvers, waiting in some discomfort until the promised barracks became available in November.

Brooke-Popham provided strong and credible leadership at a critical period in the development of the Air Battalion and RFC. He also brought a

powerful intellect and exceptional writing skills. The most important document to emerge during these formative years was the RFC *Training Manual*,
the initiative of Colonel Frederick Sykes, commanding the Military Wing.[37]
Part I, produced by CFS, covered airmanship, principles of flight, and so
forth. Part II, also known as the *War Manual*, was to contain instructions for
the Military Wing on the administration, organization, and strategical and
tactical employment of military aviation, as well as explaining its practices
and principles.[38] Although the primary aim of the *War Manual* was to guide
and instruct members of the RFC, it was also intended to inform the rest of
the Army about the employment of airplanes in wartime. It was, in effect,
the first attempt to articulate the RFC's doctrine—even if the term was not
yet in common use.[39] Work started immediately, before the War Office had
given formal approval, and a draft version was circulated for comment in
April 1913.[40] Although Sykes was the sponsor and prime mover, the writing of the manual was Brooke-Popham's responsibility, with Brancker (on
behalf of the War Office) acting as the editor.[41] When the final daft was
forwarded to the RFC's adjutant for printing, Brooke-Popham added a short
note in his own hand: "[P]lease don't lose it, it represents the expenditure of
numerous hours of toil, much sweat and many tears."[42] As the author of the
War Manual, Brooke-Popham was the first writer to offer a coherent strategy
for the employment of military airplanes. Subsequent editions (including the
provisional version issued by the War Office in 1915) provided the basis for
RFC operations throughout World War I.[43] Brooke-Popham's foresight and
imagination, together with his ability to write in clear and accessible English,
meant that he played a leading role in both creating and communicating
British airpower doctrine.[44]

At the beginning of 1914, No. 3 Squadron was re-equipped with improved
Blériot single-seat and two-seat monoplanes. Brooke-Popham flew the first
example on 16 January. The 80 hp Blériot offered a much better performance than the machines he had previously flown. He was able to reach an
altitude of more than seven thousand feet on several occasions (and kept the
barostat paper to confirm the achievement). This was still well below the
existing world height record (already more than 20,000 feet), but a major
achievement for a military airplane. The rapidly improving performance of
the RFC's aircraft offered new possibilities—such as the carriage of weapons
and wireless equipment—but it did not necessarily make flying any safer. In
March 1914, there were three accidents involving pilots of No. 3 Squadron

that claimed a total of four lives. The first occurred on 10 March when Captain C. P. Downer crashed after structural failure in the air. He was killed instantly. The cause was put down to pilot error. A further crash occurred the following day, when Captain W. R. Allen and Lieutenant J. E. G. Burroughs were flying at Netheravon. Having completed a circuit of the airfield, the entire rudder fell from the machine, which then spun into the ground—killing both occupants. An investigation concluded that the structural failure had been caused by previous damage and, possibly, an unauthorized repair. A third accident happened on 19 March when Lieutenant H. F. Treeby crashed on landing at Upavon. Once again, pilot error was suggested as the cause. These deaths were a brutal reminder of the dangers faced by military aviators and underscored the importance of training and the adoption of rigorous maintenance standards. They also highlighted the importance of the *Training Manual* in developing aviation professionalism.

From early 1914, the squadron started to conduct experiments in aerial photography. Progress was limited by the need to purchase the cameras privately, although the War Office did furnish the photographic paper and plates. Some of this work was far in advance of anything achieved later, including developing negatives in the air. On the other hand, it was not until 1915 that the RFC created an effective system for taking, interpreting, and distributing photographs.[45] There were no Army maneuvers planned for 1914. Instead, the RFC's five airplane squadrons, together with the Headquarters Flight, Repair Park, and a detachment of the Kite Section, were gathered together at Netheravon on 30 May 1914 for a "Concentration Camp" comprising a mixture of exercises, training, lectures, and field trials.[46] No. 3 Squadron was an active participant in what proved to be the last opportunity to prepare for the forthcoming war. Brooke-Popham flew and lectured, including a talk on reconnaissance, "the class of work in which aeroplanes will be principally engaged in actual warfare."[47]

On 30 June 1914, while still at Netheravon, Brooke-Popham had a lucky escape when the engine failed in his Blériot after less than forty minutes' flying during a cross-country race after a balloon. He made a forced landing in a field at Driffield (Gloucestershire), but crashed into the boundary wall. The aircraft was badly damaged and recovered by road, only to be struck off charge as beyond repair. Unfortunately, four other members of the squadron landed nearby to see if anyone was hurt and two of them also crashed. "The net result was that my squadron in one day was suddenly reduced to about half its effective strength as one or two other accidents had happened just about at the same time."⁴⁸ The incident vividly demonstrated the high wastage that accompanied routine flying and the importance of reserves if operations were to be sustained. It was a lesson that Brooke-Popham would not forget in planning the logistic support arrangements for the RFC on the Western Front. Joubert de la Ferté recalled the briefing that Brooke-Popham gave to his officers:

> It was at this Camp that we were first told officially, but secretly, of the imminence of war with Germany. I shall never forget the solemn meeting of No. 3 Sqn when our Squadron Commander, Major R. Brooke-Popham, told us what was expected. Up till then it is unlikely any but the more seriously minded of us young ones, even after the Agadir scare in 1911, had thought very much about war with Germany, but here we were faced with it in the near future and we knew that although we had plenty of energy and confidence, our equipment was woefully bad.⁴⁹

During the Concentration Camp Brooke-Popham was warned that, if mobilization were declared, he would be attached to Headquarters (HQ) RFC when it deployed in support of the British Expeditionary Force (BEF). Having commanded No. 3 Squadron for more than two years, this was neither unexpected nor exceptional, but it brought an end to his active flying and, other than a short period in 1915, his time as an operational commander.

4

THE WESTERN FRONT
1914–1915

On 28 June 1914, the Archduke Franz Ferdinand and his wife, the Duchess of Hohenberg, were assassinated in Sarajevo by a Bosnian-Serb nationalist. Austria-Hungary held Serbia responsible and as relations between the two countries worsened, so the great powers were drawn into the crisis. Threats were made, alliances dusted off, ultimatums issued, and armies mobilized. Britain's position was uncertain, but the deteriorating international situation caused the War Office to prepare quietly for the imminent deployment of the BEF. On Monday 27 July 1914, Brooke-Popham was instructed to hand over command of No. 3 Squadron to John "Jack" Salmond and assume responsibility for the RFC's training and mobilization at Farnborough. The next eight days were a mixture of anxiety and frustration. The popular view among the young officers of the RFC was that the government was dragging its heels: "Much ill feeling that no mobilization has been ordered. Fear that government intends to play the dirty on France or to creep out of the trouble. Talk of flying aeroplanes over and joining French army and, at any rate, of resigning commissions after the trouble is over."[1]

Emotions were running high with Barrington-Kennett announcing, "How can anyone with any self-respect ever vote for a Liberal again?" At this distance, and with full knowledge of what was to come, it may seem strange that there was rejoicing when war was declared on 4 August 1914 and the RFC was formally ordered to mobilize. "War brought with it a wave of exhilaration and relief; our honour was saved, and we were embarked on the great adventure about which we had dreamt so long."[2] With mobilization declared, Brooke-Popham was appointed deputy assistant adjutant and quartermaster general (DAA & QMG) with responsibility for the RFC's logistic and personnel matters.[3] This reflected his status as one of a handful of Staff College–trained officers with aviation experience. Of the 126 officers of the RFC (including Special Reserve) on the outbreak of war, just ten were staff qualified (Camberley or Quetta).[4] The post was well suited to Brooke-Popham's energy, intellect, and eye for detail. According to Philip Game, who worked closely with "Brookham" for nearly two years, he was "a scientist by nature and choice."[5] If Brooke-Popham regretted not being able to take the squadron he had created to war, he had little time to indulge in such feelings as he was kept busy resolving a myriad of supply and administrative questions. There was considerable uncertainty about the arrangements for the RFC squadrons being deployed with the BEF. It had been thought that Sykes would retain command, but Henderson decided that this role should fall to him, with Sykes and Brooke-Popham directing operations from Whitehall. In the end, it was agreed that both should accompany the RFC to France, with Sykes as Henderson's chief of staff (GSO1) and Brooke-Popham as DAA & QMG. Brancker was to remain in London, and Trenchard to take over the residual elements of the Military Wing at Farnborough. The uncertainty and constant changes created some lingering ill-feeling on Trenchard's part that would ultimately undermine his relationship with Sykes.[6]

The night that the RFC was mobilized there was a Zeppelin scare and Brooke-Popham, together with Captain John Becke, slept by their aircraft—ready to intercept any aerial intruders. In the absence of armament, it was not clear what the two airmen could have achieved—unless they had used their entire machine as a weapon. "Wonder whether I really should have charged it, as I intended to. Would have been worth a squadron of aeroplanes or a brigade or any other arm if I had."[7] Pip Playfair says that this was entirely Brooke-Popham's idea and revealed "the fiery spirit beneath his gentle and dreamy exterior."[8] No Zeppelins were reported and the next day, the first full day of mobilization, went smoothly, although securing the motor vehicles assigned to the RFC under the War Office subsidy scheme proved more difficult than expected. On 7 August, the RFC was warned to be ready to move five days later. Brooke-Popham used the time to put his affairs in order, writing to Polly about the financial arrangements for their mother, the packing of his personal possessions remaining at Netheravon, the fate of his horses (likely to be purchased for government service), the employment of his groom (Percy Threadkell), and the disposal of his motor car. Percy Threadkell soon joined Brooke-Popham in France as his personal batman.[9] By now some of the initial excitement was beginning to wear off and he found the endless questions of No. 4 Squadron rather trying, as he did the continued false alarms: "Frightful rumours about Germans poisoning the water supply at North Camp. Fire alarm about 10.30 p.m., turned out to be a bonfire at Fleet Pond. If people's nerves are as bad as this already, we shan't get much sleep on service. Spent the night under Sopwith waiting for Zeppelins."[10]

There is no reference in Brooke-Popham's personal letters or his war journal to the incident described in Trenchard's biography—the confidential box left by Sykes for Trenchard at Farnborough supposedly holding detailed orders but found only to contain shoes.[11] Whatever exactly happened, the story highlights the incipient antagonism between Sykes and Trenchard.[12] Orders and counterorders characterized the next few days but, on the early morning of 12 August, HQ RFC finally left by train for Southampton, where they embarked on the London & South Western Railway Company's SS *Laura*, arriving at Boulogne at 6 p.m. that day—much to Brooke-Popham's relief as he had been seasick throughout the voyage.[13] The RFC was warmly welcomed by the French, as was the entire BEF. The manager of the buffet at the Gare Maritime happily fed everyone (officers and men) but refused payment.[14] The bulk of the headquarters went to Amiens by train but Brooke-Popham and Barrington-Kennett travelled separately by motorcar, setting out landing marks and arranging for stores. When they got to Amiens they found that most of the RFC's aircraft had already arrived.

The next week was a flurry of activity as Brooke-Popham struggled to secure rations and petrol. He was soon ordered up to Maubeuge, where the 1st and 2nd Corps were concentrating, staying at Le Cateau on the night of 15 August in company with Captain Claude Buchanan (Signals) and Lieutenant Maurice Baring (Interpreter).[15] Early the next morning, they marked out landing grounds at Maubeuge and arranged for billets, shortly before the first aircraft arrived—much to the surprise of the French. "Brooke-Popham worked like a slave. He did most of the work himself."[16] The RFC suffered its first casualties in France during the flight to Maubeuge when Lieutenant E. W. C. Perry, and his mechanic, H. E. Parfitt, from Brooke-Popham's old squadron, were killed at Amiens when their machine crashed and caught fire.[17] By 17 August, all the RFC's aircraft had reached Maubeuge, but the petrol situation was becoming serious and Brooke-Popham was forced to stop all issues other than urgent requirements. With Henderson's support, he arranged for supplies to be sent to the railheads of both corps. This was wasteful, as they never drew on more than one of them, but as the movements of the RFC were so uncertain it was the only effective solution. The RFC was now actively involved in providing strategic reconnaissance for General Headquarters (GHQ). On 22 August, the RFC carried out ten separate reconnaissance flights, bringing back valuable information, although Sergeant Jillings was wounded and Lionel Charlton and Vivian Wadham were forced to land briefly near German troops and were almost captured before flying off.[18] A lack of suitable maps was beginning to hinder operations (those previously provided covered only Belgium), so Brooke-Popham was sent to Paris to purchase anything he could find.[19]

If Brooke-Popham kept a diary during his years in France it has not survived, but he did keep several notebooks during his first few months, including carbon copies of official correspondence (Army Book 152). The earliest entry, dated 8 August 1914, instructs the Wireless Detachment (a flight of No. 4 Squadron) to adopt predetermined wireless procedures. Subsequent orders detail the drawing down of rations, the deployment of motorcycle orderlies, postal instructions ("picture postcards bearing the name of any place will not be passed by the censor"), and the allocation of duties. The responsibilities that fell to Brooke-Popham were broad and complex, ranging from the visit of a French engine specialist to the handling of aircraft and lorry spares. The shortage of petrol features prominently, as does, with increasing urgency, the need for more bombs and grenades. Other tasks included demands for additional vehicles, the collection of new aircraft from French manufacturers, and the creation of a forward repair base. The last order is dated 11 September 1914 and instructs the RFC detachment at Étampes to send aircraft and transport destined for the front to Coulommiers, rather than Melun as previously directed. The standard working day for the squadrons and HQ RFC was more than sixteen hours (from 5:00 a.m. to 9:15 p.m.), but it could be even longer, particularly when the German advance forced the BEF to retire and the optimism of early August turned to uncertainty: "It was during this retreat that I first appreciated what a really tired man looks like; it was quite marvellous how the infantry were able to stick it out as they did. It was hot and dusty and they were short of food and water and had had no sleep for days. I shall always remember the awful ashen look on some of their faces."[20]

During the next few months Brooke-Popham laid the foundations for the RFC's logistic organization in France while coping with unprecedented rates of consumption. Within three days of landing in France there had been nineteen crashes, leaving one pilot to wonder: "If we have all these accidents now what will it be like when we go into action?"[21] Jack Salmond was fulsome about the "miracles" Brooke-Popham performed in ensuring the retreating squadrons were never short of spares or ammunition.[22] The difficulties of maintaining the RFC's aircraft serviceable during this period of constant movement, when aircraft and lorries became separated for days at a time, cannot be exaggerated.[23] In recognition, Brooke-Popham was awarded the Croix d'Officier of the French Legion d'Honneur. Although he was working behind the lines, the impact of the war was only too visible:

> The French were afraid of the Germans and that is why they hated them far more than we ever did, at least it is one of the reasons, and it is also at the bottom of their ill treatment of German prisoners. I remember so well one day during September 1914 on the Aisne bringing back some wounded men, British and Germans, in my car to a casualty clearing station. One German had both legs shattered and he was so brave. I remember now the look of gratitude he gave me when I put a coat or something under his head. And then when we were taking them out at the clearing station there were a lot of French women and old men round and when they saw my German they howled at him and cried "*Coupez la gorge.*" ["Cut his throat."] I was furious and cursed them roundly in my worst French.[24]

Such scenes were not exceptional (Baring witnessed similar events),[25] but they were unsettling and left their mark: "I pondered over the strange combination of circumstances that could lead to a lad from an Oxfordshire village to be lying by the side of a youth from Pomerania, both terribly wounded, and being taken in a RFC car over a road in Northern France. What is wrong with the world, I thought then, that this can happen? I haven't found a complete answer to that question yet."[26]

By November, the front had stabilized, with HQ RFC based at St-Omer, close to GHQ, where there was a large airfield with space for expansion. The headquarters was based in a small chateau, located between the airfield and the town. Once the fighting had settled down, and it was realized that the war was not going to end quickly, the lack of trained staff officers began to cause concerns. At the RFC's formation, all its officers were required to possess an airplane certificate. As a result, most officers were quite junior, although there were notable exceptions (such as Henderson and Trenchard). Over time, this imbalance would have been resolved, but at the beginning of the war there were simply too few individuals senior enough to have the skills and experience needed to support a highly technical organization embarked on a rapid expansion program. These difficulties were exacerbated by the decision of several very capable individuals (including Barrington-Kennett, Burke, and Herbert Musgrave) to return to their "parent" regiments. There was a widespread view (inside and outside the RFC) that the real war was to be found in the trenches. Henderson was now seriously concerned by the lack of senior RFC officers, in both France and Whitehall. Brancker felt that the RFC was being left behind in the struggle for resources and that he did not have the necessary authority to reverse the position. In July 1915 he wrote to Henderson, "We must wake up in the senior officer line or get left." However, there was no getting around the problem that there were simply not enough individuals with the skills and experience to fill all the RFC's leadership roles.[27] The headquarters had already been bolstered by recruiting officers from other parts of the army, such as Richard Pope-Hennessy, who joined as GSO3 on 19 March 1915 (a move facilitated by Brooke-Popham at Una Pope-Hennessy's instigation).[28] Pope-Hennessy quickly settled down and found Sykes a congenial boss, although "he is very much disliked and astonishingly young to be a full colonel, but he is quick and intelligent."[29] Pope-Hennessy's initial duties ranged from plotting the position of German airfields and batteries to assisting Sykes with revisions to the *War Manual*.[30]

During its first year on the Western Front the RFC worked hard to develop a range of offensive capabilities, including aerial photography, bombing, and artillery cooperation. Although much was learned from the French Air Service, the prewar experiments conducted by No. 3 Squadron provided the foundation for many of these developments.[31] Rapidly improving capabilities, and the consequent demand for more aircraft to support the BEF, saw the number of RFC squadrons on the Western Front steadily increase, with consequent organizational changes. In November 1914, the frontline squadrons were grouped into "wings," to improve cooperation with the BEF's individual corps. Trenchard (brought from Farnborough) and Burke were appointed to command the first two wings. When Third Wing was formed in March 1915, Brooke-Popham was given command in the temporary rank of lieutenant-colonel.[32] Although there is no doubt that this was a well-deserved promotion, Brancker intimates that Brooke-Popham's move was part of a wider effort to grow a cadre of senior RFC officers.[33] Following his departure, Major Francis Festing assumed the role of DAA & QMG. According to Brooke-Popham, Festing was "loyal and straight with single-minded devotion to his job.... I couldn't have asked for a better man to work with. Trenchard had full confidence in him."[34]

Third Wing was based at St-Omer and comprised two squadrons with a mixture of aircraft types. Their role was to provide strategic reconnaissance and special missions on behalf of GHQ. Shortly after Brooke-Popham's arrival all three RFC wings were engaged in the battles of Neuve Chapelle and Aubers Ridge that opened on 10 March 1915. Brooke-Popham's time in command proved disappointingly short as he returned to HQ RFC less than nine weeks later to replace Sykes as GSO1. Sykes' relationship with Henderson had deteriorated badly since the turn of the year. This was partly Henderson's fault, as he had insisted on remaining as DMA while commanding in France.[35] The position was patently unsustainable and had undoubtedly impeded the expansion of the RFC. Brancker, left to manage the department in Henderson's absence, lacked the staff or authority to meet the RFC's demands.[36] Matters were not helped by Henderson's brief illness (Sykes deputized in his absence) and an abortive decision to send him to command the First Division (Sykes' hand was suspected). Unfortunately, Sykes had made it only too obvious that the best solution was for him to take command of the RFC and Henderson to return to London. Sykes' sudden return to England at the end of April, to study air operations at Gallipoli, removed a disruptive figure, but it meant that a replacement chief of staff had to be found quickly. Brooke-Popham was recalled to HQ RFC on a temporary basis, but this became a permanent appointment on 26 May 1915 when Josh Higgins took over Third Wing and Brooke-Popham was promoted to full colonel, as GSO1 HQ RFC.

Although he had little time with Third Wing, Brooke-Popham was regarded as "no mean commanding officer."[37] Indeed, he was awarded the Distinguished Service Order (DSO) on 23 June 1915 for his leadership, as well as being mentioned in dispatches.[38] Trenchard's biographer suggests that Henderson selected Brooke-Popham at the former's instigation. Trenchard may well have recommended Brooke-Popham, but Henderson needed little prompting, having observed Brooke-Popham at close hand during the RFC's difficult first months in France. For his part, Brooke-Popham had a great admiration for Henderson, whom he credited as being the first senior Army officer to realize the value of the air in war and a great example of loyalty and chivalry.[39] He was also impressed by Henderson's operational innovations, such as concentrating aircraft rather than dispersing them to lower formations and grouping fighter aircraft into offensive squadrons, rather than allocating them to individual squadrons for self-defense (as Trenchard had wanted).[40] Henderson and Brooke-Popham got on well together, which made for a harmonious headquarters. According to Henderson's widow, the two had similar characters and always saw the best in everyone they met, however "mean or small-minded."[41] Sykes' departure had not diminished the need to strengthen the RFC's influence in the War Office. The only realistic solution was for Henderson to reassume direct oversight of the Military Aeronautics Directorate and represent the RFC on the Air Council. Trenchard, as the most senior officer in the RFC after Henderson, was the logical choice as his successor,[42] a decision undoubtedly facilitated by the close relationship that Trenchard had established at First Wing with Douglas Haig, commanding the First Army. "Trenchard worked well with Haig and Haig worked well with Trenchard."[43] On 19 August 1915, Henderson returned to London. Three days later, Trenchard was appointed to command the RFC.

5

WORKING FOR TRENCHARD
1915–1918

Brooke-Popham took a short period of leave in late September (nominally for a tour of RFC training stations) to attend his mother's funeral. She had died on 17 September 1915, at Sutton-on-Sea, Lincolnshire. Her death, after more than twenty-five years in a succession of nursing homes, may have been cause for relief rather than distress. On Brooke-Popham's return to St-Omer, he found Trenchard already making his mark. The latter's personality has been described as tyrannical and unconventional—even by his official biographer.[1] On the positive side, Trenchard's proactive and energetic approach, demonstrated by regular visits to squadrons, wings, and depots, brought a focus and coherence to RFC operations during a period of rapid expansion. It is an exaggeration to claim that the headquarters' staff "adapted themselves without demur to Trenchard's autocratic yet flexible methods."[2] Pope-Hennessy, for one, did not enjoy the experience, complaining that Trenchard created "a horrible atmosphere around him and making both work and social relations quite intolerable to most of his staff."[3] Brooke-Popham did not share his friend's antipathy, which was largely owed to differing personalities, and enjoyed a successful working relationship with Trenchard that endured for nearly forty years.[4] Trenchard gave his subordinates considerable leeway—when he was confident about their judgment. He encouraged them to communicate directly with their counterparts through personal and demi-official letters, alongside the formal system of correspondence. It was a technique that he used later as chief of the Air Staff (CAS) and one that Brooke-Popham would emulate in Singapore. Trenchard believed that this was a more effective way of progressing the war, but it relied on an implicit trust between commander and subordinate. Hugh Dowding's failure to observe this protocol greatly annoyed him.[5] Their subsequent falling out has been credited to an argument over the fitting of incorrect propellers, but the real reason was that Trenchard did not see Dowding as a team player, rather as someone who preferred to write caustic letters and create difficulties.[6] Despite these misgivings, Trenchard still agreed to accept Dowding as a wing commander in France, only to send him home after six months for being "too much of a 'dismal Jimmy.'"[7]

Brooke-Popham remained as GSO1 for a little under a year. He proved to be a thoroughly competent and efficient chief of staff, gaining both Henderson's and Trenchard's trust. "Brooke-Popham is doing splendidly here."[8] He was in constant correspondence with the War Office, chivvying the staffs on the need for new squadrons, the replacement of pilots and machines, and the progression of urgent supplies. He also found time to analyze the operational lessons from the air fighting of the previous year—for inclusion in the revised *Training Manual*.[9] With Brooke-Popham safely running the headquarters, Trenchard could spend more time touring the front line and in meetings with senior British and French military commanders.[10] For his part, Trenchard was extremely complimentary about the "wonderful staff" he had inherited from David Henderson.[11] At the time there was some uncertainty about the outcome, as Brooke-Popham recalled. "When he took over from David Henderson in 1915, he and I were potential, if not actual, enemies and he told me later on that he did not expect to get on with me and that he'd have to get me posted somewhere else. However, he felt that would be unfair without giving me a chance and as you know I worked with him till he went to the Air Ministry in 1918 and we've remained firm friends ever since."[12]

The importance of Trenchard's close relationship with Douglas Haig became clear when the latter replaced Field Marshal Sir John French as GOC BEF on 10 December 1915. The RFC featured heavily in Haig's proposals for a major offensive in 1916. To support these plans, Trenchard argued for an urgent program to increase the size of the front line. This saw the strength of the RFC on the Western Front rise from four squadrons and 860 personnel in November 1914 to twenty-three squadrons and 6,506 personnel by March 1916.[13] Although the BEF had grown substantially through 1915, the RFC had not matched this growth, even though the demands for air support had increased substantially. Brooke-Popham was among the first to identify the need for more squadrons in France. In August 1915, he had highlighted the disparity between the size of the BEF and the RFC, arguing that the Army's needs could not be met without air superiority. "If the enemy brings troops over from the Eastern front and resumes his offensive, he will doubtless make a determined effort to prevent our discovering his movements. Then will commence the real struggle for air supremacy where numbers will be one of the essentials for success."[14]

With the expansion of the RFC under way, Trenchard determined to reorganize the squadrons on a decentralized basis. These changes came into effect in January 1916. Each army was to have a brigade comprising two wings (for corps and army duties respectively), an aircraft park (for logistic support), and a kite balloon squadron.[15] Consequent on these changes, it became necessary to reorganize and upgrade the headquarters staff. Trenchard was promoted to major-general and appointed GOC RFC on 24 March 1916. At the same time, two new one-star appointments were created to manage the greater volume of staff work that accompanied the increase in flying operations. The continuing shortage of experienced staff officers meant that Trenchard was forced to look outside the RFC to fill some of these posts. While operational matters might be managed effectively by a competent officer without aviation experience, the same could not be said for technical matters. Brigadier-General (later Air Vice-Marshal Sir) Philip Game from the Forty-Fifth Division was appointed as chief of staff in place of Brooke-Popham, who returned to his previous duties, but this time as deputy adjutant and quartermaster general (DA & QMG), with the temporary rank of brigadier-general.[16]

Game, who was not happy at being ordered to join the RFC, was quite depressed at being so far out of his element: "It is a very big organisation and is growing daily but the whole thing is so intimately bound up with all sorts of technical matters of which I have no more knowledge of than a babe unborn and I don't see how one can ever do the General Staff bit of it with any success without a great deal of technical knowledge which I have neither the will nor the power to imbibe."[17] The description of the challenges faced by the chief of staff provides some indication of what Brooke-Popham had achieved over the previous year; however, the latter's real strength lay in managing both the scale and detail of the myriad activities needed to sustain air operations on the Western Front.[18] The rapid advancement available to a handful of officers in the RFC gave rise to criticism, particularly within the regular army where military aviation was regarded as an alien institution. At age thirty-seven, Brooke-Popham was one of the youngest brigadiers in the BEF. Even his friend

Pope-Hennessy raged. "I must say it is a comfort to be on a real fighting staff at last and well away from that sham Flying Corps staff. Williams said what damned rot it was having these ridiculous Flying Corps generals commanding two men and a boy, and they themselves children in war."[19] Not everyone prospered at HQ RFC. Pope-Hennessy, who arrived as a willing volunteer, came to abhor the environment, whereas Game, who arrived under protest, eventually enjoyed the challenges it offered. Neither officer was aviation-experienced and both were good friends with Brooke-Popham, during and after the war. The disparity in their experience can only be attributed to Trenchard, who was not an easy person to work for. "He [Pope-Hennessy] would have done very well under David Henderson, but was useless with Trenchard and was soon posted to III Wing HQ on Higgins' staff where he did very well."[20] Brooke-Popham went on to explain that "Trenchard often found it difficult to explain to others why he acted or thought as he did; he just knew he was right but had not memorised how he got there. So, like [Field Marshal Herbert Lord] Kitchener, he sometimes passed for being a stupid man because he couldn't explain his reasons. Added, to this, Trenchard usually found difficulty in choosing the right words or phrases in speech or writing."[21]

Trenchard, Game, and Brooke-Popham made a formidable team, the "Bow and Arrow" brigade,[22] but it took time for their relationship to settle down. Shortly after the Somme offensive had ended, Brancker proposed that Game (and then Brooke-Popham) be moved, but Trenchard strongly resisted the idea.[23] He felt that Game's departure would be disastrous for the RFC, although Game had expressed privately his ambition to return to the Army (this may even have triggered Brancker's suggestion).[24] Part of the problem was Trenchard's behavior. Game found him impulsive and impatient, with occasional depressive phases.[25] Trenchard was equally vehement about retaining Brooke-Popham, who not only undertook "Q" (quartermaster general) work, but also provided technical advice on airplanes and engines, including developing specifications for new machines.[26] Brooke-Popham had an eye for detail and an impressive knowledge of engineering and supply—his deep knowledge could sometimes disconcert junior officers.[27] The efficient functioning of the headquarters was not simply about professional competence, however. The small size of the staff meant that personality and temperament were equally important. There was literally no room for privacy or quiet routine. For most of 1916, the headquarters comprised just seven officers (including Trenchard, but excluding attached officers).[28] Their accommodation was cramped and the activity hectic. "A stuffy office, full of clerks and candles and a deafening noise of typewriters. A constant stream of pilots arriving in the evening in burberries with maps talking over reconnaissances; a perpetual stream of guests and people sleeping on the floor."[29] Trenchard valued staff who knew everybody and got on with everybody. Game and Brooke-Popham showed themselves skilled in this respect, as well as capable, robust, and intuitive officers. As a result, both remained with the headquarters—until well after Trenchard had left for London to lead the newly created RAF.

The RFC was now engaged in a major expansion program, as part of the preparations for the Battle of the Somme, involving "an enormous amount of re-arrangements of the Air Force and demands made on the authorities at home were for more machines and improvements for spotters for the Royal Artillery counter-battery work, low flying, dive bombing and fighting in the air."[30] Brooke-Popham was central to these efforts, juggling competing demands while building up the infrastructure needed to support a rapidly growing front line. An efficient and hardworking administrator, he was not necessarily the tidiest of staff officers. Baring refers to Brooke-Popham's desk as "littered with papers."[31] In June 1916, the scientist Henry Tizard (later to be closely involved in the development of radar) visited HQ RFC to discuss bombing accuracy.[32] His interview with Trenchard started off badly as he could not immediately produce his credentials (having passed them earlier to Brooke-Popham). The missing documents were eventually found, but only after Tizard suggested that, as Brooke-Popham's table was very untidy, someone might be sent to look through his papers. Despite this unfortunate beginning, Brooke-Popham and Tizard struck up a strong friendship that proved critical in the development of the UK air defense system during the 1930s.[33]

In March 1916, Trenchard relocated his headquarters from St-Omer to St-Andre, where he was closer to GHQ at Montreuil and the planned area of operations.[34] The RFC now occupied "a huge and imposing chateau with walled grounds set amongst avenues and belts of tall trees. On one side is a spacious stable yard surrounded by buildings that could hold perhaps a hundred horses. The whole place has fallen into disrepair and there is an atmosphere of decayed prosperity."[35] Three months later, on 27 June, Trenchard and his immediate staff moved to a small advanced headquarters at Fienvillers, to be as close as possible to the squadrons involved in the offensive. The bulk of the headquarters, including Brooke-Popham and the logistic staff, remained behind.[36] The Somme offensive opened on 1 July and continued until 17 November 1916. Although the RFC's contribution was judged a success, very little progress was made on the ground and certainly not the breakthrough that Haig had anticipated. Casualties were extremely high, although the Germans suffered almost as badly. Throughout the fighting, Brooke-Popham could bring new squadrons into the line while maintaining the strength of existing units.[37] The RFC enjoyed air superiority for much of the battle, but the high operational tempo meant that 370 aircraft and 500 aircrew were lost in combat. Even so, a steady supply of new and repaired machines meant that at the end of the year the front line was stronger by nineteen squadrons and some four hundred machines compared to twelve months earlier.[38] Increasing rates of aircraft production facilitated this outcome, but it was the creation of a network of repair depots and forward supply parks that made the critical difference, allowing the RFC to sustain the constant offensive demanded by Trenchard. It was a point that Brooke-Popham never lost sight of. "I was General Trenchard's staff officer from the day he took command and I am able to say absolutely definitely that General Trenchard's one idea was offence, offence, offence the whole time."[39] It was a strategy based on "organisation and discipline" and the creation of a firm foundation that was "unmoved by temporary setbacks or by drastic reduction, able to face with calmness an indef-inite expansion."[40]

In the new year, the RFC faced a rejuvenated German air service that had reorganized and reequipped because of their experiences on the Somme. The RFC had also started their own reequipment program, but for several months had to fight an enemy flying much superior aircraft. As a result, the RFC suffered heavily during the Battle of Arras (9 April–16 May 1917). "Bloody April" saw the RFC lose 245 aircraft and 319 aircrew in a single month. Even so, Brooke-Popham could make good the wastage, while replacing almost every type of British aircraft employed on the Western Front. The heavy losses in the air were difficult to bear, but there was also a personal tragedy in the death of his great friend Charles Burke on the opening day of the battle—one of 150,000 ground casualties suffered by the BEF. Brooke-Popham retained only a handful of letters from World War I but two of them were from Burke (the last dated three weeks before his death) and one from his widow Beatrice. Burke had expressed his delight at the success of his RFC friends and colleagues, although was sorry to see the daily losses: "I think I have now had the worst the weather can do when combined with seven feet of mud and no cover: and during the fighting I think I touched bottom as regards casualties. The Hun aeroplanes provided me with a considerably added interest, especially when they dived at us with their machine gun going—It would seem a poor end if I had been knocked out by a Hun aeroplane while in a shell hole."[41]

By the opening of the Third Battle of Ypres, on 31 July 1917, the RFC had further grown in strength, to a total of fifty-one squadrons and nearly nine hundred aircraft, more than twice its size at the battle of the Somme. This time, however, the RFC would have to fight for air superiority. The RFC offered considerable support to the ground offensive, particularly in artillery cooperation, but the poor weather and dogged German resistance resulted in only a modest advance and very high casualties. When the fighting ground to a halt in November, the RFC had lost more than seven hundred aircraft and one thousand aircrew in combat, considerably more than it had over the Somme. However, the efficiency of the logistic system ensured that the frontline squadrons were never short of machines or replacement aircrew. The success of the RFC in solving the operational, administrative, and logistic problems inherent in turning military aviation into operational capability encouraged Boney Fuller, his regimental colleague and now a colonel in the Tank Corps, to contact Brooke-Popham about placing it under the RFC. "He maintained that no-one at the Head of the Armies had any mechanical turn of mind, could not, or would not, understand the special problems of a mechanized force and that the army system of spare parts for tanks was hopelessly out of date. I told him that the RFC had their hands and brains fully worked over their own problems and couldn't take on anything else; all we did was to lend Tank HQ one or two of our best equipment officers."[42]

During 1917, it was increasingly clear that the supply and administrative functions at HQ RFC were too much for a single individual to manage. From October 1917, the role of DA & QMG was split, with Brooke-Popham focusing on logistic issues—as deputy quartermaster general—and his erstwhile deputy, Francis Festing, promoted to brigadier-general with responsibility for personnel matters—as deputy adjutant general.[43] At the same time, the aircraft repair sections of the two main depots at Candas and St-Omer were expanded into separate airplane supply depots, responsible for the issue, storage, repair, and salvage of aircraft—leaving the main depots to concentrate on the storage and issue of aeronautical spares. As we have seen, Brooke-Popham's ability to work with Trenchard was as much about knowing the latter's mind as about professional competence. During the Ypres fighting, Brancker (with whom Trenchard maintained a close and friendly correspondence) intimated that Trenchard and Brooke-Popham were at odds. Trenchard responded forcefully, "It is no good [Brigadier-General Walter] Caddell [director, Aircraft Equipment in the Ministry of Munitions] trying to pretend that Brooke-Popham and I do not know what each other is doing. We both know and Brooke-Popham told me a long time ago that these engines wanted special fittings. Caddell has made several attempts lately to prove that Brooke-Popham and I do not know what the other is talking about." The issue in question was the Ministry's failure to provide the equipment needed to fit the Rolls Royce Eagle aero-engine to the D.H.4 bomber. The circumstances of the argument are less important than Trenchard's vehement insistence that he and Brooke-Popham were as one.[44] The closeness of Trenchard's staff was noticeable to both subordinate headquarters and front-line units. "He was beautifully served by a small but highly efficient staff, between whom and his command there was complete liaison and sympathy."[45]

The German 1918 Spring Offensive, although anticipated, came as a great shock. The ferocity of the attack, and the employment of innovative tactics, saw the Germans advance rapidly and threaten to break the Allied line and capture the Channel ports. Throughout the emerging crisis, Brooke-Popham worked calmly and efficiently to maintain the supply of machines. He directed the evacuation and relocation of logistic units while changing supply procedures to ensure that the operational squadrons were never short of stores. Jack Salmond, who had replaced Trenchard as GOC RFC on 20 January 1918, was effusive about Brooke-Popham's contribution:

> The sagacity and foresight of Brigadier-General Brooke-Popham was equal to the emergency. The two offensives had led him to plan for the possibility of a rapid evacuation. At the beginning of April all supplies for one month necessary to two brigades at our depot at St-Omer were made ready for immediate evacuation to Guines near Calais. Thus, Guines would be able to supply all their demands without interruption. The final evacuation of St-Omer was completed by the middle of May and two nights later, on the 18th, it was bombed to destruction—although empty of stores.[46]

On the formation of the RAF (1 April 1918), Brooke-Popham's staff were restyled the "Equipment Branch," comprising more than twenty officers organized into seven sections with duties ranging from the allotment and repair of airplanes to motor transport, stationery, the supply of petrol, and technical matters of kites and parachutes.[47] Brooke-Popham himself was scheduled to return to London, as controller of aircraft production in the Ministry of Munitions, but this was deferred by Salmond, who needed his experience in France. In the event, Brooke-Popham remained at HQ RAF until well after the armistice.[48] During the height of the offensive, King George V had visited the headquarters. Game wrote to his wife: "I could not help feeling that monarchs are a bit of a nuisance in the middle of a battle. Salmond took him into Brooke-Popham's office and Brooke-Popham, who was busy telephoning, just looked up and went calmly on and finished his business, which was very sensible. His Majesty remarked that he seemed to be disturbing him, which was quite true."[49]

Brooke-Popham's calmness during these difficult days is captured in a letter that he sent to Brigadier Alfred Huggins (deputy controller-general of equipment in the Ministry of Munitions) about the delivery of stores to France. "I really don't know whether you are being engulfed in this catastrophe which seems to be overtaking the RAF. However, you are the only person of those at the head that I have not heard of resigning, so I want to explain what our position is out here now."[50] He went on to describe the relocation of the depots and stores, the thinking behind these changes, and the various options for sustaining supplies if the Germans advanced farther. For his work during this critical period Brooke-Popham received his fourth mention in dispatches (7 April 1918). Despite his heavy workload, Brooke-Popham still found time to help Lieutenant Auguste Desclos, one of the French Army liaison officers, who had been attached to HQ RFC.[51] The pair had worked closely together for over two years:

> Believe me, I have forgotten none of the days I spent as your helper and none of their kindnesses. There is one, which I know you would not like me to mention but which the circumstances allow me to recall just for once. In the dark days of March '18 you found time in the midst of your labours to notice my distress at the peril in which my wife then stood before the advancing Germans and to give me an opportunity of removing her to safety.[52]

It is a rare individual who, in a period of great stress and personal danger, can think of the needs of others. On the other hand, it was this sense of compassion that caused Brooke-Popham to hesitate over the evacuation of the aircraft depot at Fienvillers on 27 March 1918:

> It was an unpleasant evening, gusty and with low clouds, and he gave orders that the remaining aeroplanes were to be flown to St-Andre next morning. The officer in charge of the issue section, however, pleaded for permission to fly them away at once. Brigadier Brooke-Popham demurred because it was already late and the depot pilots, who would be required to make two trips, might be unable to complete their second journey before dark. The officer, however, was insistent and Brigadier Brooke-Popham yielded. All the aeroplanes were got away safely and that night the sheds in which they had been housed were heavily bombed by German aircraft and partly demolished.[53]

While this incident speaks to Brooke-Popham's willingness to listen to his juniors, particularly if their views were forcefully argued, it also suggests that a lack of emotional detachment could impede his decision-making. It is tempting to think ahead to the events of 1941, when he was again confronted by the need to take timely and decisive action. Suffice to say that, during World War I, Brooke-Popham benefitted from a hand-picked team, familiar with his style of command, honest in their opinions, and willing to speak openly. His subordinate commanders were empowered to use their initiative and improvise where necessary. Brooke-Popham was particularly close to Colonel Ralph Donaldson-Hudson (commanding No. 2 Aircraft Depot), but had a good relationship with all his depot commanders, including Colonel Alfred Huggins (commanding No. 1 Aircraft Depot) and Colonel George Hynes (commanding the Engine Repair Shops)—all three were awarded the DSO in the January 1917 New Year's Honours List for their work in France, and all readily acknowledged the help and assistance and kindness that he had afforded them.[54] There are many accounts of Brooke-Popham's generosity toward his subordinates, both officers and airmen.[55] When Brooke-Popham's personal driver at HQ RAF, Air Mechanic W. Margerison, was demobilized in 1919, he was given a wristwatch, as well as a reference.[56] Charles Grey, the editor of *The Aeroplane*, and sometime critic of senior RFC officers, was unstinting in his praise. "I have known few senior officers in the RFC or RAF who inspired so much affection or carried so much influence as he did, both with officers and men."[57]

Once the German offensive had been halted, the Allies returned to the attack. Starting with the Battle of Amiens, on 8 August 1918, the BEF soon recaptured all the territory it had lost and steadily advanced against a weakening German Army. Paradoxically, the Hundred Days campaign tested the RAF's logistic organization almost as much as the German Spring Offensive.[58] A relatively static organization had to transform itself into a flexible and mobile system of supply. The rapidly advancing armies meant that large quantities of stores had to be moved forward from the depots over increasingly greater distances. Advanced issues sections were created to maintain an uninterrupted supply of stores and consumables, but the failure to advance the railheads at the same speed meant that greater use had to be made of motor transport. Brooke-Popham responded by moving a substantial quantity of stores forward to the railheads while placing the frontline squadrons closer to the air parks—to minimize the strain on the supply chain. Although wastage rates were even higher than those experienced during Third Ypres, the frontline squadrons never suffered from want of aircraft, equipment or supplies and could maintain their relentless pressure on the retreating Germans.

The armistice, on 11 November 1918, did not represent the end of Brooke-Popham's efforts. One of his first tasks was to create an inventory of the German machines to be surrendered.[59] The depots were kept busy salvaging and sorting the vast range of equipment scattered across France and Belgium. Once assessed, these stores were either returned to the UK or disposed of locally. Demobilization was soon under way, although it took until 1920 for the last RAF personnel to return to the UK. Gradually, however, the immense logistic organization that had sustained air operations so effectively for more than four years was dismantled. Wing Commander William Havers, who served in France for three years, was adamant that the success that had been achieved was down to the quality of the staff involved. "As a result, the whole system was sound, elastic, economical and never failed, so far as I am aware, to cater for every need."[60] In 1944, Havers (by then an air vice-marshal commanding No. 40 Group) stressed the importance of Brooke-Popham's personal example, adding that in his view "no equipment service ever ran quite so smoothly and efficiently as the one you directed in France, and I often think that we have forgotten many of the wise practices we then learned."[61]

For those leading the RAF's logistic organization in World War II, Brooke-Popham had brought "a tone of distinction to our functions."[62] According to Lieutenant-Colonel Louis Fell, chief engineer at the Engine Repair Shops, Brooke-Popham "did everything he could to encourage us and make sure that if we asked for anything it was provided without question and with the absolute minimum of delay."[63] Major George Bulman, who worked in the Aeronautical Inspection Department, was equally forthright:

> "Brookham" used to fly in every few weeks and from the pockets of his British Warm strewed our tables with bits of broken engine, recalling in that high-pitched voice the number of the engine, how long it had run, the circumstances of the failure, and such ideas as he might have as to the cause, especially if it were the first of the kind. For that might mark the start of an epidemic demanding immediate investigation; or it might just be a freak. Thus, failures which otherwise would have taken reams of Army forms and months of time to arrive, and possibly have been disregarded, were dealt with "forthwith," and sometimes remedial action taken within hours. What a grand man "Brookham" was. We were understanding friends until he died, almost forgotten in his last few years, and rejected.[64]

The achievements of this energetic, hardworking, and modest man were recognized by a cascade of honors. He was awarded the Russian Knighthood of St. Stanislaus (Second Degree) in January 1916 and the Air Force Cross (AFC), Companion of the Order of St. Michael and St. George (CMG), and Commander of the Order of the Bath (CB) in 1919. Brooke-Popham's success (which he typically insisted was owed to the efforts of others) was more than a personal triumph—it provided the BEF with the airpower it needed to help win the war and created the conditions for an independent air service. It was his leadership, energy, and determination that created the complex, sophisticated, and highly effective logistic system that sustained RFC and RAF air operations on the Western Front. In coping with high wastage rates, technical obsolescence, tactical innovation, and operational shock, he also developed the first truly modern supply chain. This was achieved through a process of evolution and pragmatism—allied to a willingness to approach problems with an open mind.

Brooke-Popham was at heart a team player, able to work successfully and harmoniously with a succession of RFC commanders. Sykes, Henderson, Trenchard, and Salmond all found him, in turn, a loyal and energetic subordinate. Neither Sykes nor Trenchard were the easiest individuals to please, but Brooke-Popham's obvious competence, hard work, and lack of ego made him an ideal staff officer. According to Philip Game, Brooke-Popham's efforts "were always so utterly unselfish and always made with cheerfulness."[65] His willingness to see the best in people and his equanimity under pressure were valuable attributes, but they also meant that he was rarely impulsive. Part of Brooke-Popham's success in France was owed to his relentless hard work: "He always believed that everybody else worked much harder than he did himself and must be much more tired. Those that worked with him knew that he never did less than the work of three men and generally rather more, and they all marveled how he survived the war. He must have been very nearly dead at the end of it. One believes that his sole and only real rest and recreation was when he went flying from one RFC park or depot in France to another."[66]

It says a great deal about Brooke-Popham's character, and his professionalism, that he could forge productive working relationships under the most testing of circumstances. However, in terms of his own career, it was the two years that he spent with Trenchard at HQ RFC that proved the most influential. In Trenchard's words, Brookham was "my old and one of my main supports through the whole of the war."[67] Some idea of what this involved is provided by a postwar discussion between Brooke-Popham and Thomas Marson (Trenchard's private secretary) about finding a suitable replacement for Air Vice-Marshal John Steel (deputy chief of the Air Staff and director of Operations and Intelligence).[68] Steel had been responsible for interpreting, organizing, and presenting Trenchard's views for the previous five years. "He does want somebody who is quick to grasp what he is driving at, and who is capable of translating the idea into suitable language."[69] Brooke-Popham felt that the necessary qualities included: a willingness to speak one's mind; loyalty to the chief; a sense of humor; sound common sense; an ability to analyze the fundamentals of a problem without preconceived notions; and steadiness in a crisis.[70] It is not too far-fetched to see his own relationship with Trenchard reflected in this description.

Brooke-Popham left France in February 1919 to head the Technical Department at the Ministry of Munitions. He had spent fifty-three months continuously on the Western Front. For more than four years he had provided the RFC (and later the RAF) with an incisive and intuitive grasp of its needs.[71] His instinctive, intelligent, and seemingly instantaneous reactions in dealing with multitudinous problems and difficulties provided the essential foundation for air operations on the Western Font, creating the vital bridge between the nation's economy and airpower.

6

DIRECTOR OF RESEARCH
1919–1921

Brooke-Popham had considered retiring immediately after the war but, offered a permanent commission, decided to pursue a full career in the newly independent Air Force. There was no doubt that he had had a "successful war," but he had also found friendship, belonging, and a sense of purpose. "For the most part war, when it is not terrifying, is sordid and dull, but running through its grim, grey fabrics are golden threads—threads of gallantry, comradeship, self-sacrifice and high-hearted happiness."[1] Unlike his contemporaries, the Salmond brothers (Jack and Geoffrey) and Edward Ellington, all of whom were confirmed as major-generals, he was retained as a colonel (group captain).[2] Since the former had all reached two-star rank during the war, this was no slight, although the situation might have been different had he been able to take up the appointment of controller of aircraft production in April 1918. With his future now tied to the RAF, there seemed little sense in retaining the Popham estate. He had first attempted to dispose of it during the war, although this subsequently resulted in a court case (heard in July 1918) when he had to defend his actions in not proceeding with its sale for £43,000.[3] As a serving officer, it was highly unlikely that he would be able to live at Bagborough House during any of his prospective postings. Without a wife or immediate family, there was no benefit in renting it out against the unlikely day when he might need it. Even so, he regretted breaking the family's link with the area and funded a large community hall for the benefit of the village that was formally unveiled in August 1922, shortly after the estate was sold. As it turned out, the Brooke-Pophams did return to Bagborough, but only after his death.

Brooke-Popham's first peacetime appointment was as controller of the Technical Department, Department of Aircraft Production—within the Ministry of Munitions—on 1 March 1919 (with the temporary rank of brigadier-general).[4] The department comprised three branches: Design (Aeroplanes, Seaplanes, Engines, Materials, and Aerodynamic Investigations); Armament (Guns, Explosives, and Torpedoes); and Instruments (Wireless Telegraphy and Photography), together with a Drawing Office and Technical Library. He also had command of three experimental stations (Biggin Hill, Farnborough, and Felixstowe), as well as responsibility for the work of the Royal Aircraft Establishment (RAE). This gave him a comparatively large staff to administer, comprising both officers and civilians. Several of the department heads were familiar from his time in France, including Louis Fell, George Bulman, and Frederick "Daddy" Laws.[5] This was a period of organizational turmoil across Whitehall as wartime arrangements were dismantled and considerably smaller departments were created to support the three services. Notwithstanding these challenges, Alfred Warrington-Morris, who headed the Instrument Branch, felt that Brooke-Popham's conscientiousness and hard work set a wonderful example to his staff.[6] Less than six months after his arrival, the Technical Department was transferred to the newly formed Directorate-General of Supply and Research (DGSR)—within the Air Ministry—with Brooke-Popham appointed director of research.[7] His immediate superior was Edward Ellington, the director general of supply and research and a member of the Air Council. Brooke-Popham remained as director of research until 14 November 1921, taking on additional responsibilities for aircraft production from January 1920. This was neither a holding post nor a sinecure for an old friend. In setting out his vision for the peacetime RAF, Trenchard had stressed the supreme importance of research and the need for steady and uninterrupted progress if the RAF was to retain "the leading position we have established at such heavy cost during the war."[8]

The early 1920s were a particularly difficult time as the peacetime RAF tried to sustain an effective research program on a greatly reduced budget, while coping with the loss of key personnel. There was insufficient money to support new development and so much of the department's effort focused on those designs that showed the most promise. Wherever possible, direct competition between manufacturers was discouraged to ensure the best use of limited funds. The introduction of the "ten-year rule" in 1919 (the assumption that the British Empire would not be engaged in any great war during

the next ten years) created an understandable reluctance to commit to specu-
lative development programs. For his part, Brooke-Popham, who managed
the research vote, was never clear how this was accommodated within the
annual estimates process.[9] The outcome, however, was that his budget for
experimental research fell steadily, from some £2 million in FY 19/20 to
£1.84 million in FY 20/21 and £1.71 million in FY 21/22.[10] Some indication
of the challenges that this created can be found in a lecture that he delivered
in December 1919. Describing the huge advances achieved in military aviation during World War I, he stressed the need to invest in laborious, lengthy,
and expensive aerodynamic research and the associated study of chemistry,
physics, and allied sciences, if further improvements in performance were to
be achieved.[11] Since a modern wind tunnel cost in the region of £20,000 to
install, and required some 200 hp when running, it was evident that the directorate's budget was not going to stretch very far. Managing a research program on such a tight budget demanded a collaborative approach: "We shall
never be able to have a sufficiently large staff, nor shall we be in a position to
attract sufficiently capable brains into the Directorate of Research to ensure
that we shall be able to carry out and initiate all the research and experiments
ourselves. We must depend very largely on outside bodies."[12]

Aeronautical research was still in its infancy, notwithstanding the rapid
technological progress of wartime. The use of wind tunnels and computa-
tional models had yet to make a significant impact on aircraft design and
testing. During his time in France, Brooke-Popham had shown an instinct
for engineering and a flair for resolving technical problems but his weakness in mathematics meant that he struggled to keep abreast of aeronautical
advances. George Bulman recalled that he seemed to be overwhelmed with
the increasing abstruseness of aircraft design, even though he spent several
hours each week with a tutor in pure mathematics "in the vain hope that he
would become better able to understand the aerodynamicists who flooded
him with their involved calculations and devious curves."[13] Typical of the
practical challenges that had to be faced was the Tarrant Tabor, a large triplane
bomber (and briefly the largest aircraft in the world) originally intended to
bomb Berlin but delayed by power-plant problems and subsequent design
changes. On 26 May 1919, the prototype, fitted with six Napier Lion engines,
crashed at Farnborough while attempting its maiden flight. The pilots—
Captain Frederick George "Dusty" Dunn and Captain Percy Townley
Rawlings—were both killed but the four passengers survived, including staff

from the Technical Department and the RAE. This was both a professional and a personal tragedy. Brooke-Popham knew Dunn extremely well, having served with him since the beginning of the war.[14] In his letter of condolence to Dunn's father, he wrote that Dusty "was undoubtedly the best all-round pilot I had ever seen and was equally at home on every type of machine, whether large or small, British or Foreign. His death is a distinct loss to British aviation."[15] There was considerable controversy about the cause of the crash as there had been a dispute between the National Physical Laboratory (NPL) and the RAE over the machine's center of gravity, resulting in the addition of one thousand pounds of ballast in the nose—against the advice of the NPL and the manufacturer. Neither the report of the Board of Inquiry nor the Accidents Investigation Committee were released to the coroner. According to some, this was because the Air Ministry's Technical Department had blundered in allowing the flight to take place.[16] The controversy was exacerbated by a subsequent argument between the relatives of those killed and the insurers regarding the legal definition of "flight."

One of Brooke-Popham's many committee duties was as the RAF member of the Advisory Committee for Aeronautics, and its successor body, the Aeronautical Research Committee (ARC).[17] The ARC supervised a wide range of work, from aerodynamics to fire protection and meteorology. His staff were closely involved in these experiments and, although the NPL and RAE conducted the actual research, Brooke-Popham was not shy about instigating new work. For example, in 1920, he proposed that the ARC undertake a comparative study of wind tunnels. This became a decade-long international trials project, although the participation of the Göttingen laboratory in Germany was blocked by the Air Council.[18] He also suggested that they consider the "Aeroplane of 1930" to help identify the supporting research goals.[19] During Brooke-Popham's tenure, the first experiments were conducted with remote-controlled aircraft, while considerable progress was made with wireless telephony and navigation using wireless signals.[20] A further area of interest was the residual airship fleet, although new work on military airships was severely reduced for financial reasons from 1921 onward. He was involved in the flight of the wooden-framed R32, and the larger aluminum-framed R33, over Belgium, Holland, and northern France in September 1919, shortly before the ex-RNAS fleet was handed over to RAF control. He was also something of a troubleshooter where technical matters were concerned. In March 1920, he travelled to Berlin to report on a new method for transmitting power that its inventor (Professor Rudolph Goldschmidt) believed would revolutionize powered flight via a flapping mechanism.[21] His subsequent report was justifiably cautious, if not skeptical, and advised the Air Ministry to avoid any commitment or direct involvement.[22] The trip was not entirely wasted, however, as he took the opportunity to provide a detailed report to CAS on the economic, political, and social conditions in Germany.[23]

In the summer of 1921 Brooke-Popham arranged to be involved in the efforts to develop a practical air route across the Middle East. RAF aircraft had carried out several pioneering flights in 1919, including the flight of a Handley Page O/400 twin-engine bomber from Cairo to Baghdad (and later to India). Travelling in a Handley Page O/400 and accompanied by two other aircraft, Brooke-Popham left Amman on 18 July, following a track marked across the desert earlier in the month by an RAF ground party. Baghdad was safely reached on 20 July, but not without various adventures due to reliability problems and the heat. The return flight from Baghdad to Cairo a week later was equally challenging; however, important lessons were learned and the expedition proved a vital step in opening the region.[24] His only complaint was about the food. "The regulation emergency rations of bully beef and biscuits is very discouraging to the average stomach on a hot day in the desert."[25] The track from Egypt to Iraq was later ploughed and provided with landing grounds and stockpiles of fuel and water to facilitate regular communications. The air route became a vital element in maintaining British control of the region through airpower. It also provided the foundation for the Empire Air Routes that were developed through the 1930s, linking the UK to the Far East and Australia. Brooke-Popham's time in the Middle East had rekindled an interest in the region that endured for over thirty years. He was particularly fascinated by Mesopotamia, its history and peoples, becoming a lifelong member of the Royal Central Asian Society.[26] On his return to London, Brooke-Popham provided CAS with a personal report on conditions in the Middle East and the organization of the RAF in Egypt, Palestine, and Mesopotamia—focusing on the operational and support aspects.[27] He gave at least two public lectures about these experiences, highlighting the effect of extreme climate on aircraft structures and equipment.[28] This had confirmed to him the benefits of employing metal in aircraft construction, an interest that stemmed from an examination he carried out on a captured German all-metal Junkers J1 monoplane in 1919.[29] The machine had been abandoned in the open for some time, but had hardly deteriorated. Brooke-Popham became

an early advocate for the use of metal in aircraft design to improve performance and reliability.[30] In 1925, the Air Ministry directed manufacturers to
employ metal rather than wood in the construction of military aircraft,[31]
although it was not until 1930 that the first steps were taken in developing
an operational requirement that saw the RAF gradually move from biplanes
to monoplanes.[32]

Brooke-Popham's period as director of research was something of a hiatus
in his career. He had chosen to remain with the new service, but there was
no one-star appointment in the offing. He found that he was well suited to
his new responsibilities, but complained he had too many administrative
duties and that there were few individuals in the Air Ministry with the scientific or engineering experience to appreciate the nature of the problems faced
by his directorate.[33] This may explain why he was asked to undertake a number of external studies and reports, such as investigating the loss of several
Handley Page O/400 bombers when deploying to the Middle East in 1920,
and drafting detailed replies for Trenchard in response to the Balfour Report.[34]
In retrospect, it is difficult to avoid the conclusion that he was biding his
time. His close association with the RAF Staff College has meant that the
move to Andover seems inevitable, if not preordained, but Charles Grey says
that Brooke-Popham was at first unwilling to accept the post: "When he was
pressed still further he asked modestly whether he might see the names of the
alternative possible appointees. He contemplated the list for a few moments
and then said resignedly: 'Well, I suppose I had better take it.'"[35]

7

ROYAL AIR FORCE
STAFF COLLEGE
1922–1926

The creation of a staff college had been presaged in Trenchard's 1919 memorandum that laid out a blueprint for the peacetime RAF. The importance of creating institutional organizations that gave the service credibility and a distinct identity was acknowledged, but Trenchard also recognized the need to create the intellectual underpinning and professionalism that would sustain the RAF in the struggle for resources and influence. It was not until 1922 that the enabling arrangements and budget were in place to realize this ambition.[1] The selection of Andover was driven by practical considerations. The original choice, Halton, was no longer feasible, but surplus accommodation was available at Andover where there was an adjacent airfield to house the small flight that allowed students to maintain their flying skills. Andover was also close enough to London to attract prominent guest speakers and allow interaction with the other staff colleges, but far enough away to allow the college to develop without regular interruption from Whitehall. The choice of Brooke-Popham as the first commandant at Andover reflected Trenchard's confidence in an individual with considerable organizational skills who had shown energy and loyalty in France. Just as importantly, he was one of the few Army Staff College graduates in the RAF and a prominent airpower theorist. His authorship of prewar papers on the potential for military aviation, close involvement in the creation of the *Training Manual*, and regular lectures at the Royal Aeronautical Society and RUSI had cemented his reputation as a military intellectual.

Brooke-Popham arrived at Andover in November 1921 and set about the immense task of creating a functioning college in time for the first intake—scheduled to arrive in less than six months.[2] "Next morning, after some delay caused by locking myself in a bathroom with a spring lock on the outside, I proceeded to the small office allotted to me and sat down to an inkstand with no ink and a penholder without a nib. However, with the aid of Sergeant Major [Henry] Bethell, who had been with me since 1914, a form for indent of stationery was filled up and with its signature I felt that the formation of the Staff College had commenced."[3] Buildings had to be renovated and modified, staff recruited, housing arranged, and, most importantly, a syllabus devised. Once this was under way, instructional material had to be prepared and practical exercises developed. Completing these tasks in time for the official opening, on 4 April 1922, was a credit to Brooke-Popham and the directing staff (most of whom only arrived in late January).[4] Notwithstanding the time pressure, Brooke-Popham kept an open mind about instructional methods. An early visit was made to the French staff college in Paris (École supérieure de guerre) to study their staff training arrangements and evaluate alternative teaching methods. Brooke-Popham was disappointed in what he found, feeling that it was more of a school for tactics than for staff duties.[5] More practical help was gained from Hugh Cecil's report on the education of officer candidates for the RAF.[6] According to Joubert de la Ferté, who accompanied Brooke-Popham during their time in France, it was decided not to adopt the French approach with its excessive formality and lack of debate—in comparison to the informality of Camberley.[7] The opening address to the First Course (comprising twenty hand-picked students) was given by Jack Salmond, on behalf of Trenchard. Brooke-Popham also spoke and used the occasion to lay out his personal objectives. All the students were RAF, although it was hoped that the other services and overseas air forces would participate in subsequent years (just as Camberley and Greenwich offered a small number of places to students from the other services). A conscious decision was taken to limit the course to one year, rather than the two years of the Army Staff Course, allowing the largest number of suitable officers to be trained as quickly as possible. Other than the first two intakes, students were to be selected through competitive examination.

It is difficult to exaggerate Brooke-Popham's impact on the RAF—as an institution and a fighting service—during his time at Andover. The students were, by definition, individuals of considerable potential, but Brooke-Popham provided the intellectual framework and leadership that shaped their subsequent personal and professional development. Not only did he set the program and institutional ethos, but he also remained in post for more than four years—influencing an entire generation of RAF leaders. A little more than one hundred young officers (largely Air Force, but including Army, Navy, and Commonwealth students) attended Andover between 1922 and 1926, providing senior air force leadership in the key air campaigns of World War II. Among this group were two future chiefs of the Air Staff (Peter Portal and Jack Slessor) and more than twenty future air officers, including John Baldwin, Geoffrey Bromet, Ralph Cochrane, Sholto Douglas, Leslie Hollinghurst, Trafford Leigh-Mallory, Charles Medhurst, Keith Park, and Richard Peirse. Both air commanders in Malaya during Brooke-Popham's time as CinC Far East were ex-Andover students (John Babington and Conway Pulford). Brooke-Popham also benefitted from high-quality directing staff—all of whom rose to high rank, including Christopher Courtney, Wilfrid Freeman, Philip Joubert de la Ferté, and Bertie Sutton. The choice of these officers was as important as the selection of students. Those few who did not reach the highest rank still found positions of influence, such as Bentley Beauman, who became Brooke-Popham's friend and later served as Trenchard's private secretary.[8] Although the RAF Staff College drew on the traditions and ethos of Camberley and Greenwich, the institution was Brooke-Popham's personal creation and bore the imprint of his personality as well as his intellectual interests and strategic perspective. "A staff college is not a school, it is a cooperative society where instructors and students work as part of one team."[9] He was determined to recreate the family atmosphere he had known at Camberley. Squadron Leader (later Air Marshal) John Baldwin,[10] a student on the First Course, recalled, "I don't think I was alone in missing the family life of the Regiment, once we had thrown in our lot with the RAF. Brookham was the outstanding personality in the RAF who kept the family spirit going."[11]

Squadron Leader (later Air Commodore) Andre Walser, a student on the Second Course, recalled that Brooke-Popham had made an impression on him that had "lasted throughout the years."[12] Squadron Leader (later Wing Commander Sir) Norman Leslie, also on the Second Course, had a similar experience, as did Squadron Leader (later Air Chief Marshal Sir) Norman Bottomley, a student on the Third Course, who had "the privilege of sitting at his feet."[13] It wasn't just the students who benefitted from Brooke-Popham's character and quality of mind. Squadron Leader (later Air Marshal Sir) Guy Garrod served for three and a half years on the directing staff, "the most rewarding years of my life," and recalled Brooke-Popham's personal generosity to the college staff and their families.[14] For Group Captain (later Air Chief Marshal Sir) Christopher Courtney, who joined the directing staff in 1925, Brooke-Popham was a "tremendous inspiration to all who were there."[15] These warm sentiments, full of affection, belie the assertion that Brooke-Popham's dour public manner at Andover did not bring him easy popularity or that "his universal nickname 'Brookham' was no more than a convenient, if later an affectionate, contraction."[16] Charles Grey, who knew Brooke-Popham for more than forty years, insisted that "Brookham" was a mark of esteem. His public persona aside, Brooke-Popham was one of those rare individuals who can recognize their weaknesses as well as their strengths. He was conscious that his shyness made him seem aloof and detached. "I remember a very good friend of mine once telling me that there was nobody in the world whose absence or presence really made any difference to me, no-one whom I couldn't do without."[17] This self-awareness is evident throughout his private letters: "I remember when Trenchard told me I'd got a CB. He said, 'of course it's very nice to have eleven letters after your name, but remember that you're just Brookham after all.' . . . I know that all my people here call me Brookham amongst themselves, however polite and full of deference they may be to my face, and I wouldn't have it otherwise."[18]

Trenchard and Brooke-Popham had laid down three objectives for the RAF Staff College:

- To train officers for work on the staff.
- To give future commanders some instruction on the broader aspects of war.
- To found a school of thought and assist in solving problems regarding the organization, training, and employment of the Air Force.

It has been argued that the Staff College lamentably failed to develop airpower thinking, discouraged independent thought, and focused on social and leisure aspects at the expense of genuine learning.[19] As Ross Mahoney comments, these criticisms are misplaced and reflect a misunderstanding about Andover's role.[20] It was designed primarily, but not exclusively, to provide the RAF with individuals capable of functioning effectively in Whitehall—alongside their counterparts from the other services. The staff college's other important task was to nurture and develop future leaders. Brooke-Popham took a close interest in both aspects, delivering lectures and leading discussions on topics that ranged from Army cooperation to leadership and morale. He regarded the last two subjects as being critical to the future of the service. Students were not spoon-fed formulaic views but offered the latest scientific thinking. James Birley, who had extensive experience in treating stress-related illness among aircrew on the Western Front, lectured on the "Psychology of Courage," including the subject of fear, "a most reprehensible and dangerous subject for discussion in a school of military instruction."[21] Andover's innovative and forward-looking curriculum set it apart from the other staff colleges. Brooke-Popham has been mocked in some quarters for believing that horse riding was an important attribute for an officer: "There are good men who do not hunt and bad ones that do, but every man is improved by hunting."[22] Such sentiments may appear quaint at this distance, but they say more about Brooke-Popham's social background and personal interests than the quality and relevance of the teaching at Andover. Eighty years later, Brooke-Popham's views on airpower were described as "well thought out and compelling."[23]

Throughout his time as commandant, Brooke-Popham stressed the need to work closely with the other services and the importance of breaking free of rigid thinking. He believed that students should be taught how to think rather than what to think, and was careful to emphasize that the RAF did not have a monopoly of new ideas but should keep abreast of scientific progress and social conditions, "even art and music will give new ideas and conduce to originality."[24] The RAF needed officers who could think and act quickly. "We must have a mobile brain. This does not mean changing one's mind but that one must be receptive of new ideas, envisage their effect on air operations and foresee future developments."[25] He also warned that merely wearing a blue uniform and employing novel titles was not enough, and that a severe mental effort was required to grasp what this new power meant. It was hoped that the RAF Staff College would become a school of thought, but this was not so much about defining doctrine as creating a common way of thinking about problems—as developed at Camberley.[26] There was also a practical dimension—in the assistance provided to those writing the Air Force's early doctrine. Neville Parton has provided a detailed picture of how this was developed and the central role of the Air Staff in the writing process.[27] Andover did not set out to create doctrine—unlike the United States Air Corps Tactical School at Langley. It is true that students on the first two courses were involved in reviewing the RAF Operations Manual (Confidential Document 22) and contributing to the wider work of the Air Staff, but this initiative was not sustained. The problem was capacity rather than a deliberate change in policy. There was simply not enough time in the curriculum to deliver everything that had been hoped. Brooke-Popham acknowledged as much in his final address to the First Course. He was delighted with how much had been achieved and believed that the staff college was now on a firm footing, but there were also disappointments: "We'd formed such high ideals of how we were going to solve all the problems of employment of the Air Force and establish firm principles to be a guide to future generations. And now we have come to the end of those twelve months and so little has been accomplished."[28]

It must be questioned whether a newly created air service, fighting for its independence, would seriously consider outsourcing the development of doctrine to a staff college, however well respected. It was not a role enjoyed by either Camberley or Greenwich. Indeed, it is quite remarkable that the students at Andover were ever involved in writing doctrine, given the Air Ministry's sensitivity about the need to speak with a single, coherent voice—as reflected in their insistence that students should not publish articles, other than their collected war experiences (issued as air publications or published in the college journal).[29] This is not to suggest that doctrine, in the form of policies and practices, was absent from the curriculum. The role of airpower was at the heart of Andover's teaching. The need for inter-service cooperation was repeatedly highlighted, as was the need for unity in doctrine and the importance of learning from operational experience, but Brooke-Popham also wanted to stretch the minds of his students.[30] While at Andover, his interest in historic landscapes led to the first use of aerial photography to identify ancient sites on Salisbury Plain, the "birth of archaeology from the air."[31] This deep and abiding intellectual curiosity was reflected in the range and diversity of lectures:

> The Royal Air Force Staff College was, from the start, the home of original thought and frequently of heresy. The students were allowed great latitude in their views and, as a result, the College has done [an] incalculable amount of good in the Service. Although the teachers drove the students hard, they drove themselves even harder and, with

the help of many brilliant lecturers unconnected with the College such as Trades Union leaders, scientists, economists and financiers, produced a year's course of really deep interest. There must be very few students who have passed through Andover who do not look back to their time there as amongst the happiest and most useful of their career.[32]

Inevitably, there were some dissenting voices. Raymond Collishaw, a distinguished Canadian World War I fighter pilot on the Third Course, believed that the staff solutions were too formulaic and that there was a tendency toward "stereotype thinking."[33] He also felt that there was not enough imagination and vision in developing airpower concepts, although this was largely directed at the perceived failure to promote the deterrent effect of a large striking force. This argument sits uneasily with the suggestion that Andover was complicit in sustaining the RAF's fixation on the war-winning potential of strategic bombing.[34] William Barker, another distinguished Canadian fighter pilot (Fourth Course) was concerned about deficiencies in RAF tactics, particularly anti-shipping, and the need for multiple-gun fighters. He was persistent on the latter point, to the annoyance of the directing staff, but Brooke-Popham respected his opinions, and in Barker's graduation report gave him "the most accurate assessment he ever received."[35] There were also critical voices among the directing staff: Wilfrid Freeman reportedly found it a dull job, although he still performed well enough to be promoted in situ and made the senior instructor for the Third Course.[36] These views are exceptional—the majority of students and staff paint a picture of a happy and productive environment. Squadron Leader (later Marshal of the Royal Air Force) Peter Portal had known Brooke-Popham since 1912. When Portal retired in 1946 he wrote to his friend Brookham. "Whatever happens, I owe the chance directly to my being selected for the First Course at Andover (I should never have got in by exam)! It was then that I began working for the first time in my life and you were the inspiration."[37] It was not just the RAF students who were full of positive words about their commandant. Major (later Field Marshal Sir) Hastings Ismay was adamant that he owed a great deal of the luck that had come his way to "a very happy and very instructive year at Andover under your charge."[38] Major (later Colonel) James Powell— another Army student (1925–26)—regarded Brookham as a friend "to whom one could always turn for advice, knowing full well that it would be sound and that it would be given with much care and kindness."[39] The respect was mutual. He routinely referred to the students at Andover as "his children" (a term he also employed at the Imperial Defence College). This was no casual affectation or the dry humor of a confirmed bachelor. He felt a deep sense of responsibility for those in his charge: "One of my former students on whom I had reported badly and turned down flew over from Northolt to ask my advice. I was so touched, that's the third one of those I've failed who've asked me to help them and I appreciate that more than anything."[40]

Brooke-Popham spent a great deal of time marking essays and preparing lectures, often working late into the night. He was a hands-on commandant and put considerable effort into communicating his experience and the ideas that he had formed on the employment of airpower. The staff college records for this period show that he was involved in every aspect of the curriculum.[41] As commandant of the RAF Staff College, he also became the public advocate of airpower through lectures, papers, and interviews. Not surprisingly his views reflected those of the Air Staff and emphasized the importance of the striking power of the Air Force. However, he also stressed the importance of coordination between sea, land, and air.[42] His personal correspondence with Basil Liddell Hart reveals an individual closely interested in military strategic affairs and a willingness to test these ideas in public and private. Although historical campaigns, and the great leaders of the past, were undoubtedly part of the Andover curriculum, the writings of Boney Fuller and Liddell Hart also featured. Brooke-Popham acknowledged the debt he owed to Fuller when lecturing on the principles of war,[43] and confided to Liddell Hart that his *Paris or The Future of War* was virtually what was taught at Andover.[44] Such was Brooke-Popham's enthusiasm that he even recommended the book to Trenchard, although the latter had some criticisms of the work.[45]

Brooke-Popham's contribution to the development of airpower doctrine had begun long before Andover. Writing to Guy Garrod in 1949, shortly after the latter had become chairman of the Air League, Brooke-Popham identified the key steps in the development of RAF doctrine.[46] In his view, thinking about the air offensive had followed a logical and consistent sequence since the days of the Air Battalion.[47] Starting with his lectures to the Staff College in 1911 and 1912, Brooke-Popham highlighted how fighting between aircraft was the inevitable outcome in the struggle to achieve command of the air. Together with Brancker, he developed these ideas in successive drafts of the RFC *Training Manual* that identified the potential for carrying offensive weapons, including guns and bombs. Refined and informed by wartime experience, these principles were codified in the booklet *Fighting in the Air*, issued by HQ RFC in March 1917. Air fighting had gone through three phases prior to 1916: the defense of a small area by circling aircraft; the protection of Army cooperation aircraft by individual close escort fighters; and the employment of fighter barrages to block enemy aircraft. None of these had been successful. It was only the employment of aircraft in an offensive capacity, as demonstrated at the Battle of the Somme, that had achieved results.[48] In Brooke-Popham's opinion it was a short step from this document to what was taught at the RAF Staff College from 1922 onward.[49]

His long tour at Andover was the result of a conscious strategy to provide sufficient time for the directing staff to develop a standardized course.[50] In retrospect he felt that this had been a mistake. "Wing Commander Sutton and I are the only two members of the directing staff who have, up to the present, been here for the full period of four years and both of us feel that it is too long."[51] This was undoubtedly true, but the effect was to ensure that Brooke-Popham's impact on the RAF Staff College extended far beyond his departure, creating a structure and direction that lasted until at least World War II.[52] Trenchard was delighted with the quality of the staff officers sent to the Air Ministry and felt that "the results of your training, from every point of view, will create in the post-war Air Force the backbone which is so essential to it."[53] Over a quarter of those graduating from Andover between 1921 and 1926 were posted to the Air Ministry, where they formed 40 percent of the Deputy-Directorate of Operations and Intelligence, a figure that had risen to 88 percent by 1938.[54] A more modest legacy was Brooke-Popham's decision to leave his extensive library, some six hundred books on military history and the theory of war, for the use of the directing staff. Although this was dispersed during World War II, to the Air Ministry Library and the new Royal Canadian Air Force Staff College among others, it reflected his belief that senior leaders had much to learn from the great commanders of the past.[55]

In January 1925 Brooke-Popham had attended three hunt balls in Gloucestershire (on successive nights), starting with the Vale of the White Horse Hunt (Bathurst Ball) at Cirencester.[56] Because of the distances involved, he arranged to stay with John and Adela Birchall at Bowden Hall, near Gloucester.[57] Arriving late, and needing to change, he was welcomed by another houseguest, the twenty-four-year-old Opal Mary Hugonin—the rest of the party having left for Cirencester. Opal, the niece of Sir Granville Wheler, was also staying with the Birchalls, who were friends of her uncle.[58] According to family tradition, Opal knew immediately that she had met the man she would marry. Whether or not it was love at first sight, the two became very close during the remainder of their stay at Bowden Hall. By the third ball, at Cricklade, Brooke-Popham was confident enough to claim eleven dances before the evening had finished. When she left on Friday, Opal presented a violet to Brooke-Popham as a keepsake. By August 1925, their relationship had advanced to the point when Brooke-Popham was determined on marriage. The courtship had not been without difficulty, although some obstacles were more obvious than others. There was the age gap (twenty-two years). There was the inevitable question about whether Opal could play the role of a senior officer's wife. There were also suggestions (from within his family) that Opal was simply a young girl leading on an older man. The same voices warned about Brooke-Popham's aloof character, that he could be fierce, critical, and contemptuous. On the other hand, the couple had similar interests, including riding and a love of horses. They had well-matched temperaments and intellectual curiosity, as well as strong religious beliefs. They had also both lost a parent at a young age. Their letters were initially hesitant and avoided any salutation—as if this might presume on something deeper. "Not knowing how to address you in a manner duly respectful to your lofty position, I will follow your example and omit same!"[59] As time passed, their signatures gradually evolved, from "Opal M. Hugonin" to just "Opal" and from "RBP" to "Bob." The relationship warmed, despite occasional misunderstandings and Brooke-Popham's heavy-handed advice on matters such as the correct postal address for Andover, and the employment of the expression "12 p.m." Books were exchanged, favorite verses shared, and weekends organized. Their correspondence is full of improbable lines such as, "When not engaged with hunting my mind is occupied with the pros and cons of Socialism!"[60] Brooke-Popham found a ready listener in Opal and increasingly shared his work and private concerns with her. "Such a lot of silly official papers in my tray: 'Report on Aircraft for the Locating of Herring Shoals in Scottish Waters', 'Report on the Minimum Consumption of Petrol for a Long Flight', 'Air Speed Correction at Heights', all very dull."[61]

Brooke-Popham spent the weekend of 15–16 August 1925 with Opal at Otterden Place, Granville Wheler's estate in Kent.[62] On the Monday, before

Opal returned to Yorkshire, the couple took her donkey, David, for a walk. Opal would recall that her future husband chose to propose over an animal's back. Although the question was not unexpected, Opal delayed answering— claiming that she needed to speak with her family. The forty-seven-year-old bachelor spent the next few days beset by worry. "Please don't think that it's an Air Vice-Marshal CB CMG DSO AFC three brevets and four mentions that you have to give an answer to, it's just plain Bob."[63] On the Wednesday, he received her written reply, but such was his emotional turmoil that he walked out of his office into the countryside before he dared to open the let- ter. To his immense relief, Opal had accepted and "now everything is all too wonderful and all the people and all the world and the people in it are misty and unreal."[64]

Robert Brooke-Popham and Opal Hugonin's engagement was formally announced on 25 August 1925 with the wedding set for 5 January 1926. The news was greeted with warm congratulations (and some shock) by his many friends and the college staff. Sergeant Major Bethell announced that he had "never been so surprised in my life before. We'd made certain that you were a confirmed bachelor."[65] In sending his best wishes, Trenchard could not resist the temptation to add "better late than never."[66] This was somewhat tongue- in-cheek, as Trenchard had himself only married five years earlier (at almost the same age). Brooke-Popham believed that meeting Opal had saved him "from cultivating an attitude of indifference to the rest of the world and rap- idly strengthening the shell into which he loved to retire."[67] His love for Opal was deep and transformational. He shared his innermost thoughts with her: "Sometimes I used to feel so depressed at all my life's work, it seemed that I spent it all either in training men to kill others or else in taking an active part in doing so. And it all seemed such a waste or even worse. Now I'm beginning to feel that it's not."[68]

He also reflected on his behavior and motives, sometimes with brutal honesty:

> It is funny how things change; years (many years) ago I was at school with a man who was a bit older than I was and whom I always looked upon as a silly conceited ass. He on his part looked down on me as being a small boy. Then came the war and I got up to brigadier gen- eral whilst he was still a lieutenant-colonel. But there I stuck because there was nothing more to get at that time in the RFC but he went

> to GHQ and became a major-general (temporary) and so the big boy once again. Now he's here for the manoeuvres and back to his permanent rank of colonel and much my junior. Small minded I know dear, but though I don't mind a bit being junior to a good man, I do rather jib at seeing people whom I know to be brainless go over my head.[69]

There was no doubt that Brooke-Popham had found someone he could confide in and share his challenges. The couple's correspondence over the next twenty-eight years not only illuminates their life together but also reveals views on events and individuals that he was otherwise careful to disguise.

> I gradually realized that there could be no rest for anyone so long as he was in the air service. At one time, I thought that it would come after the war but found I was wrong, it merely meant a change in the nature of one's work. At the beginning of 1919, I thought well now, I have done something, I have proved myself on active service, others and all events think I've not done badly, surely, I can rest on my oars a bit? But no, like others I found myself in a big job organising part of the Air Force for the future, under all the limitations imposed by peace conditions. Then came the job of starting the Staff College, from nothing this time and I thought even then that after the first year it would all be running smoothly and there would be but little to do. And again, I was wrong because I found that the more one learned, the more one found there was to discuss; as one's view extended and the horizon grew ever further and further, stimulating in one sense, yet disheartening because looking forwards to the ever-receding goal, one lost sight of the path one had traversed, so felt that nothing had been achieved.[70]

Shortly after his engagement, Brooke-Popham was advised that his next posting was to be Air Officer Commanding (AOC) Fighting Area, a new group created from the existing Inland Area, responsible for the air defense of the UK. "For the first time, Great Britain will have a separately organized and administered Home Defence Force."[71] In his words, this was "the plum job" for an air vice-marshal.[72]

8

THE FIGHTING AREA
1926–1928

Robert Brooke-Popham and Opal Hugonin were married at All Saints Parish Church, Ledsham, near Castleford, on 5 January 1926. The reception was held at Ledston Hall. Air Commodore Tony Holt, Brooke-Popham's close friend and protégé, was their best man. There were more than four hundred guests, including many Army and RAF colleagues. The students at Andover had commissioned a special silver salver, engraved with their individual signatures, while one of his erstwhile "children," Flight Lieutenant Kenneth Harris (from the Second Course), was the organist. The couple honeymooned in Paris and then at Chearsley Hall for two weeks, where they spent much of the time hunting, before Brooke-Popham returned alone to the staff college and the start of his last term. They had agreed that there was no sense in Opal moving to Andover, given his imminent posting.

Air Vice-Marshal Edgar Ludlow-Hewitt took over as commandant on 28 March 1926, shortly before the start of the Fifth Course.[1] The end of Brooke-Popham's time at Andover coincided with the 1926 General Strike, called by the Trades Union Conference in support of the coal miners in dispute with mine owners over plans to reduce wages and increase working hours. The possibility of a widespread strike had been anticipated for some months and the Conservative government had made plans accordingly, including the involvement of the military in maintaining essential services and the use of volunteers.[2] Negotiations broke down on Wednesday, 1 May 1926, and the strike was called from midnight on Friday, 3 May. The action had an immediate impact, although not all industries were involved. Transport, newspapers, and the docks were hardest hit, with more than 1.5 million workers on strike.

Pending his posting to Headquarters Fighting Area, Brooke-Popham was attached to the Air Ministry in charge of the emergency organization ("Crisis") within Adastral House, responsible for coordinating the Air Ministry's efforts. The distribution of the government newspaper *The British Gazette* was regarded as a key element in sustaining public support, particularly outside London.[3] Despite the poor weather, more than half a million copies were carried in RAF aircraft to all parts of the country. A critical moment in the confrontation with the unions was the movement of a food convoy from the London docks on Saturday, 8 May 1926. From Brooke-Popham's perspective, this event was more high theater rather than class warfare:

> Three days ago, at a meeting of the Supply and Transport (S&T) sub-committee of the Cabinet there was a long talk in awed tones about moving food supplies out of the docks. It was decided to "break out" with a food convoy on Saturday, the utmost secrecy to be observed, etc., etc. A battalion of guards was moved to the docks, lorries dribbled in gradually, a couple of tanks got down under cover of darkness. Then yesterday all was got ready and, at the psychological moment, the dock gates were opened and out came a tank followed by 115 lorries, machine guns in readiness, men in tin helmets, fingers on the trigger and so forth. As soon as the crowd saw the tank they began to cheer and continued laughing and cheering as the whole convoy went by. They regarded it as a sort of Lord Mayor's Show and made not the slightest attempt to stop anyone.[4]

He also questioned the competence of the S&T committee (chaired by the home secretary) that included a bellicose and somewhat theatrical Winston Churchill.[5] "I was not impressed and I feel that if they'd all clear out, and let the three services run the business, we should have a better chance of settling it all."[6] If anything, Brooke-Popham admired the strikers, although he regarded the strike as "quite Gilbertian": "A night or two back, I sent one of my staff down to Uxbridge by car. On his way, he picked up a couple of navvies who wanted a lift there. In Hammersmith Broadway, he was stopped by a big crowd and one of them jumped on the car, presumably to damage it. One of the navvies picked up the man by the seat of his trousers and heaved him back into the crowd, which merely jeered at the man and let the car pass through."[7]

By Monday (10 May) it was evident that the strike was weakening, as people drifted back to work. "I do hope that the government will be generous not harsh when it's all over. Because it is not the mens' fault, if one wants to get to the root of the trouble, one must go to Moscow."[8] For most of this period Brooke-Popham was accommodated with four other RAF officers (including Philip Game) at Sir Philip Sassoon's London flat in Mayfair.[9] The luxury of his existence, compared to the conditions on the streets, depressed him:

> It was in Piccadilly, crowds of luxurious cars passing along and suddenly I met a ragged man pushing a decrepit perambulator with a few bits of stuff in it and followed by a woman, weary and footsore, helping herself along with a stick. And they were both glancing at the cars and the crowd, nervously and half-afraid. I wished I'd stopped and given them something, but I just passed by. Where they were going to, where they would sleep, when did they last get anything to eat? And then I came in here, with all its wealth and luxury. Something wrong somewhere. I wish people weren't getting so harsh and vindictive over this strike; after all, they are our own kith and kin.[10]

The strike was called off on 11 May, although the miners' dispute continued until November when they went back to work, having accepted all the mine owners' demands. The emergency organization's work earned the congratulations of Secretary of State for Air Samuel Hoare, as well as the appreciation of the Cabinet.[11] Although the General Strike did not last long, and Brooke-Popham's role was on the margins, it did serve to reveal his natural sympathy for the working classes and belief that they were as much part of the nation as those in power or in positions of authority. There may have been a feudal element in these feelings, but they were genuine and heartfelt. It also aligned him with the more egalitarian principles exhibited by the RAF and the belief that ability should be the basis for advancement, rather than background or class. This was not so much about achieving social equality as a rational response by the new service to an environment where military efficiency depended on technological expertise and professional excellence. Under these conditions "a structure of command based on rigid distinctions between officers and other ranks simply did not work."[12]

Brooke-Popham took over as AOC Fighting Area on 25 May 1926, his first operational command since 1915 and the first officer to lead an organization that would eventually (in 1936) become Fighter Command.[13] The

Fighting Area had been created in response to the Salisbury Committee, set up by the government in March 1923, to inquire into the question of national and imperial defense.[14] Following its interim report, Prime Minister Stanley Baldwin announced that a Home Defence Air Force would be created to defend the country against air attack and that this should, in the first instance, consist of fifty-two squadrons (including seventeen fighter squadrons) to be created with as little delay as possible.[15] The first step in realizing these ambitions was the formation of Air Defence of Great Britain (ADGB) under the command of Jack Salmond. ADGB comprised Fighting Area, Wessex Bombing Area, and No. 1 Air Defence Group (reserve and auxiliary air force units).[16]

The plan of air defense inherited by Brooke-Popham had been drawn up in 1923 and featured a defensive aircraft belt (the Aircraft Fighting Zone) about fifteen miles deep, parallel to the English coast and approximately thirty-five miles inland, equipped with searchlights to aid night fighting. Beyond this belt was an Outer Artillery Zone designed to break up attacking formations before enemy aircraft reached the defending fighters. The whole provided a cordon around the east, south, and southwest approaches to London, with an Inner Artillery Zone protecting the capital itself.[17] The system was based on the need to provide defending fighters with sufficient warning time—provided by the Observer Corps—to be able to climb to height and intercept an attacking bomber formation, while giving antiaircraft guns the freedom to attack aircraft outside the Fighting Zone.[18] This arrangement would remain largely the same until the formation of Fighter Command.[19] The Fighting Area was divided into the Advanced Fighting Squadrons RAF, ten aircraft sectors, and GOC Ground Troops (responsible for the Inner and Outer Artillery Zones, the Observer Corps, and searchlights).[20] In all, there were ten squadrons of single-seat fighters (and a night-fighting flight), all based in the south of England.[21] The total of seventeen fighter squadrons needed to secure Great Britain's air defense would not be reached until 1935, by which time rearmament would be well under way.[22] When Brooke-Popham arrived at Kenley, he had a little more than one hundred biplane fighters responsible for defending the entire country.

Brooke-Popham relished the opportunity to get involved in the day-to-day work of his stations and regularly flew from the headquarters to visit them. His chief staff officer was Group Captain Philip "Erb" Herbert, who had been one of his flight commanders in 1913. Erb would remain a close friend until his untimely death in 1936.[23] The AOC's schedule was hectic, leaving little time for Opal. Matters were further complicated by the need to sort out their domestic accommodation and the imminent transfer of Headquarters Fighting Area to Hillingdon House, Uxbridge (from 7 July 1926).[24] Opal, who was by now pregnant with their first child, remained with her family at Ledston, while the house they planned to rent near Uxbridge (Riverdale) was redecorated. There was also some trepidation on Opal's part as to what awaited her at Uxbridge. Air Vice-Marshal Sir Tom Webb-Bowen (AOC Inland Area), who had been based at Uxbridge for the previous two years, had claimed that there was no local society. Brooke-Popham was at pains to explain that this was unlikely to be an issue for them. "Webb-Bowen is a really good officer and his own staff like him but for some reason he's not popular in the RAF as a whole, as his wife is a bit difficult."[25] Typical of these days was the week of 30 May 1926:

Monday, I spent in the office till 5, then after a hasty tea flew down to Upavon. Lovely evening and the air so clear. Stayed with the Freemans and went up to the aerodrome after dinner to watch some night flying going on.[26] Next morning I went round the squadron there and at 10 o'clock started off and flew to Biggin Hill to criticise formation flying by three squadrons together. Flew back here [Kenley] for luncheon, spent a couple of hours in my office and then flew down to Lympne to see a night flying flight of mine which has just gone there. Then spent an hour looking at some acoustical apparatus for picking up aeroplanes at a distance. Flew back here, making a fearfully bad landing I think because I was tired, just time to change and go out for dinner with the Goulds.[27]

Experiments with acoustic detection had begun in World War I in response to the German aerial campaign against British cities.[28] The technology offered the possibility of long-range detection of enemy aircraft and inland tracking. Brooke-Popham was already familiar with the technique since the Signals Experimental Establishment, responsible for postwar research into acoustic mirrors, had been based at RAF Biggin Hill during his time as director of research. Experiments would continue for the next decade and the installation of an acoustic mirror early-warning system was only halted in the summer of 1935, and finally cancelled in May 1936, when the greater potential of radar became clear.[29] In the meantime, acoustic detection, allied to visual tracking, offered the best means of intercepting enemy bombers that were in some cases as fast as the defending fighters. In the absence of standing patrols (hugely expensive in time and resources), some form of early warning was essential if fighters were to be able to climb to altitude and position themselves for an attack. Brooke-Popham's interest in these experiments was no idle curiosity. He genuinely believed that there were technical solutions to be found for the operational challenges faced by the Fighting Area. In Park's opinion, he was "the first senior officer to appreciate the value of scientists in the Service."[30]

It has been said that "hearts were young and life was good in the air defence squadrons of ADGB."[31] It is certainly tempting to regard the 1920s as a golden age that encouraged the art of pure flying in gaily painted stubby biplane fighters above sun-drenched grass airfields. It is a picture encouraged by images of the exciting aerobatic displays performed by Brooke-Popham's fighter squadrons during the RAF Aerial Pageant at Hendon in 1927 and 1928.[32] In fact, there was growing public concern about the state of Britain's air defenses (exemplified by Stanley Baldwin's comment in the House of Commons that "the bomber will always get through")[33] and mounting pressure to demonstrate that progress was being made. The ADGB air exercises, conducted in the summer of 1927 and 1928, were closely covered by the national press, eager to discover whether the country could defend itself against air attack.[34] On both occasions, Wessex Bombing Area provided the attacking bombers while Brooke-Popham provided the defending fighters. Most of the targets were in London, although it was stressed that the aim was not to test the city's air defenses but to practice tactics, communications, coordination of air and ground defenses, and the functioning of the operations rooms.[35] The 1927 exercise was reportedly "the first actual air manoeuvres ever held in any country on a large scale."[36]

This pattern of office work and flying visits to his squadrons characterized much of Brooke-Popham's tour as AOC Fighting Area. His interest was both personal and professional. He took his command responsibilities seriously and saw the Fighting Area as an extended family. "All so sunny and lovely and then went to Uxbridge where I got a message to say that a pilot in one of my squadrons had just been killed. It was such a shock coming just then. And coming back I ran into all the Ascot traffic—all out of touch with reality."[37] Opal was understandably nervous about her husband's flying, but he robustly defended the need to share the same risks as his subordinates:

> If I'd been a squadron leader or a flight lieutenant you'd have married me just the same, wouldn't you? If I'd said, in such a case, that I wasn't going to fly any more after I married, I should have had to leave the service. That would not apply to an air vice-marshal, and for that very reason it is all the more essential that I should go on flying and that you should want me to, so that you can be in real sympathy with all the wives of the junior officers we shall have under us in the future.[38]

Opal's concerns had some substance. The RAF suffered fifty-four fatal flying accidents in 1926, the highest rate since the war, although matters would improve over the next few years. The causes varied,[39] but ill-discipline undoubtedly played its part: "I had a long thing to go into over an accident that occurred at Kenley before I took over. A nasty case with a remote possibility of a trial for manslaughter and it's been dragging on at the Air Ministry for weeks and I was determined there should be no delay on the part of my Fighting Area. I was in my office till after 7 p.m. and then again after dinner."[40] Brooke-Popham had every reason to be concerned about flying discipline within his command. Only a few months later, Warrant Officer Erik Haug (a World War I veteran) was killed in his Gloster Grebe at Kenley, after a particularly long and incapacitating retirement lunch, when he stalled from a steep climbing turn immediately after takeoff.[41]

Officers' wives played an important role in the interwar RAF. They were expected not to work, but to contribute to the social and professional life of a unit. At one level, this comprised innocuous activities such as presenting prizes at sports days, organizing children's Christmas parties, or chairing welfare committees, but at another it involved strengthening the bonds within the officer corps and between officers and airmen. These responsibilities could be onerous, even for the wives of junior officers.[42] Senior officers (and their wives) were expected to entertain their subordinates, contemporaries, figures in the local community, and official visitors—including providing overnight hospitality. As such, they were entitled to a residence (and appropriate staff). This was not an endless stream of parties and socializing, but a deliberate process that sought to create a shared identity—within and outside the service—that blurred the distinction between airman and family man. Unlike the other services, the RAF was distinct in that its operations often took place from its home airfield, meaning that work and family lives existed in close proximity.[43] The British military has been described as behaving like a "total institution"—alienating individuals from society and demanding that they, and their families, conform to set rules.[44] Such criticism, based on modern social norms, ignores the support structures and welfare facilities provided by the military for its personnel that (for much of the twentieth century) exceeded anything available in the wider community. In a service where the main professional activity was undertaken by individuals (or a small group of individuals), it was even more important to find opportunities to demonstrate that everyone in uniform functioned as part of a larger "team," in the air and on the ground. The idea that the regiment was both your home and family had emerged in the Victorian era and found ready acceptance in the RAF.[45] While this concept may seem paternalistic, it was a strongly held belief that resulted in a substantial and sustained investment in domestic accommodation and associated infrastructure (messes, canteens, recreational facilities, married quarters, etc.), well beyond similar efforts by the Army and Royal Navy. The remoteness and self-sufficiency of RAF stations, at home and overseas, underscored the importance of the "family'" in sustaining what was, in effect, a closed community.[46] Admittedly, it also created a hierarchy of wives but this was a by-product, rather than the primary aim of the system.[47]

This then was the carefully crafted world that Opal had chosen to join. Understanding and adapting to the social mores of the RAF presented a challenge but she faced a further obstacle. In marrying a senior officer, without braving the rigors faced by the family of a junior officer, she was also vulnerable to the criticism that she did not understand the daily lives of those working for her husband. It should be stressed, however, that it was Opal's choice to "follow" her husband. It was certainly not unknown for wives to decide that service life was not for them, such as Marjorie Denison, who married Philip Joubert de la Ferté in 1915. Her absence during much of his RAF career did not overtly hinder his promotion to the highest ranks.[48] On the other hand, Air Vice-Marshal Charles Longcroft felt obligated to retire from the RAF in 1929 when his wife made it clear that she would neither go abroad with him nor let him go without her.[49]

While at Andover, Brooke-Popham routinely "called upon" the wives of new students to welcome them to the college—a task that would have fallen to his spouse, had he been married. This ritual, which disappeared during World War II, established a corporate intimacy—although it has been described as "socially fastidious."[50] The choice of wife (as opposed to a girlfriend) had significant implications for the individual and the institution. Remaining single was not necessarily an obstacle to a successful career—Edward Ellington was a bachelor but still rose to command the RAF. Early marriage was actively discouraged for a young officer (allowances and entitlements to housing were designed to reinforce this principle). On the other hand, marrying badly or getting involved in a messy divorce could stall a career. In 1932, Brooke-Popham would advise Flight Lieutenant Guy Carter that his divorce and remarriage to a "dancing girl" would undoubtedly militate against his career.[51] It was in this context that Brooke-Popham was asked to intervene in Christopher Courtney's choice of fiancée, Constance "Micky" Rayson, whom he had brought to several Andover dances.

> Had a very tiresome letter today begging me to use my influence to break off Courtney's engagement, as she is reported to be quite impossible. I don't know what to do. To begin with, although I didn't think much of her, she's probably not so bad as she's painted; secondly a man like Courtney knows his own business best; thirdly if [a] man's really in love no arguments have the slightest effect. On the other hand, it would be horrible to see him made miserable without moving a finger and my correspondent says, "If anyone can do anything you can." And there's the Staff College to consider, she might do untold harm there.[52]

Brooke-Popham had initially viewed Constance as a "flash lady," but he soon concluded that while she may have frequented night clubs a bit too frequently, and mixed with the wrong set, he should not intervene.[53] What may have excited his anonymous correspondent was that Constance Rayson was a divorcée—something that would later cause problems with the royal family when her presentation at court was retrospectively cancelled in 1930, even though Lady Salmond (wife of Jack Salmond) had been her sponsor. According to one report, the episode demonstrated the peculiarly variegated and paradoxical quality of the British society scene that had otherwise moved toward a freer and more liberal regime since the war.[54] The Courtneys married in September 1926 and lived happily together for nearly fifty years. The couple became lifelong friends with the Brooke-Pophams.

The relocation from Kenley to Uxbridge coincided with the arrival of Flying Officer (later Group Captain) Rudolph Trevor "Taffy" Taaffe as Brooke-Popham's personal assistant (PA).[55] The two would later work together in Iraq and Kenya. A familiar face was Air Commodore Tony Holt, who was appointed Jack Salmond's chief Air Staff officer in July 1926. He proved an able ally, together with Squadron Leader (later Air Chief Marshal Sir) Keith Park, who also worked at the headquarters before he returned to flying duties, in command of No. 111 Squadron (Siskin fighters) at Hornchurch. In May 1928, Jack Salmond was detached for duty in Australia and New Zealand, tasked with inspecting their respective Air Forces and advising on future development.[56] Air Vice-Marshal Francis Scarlett was temporarily drafted in as AOCinC. This meant that one two-star was reporting to another, but Scarlett was full of praise for Brooke-Popham and the support he had offered him "in my somewhat difficult position."[57]

The two years spent at Uxbridge proved a happy and fulfilling period for the newly married couple. Their family increased to four, with the birth of Diana Mary Brooke-Popham ("Didie") on 15 December 1926 and Francis Philip ("Phil"), on 8 July 1928.[58] There was also good news in the Birthday Honours List, with the announcement of their father's knighthood.[59] This was customary for RAF two-stars in a command appointment, but Brooke-Popham was still delighted.[60] He broke the news to Opal early that morning by sending up their maid, Bertha, to ask "whether Her Ladyship wanted tea or coffee for breakfast." Life may have been good, but it still offered its share of tragedy and difficulties. There was a brief but bitter argument between husband and wife following Diana's birth. Opal wrote accusing him of showing more interest in his career than his new family.[61] It would be speculation to put the episode down to postnatal depression, but it was only one of two occasions in nearly thirty years when the two are known to have violently disagreed (at least on paper). The normally imperturbable Brooke-Popham was greatly upset by Opal's criticism and somewhat theatrical in his response, although his sense of humor did not entirely desert him. "I thought about running away from it all, not like Miss Linton but just disappearing in Canada or somewhere, I'm too old for the Foreign Legion."[62] He attempted, in a rough penciled draft (revealing qualities of self-deprecation but not poetic skill), to acknowledge his failings:

Now I am a K.C.B.
The rules of life apply to me
So hence to my office I repair
I must recline upon my chair
I then must ring my bell and say
I really cannot work today
For what use is my staff to me
When I do all the work you see

The hours I keep are far too long
Although I am so very strong
In future, I will come at ten
And with an effort wield my pen
Until the hour of lunch draws nigh
Then to my house the car will fly
And after lunch a long cigar
So puffed at ease beside my fire

And more a week I may just go
Unto my office for a blow
But afternoons are made for ease
Aside perhaps for felling trees[63]

A more serious and distressing event was the sudden death of Granville Wheler, aged just fifty-five.[64] Opal's aunt and uncle had been a second family to her. Much of her childhood had been spent at either Otterden Place or Ledston Hall (where she was home-educated).[65] Although Opal's father had attended her wedding two years earlier, it was her uncle who had given her away. Granville had been ill since August, but it was confidently expected that he would recover. Opal had spent an increasing amount of time in the autumn at Otterden helping to nurse him, but his death still took her by surprise.

As much as Brooke-Popham's career was in the ascendancy, the same could not be said of his chief staff officer Erb Herbert, who was increasingly unhappy at being overlooked for promotion. The pair rode regularly together, and although he encouraged him to be patient, Herbert resigned his commission in 1929—suggesting that there was a limit to Brooke-Popham's powers of persuasion (and patronage) however highly he rated his friend.[66] For his part, Brooke-Popham had proved to be a successful and respected AOC, bringing the Fighting Area to "a high state of efficiency."[67] Flight Lieutenant (later Air Vice-Marshal Sir) Cecil Bouchier was just one of many junior officers who had benefitted from his leadership and encouragement.[68] Although Brooke-Popham had thrown himself into the role, he still found time to write a sixty-eight-page history of the RAF for use in flying schools (with an extensive appendix detailing reading material).[69] During his two and a half years in command of the Fighting Area, the number of single-seat fighter squadrons had remained largely constant (increasing by just two),[70] but the slow growth in frontline strength was less important than the operational developments that he had overseen, including: air-to-air communications; experiments in controlling fighters from the ground; improved night interception tactics; regular air exercises (integrating visual and acoustic detection techniques); the establishment of observation centers; and a robust system for collecting and sifting telephone reports from remote observation posts (plotting the progress of raids on large, squared, table maps using counters) before passing the information to the Headquarters Operations Room.[71] Just as importantly, Brooke-Popham had established a vibrant esprit de corps among the fighter squadrons and a command style that would be imitated by his successors, routinely flying himself to his stations to meet squadron pilots.[72] He was energetic at finding ways to increase their flying skills, while improving professionalism.[73] Keith Park was not alone in admiring his AOC, whose "enthusiasm and hard work were vital to training and morale, helping lay the foundations for Fighter Command."[74] There was no surprise, therefore, when in July 1928, it was announced that he had been selected for the RAF's most important overseas appointment, AOC Iraq Command.[75]

9

IRAQ COMMAND
1928–1930

Having completed his tour as AOC Fighting Area in October 1928, Brooke-Popham travelled to Iraq to take over his new command from Edward Ellington. The post was accompanied, but with two young children (the youngest less than four months old) the couple decided that Opal should wait until October of the following year to join him (without their family), before returning to England at Easter, when the heat became oppressive. It would be the first, but not the last, time that husband and wife were separated for an extended period. Iraq was the most important overseas command in the RAF. Britain had been designated the protecting power for Mesopotamia at the San Remo Conference in April 1920, convened to deal with the peace terms to be offered to Turkey.[1] The conference had recognized the independence of Iraq (as Mesopotamia would be called from 1921) and Syria but, under the auspices of the League of Nations, awarded Britain and France mandates for the respective countries—the boundary lines to be resolved between the protecting powers. The delay in awarding independence was the primary cause of the Iraq Revolt, involving both Shia and Sunni communities, that broke out in July 1920.[2] The rebellion, a mixture of tribal uprisings and civil disobedience, forced the British military commander, General Sir Aylmer Haldane, to call for reinforcements. At one stage, the government considered evacuating the country, but Haldane had regained the initiative by August and the rebellion petered out in the autumn, although not before some ten thousand military and civilians had become casualties (including 2,500 British and Indian troops).[3]

The RAF had argued at the Cairo Conference, held in March 1921, that the most cost-effective solution to meeting Britain's responsibilities in Iraq was the use of airpower.[4] A relatively small RAF presence (eight squadrons) could provide the necessary reach and rapid strategic effect—allowing a considerable reduction in the size of the military garrison and a significant saving to the Treasury. These proposals were agreed (with Churchill's enthusiastic support—in his role as secretary of state for the colonies), although RAF control in Iraq was not assumed until October 1922, when Jack Salmond arrived as GOC Military and Air Forces.[5] The doctrine of "air control" involved the use of aircraft to enforce government authority on uncooperative tribes through warnings, blockades and, where necessary, bombing of villages and livestock.[6]

The Cairo Conference had also agreed that Iraq should become a constitutional monarchy and that the crown should be offered to Faisal, one of the main leaders in the Arab Revolt that had helped defeat the Ottoman armies in the Middle East.[7] Faisal, who had been ejected from Syria by the French, enjoyed some popular support, but there was considerable political uncertainty and resentment throughout Iraq at the continuing British occupation. The high commissioner nominally advised and guided the king but his government could not act without British authority. On the other hand, continuing threats to the government's authority required regular RAF intervention. A resurgent Turkey threatened to occupy Mosul, while there was unrest in Kurdistan and in southern Iraq. A further threat had emerged in the form of Syrian and Ikhwan raiders (irregular forces that had rebelled against the authority of Ibn Saud, who was rapidly consolidating his own power in the Arabian Peninsula).[8] The Ikhwan were responsible for several serious raids in the Najd (the desert area lying between Iraq and the Arabian Peninsula). Although the RAF could deal with these through air action, there was sensitivity about infringing the sovereignty of Kuwait—a British protectorate since 1899—that constrained offensive operations.[9] Iraq remained a troubled country with complex problems that attracted political controversy at home. While it remained Britain's long-term aim to grant Iraq its full independence (particularly after the Iraq Revolt), the route to this outcome was not going to be easy or without setbacks.

Brooke-Popham met with Trenchard in October 1928 to discuss the challenges he would face.[10] Trenchard followed this up with a personal letter: "I hope that when you get out in Iraq you will remember that the situation at home is liable to violent fluctuations and it is sometimes impossible for you to appreciate all the difficulties of the position. If the parties are pretty evenly balanced after the next election, i.e. the Conservatives, Liberals and Labour, we shall have, I fear, a constant series of crises and so-called changes of policy. This will make my job very difficult and will not ease your own."[11]

He also took the opportunity to speak with Sir Gilbert Clayton, who was due to take over from Sir Henry Dobbs as the high commissioner in the new year. Clayton was extremely knowledgeable about the Middle East, having acted as Field Marshal Edmund Allenby's chief of intelligence in Cairo during World War I and, as one of the main instigators of the Arab Revolt, was respected by the Arab leaders.[12] During his time in Iraq, Brooke-Popham kept up a regular correspondence with Trenchard (and later Jack Salmond), as well as Cyril Newall (director, operations and intelligence). These private letters supplemented his official correspondence with the Air Ministry and Colonial Office.

Leaving London on 1 November, Brooke-Popham arrived at Port Said on 7 November before travelling by rail to Cairo where he stayed with Tom Webb-Bowen, AOC Middle East. The onward journey was by air, part of a flight of four D.H. 9A day bombers that flew via Amman, following the route he had first used seven years earlier.[13] On arrival at Baghdad, he was met by Ellington, who was leaving on promotion to replace Jack Salmond as CinC ADGB in the New Year. Brooke-Popham had few illusions about what awaited him. He had previously described Baghdad as "simply a glorified mud village and hardly distinguishable at evening from the desert."[14] While he was prepared for the oppressive heat and lack of comfort, the isolation was more difficult to handle. He was lonely without his new family or any old friends like Erb Herbert or Tony Holt to go about with.[15] Opal's weekly letters provided an important, if not vital, link to home. "Letters are so much more important to one out here than they are in England."[16]

Brooke-Popham was lucky in his headquarters staff who were, by and large, extremely competent. Air Commodore (later Air Chief Marshal Sir) Frederick Bowhill was chief of staff (replaced by the equally capable Charles "Ugly" Burnett in February 1929), Group Captain (later Air Commodore) James Bowen was head of technical services, Wing Commander Douglas Oliver was chief of operations, Wing Commander Kenneth Buss was head of intelligence,[17] Wing Commander (later Air Marshal Sir) John Babington was station commander, and Flight Lieutenant (later Air Commodore)

Sydney Toomer was in the intelligence section—the last two were ex-students from Andover. Most of the HQ staff, together with the chief doctor, lived with Brooke-Popham in the AOC's residence. His aide-de-camp (ADC) was Flight Lieutenant (later Air Commodore) Guy Carter,[18] who had been a flight commander in the Fighting Area, although Brooke-Popham thought (perhaps unfairly) that he was not as good as Taaffe. Over the next few years, Brooke-Popham would become both his mentor and confidant. The squadron commanders were equally able, although he had some concerns:

> One of my squadron commanders, on whom I had reported badly, told me his life history the other day; I already knew some of it. He's been married some time and has two children. In 1920, his wife went off with another man whilst he was in India and when he came back he gave the man such a thrashing that he died. He was tried for murder and acquitted. He then took his wife back and set her up in a house and went back to India. She went off the rails again and so he arranged for the children and subsequently finding his wife was more or less penniless set her upon another house and gave her a decent allowance. Now she's keeping running [*sic*] into debt and he keeps paying up.[19]

The political and security situation in Iraq during the late 1920s was complex and uncertain. The policing of Iraq's borders was a difficult task at the best of times, even with the RAF's help. In the absence of natural features or habitation, it was possible to cross from one country to another without hindrance or the knowledge of the authorities. It was also arguable that these boundaries meant little to the nomadic tribes of the region. The construction of forts, close to the border with the Najd and intended to deter tribal raids, had incensed Ibn Saud who believed, with some justification, that they broke the terms of his treaties with the British.[20] Ibn Saud's victory in the Hijaz, forcing the abdication of Faisal's father (Hussein) and his older brother (Ali), had generated considerable enmity between the two kings.[21] A further complication was that multiple government departments (Air Ministry, War Office, Admiralty, Colonial Office, Foreign Office, and India Office) had legitimate interests in Iraq, creating a further layer of uncertainty.

The RAF's role in Iraq attracted controversy from the very moment it was first suggested. This was not driven by ethical or moral considerations

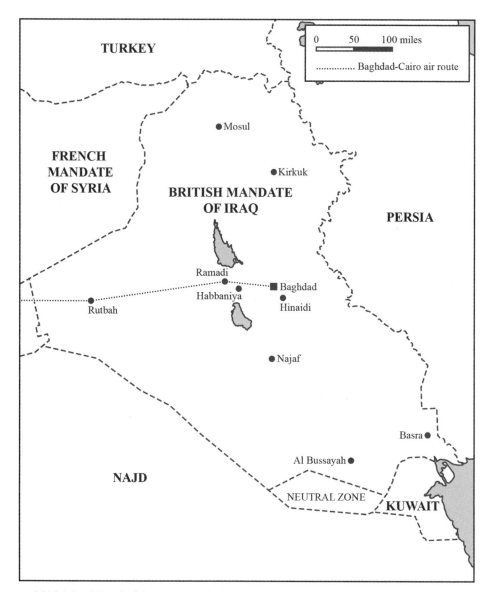

MAP I. RAF IRAQ COMMAND, 1929

(at least not at the beginning), but by a combination of declining defense budgets and inter-service rivalry. The debate about how to maintain security in Iraq became drawn into the wider argument about the future of the RAF as an independent service. The Balfour Report had supposedly resolved this question in the RAF's favor,[22] but the Army fought back, refuting the claims made for airpower. Henry Wilson, chief of the Imperial General Staff (CIGS), derided the idea of employing the Air Force in the Middle East as "hot air, aeroplanes and Arabs."[23] Wilson, who believed that garrisoning Iraq was unaffordable and Britain should withdraw (an opinion supported by the Beaverbrook press), described the RAF's role as "coming from God knows where, dropping its bombs on God knows what and going off God knows where."[24] It was the Army that first denounced air control as inhumane, "the development of a means of killing women and children."[25] The Air Ministry was sensitive to such criticism and forcefully argued the case for the "humanity" of air control through public and private media.[26] Nevertheless, accusations of inhumanity would continue to be leveled, driven by "a curious alliance of sentimentalists and die-hards."[27] In general, such views were not shared by those serving in Iraq.[28] The notable exception was Air Commodore Lionel Charlton, who had served as Jack Salmond's chief staff officer at Headquarters Iraq Command.[29] Charlton resigned over the bombing of Iraqi villages, arguing that the practice of air control was indiscriminate and inflicted unnecessary suffering.[30] Charlton was a lone voice, indeed a number of influential figures actively supported the use of air control.[31] T. E. Lawrence took the pragmatic line that "British and native casualties in the five years since the treaty was made with Iraq have only been a few tens, whereas each year before the treaty they had run to thousands."[32] Sir Henry Dobbs, the high commissioner from 1923 to 1929, strongly defended the policy and rejected the accusation that the Air Force "works by bombing only, that such bombing is indiscriminate, killing women and children, and that air operations leave a legacy of hate and resentment."[33]

Nevertheless, there continue to be questions about the efficacy and morality of the air control regime. One social historian has described the period as a "horrific episode of state-sanctioned violence."[34] Others have alleged (incorrectly) that the RAF employed poison gas and that the firestorms of Hamburg and Dresden could be traced directly to the RAF's experiences in Iraq.[35] The reality of air control was rather different, and bombing was never indiscriminate or precipitate. Toward the end of December 1928, shortly after Brooke-Popham's arrival, an Ikhwan raiding party was spotted in the southern desert a few miles inside Iraq:

> The aeroplanes, which were carrying four bombs each, circled round to make sure who the party was and were fired upon. So, they let their bombs go and the raiders scattered at once and fled back to Najd for all they were worth, leaving three men killed behind. None

of our people were touched, so it was a pretty cheap victory; the raiders numbered 130 by the way. I suppose the *Daily Herald* will cry
out against the brutality of the RAF, but they might remember that
these raiders are not merely out to steal camels, they murder every
man and every male child they catch, even babies; women they don't
touch as a rule.[36]

These raids had commenced in early 1928 and continued throughout 1929.[37]
A coordinated effort by aircraft and ground forces, including the employment
of armored cars and advance posts, saw the Najd tribes driven back from the
frontier.[38] The British action was motivated by the need to demonstrate that
it was discharging its responsibilities as the mandated power and supporting
the Iraqi government.[39] Minimum force was employed, and only when the
RAF had been fired upon first. In one instance, on 3 March 1929, this led to
the death of a wireless operator that might have been avoided—if the rules of
engagement had not been followed. During the twelve months from 1 July
1928, the RAF dropped a total of forty Cooper bombs (each weighing twenty
pounds). The total number of rounds fired from the air was a little more than
two thousand.[40] This very small expenditure, together with constant patrols
by aircraft and armored cars, was sufficient to keep five hundred miles of
frontier secure.

After his first visit to Iraq, in 1921, Brooke-Popham had commented to
Trenchard that Henry Wilson's remarks at the RAF Staff College, intended
as criticism, had only served to express the ubiquity of airpower and the reason for the immense morale effect that airplanes had had on the Arabs in
Mesopotamia.[41] These views were strengthened when he visited the town of
Najaf, staying overnight with a local landowner, Said Abbas. As part of the
entertainment, they were given an exhibition of mimicry by another of the
guests: "One of the things he imitated was a bombing attack by aeroplanes
on a body of Arabs. Rather significant, first the Arabs shouting and boasting,
then the noise of aeroplanes approaching, then the fall of bombs and finally
the Arabs screaming with terror. I don't think it was staged for our benefit at
all, anyway the audience were all most amused."[42]

Brooke-Popham spent a great deal of time flying around the country, using
his personal aircraft to visit military units, as well as places of antiquity.[43] It
has been inferred that his nerves were affected as a result. "I know I felt as if
the end of the world had really come and there was no-one left alive except

my pilot and myself."[44] However, this comment relates to his first transit of
the lava field east of Amman in 1921 and was an expression of deep wonder
rather than troubling worry. During his time in Iraq, Brooke-Popham travelled the Baghdad-Amman air route over a dozen times, without incident
or trauma. His letters to Opal routinely describe the excitement of flying
over Iraq. One of his early visits was to Basra, where he stayed with No. 84
Squadron, before flying out to the desert outpost of Busaiyah (now known
as Al Bussayah), one hundred miles to the west: "It's exactly one's idea of
Zinderneuf [the desert fort in P. C. Wren's novel *Beau Geste*] about 100 Iraqi
infantry, some Ford cars to carry machine guns, 20–30 desert police (natives
on camels) and two Englishmen. Barbed wire, a thick mud brick wall with
loopholes and sentries pacing along the top and all around the flat desert as
far as the horizon."[45]

Christmas without Opal and the children was difficult, but he was distracted by the need to deal with a crisis in Afghanistan where a force of one
thousand rebels threatened British civilians trapped in the Legation.[46] The
RAF mounted a successful rescue attempt using transport aircraft secured
from Iraq. Brooke-Popham provided pilots as well as aircraft (initially three
Vickers Victoria transports).[47] By New Year's day, 586 people had been evacuated from Kabul, including the Afghan royal family, together with 24,193
pounds of luggage.[48] Early in the New Year, RAF Headquarters was moved
from Baghdad to the airfield at Hinaidi (about four miles away), where the
climate was better, although the AOC's residence remained in Baghdad—to
stay close to the High Commission.[49] In March, Clayton arrived to replace
Dobbs, his reception at Baghdad West organized by Brooke-Popham.[50] The
new high commissioner was impressed by the RAF personnel he encountered, commenting that they had entered into the spirit of the country and
were dealing with the Iraqis "with sympathy and understanding"—an attitude that was uncommon in the other services.[51] He got on particularly well
with Brooke-Popham: "[W]e are in close and constant touch, and I am ready
to take responsibility for any decision he may take."[52] For his part, Brooke-
Popham regarded Clayton as a charming man and valued his friendship.[53] He
would later write, "He and I were such close personal friends. I will only say
this: that as regards his work there's no one I would sooner have worked with
in a crisis and that as regards his character, he was all I should like my son to
develop into."[54]

One of the earliest problems that the pair had to address was the quality of the Iraqi army. The most effective ground forces in Iraq were two battalions of Levies,[55] and the RAF Armoured Car sections.[56] It had been hoped that the Iraqi army, advised by British officers, could perform many of the country's internal security activities, but Brooke-Popham rapidly realized that the army's efficiency was poor and its officers inadequate.[57] He suggested several improvements, including giving greater authority to the (British) inspector general. Trenchard responded that, while the Levies remained under British control, the efficiency of the Iraqi army was not a serious concern. He also reminded him "that there must be only one Commander in Chief in Iraq, and that is you."[58] Brooke-Popham became an enthusiastic supporter of the Levies and encouraged their development, including the Bedouin Southern Desert Camel Corps. In this respect, he was more open-minded than his predecessor, who had initially opposed the employment of machine guns by the police.[59] One of their officers, Major (later Major-General Sir) John Glubb, acknowledged that "I owe the greater part of any reputation which I may possess—firstly to the RAF as a whole and secondly to yourself in particular, who acted as so understanding and indulgent a chief at a time when I must often have seemed very troublesome to you."[60] Glubb persuaded Brooke-Popham to be much more proactive in mounting patrols and, although the practical results were small, they produced considerable morale effect. For the first time "the Iraqi forces, the tribes and the RAF were working in perfect cooperation."[61] Even so, relations did not always run smoothly and Glubb's lack of patience created annoyance among the RAF staff. He would later admit to some sympathy for Brooke-Popham's position. "[A]ir officers commanding could scarcely be expected to follow the advice of such a young man, especially on the subject of how to use their forces on active operations."[62] In March, Brooke-Popham paid a "private" visit to Abadan and the Persian oilfields, hosted by the Anglo-Persian Oil Company, however, his real objective was to review the area's defenses and produce a suitable plan in the event of an attempted coup.[63] The same month, he attended the unveiling of the British war memorial at Basra, commemorating the nearly 40,000 officers and men who had died in World War I without a known grave: "To my mind that's quite a sufficient answer to those who ask why we don't clear out of Iraq; if we've spent all those lives in getting the country free of the Turks, surely we ought to stop and see them firmly on their feet before we leave? Certainly, a large proportion of that 40,000 were Indian troops, but they were all serving under the British flag."[64]

Early in July, Brooke-Popham was asked by Trenchard to return to London for discussions. Clayton felt that this was a timely call as Brooke-Popham was in need of a complete rest, having suffered a range of ailments since his arrival (including lumbago, tonsillitis, an infected eye, and a poisoned finger), spending several weeks in hospital.[65] Life in Iraq was physically and mentally hard—not just the monotony but also the psychological effect of dead level plains, the drab colors, the lack of normal amenities, and the absence of places to go or friends to stay with.[66] Brooke-Popham left Baghdad on 11 July and reached London six days later. The break allowed him to spend three weeks with his family before returning to the Middle East in early August. Although she would join him in October, Brooke-Popham was torn between leaving Opal and his eagerness to return to Iraq: "Such a lot of England seems artificial somehow, people worrying about the things that don't matter. Too many houses and roads and too much machinery. It's very hard though, isn't it, to know what reality is. Is it the desert or Mayfair or a slum in Leeds? I hanker after the desert; the result I suppose of the Pophams originating on the Hampshire Downs. Then I suppose, I want to get to work again."[67]

Like many of his generation, Brooke-Popham had fallen under the spell of Arabia. "There appears to be a sort of natural fellow feeling between these nomad Arabs and the Air Force. Perhaps both feel that they are at times in conflict with the vast elemental forces of nature."[68] It has been asserted that such claims to empathy with the nomadic tribes were illusory, and only served to disguise the inhumanity of bombing from the air.[69] Brooke-Popham's private letters do not support this view, nor do they suggest that his love of the desert somehow upset his moral compass:

> There's a lot of talk in Baghdad about the financial and military agreements between Britain and Iraq, the Cabinet have resigned and the newspapers are blatant, but outside Baghdad no one minds in the least, the only danger is that if the central authority in Baghdad lets things slide in the country and eases up on the control, some of the districts are very likely to seize the opportunity to break away from the present regime altogether. Many of them hate the Baghdad politicians and would much prefer to be administered direct by Great Britain, but I shall have to force them to go back to the Baghdad fold and if there are any casualties shall get execrated by the Baghdad politicians for brutality. Are we idealists or just fools?[70]

The voyage from Marseilles to Port Said, via Genoa, was uneventful, although it was not unknown to be lobbied by those looking for favors at their final destination. As no one else was travelling to Iraq, Brooke-Popham should have enjoyed a restful journey, but for the presence of Major-General Edmund "Tiny" Ironside and Hardwicke Forster Stanford, a journalist who had written about the South African War under the nom de plume "Matilda Chiffon." Ironside, who would become CIGS in 1940, was travelling to India to take command of the Meerut district. Nearly thirty years earlier a group of young officers (including Ironside) had ragged Stanford at the Mount Nelson Hotel, Cape Town, on Christmas Eve. The officers (less Ironside) were subsequently court-martialed for assault but found not guilty. Newspaper reports of the trial expressed surprise at the acquittal while contrasting the manly looks of the accused ("fresh complexioned, sturdily-built with curling blond moustaches") with the hollow-chested languor and lisp of the injured journalist.[71] Brooke-Popham was greatly amused by the turn of events, and the tension it created on board, although he confided to Opal that Stanford was "a most horrible type."[72]

Before the end of his first year in Iraq, and less than six months after Clayton had taken over as high commissioner, Brooke-Popham found himself thrust center-stage when Clayton had a fatal heart attack. "This is a hard country. At 5.30 p.m. on Wednesday I was playing polo with poor Sir Gilbert; at 7.30 p.m. I was watching his body being carried out of the hall in the Residency." In the absence of the counsellor and four out of the six secretaries, Brooke-Popham took over the duties of high commissioner, his first task being to organize Clayton's funeral. He had no illusions about his skills as a diplomat, believing that Clayton would "have made so much more of it than I shall be able to."[73] Brooke-Popham's period as acting high commissioner lasted a few weeks, until the arrival of Major Hubert Young, the new counsellor.[74] Sir Francis Humphrys was formally appointed as Clayton's replacement in October, but did not reach Iraq until 10 December 1929. Underscoring the importance of airpower in securing British control of Iraq, Humphrys flew into Baghdad escorted by eight aircraft.

The most important issue for Faisal, and one that had taken much of Clayton's time, was Iraq's independence. Faisal had only agreed to the Anglo-Iraqi Treaty of 1926, extending the mandate for a further twenty-five years, because it secured the province of Mosul, otherwise claimed by Turkey. Even so, he had persuaded the British government to agree that Iraq's progress toward admission to the League of Nations should be reviewed every four years.[75] Clayton fought hard on Faisal's behalf to achieve early independence, although continuing disagreement over the financial and military accords that underpinned British power in Iraq slowed progress. The election of a Labour government in May 1929, and Clayton's personal efforts, saw the Colonial Office change its position and agree to Iraq's independence. It fell to Brooke-Popham to announce the good news to Faisal (the telegram announcing the British government's decision was in transit when Clayton died).[76] The shift in policy allowed Faisal to appoint a new government, although Brooke-Popham was less than impressed. "They nearly all look upon politics from the purely personal point of view, how to enhance their own or their friend's prestige, how to curb their rival's ambitions, and appeals to do things for the good of the country leave them cold."[77] He felt that the prime minister, 'Abd al-Muhsin al-Sa'adoun, was better than most. His subsequent suicide was a huge setback, as Muhsin was "the one politician who was trusted both by the British and the Iraqis. I am quite certain his personal influence has prevented many crises in the past."[78] Matters were not helped by a hurried and partial translation of Muhsin's suicide note that implied the British were to blame. Brooke-Popham's period as acting high commissioner brought him closer to Faisal, and also to his brother Ali, whom he found a sympathetic but timid character.[79] His views on Faisal were more mixed. He admired the king in many ways but was also critical of some of his behavior. "A long talk with King Faisal this morning. He's become inoculated with the Mussolini doctrine that any opposition to government policy must be wiped off the slate."[80] On a happier note, however, Opal had arrived safely in Baghdad on 19 October 1929, via the overland route from Syria, and would remain at the Residence until the spring. The next week, No. 6 Squadron was redeployed from Mosul to Egypt, for employment in Palestine. Brooke-Popham met them at Ramadi: "The AOC had flown there to say good-bye. Pretty nice of him, but he seems to have the knack of doing the right thing. Guy Carter had flown him there in his 'red devil,' a 'Ninak' painted all red."[81]

During 1929, Ibn Saud had fought two major battles with the Ikhwan, forcing them to take refuge in the neutral zone, close to Kuwait, where there was some sympathy for their cause and a wariness about Ibn Saud's intentions. In January 1930, the remaining Ikhwan forces, including the main rebel leader, Faysal al-Dawish, surrendered to the British.[82] The rebels had been prevented from scattering and restricted to an increasingly small area of

Kuwait by the RAF's armored cars and airplanes at a cost of two casualties (both camels) under the direction of Ugly Burnett, Brooke-Popham's chief of staff. Burnett was part of the British delegation that met with Ibn Saud from 20 to 28 January 1930 to decide on the fate of the rebels.[83] The defeat of the Ikhwan provided Faisal with an opportunity to build bridges with Ibn Saud, notwithstanding their personal animosity.[84] Early in 1930, Faisal proposed a meeting to resolve their outstanding differences and determine the fate of the remaining Ikhwan rebels. Brooke-Popham was invited to observe the discussions, to be held on a British warship anchored at the mouth of the Shatt al-Arab waterway. Never one to miss an opportunity, he left Baghdad a fortnight in advance with the aim of identifying potential landing grounds for the air route to India. Since the inauguration of regular flights between Cairo and Baghdad there had been uncertainty about the best route from Iraq to India. The Persian government had agreed to allow Imperial Airways to fly across their territory in 1925, but ratification had been delayed and an alternative route was needed along the Trucial coast. Brooke-Popham visited Bahrein, Sharjah, Abu Dhabi, and Dubai to identify suitable airfields, before joining the high commissioner at Basra.

The ships carrying the two kings rendezvoused on Friday, 21 February 1930. Faisal was accommodated on the Basra Port Authority's ship *Nearchus*, Humphrys and Brooke-Popham on HMS *Lupin*, and Ibn Saud on the European Telegraph Company's ship *Patrick Stewart*.[85] Most of the discussions were held on *Lupin*. "Faisal appeared nervous and anxious to create a good impression; Ibn Saud was quite at ease and gave the impression from the start of being master of the situation." Brooke-Popham commented that Ibn Saud almost always got what he wanted from any meeting or conference by "his charm of manner, combined with the strength of his personality." He also felt that Ibn Saud's advisers were far superior to those accompanying Faisal. According to Fuad Hamza, Ibn Saud's foreign minister, his master wanted to absorb three things from Englishmen: their politeness; their resolution; and their mechanical ability.[86] The meeting was amicable (at least to outward appearances) and concluded on Sunday 23 February, with the two rulers having agreed on a form of arbitration over the desert outposts, the rough outline of a *bon voisinage* [good neighborliness] treaty (in which Faisal acknowledged Ibn Saud as king of the Najd and the Hijaz, and Ibn Saud acknowledged Faisal as king of Iraq), promises of a pardon for Farhan bin Mashur (the remaining Ikhwan rebel leader), and a tribunal to assess respective claims for damages (caused by the Ikhwan raids and retaliatory RAF bombing). According to Brooke-Popham, "the man who gains most appears to be Mashur, who ought to be hung." Notwithstanding their "amicable" meeting, "Ibn Saud appears to be much incensed against Faisal whom he accuses of deceitfulness. . . . [H]e also complained that he couldn't stand being left alone with Faisal because he at once commenced to whine about having been deprived of family possessions by Ibn Saud. Is it possible that Faisal proposed the meeting in the hope of getting some personal compensation out of Ibn Saud?"[87]

During May 1930 Brooke-Popham was drawn into a public argument between Admiral of the Fleet Earl Beatty and Trenchard.[88] The ostensible cause was the RAF's decision in 1928 to deploy a squadron of Southampton flying boats to Basra. Brooke-Popham had successfully employed the aircraft to survey the Gulf coast for potential landing grounds. For their part, the Admiralty complained that the flying boats had upset a delicate situation, although their real concern was the RAF's presence in what had been their bailiwick.[89] The controversy was part of a long-running and bitter battle between the Navy and the RAF over control of the Fleet Air Arm—itself a legacy of the Navy and Army's attempts in the immediate postwar years to have the RAF disbanded. Although this question had been resolved in the Air Force's favor by the Balfour Report, it remained a sensitive issue and one that continued to attract attention.[90] As a result, the RAF's performance in Iraq, including the effectiveness and morality of air control, came under close and continued scrutiny.[91]

It has since become convenient to describe the use of aircraft in Iraq as some sort of experiment. "It was in Iraq that the British would rigorously practice, if never perfect, the technology of bombardment as a permanent method of colonial administration and surveillance and there that they would fully theorise the value of airpower as an independent arm of the military."[92] The RAF's success in maintaining security in Iraq strengthened the case for a separate air service, but this argument had largely been won by 1930. It is therefore misleading to suggest that, in the struggle to retain independence and demonstrate relevance, RAF commanders were somehow oblivious to the fact that air control caused casualties. The use of bombing was a last resort, even where British pilots were shot down and killed, as occurred in both April and August 1924. On neither occasion was air action taken, instead the Iraqi police were dispatched to arrest those responsible.[93] Brooke-Popham had no sympathy for the argument that air policing inflicted excessive casualties or disproportionate damage, but he understood there were those who did not agree. "Women and children will get killed accidentally in war, even by shells, but the RAF have found other objectives."[94] All the evidence suggests that the RAF was exceptionally efficient at maintaining order and avoiding sowing the seeds for ever greater disorder.[95] Whatever the intrinsic merits of air control, airpower offered Faisal the opportunity to create a modern, functioning state. "What kept the country physically and politically united was the power and reach of the RAF, and beyond it the might of an imperial power."[96] Ultimately, the RAF's actions can only be judged by Iraq's progress toward a stable, secure, and functioning democracy. For good or bad, the modern frontiers of Jordan and Iraq are, in part, the legacy of air policing.[97]

Brooke-Popham's time as AOC was now ending. The end of the Ikhwan revolt ensured that the southern frontier was for the moment quiet. The same could not be said for Iraqi politicians. Independence meant that a new Anglo-Iraqi treaty was required. Faisal recognized that a British presence beyond 1932 was essential to ensure the country's security. Not all Iraqis agreed, and there was considerable turmoil over the issue. Brooke-Popham continued to find Iraqi politics a depressing affair. "The Iraq Cabinet are being very tiresome over the treaty and refusing to agree to publication of the text, however, they may see reason before it is too late."[98] In the event, the treaty was published in London on 18 July and the following day in the Baghdad press. These frustrations did not weaken his love of the country. "When I'm feeling utterly fed up with Iraqi politicians and the apparent impossibility of instilling any idea of loyalty or patriotism into their heads, I sit on the veranda and gaze at the sunset."[99] There were also some niggling issues to be resolved with the Air Staff. He was more pragmatic and flexible than some in London, confessing to Opal that he didn't see eye to eye with them over the defense treaty.[100] To Brooke-Popham's mind, the proposed move to a new airfield at Habbaniya, and the withdrawal from Mosul, did not represent a major weakening of the RAF's position in Iraq and actually offered some advantages.[101] He was insistent that Habbaniya provided a more secure location compared to Hinaidi ("practicably indefensible") in the event of civil disorder, a prediction that was borne out by the events of 1941 when Habbaniya withstood a long siege by the Iraqi army.[102] It is highly unlikely that the garrison would have fared as well had it still been based at Hinaidi.[103] In the end, the Air Ministry gave way and the Anglo-Iraqi treaty was signed on 30 June 1930. Shortly afterward came the news that Brooke-Popham was to be appointed, on promotion, to the Imperial Defence College (IDC), as the first RAF commandant. With two years in central London ahead of them, he and Opal decided to purchase a flat locally and moved into 30 Chester Terrace, Regents Park, in early October 1930. The family would live here throughout his time as commandant. The only drawback was that they would have to give up hunting and "we shall be reduced to that awful position of a motor car but no horses."[104]

Brooke-Popham's achievements in Iraq were substantial and significant. Francis Humphrys was especially grateful for all that he had achieved and his "guiding hand."[105] The high commissioner felt that much of the credit he had received for the successful treaty negotiations was actually owed to Brooke-Popham and Young.[106] At a personal level, Brooke-Popham's two years in Iraq had cemented his fascination for the ancient Middle East and his admiration for the Assyrians, "a fine lot of men, Christians and good fighters,"[107] although they were to fare badly at the hands of a newly independent Iraq.[108] He would later become active in their cause and the struggle to find a secure homeland. From a professional perspective, Brooke-Popham had held down an important post, gaining a reputation as a considerate and well-respected AOC. He had also shown an ability to deal with high-level military-strategic issues as well as operating (briefly) as a diplomat. Jack Salmond was particularly grateful for the great tact he had used in some very difficult negotiations.[109] Significantly, in view of his next appointment, he had actively promoted joint air and ground operations. It has been said that the RAF of the period endeavored to ignore the role of ground forces in maintaining internal security.[110] This was not the view of Jack Salmond, the first AOC Iraq Command, who was adamant that air policing was part of a combined policy.[111] Brooke-Popham was equally clear: "I think it has always been the Air Staff policy that the RAF cannot quell rioting in towns, e.g., Jerusalem and Haifa—and that this must be the work of the police and infantry."[112] Brooke-Popham wrote to Liddell Hart soon after returning from Iraq, arguing that although airpower was the primary arm in maintaining Iraq's security, this did not exclude ground forces. "One will always get the best results in control of underdeveloped countries by a proper combination of army troops and air forces."[113] This perspective was not limited to the circumstances of the Middle East. Brooke-Popham never believed that the RAF should work separately to the other two services. In a talk broadcast in 1940, he stressed to his audience that "air forces are fully capable of action independent of either an army or a navy but to bring about the most effective results their action must be related to that being carried out on the ground or on the sea."[114] Jack Slessor, a member of the First Course at Andover, vigorously rejected the idea that the Air Staff were guilty of extravagant claims for airpower during the interwar period or that RAF officers had been indoctrinated in the works of General Giulio Douhet. "When I was a student at Staff College in 1924, we were not taught that the RAF could win wars by itself."[115]

10

IMPERIAL DEFENCE COLLEGE
1931–1933

Brooke-Popham returned from Iraq to a nation facing severe austerity and a continent that was increasingly unstable. Britain's economic position had deteriorated with the onset of the Great Depression. The rapid contraction in trade, and high unemployment, created a succession of financial crises. The new Labour government, elected in May 1929, was confronted by demands to cut expenditure just as welfare costs were rapidly rising. Failure to resolve these conflicting claims saw the Cabinet resign two years later, replaced by a coalition government. Elsewhere in Europe, economic problems were even worse, creating an unsettled political environment and encouraging the emergence of authoritarian regimes. He also returned to a new CAS, Jack Salmond, who had replaced Trenchard in January 1930. The latter's retirement had been announced shortly after he had left for Iraq, providing Brooke-Popham with the time and distance to reflect on their relationship. His farewell letter to Trenchard was a touching mixture of affection and respect:

> I have now written my last private official letter to you, so a big break has occurred in my life and I feel rather like a new boy at school. I've served under you now for fifteen years in peace and war, and that's a big slice in one's useful life. I suppose one doesn't fully realize the value of anything, till one's lost it; and it's been such an enormous help both here and in England to have someone to fall back on when things got difficult, someone who was a friend as well as a senior officer and whom one knew would be sympathetic, give a sound decision

and see that decision through. I remember you often used to say in France that the best is the enemy of the good and I'm sure it was the strongest of all your good points that you always made up your mind to a definite course of action and stuck to it. It gave just that element of stability to the RAF which was what we wanted above all else. I want to thank you for all you've done for me. I'm not referring now to promotions or decorations but to the help you've given by your example, towards moulding my own character. So, goodbye to the senior officer half of you but I hope the friend half will remain.[1]

The IDC had emerged from a post–World War I debate, encouraged by the Geddes Committee on National Expenditure, on the benefits of creating a joint Ministry of Defence that would produce less duplication and greater coordination and economy in the functions of the Fighting Services.[2] Churchill, who chaired a Cabinet committee on the subject in 1922, felt that a joint ministry was a step too far, but suggested the creation of a Joint Services College. For a variety of reasons, it took until 1927 for this to become a reality. The function of the new college was to:

- train a body of officers and civil officials in the broadest aspects of Imperial Strategy, and
- in order to ensure that the courses of study shall not become wholly academic and lose touch with realities, the occasional examination of concrete problems of Imperial Defence which are referred to them by the Chiefs of Staff Committee.[3]

Each course, which lasted a calendar year, comprised up to thirty students drawn from the military and civil service, as well as overseas. There were four directing staff, also drawn from the military and civil service, and a three-star commandant. The curriculum was aimed at middle-ranking officers with clear potential for senior rank. Many of those who attended during Brooke-Popham's time as commandant went on to occupy high positions during World War II.[4] The directing staff was of equal caliber.[5] The syllabus comprised a mixture of lectures and visits that embraced military, political, economic, industrial, and scientific issues. The strategic management of defense provided the academic foundation, together with several week-long visits to the armed services, but the overriding aim was to prepare students for the global challenges they would face in the future.

Located initially at 9 Buckingham Gate (adjacent to St. James' Park), the college occupied somewhat cramped accommodation with modest facilities.[6] Even so, it soon won a high reputation and attracted strong support from all three services. Much of the credit must go to the first commandant, Admiral Sir Herbert Richmond, an able but not the most tolerant of senior officers, who was regarded as one of the foremost military thinkers of his day.[7] Although he had fallen out of favor with the Admiralty, Richmond ensured that his students used their time at Buckingham Gate to think deeply about their profession, to analyze problems rigorously, and to develop a better understanding of the strategic management of war.[8] He also used the opportunity, as have succeeding commandants, to press home his personal views, such as the need for a common doctrine of war. Unfortunately, he also exhibited a profound skepticism about the RAF.[9] It has been argued that Richmond's hostility was a reaction to the arguments of the airpower theorists, who advocated "massive terroristic" attacks on large urban and industrial targets, and that this accounted for his blindness to the potential impact of aviation on naval warfare. Richmond was later taken to task by Wilfrid Freeman about this oversight.[10] In response, Richmond argued that the RAF was not without fault, in claiming that offense was the best form of defense, and for asserting that the principles of war did not apply to air forces. Richmond's most bitter antagonist was Trenchard, who believed passionately that an enemy could be defeated without first destroying his military capability.[11] Their argument was less about principles and more about practice (the RAF Staff College, under Brooke-Popham, had taught the need for doctrinal unity since 1921), but the controversy created ill-feeling and left a difficult legacy at the IDC. The irony is that the Royal Navy would later be accused (with some justification) of short-changing the IDC by failing to send their share of students.[12] The Royal Navy's attitude to staff training during the interwar period was at best ambivalent and often confused. It was popularly believed that attendance at Staff College slowed career advancement.[13]

More worrying, perhaps, was Richmond's overt prejudice toward his RAF students, who he privately described as "mentally inferior." Joubert de la Ferté, the RAF senior instructor at IDC for three years, regarded the commandant's lectures as tendentious. His attacks on the air force were resented by the student body and led to some embarrassing moments.[14] Brooke-Popham was aware of Richmond's reputation in this regard. "One does not want a brilliant scholar for that job; Richmond was and did not make a great success of it. What one does want is a man with tact, sense and balanced judgement."[15] For his part, Richmond viewed Brooke-Popham's appointment with trepidation and wanted the best naval directing staff to counter "the possible extremist views of the Air Officer who will be in charge of the IDC in January 1931."[16] A great deal rested therefore on Brooke-Popham's shoulders. His record at the RAF Staff College suggested little reason for concern, but unlike Andover (where only RAF students attended the first course), any shortcomings or missteps would be readily visible. In the torrid world of inter-service rivalry that characterized much of the interwar period, failure could have had significant repercussions. It is hardly surprising, therefore, that Brooke-Popham (who had been enlisted to prepare the RAF students attending the first courses, including Peter Portal),[17] was brought home early from Iraq to see the IDC's work at firsthand, joining the 1930 course for their last few weeks.[18]

Brooke-Popham's time at the IDC coincided with a period of rapidly increasing national and international uncertainty. The Labour government had been battling the effects of the Depression for two years, but a budget crisis in August saw it resign—to be replaced by a National government. The pound left the gold standard and the Treasury introduced additional cuts in public spending. "Air Marshals go down 10% in payment over and above what's already been cut, makes nearly 20% altogether quite apart from the extra income tax. However, it's no good grumbling, we've all got to take our share in getting the country's finances straight."[19] There were ominous developments overseas that suggested worse was to come. Spain declared a republic, Japanese troops occupied Manchuria, and Germany would "either go 'Hitlerite' or Communist."[20]

The course comprised a mixture of lectures and external visits. Every effort was made to expand the students' knowledge and to broaden their professional experience. Trips to Fleet Street, the docks, and gas plants were interposed with visits to the services, included inspecting new tanks at Aldershot and several periods of sea time with the Royal Navy at Portsmouth and Invergordon. There was also a battlefield tour to the Western Front. This was not the first time that Brooke-Popham had returned to France—he had recently joined Trenchard and Jack Salmond at Montreuil for the unveiling of a commemorative tablet at Haig's old headquarters and a memorial statue in

Montreuil (he thought the horse first-class, but that Haig stooped rather too much),[21] however, this was his first opportunity to revisit the battlefields. "No sign of barbed wire or trenches or dug outs, all under cultivation again. And all the villages rebuilt much better than they were before."[22]

The Brooke-Pophams enjoyed their time in London, although they regularly took the opportunity to get out of town on the weekends, to ride and visit family. Early in their stay at Chester Terrace came the shocking news of Tony Holt's death in a mid-air collision. This was a bitter blow; he had been their best man and a friend for nearly twenty-five years.[23] There was also a deep sense of loss. Holt would undoubtedly have risen to higher rank and, quite possibly, could have led Fighter Command in 1940, rather than Hugh Dowding.[24] It was at this time that Brooke-Popham took the opportunity to renew his correspondence with Basil Liddell Hart, writing complimentary letters about the latter's biography of Ferdinand Foch. Brooke-Popham had met Foch before the war and felt that he should have received more credit for the Allied success in 1918.[25] He also praised Liddell Hart for his book *The British Way in Warfare*.[26] "I am so glad that you have stressed the American Civil War. It is extraordinary how everybody missed the real lessons of that war. It makes one wonder how many lessons of 1914 we shall fail to grasp until the next war brings them to our notice."[27] In the same month, Brooke-Popham returned to Haileybury for the opening of the War Memorial Hall. The Duke of York (the future King George VI) performed the opening ceremony but his speech was very hesitating and "stopped completely once and never ended a sentence at all."[28]

The IDC attracted a wide range of speakers, although the commandant had to use his personal contacts and reputation to secure many of them (such as Stanley Bruce, the Australian resident minister in London and Australian high commissioner, 1933–45).[29] Sir Denys Bray, a long-serving diplomat in the Indian Civil Service, discussed the political situation in India, providing an informed view on the key personalities (including Gandhi) and the League of Nations. "When they talk about the Great Powers there, they mean France and the USA, England fell out of that category with the pound."[30] Brooke-Popham had a free hand and was keen to secure those who would both inform and test the students, such as Lord Lloyd,[31] who spoke on communistic propaganda in the East. "He's a very live wire, but rather a trial to governments."[32] Other lecturers included Sir Maurice Hankey (Cabinet secretary and secretary to the Committee for Imperial Defence) on the role of the CID, and Captain (later Admiral of the Fleet, Viscount) Andrew Cunningham on the naval situation. A large circle of friends and acquaintances was a "great advantage in getting hold of the right people to lecture."[33]

From the very first course, the subject of Japan and the British Empire featured as one of the main syndicate exercises.[34] Japan's overwhelming victory at Tsushima in 1905, when the Russian fleet was destroyed, had upset the balance of power in the Pacific. The possibility that Japan might seize Hong Kong and Singapore dominated the 1911 Imperial Conference.[35] Japan had fought on the side of the Allies in World War I, but Britain's abrogation of the Anglo-Japanese Alliance in 1921 in favor of the United States, and Japan's aggressive ambitions in China, saw postwar relations steadily worsen.[36] By 1931, Japan was a serious and growing threat. Borneo, Burma, and Malaya (the "Dollar Arsenal" of the empire) were hugely valuable to the Exchequer, generating significant amounts of foreign exchange from the export of oil, tin, and rubber. As the center for British trade in the region, and a major port, Singapore became the focus for British defense policy, as well as being critical to the relationship with Australia and New Zealand. The need to protect sea communications in the Far East led the CID to recommend as early as 1921 that a large, well-defended naval base be constructed at Singapore, although the fleet would be retained in European waters, to be deployed when required.[37] The importance of Singapore in securing British and Dominion interests in the region had been identified as early as 1919, in Lord Jellicoe's report on the Naval Mission to the Dominions.[38] He anticipated that Britain would not be able to dispatch significant naval forces to the Far East prior to the outbreak of a future war and that the Japanese would attempt to seize advanced bases at Hong Kong and Singapore in order to paralyze the Navy's operations. The Admiralty rejected many of his recommendations, but they did support the idea of creating a large naval base at Singapore that could be defended pending the arrival of the fleet. Changes in government and budgetary problems meant that construction progressed slowly. The project was reviewed in 1923 to consider, inter alia, the employment of aircraft rather than fixed batteries in defending the naval base. The suggestion that aircraft might take the place of coastal artillery led, in the words of the Official History, "to a difference of opinion among the Chiefs of Staff, and started a controversy which lasted for ten years."[39] This argument pitted the Air Ministry against the War Office and the Admiralty.

A compromise solution was reached in 1926, allowing the first stage of construction to proceed while action was taken to extend the air reinforcement route pending evidence that aircraft could provide an effective defense against seaborne attack. Progress in building the naval base remained slow, however, partly because of the ten-year rule and partly because it was hoped to restrict naval expansion in the Far East through a binding treaty. When the 1931 and 1932 courses came to study the problem, Japanese actions in China and Manchuria had already led to calls for the ten-year rule to be abandoned as "it would be the height of folly to perpetuate our defenceless state in the Far East."[40] In May 1932, the Baldwin Committee (reporting to the CID) recommended that Singapore's coast defenses should be organized "on the basis of co-operation between the three Services . . . and that air forces were to be considered as a valuable and essential addition to the fixed defences, as well as a means of attack."[41] It was in this context that IDC students were required to consider how to protect British and Commonwealth interests in the Far East. Supporting material included the most recent CID papers, CID 883-B "Supreme Control in War" and CID Paper 1009B "A Review of Imperial Defence." Background lectures were provided by experts in their respective fields, including Major-General Harry Pritchard, GOC Malaya Command (lecturing on Singapore), who offered a possible timetable for a Japanese move on Singapore (Z+6), and 30,000 troops (Z+22),[42] Sir Louis Beale,[43] Sir Meyrick Hewlett,[44] and Lieutenant-Colonel Hugh James "Banzai" Simson,[45] spoke respectively on British trade in the Far East, China, and Japan. The latter advised ominously that "speed is the essence of Japanese tactics and strategy. They believe in seizing the initiative and in flank attacks."[46] The outcome to these deliberations generally followed the lines of the 1925 appreciation, produced by the CID Singapore Sub-Committee, which had concluded that the Singapore defenses could survive a direct Japanese attack until the main fleet arrived.[47] This scenario assumed adequate intelligence of Japanese intentions; that the period before relief would not be increased, that Siam (Thailand) would remain neutral, and that the Japanese would not be able to establish advanced naval and air bases. The only uncertainty highlighted in the IDC appreciation was the potential delay in the arrival of the British fleet—the period before relief had been set at forty-two days in 1921.[48] Richmond later wrote scathingly about the discredited Singapore Strategy, pointing out the fallacy of creating a one-hemisphere navy to defend a two-hemisphere empire.[49] This conveniently ignored the fact that Britain could not afford the investment needed to support two great fleets against the possibility of a two-hemisphere war. The building of the naval base at Singapore (at considerable cost) was therefore a gamble, the assumption being that Britain would not face the German, Italian, and Japanese navies simultaneously—at least not without the support of the French navy. The use of airpower to bolster the defenses pending the arrival of the fleet was a sensible step, although Trenchard had consistently argued vigorously against the plan to send a battle fleet to Singapore, believing that aircraft offered a more secure and affordable defense. It was a view that he maintained long after he had left office.[50] Following the 1933 IDC Far East exercise, Brooke-Popham's successor (Vice-Admiral Sir Lionel Preston) remarked that "as matters stand, we are so situated in the Far East that we cannot hope to exercise any substantial degree of pressure on Japan without the active cooperation of any ally, but with the USA as our allies, the situation would be materially altered."[51] There is no evidence to suggest that Brooke-Popham was unduly influenced by these arguments, but the discussions provided him with an invaluable grounding in the complexities of British policy in the Far East, the uncertainties surrounding the defense of Singapore, and the need for allies if the Japanese had to be confronted. It would prove to be an important education.[52]

The performance of the IDC prior to 1939 has been criticized in some quarters for failing to challenge defense orthodoxy or generate controversy.[53] This is hardly fair since, as at Andover, the IDC had not been created to generate defense policy or establish a school of thought. Joubert de la Ferté acknowledged the criticism but felt that the IDC had more than proved a success in encouraging collaboration and a common language across the three services.[54] On this basis, Brooke-Popham's tenure at the IDC was undoubtedly successful. He offered a positive role model and worked hard to create greater understanding between the services.[55] His influence was all the greater for having consistently advocated a collaborative approach in defense matters. When the inter-service controversy was at its height, with the Army and Navy intent on abolishing the RAF,[56] he had still argued for close relations with the Admiralty "to show them that we are really doing our level best to produce the machines they want."[57] Indeed, while commandant, he lectured the Royal Navy (RN) War College at Greenwich on the importance of "Cooperation."[58] Brooke-Popham's good humor and open-mindedness created a positive working environment that both students and directing staff, including the naval historian C. E. "Ernest" Fayle, found productive and enjoyable.[59] Just as importantly, he gained the confidence and respect of a future generation of senior Allied leaders. This provided an unparalleled network of friends in high places that would prove particularly helpful in the years to come, including facilitating the smooth working of the three services in the Near East during the Italian Crisis of 1935–36, where "several senior officers on the different staffs had been to the Imperial Defence College."[60]

It was during Brooke-Popham's final year at Buckingham Gate that Jack Salmond's successor as CAS was chosen. There is no indication in any of his writings (public or private) that he had ever harbored expectations in this respect, but the outcome would be critical to his career. The appointment of CAS was the responsibility of Secretary of State for Air Charles Vane-Tempest-Stewart, Marquess of Londonderry, but it would be naïve to think that Trenchard had no hand in the process. In controlling the most senior RAF appointments for more than ten years, he had determined the pool of likely candidates.[61] When Trenchard had announced his retirement in December 1928, Jack Salmond had been the obvious successor.[62] His appointment was settled in the early summer of 1929, with the agreement of the then–secretary of state for Air, Lord Thompson. At the time, there were no other officers of comparable experience or the required rank (unless a younger man was to be promoted over the heads of his seniors). However, when Jack Salmond unexpectedly retired in early 1933, there were three possible choices, in addition to Brooke-Popham: Edward Ellington (Air Member for Personnel); Geoffrey Salmond (CinC Air Defence of Great Britain and Jack Salmond's older brother); and John Steel (AOC India). All four were roughly the same age (fifty-four to fifty-five), and all were slightly older than Jack Salmond. By choosing to leave when he did, Salmond effectively guaranteed that his successor would be from the same generation.[63] Trenchard, who claimed not to have been involved in the decision, believed that Salmond's early retirement broke the planned line of succession and failed to clear the way for younger officers.[64]

The discussion about Jack Salmond's successor took place in the early summer of 1932. It is difficult to imagine that Trenchard was excluded, but ultimately the decision lay with the secretary of state, who felt that the choice lay between Ellington and Geoffrey Salmond.[65] Londonderry selected Geoffrey, but not before he had spoken to Ellington, "the only other man who could have been asked to succeed him at that time." Sadly, Geoffrey Salmond was diagnosed with terminal cancer shortly afterwards, dying a month after taking up his new appointment.[66] Jack Salmond temporarily returned as CAS while a replacement was found. Once again, Brooke-Popham was overlooked, in favor of Ellington. On this occasion, it appears that Trenchard was consulted. He admitted as much, some fifteen years later, in a private letter to Wilfrid Freeman, who had directly criticized Trenchard for appointing Ellington, "our worst CAS." Trenchard did not demur, commenting that "I still think he had a great brain, but was ruined by being appallingly shy and very keen to get an important position. I agree he never understood a big job—or any job except detail, and that not too well."[67] These criticisms echo a much earlier private conversation between Group Captain (later Air Marshal Sir) Richard Hallam Peck and Liddell Hart. According to Peck, Ellington was "a very shy man with an aloof temperament and a temperament which requires a great deal of understanding with the result that, though personally most charming, he is not a good or quick mixer and does not capture the imagination of his subordinates." Peck's opinion carries some weight, not only because he proved a highly effective assistant chief of the Air Staff (General) during World War II, but also because his assessment of other senior officers proved particularly sound. For example, he correctly identified the high potential of Wilfrid Freeman, Charles Courtney, and Peter Portal.

Why was Brooke-Popham not selected as CAS? Chance and opportunity undoubtedly played their part. Geoffrey Salmond and Edward Ellington both had major operational appointments under their belt. Each had been appointed air vice-marshals four years earlier than Brooke-Popham, who because of his long tenure at Andover, was also a "tour" behind them. Geoffrey Salmond had commanded the RAF in the Middle East during World War I, served as AOC India, and, when appointed CAS, was CinC ADGB. Ellington, like Brooke-Popham, had served as AOC Iraq; however, he had also commanded ADGB and served on the Air Council (unlike Brooke-Popham). ADGB was regarded as the most important RAF position at home, second only to CAS and ranking higher than Iraq Command.[68] Other than his time as director of research, Brooke-Popham had not spent any significant time in the Air Ministry or worked closely with ministers and their senior civil servants. From what we know of Brooke-Popham's character, it may have been thought that he lacked the ruthlessness and single-minded determination needed to succeed in Whitehall. Peck's description of Brooke-Popham's leadership style bears out the views of many others: "He is particularly pleasant and easy to work with and gives subordinates a feeling that they are absolutely free to put forward any idea they have got and he makes them feel at ease in doing so without obtruding his seniority. This is of particular value in a developing Service like the Air Force. You never feel when dealing with him that he is a very senior officer standing on his dignity."[69]

If Trenchard believed Ellington a better choice than Brooke-Popham, he had come to this conclusion based on firsthand knowledge and an appreciation of the strengths and weaknesses of both individuals. It is a judgment that he was qualified to make—even if he came to regret it, and even if there were voices in support of Brooke-Popham's candidacy: "In many quarters the possibility that he might became Chief of the Air Staff is not immediately welcomed, but I think for myself, that he would make a very good Chief of the Air Staff. At a time when the inter-Service controversy was at its height he did very well at the IDC. He is a very keen co-operator with the other Services and has a way of understanding the outlook of the practical pilot."[70]

We will never know how close Brooke-Popham came to getting the RAF's top job. His letters and diaries reveal no hint of anticipation or disappointment. Whatever hopes Brooke-Popham had entertained, if he was not to be CAS only one question remained: would he be warned for retirement or offered further employment? On 26 September, the Air Ministry advised that he had been selected to succeed Geoffrey Salmond, as CinC ADGB.[71] He was delighted at the prospect and, without any sign of rancor, wrote delightedly to Opal. "I'm awfully pleased we've got ADGB, are you? It will be great for being in touch with all the Air Force people again."[72]

11

AIR DEFENSE OF
GREAT BRITAIN
1933–1935

B ecause of the fixed tour length at IDC, Brooke-Popham had three months to wait before taking up his appointment at ADGB. He spent the time engaged in a review of the Air Ministry and, in particular, its wartime organization.[1] His subsequent report made a number of important recommendations, including the need to create a dedicated directorate to deal with the rapid increase in work generated by operational requirements for new aircraft and armament, a proposal that was implemented in April 1934.[2] In the meantime, he and Opal sold their flat at Chester Terrace and moved the family to Woodlands, an Air Ministry hiring at Stoke Poges, some seven miles from the ADGB Headquarters at Uxbridge. Command of ADGB, a two-year tour in the rank of air marshal, was destined to be Brooke-Popham's last operational appointment.[3]

Installed at RAF Uxbridge, he found himself at the center of a close-knit team. Following Tony Holt's untimely death, the Fighting Area was temporarily under the command of Air Commodore John Baldwin (one of his original staff college students). Holt's successor was his old friend, Philip Joubert de la Ferté, who took up the post in January 1934. The other major component of the ADGB, the Wessex Bombing Area, was under the command of Tom Webb-Bowen—yet another longstanding colleague. The Wessex Bombing Area would split later in the year into two separate groups, the "Western Area" and the "Central Area."[4] His PA was Flight Lieutenant (later Air Marshal Sir) Frank Fressanges, who never forgot the advice and guidance that he received while working for Brooke-Popham. "Whatever success I have attained since was founded on your unfailing help and kindness."[5]

Brooke-Popham's arrival at the ADGB coincided with the British government's reluctant commitment to rearmament. Serious financial constraints, and the debilitating impact of the ten-year rule, had restricted investment in the RAF, notwithstanding the commitments made in 1923.[6] The ten-year rule had been abandoned in 1932 but any expansion of home defense remained stalled while the Disarmament Conference was under way, and the government observed a voluntary armaments truce.[7] The rise of Hitler, and wider international uncertainty, finally forced action, but not before a last attempt to secure an agreement on world disarmament at Geneva. By the end of 1933 these efforts had proved fruitless and Britain reluctantly prepared for a possible war. The first plans, produced in early 1934 by the Cabinet's Defence Requirements Committee (DRC), were relatively unambitious, based as they were on Britain's existing industrial capacity and the RAF's limited ability to expand from a standing start.[8] The Cabinet agreed to these proposals, with some refinements, in July 1934. The initial program, which would be followed by a succession of more ambitious programs over the next few years, envisaged the creation of seventy-five Home Defence squadrons by 1940 and the extension of the Air Defence scheme to cover the wider area now threatened by air attack.[9]

The first air defense exercises under Brooke-Popham's direction, as CinC ADGB, were held from 17 to 21 July 1933. These short summer exercises were part of a series that had begun in 1927, when he was AOC Fighting Area.[10] Because of political sensitivities (while the Disarmament Conference was under way), no major cities were involved. Instead, a series of tactical exercises were carried out.[11] Press coverage of the 1933 exercises was relatively low-key, but the 1934 exercises (held from 23 to 26 July) created a great deal of comment. Unlike the previous year, London was a target for enemy bombers and the press were invited into the ground centers to observe the outcome.[12] From Brooke-Popham's perspective the exercises went well. "They were quite successful, no accidents or anything, but the papers are very bad in their reports."[13] The *Times* pointed out the artificial nature of the exercises, and reminded its readers that the primary aim had been to improve coordination between the Observer Corps and the air and ground defenses,[14] but there was considerable alarm at the Air Ministry's official communiqués stating that 70 percent of the raiders had reached their targets. On the positive side, the exercises had identified improvements to training and communications, as well as the utility of sound mirrors.[15] With Brooke-Popham's support, it was agreed to go ahead and install a ten-mirror scheme covering the Thames estuary, even though the limited information produced by the existing mirrors had proved difficult to handle.[16] At this distance, the concept of sound mirrors may seem quaint, but it did provide an improvement over visual methods and, although it turned out to be a technological dead-end, cannot be dismissed as either misguided or fantastical. The possibility of other technical solutions was not lost on the ADGB staff, but they had to work with the available technologies. Moreover, irrespective of the sensors employed (optical, audio or electromagnetic), they faced the same problem of how to process the data quickly enough to provide timely information to the air defenses. Brooke-Popham put his finger on the heart of the issue: "The mirrors were transmitting a wealth of information which proved an embarrassment because of its volume and the difficulty in sorting out the steady flow of reports."[17]

It has been implied that there was no effective air defense system before 1934, yet the arrangements created by ADGB were probably the best in the world at that time. Moreover, by developing a system able to handle large volumes of data, and capable of merging varied information sources into a "recognised picture," ADGB established the basis for the first fully integrated air defense network.[18] John Ferris has identified the importance of these arrangements, but attributed much of the credit to Charles Higgins and Geoffrey Salmond (Brooke-Popham's predecessor as CinC).[19] This is unfair to both Brooke-Popham and Tony Holt—a point stressed by Keith Park, who commanded No. 11 Group during the Battle of Britain.[20] For his part, Brooke-Popham felt that Higgins had achieved very little and was merely the beneficiary of Holt's work in creating the Home Defence Wing in 1916,[21] a view shared by Brancker, who commended Holt's air defense efforts to Trenchard.[22] It was Holt who led the 1929 study that provided the basis for the information handling system implemented by ADGB and, in particular, the use of raid intelligence and the unification of information.[23] Park also felt that Holt should have received more credit and would likely have become CinC Fighter Command, rather than Dowding, had he not been killed in 1931.[24] Brooke-Popham's particular contribution was to refine the system that he inherited from Salmond and to provide a clear vision of how the air defense system needed to evolve if it was to defeat the Luftwaffe.

While ADGB and the Fighting Area were digesting the lessons from the 1934 air exercises, the Air Staff pressed hard for a full review of Britain's air defenses. A joint RAF and War Office group, the Sub-committee for the Reorientation of the Air Defence of Great Britain (the ADGB Sub-Committee), was established by the CID on 2 August 1934 for this purpose, under the chairmanship of Brooke-Popham.[25] For the next year (until he handed over command of ADGB), Brooke-Popham led the work to provide Britain with a modern air defense system. He met with the CID Home Defence Committee on at least a dozen occasions, between October 1934 and March 1935, to discuss progress. The work moved quickly and an interim report was ready by January.[26] At the heart of the committee's proposals was a continuous defensive system, to a depth of twenty-six miles, circling to the east of London, from Portsmouth in the southwest to the Tees River in the northeast. Their final recommendations, including extensive annexes detailing equipment and personnel requirements,[27] were considered by the CID on 11 April 1935 (Brooke-Popham briefed the report in person) and accepted by the Cabinet on 24 July 1935.[28] The delay was caused by the need for the DRC to consider the resource requirements against the expansion program agreed the previous year. The scope and rigor of the work completed by the ADGB Sub-Committee marked "a critical stage in the development of the air defences of the country, and of Fighter Command in particular, and all subsequent changes in our air defences were only commentaries upon it."[29] Brooke-Popham never attempted to take credit for any of this work, although he was proud of what had been achieved. The most he would say, in commenting on Britain's air defences shortly before the Battle of Britain opened, was that "a few years ago, I was Commander-in-Chief of the Air Defences of Great Britain, and since then have watched developments which my staff and I were planning and thinking of come to fruition."[30]

One of the papers considered by Brooke-Popham's committee was an analysis of early warning requirements, prepared by the ADGB staff.[31] The fundamental challenge facing the air defenses was how to secure adequate notice of an enemy raid. Because there was a relatively small speed difference between fighters and bombers, there was little chance that the defending fighters could climb to altitude in time to intercept enemy bombing raids without advance warning. Standing patrols were impracticable because of the excessive resources that would be required. Acoustic mirrors could, under the right conditions, provide some warning, but only out to twenty to twenty-five miles in good weather.[32] What was needed was a system to identify enemy targets at a distance of at least fifty miles, to allow fighters time to take up their defensive positions. The press coverage of the 1934 air exercises had encouraged Frederick Lindemann (later Lord Cherwell), an influential scientist and Churchill's scientific adviser, to write to the *Times* arguing that the widespread belief that there could be no defense against the bomber was misplaced, and that the government should commission a research program to find a technical solution.[33] Lindemann encouraged Churchill to raise the issue in the House of Commons and met with Brooke-Popham in October to suggest various possibilities for finding a defense against the bomber.[34] Lindemann was skeptical of departmental committees in general and Brooke-Popham's committee in particular. He believed that their attitude was that "the bomber would always get through."[35] In deference to Lindemann's wishes, and with Baldwin's encouragement, Brooke-Popham would later recommend the creation of a CID sub-committee on air defense.[36] This was formed in April 1935 as the Air Defence Research Committee (ADRC).[37]

The possibility that a technological answer could be found to the air defense problem had already prompted Henry "Harry" Wimperis, the director of scientific research at the Air Ministry, to propose the creation of a scientific committee to study the problem. The Committee for the Scientific Survey of Air Defence—otherwise known as the Tizard Committee—was formed by the Air Ministry in December 1934 under the chairmanship of Sir Henry Tizard.[38] There is some confusion over exactly when Brooke-Popham first met the Tizard Committee. His personal diary records a meeting with the "Scientists Committee" (including Tizard) on 21 February 1935. However, Joubert states that he and Brooke-Popham met Tizard at ADGB Headquarters in the autumn of 1934.[39] There is no record of such a meeting and, although it is possible it did take place, it appears that Joubert misremembered the date. On the other hand, it seems highly unlikely that Brooke-Popham was unaware of the existence of the Tizard Committee before he submitted his interim report in January.[40]

The meeting between Brooke-Popham, Joubert, and the Tizard Committee proved highly productive and far-reaching in its long-term impact. According to Joubert, they discussed various ways of obtaining early warning of enemy air attack before Tizard wound up the discussion by saying: "I think I know the answer. I will let you know after I have made some further enquiries." In Joubert's words this was the instigation "of some most-needed research into a vital defence problem" that would lead to radio direction finding (RDF).[41] The conduct of the meeting was undoubtedly helped by the fact that Brooke-Popham knew many of the scientists. Tizard had been a colleague since World War I. They had both served on the ARC in 1921 and subsequently were fellow members of the Council of the Royal Aeronautical Society (Wimperis was also a member). Brooke-Popham had known Wimperis and A. P. "Jimmy" Rowe since 1919, when they were both employed in the Air Ministry Laboratory and worked under him when he was the director of research. The key step in the development of RDF occurred shortly after Brooke-Popham's meeting with the Tizard Committee. Wimperis had been in contact with Robert Watson-Watt, superintendent of the Radio Department at the NPL, in January 1928 regarding the potential for employing rays to defend against air attack. Watson-Watt reported that this was impracticable but suggested that radio-detection was a "less unpromising problem." From this conversation emerged the first successful demonstration on 25–26 February 1935 of radar principles, using an RAF Heyford bomber and the BBC's Daventry transmitter.[42] Watson-Watt's subsequent memorandum, "Detection and Location of Aircraft by Radio Methods," is regarded as the founding charter for radar.[43]

Much of the credit for the development of radar has properly gone to the Tizard Committee and, in particular, to Watson-Watt.[44] The latter identified several RAF "champions" in the development process. Brooke-Popham is not one of them—he had retired well before Fighter Command's radar system became operational.[45] However, he does deserve credit for creating the permissive environment in which radar was conceived and developed. Brooke-Popham's willingness to work with scientists, as partners and colleagues, generated a collaborative mindset within the RAF. As the RAF's first director of research, he had insisted that the Air Ministry get as close as possible not only to the ARC and NPL but also to the universities, engineering colleges, and technical schools.[46] It is taken for granted that such open and productive conversations were normal, but they were exceptional—if not unique to Britain. Phil Judkins points out that British radar was the subject of major debate between senior RAF commanders in chief, scientists, and key politicians, and that this had had no parallels in either Germany or the United States.[47] Woodburn Kirby and Capey make the same argument, commentating how Germany, well endowed with scientists and research institutions, failed to deploy these resources effectively because scientists and the military did not work closely together.[48] Even so, it has also been suggested that the RAF was hostile to scientists during the 1920s.[49] This picture is misleading and confuses practice with policy. Investment in scientific research was certainly limited during the immediate interwar years, but this was driven by austerity rather than prejudice. Brooke-Popham's teaching at Andover stressed the role of scientists in creating airpower ("the development of scientific warfare"); indeed, Tizard was one of a number of external lecturers brought in to broaden the students' education.[50] "Above all, it is necessary to keep in touch with scientific progress: not merely with recent experiments in aeroplanes and engines, but with the latest developments in all branches of science."[51] Watson-Watt stresses the important role of the Air Ministry in supporting his research and persuading the Treasury to provide the required funding. Although some notable individuals (including Rowe, R. V. Jones, and Solly Zuckerman) have criticized the quality of military research during the interwar years, suggesting that it was a backwater staffed by second-rate scientists, David Edgerton has demonstrated that this was far from the case.[52] In Tizard's opinion, the scientific branches were generally well in front in scientific developments, while the Air Staff were receptive of new scientific ideas, although admittedly implementation was handicapped by the shortage of engineer officers.[53] Another misrepresentation is the claim that the Air Ministry was uninterested in air defense prior to 1934 (and Rowe's intervention). The latter has been accused of "dubious assertions" in his personal memoir that presented the development of radar as an isolated process, driven by a few individuals, rather than the product of longstanding Air Ministry and ADGB interest in scientific methods of air defense.[54]

Most narratives about the Battle of Britain scarcely mention Brooke-Popham, preferring to focus on the period after the creation of Fighter Command. When he is discussed, it is generally in the context of the machine-gun controversy of 1934. According to Brian Bond, the suggestion that eight Browning 0.303-inch guns be fitted to the Hurricane and Spitfire "created furore amongst senior officers," including Brooke-Popham.[55] This is a misleading picture, encouraged by Dempster and Wood's *Narrow Margin* and Wykeham's *Fighter Command*.[56] Colin Sinnott has demonstrated that these authors misrepresented the discussion within ADGB.[57] In a comprehensive review of the history of operational requirements during the interwar period, he notes that Brooke-Popham's views were generally forward-looking and that he was willing to accede to specialist advice (in areas such as the introduction of tail turrets).[58] The particular comment on the proposal for eight guns (within a long letter responding to a draft operational requirement circulated in 1934) has been used to imply that there was widespread opposition to the idea. When added to the self-serving recollections of Wing Commander (later Air Marshal Sir) Ralph Sorley, we are invited to believe that a far-sighted individual had to fight out-of-date, elderly officers to achieve progress.[59] In fact, a reading of the relevant documents shows that there was a lively but well-informed discussion about the need for multiple guns to give the best chance of bringing down an enemy bomber. The potential for cannon in fighter aircraft was not discussed—in some ways a more serious omission, since the heavier weapon was considerably more effective against metal structures than the machine gun.[60] Brooke-Popham's reasonable question regarding the number of guns was driven by staff concerns about head resistance and stoppages.[61] Installing the guns in the wings necessitated a considerable amount of redesign to achieve the necessary reliability.[62] It seems a little unfair to criticize Brooke-Popham for his contribution to a staffing process that he had helped to develop and for raising concerns that led to a more robust design. In fact, he had argued (as early as 1921) for a larger caliber (.5-inch) machine gun to be fitted to fighter aircraft, even though it was heavier and less ammunition could be carried, noting the extraordinary success of the 11-mm Vickers balloon guns employed against German aircraft during the war.[63] Brooke-Popham's views on future technical development were not always without flaws, but they were never the product of prejudice. As director of research he had recognized the utility of metal structures, fuel injection, and high-compression engines, although he was excessively skeptical about enclosed cockpits. As late as 1935, he argued that more research was needed because of concerns that night vision would be adversely affected.[64] In general, however, his instinct was to allow the experimental evidence to drive progress rather than resisting technological developments just because they were new or unfamiliar.

The increasing importance of ADGB saw Brooke-Popham promoted to four-star rank in January 1935. This brought many letters of congratulations, including one from a serving corporal at RAF North Weald, who had been in G Company at Tidworth, expressing his great pleasure at Captain Brooke-Popham's success since 1909.[65] Promotion also meant that his tour at ADGB would be extended by a year, to March 1936.[66] An equally pleasant surprise was his appointment as a Knight Grand Cross of the Victorian Order (GCVO), an award in the gift of the monarch, in the king's Birthday

Honours List. The investiture was held during the Royal Review of the RAF, organized by Brooke-Popham and held on 6 July 1935 at Mildenhall and Duxford, as part of the king's Jubilee Year.[67] The review was hugely successful, involving 1,750 personnel and 350 airplanes on parade followed by a flypast of 180 machines. "Its planning was so efficient, its precision so perfect, as to appear effortless."[68] The administrative and logistics effort was immense, making heavy demands of the ADGB Headquarters staff, who were responsible for the largest movement of personnel since the RAF had been formed.[69] It is tempting to wonder whether, watching the flypast, Brooke-Popham recalled his involvement in the RFC's first Royal Review when a total of seventeen aircraft (all that could get airborne) flew past the king.

The end of Brooke-Popham's time with the ADGB was now in sight and retirement beckoned. However, with RAF expansion gaining momentum, and a shortage of senior officers, Ellington decided to revive the post of inspector general (not filled since 1919) to assist him in supervising the expansion of the RAF and "in identifying and resolving issues that crossed command boundaries."[70] Brooke-Popham was the natural choice for this role, given his deep knowledge of the service, personal qualities, and diplomatic skills. The decision not only reflected Ellington's confidence in Brooke-Popham's abilities but also his respect for his colleague of twenty-five years. Had war broken out, it was Ellington's intention to make Brooke-Popham deputy CAS.[71] In June 1935, the Air Council formally advised Brooke-Popham that he would be appointed inspector general, with effect from 1 August 1935.[72] His successor at ADGB would be Air Marshal Sir John Steel. A year later, ADGB was split into Bomber and Fighter Commands. Steel took command of Bomber Command and Hugh Dowding took command of Fighter Command, both in the rank of air chief marshal.

Brooke-Popham's achievements at ADGB were substantial and enduring. He played a major role in the development of Britain's air defenses for more than a decade. As AOC Fighting Area, he helped reestablish the air defense system of 1918, improving its communications and squadron performance. As CinC ADGB, he systematically improved that system, melding science, technology, and information management to serve the task of intercepting daylight raids.[73] As chairman of the ADGB Sub-Committee, he laid the foundation for a comprehensive and robust air defense network that would be validated under the most testing of conditions. Through his leadership style he encouraged an open-mindedness and determination that gave life to Fighter Command. Just as importantly, he demonstrated the importance of working with scientists to solve the most challenging technical problems. He was the first senior officer to appreciate the value of scientists when others were still refusing to admit them to their headquarters.[74] Brooke-Popham was neither the architect of victory in 1940 nor the instigator of radar, but without his personal contribution both achievements would have been jeopardized.

12

INSPECTOR GENERAL
1935–1937

B rooke-Popham took some well-earned leave in August, pending taking up his post as inspector general. It made sense for the family to remain at Woodlands, where they were well settled and could ride, rather than searching for a new house and stabling. They had anticipated that his new role would involve considerable travel, but less than a month later he was in Egypt. The reason was the British Cabinet's increasing concerns over Italian behavior in Abyssinia.[1] The Abyssinia Crisis arose from a border incident between Italy and Ethiopia in November 1934 that escalated into an opportunity for Benito Mussolini to expand the Italian Empire and redress the embarrassment of the first Italo-Ethiopian war. The League of Nations proved unable to intervene and, although Britain and France attempted to mediate, the Italians refused to back down. At an emergency Cabinet meeting on 22 August 1935, the British government agreed to send urgent reinforcements to Aden, Egypt, Kenya, and Sudan to strengthen their defenses.[2] This failed to deter Mussolini, who ordered his forces in Eritrea and Somaliland to invade Ethiopia on 3 October 1935. The fighting ended in May 1936 with the capture of the capital, Addis Ababa.

Although the bulk of the Home Fleet had been sent to the eastern Mediterranean together with additional RAF aircraft (equivalent to six, and later eleven, squadrons),[3] the chiefs of staff did not believe there was a serious military threat from the Italians. Admiral Ernle Chatfield (First Sea Lord) and Field Marshal Sir Archibald Montgomery-Massingberd (CIGS) were particularly skeptical, although the transfer of two Italian divisions to Libya in September 1935 highlighted the potential danger to Egypt.[4] Ellington decided that he needed Brooke-Popham in Cairo to oversee the RAF squadrons across the region and to develop operational plans in the event of war. His directive was "to defend British territory, and British-protected territories, against all forms of attack, whether by sea, land, or air."[5] On 24 September, Brooke-Popham lunched with Viscount Swinton, the secretary of state for air, to discuss his mission.[6] Two days later he met with Chatfield and Montgomery-Massingberd before joining the SS *Kaisar-i-Hind* at Tilbury, bound for Bombay. They called at Tangier, Gibraltar, and Malta, where he transferred to HMS *Queen Elizabeth* for the journey to Alexandria, arriving on 10 October, by which time the Italian offensive had been under way for a week. The newspapers initially reported that Brooke-Popham was making a tour of inspection of RAF stations; however, in December it was announced that he had been appointed to command Royal Air Force Middle East.[7]

Brooke-Popham was acutely aware that the uncertainty surrounding his responsibilities could create difficulties with the existing AOC Middle East, Air Vice-Marshal Cuthbert MacLean, also based in Cairo. "My functions are, at present, a little bit vague but I am in charge of the coordination of all RAF activities in the Middle East, apparently including Malta and Gibraltar as well as Aden and Iraq."[8] Ellington would later describe Brooke-Popham's role as exercising "general supervision over the Middle East."[9] Pending greater clarification, he spent the first few months visiting the RAF units in Egypt as well as meeting the recently deployed squadrons in Aden (where he stayed with Air Commodore Peter Portal), Somaliland, and Sudan (where the energetic and capable Raymond Collishaw commanded No. 5 Wing).[10] These visits were uneventful, other than Aden, where Portal's driver ran over Brooke-Popham's dispatch case and crushed the contents.[11] It would take him several months to acquire replacement reading glasses from England. For the next few weeks he continued his tour of the region, including visiting the frontier with Italian Libya and historic sites, such as the Siwa Oasis. Early discussions with his military and naval counterparts focused both on defensive arrangements and potential offensive action in the event of war, including an assault by armored forces on Tobruk with air support.[12]

In late November Brooke-Popham was in Jerusalem, where he stayed with Air Commodore Richard Peirse (another of his ex-Andover students), before travelling to Iraq. He found his return to Baghdad a bittersweet experience. He was delighted to meet old friends but felt that there was "a sad lack of dignity and savoir faire about the place." It is rare to find Brooke-Popham quite so critical, even in his private letters. "The Embassy counsellor looked more like a head clerk" and the other secretaries were "typical caricatures of the pale willowy Foreign Office youth." He was marginally more impressed by the ambassador, Sir Archibald Clark Kerr, who reminded him of Young, the counsellor under Francis Humphrys, who "was unable to realize that any Iraqi could be so unfriendly or so clever as to double-cross him."[13] He also had an opportunity to meet King Faisal's successor, his son Ghazi. "For a lad of 23 he certainly is wearing very badly and shows definite marks of dissipation." Ghazi did not attract the same respect as his father and as a result British influence had declined. "In the former days one could always see King Faisal and get him to stop some silly decree the Cabinet was about to issue."[14] He confided to Opal that "I thought of Francis Humphrys or Gilbert Clayton and sighed."[15]

Just after Christmas Brooke-Popham returned to Siwa to explore the Great Sand Sea, spending five nights in the desert and covering a little more than five hundred miles. He was one of a party of ten, travelling in Ford cars with low-pressure tires that explored the central part of the northern sea— a region that reportedly had never been successfully crossed before.[16] Returning to Cairo, Brooke-Popham flew to Kenya for a tour of inspection, visiting the detached RAF flight at Nairobi where the governor, Sir Joseph Byrne, had raised concerns about the high accident rate.[17] He was also aware that Byrne had proved reluctant to employ the aircraft deployed to Kenya to help maintain order. "Byrne has a rooted objection to the word 'bomb' or its use."[18] While staying in Nairobi, Brooke-Popham took the opportunity to tour the northern frontier with Abyssinia. Returning from Moyale, in company with District Commissioner Vincent Glenday, the brakes failed in his car while descending a steep hill. The vehicle was eventually stopped by a large boulder and no one was injured, other than Brooke-Popham who broke his left arm. He needed immediate treatment in Nairobi and had to spend several further weeks in hospital on his return to Cairo. He declined Ellington's suggestion that he return home to recuperate, typically making light of the incident: "We should have made a grand picture for the films—I, in my torn khaki uniform lying on the side of the road with my head in Glenday's lap, half a dozen Somali policemen looking on, the sun just rising; a beautiful part of the bush and all sorts of strange birds singing."[19] Before leaving for Egypt, Brooke-Popham and Opal had discussed the possibility that she would join him in the new year. She remained keen to travel, but he was concerned about the high level of entertaining that would be expected. "People seem to have such exaggerated ideas out here as to the standard of comfort necessary and entertaining on a big scale has become a perfect mania; it's all out of propor-tion, social requirements come far above everything, and work, or getting to know the country and the people, come low down on the scale."[20] Once the prospect of war with Italy had receded in February, it was agreed that Opal would come out to Cairo, returning to England at Easter.[21]

Unlike his reaction to the British embassy in Baghdad, Brooke-Popham had been impressed by the High Commission in Cairo. He instinctively liked Sir Miles Lampson (later Lord Killearn), "a huge, big, cheery man, weight 19 stone,"[22] the recently appointed high commissioner for Egypt and the Sudan. Lampson was keen to restart the 1930 treaty negotiations, which had ended in deadlock.[23] The previous discussions had stalled over the question of the Sudan, but the Abyssinia Crisis encouraged the Foreign Office to try again to secure an alliance with Egypt.[24] Brooke-Popham was appointed as one of three technical advisers supporting Lampson. The others were: Lieutenant-General Sir George Weir (GOC Egypt), Admiral Sir William Fisher (CinC Mediterranean Fleet), and Rear-Admiral Robert Raikes, who deputized for Fisher when required.[25] By all accounts, Brooke-Popham was Lampson's favored adviser.[26] The Egyptian delegation was led by the Egyptian prime minister, Mostafa el-Nahhas Pasha. The negotiations, which began on 2 March 1936, proved extremely difficult. The War Office wanted to retain forces close to the main cities to safeguard imperial communications, but this was regarded as unacceptable by the Egyptians. There was also a desire by the chiefs of staff to secure arrangements that provided an absolute guarantee of security.[27] The treaty conversations continued until 17 April, when they were adjourned until after the parliamentary elections. In the meantime, the British Cabinet created an Anglo-Egyptian Conversations Committee to review the question of further concessions and whether the treaty should be time limited. There was a valiant effort to find a form of words that addressed the concerns of both sides. Brooke-Popham was dismissive of such legalistic wordsmithing. "Whilst being tactful in wording, let's don't resort to phraseology purposely designed to be interpreted in two different ways. For one thing, when it comes to verbal subterfuge, we are chicken in the hands of the Egyptian past masters. The strength of England lies in telling the truth. Let's stick to it."[28]

Ellington had wanted Brooke-Popham to return home once the war in Ethiopia had ended (the Italians occupied Addis Ababa on 5 May 1936), but Lampson was keen to retain him while the negotiations on the military clauses continued.[29] Brooke-Popham used the break in the talks to visit Palestine with Opal before she left for England. On his return, as the negotiations were still postponed, Brooke-Popham took the opportunity to visit the Sudan and travel to Lebanon to meet his French counterparts. The impasse that had developed between the Foreign Office and the service chiefs led Foreign Secretary Anthony Eden to recall Lampson, accompanied by Brooke-Popham, in early June. The latter was considerably more pragmatic about the Egyptian proposals than the chiefs of staff. Brooke-Popham vigorously supported Lampson, including rebutting strong criticism from Ellington.[30] As he pointed out, similar arrangements had proved effective in Iraq.[31] The London discussions were facilitated by an Egyptian offer of a permanent treaty of alliance that helped secure Cabinet support in the face of continuing military objections. Lampson, with Brooke-Popham in attendance, briefed the Cabinet Committee (chaired by the prime minister) on 12 June and subsequently attended three meetings of the Conversations Committee (its membership had by now been expanded to include the service ministers and chiefs of staff).[32] Despite continuing reservations, it was agreed that it was vital to Britain's interests to secure a treaty, even if this necessitated concessions, given the possibility of unrest in the Middle East and the growing dangers in Europe.

Lampson and Brooke-Popham returned to Cairo on 27 June 1935 and quickly secured agreement on the military clauses. On 24 July, Brooke-Popham noted that "[t]he military clauses of the treaty were initialled this evening at the Zafaran Palace, 20 weeks and four days from the start of the negotiations. I feel we've got all that we really want. There are various other parts of the treaty still to be settled, e.g., the Sudan and capitulations, happily, I don't come into these."[33] The military clauses were the key to the treaty and had taken up the bulk (88 percent) of the negotiations.[34] The fundamental difficulty was London's unrealistic demand for security guarantees. Brooke-Popham understood this and felt that the looser arrangements implemented in Iraq (in which he had played a large part) should be sufficient. His advice, and reputation,[35] helped counter the more inflexible line taken by the service chiefs.[36] The role of the military advisers in securing the 1936 Anglo-Egyptian Treaty has never been properly recognized. Between them, Brooke-Popham and Weir were able to persuade the British government to concede the changes needed to secure an agreement. Without their efforts, Britain's position in the Middle East during World War II would have been weaker and could well have been fatally compromised. The outcome was a treaty that respected Egypt's independence, did not excite nationalist passions, and regularized the continuing British military presence. In the process, it extended the area of the Canal Zone, increased the standing garrison from eight thousand to ten thousand troops, and secured stationing and overflying rights for the RAF. The treaty was finalized on 13 August 1936 and was followed by a large dinner party in celebration, hosted by Lampson at the Alexandria Yacht Club. "It really is rather a triumph for him in view of the many abortive attempts to conclude one in the past."[37] For his part, Lampson readily acknowledged Brooke-Popham's contribution. "Without your most generous assistance and readiness to meet all difficulties and suggestions, we should certainly never have got through. . . . I only wish we were to have the same team over our other problems, for I have found your shrewd criticism the greatest asset."[38] In his contribution to the treaty negotiations, Brooke-Popham had demonstrated an open-mindedness and astuteness that helped secure a successful outcome. He had also shown he was not afraid to challenge the service chiefs when he felt they were wrong. While recognizing that their collective aim was to protect Britain's interests, he was equally adamant that this should not mean abandoning honesty. Throughout Brooke-Popham's time in Egypt, his Iraq experience engendered a willingness to consider other views and to adopt a more trusting and confident approach than many in Whitehall.

With the signing of the treaty there was no reason for Brooke-Popham to remain in the Middle East. There was increasing concern about the situation in Palestine, where disturbances had broken out in April 1936, but the task of restoring law and order fell to AOC Palestine and his successor, following the appointment of Lieutenant-General (later Field Marshal Sir) John Dill to supreme military command.[39] Peirse had wanted a free hand to deal with the violence, but the high commissioner and London had stalled, only to decide later to declare martial law and send in substantial ground forces. "I'm sorry for Peirse over this Palestine business, rather heart-breaking to see another man succeed owing to him being allowed to do what you'd been begging for months' past."[40] It had originally been planned that Brooke-Popham's time as inspector general would end in April 1937.[41] During 1936, he and Opal had started to think about his future employment and finding somewhere to live. Having sold Bagborough House in 1921, there was no family home. Since their marriage, they had lived in a succession of houses rented by the

Air Ministry. In July, Opal announced that she had found the perfect property near Bicester.[42] Cottisford House (then located in Northamptonshire, but now in Oxfordshire) needed a great deal of work, but the location meant that they could both ride and the proximity to Bicester made it relatively easy to get into London by train. The purchase (for nine thousand pounds) was completed in October, just before Brooke-Popham arrived back from Egypt. The only concern was that, without a job, his income would be restricted and they might not be able to afford to hunt.[43] It was at this critical moment that Brooke-Popham was approached about taking the post of governor in Kenya. "There is an Imperial job to be done there and it requires someone with wide and varied experience and outlook."[44] Having discussed the question with Opal, he replied on 4 November agreeing to have his name put forward. Ten days later, it was announced that Air Chief Marshal Sir Robert Brooke-Popham was to become governor and commander in chief of the Colony and Protectorate of Kenya, in succession to Brigadier-General Sir Joseph Byrne, in March 1937.[45]

It was during his first few months back in England that Brooke-Popham was drawn into the debate about Ellington's successor as CAS. Past practice had been to look to the most senior air marshal. Ellington wrote to Dowding in February 1937 to advise him that Newall had been selected by the secretary of state.[46] While this was strictly correct, Ellington was closely involved in the decision to appoint Newall, who was the most junior of the RAF's four air marshals—the most senior being Dowding. Brooke-Popham thought it a good thing to break with the custom that CAS should always be the most senior officer, but was concerned that the lack of seniority might undermine his ability to act as a final court of appeal. "The CAS, who is junior to three or four other officers in the RAF, including two commanders in England, cannot give personal decisions carrying the same weight as in the past."[47] The episode is important in underscoring the close relationship between Ellington and Brooke-Popham and in highlighting the latter's role, albeit at the margins, in ensuring that Dowding was CinC Fighter Command rather than CAS during the Battle of Britain.

On his formal retirement from the RAF, Brooke-Popham received an official letter of appreciation from the Air Ministry. Such documents are formulaic and drafted from a summary of the individual's career provided by the Air Secretary's department. Nevertheless, the narrative properly highlighted Brooke-Popham's work for the RFC and RAF, in war and in peace, including his service as the first commandant of the Staff College and the first RAF commandant of IDC, as well as his role as CinC ADGB and the RAF's inspector general.[48] For his work in Egypt, he also received the secretary of state's public thanks and a personal letter of appreciation from Eden. The latter was more than formulaic; it was a genuine expression of gratitude. When Eden ran into Brooke-Popham in 1939, shortly after the war had started, he greeted him as "the man who got us the Egyptian Treaty."[49]

13

GOVERNOR OF KENYA
1937–1939

There was no laid-down process for the selection of a colonial governor, although ultimately it was a decision for the secretary of state at the Colonial Office, after consulting the prime minister (and seeking the king's approval).[1] In forwarding Brooke-Popham's name to His Majesty, Secretary of State William Ormsby-Gore pointed out that the appointment presented special and exceptional difficulties. He went on to highlight Sir Robert's distinguished military record and his wide experience of different parts of the empire.[2] In a passage subsequently removed from the final draft, Ormsby-Gore added that in his opinion, "there is no officer at present in the Colonial Service who can be regarded as in any way qualified for the appointment." He also believed that Brooke-Popham, unlike his predecessor, would be better socially with the necessary self-reliance and sense of humor.[3] By coincidence, Brooke-Popham had stayed with Byrne earlier in the year. "He is very nice, but lacks confidence and also a sense of humour. So, he finds it somewhat difficult to deal with the British settlers, who I imagine are a pretty troublesome lot."[4]

Robert and Opal arrived in Kenya on 6 April 1937, having taken a month to travel to Egypt (via Marseilles and Malta), and then by air to Nairobi (landing en route at Khartoum and Entebbe). The couple took the opportunity to spend a week in Egypt, visiting Miles Lampson—now the British ambassador—and other friends. The children followed separately with their governess. The two years that the family spent in Kenya would prove both happy and productive. It was also an opportunity for Opal to play a larger role than simply supporting her husband's social obligations. "I'm afraid we shall never have a job, which we were able to do together in the same way, as we were able in Kenya. Looking back on it now, I think that's the real reason why we enjoyed it so much, in spite of the setbacks and the Colonial Office and the Ailsa Turners."[5]

The role of governor in British Africa was a combination of sovereign, prime minister, and head of the Civil Service, as well as the leader of the colony's social life.[6] Governors were appointed for five years with a possible two-year extension. By the late 1930s the governorship of Kenya was one of the most important appointments in the empire, graded alongside Ceylon, Hong Kong, Malaya, and Palestine.[7] The salary (£7,500 per annum) reflected this status and was considerably more than the pay of an air chief marshal (£2,300), let alone a retired officer on a pension (equivalent to half-pay). The selection of Brooke-Popham as governor of Kenya was regarded as a happy choice. "Brookham had ability, vision, enterprise, tact, persuasiveness and determination and he quickly brought harmony to a sadly disunited Kenya, for he was a good conciliator."[8] He was undoubtedly more popular than his predecessor, who had introduced several measures, including income tax, that were disliked by the European settlers, and had resisted their demands for greater influence. Byrne was regarded as tough and uncompromising. While Brooke-Popham was much more to the settlers' liking, the difference between the two was more about style than substance.[9] Brooke-Popham inherited an efficient and experienced staff including the deputy governor and chief secretary to the Kenya government, Sir Armigel de V. Wade, who was highly respected and had considerable experience, having served in East Africa since 1912. Wade provided both continuity and local knowledge. Before he left England, Brooke-Popham had selected Flight Lieutenant Reggie Elsmie, a Cranwell Sword of Honour recipient, as his ADC. Elsmie was an outstanding officer and destined to achieve high rank in the RAF but was shot down and killed over Greece in 1941.

Although the governor exercised full authority in the colony, he was advised by an executive council of eight ex officio members together with a number (usually four) of unofficial members. The governor was also president of the Legislative Council (commonly referred to as the "LegCo"), comprising both ex officio and unofficial members representing European, Indian,

Arab, and African communities.[10] Kenya was one of the largest and most prosperous of Britain's colonies. Covering 225,000 square miles, it had an estimated population of 3,335,000—of which some 42,000 were Europeans—and an administrative staff of around 350 civil servants.[11] Relations between the European settlers and the Colonial Office had been increasingly strained during the 1930s. The settlers' efforts to claim a greater economic and political role in the colony had been largely rebuffed. There were also long-running problems relating to land and labor management that had proved intractable—even more so as they impinged on the rights of the African population.

One of these issues was colonial labor policy and the position of contract labor employed on white-owned farms. This had attracted considerable public attention in Britain and was the subject of extensive correspondence between the governor and the Colonial Office. Because the problem was partly cultural and partly economic, there was no easy or immediate solution. British concepts of work and wages undermined traditional tribal values, while the growing population and pressure on land meant that maintaining the status quo was not a realistic strategy. According to one study, Brooke-Popham sided with the settlers, although the colonial secretary, Ormsby-Gore, had urged him to find a humane solution.[12] The status of African labor in the major towns was also a concern and after riots in Mombasa, Brooke-Popham took steps to improve workers' accommodation, particularly in Nairobi.[13]

Another of the major challenges faced by the Kenya government was how to halt the extensive soil erosion caused by excessive cattle numbers. This was not just a problem in East Africa. Soil conservation had become a major environmental concern in many British colonies, driven by the American Dust Bowl catastrophe that reached its height in 1935.[14] The preferred solution was to reduce the size of the herds by destocking, but this was strongly opposed by the tribes—for economic and cultural reasons.[15] In February 1938, Brooke-Popham determined on "drastic action" to destock and recondition the Machakos reserve, used as grazing land by the Kamba tribe. The government believed the carrying capacity of the reserve was only 25,000 head of cattle (and possibly 100,000 after reconditioning) rather than the existing 250,000.[16] He had first visited the reserve shortly after arriving in Kenya and was convinced that "unless we take action in the very near future, we shall have a large population who will have to be located elsewhere if they are not going to starve."[17] The destocking policy saw the forced sale of over 22,000 cattle between April and August 1938. The Kamba petitioned the Colonial Office and some three thousand marched to Nairobi in protest, demanding to meet the governor. Brooke-Popham was sympathetic to Kamba concerns, but argued that destocking was in their best interest—if soil erosion was to be controlled. Henry Gurney, chief secretary of the East Africa Governors' Conference, was adamant that the policy was not a mistake and that, in the end, there was a grudging recognition that a "difficult problem was tackled for their own good and not shirked because of its difficulty."[18] Although Brooke-Popham refused to meet with the protestors in Nairobi, believing that this would set a precedent, he travelled to Machakos on 25 August 1938 where he announced at a *baraza* (public meeting) that the forced sales would be halted in favor of voluntary sales.[19] The decision was interpreted in some quarters as a defeat, but Brooke-Popham preferred to describe it as a "slowing down" rather than a change in methods.[20] He remained determined to gain the trust of the Kamba and directed that work continue in the reserve to restore the fertility of the soil and eliminate the tsetse fly.[21]

There is little doubt that the government had been clumsy in its actions rather than "incredible in its stupidity," but there were strong and compelling reasons to act on soil erosion.[22] Moreover, the policy had already been success-fully implemented the previous year on the Yatta plains.[23] Brooke-Popham's speech at Machakos has been portrayed as a Kamba victory, but the decision was a tactical retreat; the government was still intent on reconditioning the land. By 1940, substantial progress had been made in halting soil erosion in the reserve.[24] Even so, the episode had caused embarrassment and excited criticism in London. The subsequent debate in the national press and Par-liament put pressure on both the Colonial Office and the Kenyan govern-ment.[25] Responsibility must lie with Brooke-Popham, but it is to his credit that he changed tack, once he understood the strength of the opposition, and that he did so at a public forum in the heart of the Kamba tribal lands. He spoke later about the need for balance in developing East Africa, between speed and the need for dalliance: "It was so easy to motor round a place and come back with the idea that something must be done immediately, but it must be remembered that we could not ride rough-shod over native tradi-tions, customs and habits: that would only lead to the use of machine guns."[26]

Brooke-Popham was more than just a friend to the colonist and defender of the status quo. He was an able administrator and innovator, who antici-pated wider political and social changes. In October 1937, he addressed the

LegCo about the vital importance of "constructive development." This was followed by a memorandum to the Executive Council, proposing the creation of a long-term plan for Kenya that anticipated the creation of the Colonial Development and Welfare Act of 1940 and recognized the role of government in addressing economic and welfare issues of benefit to the country as a whole.[27] To support these aims, he also announced that the newly reconstituted Executive Council would meet fortnightly as a development committee.[28] Brooke-Popham's plans have been criticized for failing to provide a "constructive formulation of native policy."[29] In fact, his proposals embraced education objectives for all races (African, European, Goans, and Indians)—including the specific issue of "female education for Africans," agriculture (coffee and cash crops for Africans), and "Native Affairs." The latter objective identified the need to develop African responsibilities, including representation on the LegCo.[30] He can be criticized for his role in a colonial system that favored European settlers, but he genuinely believed it was his responsibility to protect African interests (the "Trust Principle").[31] "I was responsible for the welfare and guidance of something over three million people in East Africa, so I would be quite ready to admit that our methods are not perfect. But those who make no mistakes will never make anything."[32] In the postcolonial era such sentiments have been dismissed as a fig-leaf for European self-interest, but Brooke-Popham's record shows that he was never the pompous reactionary suggested by some commentators, and in many ways was more open-minded and fair-handed than his predecessors.[33]

Another problem confronting the governor was how to manage the large number of refugees who had fled Abyssinia and Eritrea following the Italian invasion. More than six thousand were living in Northern Kenya, at Isiolo, under difficult conditions.[34] The Kenyan government was desperate to find a solution that did not involve resettlement in the country, while the Colonial Office was determined that any Kenyan "solution" did not have wider implications. Meanwhile, unrest grew in the camps because of the British decision to recognize Italian sovereignty in Abyssinia.[35] It was eventually agreed to resettle the refugees in Kenya, but by the time this was put into effect war had broken out. Early in his tenure, Brooke-Popham unwittingly participated in a charade perpetrated by Mervyn Cowie, an enthusiastic and vociferous advocate of game preservation. The pair visited the Mbagathi grasslands in the Kiserian Valley, some fifteen miles from Nairobi, to see lions that had been lured there by regular feeding. Brooke-Popham was unaware of the subter-fuge.[36] Cowie's aim was to get the new governor's support for the creation of a national park system. "I felt confident that I could now make a bold attempt to convert the Governor of Kenya to the virtues of game preservation."[37] The outcome was in the balance when Cowie became lost in the dark, but he was eventually able to return his guest to Nairobi unscathed and impressed by their shared adventure. "The Governor was full of praise, and asked how a scheme could be promoted to enable visitors from overseas to enjoy the same exciting afternoon which he had experienced."[38] Brooke-Popham advanced Cowie's efforts, through the Game Policy Committee, to establish a national parks system in Kenya and by encouraging schemes to attract foreign visitors. His support opened many doors and gradually helped to change opinion in the colony. Cowie was undoubtedly a shrewd and influential advocate but, although the outbreak of war slowed the process, Brooke-Popham should certainly receive some credit for the first national parks in British East Africa, created at Nairobi in 1946 and Tsavo in 1948.

During the summer of 1938, the Duke and Duchess of Gloucester vis-ited Kenya. The duke was the younger brother of King George VI. His wife, Alice Montague-Douglas-Scott, was the niece of Lord Francis Scott, who farmed in the colony and was the unofficial leader of the European settlers. The duchess had been advised by her doctors in July to take a complete rest. It was hoped that three months in Kenya would provide the necessary respite. The couple arrived at Port Bell, Uganda, by Imperial Airways flying boat on 19 August 1938. They left the next day for Nakuru where they were met by the Brooke-Pophams before travelling to Francis Scott's farm, Deloraine, where they spent several weeks without any official duties. The couple returned to England on 5 November 1938 after a highly successful visit. Shortly before his departure, the duke joined Brooke-Popham and Joss Erroll in winning the Nairobi Polo Club's Captain's Pot.

Brooke-Popham's main achievement in the two years he spent in Kenya was to revitalize the local defense organization, created to supplement and support the King's African Rifles. The Kenya Defence Force (KDF) had been created in 1928 from volunteers—many of whom had served in World War I. The KDF was organized on a territorial basis and members attended training only when they could. By 1936, it had reached a low state of efficiency.[39] At the same time, the Italian occupation of Abyssinia and growing uncertainty about Hitler's ambitions meant that the defense of the colony was a serious and pressing concern for the governor and the Colonial Office. Although the enabling legislation had been passed shortly before Brooke-Popham arrived, it was under his tenure that the Kenya Regiment (Territorial Force) came into being. It took some months for the first two companies to be recruited and trained, but Brooke-Popham was able to inspect the new regiment at its first annual camp in March 1938.[40] There is no doubt that Brooke-Popham's military background assisted in preparing Kenya for a future war, devising a plan to defend the strategically important port of Mombasa while leaving Nairobi and the highlands lightly defended. His assessment was that an attack by land from the north was unlikely, as Italian troops would have had to cross hundreds of miles of barren wasteland before reaching these inland targets. Several precautionary measures were initiated to move the colony toward a war footing. When the LegCo reconvened on 5 August 1938, Brooke-Popham announced the formation of a Manpower Committee to examine the utilization of the colony's manpower in time of war, together with the creation of a Communications Committee to explore the adaptation of existing communication systems to meet military requirements. These measures also helped reassure the settler community that London was concerned about the colony's defense. Other initiatives included the creation of a volunteer naval unit at Mombasa and the establishment of an auxiliary air unit. Opal also played her part, setting up the Kenya Women's Emergency Organisation (KWEO) in 1938 to undertake war work once mobilization had been declared. By 1942, the KWEO had registered 6,500 European women, of whom 2,300 were doing war work outside of their homes.[41] Opal was also active in supporting social work throughout the colony and the activities of the East African Women's League (EAWL).

As the possibility of war in Europe grew, so did the preparations to repel a possible Italian attack from Ethiopia and Italian Somaliland.[42] Brooke-Popham was criticized by the Foreign Office in May 1939 over his skepticism about the potential for an uprising in Ethiopia and for raising moral concerns about encouraging the tribes to revolt against the Italian occupation when there was no prospect of British intervention.[43] His position was supported by Sir Stewart Symes, the governor of Sudan. Their attitude was likely influenced by a shared concern about the stability of their own areas if insurrections were actively encouraged and the border destabilized. Realistically, however, there was little prospect that the British government would encourage a revolt before the outbreak of war. Brooke-Popham may also have been influenced by discussions with Katharine Fannin, who travelled from Kenya through Ethiopia collecting valuable intelligence in 1938. She met with him before setting out and, on her return from her second visit to Ethiopia in March 1939, provided a detailed report on conditions in the country.[44] Brooke-Popham's concerns about precipitate action in Abyssinia did not diminish with the outbreak of war. "I feel very strongly that we shall be leaning on a broken reed if we rely on a revolt by itself to achieve anything big. It must be done in conjunction with an offensive and not as a separate action."[45] Interestingly, this was the view of M. R. D. Foot, writing about later efforts to foment revolt in Abyssinia: "The main lesson of interest remained: that a major guerrilla war could be mounted with effect, provided it was timed to join in with the efforts of more regular forces in the same theatre of war."[46]

The Brooke-Pophams fully embraced the life of the colony. Didie and Phil went to local schools while Opal threw herself into the many and varied activities demanded of a governor's wife, including welfare and social organizations. Opal had been prominent in girl guiding for many years and did much to diversify the movement in Kenya, helping to establish the first African girl guide troop in Kenya.[47] She was delighted, therefore, when Lord Robert and Lady Olave Baden-Powell, who knew Kenya well, chose to retire to Nyeri in 1938.[48] The two couples had much in common, beyond double twin initials (R. B. P. and O. B. P.).[49] When Baden-Powell died in January 1941, Brooke-Popham wrote to Olave Baden-Powell extending his condolences and mentioning the privilege it had been to meet and talk with them. For her part, Olave spoke of her husband's admiration for Brooke-Popham and recalled the calm peace and loveliness of Government House at Nairobi.[50] Kenya also brought a personal tragedy for the Brooke-Pophams. Opal became pregnant in August 1938 and returned to England shortly afterward. Sadly, it proved to be an ectopic pregnancy and she lost the baby. She did not return to Kenya until after Christmas, following an operation and an extended period of recovery. Brooke-Popham regretted the loss of their "Kenyan baby" but was more concerned about Opal's health and well-being. Determined and energetic in equal measure, Opal used her "exile" in England to give lectures about the colony before she was allowed by the doctors to return to Kenya and rejoin her family.

There was a darker side to life in Kenya—reflected in the behavior of the "Happy Valley" set and the events that led to the death of Josslyn "Joss" Hay, the Earl of Erroll, in the same month that Baden-Powell died.[51] Erroll was a well-known figure in Kenya's social life and a fellow polo player.[52] He had joined the Manpower Committee on its formation and became deputy director (and assistant military secretary), where he proved to be an energetic and capable administrator. When war was declared some three thousand Europeans (out of just nine thousand eligible) joined the armed services. Erroll had asked for help finding a job with the Foreign Office, but this proved fruitless and Brooke-Popham advised that he should join the fighting forces in some capacity.[53] "Sad news about poor Joss Erroll's death, such a pity when he was just beginning to become a useful citizen of Kenya. One couldn't help loving him in a way." "What a waste of a brain and a kind heart."[54] The mystery surrounding his death, and the hedonistic lifestyle that he and a small group of white settlers enjoyed in the highlands, have continued to dominate the public imagination, generating a series of books and films.

During the summer of 1939, events in Europe took a turn for the worse. Kenya, as with all parts of the British Empire, moved through a series of preplanned stages—initiated by abbreviated messages detailing the precautions to be taken. The first "alert" stage was declared on 22 August, followed by the "precautionary" stage on 1 September (the day that Germany invaded Poland). When war was declared on 3 September 1939, Brooke-Popham had already interned every German national in the colony,[55] and commandeered all aircraft, as well as issuing a plan to keep farms operating. A total of seven hundred German civilians (male and female) were interned, although this was done in a good-humored manner. By October, six hundred had been released from internment.[56] Brooke-Popham later told his son that he had been extremely nervous in taking this step, before the actual outbreak of war, for fear of the diplomatic and political repercussions if it turned out he had acted prematurely. Once again, there is an intimation of the predicament he would face in December 1941, in determining whether to invade Thailand.

On 21 September 1939, less than three weeks after war had been declared, Brooke-Popham was warned by the Air Ministry that he would be required to return to England. This is likely to have been his decision, notwithstanding the formality of the request. The RAF certainly wanted him back, and there was a legal obligation (as a reservist), but he could likely have stayed in Kenya and still contributed to the war effort. His family were settled and enjoying life in East Africa. Moreover, resignation came at considerable financial cost—more than £5,000 per annum.[57] A year later, and another Christmas away from home, he reflected on his decision. "Of course, we should still have been together if I'd stayed on in Kenya, but I'm sure we should have felt awfully out of the picture. Ailsa and her fulminations in place of bombs; deputations from disgruntled Indians in place of air raid warnings. . . . we shouldn't really have been able to do much constructive work after the war had started."[58] As he explained to his neighboring governor, Sir Mark Young (Tanganyika), "I feel that, at any rate from the defence point of view, East Africa is now safe and I should be doing more good towards winning the war as an airman in England than as a governor in Kenya."[59]

The king approved Brooke-Popham's departure on 25 September 1939,[60] although the formal notice that he had been recalled for permanent service was not issued until 2 November 1939.[61] In the interim, the attorney general of Kenya, Walter Harrigan,[62] served as acting governor until Brooke-Popham's successor, Sir Henry Monck-Mason Moore, arrived in January 1940. Moore (who had previously served as the colony's colonial secretary) was the first governor of Kenya to have spent his entire career in the Colonial Service. He adopted similar policies to Brooke-Popham and allowed the European settlers to make significant political and economic gains during his tenure.[63] During his time in Kenya, Brooke-Popham improved relations with the settlers, whose conservative leaders had repeatedly clashed with his predecessor to establish their dominance over the political and economic life of the colony. Some postcolonial historians have accused him of weak leadership for failing to confront those who wanted to restrict African and Asian rights in Kenya. Others have described his tenure as undistinguished.[64] This is unfair, not only because his time as governor was cut short, but also because it ignores the importance to the entire colony of creating better relations with London and the long-term benefits of his forward-looking initiatives, such as "constructive development" and the Game Policy Committee. It is true that he made little progress with African political development, educational opportunities, land ownership, and economic policies,[65] but it is wrong to saddle Brooke-Popham with all the problems of the British Empire. He was not responsible for the decision to invite white settlers to Kenya, but he tried to balance the needs and aspirations of all communities in Kenya. This is not to suggest that he was embarrassed by colonial rule. Brooke-Popham was convinced that the white settler community had much to offer Kenya and that traditional British values should underpin the colony. He was concerned, however, that Kenya should look to the north (England) rather than the south (Union of South Africa) for a role model.[66] He was also willing to challenge the status quo and

vested interests as, for example, when he allowed an expansion in tea plant-
ing, contrary to international agreements.[67] Unusually perhaps, as the king's
representative, he was also prepared to change his mind, as he did over the
Kamba destocking protest—against the views of the settlers.

Brooke-Popham's tenure in Kenya was overshadowed by events in Europe.
He had served less than half the normal tenure of a colonial governor and
spent much of this time focused on preparing the colony for war. Significant
progress had been made but several major issues remained unresolved.[68] He
had no illusions in this respect. "After I had been out in Kenya a fortnight,
I wrote to Ormsby Gore and told him there were two things I was setting
out to do, first, to bring about cooperation between officials and unofficials
and second, having done that, to develop Kenya. I think it is fair to say that
I did achieve the first. The second I had only started and I do hope this development will continue."[69] There was genuine regret across the colony at
his departure. Several newspapers commented on how he had transformed
public opinion and addressed longstanding grievances. Commending all that
he had achieved, emphasis was placed on Brooke-Popham's enthusiasm for
education and the social advancement of the African and Indian communities. "He has never once placed anything before the public interest. No effort
has been too much, no attention to detail too great, in understanding the
problems of all races." He was also congratulated for his remarkable record in
so short a time, while Opal's energy, enthusiasm, and organizing ability were
singled out, particularly her efforts in creating the KWEO. Noting that the
governor would be leaving the colony in a few days' time, and while observ-
ing that no one would dispute the decision, "we cannot pretend that it will be
received throughout Kenya with any other sentiment than regret."[70]

14

WORLD WAR II
1939–1940

Brooke-Popham flew back to the UK via Egypt, Malta, and France while his family sailed home from Mombasa (via Port Said), having packed their possessions and said their farewells.[1] Because of the speed of events, it was left to Opal to handle the extensive correspondence that followed news of the governor's departure. During the journey, he produced several *poste restante* letters, to be read when she reached Egypt, much as he had written to his sister twenty-five years earlier when putting his affairs in order at the beginning of the Great War. The contents were largely about household matters (including their tax affairs), but faced with the prospect of another world war, he was also in a reflective mood, wondering whether it might see "the end of European dominance over Asian and African races?"[2] It may not have crossed his mind that he would play a central role in this process, but he had some sense of what lay ahead for the empire he served.

Arriving in London on 5 October 1939, Brooke-Popham met with Air Member for Personnel Peter Portal, who was accompanied by Rear-Admiral Arthur Bromley from the Dominions Office. Portal offered him the task of starting up the RAF's new air training organization in Canada. A variety of flying training schemes based in Canada had been mooted before the outbreak of war, but all had encountered political opposition, notably from Mackenzie King, the Canadian prime minister, who was wary about his country's potential involvement in an imperial war.[3] Early in the rearmament process, the Air Ministry had identified training capacity as the critical path to sustaining wartime operations (and the loss of 50 percent of crews per month).[4] Canada was seen as an ideal location—out of range of enemy aircraft while offering the suitable terrain, weather, and accessibility.[5] When these ideas were first raised in 1936, the Canadian government had concluded that it was inadvisable "to have Canadian territory used by the British Government to establish training schools of its own."[6] An attempt was made to table the question at the 1937 Imperial Conference, but Mackenzie King steadfastly refused.[7]

The outbreak of war meant that finding a solution to the RAF's training needs was even more urgent. The Air Ministry once again looked to Canada. While the political climate had improved, there were still obstacles to be overcome, both financial and practical. Overshadowing everything, however, were the tension and contradictions that characterized Britain's relationship with the Dominions.[8] Before his departure for Canada, Brooke-Popham had lengthy discussions on the Air Ministry's requirements (and its red lines) with Secretary of State for Air Kingsley Wood and Chief of the Air Staff Cyril Newall.[9] He toured a number of flying training establishments, to acquaint himself with the latest training methods and standards, as well as visiting the RAF's Advanced Air Striking Force (AASF) in France with Air Marshal Sir Charles Burnett (his successor as inspector general), providing a private report for Newall on morale and organization.[10] While at the AASF Headquarters in Rheims, he used the opportunity to look around the cathedral: "I saw it in 1910 in all its beauty and again in 1918 when it was partly in ruins, no roof and the upper part of some of the walls knocked down by German shellfire. Now the restoration is finished, very well too, but they are sandbagging the main entrances and removing what was left of the stained glass. Few things have brought home to me the futility of war as seeing it again."[11]

The importance of the training mission was not lost on Brooke-Popham but, as he confided to Opal, he "would have preferred a command closer to the war."[12] On the other hand, he enjoyed being back in uniform and was delighted at the warm welcome he encountered.[13] He had planned to leave for Canada on 27 October, but this was delayed, allowing a brief reunion with Opal, who arrived in the UK by air on 2 November, just as he set off by train for Liverpool. Brooke-Popham was officially appointed "Chief RAF Member of the British Air Mission to Canada" the day that he sailed from Liverpool, on the *Duchess of Richmond*. The other members of the air mission, notably Lord Riverdale and Air Marshal Sir Christopher Courtney, were already in Canada.[14] The crossing was uneventful and he arrived in Montréal, Québec, ten days later—to be met by Billy Bishop, a Canadian fighter ace who had served with him in the RFC and was now an air marshal in the Royal

Canadian Air Force (RCAF). Travelling by train from Montréal, they reached Ottawa on 13 November 1939 where Brooke-Popham went to work immediately, attending a joint conference that evening. The next day was also busy, with a full schedule of meetings (including dinner with Mackenzie King) and an extended discussion with the Air Ministry via telegraphic dispatch. Brooke-Popham was attracted by much of what he found in Canada, especially the warmth of individual Canadians, but he had little time for their politics:

> The service departments, especially their Air Force, carry very little weight in government circles and their CAS merely does what his Minister tells him. The Prime Minister is very nervous about his own position and is swayed mainly by what he thinks the country would like him to do irrespective of what's the right course. No one will give a decision and I fancy the people as a whole are getting very restive at the slow progress in all directions. The ministers as a whole don't impress one either for their ability or driving power, though they certainly work hard. Socially, most of them are very nice and everyone is very friendly.[15]

Mackenzie King noted in his private diary that "I quite enjoyed the evening's talk with different members of the Mission, including Sir Robert Brooke-Popham, ex-Governor of Kenya. He did not make quite as favourable an impression as the others; has a bit of the Englishman's tranquil, self-satisfied way."[16]

The Air Mission was based in the Parliament building. Brooke-Popham's fears about decision-making were soon realized as the negotiations dragged on. "Things move very slowly here, far too much argument over the exact wording of agreements and memoranda and far too little action towards winning the war. I'm getting fed up with it all."[17] Negotiating the scheme proved complicated and often tense. By and large, Australia and New Zealand were supportive and prepared to subordinate national interest to the wider good, but the Canadians worried over the detail and threatened to abandon the entire process. On at least one occasion, an angered Mackenzie King shocked the British by announcing, "This is not our war."[18] Brooke-Popham met the governor-general (Lord Tweedsmuir) at the end of his first week in Ottawa,[19] and had an opportunity to compare the role with his experience in Kenya:

The Governor General here has a pretty rotten time. He hardly comes into the affairs of Canada at all, for instance we've never dealt through him in any way over the air-training scheme. He's not much more than a figurehead . . . there's a High Commissioner for the United Kingdom, a very good chap, Gerald Campbell, he and his office really do all the work. I'd hate to have Tweedsmuir's job. It rather amused me to hear the Prime Minister, in referring to me, say what an example I'd set by giving up a life of ease and retirement as a governor and once more resuming burdens of responsibility, etc., etc.[20]

Riverdale, as leader of the Air Mission, was key to achieving an agreement, but Brooke-Popham felt that the popular and generous Riverdale was not ideally suited to running the negotiations.[21] Nevertheless, the main elements of the scheme were resolved (finance and manpower) over the next two weeks, including securing the agreement of the Australian and New Zealand missions. There was a danger, however, that "someone with a legal turn of mind would throw a spanner in the works."[22] A week later, the Canadian Cabinet had yet to agree to the proposals. When Brooke-Popham left for a planned visit to Toronto, visiting factories and military installations, Riverdale remained in Ottawa in case there was a breakthrough. The following Monday, matters were still stalled. Everything hinged on whether the word "the" was to be added or not. This was no arcane argument about grammar (or the correct employment of the definite article), but a question of war finance. The issue was whether the RAF would agree to form sufficient Canadian squadrons to absorb "the" entire Canadian output from the Training Scheme or just "some" output. "The Canadians, perhaps rightly, regarded me as the one obstacle in the way of getting what they wanted, Riverdale being ready to concede the point, until last night. Thursday evening, long argument, heated at times."[23] Brooke-Popham was upbraided by the finance minister (James Ralston) for being so particular over words, "when sensible men realized that they could not be interpreted too literally if there were difficulties."[24] This had not been his experience in Baghdad and Cairo, where words (and their interpretation) meant everything in building an understanding that would survive beyond the signing ceremony. There was also a related argument over exactly what comprised a "Canadian" squadron. Brooke-Popham was pragmatic about the distinction but felt that it logically meant both air and groundcrew. Mackenzie King disagreed and felt that a squadron could be "Canadian" even if the groundcrew were not. In truth, the issue that divided the two sides was money. The Air Ministry did not want to fund more Canadian squadrons than they had to, while the Canadian government felt that they were contributing more than enough in human capital.[25] A compromise proved elusive as the emphasis on "Canadianization" was driven by political rather than operational concerns. Australia and New Zealand recognized that it was neither practical nor effective to place all their aircrew in "national" squadrons. Brooke-Popham's concerns over the provision of groundcrew (largely British personnel) proved prescient and ultimately restricted the number of Canadian squadrons that could be created, notwithstanding the trained aircrew available. The Air Ministry would later complain that the scheme was "bogged down in apples" because of arguments between the respective treasuries over offsetting Canadian apple exports against their financial contribution.[26]

Mackenzie King has left his own account of the hectic forty-eight hours leading to the signature of the agreement just after midnight on Sunday, 17 December 1939.[27] He regarded Brooke-Popham as the main obstacle. Realizing that Riverdale was the weak point, and that Campbell was "an incorrigible obstructionist," the prime minister maneuvered to isolate Riverdale from the influence of the other members of the Air Mission.[28] At one stage Riverdale, on his own with the Canadians, agreed to a formula that "gave our position away." He was induced by the high commissioner and Brooke-Popham to withdraw his assent, on the promise of a telephone call to Kingsley Wood. A flurry of calls and telegrams between Ottawa and London followed, but a consensus on the wording still seemed to be far away on the Saturday evening when Brooke-Popham took the opportunity to attend an ice hockey match. At 10 p.m., as the match was nearing the end, he was summoned (over the public-address system) to Government House. Mackenzie King had spoken with Tweedsmuir and persuaded him to get Brooke-Popham to back down. There followed an uncomfortable discussion between the governor-general, in his dressing-gown, and Brooke-Popham, fresh from the stadium: "I bowed my farewell to the pyjama'ed reflection of royalty and departed, feeling very tired, lonely and troubled. His ADC told me I was now wanted urgently at the Prime Minister's office where Riverdale had already gone. However, I meant to prove to them that though the Canadian Cabinet might be in a hurry I wasn't, so I had a drink and a cigarette before I left Government House."[29]

Mackenzie King regarded the subsequent signing as a great triumph for himself and a defeat for Brooke-Popham, even though the latter was largely content with the outcome. "Riverdale had (most loyally to me) refused to sign unless the Prime Minister agreed to the omission of that offending particle 'the,' and that the Prime Minister had given way and all was well." While they were busy with the pens (noting that it was now past midnight), Brooke-Popham wished Mackenzie King very many happy returns of the day. "He was so surprised and pleased at my remembering his birthday."[30] According to Mackenzie King: "I never saw a man look so deflated in a way than Sir Robert Brooke-Popham did. He looked indeed as if he had been spanked. His face was very red and his manner very crushed. I think having the Governor General speak with him was something he never anticipated and, having been Governor of a Crown Colony himself, he would realize the significance of the word of a Governor in a self-governing dominion, given in the name of the King."[31] Brooke-Popham was indeed upset (Campbell thought he looked a broken man), but only because he deeply resented Tweedsmuir's intervention, believing that the governor-general had overstepped his authority in insisting that he ignore the interests of his service and the instructions of his ministers.[32] The high commissioner and the Dominions Office were appalled by the involvement of the governor-general and believed that the agreement could have been signed two weeks earlier, but for Mackenzie King's actions.[33] Brooke-Popham readily acknowledged that he was regarded by the Canadians as the cause for the delay, but insisted that it had only arisen because of last-minute changes tabled by Ralston. On his return to London, he raised these concerns with the Air Ministry and the Dominions Office, but with Tweedsmuir's sudden death on 11 February 1940 (having suffered a stroke), there was little appetite to pursue the matter. Moreover, in the intervening two months, relations had largely been patched up. "I'm glad we'd got on good terms again after that tiresome bedroom scene in December, as you know, I was a bit upset with him at the time."[34] In retrospect, Brooke-Popham felt that many of the problems faced in Canada could have been avoided, if terms of reference had been provided for the Air Mission. He remained unforgiving, however, about what he saw as some unpleasant remarks by Canadian ministers and their deliberate deception. He was particularly critical of Ralston, whom he blamed for much of the delay. "He concentrates on details and sticks to his opinions as an article of faith and is not amenable to argument."[35]

Riverdale and Courtney returned to England as soon as the agreement was signed, but Brooke-Popham remained in Canada as head of the training mission and a member of the supervisory board set up to administer the plan.[36] For the next three months, he travelled across the country, visiting RCAF units and touring defense factories. This meant another Christmas without his family, but he threw himself into his new role with energy and enthusiasm. He was impressed by everyone he met, civil and military, although he still found it difficult to warm to Canadian politics. "The election campaign is in full swing—at least if you can dignify it by the name of a campaign. No-one has any constructive policy and neither side has any programmes, the fight is purely personal—abuse, accusation, retorts and counter-charges; all on a low level but the opposition has dug itself rather deeper into slime than the government."[37] After a false start, due to poor weather, he arrived in Vancouver on 17 January 1940 to tour RCAF's Western Air Command. There was widespread coverage in the press that stressed his considerable experience and high reputation.[38] In return, he was fulsome in praising the contribution made by Canadian aviators in both world wars. By now, his time in Canada was coming to an end. The Air Training Scheme—subsequently known as the British Commonwealth Air Training Plan (BCATP)—was gradually moving forward, notwithstanding arguments about many of the details. The first Canadian-trained pilots would not reach Europe until November 1941, almost two years after the initial agreement had been signed. It took until 1942 for the BCATP to get into full stride, once equipment and personnel issues had been resolved and the infrastructure in place, but when it did the results were impressive. By April 1945, when the scheme ended, a total of 131,553 aircrew (including 42,000 RAF) had been trained.[39] The BCATP proved vital in providing the Commonwealth air forces with the trained aircrew they needed to help establish Allied air superiority. It was an achievement that Brooke-Popham was proud to have been associated with.[40]

The sensitivities and misunderstandings that had characterized the discussions between the respective governments did not disappear with the signing of the agreement. Anglo-Canadian relations remained difficult throughout the war and were always liable to descend into acrimony—as was shown when ill-judged comments made by Lord Beaverbrook threatened to derail the entire project before it had even really started.[41] It would be unfair, therefore, to criticize either Brooke-Popham or Campbell. Indeed, the Dominion Office and the British Cabinet rapidly came to see Mackenzie King as the "problem." On the other hand, the British official history is wrong to absolve the RAF from all culpability in failing to obtain a prewar agreement with the Canadians.[42] It was only the coming of war, and the need to confront the magnitude of the training task, that forced the Air Ministry and the Treasury to spell out in detail what they needed from Canada. There was also a personal cost. When Brooke-Popham suggested, in December 1941, that he return from Singapore to the UK via Canada and report on the Air Training Scheme, the vice chief of the Air Staff (Wilfrid Freeman) minuted that this would be a great mistake as "he was not a success in Canada."[43] Brooke-Popham was not blind to his reputation among some Canadian ministers and advised Arthur Street, the permanent undersecretary of state for air, that his early replacement might ease the situation and dispel the latent suspicion that the Air Ministry wanted more control over the scheme.[44]

While he was visiting Halifax in February 1940, the Air Ministry telegrammed the high commission proposing that Brooke-Popham lead an aviation mission to South Africa to negotiate a similar training scheme to the BCATP. General Jan Smuts, the South African prime minister, had concluded that a Commonwealth flying training program could allow South Africa to play an immediate part in the war, while developing the capabilities of the South African Air Force (SAAF).[45] Returning to Ottawa, Brooke-Popham accepted the position and set about making the necessary arrangements. His replacement was to be Air Vice-Marshal Lionel McKean, who arrived in Ottawa on 20 March 1940.[46] The previous day, Brooke-Popham had a long and amiable conversation with Mackenzie King. The former was at his diplomatic best, expressing pleasure at the progress of the air training scheme and strongly endorsing Norman Rogers' performance as defense minister.[47] Brooke-Popham left Canada a week later, sailing on *The Duchess of York*, and landed at Liverpool on 5 April. After the weekend with his family, he spent the next ten days in a succession of meetings. In addition to discussions with the secretary of state and CAS, he met with Sholto Douglas (assistant chief of the Air Staff), Anthony Eden (secretary of state for Dominion affairs), and Tizard. The latter was keen to discuss the exchange of scientific information with the United States and Canada—an initiative that would result in the Tizard Mission of August 1940.[48] The following Tuesday (16 April 1940), he met all four Dominion high commissioners, one after the other, followed by Sir William Clark, the former British high commissioner to South Africa. Drawing on his recent experience, Brooke-Popham insisted that the

Air Ministry provide him with full written instructions to avoid the misunderstandings and divisions that had marred the Canadian mission.[49]

On 11 April 1940, while Brooke-Popham was still in London, Smuts announced that the British government had accepted his offer of flying training facilities. Brooke-Popham, accompanied by Opal, flew out from Heston nine days later, travelling via Marseilles, Tunis, Malta, and Cairo.[50] Other members of the mission included Sir James Ross (deputy undersecretary of the Air Ministry) and Group Captain (later Air Vice-Marshal Sir) Anthony Paxton (Directorate of Training).[51] From Egypt they followed the imperial air route south, via Khartoum and Nairobi, before reaching Cape Town on 30 April. Brooke-Popham went to work immediately, meeting Smuts the next morning, together with Lieutenant-General Sir Pierre van Ryneveld, the chief of the General Staff for the Union (an ex-RFC pilot who had served in the Middle East and on the Western Front). Discussions progressed rapidly, with none of the problems that had characterized the Canadian negotiations. Not surprisingly, van Ryneveld and Brooke-Popham got on well together. He also struck up a good relationship with Smuts, spending time with the premier at his farm at Irene. "I do find the Prime Minister and van Ryneveld, the Chief of the General Staff, full out to do everything they can to help in the war."[52] In offering training facilities, Smuts also proposed to send three SAAF squadrons to Kenya to help bolster the defenses. Brooke-Popham and Smuts resolved the necessary command arrangements and the first SAAF aircraft, from No. 1 Bomber Brigade, arrived in Nairobi on 23 May 1940, less than three weeks before the Italian declaration of war.[53]

The mission moved to Pretoria on 15 May for more detailed discussions with the staff (only cabinet ministers and heads of department had been available in Cape Town). While there, Brooke-Popham was invited to broadcast about air defense. The scripted talk drew on his experience with the Fighting Area and ADGB.[54] By now, however, the situation in France was rapidly deteriorating and he decided that Opal should return home.[55] During a break in the discussions, he flew to Southern Rhodesia to inspect the flying training facilities that had been under development since October 1939, formally opening the first Elementary Flying Training School.[56] The Rhodesia Air Training Group became operational earlier than the BCATP and would train more than ten thousand aircrew between 1940 and 1945. All the while, the news from France was getting worse: "[I]t's rather dreadful to be sitting here in comfort and doing nothing to help, still as Winston said, 'we've got to win the war as well as the battle' so the training scheme will be of value."[57] Brooke-Popham returned from Bulawayo before the end of the month to finalize the "Memorandum on the Expansion of Training Facilities in South Africa." The document, jointly signed with van Ryneveld on 1 June 1940, became known as the "Van Brookham Agreement."[58] Although it had been planned that there would be separate RAF and SAAF flying training units, these were merged in June 1941 to form the Joint Air Training Scheme (JATS). The JATS was one of South Africa's great success stories in World War II and played a major part in the transformation of the SAAF. By 31 December 1945, it had passed out 33,347 aircrew at fifty-seven flying schools and depots, including nearly 21,000 for the RAF.[59] His mission completed, Brooke-Popham left Pretoria for England on 3 June 1940, carrying a personal letter from Smuts expressing his satisfaction with the mission's outcome. By the time Brooke-Popham reached Malta, on 10 June, the Battle of France was all but over. Although direct passage to London was no longer possible, he found a seat on a flying boat that reached Poole, via Biscarrosse (southwest of Bordeaux), on Tuesday 11 June 1940.

For the next four months Brooke-Popham found himself as CAS's unofficial troubleshooter.[60] His immediate task was to chair a committee to consider lessons learned from the RAF's disastrous campaign in France. Appointed on 22 June 1940, the committee first sat on the afternoon of 26 June. It would be significant for its speed (the final report was submitted on 16 July 1940) and inclusivity. Participants ranged from senior to junior officers and included those employed on the ground as well as in the air. It proved a comprehensive and insightful study, notwithstanding the limitations imposed by the three-week deadline. The RAF's review differed considerably from the parallel Army study in that it took evidence from junior officers and noncommissioned officers. Byford believes that this was because there was no desire to identify strategic lessons, but it is more likely that it reflected the importance of identifying potential tactical and operational improvements before the start of the Battle of Britain.[61] The final report was circulated widely within the RAF and, although there was some hostility from those who felt they had been unfairly criticized, it was regarded as identifying valuable lessons. During August, Newall asked Brooke-Popham to undertake an organizational and operational study of RAF stations, building on his recently completed report.[62] This involved visits to all the major UK commands and many of their operational units. Given the scale of the task, he was allocated a PA, Flight Lieutenant

Roderick "Babe" Learoyd.[63] During the height of the Battle of Britain, Brooke-Popham toured the fighter stations at Hornchurch and Biggin Hill, as well as the headquarters at Uxbridge and Bentley Priory. He addressed a variety of issues, including changes in maintenance arrangements, ground defense requirements, preparation standards for new aircraft, the distribution of combat reports, the use of teleprinters, signals staff numbers, the establishment of armorers, and the fatigue experienced by station commanders of units operating by day and night.[64] It was later argued, in the context of Singapore, that Brooke-Popham lacked up-to-date experience and was not "au fait with modern warfare." It is questionable whether there was any airman at the time who could have qualified for such an accolade, but Brooke-Popham's work for CAS during the summer of 1940 provided him with some insight into the tactical and operational realities of the Blitzkrieg.

In late September 1940, Opal offered Cottisford House as a residential nursery. These war nurseries had sprung up across the country in response to the increasing number of homeless or orphaned families created by the Blitz. The first evacuee children arrived just a week later.[65] Cottisford was one of 167 nurseries organized by the Waifs and Strays Society (now the Children's' Society) during World War II. The family continued to live at Cottisford but most of the rooms were given over to the children. This involved considerable disruption to the household. Didie and Phil's bedrooms were turned into nurseries and they were banished to the stables. On his final visit home, Brooke-Popham was kept busy taking up stair carpets and helping to prepare the house. By January 1941 there were more than thirty children, aged one to five years, living at Cottisford with their nurses. Seven of the children were nameless. Their homes had been completely destroyed and no one knew who they were or where they came from. When the evacuees (Opal would refer to them as "Our Bombed Babies") reached the age of five, they were placed locally with foster families or moved to other homes so they could attend infants school.[66] The number of children had dropped to around twenty by June 1941, but the home continued to operate for a further three years, until it was closed due to the improved war situation. Between 5 October 1940 and 23 November 1944, nearly one hundred children were cared for at Cottisford—a testament to Opal's generosity and hard work.[67]

Brooke-Popham missed much of the disruption at Cottisford as he was almost constantly on the road, visiting RAF stations and depots across the UK. It was only when he returned to the Air Ministry, on 14 October 1940, that Newall warned him that he was likely to be offered the post of CinC Far East.[68] There is no indication that he was even aware his name had been put forward. The previous day, the prime minister had approved the chiefs of staff recommendation that a unified system of command in the Far East be set up under a new four-star appointee.[69] This followed an extensive Cabinet discussion following receipt of the latest Far East appreciation. Brooke-Popham's appointment was not confirmed until after he had met with Churchill for lunch at 10 Downing Street on 17 October.[70] Dill and Newall joined them in what became a wide-ranging discussion about the Far East and the importance of Singapore.[71] Just eleven days later, he left England by flying boat. Although Brooke-Popham may have had preliminary meetings with key Whitehall staff immediately before his meeting with the prime minister, this provided just two weeks to be briefed, select his staff, agree on lines of communication, and complete any domestic and personal arrangements.

15

COMMANDER-IN-CHIEF
FAR EAST
1940

Britain and Japan had signed a treaty of alliance in 1902 (renewed and extended in 1905 and 1911) and were allies during World War I, but relations had become increasingly problematic during the immediate postwar years.[1] The abrogation of the Anglo-Japanese Alliance, as a result of the 1921 Washington Conference Four-Power Treaty, and increasing Japanese involvement in Manchuria and subsequently China, reflected divergent interests and revealed two nations that were more rivals than friends. The Foreign Office later concluded that Japan had been preparing to go to war for at least a decade prior to 1941, "although until that year she had not decided when or whom to attack."[2] Until 1934, it had been believed that Japan represented the greatest threat to British interests, but with Hitler's rise to power, Germany rapidly became the overriding concern.[3] Britain could not afford the cost of rearming against two potential enemies. Unable to maintain significant forces in the Far East, Britain endeavored to maintain the status quo through diplomacy and propaganda. As relations between Britain and Japan deteriorated, so Britain and the United States grew closer. The United States, as the other great Pacific power, was in a position to counter Japanese ambitions and was determined to safeguard China's integrity. With Britain fighting fascism in Europe, anything that weakened her military effort increased the potential threat to the United States from the Axis powers. The appointment of Brooke-Popham as CinC Far East arose from these longstanding concerns about Japan's intentions—exacerbated by the partial occupation of French Indochina in September 1940 that brought Japanese forces within striking distance of Malaya and Burma, and, a few days later, by the signing of the Tripartite Pact between Germany, Italy, and Japan.

The concept of creating a base in Singapore to secure Britain's Far East colonies had emerged in the early 1920s. Control of the sea lanes was vital to Britain's economic interests and defeating a potential aggressor; however, maintaining a resident fleet in the Far East was prohibitively expensive (and would also potentially weaken defenses in other areas). The solution was to create a major naval base at Singapore, capable of sustaining the main fleet— when deployed. The "Main Fleet to Singapore" strategy was formally endorsed by the Cabinet in June 1921.[4] Although substantial investment was required, the policy was made more affordable at a time of financial stringency by taking a piecemeal approach in creating the required infrastructure. The outbreak of war in Europe fatally undermined these plans, but the naval base continued to exercise a powerful influence on strategic thinking in Britain and Australia. It soon became clear that the Royal Navy did not have the resources to send any significant assets to the Far East while it was heavily engaged in the Atlantic and Mediterranean. The naval option was never abandoned, but operational realities meant that an air/land approach offered the only credible route for defending British and Dominion interests. The need for a senior commander to organize the region's defenses emerged following a review of the situation in the Far East commissioned by the chiefs of staff in July 1940.[5] This was the first strategic appreciation since June 1939, when the world was very different. Because of the collapse of France, and the need to keep a fleet in European waters to counter the German and Italian navies, two previous assumptions were no longer valid—that any threat to Singapore would be seaborne and that Britain would be able to send a fleet of sufficient strength to the Far East within three months. The necessary analysis was undertaken by the Chiefs of Staff Joint Planning Sub-Committee (JPS) and was completed by 31 July 1940. The JPS concluded that an open clash with Japan should be avoided since British interests in the Far East would inevitably be damaged.[6] As a result, it was no longer adequate to focus solely on the defense of Singapore; it would now be necessary to hold the whole of Malaya. This, in turn, required an increase in army and air forces. Indeed, in the absence of a fleet, the primary defense of Malaya would rely on airpower. Hong Kong was not regarded as a vital interest and any pressure to reinforce the garrison was to be resisted. For similar reasons, it was not seen as feasible to defend

British Borneo. This stark assessment was less radical than might first appear. The view that Singapore was not a fortress, and that its defense depended on holding the greater part of the Malay peninsula, especially the airfields of the northeast, was one of the major conclusions of the 1939 Singapore planning conference.[7] Indeed, the first thoughts along these lines had emerged as early as 1937.[8]

The JPS further noted that the problem of defending Malaya would be made easier by working in cooperation with the Dutch, nevertheless there were concerns (shared by Churchill), about Britain's position should the Japanese *only* attack Dutch possessions in the Far East.[9] Unable to agree, the chiefs of staff commissioned a further report on the question. Both papers were considered by the War Cabinet on the morning of 8 August 1940.[10] There was very little argument about the conclusions, although the prime minister thought it premature to make a decision on support for the Dutch. In his view, a more immediate issue was whether a digest of the Far East appreciation should be communicated to the Dominion governments, given that aspects might raise concerns about Britain's ability to reinforce the Far East.[11] It was agreed that a telegram outlining the report's conclusions should be sent to Australia and New Zealand.[12] Following the meeting, the chiefs of staff sent a summary to Singapore by cipher telegram for action by the local commanders (CinC China, CinC East Indies, AOC RAF Far East, and GOC Malaya). A copy of the complete report was to be forwarded separately, but they were not to wait for the full text before making a tactical appreciation.[13] The work was completed by 16 October and formed the basis for a defense conference convened at Singapore from 22 to 31 October 1940. Attendees included the deputy chiefs of staffs of Australia and New Zealand, although there was no Dutch or American representation (other than a U.S. Navy observer).[14]

The meeting's main conclusion was that the first and immediate consideration must be to ensure the security of Malaya against Japanese attack.[15] The tactical appreciation had recommended a minimum air strength of 566 frontline aircraft (two hundred more than the chiefs of staff estimate) and a total of twenty-six battalions (eight more than the chiefs of staff estimate) to secure the defense of Malaya. Even with reinforcements, "our ability to hold Malaya beyond the immediate vicinity of Singapore in the face of a determined attack is very problematic. Moreover, in the event of a successful invasion, the survival of Singapore for more than a short period is very improbable."[16] The defense conference supported these conclusions and identified a total of 582 modern aircraft (the increase over the tactical appreciation was to provide a fighter squadron at Rangoon) as the minimum strength required for the defense of Malaya and Singapore, together with twenty-six battalions, five field regiments, and three light tank companies.[17] The chiefs of staff insisted that "they were fully alive to the weaknesses in land and air forces, particularly the latter," but nevertheless rejected these proposals, insisting that 336 aircraft and six brigades would provide an adequate level of security—given the demands of other theaters, particularly the Middle East. They also added that the "Japanese should not be overestimated."[18] One positive outcome, however, was the Australian government's decision to offer a brigade group to reinforce Singapore, together with military supplies.[19]

During the Whitehall staffing process the question had arisen about how best to organize the defense of Burma and the Bay of Bengal, considering the growing Japanese interest in Malaya. This prompted a further report by the JPS, proposing a form of unified command.[20] Their recommendations were discussed by the chiefs of staff on 6 September where it was agreed that, as the defense of Burma and the Bay of Bengal was intimately linked with the interests of Malaya and Hong Kong rather than India, responsibility for coordinating the defense of Burma and Malaya should be in the hands of the commanders in the Far East.[21] Further work by the JPS resulted in the proposal to create a joint commander. This was endorsed by the chiefs of staff and put to the prime minister by CIGS (Dill) on the evening of 12 October.[22] It seems likely that Newall and Dill had already agreed that Brooke-Popham was their preferred candidate.[23] The latter knew Dill from his time as commandant of the Army Staff College and had written to him only five months earlier about playing a larger part in the war.[24]

It has been suggested that Brooke-Popham's appointment was an example of "Jobs for the Boys."[25] In fact, he was more than qualified. Beyond a strong war record, he had excellent staff skills and an impressive intellect.[26] His time in the Middle East (where he was briefly the acting high commissioner) provided a valuable lesson in the military-political relationship and the challenging role of the professional diplomat—skills that were further refined in Egypt, Kenya, Canada, and South Africa.[27] His "joint" credentials were strong, following tenure at the RAF Staff College and the IDC.[28] Above all, he had the confidence of the chiefs of staff, the Colonial Office, the Dominions Office, and the Foreign Office. Admittedly, he had never served in the Far East, but he did have immediate family in Malaya and the Dutch

East Indies. His brother-in-law, Francis Hugonin (a colonel in the Royal Artillery), had been based in Malaya with his family since 1939, while his nephew Frederick "Fred" Pooley was a partner with Presgrave and Matthews, one of the largest legal firms in the Straits Settlement, and living in Penang where he was a subaltern in the machine-gun company of a volunteer battalion. Another nephew, Richard "Dick" Pooley was employed by Shell and working in the Dutch East Indies.

Brooke-Popham's directive, as CinC Far East, was approved by the chiefs of staff on 18 October 1940, subject to some slight changes.[29] The document was brief and to the point. He was to be responsible for the operational control (and the direction of training) of all British land and air forces in Malaya, Burma, and Hong Kong. He had two (linked) tasks: to avoid a war with Japan; and to improve political/military coordination across the region. It was not envisaged that he would be a "fighting" commander, but rather an influential figurehead able to instigate and develop joint defense arrangements. In retrospect, there were two glaring omissions. He had no authority over the colonial administration, led by Sir Shenton Thomas, the governor of the Straits Settlements and high commissioner in Malaya. In addition, the naval forces in the region, commanded by Admiral Sir Geoffrey Layton, CinC China Station, remained under the operational control of the Admiralty. This was partly in deference to the Navy's long-established primacy in Far East matters, and partly to avoid disturbing the status quo any more than strictly necessary.[30]

Based on his directive, and informed by briefings in London and Singapore, Brooke-Popham directed his efforts, and the work of General Headquarters (GHQ) Far East, to five key objectives:[31]

- Ensure effective cooperation in Malaya, not only between the Royal Navy, the Army, and the Royal Air Force but also between them and the civil services.
- Avoid any action that might be deemed provocative by Japan but at the same time to try and convince her that our strength was too great to be challenged successfully.
- Strengthen our defenses in the Far East, and especially to build up our air forces, not only by obtaining new aircraft but also by making all preparations to ensure mutual reinforcement in the Far East area.
- Stiffen the Chinese so that they could contain the maximum Japanese effort.

- Establish as close cooperation as possible with the Dutch and Americans, as well as with Australia and New Zealand, the main object being to ensure that, should an attack be made on any part of the Far East area, all the nations concerned would simultaneously enter the war against Japan, thus avoiding the risk of defeat in detail, as had happened in Europe.

Even before he had left London, Brooke-Popham wrote to Ismay, as secretary of the Chiefs of Staff Committee (COSC) giving his immediate views on his future responsibilities. The note is a curious mixture of practical observations and tongue-in-cheek rhetoric, including the statement that "should an attack on Singapore develop, its defence will be found not unworthy of record in the annals of the British Empire." It is significant that, while supporting the forward defense of Singapore, he highlighted the deficiencies in aircraft, antiaircraft guns, and artillery needed to deliver such a strategy.[32] As CinC Far East's responsibilities were intended to be limited to operational matters (without any administrative or financial authority), his staff were to be kept to a minimum.[33] A small expansion was authorized in 1941, but GHQ Far East never exceeded twenty personnel (including administrative support). Brooke-Popham's chief of staff (until April 1941) was Major-General R. H. "Dicky" Dewing. A capable and well-liked officer, his forced repatriation after just five months (due to illness) was a great blow—particularly as his replacement, Major-General Ian "Bungy" Playfair, did not arrive in-theater until June 1941. Brooke-Popham got on well with Playfair, but they had little time to forge a working relationship.[34] Colonel Walter Fawcett (Gurkha Regiment) was the senior Army staff officer, while Commander Andrew Grey and Group Captain Lawrence "Johnny" Darvall were the respective senior RN and senior RAF staff officers. Captain Terence Back, from CinC China's staff, acted as the naval liaison officer.[35] The other key member of Brooke-Popham's team was Squadron Leader Foster Cox, who served as his PA. They had known each other socially before the war—they regularly rode together—and met accidentally in London when Cox was working as a wing commander in the Maps Room of the Cabinet Office.[36] His appointment to GHQ Far East was undoubtedly owed to his friendship with Brooke-Popham (and Darvall), although the appointment necessitated a reduction in rank. Cox remained in Singapore after Brooke-Popham's departure and continued to serve in the Far East, including a period on Lord Louis Mountbatten's staff (at South East Asia Command), until the end of the war.[37]

Brooke-Popham left Plymouth (RAF Mount Batten) by flying boat on 28 October 1940, accompanied by Dewing, Darvall, and Cox. Other members of his headquarters were either already in Singapore or would be recruited later. The itinerary included stops in Gibraltar, Malta, Cairo (three days), and Delhi (four days)—the last two locations providing an opportunity to be briefed on the latest political and military developments and to establish future working relationships. During the stopover at Malta, there was time to talk with the governor, Lieutenant-General William Dobbie, who had served for four years as GOC Malaya (1935–39). Dobbie was full of helpful advice on the issues and personalities he would encounter in Malaya. Malta, under siege for six months by the Italian air force, also offered a template for the practical measures (early warning systems, dispersal arrangements, etc.) needed to defend against sustained air attack. While in Egypt, Brooke-Popham had lengthy meetings with General Sir Archibald Wavell, CinC Middle East, and Air Chief Marshal Sir Arthur Longmore, AOCinC RAF Middle East. Archie Wavell was an old acquaintance, who had been in his senior year at Staff College. The two CinCs had very different roles, but there was plenty to discuss. Wavell was an operational commander actively engaged in war fighting, while Brooke-Popham was a theater commander tasked with avoiding war; however, Wavell's headquarters had started life as a strategic planning staff before migrating into a full operational staff. Although Brooke-Popham wasn't convinced, Wavell warned that an operational staff with no administrative staff was not practicable in war.[38] They also discussed the removal of senior officers with or without adverse reports—in the context of the organizational problems that had been reported in Singapore.[39] Before he left Cairo, there was also a (secret) meeting with General Georges Catroux, the governor of French Indochina until forced to resign by the Vichy government, who revealed that little assistance would be available from the administration or individuals in French Indochina.[40]

During the final leg of his outward journey, Brooke-Popham spent four days in Burma with Sir Archibald Cochrane (coming to the end of his five years as governor) and GOC Burma, Major-General Kenneth McLeod. Cochrane, whose brother was a serving air vice-marshal, was regarded as friendly to the RAF.[41] Among the issues to be resolved were the constitutional implications arising from their shared defense responsibilities. McLeod was a fifty-five-year-old veteran of the Indian Army who had served with distinction on the Western Front as well as in India. He was well known to Brooke-Popham, having attended the IDC in 1932, during the latter's second year as commandant. McLeod had been appointed GOC Burma in 1938, shortly after Burma gained administrative independence from India. He had invested considerable effort and energy in developing the colony's defense capabilities and organizing an effective and efficient command—in the absence of any substantial resources. In most accounts of the Burma Campaign, McLeod appears only as a footnote having been abruptly removed ("lacking in energy") in late December 1941. Although he has been described as "over complacent," McLeod was a capable and conscientious officer.[42] His work was highly regarded by the Burma Office, especially in dealing with a "very sticky Defence Department," while his preparations for a potential Japanese invasion were sensible and (according to the Official History) his assessment of the forces involved was "remarkably accurate."[43] McLeod's efforts to stem the Japanese attack, while making provision for a fighting retreat, were all the more commendable given the small size of his headquarters.[44] Unfortunately, his reputation was sealed by a contemporary description that brought to mind a friendly uncle, rather than a vigorous field commander. "A sweet old gentleman, tall, a bit heavy, with perfectly white hair and all ruddy complexion. He seemed very pleased about everything but maybe the whisky sodas had something to do with it."[45]

Brooke-Popham flew from Rangoon to Singapore via Alor Star, in a Royal Australian Air Force (RAAF) Hudson. Arriving at Sembawang airfield (on the evening of 14 November 1940), he was greeted by his two immediate subordinates, Air Vice-Marshal John Babington, AOC RAF Far East, and Major-General Lionel Bond, Dobbie's successor as GOC Malaya Command. His brother-in-law, Francis Hugonin, was also part of the arrival party. Neither CinC China nor the governor were present. The former sent his liaison officer, Captain Back, but the governor (Sir Shenton Thomas) was en route from England after a seven-month absence from Singapore.[46] In retrospect, the absence of CinC China and the governor was a sign of the divided authority that would fatally weaken the colony's defense preparations. The following day, newly installed in the six offices that represented Headquarters Far East,

Brooke-Popham sent the first of his personal reports to Ismay.[47] Described as "a series of indiscrete letters from Singapore," they followed a pattern established when he was AOC Iraq. "One can express one's thoughts in a personal letter with greater freedom than in an official document. Further, one can discuss proposals which are floating through one's mind but which are not yet sufficiently concrete to become the subject of official correspondence."[48] In the next year, he would write thirteen of these demi-official reports, describing his impressions and highlighting issues of concern. He also wrote more than forty personal letters to Opal, although there was a considerable lag involved since private mail took several months to travel between the UK and Singapore. If hand-carried, the time could be reduced to twelve days (and avoid the censor).

Coincident with Brooke-Popham's arrival in Singapore, events were unfolding in Tokyo that would have a tumultuous effect on the course of World War II—Japan's decision to attack the Allies. One of the contributory factors was access to detailed intelligence on Britain's plans for defending its possessions in the Far East. This arose from a major security lapse that allowed the Far East appreciation to fall into German hands. The disaster was compounded when London failed to realize that the report's contents had been compromised. It was only when the original document was found in Berlin in 1945 (reputedly bearing Hitler's handwriting) that the enormity of the loss became apparent. The chiefs of staff had promised the Singapore commanders a copy of the Far East appreciation "by safe hand." Various sources have assumed that the document (together with the relevant War Cabinet minutes) was sent to Brooke-Popham, as CinC Far East, but as he had yet to be appointed (or the post approved by Churchill), the package would have been sent to CinC China (as chairman of the Singapore Defence Conference).[49] The point is important because it has been questioned why Newall chose not to hand the appreciation to Brooke-Popham before his departure. The explanation is that it was already en route to Singapore by sea (the normal procedure for highly classified material such as cipher tables and naval codes) on the Blue Funnel Line SS *Automedon*, which sailed from the Mersey destined for Yokohama via Penang on 25 September 1940 with a cargo of crated aircraft, machinery, vehicles, uniforms, medicine, foodstuffs, and 120 mailbags.[50] The *Automedon*'s outbound journey through the Atlantic was uneventful, arriving at Freetown on 12 October and Cape Town ten days later. The vessel departed for Durban on 29 October, bound for

Penang, where it was scheduled to arrive by 18 November. On the morning of 11 November, the German raider *Atlantis* intercepted the *Automedon* off Sumatra.[51] The bridge was shelled (killing six of the crew) and the ship was boarded before being scuttled. The surviving passengers and crew were taken off, together with the classified mail.[52] The captain of the *Atlantis* immediately recognized the importance of what he had seized and arranged for the documents to be forwarded as soon as possible to the German naval attaché in Tokyo, Vice-Admiral Paul Wennecker. "The most important item is a report of the War Cabinet about the situation in the Far East in the event of a Japanese entry into the war. Knowledge of this report, which was issued on 15 August 1940, must be of the very greatest significance for the Japanese."[53] After discussion with Berlin, the attaché passed copies to the Japanese naval staff on 12 December 1940. Admiral Nobutake Kondo, the vice-chief of the Naval Staff, "repeatedly expressed to me how valuable the information in the War Cabinet memorandum was for the Navy. Such a significant weakening of the British Empire could not have been identified (from outward appearances)."[54] Although Brooke-Popham was oblivious to the entire episode until after the end of the war, Opal wrote to him in early February to say that "a notice in the papers yesterday to say all outbound mails to Singapore and those parts had been lost owing to enemy action between November 9th and December 21st, so I expect a lot of ours to you have gone to the bottom."[55]

While the chiefs of staff analysis may not have come as a total surprise to the Japanese, it confirmed that the Far East was not a British priority and allowed the Imperial Japanese Navy planners to concentrate on a single threat, the U.S. Pacific Fleet. The intelligence provided by the *Automedon* further weakened opposition to the Imperial Japanese Army's plans for a southern offensive.[56] There is some evidence that it played a part in the decision to go to war, and was alluded to at a liaison meeting on 27 December 1940 in Tokyo.[57] The Japanese had previously discussed seizing either Hong Kong or Singapore (or both), in the event of German victory in the Battle of Britain, but hesitated in the face of the RAF's success.[58] The intelligence provided by the *Automedon* gave them the confidence to occupy all of Indochina in the knowledge that Britain would not declare war. Brooke-Popham might attempt a show of strength, but "the Japanese knew beforehand that the show was hollow."[59] At one stroke, any efforts to deter a Japanese attack on Malaya were undone, before he had even reached Singapore.

16

IMPROVING DEFENSE
COOPERATION
1940–1941

The most pressing problem in the Far East was defense cooperation. Relations between the services (particularly the Army and the RAF) had not been good for some time, while poor collaboration between the military and civil authorities continued to impede defense planning. Solving these issues would not be straightforward, even though Brooke-Popham had considerable experience in the conduct of civil/military affairs. He had worked closely with high commissioners in Canada, Iraq, and Egypt, and had governed a British colony in his own right, but Malaya proved to be a very different affair. The complex constitutional arrangements were quite unlike those in any other part of the British Empire. The governor, Sir Shenton Thomas, had multiple interlocking roles that had evolved piecemeal over the previous two centuries. As governor and CinC of the four Straits Settlements (Penang Island, Singapore Island, Malacca Settlement, and Labuan Island),[1] Shenton Thomas had direct control of all civil and military affairs. As high commissioner, he had responsibilities arising from diplomatic treaties with ten individual Malay states, the foremost being the Federated Malay States (Perak, Selangor, Negri Sembilan, and Pahang). There was a British resident in each state, but the federation had its own parliament and budget. The five Unfederated Malay States (Johore, Trengganu, Kedah, Kelatan, and Perlis) had no parliament and no British residents (although there were British advisers). Only in matters of defense or foreign affairs were there overriding British powers. The tenth state was Brunei, on the northwest coast of Borneo, which had enjoyed British protection since 1888. Finally,

Thomas was the agent for British North Borneo and Sarawak, independent states that were controlled entirely by British commercial or family interests. This cat's cradle of authority, responsibility, advice, and tradition meant that enacting legislation, and delivering action on the ground, was a slow and difficult process that required considerable patience on the part of the services and copious goodwill on the part of the Malayan Civil Service (MCS).

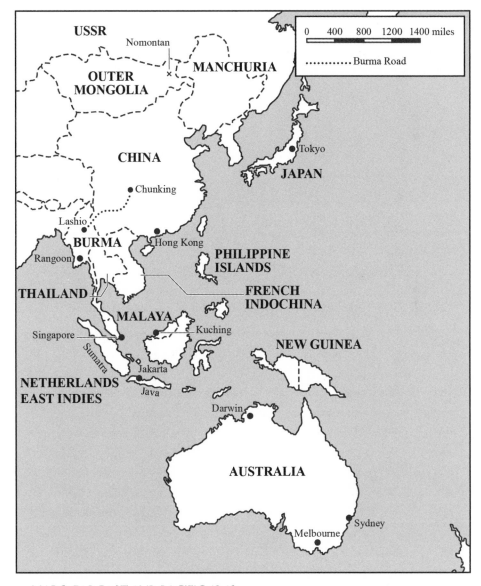

MAP 2. FAR EAST AND PACIFIC, 1940

It has been questioned whether the post of CinC Far East should have been combined with that of the governor and given supreme command of all forces in Malaya.[2] In Brooke-Popham's opinion this would have been impracticable, given the complexity of the constitutional and administrative arrangements and the need for all decisions to be channeled through the governor. A more workable solution might have been to retain the governor, but to give CinC Far East responsibility for all land, air, and local naval forces—alongside a minister of state with responsibility for external political matters.[3] Before 1941, however, there was no suggestion that any changes were required. War might be raging in Europe, but it was business as usual in the Far East. The rubber and tin produced by Malaya, and the income they generated, were vital in sustaining the British war effort. The government in Malaya gave priority to the production of these commodities (to meet increased export quotas) and attempted to avoid any actions that might reduce output. This created conflicting economic and military demands, notably in the allocation of manpower.[4] Although the governor had ultimate responsibility for the defense of the Straits Settlements and Malay States, the military still enjoyed considerable authority. Coordination between the service and civil authorities was exercised through the Defence Committee (this became the War Committee in September 1939), chaired by the governor. Membership included the single service heads, and the military secretary for Malaya—Charles Vlieland.[5] Brooke-Popham had been warned in London that he was a difficult man, according to a private letter from GOC Malaya, Lionel Bond.[6]

Until his domestic arrangements could be sorted out, Brooke-Popham and his immediate staff stayed with Singapore's chief secretary, Stanley Jones. Jones had been acting governor since May and was partly responsible for the delay in progressing war measures.[7] This may well have been at the governor's instigation since, according to Vlieland, he had instructed his staff to "hold the fort" against Bond.[8] Shenton Thomas did not return to Singapore until early December, having taken leave of absence in April. He was fully entitled to do so (having been in post continuously for six years), but it was a questionable decision in wartime.[9] At first, Brooke-Popham found Shenton Thomas "nice and friendly," but he soon became worried that the governor couldn't deliver on his promises. "He's ready, so far, to fall in with what I want; but I feel he's rather too ready to agree without argument and so when he comes up against opposition from elsewhere may be inclined to climb down because he hasn't really thought through the matter himself."[10] For his part, the governor was delighted by Brooke-Popham's arrival, confiding to the Colonial Office that he "was an immense tower of strength and he knows the difficulties of a civil government as a result of his years in Kenya and the Middle East."[11]

The work of the War Committee had been seriously handicapped by a long-running and increasingly acrimonious argument between Babington and Bond about how to defend Malaya. The ostensible cause was a debate over resources and priorities, particularly the forward defense strategy and the role of the northern airfields. It is easy to see this as an Army/Air Force spat. Babington certainly felt so, but there was undoubtedly some personal antagonism involved. Notwithstanding the conclusions of the 1939 Singapore conference, Bond was adamant that the limited resources available necessitated the close defense of Singapore, whereas Babington believed that a forward strategy was essential if any attack was to be defeated. A further argument (between Vlieland and Bond) had arisen over the competing claims between defense and economic activity. The governor had written to the Colonial Office on the subject, while Bond had sent his own (dissenting) account to the War Office. The situation was made more difficult by Vlieland's reputation, at least in Army circles, as an obstructionist. The military secretary had argued for an extended defense of Malaya (in this, he was an ally of Babington), but was blamed for delays in enacting war measures, including the introduction of conscription and the training of volunteers.[12] Vlieland claimed that all his actions were at the instance or with the active support of Shenton Thomas.[13] Brooke-Popham attended his first War Committee (chaired by Jones) on 26 November 1940, alongside Babington and Bond, together with Layton and Vlieland. There had been some debate about whether CinC Far East needed to be present, but Brooke-Popham was not inclined to sit back and wait for his commanders to report. Although the committee had no executive powers, it was vital in setting priorities and allocating responsibilities. On this occasion, the topics for discussion included the policy for evacuating Europeans, establishing camps for those evacuated from the coast, handling potential casualties from bombing, and the observation arrangements for tracking enemy aircraft.[14] He soon concluded that radical changes were required to improve the committee's effectiveness and, as a first step, determined to replace both of his subordinate commanders.[15] Babington had been in Malaya since August 1938 and the Air Ministry was happy to find a replacement (although they had initially wanted to send an officer who was "mentally and physically tired"),[16] but Bond was more problematic (he had only been in

Malaya since July 1939). Brooke-Popham hesitated to take immediate action, but Dewing forced the issue.[17] Removing two of his most senior subordinates within a month of each other was not without risk, but there were sound reasons to do so, beyond the need to end their mutual hostility. Sir Robert Menzies, the Australian prime minister, was not impressed by either officer: "General Bond commands the army, presumably. Tall, well-groomed and with that form of mental hiccups which reduces conversation to a series of unrelated ejaculations. One eye is closed, the other droops behind a monocle. If there is action, the General will no doubt die gallantly, but too many of his men will die with him. Air Vice-Marshal Babington commands the RAF. His information appeared sketchy and he also is of few words."[18] Brooke-Popham liked and admired Babington (he had been one of his earliest students at Andover and they had worked well together in Iraq), but improving relations between the Army and Air Force was vital. Babington was replaced by Air Vice-Marshal Conway Pulford on 26 April 1941 and Bond by Lieutenant-General Arthur Percival on 16 May 1941.[19] Although circumstances had dictated his actions, Brooke-Popham took care to protect the professional reputation of those involved: "Regarding Babington; he has been posted to the UK by the Air Ministry and there was no question of his being changed for inefficiency or anything of that sort. The GOC Bond is also going in a few days, he's a good friend of mine but a change there was necessary. Bond has been in this climate long enough in addition to which his wife is an invalid, not in hospital but just fading away."[20]

This left the problem of Vlieland, who was "universally distrusted, by Government officials and by the Services and, as far as I can judge, by the civilian community."[21] Dobbie had spoken highly of the military secretary, but this was unlikely to have reassured Brooke-Popham.[22] Vlieland was undoubtedly a loyal and professional civil servant, but he had become a focus for suspicion and mistrust. Even Shenton Thomas, who acknowledged Vlieland's previous excellent work, felt that he "had let his egomania get completely out of hand and was quite impossible. Obstruction and offensive criticism was his line."[23] Before leaving London, Brooke-Popham had been informed by Lord Lloyd, secretary of state for the colonies, that "any change he may recommend in this vital organization [the Malayan government] will be made at once. Our Far East position is so serious that you may feel that the risk of possible injustice to an individual should be accepted."[24] It has been claimed that

Vlieland was unique in anticipating future Japanese strategic and military intentions, but the evidence rests entirely on Vlieland's personal account, written after the events it confidently predicted.[25] The document is not supported by any official records, leading at least one author to question its authenticity.[26] In the event, Brooke-Popham did not have to sack Vlieland, he resigned on 14 December 1940, after being strongly criticized at the previous day's War Committee.[27] Brooke-Popham was greatly relieved at what he felt was the only satisfactory solution.[28] Vlieland would later present his resignation as a protest against a strategic policy based on the close defense of Singapore, rather than the forward defense of Malaya as a whole.[29] He was particularly critical of Bond and Layton, accusing their "agent" (Brooke-Popham) of exhibiting "the kind of stupidity which blinds the sufferer to his own abysmal ignorance and incomprehension." Vlieland's memoir is bitter, self-promoting, and less than honest, but it does raise questions about Brooke-Popham's own character.[30] In considering these allegations, and other personal criticisms, we would do well to remember Roskill's stricture that in writing about a disaster there is "a tendency to blame the other fellow."[31]

Sir Robert Menzies spent several days in Singapore in January 1941 while on his way to London:

> Air Chief Marshal Sir Robert Brooke-Popham looks like the late Baden-Powell. He has borne the white man's burden in many places from Kenya to Canada, and it has left his shoulders a little stooped. His hair and moustache are both sandy and wispy and a little indeterminate. His voice is thin and high-pitched, but, after a while, not unpleasant. . . . His attitude throughout our talks was courteous and benevolent; he is a first-class listener but left me with a vague feeling that his instincts favour some heroic but futile Rorke's Drift rather than clear-cut planning, realism and science.[32]

As the end neared in Malaya, he came to Brooke-Popham's defense. "When I passed through Singapore in January 1941, Sir Robert was behaving with tireless energy. He had plainly inherited a military and air situation each of which badly needed the freshening effect of active energy. From first to last, he spoke to me about the urgent and predominant need for all strength, particularly fighter strength. He was, and is, a brave man but he was in a state of the greatest possible nervous disturbance about our air weakness."[33]

Cecil Brown, a journalist with the Columbia Broadcasting System (CBS), interviewed Brooke-Popham on 11 August 1941. He found "a huge, gangling officer with a straggly, reddish moustache and thinning blond hair" with "an odd, abashed, friendly manner, and a high, breaking voice."[34] Brown was a highly regarded correspondent, but he was a persistent critic of the military public relations organization, which colored his reporting, leading him to dislike "almost every British officer above the rank of Captain."[35] Brown's behavior during one press conference caused Virgil Pinkley, European manager for United Press, to apologize for his fellow countryman's conduct.[36] Megan Spooner, the wife of Admiral Jack Spooner, who oversaw the naval base (and was Layton's deputy), encountered Brooke-Popham at a dinner in December 1941. "I found Sir Robert Brooke-Popham improved on acquaintance. I think he is a little shy. Now he feels comfortable with me. He is certainly an aloof bird by nature."[37] Foster Cox was probably the closest to Brooke-Popham in Singapore—to the extent of nursing him when he was unwell. Cox greatly liked and respected his boss (whom he called "Master"). There were times that he got impatient, but overall "he was a splendid fellow." A lengthy and insightful character sketch, published by the *Australasian*, dwelt on several of these traits:

> He is invariably charming in his manner toward subordinate officers and of an unfailing cheerfulness. He is ruddy of countenance and affects a small moustache, and his well-knit features give him the appearance of being much younger than his 62 years. Sir Robert Brooke-Popham combines tremendous efficiency with ease of manner; a flair for leadership and authority, with simplicity, kindliness and understanding. He appears, in short, to be a man with all the great traditions of the British fighting services behind him. He has no pretensions, especially social ones. In a social atmosphere, his charm of manner never fails him, but he seems to draw into himself; conversation on general topics does not come easily to him—in truth he is shy.[38]

Brooke-Popham rarely showed anger or irritability and, thus, was sometimes seen as aloof and distant. He undoubtedly had a sense of humor, but it was gently self-deprecating. There are several family photographs of Brooke-Popham with disparaging comments in his own handwriting scrawled on the back. He happily sent a note to Ismay enclosing a cutting from the *Singapore*

Free Press with an unfortunate juxtaposition of headlines that suggested the newly appointed CinC and his staff were already "wrecks."[39] Anthony Tinsley, an airman at Old Sarum in 1934, describes Brooke-Popham's grin when, in his attempts to open the car door, he fell over several half-barrels of geraniums.[40] Inspecting an Australian military guard, Brooke-Popham gamely asked each man what he had done in his civilian days: "Regrettably, not a man told the truth. Solicitors said they had plumbed, a carpenter said that he trained choir boys and gave the air marshal a very lewd look, a hardened journalist fluttered his eye lashes and announced in effeminate tones that he was a ballet dancer. By the time the air marshal had made his way as far as me, all the more reasonable occupations having gone, I could only, in answer to his query, say 'Mortician, Sir,' which he said was very interesting."[41]

The picture presented by his contemporaries, subordinates, colleagues, and friends is of a charming, friendly, energetic but reticent individual of considerable intellect. He is variously described as, "a delightful person, but he wasn't a fire-eater," and "a tall man, with a tendency to shamble. If I had been a schoolboy, I would have been delighted to have him for an uncle."[42] However, none of this explains Brooke-Popham's success in a profession where strong leadership and decisiveness are important attributes. The answer may lie with the caricature created at Sandhurst forty years earlier (see chapter 1). Although behavior evolves with time and experience, character traits are deep-seated and more resistant to change. If one strips away his self-deprecating humor, kind-heartedness, and concern for others, you are left with a powerful mind, allied to obstinacy, determination, and perseverance. In announcing his appointment as CinC Far East, the Air Ministry stressed these same qualities. "Sir Robert Brooke-Popham is tall and spare with sandy hair, a rugged face and penetrating voice. He's very methodical and never leaves a job unfinished, he is tremendously energetic in everything he does, and while expecting his subordinates to be as energetic in their work as he is in his, wouldn't dream of 'driving' them."[43] Not given to outward shows of emotion, Brooke-Popham thought deeply about issues and was interested in the world and the lives of others. This inner reflection was often mistaken for shyness or diffidence. Above all, he passionately believed that service was more important than self. He was wont to quote Chaucer's "verray, parfit, gentil knyght" when pressed to explain his motives or the philosophy that governed his life. His enthusiasm for Napoleon, and other great military leaders from history, continued into late life. Brooke-Popham's letters to Ismay and Dill are peppered with references to Napoleon's military maxims and the sayings of Moltke.[44] The extent to which other aspects of his character were sustained, or modified by time and experience, is a matter for conjecture. What the Sandhurst synopsis does highlight is that, as with all human beings, he was a complex individual and the external persona was not the total man.

In early December Brooke-Popham moved into the Sea View Hotel, on the Singapore seafront. He spent most weekends (accompanied by Foster) with Joan and Francis Hugonin at their house in Nee Soon, about forty minutes away by car. Early in the New Year he relocated his headquarters to the naval base on the north of the island. The new offices were "much pleasanter than our original ones which had advantages but were very noisy and in certain winds were filled with an all-pervading odour of rotten fish."[45] GHQ occupied a series of wooden mat-sheds within the administrative compound, adjacent to the concrete buildings housing CinC China Station and his support staff.[46] Brooke-Popham remained billeted at Sea View until April, when he and Cox moved to Draycot, Babington's old residence. The naval base offered the advantages of collocation with CinC China, but it placed him more than thirty-five minutes away from the Army and Air Force Headquarters. One of the main factors influencing Brooke-Popham's decision was the location of the Far East Combined Bureau (FECB). The FECB had been formed as an inter-service intelligence center in 1935 in response to the growing Japanese threat.[47] Originally based in Hong Kong, it was moved for greater security to Singapore in August 1939.[48] The FECB contained a cryptanalysis section, in direct contact with the Government Code and Cipher School, together with an operational intelligence center, under the command of a naval captain— responsible to both the chief of Naval Intelligence and CinC China. The FECB was the first example of an integrated interservice intelligence organization and was regarded as Naval Intelligence's most important out-station.[49]

Vice-Admiral Geoffrey "Windy" Layton had been appointed CinC China in September 1940. "A rough, tough old man, of deep religious belief well disguised, not much liked, but he knew his onions."[50] He was a World War I submariner who had extensive sea experience, and was prone to pass harsh judgments on his colleagues and contemporaries. Although Brooke-Popham's directive had been written to avoid trespassing on the authority of CinC China, the arrangement caused an underlying tension—as Brown realized when he and other members of the press corps, called together to discuss their complaints about excessive censorship, were subjected to a lecture about the ancient and honorable history of Layton's post.[51] The outburst had apparently been triggered by the appearance of Brooke-Popham's picture on the cover of *Life*.[52] Layton also made a heavy-handed attempt to secure better publicity for the Navy, compared to the Army and Air Force, who were (in his opinion) "a minor concern." Layton's jealousy over the attention given to the other services seems to have been exacerbated by a degree of personal animosity. Brooke-Popham insisted that his relations with CinC China were close and friendly, but there is plenty of evidence to the contrary.[53] Alan Michie, an American who worked for both *Time* and *Life* magazines and briefly visited Singapore in October 1941, says that Layton's jealousy was well-known in military and civil circles. Brooke-Popham was too old for his responsibilities and "had developed the habit of dropping off to sleep even in the midst of staff conferences."[54] Michie's source may well have been Layton himself since the latter was only too happy to make fun of Brooke-Popham to several other American journalists who, in relaying these remarks to Brigadier General Claire Chennault, added that they thought Layton "a fool."[55] Ed Mowrer, on a six-week intelligence mission for the Office of Strategic Services (OSS), wrote a detailed report for Colonel Bill Donovan on what he found. He did not meet Brooke-Popham, but he spoke with many of the senior officers in Malaya:

> Few of these Admirals, Generals and other Commanders spoke well of each other and none of them spoke well of Brooke-Popham. Admiral Layton went so far as to refer to him continuously as "Brooke Pop-Off"—in reference to his numerous trips about the area—and "Old Popcorn." This is a point of view that seemed to be shared by our own Admiral Hart in Manila. Generally, the Air Vice-Marshal is reproached with being a feeble old dodderer. Only two or three of the persons I met had a good word to say about Brooke and they admitted that he was "too old." Admiral Spooner insisted, however, that Brooke-Popham's job was purely preparatory and that when the balloon went up, actual command would pass to someone else. On the other hand, I heard two Army men refer to Layton as "that old fool." My own impression of the Admiral was of an aggressive fighting fellow, a fine man on the bridge, but with no great sense of politics, a matter in which he persists in meddling.[56]

High-ranking officers are no less prone to gossip and tittle-tattle than their juniors, but denigrating your senior military leadership seems a strange way to build a relationship with a major ally while fighting a world war. Layton's private views became clearer in 1947 when he circulated a private addendum to his "Report on Events in the Far East."[57] Brooke-Popham was "too old a man to deal with a situation in which it was really essential to have a commander who was right up to date with the possibilities of land, sea and air warfare in light of what had happened in Europe and Africa," adding that "he proved unfortunately to be unimpressive in personality and insufficiently strong-minded to keep a real and effective control over the members of his staff, which contained some very able men." The impact of these comments is somewhat reduced by Layton's assertion that the post of CinC Far East was only created because of his personal representation to the First Sea Lord, and that an admiral (presumably Layton) should have been appointed as supreme commander in the Far East. He also makes the (debatable) claim that his decision to leave Singapore well before its fall facilitated the arrival of vital reinforcement convoys. It is difficult to tell where objective professional judgment stops and interservice jealousy begins. Nevertheless, it would be wrong to dismiss these remarks entirely, particularly as Dewing, who was a loyal and extremely competent subordinate to Brooke-Popham, liked and respected Layton.[58] Wavell also warmed to Layton, even if he found him "a very forceful person."[59] Professional jealousy apart, it would have been a miracle if the "bullet headed, aggressive-looking and aggressive" admiral had warmed to the tall, thoughtful, and cautious air marshal.[60]

Brooke-Popham never expressed public or private criticism of his subordinates. He admired Pulford as a capable and conscientious officer; they had known each other for more than twenty years and were friends as well as colleagues.[61] He had a similarly good relationship with Percival, although this was based on the latter's professional abilities rather than a shared history. Percival was very positive about his CinC, who "was always readily accessible and my personal relations with him throughout were of the happiest."[62] Pulford and Percival worked extremely well together, a relationship that facilitated the creation of a joint (Army/Air Force) operations headquarters at Sime Road in 1941, consisting of a series of wooden huts occupying a narrow, tree-filled ravine.[63] Brooke-Popham had considerable respect for Major-General Gordon Bennett, commanding the Australian Imperial Forces (AIF) (as indeed he did for Australians in general). Admittedly, he had left Singapore before their friendship could be tested, but Bennett, who was generally contemptuous of the British (believing them soft and lacking in initiative),[64] was consistently positive about Brooke-Popham's leadership.[65] The reported friction between the two officers—described as "embarrassingly obvious"—is a case of mistaken identity (Bennett's relationship with Percival was certainly not good).[66] In a wartime letter to Brooke-Popham, Bennett wrote: "I have always wanted to thank you for your many kindnesses to me in Malaya and to let you know how I enjoyed the privilege of serving under you. One day, the world will know the truth about Singapore and your strenuous efforts will, without doubt, be fully appreciated. Cheap carping criticism dies easily but deeds live long after the criticism is forgotten."[67]

There are mixed views about Brooke-Popham's immediate staff. It has been suggested that they were guilty of suppressing opinions that diverged from their own thinking. The finger has been pointed at Darvall, who is said to have described a warning about the likely scale and location of a Japanese attack as "alarmist and defeatist."[68] This account is supported by Elphick and Aldrich (who relies on Elphick), but they have misunderstood the evidence.[69] Darvall's outburst was triggered by an FECB report, issued in July 1941, that placed the potential strength of a Japanese attack (in the first fight) at eleven divisions, even though two months earlier they had claimed Malaya would face no more than six divisions. The step change was based on the additional shipping available to the Japanese, once Allied sanctions were in place. Darvall reportedly stormed into the FECB office and told them that he refused to accept the document, since all the existing plans had been based on the need to repulse a force of six divisions.[70] Lieutenant-Colonel Gordon Grimsdale (who headed the Army section) did not greatly like Darvall or Back. "Our relations with some senior members of GHQ were sometimes strained. It was not easy to discover how or why one or two of them had been appointed." He added that Goethe must have been thinking of Back when he wrote, "There is nothing more frightful than ignorance in action."[71] Layton was also critical of Darvall's influence, although Percival was adamant that it was the RAF *and* RN staffs (naming Darvall and Back) who were too optimistic about the potential damage that could be inflicted on a Japanese landing force.[72] In his defense, Darvall put considerable effort into identifying, with some accuracy, Japanese air strength in the Far East.[73] He proved correct in determining key performance data and identifying the likely indicators for imminent action. Darvall, who had responsibility within GHQ for liaison with the Americans, also provided a valuable and insightful review of Air Corps activities in the Philippines. Following a visit in May 1941, he advised his hosts that without more airfields and greater efforts at dispersal, "a sudden determined enemy attack would reduce the effectiveness of your present air force practicably to zero."[74] Just over six months later, the Japanese destroyed nearly 40 percent of the American air strength in the Philippines in a few hours. This included twelve of the nineteen B-17 bombers based at Clark Field—aircraft that Brooke-Popham had hoped would enable the Allies to win the battle for air superiority.[75]

Estimating the fighting quality of the Japanese was a different matter. Darvall did show complacency in assessing what the Japanese Imperial Army Air Force might achieve, arguing that their likely sortie generation rates were not particularly serious.[76] In this respect, he may well have been influenced by Roy Chappell, the experienced and knowledgeable head of the FECB's air intelligence section, who was highly skeptical about Japanese aviation.[77] Claire Chennault met Brooke-Popham and his staff in Singapore during July 1941. He felt that they underestimated the Japanese and confided in his diary, "Hope their confidence in themselves is justified."[78] Ferris accuses Brooke-Popham, and the RAF in general, of vulgar racism and ethnocentrism in assessing Japanese airpower. He even asserts that Brooke-Popham's racism for Asia may have been honed by his period as governor of Kenya.[79] This is neither fair nor justified. The Japanese Army Air Force was not regarded as "first rate" because the lack of a mature technical base, poor training, low maintenance standards, and minimal reserves compared unfavorably with Western air forces.[80] By comparison, the Japanese Imperial Navy Air Force was highly regarded. Nevertheless, Chennault is right to say that GHQ was overconfident. There was a marked reluctance to take Japanese military capabilities seriously; an attitude shared by London and Washington: "Is it to be war? One's reason says 'Yes' and yet, as in 1939, one can't believe it. On Wednesday, Captain Back, one of the staff officers to Brooke-Popham seemed very confident that nothing would happen. Does he voice the opinion of Brooke-Popham or merely of Darvall?"[81]

The heart of the problem was not so much an argument about Japanese capabilities as resentment about GHQ's involvement in matters that the subordinate headquarters felt was their preserve. It was inevitable that the arrival of GHQ would ruffle some feathers, but it became more serious once Dewing was invalided home. "During his three months as Chief of Staff, he had kept GHQ strictly under control and had consistently made certain that they did not interfere with local commanders or get mixed up in administrative detail."[82] This view is supported by Lieutenant-Colonel Brenton

Ashmore, who worked in Headquarters Malaya Command. "One formed an opinion that so long as GHQ confined their activities to planning and coordination, they were of great value but unfortunately this was not entirely the case and interference in administrative details and purely domestic matters gave rise to an enormous increase in staff work and paper."[83] Air Vice-Marshal Paul Maltby made a similar point about the additional work that had fallen to Air Command. In response, Brooke-Popham argued that what was not recognized was just how much work GHQ had saved the respective staffs, although Bungy Playfair agrees that some of GHQ's efforts to coordinate and expedite may have had the opposite effect.[84] If events had turned out differently, such irritants would likely have been forgotten or at least overlooked. As it was, they became symptomatic of a wider failure. Sir Robert Scott, who was the Ministry of Information (MOI) representative in Singapore, later commented that Grey and Dewing were the only members of Brookham's staff that he had any respect for,[85] although Foster Cox attracted separate praise as a capable and conscientious staff officer (Wavell found Cox shrewd and forthright).[86] Megan Spooner met all the key figures in Singapore. While her diary entries are based on observations at social gatherings, it is likely that they owed something to her husband's professional opinion. In late November, just a week before the Japanese attack, she wrote:

> We need more brains in Singapore. Brooke-Popham is unusual but has a first-class brain. Percival may have brains but certainly is short of guts and decision. Layton has plenty of guts but not first class grey matter. Pulford is good, brain keen and subtle and character firm and steady. Keith Simmons, steady brain, great tact, considerable charm and judgement, but lacking in drive and not a first-class brain.[87] Governor seems a poor reed. Colonial Secretary reputed to be a bottleneck and obstructer and to be revengeful. Certainly unbalanced.[88]

The backbiting and personal attacks that characterize many of these accounts make for sad reading—even at this distance. Such behavior is probably inevitable when a shared endeavor goes spectacularly wrong: "No clear report has come out but quarrelling and recriminations are obviously going on, with past maladministration as the background and with the Governor and the Colonial Secretary, the military command, the civil servants, the non-official community and the journalists as protagonists. Through a haze of partial information, it is not a pleasing picture."[89]

It would be a mistake to conclude that Singapore was rent by private jealousies and professional rivalry.[90] Brooke-Popham's letters to Opal, personal notebooks, and informal correspondence with Ismay reveal an optimistic man determined to make the best use of the limited resources available and enthusiastic about the task he had been given. The changes that he made among the members of the War Committee greatly helped inter-service cooperation; indeed, the relationship between the Army and the RAF became extremely close. The Official History claims, although Brooke-Popham disagreed, that the appointment of a CinC Far East simply added another cog to an already complex machine and did nothing to improve coordination between the services and the civil authorities.[91] In his last letter to Woodburn Kirby, sent less than a month before his death, Brooke-Popham offered a spirited defense of his staff, in response to the first draft of *The War against Japan*:

> When a CinC accepts his appointment, he must accept all the responsibilities which includes shouldering the blame. But I strongly object to the implication that GHQ or my immediate subordinates were complacent or lethargic. General Dewing nearly worked himself to death in the first eight months and has never recovered his health. General Percival may have lacked certain qualities of leadership but he was an untiring worker. AVM Pulford had overworked most of his service career and was nearly at the end of his tether by December 1941. I remember a wing commander on my staff having to be carried to his office and worked from a bed there for some weeks.[92]

The fundamental difficulty was that GHQ was far too small for its stated tasks and not large enough for its implied tasks. Wavell's observations about attempting to run an operational staff without administrative support proved to be only too true. Brooke-Popham's staff never exceeded twenty-three in total (perhaps sixty, if attached personnel are included), compared to the six thousand supporting Wavell in Cairo.[93] Although he endeavored to secure additional assistance, all requests were firmly rebuffed by the chiefs of staff. "We would not wish your staff to be drawn into operational and administrative details which would lead to a need for expansion of your establishment which we cannot possibly afford."[94] Because Brooke-Popham's team was so small, sickness or absence placed an immense burden on the remaining officers. There was simply too much to do and too few to do it.[95]

17

"TOO GREAT TO BE CHALLENGED"

1941

Unaware that the Japanese had obtained a copy of the Far East appreciation,[1] Brooke-Popham believed that they were susceptible to misinformation, particularly as Hong Kong and Singapore could have been seized at little cost in the autumn of 1940, if Japan had only realized Britain's military weakness.[2] However, as he recorded in his official dispatch, GHQ Far East "failed to convince the Japanese that our strength was too great to be challenged with success."[3] This was hardly a surprising revelation, but Brooke-Popham was convinced that a lot more could have been achieved—going so far as to describe the attempts to mislead the Japanese as "pathetic."[4] In retrospect, he felt GHQ Far East lacked the skills or experience to conduct what would now be described as "information warfare."[5] He also found it a struggle to mobilize public opinion while trying to present an upbeat picture of military preparedness: "I found it very difficult to strike a happy balance between (a) boosting up the strength of our defences in order to scare off the Japanese, to influence Siam and encourage the Malays, and (b) overemphasis on our strength resulting in the civil authorities and community sitting back completely."[6]

The mixture of races and multiple languages meant that there was no single audience for the government's propaganda efforts. Malaya's population in December 1941 was around 5.4 million; the large majority were either Malays (around 2 million) or Chinese (also around 2 million), but there were substantial numbers of Indians. The European population was around nine thousand.[7] There was a wide range of Chinese, English, and (a smaller number) Malay-language daily and weekly newspapers. In addition, more than

150,000 official news bulletins and pamphlets (published in eight languages) were circulated each month. Even so, the government propaganda service was regarded as weak.[8] Strenuous efforts were under way to use radio to reach more of the population using the Malayan Broadcasting Corporation (MBC). The MBC broadcast in thirteen languages, although there were just ten thousand radio sets in Malaya on the outbreak of war, largely owned by the British and Chinese.[9]

Before reaching Singapore, Brooke-Popham had been warned by his sister-in-law about problems with the civil (European) population. "The greatest obstacles and infuriations will lie outside the services and they will be many and endless—believe me! This is a terribly selfish, money-grubbing place."[10] There were inevitable comparisons with Kenya, where the settlers at least had an affection for the country or the people. "No one would ever dream of settling down here, all they're out for is to make money quickly." The resistance to the introduction of income tax was also familiar, but he feared that the issue might become divisive as "there's some pretty strong feeling amongst the soldiers here, who are of course all paying full income tax on their pay, at the squeals these people put up when they fear their pockets are going to be touched."[11] The immediate impression given by the British community (at least in Singapore) was that they "didn't think of much, bar making a small fortune out of tin or rubber,"[12] although on the actual rubber estates "there was a much more realistic attitude as to the possibility of war and a much greater readiness to help."[13] These views, recorded well before the Japanese attack, differed little from those expressed by others in his command and by visiting journalists.[14] In as much as Britain desperately needed Malaya's output of tin, oil, and rubber (and the income it generated), there was a contradiction between maintaining "business as usual" and placing the colony on a total war footing. This tension played itself out in the difficult relationship between the military and civil authorities.

For obvious reasons, Brooke-Popham tried to strike a positive note in all his public statements. Interviewed by an Australian journalist shortly after his arrival, he offered an optimistic view on the colony's preparedness. "I cannot guarantee peace, but Britain will hold Singapore, whatever happens."[15] Even so, he refused to describe Singapore as impregnable. "No soldier would ever say that any fortress is impregnable. All I can say is that we will do our best to make it impregnable!" A few weeks later, in a briefing to journalists in Hong Kong, he was confident in the colony's ability to withstand an attack from any quarter.[16] When he returned in April, the message was still upbeat, even if much remained to be done.[17] In a radio talk, broadcast the same month from Singapore, he focused on the wider military and political scene, emphasizing the challenges that the colony would face in the future months.[18] Only toward the end did he touch on the controversial question of taxation: "There can be no comparison between any burden of taxation and the suffering that has to be borne by wives and mothers, and we might think sometimes of the degree of sacrifice that others are making for a cause that is as much ours as theirs."

By way of example, he asked his listeners to consider whether the shipping space required to provide a glass of sherry before dinner might be better used to carry airplane engines or spare parts for a Bren gun. Although this might appear a rather mild and circuitous admonition, it does indicate the difficulties faced in attempting to place the colony on a war footing through a process of consensus and debate, rather than military decree. He was aware that these policy areas were the responsibility of the governor, and not CinC Far East. Brooke-Popham also used the opportunity provided by visits to military and civil defense units to talk up the strength of Malaya's defenses (they would "put up a really good show") although his private views, expressed in a series of reports to London, were very different. Speaking at Ipoh (Perak) in March 1941, he stressed the importance of volunteers and their continuing role, even though the colony had been recently reinforced by regular troops.[19] Brooke-Popham's public pronouncements were little different (and sometimes more realistic) than those of other senior commanders in the Far East. Layton announced in a radio broadcast on 10 June 1941 that the Fleet Air Arm would arrive immediately in the event of hostilities spreading to Malaya.[20] He went on to state, "If and when trouble starts, we shall very soon see that the fleet here is capable of enjoying an engagement with any fleet it is likely to meet." Layton knew better than most that there was no serious prospect of any fleet being sent to the Far East. Speaking in Calcutta on 7 December 1941, just a few hours before the Japanese attack, Wavell sought to reassure his audience: "In view of the threatening Japanese attitude at present you may like to know that when I recently visited Burma and Malaya I was impressed by the strength of the defenses which any attackers are likely to meet. And these defenses by land, sea and air are constantly being reinforced."[21] Encouraging reports of Malaya's air defenses regularly appeared in local and international newspapers, explaining how the RAF's airpower was growing steadily stronger and highlighting the quality and experience of the aircrews, operating from all-weather aerodromes with extensive facilities, able to strike at an invading force while Japanese airfields were more than three hundred miles away.[22] Brooke-Popham knew only too well that in the absence of concrete or tarmac runways no airfield in Malaya could be described as "all-weather." On the west of the peninsula the wet season ran from April until October and on the east coast, from November to February. Thus, of the RAF's six airfields in Malaya, at least two were adversely affected by water-logged surfaces at any one time.

The importance of American public opinion—in securing political and military support—meant that American journalists were encouraged to visit the colony. This resulted in a lengthy photographic essay by Carl Mydans published in *Life* magazine in July 1941.[23] Only nine months earlier, the magazine had confidently described Singapore as a "Class A naval base" and the most strongly fortified location in the world, heavily garrisoned and well equipped with planes and antiaircraft guns that "can never be taken by surprise."[24] Mydans chose not to follow this script, and offered a mixture of praise and criticism in a narrative that ranged from bemused affection to slight disdain. Two clear themes emerged that would define much of the subsequent writing about Singapore—the "unreality" of white colonial life and the hollow rhetoric of "Fortress Singapore." Brooke-Popham was a "frail, ramrod-straight, tired 62-year-old English soldier" who had a large job and worked immensely hard at it. He was the first since Sir Stamford Raffles to breathe new life into Singapore, but "Singapore hostesses who are lucky enough to inveigle him to a formal affair have come to accept one social fact about Sir Robert. When Dinner is over, he walks quietly to a corner, sits down and goes to sleep until it is a polite time to go home." Brooke-Popham high-lighted key passages to Opal, without comment, including the line describing him as "exquisitely English—tough, tactful, thoughtful and fond of flowers."[25] A subsequent essay by Martha Gellhorn, published in *Collier's Weekly*, was less well received.[26] "Singapore Scenario" picked up where Mydans had left off, signposted by the subtitle, "a melodrama that may become an epic."[27] Gellhorn stressed the contrasts that defined Singapore: peace and war; offi-cers and other ranks; the rulers and the ruled. More damaging, however, was the implication that the colony was simply one large film set where the white elite partied in the confident knowledge that, if war came, the United States Navy would sail to the rescue. Such criticism was not seen as helpful, particu-larly as there was a belief among many in the United States that Britain was determined to safeguard its empire and prevent the postwar dislocation of its trade at the expense of American lives and matériel.[28]

Brooke-Popham recognized that his public relations efforts were struggling.[29] The problem was partly organizational and partly a lack of professionalism.[30] It had been agreed to group the press relations of all three services under a single head (Commander William Burrows, an old classmate of Layton's) working with CinC China. Brown was willing to acknowledge that much of the problem with the Services Public Relations Office (SPRO) was the result of fear about creating the wrong impression. "They seem to think that perhaps some tourists might not come to Singapore if the wrong kind of stories get out."[31] Frank Gervasi concurred: "He [Burrows] didn't know one newspaper from another and the only press association he had ever heard of was Reuters. . . . He dedicated himself to the proposition that no one, absolutely no one, old boy, should find out one damned thing about Singapore. He was eminently successful."[32] Other correspondents regarded Burrows as both incompetent and dangerous, with neither experience nor talent. His secretary, who worked in the SPRO from March 1941, agreed that he was "totally unsuited to the job, knowing little about the press world."[33] The strict censorship exercised by the SPRO, and the disparaging of those willing to take an independent line, created increasing mistrust between the military and the media.[34] Following several complaints, Brooke-Popham and Layton met with the press corps in September 1941, but the meeting did little to clear the air and, despite a further discussion with Layton, the antagonism continued. Brooke-Popham would refer to "discordant personalities" and the lack of officers experienced in dealing with the press.[35] As one of CinC Far East's key objectives was to influence public opinion, these comments are strangely muted. Duff Cooper, for one, believed that the arrangements for handling the press, particularly American reporters, were inadequate.[36] He complained that Burrows thought his main duty was "to prevent the press from finding out anything they shouldn't, rather than to assist them to find out as much as they could." Matters improved with the appointment of George Sansom as director general of Publicity in December 1941, but this was far too late in the day.[37] In Brooke-Popham's defense, Percival also found press relations difficult and struggled to find the right balance between openness and operational security, a problem that Allied commanders would struggle with in every theater.[38] As Brooke-Popham admitted, relations with the press were not taught at Staff College.[39] It should be said, however, that there was a degree of dramatization and belated posturing on the part of some reporters. Frank Gervasi, who spent barely a week in Singapore (in August 1941), wrote that: "I tried for days to meet Brooke-Popham. He was always too busy to see reporters. He didn't like reporters. He didn't like questions. I've found in years of European reporting that the men who deny themselves to newspapermen are invariably men who won't take advice and who are vain and incompetent. Brooke-Popham looked as inadequate for the task ahead as the Bren gun carriers, the old Lysander planes, and the single-shot rifles of the native infantrymen." No doubt it was convenient to contrast the brave young officers in Malaya with the "elderly placemen" who were their leaders. Gervasi took aim at several targets, calling Sir Josiah Crosby, Britain's ambassador to Thailand, defeatist, and naming Brooke-Popham as one of scores of offensive individuals "whose incompetence and utter cynicism make our task so unpalatable."[40] This was palpably untrue, but it reflected the mood of many journalists who, after the fall of Singapore, struggled to find explanations for the disaster. There may also have been a degree of embarrassment about their personal role in presenting an overly optimistic picture of Allied preparations—witness the article published by *Collier's Weekly* in June 1941 entitled "Impregnable Pearl Harbor, Our Navy Visibly Ready for Anything in the Pacific."[41] A similarly upbeat report (filed by Gervasi) from Manila in November 1941 extolled the scale and quality of the defenses, compared to Singapore.[42] Foreign journalists often lacked an understanding of the country, and the context for British rule, while some exaggerated or were prone to self-aggrandizement, but the majority tried to provide an honest and balanced view, within the constraints of military security and editorial policy.[43]

Where Brooke-Popham can be properly criticized is his failure to develop a coherent plan to deliver his propaganda objectives:

- To persuade the Japanese that we were stronger than we were.
- To hearten Asiatic people, not only in Malaya, but also in neighbouring countries.
- To maintain confidence in the Supreme Command at home.
- To check the complacency of the civilians in Singapore (recognising that this object was not entirely compatible with the first three).[44]

He recognized that success required the employment of "every resource we have, not only to the full extent but in the most effective manner."[45] The difficulty was that there was no coordination of British propaganda efforts in the Far East. He and Layton had urged a more coherent strategy of coercion against Japan in May 1941, but six months later they were still seeking guidance on lines to take.[46] There was no policy for employing official statements, briefings, visits, and interviews to achieve military or political outcomes, other than stressing the growing number of reinforcements reaching Malaya (he thought it doubtful that this had any great effect). Indeed, the Japanese were aware that the RAF's strength had been exaggerated in press reports.[47] The Foreign Office was not persuaded that the emphasis on reinforcements reaching Malaya was helpful. Sir Robert Craigie, Britain's ambassador in Tokyo, thought that it was provocative and that "all this talk leads the Japanese public to think that we are whistling to keep up our courage."[48] Part of the problem was that there were at least four agencies in Singapore, all with separate reporting chains, engaged in propaganda. To make matters worse, Brooke-Popham controlled none of them, although contemporary American doctrine suggested that the theater commander should have sole responsibility. There was considerable rivalry between the SPRO reporting to CinC China, the Special Branch Nippon Section reporting to the Malayan government, the Orient Mission (OM) reporting to the Ministry of Economic Warfare (MEW), and the Far Eastern Bureau (FEB) reporting to the MOI. The arguments between the last two organizations had already led to a turf battle between Hugh Dalton (minister for economic warfare) and Brendan Bracken (minister for information) as to who had authority for propaganda in the Far East.[49] Even without organizational rivalries, until Malaya was placed on a war footing, there were practical constraints on what could be done. Crosby vehemently objected to actual (or imagined) OM propaganda activities in Thailand, while Layton expressed similar concerns about OM plans for French Indochina. When Duff Cooper arrived, he attempted to resolve some of the overlapping responsibilities in Malaya by grouping all propaganda activities under the FEB and establishing a coordination committee, chaired by George Sansom.[50] This met weekly and helped smooth over some of the obvious inefficiencies, but did not resolve the fundamental problem: Brooke-Popham was required to deter a Japanese attack without control over the means for doing so.[51] More time might have permitted a more coordinated campaign but it is equally possible that Britain's military weakness and the desire to avoid antagonizing Japan would have continued to undermine propaganda efforts in the Far East. Unfortunately, if Brooke-Popham was successful to any extent, it was in helping persuade the Japanese that an attack on Britain would necessitate an attack on the United States.[52]

The Japanese were aware of Brooke-Popham's appointment and his responsibility for strengthening allied defenses, including the Dutch East Indies.[53] "Popham frequently stated to be plotting desperate actions against the poor harmless Japanese; a few days ago, they said that I'd been appointed to command all the Chinese armies!"[54] Such fears were heightened by reports of secret high-level staff conferences and the meetings held in Manila during April 1941. These developments persuaded the Japanese that the Allied powers were preparing concrete plans for immediate military collaboration.[55] While there is little in the Magic decrypts to indicate that Brooke-Popham's public pronouncements directly influenced the Japanese,[56] they remained particularly well informed of the state of Malaya's defenses. A message from Singapore in October 1941 stated that "though British defence measures appeared to be approaching fulfillment, the available sea power in that area was still inadequate and provided the British with a source of constant concern."[57] Even if the Japanese weren't impressed, the British press certainly were. "The new Commander-in-Chief has already expressed himself frankly on the Pacific question with a Japanese journalist and the time may not be far away when his warnings and those of the American Ambassador in Tokyo may begin to be taken to heart by the Japanese."[58]

The paradox is that Brooke-Popham privately worried that his efforts, and the economic pressure exerted by the United States and Britain, might bring war closer. In March 1941, he confided to Opal:

> It's so hard to foresee what the next step will be when one's dealing with countries that are out to double-cross you or anyone else and that are Easterners with not merely a different outlook on life but a different manner of thinking. Given certain facts, one can at least deduce what would be the logical action for a German to take, but one can't do that with the Japanese, they build up their chain of argument quite differently to our method of construction. And all the time one's got to be constantly on the watch to recognise the psychological moment at which to act, in order to stop war spreading to this area, too early would be as fatal as too late and one can't say in advance what form that action would take, it might be a telegram, or a personal interview or movement of forces.[59]

Four months later he was even more concerned about the situation: "I think it is very hard for an Englishman really to understand the Chinese or Japanese, partly because their method of expression and consequently the chain of thought they build up is so different from ours."[60] The impact of the oil embargo, imposed by the United States and Britain after Japan's occupation of southern Indochina, gave him even greater cause for concern. According to Sir Robert Scott, Brooke-Popham regarded this as a fatal mistake: "Brookham was right, of course, in forecasting that sanctions on Japan would or might drive them to war. Craigie and many of the rest of us feared the same, but Churchill was playing for big stakes. I'm not surprised that no one answered Brookham's protest. No one answered Craigie's either from Japan."[61]

Brooke-Popham's fear of unintended consequences in the conduct of international affairs was not new. In his final address to the IDC students of the sixth course (1932), he reflected on this very problem: "I believe Thucydides was the first man to say that wars have great causes and little occasions, and it is the latter to which I want to draw attention; to the psychological factors, the real or fancied affronts to national pride. By themselves they are not likely to cause wars but superimposed upon long dated disputes, economic, territorial or racial, they form the match that may set off the mine."[62] It was important to study "the psychology of other countries in order to learn, not how to climb down or how best to apologise, but how when the time has come to take a strong line, to be firm without being rude, what action to take before it is too late and how to avoid blundering into a position from which there is no escape except by war or by the sacrifice of something which affects our honour and that of future generations." It is tempting to see these words as a warning about the policy of appeasement toward Germany, pursued by the British government from 1933, but they could just as easily be an indictment of British and American actions in 1941 that had the (unintended) effect of encouraging the Japanese to believe that they had no choice but to wage war.[63]

Brooke-Popham paid a high price for his public reassurances about the strength of Malaya's defenses. Trenchard pointed out that no sensible commander would have announced the weakness of their position but this did little to still the criticism.[64] He was accused of making over-optimistic statements that had "misled public opinion in Malaya, Australia and Britain."[65] The support of those who had served in Malaya did not sway the debate. "What he said for public or enemy consumption was of no moment. What did matter was that he placed the position forcibly before the air chiefs in London."[66]

Brooke-Popham's pronouncements on the strength of Singapore's defenses, and Hong Kong's ability to withstand a siege, were seized upon as symptomatic of an over-confident, lazy commander, divorced from reality. The repeated requests for more resources, and his energetic efforts to avert war while building regional alliances, counted for little when the public needed culprits. This was regrettable although, under the circumstances, understandable. There can be no excuse, however, for those who continue to fasten on Brooke-Popham's public statements while ignoring the many private concerns and persistent warnings documented in the official record. Unfortunately, such is the pervasive belief in his fallibility that Brooke-Popham continues to be credited with comments he never made, opinions he never held, and behavior he never displayed.[67] It sometimes seems that we prefer our history in the form of a medieval morality play rather than a considered explanation of the complex events and multiple tragedies surrounding the fall of Singapore.

18

STRENGTHENING MALAYA'S DEFENSES
1941

Brooke-Popham lost little time in moving Malaya to a war footing, starting with a two-day desk-based exercise designed to shake down the headquarters and test the existing defense plans. Several significant lessons were identified including "mistakes that hopefully wouldn't be made when the fighting started."[1] The first big exercise took place from 6 to 11 March 1941. He felt that it went off quite well and had "served to bring home to some of the civilians here that war may entail discomfort, even to Malaya. They've introduced a petrol ration at last and every day one sees anonymous letters to the newspapers protesting against it, when the minimum is 17 gallons a month."[2] There were continuing frustrations, however, over the failure to mobilize the civil population, or at least to prepare seriously for war. There was no equivalent to the KWEO that had produced detailed lists of volunteers, addresses, resources, and skills—well before war broke out. "The standard here is all too low and they fail to realize even now, how incompetent they are."[3] The civil defense preparations in Singapore did receive some praise, but only in comparison to the poor progress achieved in the Philippines.[4] Duff Cooper would later defend the attitude of the civilian population, but the reality was that life in Singapore (at least among the white population) continued largely unchanged.[5] Wavell, who visited Singapore in November 1941, described the atmosphere as completely unwarlike and far from being at a war pitch, although he said the same about the peacetime leisureliness found in Delhi.[6] An important outcome of the exercise was the decision to create a shared operations room at Sime Road to allow the Air and Army staffs to work alongside each other.[7]

The most significant proposal in the October 1940 tactical appreciation, endorsed by the subsequent defense conference, was the need for an advance into southern Thailand to deny the Japanese a base for conducting ground and air attacks against British lines of communication.[8] Brooke-Popham was determined to develop this idea, although he recognized that it would infringe on Thailand's sovereignty.[9] British relations with Thailand (previously Siam) were dominated by Sir Josiah Crosby, who had lived in the country for thirteen years and served as ambassador from 1934 to 1942.[10] Brooke-Popham had several meetings with Crosby and, although he respected the minister, he found him "a queer, lonely character."[11] Crosby's intimate knowledge and personal contacts (including military officers, politicians, and members of the royal family) meant that his views carried considerable weight with the Foreign and Colonial Offices, although Brooke-Popham worried that, in a rapidly changing situation, "he [Crosby] was too much inclined to rely on his former knowledge of the Thais and the former friendship of the Thai ministers for him."[12] During Crosby's long service in Bangkok he was active in sustaining British influence, while resisting the growing power of Japan—a task complicated by Thailand's military factions, weak democracy, unequal treaties, and a general belief that British power was declining.[13] As an independent country, sandwiched between British Burma and French Indochina, Thailand's government jealously guarded its neutrality, although the geography of the Kra Isthmus meant that southern Thailand offered an invasion route south to Singapore and north to Burma, as well as an opportunity to sever the reinforcement air route by capturing the RAF airfields at Point Victoria and Alor Star. Japanese infiltration of Thailand grew rapidly through 1941 but, in the absence of military or economic assistance from Britain, there was little that could be done to stem their growing influence. Brooke-Popham advocated a carrot-and-stick approach, but warned that "further delay may mean the Thais have lost taste for carrot and feel fortified against stick."[14] When, in July 1941, a delegation of Thai officers visited Singapore seeking military support, Brooke-Popham was only able to offer the possibility of assistance at some point in 1942, given the wider war and the urgent need for equipment elsewhere.[15]

Brooke-Popham outlined his intentions for the forward defense of Malaya in his initial appreciation, sent to the chiefs of staff on 7 December 1940, following a tour of the Malaya/Thailand frontier, accompanied by Babington and Bond. With an eye to future reinforcements (including the promised

Australian brigade), GHQ developed plans to enter the Kra Isthmus—if the Japanese occupied Thailand.[16] This appeared increasingly likely after the Japanese-brokered peace that ended the fighting that broke out in January 1941 between French Indochina and Thailand. Robert Craigie, Britain's ambassador in Tokyo, suggested that the Kra Isthmus should be occupied if the Japanese entered southern Indochina, but this was vehemently opposed by Crosby, who felt that such an act would be a breach of the nonaggression pact with Thailand. Much of the subsequent debate centered on what exactly constituted a casus belli and the likely attitude of the Americans. Determining what Japanese actions might offer justification for war had been a significant concern for Brooke-Popham from the moment he had been appointed.[17] He had raised the question during his initial briefings in London and pressed the matter at successive conferences over the next year. In the meantime, GHQ continued to work on the details of an advance into Thailand, code-named "Etonian" (known as "Matador" from August 1941). Brooke-Popham was confident that he had the necessary forces to implement the operation, which comprised two separate lines of advance.[18] The main thrust would be from Jitra toward Singora on Thailand's east coast (some fifty miles) with the aim of occupying potential landing beaches and airfields, while a smaller force would move from Kroh and seize "The Ledge," a strong defensive feature thirty miles inside Thailand, on the road to Patani. Possession of the Ledge would offer Matador protection from a flank attack, as well as slowing a potential enemy advance into northern Malaya. The plan, strongly supported by the chiefs of staff, was approved by Churchill on 10 April 1941.[19] Matador had the strong support of Major-General David Murray-Lyon, commanding the Eleventh Indian Division, who was tasked with leading the operation.[20]

Although it was suspected that any Japanese attack would be via Thailand, the remainder of Malaya still had to be defended, including the beaches of the east coast. A Japanese landing in Johore could seize the airfield at Kuantan and then strike either west (cutting off north-south communications and isolating the forces on the frontier) or south (toward Singapore).[21] It was important to guard against these widely spaced threats, including the possibility of simultaneous landings. Brooke-Popham decided to place his troops forward and directly defend the beaches, rather than holding his main forces in reserve. Because of the uncertainties over Matador, and the lack of a reserve division to support the operation, Malaya Command planned a strong defensive position at Jitra, straddling the main road and rail links, where any invading forces advancing from the border down the west coast could be held. In the event, the dispositions adopted by Brooke-Popham and Percival were well placed, although this has been somewhat overshadowed by an argument about the level of attrition that might be inflicted during any landing operations. Percival later insisted that GHQ had claimed 40 percent of the enemy force could be destroyed, naming Darvall and Back as the culprits.[22] Darvall sensibly pointed out that, even if such a claim had been made, it would have been based on the full establishment of aircraft and ideal conditions. The debate is something of a distraction as the actual number of divisions employed by the Japanese closely matched the planning figure (2/3 division by land and two divisions by sea). Percival's defensive plans were therefore based on an accurate assessment of likely enemy strength—even if the underpinning math was flawed.

All defense plans, however detailed, are only as realistic as the resources to implement them. The Far East only received the equipment and troops that could be spared from the European and Mediterranean theaters. Moreover, what was available was often not of the first quality. There were also major gaps in capability, such as tanks. Even so, GHQ Far East did an excellent job in determining the likely areas for a Japanese attack and deploying their limited forces accordingly. This required a degree of pragmatism. For example, it was recognized that little could be done to protect North Borneo and Labuan. A battalion was assigned to defend Brunei and Sarawak, but otherwise the emphasis was on destroying the oil fields, associated facilities, and any infrastructure of military value (such as the airfields at Kuching and Miri).

Burma was a different matter, even though it was thought unlikely to be attacked unless Singapore fell. As a result, it was in something of a strategic and administrative "no man's land."[23] The inclusion of the colony in Brooke-Popham's command had never sat easily with the government of India or the India Office. They had argued against the proposal when CinC Far East's directive was drafted but had chosen not to press the matter. The arrival of Archie Wavell as CinC India saw the argument reopened. Wavell had been abruptly replaced as CinC Middle East in June 1941, for failings that stemmed largely from Churchill's decision to intervene in Greece. Wavell's successor was his predecessor as CinC India, General Claude Auchinleck. Wavell's appointment was welcomed by Brooke-Popham, who had seen little of Auchinleck. Wavell proved more proactive than Auchinleck and visited both Burma and Singapore within his first few months in command.[24]

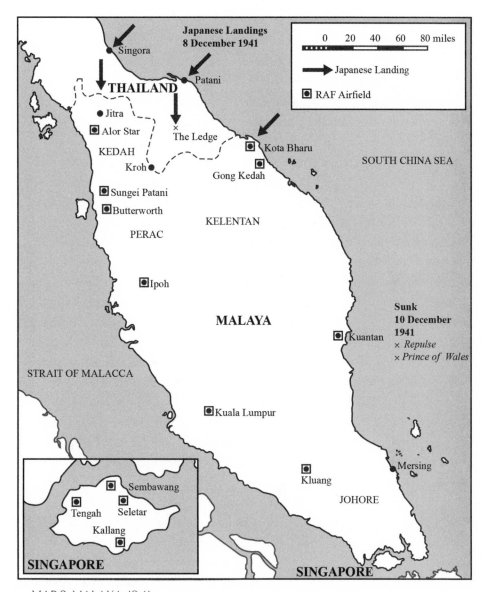

MAP 3. MALAYA, 1941

Before meeting with Brooke-Popham, Wavell asked the chiefs of staff to reconsider responsibility for the defense of Burma.[25] Brooke-Popham has been criticized for opposing this suggestion, but he had sound reasons for doing so.[26] "The defense of Burma could not be considered apart from the Far East, nor the Far East apart from the war as a whole."[27] Wavell returned to the question in his postwar dispatch, asserting that Burma should have been transferred to his command before war broke out.[28] This was tactically sound, but strategically naïve. Burma was vital in sustaining Chinese resistance. Control of the Burma Road (alongside Hong Kong) offered CinC Far East a central role in the Sino-Japanese conflict and an opportunity to leverage Chiang Kai-shek's support in deterring the Japanese. While it would have been tidier to align Burma's defense arrangements with India, the fundamental problem was a shortage of resources rather than a flawed strategy.[29] Wavell tried again in November to get the chiefs of staff to change their mind, but to no avail.[30] This second attempt may well have been encouraged by the imminent departure of Brooke-Popham—a development that was well known, but not officially announced. Wavell's focus on the defense of India, rather than the wider needs of the Far East, had damaging implications for his relationship with Chiang Kai-shek.[31] The issue came to a head in December 1941, when Wavell rejected the offer of the Chinese Fifth and Sixth Armies to help fight the Japanese in Burma.[32] He would later argue that the bad feeling this engendered was the result of injured pride, rather than his failure to comprehend Chiang Kai-shek's shared strategic objectives or to respect China as a full partner with the democratic allies.[33] Brooke-Popham had a much sounder understanding of grand strategy and the importance of maintaining relations with China, which was also a high priority for Washington. Roosevelt was annoyed by what he saw as Wavell's lack of interest and his inability to get on with the Chinese.[34] It is significant that, when American-British-Dutch-Australian Command (ABDACOM) was created on 3 January 1942, Burma (but not India) was included within the supreme commander's operational sphere for much the same reasons as argued by Brooke-Popham.[35] Burma would only be returned to operational control of GHQ India on 21 February 1942, following the fall of Singapore and the dissolution of ABDACOM.

Wavell also claimed that prewar defense preparations in Burma were inadequate because GHQ in Singapore had little strategic interest in the colony, focused as it was on Hong Kong and Malaya.[36] To his mind, more should have been done about these deficiencies at the time of Japan's move into southern Indochina (in July 1941). He also criticized the lack of organization, of military intelligence, and of planning generally to meet any Japanese attack.[37] McLeod did not feel this was justified: "I do honestly feel that I did all that could be done in the circumstances and I must thank you and your staff for the consideration you always showed us. The fact that we could get nothing from Home or India was not our fault."[38] His successor as CinC Far East, Lieutenant-General Sir Henry Pownall, acknowledged that matters were probably no worse in Burma than Malaya, even if Wavell felt that Brooke-Popham was at fault.[39] Had the command changes proposed in September 1941 been agreed, they would have made little difference to Burma's ability to defeat the Japanese. Only more aircraft, tanks, and combat-experienced troops would have helped, assets that neither Malaya nor India possessed.[40]

The Far East appreciation had identified the need for twenty-two squadrons, comprising 336 aircraft, and six brigades (some eighteen battalions) to defend Malaya against a potential Japanese attack.[41] This program was to be achieved by the end of 1941, although it fell far short of what the local commanders had wanted.[42] Even so, Churchill objected to the diversion of aircraft from the Middle East.[43] In the meantime, everything possible was to be done to strengthen the land forces in Malaya and secure the effective collaboration of the Dutch. From December 1940, Brooke-Popham fought a long battle to get the reinforcements agreed to by the chiefs of staff. He was relatively successful in building up Malaya Command, but the number (and quality) of aircraft fell far short. The RAF's front line in Malaya on the outbreak of war was just 180 (excluding reserves). If the two squadrons of obsolete Vildebeeste single-engined biplanes are excluded, the front line was 156. Even so, this flatters the position, because an additional fighter squadron had been created (from aircraft allocated as reserves) to provide for the air defense of Burma.[44] By comparison, the infantry strength in Malaya (thirty-one regular battalions) exceeded the twenty-six infantry battalions identified at the Singapore Conference (although there were significant shortfalls in antiaircraft guns, artillery, and tanks). However, the required number of battalions was predicated on a figure of 582 aircraft. When Percival reviewed the situation in August 1941, against the actual and predicted RAF strength, he estimated that he needed forty-eight infantry battalions, as well as a substantial uplift in artillery, antiaircraft guns, tanks, and antitank guns. Pending these reinforcements, only one division (Eleventh Indian) could be allocated to Matador while two divisions (Eighth Australian and Ninth Indian) defended central and southern Malaya (with a further two brigades assigned to Singapore itself).[45]

Air support for Matador (Norgroup) was to be provided by squadrons deployed forward to airfields in northern Malaya.[46] Brooke-Popham has been criticized for progressing their construction (in the absence of the promised air reinforcements) but given the considerable time it took to complete any public works in Malaya, the program could not sensibly be delayed until the additional squadrons arrived. As it was necessary to defend the whole of Malaya, Brooke-Popham was instructed to prepare airfields for up to two-thirds of planned strength (equivalent to some 220 aircraft) in both north and south Malaya.[47] The result was that Malaya had more airfields than squadrons to fill them (pending the arrival of reinforcements). A more worrying problem was the decision to site airfields with little thought for their ground defense needs. This dated back to 1937, well before Brooke-Popham's arrival, and was due to the failure of AOC Far East Command (Arthur Tedder) to consult with GOC Malaya Command (William Dobbie). Tedder, accompanied by then–Squadron Leader Johnny Darvall, determined the location of seven airfields in Malaya and Sarawak (Kluang, Kota Bharu, Kuantan, Kuching, Penang, Tengah, and Sembawang) without any reference to the Army.[48] Tedder was of the view that RAF personnel could defend the airfields if necessary, although it is clear that he never envisaged major land operations.[49] The failure to consider these broader needs was not driven by inter-service rivalry, but it does illustrate the poor inter-service cooperation that existed before November 1940.[50] Brooke-Popham was left to deal with the problem as best he could. His solution was to employ regular troops to guard the coast, and to rely on volunteers to defend the airfields.[51] Thus, although the siting and defense of the northern airfields was problematic, they did not, per se, impact on the general disposition of British forces in Malaya.[52] It is wrong to argue that their existence doomed the Army to a series of unwinnable battles.[53] The suggestion that Brooke-Popham and Percival should have abandoned the east coast (and its airfields), and transferred the garrison to bolster the west coast defenses, would have negated the RAF's ability to provide early warning of enemy convoys in the Gulf of Siam, to offer any (limited) protection to the Royal Navy, or to prevent the Japanese from seizing Kuantan at will. It would also have meant abandoning the defense plans jointly agreed at the October 1940 Singapore conference. Not only was this dangerous militarily, but also could never have been sanctioned by the governor.[54]

One initiative that did bear fruit was the decision to supply Malaya with a ground radar system, involving both fixed and mobile sets, to enable the detection and interception of enemy aircraft. Brooke-Popham had discussed this possibility with the Air Ministry before he left London and sought the advice of Assistant Chief of the Air Staff (Radio) Joubert de la Ferté on the siting, installation, and coordination issues involved.[55] The requisite personnel and equipment were identified and sent to Malaya shortly afterward. It took considerable time to prepare the sites but, by the time the Japanese attacked, the system was working well—as far as its coverage permitted.[56] Radars on Singapore Island and in the southern part of the Malayan peninsula, linked to a filter room at Kallang (and an adjacent fighter operations room), were operational and work was under way to provide sites for the airfields in the north, to cover against overland attack, although the requisite radar equipment had yet to arrive.[57] Difficulties with the Malayan telephone system were overcome by constructing new lines and installing VHF communications between the individual radar stations and Singapore, supplemented by a network of observer centers.[58] As a result, there was adequate warning of the bombing raids on Singapore, but none for the northern airfields closest to the frontier.

Throughout 1941 the chiefs of staff rebuffed successive requests by Brooke-Popham for more aircraft and pilots. When reinforcements were agreed, they arrived late or were deferred because of other priorities. The lack of modern aircraft was the fundamental weakness in the defense plans for Malaya. This was hardly a closely guarded secret. "The great flaw in the British Far Eastern military setup is weakness in the air. Japan's naval air arm has had plenty of practice in China and has proved itself far above the Japanese warring average."[59] In February 1941, the promised Australian reinforcements arrived in the form of Eighth Australian Division—although initially this comprised just the headquarters and the Twenty-Second Australian Brigade Group. The next month, Ninth Indian Division, comprising two brigade groups (less artillery), joined the Far East Command from India. The third brigade had been diverted to Iraq to deal with the rebellion that had broken out there.[60] The chiefs of staff had intended that four additional squadrons would arrive in Malaya before the end of 1940. In the end, 167 crated Brewster Buffalo fighters (equivalent to four squadrons) started to arrive from February 1941 onward. Brooke-Popham has received little credit for his persistent requests for more air reinforcements; instead he has been castigated for publicly expressing confidence in the few modern aircraft that were delivered.[61] This stems from a report by O'Dowd Gallagher, of the *Daily Express*, who attended a briefing at Sime Road on 3 December 1941. According to Gallagher, Brooke-Popham claimed that "we can get on alright with Buffaloes out here . . . let England have the super-Spitfires and the hyper-Tornadoes. Buffaloes are quite good enough for Malaya."[62] Brown, who was also present, says that the question actually put to Brooke-Popham was, "Don't you think that we need some of the machines that Britain has at home?" To which he replied,

"If we need any of these super-Spitfires and hyper-Hurricanes we can get them out here quick enough."[63] The Buffalo's poor showing in combat with Japanese fighters has meant that these remarks are regularly cited as evidence of myopic and arrogant leadership.[64] There were good reasons, however, why Brooke-Popham might express confidence in the type—beyond the fact that the Air Staff had vigorously defended the aircraft when it was suggested in March 1941 (after the first Buffaloes had started to arrive in Singapore) that Hurricanes might be preferred.[65]

The first point to make is that, through 1941 and well into 1942, the Buffalo fared extremely well in combat against the Soviet Air Force.[66] The Finnish Air Force received forty-four examples in April 1940. They were similar to the models employed in Malaya, although the Finns had introduced several minor modifications. Until superseded in 1943, the Finnish Buffaloes exercised a remarkable ascendancy over Russian fighters—the same air force that had overcome the Japanese Army Air Force during the Nomonhan Incident of August 1939.[67] It was reasonable to believe that the Buffalo (in the hands of well-trained pilots and employing the appropriate tactics) could be a match for Japanese fighters. Brooke-Popham's comments on the type—intended primarily to reassure—should not be dismissed as the product of a delusional mind or just spin and untruths intended to deceive the Australian government.[68] Before he left London, Brooke-Popham had met with Group Captain Roy Chappell, an experienced intelligence expert on the Japanese military who had served as air attaché in Tokyo for more than seven years (including duty with the Japanese navy). He also investigated the Buffalo's reported performance compared to the Spitfire (noting the higher wing loading and lack of self-sealing tanks).[69] It has been claimed that reporters such as Yates McDaniel—one of the last journalists to leave Singapore—knew that the Buffalo was "slow and cumbersome," but this owes more to postwar rationalization than to contemporary professional judgment.[70] The RAF station intelligence officer at Kallang had the opportunity to see the air fighting at close quarters. It was his view that the Buffalo "showed itself fully capable of dealing with any Japanese bomber types used in the course of the campaign," but "went down before greatly superior numbers of slightly superior fighters, armed with a wider range of projectiles."[71] These comments tally with the view of a Dutch squadron commander: "My view is that our drawback during the fighter actions was not an inferior aeroplane but that we had too few against them and also our armament was too little and too light."[72] The

Nomonhan Incident provides a benchmark for assessing the RAF's readiness to win the battle for air superiority, while remembering that the Russian air campaign was but one element in a massive (albeit limited) ground assault that annihilated the Japanese Sixth Army over a period of four weeks.[73] The Soviet Air Force employed overwhelming numbers (achieving an advantage of roughly 2:1) against a range of aircraft types, including the Ki-27 (Nate), the main Japanese fighter in the Malayan campaign. Although more modern Japanese designs were not involved, the Japanese Army Air Force had a slight qualitative edge over its Soviet counterpart. However, the key factor in achieving air superiority was neither quantity nor quality, but the supply of replacement aircraft and pilots. The Russians had the resources to sustain operations, even though their losses were greater, flying almost twice the number of sorties as the Japanese.[74]

The RAF's frontline strength in Malaya on 7 December 1941 comprised 158 aircraft (including sixty fighters), with eighty-eight in reserve.[75] Against these, the Japanese Army Air Force could field 434 aircraft (including 173 fighters) to support the 15th and 25th Armies.[76] On paper, the RAF was significantly outnumbered but the true position was even worse. Without a ready supply of replacement aircraft and crews, a significant proportion of the RAF's strength should have been held in reserve to make good operational wastage. RAF plans, detailed in Secret Document (SD) 98, anticipated losses of 100 percent of aircraft and 50 percent of pilots per month for fighter squadrons under wartime conditions.[77] Although repair facilities were established at Singapore and Rangoon to make good some of the expected wastage (including peacetime accidents), there were no further replacements; production of the Buffalo ceased in December 1941.[78] Other aircraft types would therefore need to be secured (such as Hurricanes or Spitfires),[79] however, it would take a minimum of eight to twelve weeks for these to arrive—depending on whether they were sent from England or the Middle East.[80] Further time, up to four months, would be needed to get a newly arrived squadron up to full operational readiness, a problem that reduced the effectiveness of several of the Buffalo squadrons.[81] At the very least, therefore, the RAF should have planned for two months' operations before reinforcement. On this basis, the 112 Buffaloes and eighty-eight pilots available in Malaya were adequate to sustain a front line of approximately thirty-seven fighters (three squadrons), with seventy-five aircraft in reserve. Instead, four squadrons were created (sixty frontline aircraft with fifty-two in reserve).[82] The inevitable result was that frontline strength rapidly fell as the war progressed. The position was even worse with the other types in the RAF's frontline. The Vickers Vildebeeste was obsolete, but the seven Hudson and Blenheim squadrons (seventy-one aircraft) were supported by just fifty-three aircraft in reserve. Planning assumptions envisaged monthly losses of 80 percent of aircraft and 50 percent of pilots for twin-engined bombers.[83] In the absence of additional machines (and pilots), supported by a comprehensive repair and salvage organization, a more realistic front line would have been four twin-engined squadrons operating a total of roughly fifty aircraft, with eighty aircraft in reserve.[84] Even this is a generous assessment, because there were no reserve aircrew in Malaya—against a requirement for 60 to 110 each month (all to operational training unit standard).[85]

In short, the RAF's order of battle was flattered by the simple expedient of reducing the size of the reserve and increasing the number of frontline squadrons. Rather than 158 aircraft (including twenty-seven obsolete types), the RAF's effective strength was slightly less than ninety frontline aircraft—if air operations were to be sustained for two months without reinforcement. Placing additional aircraft with the squadrons stretched the available resources and ensured that units rapidly became ineffective as losses mounted. Without a substantial increase in the number of aircraft (on the order of three hundred to four hundred machines) and a commensurate number of pilots, there was no way that the RAF—in the absence of significant qualitative superiority— could have defeated the Japanese in the air. With his extensive experience of operational logistics, Brooke-Popham knew that the RAF's front line in Malaya was a shop window designed to impress.[86] He also knew how difficult it would be to provide reinforcements once war broke out. His repeated requests to the chiefs of staff for more aircraft were echoed in private conversations with his senior commanders. "He confided to me that he was very worried, as Hurricanes and other modern aircraft types that were supposed to have been sent to Malaya were being side-tracked to the Middle East."[87] Insufficient reserves were not the only problem. The inexperience of the Buffalo pilots (most of whom had come straight from flying training schools and all of whom had to convert to type in-theater) placed the air defenses at a huge disadvantage.[88] Flying Officer Leigh Bowes arrived with No. 453 Squadron RAAF in August 1941, immediately after completing flying training. There was little time for the squadron's pilots to gain experience on the Buffalo. Reliability problems, weather, and illness meant Bowes flew less than sixty hours in three months.[89]

A further difficulty, if the RAF were to interdict any Japanese invasion fleet, was the lack of modern torpedo-carrying aircraft. This was to have been resolved by the delivery of Australian-built Beaufort bombers from May 1941 onward (equivalent to two squadrons), but production delays meant that only a handful had arrived before war broke out.[90] In retrospect, it is clear that Brooke-Popham had been given an unjustifiably rosy picture of the production situation.[91] The Beaufort had demonstrated its potential in a successful night torpedo attack against the pocket battleship *Lutzow* in June 1941, but a lack of torpedoes and trained crews would have limited its utility in Malaya, even if the original timetable had been achieved.[92] In the absence of the Beaufort, the RAF had to rely on two squadrons equipped with the Vickers Vildebeeste biplane bomber, with a top speed of 140 mph. Brooke-Popham highlighted these problems in a series of urgent signals to the chiefs of staff on 30 June, 18 August, and 20 August 1941: "At present, not only is our ability to attack shipping deplorably weak, but we have not the staying power to sustain even what we could now do. As our air effort dwindles . . . so will the enemy's chance of landing increase."[93]

It has been said that the RAF's numerical weakness was exacerbated by a failure to disseminate intelligence about the latest Japanese fighters, notably the Navy A6M (Zero) and Army Ki-43 (Oscar); however, the Zero did not see combat in the Malaya or Burma campaigns.[94] The Oscar was used, but frontline deliveries only began in October 1941—leaving little or no time for the type's performance to be assessed. The confusion between the two aircraft was understandable at the time, but authors have continued to discuss the superiority of the Zero in air combat over Malaya.[95] In fact, the bulk of the Japanese fighter force comprised the relatively old Ki-27 Nate (with its fixed undercarriage). Some 114 examples equipped the 1st, 11th, and 77th fighter groups. Fewer than sixty examples of the Oscar were used in Malaya, all with the 59th and 64th fighter groups.[96] The Official History highlights the failure of the Air Ministry and Headquarters Air Command to act on information received in July 1941, forwarded by the air attaché at Chungking, about the performance of the Zero, but says nothing about the Oscar.[97] Admittedly, the performances of the Oscar and Zero were very similar (although the latter was slightly faster and more heavily armed), but it is not fair to say that Brooke-Popham should have known his fighters were severely outclassed. This could only have been properly established by comparative testing or actual combat.[98] The Buffalo was more heavily armed than both the Nate and the Oscar and could dive faster, but it had a lower top speed than the Oscar and was appreciably slower in the climb.[99] The reason why the RAF lost air superiority was less about the performance of Japanese fighters and more about numbers, tactics, and experience. In these last three areas, the RAF was undoubtedly deficient.[100] If Brooke-Popham is to be criticized it is over the RAF's failure to adopt the dive-and-zoom tactics employed by the American Volunteer Group (AVG), which avoided turning maneuvers and relied on high-speed passes to negate the greater agility of Japanese fighters. Chennault was undoubtedly justified in believing that the Buffalo squadrons in Burma and Malaya would have benefitted from adopting the lessons he had learned in China. Indeed, the performance of the Japanese Army Air Force in the opening months of the Pacific War was good but not outstanding. Having established air superiority, the Japanese did not properly exploit their success. The RAF's failure in Malaya should not disguise the technical and tactical shortcomings of Japanese airpower.[101] As the war progressed, these flaws became more evident, leaving the Japanese army to fight largely without air support or any protection from Allied aircraft.[102] Even in the halcyon days of December 1941, very little direct assistance was provided to Japanese ground forces in Malaya. On the other hand, by destroying the RAF, the Japanese Army Air Force ensured that there was no possibility that Allied airpower could compensate for Percival's lack of mobility and firepower.

The decision not to provide Brooke-Popham with the agreed level of reinforcements lay entirely with the prime minister and the chiefs of staff. The invariable response from London was that the difficult supply position, and priority given to the Middle East and (after June 1941) Russia, meant that the Far East would have to wait.[103] However, when it looked as if Malaya would fall, significant reinforcements were diverted from the Middle East, equivalent to two divisions, a squadron of light tanks, and three squadrons of Hurricanes. A British defeat in North Africa or a German victory in Russia would undoubtedly have had serious implications for the course of World War II, but there was a deep-seated belief on the part of Churchill that Japan would not attack Britain or, if it decided to do so, that there would be adequate warning time. This view was even more strongly held because such a move was regarded as "irrational." Churchill explained his thinking to the House of Commons on 27 January 1942:

What was the likelihood of the Far Eastern Theatre being thrown into the war by a Japanese attack? I have explained how very delicately we walked and how painful it was at times and how very careful I was every time that we should not be exposed single-handed to this onslaught which we were utterly incapable of meeting. But it seemed irrational to suppose that in the last six months—which is what I am principally dealing with—the Japanese having thrown away their opportunity of attacking us in the autumn of 1940 when we were so much weaker and so much less well armed and all alone, should at this period have plunged into a desperate struggle against the combined forces of the British Empire and the United States.[104]

The Japanese attack on Malaya and at Pearl Harbor was not the first (nor likely the last) time that the American and British governments failed to anticipate the actions of a foreign power. There are many similarities with the Argentinian occupation of the Falklands in 1982 when ministers and the intelligence services, aware of increasing Argentinian frustration and nationalist fervor, simply did not believe that an invasion would take place. The cognitive behaviors that contributed to this strategic blindness included:

- "Transferred judgment": The erroneous belief that others, even non-democratic states, will be deterred by the same factors that would make you hesitate.
- "Mirror-imaging": The assumption that others are likely to act as you would act under the same circumstances.
- "Deception": The aggressor's actions to hide true intentions.
- "Perseveration": The psychological phenomenon whereby initial errors are very difficult to correct later. Such anchoring errors can prove robust, even in the face of conflicting and contradictory information.[105]

All these mental traps were present in London, Singapore, and Washington in the months prior to the Japanese attack. Brooke-Popham's public pronouncements, to the effect that if Japan opened a new offensive it would be in the north, seem naïve if not reckless, but the view that Japan's interests lay elsewhere was widely shared.[106] It was the "sensible" strategy. Why would Japan embark on a war against the United States and Britain—a war it was bound to lose? As late as the summer of 1941 it was believed by many, including the media, that Japan would not attack British possessions in the Far East.

"Japan would not move south unless there was a German move to invade England ... it looks as if Japan will not risk war with England and America until she sees a possibility of England and the U.S.A. being so occupied that they cannot oppose her adequately."[107] Even when the threat to Malaya was acknowledged, it was regarded as a remote possibility: "It would evidently have been a very improvident use of our limited resources if we had kept large masses of troops and equipment spread about the immense areas of the Pacific, or in India, Burma and the Malay Peninsula, standing idle month by month, perhaps year by year, without any war occurring."[108]

The chiefs of staff recognized that many of the criticisms directed at Brooke-Popham (and the commanders in Malaya in general) were unfair. In their opinion, "it should be made clear that the deficiencies in aircraft and equipment were not due either to lack of asking on the part of the commanders themselves, or to failure on the part of the Chiefs of Staff in this country to realize the necessity for them, but solely to the fact that there was not enough to go round and that other more important theatres had to come first."[109] Although the British had argued in Washington that the defense of Singapore was a higher priority than the Middle East, they saw defeat in North Africa as a higher risk than an attack on British possessions in the Far East. This was not a view shared by the Americans, who argued that the loss of the Middle East would be less damaging to Britain's strategic interests than defeat in the Far East.

Assessing the threat posed by Japan was the responsibility of the Secret Intelligence Service (SIS) and the FECB.[110] Brooke-Popham had flagged up problems with both organizations within a week of his arrival in Singapore.[111] His concerns about SIS were shared by the Joint Intelligence Committee (JIC) in London, who worried about the lack of functional sources covering military preparations.[112] Some, but not all, of the necessary improvements had been implemented by the time the Japanese attacked.[113] The resources available to SIS in the Far East during the early stages of the European war were grossly inadequate. In 1938, there were only two full-time representatives in the Far East.[114] Priorities inevitably lay elsewhere, but by the middle of 1940 there were seven main stations, including Singapore, where Major J. H. Green had responsibility for Burma, Malaya, Siam, and French Indochina.[115] Cooperation with the military was poor—a problem highlighted by the FECB's chief of intelligence, Captain F. J. Wylie, who strongly criticized SIS's performance and suggested that a regional director be appointed to improve liaison between the individual stations and the quality of information provided.[116] The position improved following the arrival of Godfrey Denham, a former inspector general of the Straits Settlements Police, in February 1941. Coordination between the intelligence agencies also benefitted from the appointment of Sansom as Head of "Organisation X," responsible for all secret propaganda in the region (working undercover to the MEW).[117] Unfortunately, the absence of an SIS representative within the FECB not only meant that the work of the two organizations was never fully integrated, but also created a lingering suspicion (at least on the part of the FECB) that the SIS was far too independent.[118]

In his dispatch, Brooke-Popham highlighted a number of intelligence-related problems in the conduct of the campaign in Malaya, but was careful to say (on several occasions) that the FECB had fulfilled its functions in providing operational intelligence and that his own headquarters had played a part in underestimating Japanese military capabilities.[119] He was very clear that the SIS was the weakest part of the whole intelligence system.[120] Although it was not his responsibility, Brooke-Popham might have added that the gathering of political intelligence (internal security) was equally deficient and involved at least eight separate organizations.[121] Aldrich, having documented Brooke-Popham's longstanding and repeated concerns about the intelligence organization in the Far East, and his efforts to improve both FECB and SIS coverage, argues that British intelligence forecasts were timely and accurate and accuses Brooke-Popham of using the under-resourcing issue "to distract from the fact that he had chosen to ignore what was [sic] nevertheless prescient warnings, until shortly before the outbreak of war."[122] He goes on to say that Brooke-Popham's comments were recognized as disingenuous by the official historians, although no evidence is offered, other than referencing an analysis by John Ferris.[123] Ferris makes no such claim, although he does reveal the collective failure of Whitehall and GHQ to recognize Japanese military capabilities. A careful reading of the surviving documents indicates that the FECB were as confused as any other organization about Japanese intentions.[124] The JIC was also uncertain and, although there was no strategic surprise (in respect to Japan's aggressive intentions), there was tactical surprise in the location and scale of the subsequent attack. Throughout November, multiple sources indicated imminent danger, including Brooke-Popham's own messages to London, highlighting warship movements and the buildup of aviation units in Indochina. However, both London and Singapore thought that the intended target was Thailand. At no stage was it ever believed that Japan had the capabilities or the appetite to attack the United States and Britain simultaneously.[125]

While Brooke-Popham was not directly critical of the FECB, it enjoyed a more mixed reputation with his subordinates. Malaya Command believed that the military and civil intelligence it provided was extremely incomplete. The FECB, "which one always assumed was fully in the picture, used to produce intelligence summaries which were generally noteworthy for their complete lack of intelligence."[126] Pilot Officer Edward Cox, an RAF intelligence officer in Malaya from May 1941, called the FECB "morally bankrupt." In his opinion, it routinely distributed inaccurate and misleading information, while the failure to circulate data on the latest enemy fighter types was owed to delays in translation and a belief, on the part of the FECB, that the Japanese could not possess machines of high performance. In Brooke-Popham's opinion, this was due to the lack of an effective system of collecting air intelligence, exacerbated by an embryonic organization at Air Headquarters that meant intelligence "was not effectively digested, promulgated or acted upon."[127] The picture that emerges from Cox's analysis is of a poorly organized and unbalanced organization, starved of resources, with inexperienced staff and poor leadership. As a result, there was little proactive effort to secure intelligence and the limited information that was obtained was handled erratically, although the incompetence of Air Headquarters also played its part.[128] This echoes Australian criticism about the FECB, including examples of poor training and low quality work.[129] Of course, failures in the provision of operational intelligence did not necessarily weaken the FECB's ability to deduce intent, but it is difficult to divorce the two.[130] Brooke-Popham was not blind to the possibility, if not the probability, that the Japanese would attack Malaya. "It was in the probable date of the Japanese attack that GHQ were in error, not of its probability at some time. Had GHQ really doubted the probability of a Japanese attack, it would hardly have been so insistent in its demand for reinforcements."[131] In the absence of specific intelligence, Brooke-Popham relied on the respective British ambassadors to gain some understanding of Japan's intentions and the likely response of other countries. He had considerable respect for the opinions of Clark Kerr (China), Craigie (Japan), and Crosby (Thailand).[132] Unfortunately, it was Crosby's cautionary advice and the FECB's warnings about Japanese efforts to lure Britain into an unprovoked attack on Thailand that would weigh heavily when the time came to implement Matador.

The newly qualified aviator, July 1911. Captain Robert Brooke-Popham, Oxfordshire and Buckinghamshire Light Infantry.

Major Robert Brooke-Popham (far right) briefing pilots at the 1913 Army Manoeuvres.

A B.E.2 aircraft parades in front of General Sir Horace Smith-Dorrien, Salisbury Plain, June 1914. Two months later, the RFC was at war.

RAF Staff College Andover, 1922. The commandant, Air Commodore Robert Brooke-Popham (with his terrier, Jane) is front center. Notable students and staff include: Squadron Leader (later Marshal of the RAF) Charles "Peter" Portal (back row, second from left); Squadron Leader (later Air Vice-Marshal) Conway Pulford (back row, sixth from left); Squadron Leader (later Air Chief Marshal) Keith Park (back row, eighth from left); Squadron Leader (later Marshal of the RAF) Sholto Douglas (middle row, sixth from left); and Group Captain (later Air Chief Marshal) Wilfrid Freeman (front row, second from left).

Hinaidi, Iraq, 12 September 1929. A shaken Brooke-Popham leads Sir Gilbert Clayton's military funeral procession at the RAF Cemetery.

HMS Lupin, 22 February 1930. The successful conclusion of the treaty talks. Seated, left to right: Air Vice-Marshal Sir Robert Brooke-Popham, Commander Sir John Alleyne RN (HMS Lupin), Sir Francis Humphrys, King Faisal I, King Ibn Saud, and Naji al-Suwaydi (prime minister, Iraq). Brooke-Popham contrasted Ibn Saud's charm of manner and strength of personality with Faisal's nervousness.

Imperial Defence College, 1931. The commandant, Air Marshal Sir Robert Brooke-Popham is front center. Notable students include: Lieutenant–Colonel (later General) Vernon Sturdee (middle row, fourth from left); Lieutenant–Colonel (later General) Teddy Grasett (back row, fifth from left); Squadron Leader (later Air Marshal) Paul Maltby (back row, sixth from left); and Lieutenant–Colonel (later General) Tom Hutton (back row, seventh from left).

*Nairobi, Christmas 1937. Robert and Opal Brooke-Popham with
their children, Didie and Philip, on the steps of Government House.*

*Cottisford, 1940. Opal Brooke-Popham opened her house
as a nursery for children evacuated from the London Blitz.*

Burma, November 1940. Back row (left to right): Group Captain Johnny Darvall; Squadron Leader Foster Cox; and Colonel Walter Fawcett. Front row (left to right): Major-General Dicky Dewing; Air Chief Marshal Sir Robert Brooke-Popham; His Excellency Sir Archibald Cochrane, Governor of Burma; and Lieutenant-General Kenneth McLeod.

The SS Automedon. The sinking of the Automedon by the German raider Atlantis in November 1940, and the capture of top-secret documents being carried to Singapore, gravely compromised British strategy in the Far East and negated Brooke-Popham's efforts to deter the Japanese.

CinC Far East's arrival at Singapore, 14 November 1940. (left to right): General Lionel Bond (half out of frame); Sir Robert Brooke-Popham; Air Vice-Marshal John Babington, AOC RAF Far East; and Group Captain Raymond Brownell, commanding RAF Sembawang. The antagonism between Babington and Bond would see both of Brooke-Popham's subordinates replaced within a matter of months.

The much-maligned
Brewster Buffalo Fighter.
Inferior in many ways
to the latest Japanese
fighters, it should still
have performed better
in air combat over
Malaya, with the right
equipment, tactics,
and training.

Uncomfortable body language, Manila, 16 April 1941. Air Chief Marshal Sir Robert Brooke-Popham, CinC Far East, and Admiral Thomas Hart, CinC U.S. Asiatic Fleet.

Headquarters Far East Command, May 1941. Left to right: Lieutenant Augustus Jacobs, Wing Commander Brian Yarde, Group Captain Johnny Darvall, Captain Terrence Back, Sir Robert Brooke-Popham, Colonel Walter Fawcett, Commander Andrew Grey, Major Robert Dobbin, and Captain Andrew Graham. The chief of staff post was vacant, pending the arrival of Bungy Playfair to replace Dicky Dewing.

Allied defense cooperation in Malaya—A Dutch Air Force Martin B-10 bomber at Singapore, 10 September 1941.

Toungoo, Burma, 19 September 1941. Robert Brooke-Popham and Claire Chennault (left and right center) with the pilots of the American Volunteer Group. Olga Greenlaw is at the far right.

"A regular galaxy of diplomats" attended a meeting held at Singapore on 29 September 1941 to discuss Britain's Far East strategy. Left to right: Robert Brooke-Popham, Duff Cooper, Earl Page, Clark Kerr, Shenton Thomas, and Geoffrey Layton.

Manila, 4 October 1941. Left to right: Captain Kenneth Harkness, Chief of Intelligence Staff FECB; Air Chief Marshal Sir Robert Brooke-Popham, CinC Far East; General Douglas MacArthur, commander, U.S. Army Forces Far East; and Group Captain Johnny Darvall.

A cheerful Robert Brooke-Popham with Australian journalists, Melbourne, 17 October 1941. Brooke-Popham's relations with the press became increasingly strained during 1941.

Three commanders in chief at Singapore on 3 November 1941. Air Chief Marshal Sir Robert Brooke-Popham, CinC Far East; General Sir Archibald Wavell, CinC India; and Admiral Sir Geoffrey Layton, CinC China Station. War with Japan was a little over a month away.

Air Chief Marshal Sir Robert Brooke-Popham pictured on board the ill-fated HMS Repulse, Singapore Naval Base, December 1941. Within a week, she and her sister ship, HMS Prince of Wales, would be sunk by Japanese aircraft.

19

"STIFFENING THE CHINESE"
1941

The struggle between the Allies and Japan in Southeast Asia began well before the outbreak of the Pacific War. In 1931, the Japanese had exploited the Kuomintang government's weakness to seize all of Manchuria.[1] Emboldened by this success, and encouraged by nationalists at home, the Japanese army clashed repeatedly with Chinese forces in a series of incidents until full-blown war broke out in 1937, following fighting at the Marco Polo Bridge, Wanping.[2] Japan insisted on describing the fighting as the "China Incident" rather than a war, although it involved millions of men under arms on each side. Over the next three years Japan secured large swathes of northern and eastern China and seized the main ports, although losses were heavy on both sides.[3] Continued Chinese resistance centered on Generalissimo Chiang Kai-shek, based in Chungking, who had commanded the National Revolutionary Army in the northern campaign (1925–28) that had unified much of China. Chiang Kai-shek lost many of his best-equipped and trained forces in the battle for Shanghai and looked to external powers for military assistance and supplies. At the same time, the Japanese army found it difficult to crush the remaining Chinese forces and encountered difficulties in administering and garrisoning their captured territory. The Allies had watched Japanese actions in China with increasing alarm, but it was the seizure of Hainan (and the Spratly Islands) in 1939, followed by French Indochina in 1940, that forced their hand. Neither America nor Britain wanted to deploy military forces and focused their efforts on encouraging Chinese resistance while applying diplomatic and economic pressure on Japan. The loss of China's ports on the south coast meant that maintaining the overland supply routes to the Nationalists, through French Indochina, Hong Kong, and Burma (the Burma Road) was critical. It is not difficult to see why Brooke-Popham regarded Burma and Hong Kong as key to his relationship with Chiang Kai-shek and to protecting Britain's geostrategic interests.

Within a month of his arrival, after touring Malaya to inspect its troops and defenses, Brooke-Popham set out for Hong Kong via Sarawak (ruled by the White Rajah, Vyner Brooke). He found his namesake friendly, but "his lumbago came on rather badly as soon as I started to tackle him about raising a local defence force of his own and paying for it."[4] The plan was to continue to Hong Kong by flying boat, but the diplomatic clearances could not be finalized in time. Undeterred, Brooke-Popham returned to Singapore and, accompanied by Dewing, took ship for Hong Kong, where they arrived on Friday, 27 December 1940. He just missed meeting Percy Spender, the Australian minister of war, and Lieutenant-General Vernon Sturdee, chief of the Australian General Staff, who arrived in Singapore two days later on a fact-finding visit.[5]

The acting governor of Hong Kong (Edward Norton) was unwell, so Brooke-Popham stayed with Major-General Edward "Teddy" Grasett, GOC Hong Kong, another of his IDC students. Together they toured the island and the New Territories. The Far East appreciation had described Hong Kong as an outpost to be held as long as possible with the caveat that "militarily our position in the Far East would be stronger without this unsatisfactory commitment," but Grasett was convinced that Hong Kong's defenses were strong and that the Japanese would hesitate before attacking.[6] Brooke-Popham recognized that there were wider factors to be considered. The colony was a major trading port and played a vital role in sustaining British prestige in the Far East. It was also an important route for smuggling supplies to the Chinese Nationalists, even though the Japanese had seized Canton and were in control of the mainland. Given the significance of Hong Kong to the Chinese, he sought out Madame Chiang Kai-shek, who was in Hong Kong visiting her mother and two sisters. He was impressed by her intelligence, drive, and energy, as well as command of languages. During the voyage home (by RN warship) he composed a long note to Ismay on his first impressions, including the importance of retaining a strong military presence in Hong Kong to deter potential Japanese aggression.[7] His letter also included disparaging comments about the quality of the Japanese troops he had seen at the border, leading some historians to accuse him of overconfidence tinged with racial superiority.[8] "I had a good close-up, across the barbed wire of various sub-human specimens dressed in dirty grey uniform, which I was informed were Japanese soldiers. If these represent the average of the Japanese army, the problems of their food and accommodation would be simple, but I cannot believe they would form an intelligent fighting force."[9] What is often overlooked, however, is that he had encountered second-rate conscript troops, rather than battle-hardened veterans. In a more cautious follow-up letter to Arthur Street, the permanent undersecretary of state for air, Brooke-Popham acknowledged the danger of drawing firm conclusions: "I have seen some specimens of the Japanese Army through a barbed wire fence; I was not inspired by their smartness or apparent intelligence though it is dangerous to draw deductions from such a chance meeting, but I do feel that as regards landing from the sea they have never been up against any opposition and as regards bombing, they have never been up against fighters."[10] He returned to Hong Kong by flying boat just four months later (combining it with a series of meetings in Manila). Since Government House was under repair, he again stayed with Grasett. The visit was more stressful than the previous trip and not without its difficulties. Brooke-Popham's staff caused some ructions in seeking out defense information,[11] while he was forced to show interest in a local rifle meeting before giving away the prizes in the cold and rain, "I hope I didn't look as miserable as I felt."[12] During the four days he was in the colony he held a series of meetings with the governor, Sir Geoffrey Northcote,[13] and the British ambassador to Chunking, Clark Kerr, who was well regarded by the Chinese.[14] Brooke-Popham was not particularly impressed by Northcote, who seemed "a typical colonial governor brought up in all the Colonial Office traditions, but I'm told he's got a certain bulldog tenacity. I'm sorry that Norton, the present acting governor, is going. A change for the worse, I fear."[15] While in Hong Kong, he also gave (in his words) "a very bad lecture to a large number of officers."[16] "My poor 'Master' had to address the officers and the men and there was little he could say to them. They knew, just as he knew, that we hadn't a hope of getting them away or reinforcing them if the Japanese attacked, so what could he say to them? But, anyway he did his best, he didn't pull the wool over their eyes."[17] In attempting to reassure the garrison Brooke-Popham played down the fighting abilities of the Japanese. Tony Hewitt, a captain in the Middlesex Regiment, recorded that Brooke-Popham told them that the Japanese lacked martial qualities. "Myopic creatures, he called them, incapable of night fighting, lacking in automatic weapons, inferior in the air."[18] The intemperate tone seems uncharacteristic, and at variance with his speaking notes,[19] although Sergeant Harry Hale, of the Royal Scots, also says that Brooke-Popham told them not to worry about the Japanese "because we had far better equipment and their stuff was made of cardboard and they couldn't pilot an aircraft."[20] In his defense, Brooke-Popham was just one of many who underestimated the Japanese—it was a pervasive and longstanding belief in Malaya and Whitehall.[21] As late as November 1941, Wavell wrote to Brooke-Popham, "Personally, I should be doubtful if the Japs ever tried to make an attack on Malaya and I am sure that they will get it in the neck if they do."[22] Duff Cooper made similar comments on a visit to Burma in October 1941.[23] Just two weeks before the Japanese attack, Earle Page described the defenses in the Far East as stronger than at any previous period in their history and, if the need to use them arose, they would be found impregnable.[24] Brooke-Popham never tried to hide his failure to recognize the professionalism and fighting abilities of the Japanese, but his attitude was not driven by racial animosity or cultural hostility.[25] It was based on a lack of reliable information, limited access, and the Japanese army's poor performance in China and Russia: "I met the British Military Attaché Tokyo accidentally in, I think, Hong Kong, but to the best of my recollection neither he nor the Ambassador ever communicated direct with Singapore. I remember clearly in December thinking that he gave a far more accurate impression of the Japanese than I received from other sources. I remember clearly getting a signal from London to the effect that I must not overrate the efficiency of the Japanese."[26]

Brooke-Popham knew that any attack by the Japanese on Hong Kong was likely to be in overwhelming strength, but while military defeat was inevitable (should the Japanese attack), there was still hope for diplomacy. The argument for reinforcing the Hong Kong garrison was neither irrational nor a case of strategic blindness.[27] It was certainly not an attempt to strengthen the colony so much as to make it, morally, a "Verdun" or "Port Arthur."[28] The decision to send two Canadian battalions to Hong Kong in November 1941 has to be understood in the context of Canadian domestic politics and the wider strategy to avoid war in the Far East.[29] Grasett is credited with persuading the Canadian government to support the idea, but he and Brooke-Popham had discussed the relative merits of providing one or two more additional battalions as early as December 1940.[30] Hong Kong may have been "impossible to defend adequately and impossible to abandon politically,"[31] but Brooke-Popham was convinced that visibly strengthening the garrison, coincident with American reinforcements to the Philippines and the dispatch of an Australian division to Malaya, would act as a powerful check on the Japanese. It would also encourage the Chinese Nationalists to continue fighting and avoid the possibility of a Sino-Japanese peace that would have been fatal to British interests: "The reasons might be termed political, but they had a direct effect on the military conduct of the war and to my mind give a useful example of the fact that it's impossible to draw a line between policy and strategy, they're both parts of one activity."[32] Whether there was a genuine risk that China would quit the war is questionable, although it seemed a distinct possibility in early 1940 when tentative talks were held (in Hong Kong) between senior Chinese officials and the Japanese.[33] China's capitulation would have hugely increased the threat to both Hong Kong and Singapore. The decision to reinforce Hong Kong was significant, therefore, as much for its influence on diplomatic efforts at the higher strategic level as for its potential contribution to future military operations.[34] The geopolitical impact, and the indirect support it provided to the Russians, should not be underestimated.[35]

⌒

Burma, and the Burma Road, provided the second pillar in Brooke-Popham's strategy for sustaining the Nationalists in their continued resistance. His initial visit to Burma in November 1940 had been necessarily brief, but the arrival of Reginald ("Reggie") Dorman-Smith, Cochrane's successor as governor, in May 1941 offered an opportunity to see more of the country. Brooke-Popham caught the scheduled flying boat, leaving Singapore on 3 July and reaching Rangoon (via Penang and Bangkok) the next day. Following a series of productive meetings with Dorman-Smith and McLeod, he travelled to Lashio at the start of the Burma Road, where supplies destined for the Nationalists were transferred to trucks for the journey across the border to Kunming, having arrived by rail from the Rangoon docks (some six hundred miles distant). The Burma Road had been built in 1937–38 by Chinese and Burmese laborers across 726 miles of extremely difficult terrain, including mountain ranges and deep river valleys. Heavy traffic and poor weather meant that the route required constant maintenance and repair. The quantity of supplies that reached the Nationalists was not immense and a proportion (notably petrol) was "squeezed" along the route.[36] In the five months of June–October 1941, an average of 4,700 trucks arrived each month in Kunming, carrying some 14,000–15,000 tons of freight.[37] Beyond its logistic importance, however, the Burma Road was symbolic of continued Chinese resistance and was loudly blamed by the Japanese for their failure to bring the war to a speedy conclusion.[38] The British government had agreed to close the Burma Road in July 1940 as a conciliatory gesture (knowing full well that there was little movement along the road during the wet season), hoping to avoid a war with the Japanese.[39] It was reopened in October (after the Luftwaffe's defeat in the Battle of Britain) and continued to operate until the Japanese captured Lashio in April 1942.

Brooke-Popham was determined to offer more direct support to the Chinese, although to do so, he had to negotiate some difficult policy areas. The contradictions and uncertainties that characterized the Allies' relationship with China were reflected in the creation and deployment of the AVG.[40] While Britain hesitated at providing overt support to Chiang Kai-shek, Washington was prepared to create a mercenary air force, employing Curtiss P-40 fighters and American pilots, to fight alongside the Chinese. The creation of the AVG is commonly credited to Chennault, who had worked since 1937 as an adviser on air training to the Nationalists, but it actually originated from earlier Sino-British discussions and a series of haphazard decisions in Washington and Whitehall, including an agreement to transfer to China aircraft previously allocated to the RAF.[41] By June 1941, one hundred aircraft and their pilots were on their way by sea to Rangoon, but the Chinese were not ready for them. Edward Pawley (brother of William Pawley, who had done much of the recruiting of pilots) encountered Brooke-Popham while he was at Lashio.[42] Pawley found CinC Far East "most helpful and obtained permission from the British War Office to offer facilities at Kyedaw airfield (Toungoo) and Magwe to the AVG."[43] It was agreed that the AVG could undertake full combat training, albeit with the proviso that their aircraft would not be armed and they would not attack the Japanese. Group Captain Edye Manning (an Australian), who commanded the air forces in Burma, was directed to make the necessary preparations including providing an erecting shop, maintenance facilities, and the supply of petrol and spares.[44] The AVG's pilots assembled in San Francisco in the summer of 1941 and sailed for China via Manila and Singapore, disembarking at Rangoon. For the remainder of the year, the AVG trained intensively at Toungoo, where Brooke-Popham visited them in September. He used the opportunity to talk to the pilots and discuss their tactics against the Japanese, as well as watching a flypast. According to Olga Greenlaw, who had been hired by Chennault to maintain the AVG War Diary, Brooke-Popham became affectionately known as "Popeye."[45] Although Dorman-Smith felt that Brooke-Popham was excessively cautious in not allowing the AVG to fly armed aircraft, this was the War Cabinet's decision (Brooke-Popham had already challenged this and been rebuffed).[46] In reality, Brooke-Popham greatly admired the AVG despite their "peculiar" discipline (such as a mechanic working on an aircraft "wearing a scarlet baseball cap with an enormous peak"), and was favorably impressed by Chennault who "will make a success of his air force if anyone can."[47] He readily acknowledged their major contribution to the defense of Burma, which he put down to the individual knowledge and experience of the pilots, the personality of Chennault, and the close relationship between officers and mechanics. For his part, Chennault was delighted with the assistance he had received, recording that the British had been extraordinarily helpful, stretching their policy to its limits to provide the AVG with what it needed.[48] He would later write to Brooke-Popham: "It was also a source of great satisfaction to me that you, with your much greater experience in the air, approved of my theories of air tactics and strategy. Your comments to my AVG pilots, brief though they were, emphasized the things which I had been hammering into them in our crude lecture room at Toungoo."[49] Brooke-Popham came to an understanding with Chiang Kai-shek that, should war break out, the AVG would be employed in Burma. In the event, one squadron moved to Mingaladon to defend Rangoon and the remaining two squadrons were transferred to Kunming. The creation of the AVG, and its importance to the Nationalists, enabled Brooke-Popham to champion a similar scheme involving volunteer RAF pilots. It was hoped to be able to contribute both fighter and bomber squadrons to operate alongside the AVG.[50] Only modest progress had been made to put this into effect before war broke out. In his initial appreciation, sent to the chiefs of staff in December, Brooke-Popham had highlighted the potential for supporting China more directly, beyond maintaining supplies via the Burma Road and Hong Kong.[51] As a result, Major-General Lancelot "Lance" Dennys was appointed British military attaché in Chungking in early 1941.[52] A joint Sino-British military inspection team (including Dennys) visited India, Burma, and Malaya in February 1941 to determine what mutual assistance could be provided. During the remainder of 1941, a series of Chinese delegations visited Singapore to discuss closer cooperation. "There's been a Chinese military mission here for a fortnight, nice intelligent lot and very keen to learn. Fourteen in all. I had them in to a sort of cocktail party one evening though they drank nothing but soft drinks. Chiang Kai-shek sent me his photograph signed in Chinese, a fine face."[53]

Talks with General Shang Zhen focused on collective defense of the Burma Road (including the creation of Anglo-Chinese sabotage teams) and a possible offensive against Japan in French Indochina, if Japan attacked Burma through Thailand.[54] Further Chinese officers arrived in June, including the head of their air force. In June 1941, Brooke-Popham also met with the ex-Chinese ambassador to London. "Talks excellent English and I think he's a good type and he'll be a great help to Chiang Kai-shek at Chungking where he's to be foreign minister."[55]

Brooke-Popham was particularly enthusiastic about the potential for conducting covert guerrilla activity in China. It was agreed to set up a specialist sabotage force (codenamed Detachment 204). The key figure in realizing these plans was Valentine Killery, a businessman and president of Imperial Chemical Industries (China) Ltd., who arrived in Singapore in May 1941 to establish the headquarters for the Special Operations Executive's (SOE) Orient Mission (OM). Under the auspices of the MEW, the SOE was tasked with encouraging covert resistance to the Japanese across East Asia. The decision to deploy the SOE in the Far East had been made in January, as a direct result of Dewing's lobbying for the creation of a guerrilla warfare capability.[56] He had written to the War Office on the subject within days of arriving in Singapore.[57] Brooke-Popham felt that insufficient support was subsequently provided by his headquarters. "The inadequacy of the arrangements is in no way due to lack of keenness on the part of him [Killery] or his staff. My own GHQ should have pushed the matter more forcefully."[58] Part of the problem was that Dewing, who had taken personal responsibility for the initiative, was hospitalized in April. Vital impetus was lost in this, and several other areas. "His absence just at this time is an awful nuisance."[59] Although Dennys, Brooke-Popham, and Clark Kerr strongly supported the guerrilla initiative, London decided that the SOE would not conduct active operations in China until war broke out between Britain and Japan. Killery was eventually able to obtain support for a joint Anglo-Chinese guerrilla organization, but only if it was led by non-British Europeans. The project became officially known as the China Commando Group, codename "Tulip," and based in Burma. Little was achieved, however, as Chinese suspicions, British high-handedness, and Japanese military success meant that it was abandoned after only eight months.[60] One of the contributory factors was the resentment felt by those Chinese who had lost money and family when Hong Kong fell (including Madame Chiang Kai-shek) and the consequent loss of British prestige.[61]

Killery also attempted to set up "left-behind parties," to operate behind enemy lines in the event of an invasion. CinC Far East's notebooks record regular meetings with Killery before he submitted his plans in August 1941. Brooke-Popham was initially skeptical, but eventually gave his support, only for Shenton Thomas and Percival to object.[62] There was an element of pique involved, as Percival had been unaware of the initiative, but Malaya Command was primarily concerned about the impact on scarce resources. Wavell attributed their opposition to a lack of belief "in the ability of the Japanese to invade Malaya, let alone overrun it."[63] This was demonstrably unfair, as Wavell not only shared the general skepticism about Japanese military capabilities but also actively opposed SOE operations in the Far East. Moreover, Shenton Thomas harbored deep reservations about the initiative, as did Layton who, when CinC Ceylon in 1942, gave short shrift to SOE activities.[64] As a result of these arguments, Brooke-Popham was persuaded in October to halt planning, only to relent when Killery protested.[65] Similar obstacles were encountered in Burma, where McLeod felt that there were insufficient resources.[66] Proposals to undertake covert action in Thailand, in support of Matador, made more progress, despite the opposition of Crosby. Notwithstanding these problems, Killery recognized the importance of Brooke-Popham's support, insisting that it was the only reason that he decided to persevere. He compared CinC Far East's attitude with Wavell's: "Whereas under the command of the CinC Far East military opposition to SOE was based generally on local considerations, when General Wavell assumed Supreme Command of the Northwest Pacific the situation was altered radically, and for the worse."[67]

The history of the OM in the Far East is a story of frustration, exclusion, and indecision. Even so, Killery felt that if he had been given a year, rather than seven months, an effective organization would have been operating, albeit not on the scale originally envisaged. Grimsdale may have been correct in his assertion that more progress would have been made if Killery had been replaced by a senior soldier officer working on Brooke-Popham's staff, but the potential impact of covert operations on the progress of the Japanese attack was never likely to be substantial.[68] Spencer Chapman, who led the OM training mission, believed that better support from Malaya Command would have enabled SOE to slow the Japanese and allowed the reinforcements rushed to Singapore to be deployed more effectively.[69] Whether this was ever a realistic prospect is debatable, but it would still not have saved Singapore.

Wavell mooted the idea that, had the garrison held out for a further month, the Allies could have halted the loss of further territory. This was more than wishful thinking; it steadfastly ignored the strength, endurance, and resilience of the Japanese army that destroyed American, Australian, British, Dutch, and French military power in the Far East.[70] The fate of the OM underscores the muddled thinking and prejudice that characterized much of the defense planning in Malaya. When an attack by the enemy is believed "irrational," preparations for war are inevitably compromised by the friction of "rational" disbelief.

20

BUILDING ALLIANCES
1941

Brooke-Popham knew that the security of his command, overstretched and under-resourced, depended on collaboration with the other regional powers. He put a great deal of personal effort into developing contacts with his American, Australian, and Dutch counterparts.[1] During 1941, he visited Australia twice, Manila three times, and the Netherlands East Indies (NEI) five times. He also visited Hong Kong (twice), Burma (twice), Borneo, and Thailand. The distances travelled, and frequency of these journeys, would have challenged a younger man.[2] Between December 1940 and October 1941, he covered at least 35,000 miles by sea and air, spending nearly three months away from GHQ Far East. As there was no dedicated transport available, he had to hitch lifts with the military, rely on his hosts' generosity, or travel by commercial routes.[3] "The Dutch and the Americans were very good about this but found it difficult to understand why a British air chief marshal should not possess the means of moving himself and his staff about in his own area."[4] This hectic program cannot be dismissed as "defence tourism," notwithstanding Layton's criticism. As Brooke-Popham noted, "external affairs certainly occupied the greater part of my time for the first six months and in November 1940 there was very little touch between us and the Dutch, none between us and the Americans and not much interest shown by Australia. To get things on a better footing took a great deal of personal intervention."[5]

The most problematic of Britain's allies was Australia. Not due to a lack of determination, or wavering support, but because the substantial military forces provided by Australia were employed in theaters (primarily the Middle East) distant from the homeland. The defense of Southeast Asia had been a concern of successive Australian governments, who had relied on British promises to reinforce Singapore in the event of Japanese aggression. While Australia had declined to help fund any of the work at Singapore before the war, they were more than willing to contribute men and matériel to the Allied cause in Europe, even though the Australian chiefs of staff believed that the Far East was ultimately of greater importance than the Middle East.[6] It is no coincidence that Brooke-Popham's first overseas visit was to Australia. The arrangements had been agreed in January when the Australian prime minister, Sir Robert Menzies, had stopped in Singapore en route to the Middle East and London, where he intended to discuss the state of Singapore's defenses.[7] Brooke-Popham had briefed him on the military situation, including the emerging plans for an advance into southern Thailand. Menzies was greatly concerned by the shortfalls in equipment and disconcerted by the lack of energy and insular outlook: "Brooke-Popham is I gather active and a disciplinarian. He must ginger up these other people, who have a more garrison outlook. Why the devil these generals and people should be ignorant of and not interested in the broad principles of international strategy I cannot understand."[8]

Before he left for Bangkok, Menzies agreed that staff talks (between Australian, British, and Dutch officers) should be held in Singapore as soon as possible. Shortly afterward, Brooke-Popham flew to Melbourne for preparatory discussions with the Australian chiefs of staff.[9] While he was in conference on 13 February, the Australian Cabinet asked for an immediate meeting. Brooke-Popham spent an uncomfortable night travelling by train to Sydney. The urgency had as much to do with local politics as a deterioration in the international situation. The ruling coalition government had a slender working majority and, with Menzies out of the country, the Labour opposition was not slow to raise concerns about the conduct of the war.[10] At the War Council meeting on 14 February, Brooke-Popham explained the basis for his defense plans, including the need to secure the entire Malay Peninsula in the absence of fixed defenses on the north side of Singapore, and his belief that the city could hold out for six months.[11] He outlined the likely Japanese strategy (infiltration of Malaya from the north via Thailand), stressing that his most pressing needs were additional aircraft and equipment. In doing so, he made clear that he did not rate Japanese airpower very highly. The remainder of the discussion centered on how Australian industry could help make good these deficiencies. Woodburn Kirby says that Brooke-Popham's comments were "palpably over-optimistic," and that they undermined confidence in Britain's ability to hold the Far East.[12] Although Brooke-Popham's views about Japanese aviation were misplaced, they were widely shared; moreover, Australian concerns about the defense of the Far East were longstanding (hence the Menzies mission to London).[13] Brooke-Popham's visit, and his involvement in the War Cabinet deliberations, played an important part in calming the public mood following the "alarmist statements" that had appeared in the press. "To my mind the newspapers here carry far too much influence and everyone seems to be afraid of what the papers will say."[14] He welcomed the Cabinet's suggestion that the remainder of the Eighth Division be sent to Malaya and was impressed by "their sensible questions and definite decisions."[15] From the Australian perspective, Brooke-Popham had made a good impression and was celebrated in the press as a man of action with "none of the haughty aloofness once so common among men of high military rank."[16] Brooke-Popham left Australia on 18 February, reaching Singapore three days later, in time to prepare for the Anglo-Dutch-Australian (ADA) staff conference that took place from 25 to 29 February 1941. The meeting drew up an agreement, without commitment to their respective governments, for mutual reinforcement in the event of aggression.[17] The Dutch were to provide submarines for operations in the South China Sea, and one fighter squadron and three bomber squadrons to reinforce Malaya. Four RAF bomber squadrons, it was estimated, would be available from Malaya to reinforce the NEI. These collaborative actions, to be implemented on the outbreak of war, became the "Plan for the Employment of Naval and Air Forces of the Associated Powers in the Eastern Theatre in the Event of War with Japan" (PLENAPS).[18]

Brooke-Popham travelled to Australia for the second time in October 1941.[19] He cancelled his planned onward leg to New Zealand because of the deteriorating international situation. During this final visit, he sought to reassure the new prime minister, John Curtin, about the position in Malaya, while expressing gratitude for the support Australia had already provided. "At Malaya, we had more aeroplanes, many more troops and more equipment than we had earlier this year."[20] He attended a meeting of the War Advisory Council in Melbourne on 16 October 1941 and provided a generally upbeat briefing on the military situation but highlighted the worrying shortfalls in aircraft.[21] In seeking reinforcements, "he had made all representations short of resigning."The subsequent discussion reflected a belief that there was still time to build up the defenses, while the Japanese were focused on Russia. Meanwhile, the supply position was steadily improving, particularly as Allied equipment (including the Buffalo fighter) was superior, even if numerically inferior. A more accurate assessment was his suggestion that the Japanese would invade Thailand and advance on Malaya down the Kra Isthmus, supported by a seaborne attack from Indochina. Once again, his geostrategic appreciation was impressive, even if his operational confidence was badly misjudged. At the subsequent press conference, Brooke-Popham offered a mixture of conciliation and defiance. "We don't want war with Japan. We have enough on our hands in dealing with Hitler. We don't want to assume any more commitments; but if Japan insists on war with us we are going to be ready." Mindful of his audience, he also tried to provide some reassurance, adding that "the probability of immediate attack had receded—but only the immediate probability."[22] While these sentiments appear misplaced (in view of subsequent events), they aimed to encourage Australian military and industrial efforts while deterring the Japanese. Although the Australian press would later criticize his public statements, Brooke-Popham never attempted to conceal the weakness of his forces or the threat posed by Japan in his conversations with the Australian government. He was undoubtedly an optimist about the forces he had available, an attitude encouraged by his encounters with Australian troops ("a fine body of men and a very good type"), but his belief that there was still time to build up Malaya's defenses was widely shared.[23]

Brooke-Popham's efforts facilitated generous Australian support in the defense of Malaya. The deployment of the Eighth Division is credited to the influence of Percy Spender, the Australian minister for the army, following his earlier visit to Singapore, but Brooke-Popham's advocacy was also important, particularly as Churchill would have preferred the division in the Middle East.[24] Without the contribution of four RAAF squadrons, the RAF's front line in Malaya would have been even thinner. Had time allowed, Australia would also have provided additional squadrons of Beaufort torpedo bombers—to replace the obsolete Vickers Vildebeestes. The Australian government readily acknowledged Brooke-Popham's important role in improving defenses in the Far East.[25] When the news broke that he was to be replaced, Curtin cabled: "We would like you to know that the Government and people of Australia are deeply indebted to you for the unsparing manner in which you have devoted yourself to strengthening the defences of the area commanded by you, the results which you have achieved and the manner in which you have collaborated with the Governments of the adjacent parts of the Empire and other neighbourhood countries."[26]

Britain's relationship with the NEI was equally challenging, but for very different reasons. Although the Dutch government was publicly committed to a policy of neutrality, the Dutch prime minister had approached Britain in 1936 about the possibility of an Anglo-Dutch defense scheme in the East Indies. This was rejected because the British government did not want to become committed to the defense of the NEI, but a series of informal discussions were held between the respective army and air staffs in the Far East.[27] The occupation of Holland in May 1940, and the exile of the Dutch government, encouraged the Japanese to believe that they could pressure the Dutch into agreeing to preferential terms for the supply of rubber and oil. The chiefs of staff had authorized staff conversations with the Dutch shortly after the War Cabinet's discussion on the Far East, but the first meeting did not take place until late November, as the governor general of NEI, Jonkheer Tjarda van Starkenborgh Stachouwer, was reluctant to do anything that might provoke the Japanese.[28] British–Dutch conversations took place in Singapore on 26–28 November (with an American observer), but the scope was limited to agreements on patrolling, the use of airfields, and the exchange of liaison officers. The governor general continued to resist any weakening of Dutch neutrality, although the Dutch government in London was convinced that military cooperation was essential. Within two months, however, he had reversed his decision.[29]

The large number of visits made by Brooke-Popham to Batavia, between February and October 1941, reflected his view that Malaya and the NEI shared the same threat and were stronger working together than standing alone. Notwithstanding the caution of the War Cabinet in pledging support in the event of a Japanese attack on the NEI, Brooke-Popham saw little reason to be hesitant and worked hard to develop joint defense plans based on mutual assistance. In this task, he was encouraged by the recent meeting between Spender (on his way back from Singapore) and van Starkenborgh and their agreement on the need for early Australian–Dutch staff talks.[30] The governor general, alarmed by increasing Japanese demands, was worried about the lack of arms, aircraft, and ammunition to resist any aggression. Brooke-Popham was attracted by the prospect of gaining the support of Dutch air and sea forces, but also feared that the Japanese would attempt to absorb the NEI as they had French Indochina.[31] The two men met in Java in February 1941 (when Brooke-Popham was en route to Australia),[32] and discussed the potential for greater cooperation, including preparing a joint declaration that the two countries would stand together if the NEI were attacked.[33] This meeting (and Brooke-Popham's subsequent discussions in Australia) paved the way for the ADA conference held the same month in Singapore.[34] He reported to Ismay, "I consider that reports to the effect that the Governor-General is lukewarm are misleading. He was determined to maintain the status quo for the Netherlands East Indies for as long as possible and therefore was opposed to giving the Japanese any opening for lodging any complaints about the Netherlands East Indies. I believe he is fully determined to resist aggression should it occur with all the resources he can utilize. The Governor-General was very frank during his conversations with me and there is much soundness in his argument."[35]

Neither the Americans nor the British had offered any formal security guarantees but Brooke-Popham's personal assurances, pressure from the Australians, and the momentum created by successive Singapore conferences persuaded the Dutch that their best interests lay in abandoning any pretense at neutrality. Brooke-Popham's pronouncement that "Malaya-NEI-Australia should be considered as a whole, and that an attack on one part must be considered as an attack on the whole" was warmly welcomed by the Dutch foreign minister, Eelco van Kleffens.[36] From February 1941 onward, the Dutch played an active role in Allied defense planning and in June 1941 enthusiastically supported the American-led oil embargo imposed on Japan. The first military benefits became apparent on 10 September 1941 when an NEI squadron, equipped with the Martin B-10 bomber, arrived at Sembawang for a week's detachment—demonstrating Dutch willingness to stand alongside Britain in the defense of the Far East. One of Brooke-Popham's final actions, before news of his recall emerged, was to attend an Anglo-Dutch planning conference, with Lieutenant-General Johannes Berenschot, CinC NEI, in Batavia on 13 October 1941.[37] When the Japanese attacked Malaya, the Dutch fulfilled all their commitments; indeed, they went beyond what had been agreed, declaring war on Japan before any part of the NEI had been attacked. Brooke-Popham took care to acknowledge the "prompt and wholehearted assistance they rendered to us."[38] For their part, the Dutch felt that he deserved full credit for instigating Allied cooperation in the Far East.[39]

Relations with the United States were not so much challenging as hesitant and confused. Ever since the Washington Treaty, and the abrogation of the Anglo-Japanese Alliance, Britain had attempted to work with the United States to maintain stability and security in the Far East. For a variety of reasons, including political uncertainty and mistrust dating back to World War I, military cooperation remained stalled for much of the interwar period.[40] Although Japanese intentions had been of increasing concern since the invasion of Manchuria in 1931, it was the China Incident (and the sinking of the USS *Panay* in December 1937) that precipitated the first serious effort in joint planning. Although little of immediate substance emerged from the subsequent naval and army conversations, they were the first step in creating the Anglo-American Grand Alliance.[41] By the outbreak of war in September 1939, cooperation had progressed from discussions on undertaking parallel action in the Far East to planning for active cooperation between naval forces. What was absent, however, was political commitment to combined military action. The stunning German victories in Europe provided a fresh impetus for military talks. American support was essential if Britain was to survive, but President Roosevelt, who was deeply concerned by the threat posed by the fascist powers, had to consider public opinion and Congress, neither of which was prepared to support military intervention. On the other hand, American matériel support provided a vital lifeline at a critical period, particularly the substantial aircraft contracts raised by the British and French purchasing commissions in 1939 (the latter's orders being transferred to Britain in June 1940). Although many of the designs (such as the Curtiss P-40 and the Brewster Buffalo) were no longer regarded as the most modern combat types, they offered a marked improvement over the aircraft previously employed in the Far East. During meetings with the Anglo-American Standardization of Arms Committee in August 1940, Newall (on behalf of the chiefs of staff) made clear Britain's view that Germany was the main enemy and that the loss of the French fleet meant it was no longer possible to send a battle fleet to Singapore. The defense of the Far East would depend on airpower and the Army's ability to hold the Malay Peninsula. He did observe, however, that "the support of the American battle fleet would obviously transform the whole strategic position in the Far East."[42]

A series of meetings and conferences over the next year paved the way for increasingly closer military cooperation, based on a shared strategy for defeating the Axis, once the United States joined the war. Although agreement was reached rapidly in many areas, the Far East proved problematic. Misunderstanding and misapprehension meant that an agreed position on the joint employment of (largely naval) forces proved elusive. The American-British Conference (ABC-1), held in Washington between 29 January and 29 March 1941, failed to develop a practical plan and recommended that a commanders' conference (of associated and Allied forces) should be convened in the Far East as soon as possible.[43] This would be the fourth conference, since October 1940, involving American military representatives. Despite British promptings, neither Admiral Thomas Hart, CinC U.S. Asiatic Fleet, nor Major-General George Grunert, Commander, U.S. Army Philippine Department, the senior American commanders in the Far East, had attended any of the previous meetings. Brooke-Popham's decision to travel unannounced to the Philippines seems to have been partly driven by a desire to engage more closely with his counterparts—as the ABC-1 planners had intended.

Brooke-Popham arrived at Cavite (Manila) on 2 April 1941, aboard the Imperial Airways flying boat *Cleopatra*, to be met by Hart and the British consul general. A series of discussions were held the same day with Hart and Francis Sayre, the United States' high commissioner for the Philippines. Hart, who had been in post since June 1939 and was approaching retirement, had the unenviable task of building a credible response to a growing Japanese threat without adequate resources or modern equipment.[44] The two commanders-in-chief should have found that they had much in common, but their discussions achieved little. Hart was dismissive of his visitor, whom he regarded as muddle-headed and showing his years (even though Hart was the older man).[45] During his brief stay Brooke-Popham had time to tour the nearby Nichols Field with Grunert and to meet with General Douglas MacArthur, military adviser to the Commonwealth government. According to "informed Washington quarters," the visit was "part of the general programme of increased Anglo-American cooperation . . . emphasizing the parallel United States and British interests in the Pacific area."[46] Brooke-Popham left Manila for Hong Kong on 4 April 1941 but returned four days later for further discussions with Sayre and van Kleffens. He was impressed by Sayre, who had great personal charm and was "a most attractive personality and the sort of person one can talk to, but I feel he's a little too gentle for the post he holds. He wants to do everything by persuasion and hates the use of force."[47] From the British perspective, it was important to publicize these gatherings as part of the strategy to deter further Japanese aggression.[48] The *New York Times* reported that Brooke-Popham's presence was a "natural and logical consequence of the situation in East Asia," while the *Brooklyn Eagle* noted, "[T]his seems to be a good time for a demonstration of Anglo-Dutch-Filipino-American cooperation in the Far East."[49] The *Manila Daily Bulletin* also highlighted the presence of the Netherlands foreign minister and speculated that "the bulk of the talks last week between the British air marshal, High Commissioner Sayre and U.S. military and naval staffs presumably dealt with the role that the United States and Britain will play in defense of the Pacific in which the Netherlands East Indies is an essential part."[50] The timing of the visit was also helpful, being interpreted as a riposte to Yosuke Matsuoka, the Japanese foreign minister, who had recently held discussions in Berlin and Moscow.[51] On the face of it, Brooke-Popham's visits to the Philippines had the desired effect. Japanese newspapers expressed concern about an Anglo-American-Dutch conspiracy to check Japan's advance. "If Japanese editors, with such material to work with, couldn't build a pyramidal and diabolical plot to check their country's aggression in Greater East Asia, they would be surprisingly lacking in imagination."[52]

Hart saw it rather differently. In his opinion, such meetings should have been kept secret in case they encouraged Japanese military action.[53] It also seems that he was taken aback by Brooke-Popham's impromptu "military reconnaissance," complaining that the air marshal had arrived without warning. Although Hart had been instructed by Chief Naval Operations Harold Stark to meet with local Allied commanders to coordinate operations, he was told to do so secretly and not to promise specific help.[54] Hart went on to describe Brooke-Popham as a "politico" who had engaged in noisy flamboyance around town that widely advertised to the Japanese the probability of joint Anglo-American planning.[55] Once Brooke-Popham had left, Hart complained to Washington, who relayed this to London via the Joint Staff Mission. Hart's concerns do not appear to have been shared by Grunert, but the former was in a particularly exposed position and opposed anything (including American speeches) that might be regarded by the Japanese as provocative. "He thinks they only get the Japs' back up. I suggested that in 1940 Singapore was perhaps saved by big words. But the Admiral considered that time was on our side and that we ought to postpone the 'probably inevitable' struggle as long as possible."[56] It seems that the Navy Department had not kept Hart up to speed on the progress of the Anglo-American talks or the latest strategic thinking.[57] It is also possible that there was some professional and personal antipathy involved. Hart had a reputation for disliking the British, although he found fellow sailors Phillips ("good stuff") and Layton ("a fine example of the blue-water school") more congenial visitors.[58] Layton did not feel the same way, describing Hart as an officer approaching retirement age and only anxious to withdraw from the scene of active service.[59] Whatever the cause, and whether justified or not, Hart's complaints would weigh heavily when the chiefs of staff had to decide on Brooke-Popham's continued tenure as CinC Far East. As fate would have it, Hart was "retired" only a few months later, on the grounds of ill health, following a private and confidential telegram about his performance sent by Wavell to Churchill, who promptly copied it to Roosevelt.[60]

The Australian-Dutch-British (ADB) staff discussions in Singapore were notable for exposing the continuing fault lines in Anglo-American strategy. Brooke-Popham must take some of the blame, although the lack of senior American participation did not help, and neither did the absence of specific political guidance. British preparatory work had been thorough, but Hart and Grunert's representatives were less well prepared.[61] The ADB delegates were tasked with preparing plans for the conduct of military operations in the Far East based on the ABC-1 report. Brooke-Popham was also required to seek agreement on the employment and disposition of forces before the arrival of the British Far East Fleet.[62] The conference report (ADB-1), produced after six days' work, has been criticized for its optimism regarding coalition offensive capabilities and a failure to appreciate that the Japanese might pursue a more ambitious course of action. It also contained explicit political commitments that went well beyond the agreed terms of reference. The British chiefs of staff were generally supportive of the recommendations, but Washington was less happy and, when the detailed report was received in July, raised vehement objections. They felt that the plans were not practical (in that the resources were not available), concentrated too much on airpower, and sought to employ the U.S. Asiatic Fleet solely to defend British interests. There was also criticism about the proposed command arrangements, although the British regarded this as an internal matter. The difficulty faced by the Singapore planners was overcoming wishful British thinking and American suspicions, while coping with a rapidly changing political and strategic environment.[63] The original ADB-1 report was rewritten by the JPS (and issued as ADB-2), but it proved to be no more palatable to the Americans. In the end, both

ADB-1 and ADB-2 were abandoned and it was agreed to convene a further conference between the respective naval planners (since this was where most of the outstanding issues lay).[64]

Brooke-Popham's third visit to the Philippines took place in early October. In the intervening five months Anglo-American cooperation had rapidly advanced. The German invasion of Russia and Japan's occupation of southern Indochina had contributed to a growing sense of urgency, underscored by the unprecedented meeting of Churchill and Roosevelt at Placentia Bay in August 1941. Accompanied by Darvall and Cox, Brooke-Popham hitched a lift in an RAF Catalina as far as Labuan, from where the U.S. Navy took him on to Manila. The next two days were spent in detailed talks, including meetings with MacArthur and President Manuel Quezon, who "has his faults, but the heart of a lion in a frail, sick body."[65] Since their last meeting, MacArthur had been recalled from retirement, replacing Grunert in command of the United States Army Forces in the Far East. He envied MacArthur, who was an "actual commander, not a strategic director like me." The pair got on well, although MacArthur had a "tendency to deliver a speech to a hundred instead of answering a simple question in a few words."[66] A range of issues was covered, including Brooke-Popham's ideas for defeating Japan and the potential deployment of American heavy bombers to British bases in the Far East.[67]

These discussions marked the start of Anglo-American military collaboration in the Far East. Brooke-Popham was delighted that MacArthur ("a brilliant brain even if he lacked adequate wisdom to make up a balanced character") was willing to look beyond the immediate defense of the Philippines and consider the wider strategic options.[68] Brooke-Popham's instincts were always to look to the wider picture. "When I was Commandant of the Imperial Defence College we laid down that, when drawing up a big combined appreciation, the first step was to decide on, or to get a ruling as to, the method by which the war was to be won; I have sometimes wondered whether this has been carried out in practice. Being a fly on the circumference instead of oil at the centre, it does sometimes look to me as if we are merely thinking how to avoid losing the war, instead of how to win it actively."[69] By contrast, he had a single brief meeting with Hart, who felt that "there seemed to be little to talk over."[70] Hart regarded Brooke-Popham as a "dunderhead," who should be replaced because of shortcomings that included falling asleep in meetings and believing that one of the worst things about the war was that it would finish fox-hunting. As the source for these views can only have been the liaison officer on Layton's staff in Singapore, the hand of CinC China may be detected.[71] To make matters worse, Hart and MacArthur were markedly different personalities and heartily detested each other, an attitude that pervaded their respective staffs.[72] Whatever the cause, such ill-feeling had serious implications for the joint planning process. By December 1941, after many months of hard work, there was little to show by way of credible Anglo-American plans for the defense of the Far East. Hart claimed that this was not a serious disadvantage to his command, other than a lack of familiarity with NEI and Malayan waters and incomplete preparation for tactical operations.[73] This studiously ignores the fact that the lack of a shared strategic concept, and any agreement on joint operations, doomed the Allied navies to piecemeal destruction. As a result, Brooke-Popham and Layton fell back on the PLENAPS arrangements, agreed at the ADB conference, to guide their actions in the first weeks of the war.

"It is tempting to blame the local commanders in the Far East for this state of affairs. Their personal differences were certainly unhelpful, but without agreement in Washington and London, it was unrealistic to expect them to conceive, and implement, a comprehensive plan for the defence of the region."[74] For his part, Brooke-Popham was satisfied with what he had achieved in improving collaboration with the Australians and the Dutch, notably the plans for mutual reinforcement.[75] According to Lieutenant-General Lewis Heath, commanding III Indian Corps (Ninth and Eleventh Indian Divisions), he did much good work, "more than mere conversation."[76] Perhaps the final word should be left to the U.S. naval advisor in Singapore: "Brooke-Popham is a man who favors action and he's done a good job. Australia, Malaya and the Dutch East Indies are now working together, which wasn't the case six months ago. Brooke-Popham has accomplished that."[77]

21

"AN ARMY OFFICER WITH MORE RECENT EXPERIENCE"
1941

By the middle of 1941, just six months after arriving in Singapore, Brooke-Popham could look back on some significant achievements. Relations with the Dutch were much closer, considerable progress had been made in coordinating Allied defense planning, reinforcements had started to arrive in Malaya, the forward defense strategy had been strengthened by Churchill's approval of the preemptive occupation of Singora (in the event of a Japanese invasion of Thailand), and military cooperation with the Chinese was steadily improving. These changes had enhanced Britain's strategic position in the Far East, although there were still important shortfalls in equipment—notably aircraft, tanks and artillery.

Behind the scenes, however, all was not well. The first sign of trouble emerged with the appointment of Reggie Dorman-Smith as governor of Burma. Dorman-Smith was something of an outcast, banished to the colonies by the prime minister.[1] He had been one of fifteen public figures attacked in the polemical book *Guilty Men* for their role in appeasing Germany.[2] Dorman-Smith was by no means an appeaser but he had been a member of the Chamberlain government.[3] He was a politician, rather than an inspired leader, with no service affiliation (although his older brother, Eric "Chink" Dorman-Smith, was a major-general on Auchinleck's staff in Cairo) and not minded to follow protocol.[4] "He's burly, full of 'old buck' as we say in Lancashire, and he's got a glint and a twinkle in his eye."[5] In August 1941, just three months into his new job, he sent a private and personal telegram to Leo Amery, secretary of state at the Burma Office, expressing his concerns about the large number of Army officers in Burma who lacked experience of modern warfare.[6] He went on to add: "For my part I would like to see someone like [General Sir Bernard] Paget as Commander-in-Chief Far East. I have the greatest admiration for the present Commander-in-Chief, but I think a younger man is now necessary. This view I advance with all humility knowing what a fine person Brooke-Popham is. This may be going far beyond my province, but I consider that I should tell you this is not confined merely to me but is widespread in Burma." The telegram ended, "I fully appreciate that some changes have been carried out recently at Singapore but from my limited information I do not think they meet our needs." It is unclear how Dorman-Smith arrived at these views, although he hints that it was the result of a recent defense exercise.[7] For his part, Brooke-Popham thought that he had got on well with the governor and that the exercise had gone well, although many faults and omissions had been discovered: "I paid a visit to Burma early in June mainly to make my number with the new Governor, Sir Reginald Dorman-Smith. I spent two days and one night with him at Maymyo and I'm sure we shall work together well. The Governor has a high opinion of McLeod, both of his character as a man and of his ability as a soldier."[8] Writing privately to Dorman-Smith, Amery expressed concern about the desirability for changes but then added, "I confess that when I saw Brooke-Popham before he left I thought that he had aged a good bit since I had seen anything of him." He then pressed the governor to say whether his concerns included GOC Burma.[9] In response, Dorman-Smith acknowledged McLeod's energy and ability (as well as his valuable knowledge of the country and people) but expressed a preference for someone who had more recent experience of fighting. "I imagine that East Africa experience would be most akin to our type of fighting."[10] McLeod, who was close to Brooke-Popham, can hardly have been the governor's informant or the source for the "widespread" concern in Burma. The culprit was most likely Lieutenant George "Wally" Richmond, who had joined Dorman-Smith as his military assistant in August 1941.[11] Richmond was a forty-two-year-old forestry official and long-term Burma resident with a reserve commission in the Burma army. His military experience was limited to two years' postwar service with the RAF on the North-West Frontier, where he had met Dorman-Smith (shortly after he had been shot down and ransomed).[12] McLeod was adamant that Richmond had influenced the governor against him.[13] Why Richmond should have done so, and why Dorman-Smith felt Richmond's views were credible, can only be surmised. Two years later, "Colonel" Richmond (then serving as an SOE liaison officer with Detachment 101, Office of Strategic Services) was dismissed for graft through Army contracts.[14] Brooke-Popham was very much aware of Richmond's influence over the governor and the problems that this created: "Sir R. Dorman-Smith established a military liaison officer on his personal staff. There were obvious advantages in this and it would doubtless have worked well had the facts and figures always been obtained from the responsible authorities. As it was, information was sometimes sought through other channels, with the result that at times inaccurate or incomplete information was given to the Governor, leading to misunderstandings."[15]

Dorman-Smith's telegram arrived just as there was a shift in London's strategic thinking, triggered by the British ambassador to China, Sir Archibald Clark Kerr, who raised concerns, shortly after the German invasion of Russia, about the difficulty of coordinating military, economic, and political activities in the Far East: "The problem is complicated as the Dominions, Colonies and India are all concerned as well as the Foreign Office and the Treasury and a number of other departments. At present coordination is affected in London, but with increasing difficulty of rapid communication detailed coordination from that centre as in peacetime is already becoming more difficult and may become impossible."[16] After discussion with Canberra and Wellington, it was decided that someone of ministerial rank should lead a mission to investigate the question. The War Cabinet agreed to appoint Alfred "Duff" Cooper, recently minister of information, to head the inquiry. His task was to "examine the present arrangements for consultation and communication between the various British authorities in that area [the Far East] military, administrative and political and to report to the War Cabinet how these arrangements can be made more effective."[17] Duff Cooper's qualifications for the role were largely nonexistent, but he was available and, like Dorman-Smith, it was convenient to get him out of the country. Duff Cooper was seen to have failed at the MOI and was widely regarded as indolent.[18] He was, however, a very able man, who had access to the prime minister.[19] In considering how to deal with Dorman-Smith's criticisms,[20] the permanent undersecretary at the Burma Office, Sir David Monteith, pointed out that Brooke-Popham's selection had not been based on war fighting, but on the pressing need to develop a more proactive defensive alliance.[21] Amery decided to forward the telegram to the prime minister, who directed that the chiefs of staff were to consider the matter. Not surprisingly, they were robust in defending Brooke-Popham and asserted that, from their perspective, "he has shown energy, resource and vision in handling the many difficult problems which have confronted him since taking up his appointment."[22] They also argued that they could not undertake any large-scale transfer of officers who have served in modern campaigns without denuding other theaters. However, they did not entirely close the door and went on to suggest that Duff Cooper, who would shortly arrive in Singapore, might be in a better position to advise on the matter—once he had had time to take stock of the situation.[23]

Brooke-Popham became aware of Dorman-Smith's intervention within a few weeks—in a private letter from Babington, who had evidently discussed the matter with Portal. "Advancing to more delicate ground. There is reason to suppose (on the very highest authority) that an important and recent arrival in Burma is no great friend of yours. I infer, but this is only a guess—that he may have leanings towards the Army outlook." Not surprisingly, Babington feared the reemergence of the Army/Air Force struggle over defense priorities in Malaya. "I told CAS point-blank that I personally regarded your continued presence at Singapore as absolutely indispensable, since your departure from the scene would run the risk of the next CinC being a War Office nominee—in which we would be back in the bad old days of evacuations, retirements, withdrawals and demolitions."[24] It seems likely that Brooke-Popham's decision to return to Burma so soon was linked to Babington's warning (although it also offered an opportunity to meet with Clark Kerr who was on a brief visit from Chungking). Arriving in Rangoon on the evening of 18 September 1941, Brooke-Popham wrote in his private notebook (under the title "Burma—McLeod"), "Does Dorman-Smith consult with him [McLeod] before sending off telegrams?" He did not tackle the governor directly, instead he casually mentioned his concern that military matters had been raised with London without involving the GOC or the senior RAF officer. "I think he appreciated the point."[25]

Duff Cooper, together with his wife, Lady Diana Cooper, reached Singapore by flying boat in early September (having travelled via Washington and Manila). Unlike Brooke-Popham's low-key arrival the previous November, the couple was greeted with an aerial escort (of Buffalo fighters) and met by the governor, as well as by both CinCs. Duff Cooper's presence in Singapore was not universally welcomed. Shenton Thomas felt that they had been saddled with a failure. Duff Cooper was an accomplished author, whose books on Haig and Talleyrand were well regarded, but his personal reputation was more mixed. A cabinet minister in Chamberlain's government, he resigned over Munich, as did Eden, but never gained the moral authority that the latter enjoyed.[26] He was not well liked, in or out of Parliament ("pipsqueak" was one of the politer epithets), while his private life, including numerous affairs, absence from London during the Blitz, and his decision to send his son to school in Canada for the duration of the war made him a controversial figure. Their presence in Singapore generated a mixture of jealousy and resentment. He was reportedly referred to as "Fluff Goofy," but it was Diana who excited the most criticism.[27] Her reputation as a society beauty meant that she was the object of scrutiny, including by the ever-observant Megan Spooner. "She [Diana] looks very well preserved. Her eyes which she lines heavily in black are very pale, blue and large. At certain angles, they look lovely but when focused on one, are cold, bold and old."[28] By early December, the description had become more clinical. "Every whim is gratified. Her manners are not very polished. She looked remarkably lovely, but her face is unattractive and after the enamel had worn off, an hour or two, the face fell away."[29] Lady Doreen Dorman-Smith, who hosted the Duff Coopers in Burma, wrote that "she [Diana] didn't appear till nearly lunchtime. She is very 'la-did-da' and stares, never blinking her eyes, which is not attractive."[30] It may be an exaggeration that Diana brought one hundred pieces of luggage with her, but the rumor was eagerly repeated.[31] The Japanese were certainly impressed and deduced from the size of Duff Cooper's party that he was expected to coordinate the British defense organization in Malaya, as well as being involved in the administration of foreign affairs in the Far East.[32] They would have been surprised to learn that, for his part, Duff Cooper was not entirely certain what he was doing in Singapore.[33]

Once suitable accommodation had been found for his six staff, Duff Cooper embarked on a tour of the region. After visiting Batavia, he set out for Burma, reaching Rangoon on 3 October.[34] Ominously for Brooke-Popham, the governor's military assistant, Wally Richmond, provided escort throughout their visit.[35] Two days later, shortly before he left for India, Duff Cooper dispatched a short message to the Burma Office supporting Dorman-Smith's views about Brooke-Popham, "having come separately to precisely the same conclusion."[36] He had previously described Brooke-Popham to David Margesson, secretary of state for war, as "damned near gaga." On his return to Singapore, he advised Amery that "both D-S and I are convinced that Brooke-Popham is no longer up to the job of CinC Far East. This view is shared by the Viceroy. I am sorry to express it because I have great admiration for the man who is working with the utmost devotion. In my opinion, he is over-working, but his conscience will not allow him to take things easier."[37] Amery wrote again to the prime minister, commenting that, although both Dorman-Smith and Duff Cooper might be mistaken, the matter deserved his serious consideration.[38] This time, the chiefs of staff bowed to the inevitable. Noting that the opinions of the governor of Burma and the minister of state could not be set aside, they proposed that Brooke-Popham should be relieved, adding that he had not "at all times made a favourable impression on the Americans."[39] Churchill was also advised that "it was essential to have a soldier on account of American susceptibilities re independent Air."[40] It was recommended that if a soldier was to succeed Brooke-Popham it should be General Bernard Paget and, if an airman, it should be Air Chief Marshal Sir Arthur Longmore. Churchill challenged this on the grounds of Longmore's age (he was fifty-eight) and that Paget was "a fighting man" and could not be spared for what was "an extended supervisory job."[41] The last comment is interesting, not so much because of Churchill's high opinion of Paget, but because it reveals that, even at this stage, he still did not believe the Japanese would attack. Churchill later relented and Brooke-Popham was informed on 6 November 1941 that Paget was to take over as CinC Far East.[42]

Throughout September and October Brooke-Popham had become increasingly worried about his position. The arrival of Duff Cooper only added to his sense of insecurity. "I know what will happen. As soon as Duff Cooper comes he'll report that I ought to be replaced."[43] The fate of Newall, Ironside, and Wavell (all sacked in the previous twelve months) demonstrated the difficulty of retaining Churchill's confidence. Sir Frederic Eggleston, the Australian minister to China, visited Singapore in September, en route to Chungking. He found Duff Cooper grumpy and silent, Bennett distracted (speaking only to complain about the British), and Brooke-Popham lacking presence, but relentlessly optimistic.[44] On 5 November, just a few days short of a year since he had first arrived in the Far East, Brooke-Popham received the news that he was expecting—in the form of an immediate cipher telegram from the prime minister. "It has been decided, in view of ongoing developments in the Far East, that the duties of Commander in Chief Far East should be entrusted to an army officer with up-to-date experience." To soften the blow, Churchill congratulated Brooke-Popham on his work and offered a baronetcy.[45] The next day, Brooke-Popham was told by the Air Ministry that his successor would be Paget, with the proviso that "his [Paget's] arrival might be delayed by the need to make visits on his way out."[46] Giving no sign of any personal disappointment, Brooke-Popham acknowledged the prime minister's decision, and accepted the baronetcy, although he requested that he be considered for other jobs contributing to the war effort.[47] Amery wrote to congratulate Dorman-Smith. "Your representation and Duff's, as to the Commander-in-Chief Far East, have had their effect and you are going to get the man whom you yourself mentioned as the right sort of person for the job."[48]

The Australian government was unsettled by the news of Brooke-Popham's sudden replacement and complained that they had not been consulted. Churchill attempted to get Duff Cooper to explain his reasons to Curtin, "as your adverse opinion was one of the factors which influenced the decision," however, as Cooper was away from Singapore (travelling to New Zealand), the matter was not pursued.[49] Brooke-Popham's immediate concern was for the defense of Malaya, rather than his personal circumstances. This included the issue of how the air aspects were going to be addressed (with the Army providing both CinC and chief of staff) and how news of his recall could be delayed.[50] He worried that once the change was publicly known, any delay in Paget's arrival would weaken the authority of GHQ and undermine the defense relationships he had established.[51] Even so, rumors soon started that he had been recalled. Duff Cooper, who was largely to blame, tried to disguise his role when Brooke-Popham raised the matter, claiming that Curtin was the source for his information (by long-distance telephone call).[52] The minister of state failed to mention that he had already discussed Brooke-Popham's performance with Layton (and likely shared Dorman-Smith's opinion with him). Layton advised that there was very little for CinC Far East to do and that, as far as he could see, "Brooke-Popham had completed his task when he settled the differences between the GOC and AOC." No doubt Layton and Duff Cooper felt they were acting in the national interest, and that their views were honest and objective, but it is difficult to reconcile the latter's behavior with the man described in his official biography as possessing an extravagant degree of "integrity and moral courage."[53] Sir Archibald James, who knew Duff Cooper well, felt that he was a bad administrator and an unfortunate choice for Singapore. In his opinion, Duff Cooper entirely misjudged Brooke-Popham (whom James had worked with in France), leading to a grave injustice.[54] Unfortunately, Duff Cooper's assertions about Brooke-Popham have become the basis for a popular narrative that portrays all the British senior commanders in the Far East as either mad, bad, or both. Even Woodburn Kirby, the official historian, fell victim to this prejudice.[55] Borrowing Churchill's phrasing, he concluded that Brooke-Popham:

could not be said to be entirely au fait with sea, land and air warfare in the form it had taken in Europe and the Middle East. He was also very dependent on his staff, for he had developed a habit of falling asleep at any time of day and often in the middle of a conference at which he presided, therefore often missing much of the subject under discussion. Although a man of great charm, he had clearly passed his prime and was not a forceful enough personality to deal with this complicated and difficult situation.[56]

No sources are quoted, although Woodburn Kirby had access to a wide range of material and individuals. The image of a somnolent and ineffectual air marshal, well past his prime, struggling to cope with the heavy demands of command, seems to sum up all that was wrong with Britain's strategy in the Far East. Yet this same individual, according to the chiefs of staff, had shown energy, resource, and vision during the brief time he was in Malaya.

To be fair, there is a grain of truth in the picture presented by Duff Cooper and Woodburn Kirby, although it is not related to old age. Maurice Baring tells of a dinner at St-Omer in 1915 where chaos reigned due to a drunken mess sergeant.[57] After a series of culinary catastrophes, including the noisy destruction of an entire course, the host (Brooke-Popham) had to be pinched awake. Charles Grey, the outspoken editor of *The Aeroplane*, fell asleep in company with him at a dinner in 1918, although he insisted that, in Brooke-Popham's case, it was down to years of overwork.[58] We may infer that there were other incidents, to judge from comments published in the *Oxfordshire Light Infantry Chronicle*. "He owed his rapid advancement to a more than ordinarily good brain, and an infinite capacity for work. More often than not, he was known to continue his labours into the small hours of the morning and then fall sound asleep during dinner next day."[59] Singapore's conqueror, General Tomoyuki Yamashita (the "Tiger of Malaya"), and seven years younger than Brooke-Popham, was renowned for taking a nap at work or in military lectures, and snoring loudly, sometimes at critical moments.[60] There is no evidence that Brooke-Popham ever nodded off during meetings. It is not mentioned by any of his staff, and Andrew Gilchrist, who was head of the News Bureau at the British embassy at Bangkok and encountered Brooke-Popham several times in 1941, says that he is not persuaded of Woodburn Kirby's claim.[61] Diana Duff Cooper, aware of Brooke-Popham's reputation, became frustrated when he failed to oblige: "I entertained General Brooke-Popham, Commander-in-Chief Far East, last night. He can be relied upon to go to sleep directly after dinner, but stupidly I let him talk instead of talking to him and he stayed and stayed. I also had a Chinese couple, Mr and Mrs Kau, both completely speechless—it was dreadful."[62]

Brooke-Popham's postprandial habit (the subject of gossip among journalists as far away as Cairo) became a stick to beat him with when the war started to go wrong, leading *Time* magazine to describe him as "sleepy and over-confident."[63] A social foible had now become a sign of advancing senility. Brooke-Popham was marginally younger than Hart, and only slightly older than MacArthur, but he was at least five years older than other British commanders in the region.[64] As Dewing pointed out, this was a compliment rather than an embarrassment:

> I know how bitterly disappointing it must be to be asked to hand over now, when your grasp of the situation and conflicting interests throughout the vast area in which you work is so complete and when the crisis for which you have prepared for over a year seems so imminent. I am afraid that you will find small consolation in the fact that changes based on men's age are being made in many other places. Your appointment a year ago was a personal tribute to your physical and mental fitness such as even then was not being paid to your contemporaries.[65]

It was not just Dewing who subscribed to this view. Denis Richards was impressed by Brooke-Popham's writing skills (in comparison to other senior officers), adding that "he was a fine old boy—in fact only in his early sixties, but he had very white hair . . . doubtless he had not been quite up to his impossible job in the Far East, but who else could have done much with such patently inadequate forces in so vast an area of command?"[66] A junior RAF radar officer in Singapore recalled that "he was a delightful person to talk with: you didn't feel you were just a 23-year-old jumped up volunteer reservist. He was there listening to you and asking you for your advice on this and that and making a clear decision about where we wanted to have radar cover."[67] Brooke-Popham was unusual among his contemporaries in his willingness to treat subordinates with respect and to listen to their ideas. To his mind, decision-making was a shared intellectual challenge rather than an opportunity to exercise power. Gilchrist recalls "feeling not the slightest twinge of apprehension or fear when I was first ushered into his presence."[68]

Brooke-Popham was not a force of nature, yet he still had presence. He was often described as "large," even though he was under six feet tall and slender in build.

As tensions grew and war became more likely, so Brooke-Popham's age and personality became a lightning rod for the high command's collective anxiety. Constant travel and growing demands meant that he was increasingly tired. The climate and the absence of a chief of staff, in an already overstretched headquarters, took a heavy toll.[69] "My days in Singapore are pretty regular, leave the house about 8.15, in the office all the morning—papers, interviews, conferences—luncheon with Admiral and Lady Layton, office or local visits in the afternoon and back to the house any time between 6.30 and 8. I shall be pretty well stuck to that with Dewing sick."[70] In August, he had a feeling that his time in Singapore might be coming to an end. "My birthday next month and I shall be 63, I ought to feel much older than I do as I sometimes feel it's all wrong for a man of my age to be a CinC in these days and if they did decide to put someone in my place there'd be nothing to complain about."[71] The pressure on Brooke-Popham grew relentlessly over the next few months. "Things have been a bit busy here lately and I have had to work the last three Sundays which is against all my principles and does lead to a fogged brain."[72] By early December, he was looking more tired than at any time in the previous three months.[73]

Brooke-Popham was neither gaga nor incompetent, but it is difficult to disagree with the decision to replace him with a younger man. The argument for doing so may have been based on questionable evidence, but it was nevertheless a timely and sensible step. He recognized the logic (even before Dorman-Smith's intervention), but the subsequent uncertainty about who would take over and when they would arrive made a bad situation even worse.[74] Within three weeks, it was decided to replace Paget by Henry Pownall. Field Marshal Alan Brooke's appointment as CIGS (replacing Dill) meant that Paget was now needed as CinC Home Command, in succession to Brooke.[75] The chopping and changing in Whitehall wasted valuable time and Pownall had only reached Cairo when the Japanese attacked. This raised the reasonable question of whether it was clever to change the CinC once fighting had broken out—a problem that Dorman-Smith had highlighted back in August.[76] Churchill hesitated, and again sought Duff Cooper's advice. The latter's response was unequivocal: "I consider the very great strain and shocking recent events have greatly increased reasons, which already existed for Brooke-Popham's supersession. In addition, I am not satisfied with the manner in which the land campaign is being conducted and I feel that the defenses of the naval base against superiority of numbers and without command either of the sea or air require the presence of the best soldier the Empire can provide."[77]

When Brooke-Popham had left England in October 1940 he had hoped that Opal might be able to join him at the end of 1941. Joan Hugonin had written to her sister-in-law advising that she try to join her husband in Singapore. "He will, of course travel and get away a lot, which will help a great deal but he is in for a *very* difficult time and you ought to come if you possibly can."[78] By spring 1941, this seemed increasingly unlikely: "You mustn't make any definite arrangements to come out here yet; one reason is that no wives are allowed out except for those permanently stationed here; the wife of a senior naval officer who came out was sent away within a week. I can't have you regarded as a second Lady Blamey. And remember it's two months here and two months back. A lot will have happened by the end of June and I may be elsewhere."[79] The problem had been compounded by the decision, in June 1940, to evacuate all British women and children from Hong Kong.[80] This had caused considerable controversy and was not a step that the Singapore government was willing to contemplate, although all new military personnel posted to Malaya were unaccompanied. In July, Brooke-Popham received a telegram from Opal announcing that she was travelling to Kenya to help set up a war babies scheme, like that at Cottisford, and hoped to be with him by the end of the year. Once again, he warned that it would be unwise to plan on travelling on to Singapore. London had ruled that no more wives were to be allowed to come and "with the Far East in its present uneasy condition . . . none of us can forecast with any degree of certainty what will have happened by then."[81] He repeated these concerns just a few weeks later: "I'm really not going to set a bad example to young subalterns and start here all the strife and bitterness that the problem of wives has started in Hong Kong. Duff Cooper, who's on his way here, is bringing Lady Diana with him, but we needn't take either of them as examples to follow."[82] Opal was not to be deterred and set out for South Africa in early September. She duly arrived in Singapore on 8 November 1941, via Kenya and Burma.[83] Her plans for establishing an adoption scheme for war babies, organized through the EAWL, had faltered in the face of the worsening war situation and a lack of shipping, but she pressed on to Singapore regardless.[84] By this time they knew that he had only a few weeks left to serve as CinC Far East, although Opal threw herself into organizing service welfare programs with her customary energy and enthusiasm, much as she had as a member of the RAF Comforts Committee in England.[85] According to Foster Cox, "Opal was a very formidable person and she started throwing her weight about a lot. A lot of it was necessary."[86]

While London was making up its mind about Brooke-Popham's replacement, Duff Cooper continued with his inquiry.[87] As part of this process, he convened a conference in Singapore on 29 September 1941 to discuss military and civil coordination. Participants included Brooke-Popham, Layton, Crosby, Clark Kerr, Shenton Thomas, and Sir Earle Page, the Australian special envoy to London. The simultaneous visit by this "regular galaxy, or should I say gaggle, of diplomats in Singapore" proved quite helpful as it was the first occasion, since the Japanese occupation of southern Indochina and the German invasion of Russia, that Britain's senior leadership in the Far East (only Craigie was absent) could meet.[88] In their collective view, it was improbable that Japan would consider war in the south before January 1942—based on the poor weather in the Gulf of Siam between November and January and the opportunities in the north. Although this assessment has been described as misguided and optimistic, we now know that the Japanese were still uncertain about where to strike.[89] The meeting concluded that the best course of action was to attempt to disengage Japan from Indochina, which would help bolster Thailand's resistance, and to increase military cooperation with China. To exert further pressure, it was strongly recommended that a British fleet be dispatched to the Far East, where even one or two warships would have a major propaganda value.[90] Duff Cooper was privately dismissive of Brooke-Popham and Layton's telegram to the chiefs of staff summarizing the conference's conclusions, which he compared to *Gone with the Wind*, adding that "we hardly thought it necessary to inform H.M.G. at such great length that battleships might be useful at Singapore and that the Japs are beggars." The commanders in Malaya have been accused of willfully ignoring evidence that landings were possible in the northeast monsoon, but both Brooke-Popham and Playfair were adamant that this was not the case. From their perspective, saying that landings would be difficult (and involve a considerable element of risk) was not the same as saying they were impossible, hence the decision to retain a strong force to defend the beaches on the east coast rather than redeploying them.[91]

The idea of sending warships to the Far East had been under discussion since August 1941.[92] The Defence Committee (Operations) of the War

Cabinet decided on 20 October to deploy "Force Z," the battleship HMS *Prince of Wales*, the battle-cruiser HMS *Repulse*, and four destroyers.[93] This was not the main fleet envisaged by prewar plans, but it reflected the improved naval situation following the sinking of the *Bismarck* and the heavy losses inflicted on the Italian navy.[94] It is traditionally argued that this decision was forced on the Admiralty by Churchill, who was oblivious to the dangers involved, but it should also be seen in the context of the forward naval strategy set out in ABC-1.[95] It is true that the deployment of Force Z was regarded by Eden (the foreign secretary) as an important step in influencing the Japanese, who were already in a hesitant mood "brought about by the contemplation of the forces that may possibly confront them," but it was also influenced by the Admiralty's desire to improve naval cooperation with the Americans.[96] Failure to achieve agreement on ABC-1 and ABC-2 had largely been due to Britain's persistent naval weakness in the Far East.[97] The Admiralty was now prepared to consider operations north of the Malay Barrier, rather than focusing simply on trade protection, if necessary using Manila as a forward base.[98]

Force Z, commanded by Admiral Tom Phillips, arrived in Singapore on the evening of 2 December 1941, to considerable publicity and a growing confidence that the defense of the Far East was at last receiving the attention it demanded.[99] "When they came to the Johore Straits the evening was still and clear and the ships with their strange exotic camouflage looked very fine against the green hills of Johore. Never before can [*sic*] two ships of H.M. Navy have been more welcome nor given more confidence. Malaya is pleased."[100] Phillips had flown into Singapore on 29 November, ahead of his ships, to prepare for discussions with Allied naval chiefs. As CinC Eastern Fleet, he was directed to assume responsibility for all ships and establishments of the China Station in place of Layton, who was scheduled to return home on appointment as CinC Portsmouth.[101] Layton, who did not particularly like Phillips, was offended at being replaced by a younger man with little sea experience, and felt that he would have been a better choice to command Force Z. Indeed, Phillips was regarded by many of his colleagues as an armchair sailor who enjoyed the confidence of the prime minister but suffered from a willingness to "push on regardless." While it was generally acknowledged that he was an intelligent and energetic officer, he was also seen as opinionated and lacking in inspirational qualities.[102] More significantly, considering future events, he had a reputation for downplaying the effect of airpower on naval operations.[103]

22

MATADOR
1941

Although there was a widespread feeling that Japan had "missed the boat" in 1940, neither GHQ nor Whitehall was oblivious to the possibility of a Japanese attack on Malaya. The German invasion of Russia led to a growing nervousness about Japan's intentions, although there was no firm view on where their next move would be. There were many, including Brooke-Popham, who rationalized that Japan would renew operations along the Soviet border, to erase the crushing defeat suffered at Nomonhan in 1939. As the Wehrmacht approached Moscow this seemed an ever more likely scenario, notwithstanding the Soviet-Japanese Neutrality Treaty signed in April 1941. We now know that the Japanese were also uncertain about where they should strike.[1] Throughout June 1941 a series of conferences and liaison meetings were held in Tokyo to agree on their future military strategy. The Army preferred active involvement in the Germany-Russia war while the Navy advocated a more cautious approach that kept open the possibility of a southern advance against the European possessions in the Far East. Despite German encouragement for an immediate intervention, the General Staff decided to wait while developing opportunities in the south, including the occupation of French Indochina. By August 1941, with a slowing German advance and without any sign that the Soviet Union was close to imminent collapse, the planned operation in the north was abandoned.[2] The serious weakening in Russia's military position meant that there was little prospect they would open a second front. Under these circumstances, the Japanese High Command was persuaded that the "Southern Advance" would achieve two of Japan's key policy goals: closure of the China Incident, and economic independence—in the form of secure access to oil and raw materials.[3]

Japan's formal decision to wage war against the Allies was made at the Imperial Conference held on 1 December 1941, but planning for the Southern Advance had begun more than a year before, when the outcome to the Battle of Britain was still uncertain.[4] By the summer of 1941, the Japanese had concluded that any move against the British and Dutch would almost certainly bring the Americans into the war, and thus the scale of the planned operation was expanded to include simultaneous attacks against Britain and the United States.[5] Army units earmarked for the Malaya operation underwent intensive training from early October and started to move from 17 November, with embarkation commencing three days later.[6] By 4 December 1941, the assembly of the invasion forces was complete and the advance formations sailed from Hainan. A total of eleven divisions were to be employed (of which four, under the command of General Tomoyuki Yamashita, were allocated to the Malayan and Burmese operations). Although their numbers were not large compared to the forces opposing them, the Japanese were confident of achieving local superiority against "colonial troops of inferior quality." They were also confident that the Malayan operation could be completed within one hundred days.[7] Nearly seven hundred army aircraft, including reserves, were available, compared to a similar number of Allied aircraft. However, as the latter were spread across the entire area of operations, the Japanese expected to be able to achieve local air superiority and to eliminate Allied airpower in the first few days of fighting. In the Philippines, it was decided to attack air installations in advance of landings, whereas in Malaya they were forced to conduct simultaneous air and landing operations—to forestall an immediate British move into Thailand. The Japanese navy allocated the faster transport ships to the landings in Malaya and Thailand, to minimize potential losses to air attack.[8] Japanese intelligence reports identified RAF strength in Malaya as being in the order of 300–350 aircraft (including reserves).[9] This was well above the number available and was based on the numbers predicted in the Far East appreciation.[10]

Even at this late stage, there was a widespread belief in Singapore and London that the Japanese would not attack. According to Dorman-Smith, Duff Cooper assured him that war would never come to Burma. "Not for one moment do I blame Duff-Cooper whose opinion could only have been based on information which he had received from our Intelligence in Singapore."[11] The British press were also optimistic that the worst had passed. "Quietly and unostentatiously a system of consultation and cooperation is being built up round the poles of Singapore and Manila. If the Japanese hoped to strike in this area before the democracies had concerted their defence they may well have delayed too long."[12] It was believed that diplomacy, and American economic measures, would be enough to deter the Japanese. Moreover, Washington's robust response to the occupation of southern Indochina encouraged the belief that U.S. military assistance would be forthcoming if Japan attacked Malaya. Even so, the oil embargo and the subsequent American-Japanese talks in Washington created a sense of urgency. Brooke-Popham's private letters and notebook testify to growing unease—reflected in increased signal traffic and longer working days.[13]

November brought the realization that war was progressively more likely, although it was still thought that the Japanese would strike in the north. Toward the end of the month it became abundantly clear that this confidence was misplaced and that the Japanese were planning to move in the south.[14] American and British intelligence sources revealed a buildup of forces in Indochina, including aircraft, troops, and warships. The FECB could provide an accurate assessment of the numbers involved, but not the target. The Chinese believed that the Japanese would advance from northern Indochina against the Burma Road, while GHQ felt it more likely that they would attack Thailand from southern Indochina. The Dutch feared that the Japanese might strike south, as the chiefs of staff had previously speculated, to secure the oilfields of Borneo and Sumatra.[15] Even so, the possibility of a direct move against Malaya was not ruled out. On 22 November, Brooke-Popham ordered that all vulnerable points in Malaya be secured and the Army and RAF be prepared to implement Operation Matador at seventy-two hours' notice. The northern airfields were reinforced and daily reconnaissance flights commenced, using Dutch and British aircraft (under the PLENAPS agreement). The involvement of the Dutch enabled much of the South China Sea to be covered, well beyond what Brooke-Popham's limited resources could have achieved on their own.[16] On 29 November, following reports from Saigon of an imminent landing in southern Thailand, the warning notice for Matador was reduced to twelve hours. Two days later, Brooke-Popham ordered Far East Command to be brought to enhanced readiness, including the mobilization of volunteer forces, further air patrols, and the manning of beach defenses.

As Malaya prepared for war, there was intense diplomatic effort to secure American support. Brooke-Popham had pressed the chiefs of staff several times during 1941 to establish exactly what would comprise a casus belli. The ADA conference suggested a "chalk line" (as a trigger for action), while the subsequent ADB conference sought authority to attack Japanese troop convoys approaching Malaya; both proposals were rejected.[17] As late as 24 November, the chiefs of staff insisted that they could offer no prior definition of casus belli, however, the very real possibility that Matador might be implemented focused minds in London and Washington.[18] On 5 December the chiefs of staff advised that they had been assured of American support if Japan launched an attack against British or Dutch possessions or against Thailand.[19] The United States naval attaché in Singapore, Captain John M. Creighton, repeated this wording in a telegram sent the next day to Hart, although it seems likely that the immediate source was Lieutenant-Colonel Francis Brink, the U.S. military liaison officer attached to CinC Far East's staff.[20] The president's decision had not been communicated to either Hart or MacArthur.[21] In advising Brooke-Popham of these developments, the chiefs of staff also acceded to his longstanding request to be allowed to launch Matador without reference to London. He was authorized to enter Thailand, if

- he had good information that a Japanese expedition was advancing with the apparent intention of landing on the Kra Isthmus, or
- The Japanese violated any other part of Thailand.[22]

Given the intelligence reports and the heightened alert state, it is difficult to comprehend why Phillips should have chosen this moment to fly to Manila for naval talks, even if it was with the Admiralty's encouragement (Creighton says that it was Phillips' personal choice).[23] Hart may have realized that it was a questionable decision and later made a specific point of saying he would have gone to Singapore for their meeting, if he had been given the necessary information.[24] To compound the problem, Phillips sent the *Repulse* to Darwin for a goodwill visit, and placed the *Prince of Wales* in maintenance, including the fitting of additional antiaircraft guns, while two of the accompanying destroyers went into dock for essential repairs. Boiler work on the *Prince of Wales* was scheduled to take seven days and meant that it could not be made ready for sea in under forty-eight hours.[25] Thus, at the very time that the

Japanese invasion fleet was assembling, and with Malaya at enhanced readiness, Force Z found itself without its commander-in-chief and in no position to conduct operations. Phillips' rapid departure also meant that there was only a short meeting with Brooke-Popham and no opportunity to be briefed on the local situation or to discuss joint plans.[26]

At about 2 p.m. (local) on 6 December, GHQ received information that two RAAF Hudsons flying from Kota Bahru, and at the furthest extent of their range, had spotted three large Japanese convoys. The first of these appeared to have rounded Cape Cambodia and was steering northwest into the Gulf of Siam while the other two were southeast of Cape Cambodia and steering west. They might, or might not, be following the first convoy into the Gulf of Siam. Brooke-Popham was now faced with the most important decision of his career. Less than twenty-four hours had passed since he received authority to launch Matador and, potentially, commit his country to war in the Far East. He was not by nature an impulsive man, and had invariably shown calmness in a crisis, but it was widely known that he had lost the confidence of the prime minister and the chiefs of staff. Ong goes too far in asserting that "a man cowed, humiliated and due to leave office was not one who would make such a momentous decision," but the widespread knowledge of the change, and the delay in the arrival of a successor, had without a doubt undermined his authority and induced even more caution in a naturally cautious man.[27] With Phillips in Manila, Percival away from his headquarters (meeting with Lewis Heath), and Pulford at Air Headquarters, it was left to two time-expired CinCs (Brooke-Popham and Layton), together with the recently arrived Admiral Arthur Palliser (Phillips' chief of staff), to decide whether to launch Matador. Were the sightings sufficient evidence of an intended landing on the Kra Isthmus? To confuse the issue, the Japanese did their very best to disguise their intention and headed into the Gulf of Siam before splitting into individual landing operations.[28] It has been said that Brooke-Popham was not "ready to reach out and grasp responsibility with an eager hand,"[29] but this would have required him to act, at best, on slim evidence. The Australian Official History suggests that the presence of a strong navy escort should have enabled him to deduce the destination.[30] A more impetuous and aggressive commander might have reacted differently, but London's instructions authorizing Matador had been worded in such a way that the chances of the operation succeeding were greatly reduced.[31] Brooke-Popham had no authority to order an all-out attack against the transports at sea, which anyway were well beyond the range of even his forward squadrons.[32] The chiefs of staff, given the same information, were no more prescient. "We examined the situation carefully, but from the position of the transports, it was not possible to tell whether they were going to Bangkok, to the Kra peninsula or whether they were just cruising around as a bluff."[33]

There was a further meeting late that evening at Draycot, this time with Percival, who had flown back from Kuala Lumpur. Brooke-Popham explained that he believed the convoys would very likely turn northeast and anchor at Kau Rong Bay, off the west coast of Indochina, and that "the Japanese expedition might very well be directed against Thailand, rather than Malaya and might even be only a demonstration aimed at frightening the Thais into submission."[34] Percival makes the point that Malaya Command believed that the Japanese were more likely to land in the Mersing/Endau area (on the north-east coast of Johore) and that the apparent move against Thailand could have been designed to draw off the Australian forces defending Johore. As Brooke-Popham hesitated, a further factor may have loomed large—the prospect of losing American support. If the Japanese did not land, and he attacked a neutral country on spurious grounds, where would this place the American commitment to fight alongside Britain?[35] Neither London nor Washington expected Japan to attack them simultaneously. Without the attack on Pearl Harbor, would the president really have been able to mobilize American opinion and intervene militarily on the side of the British and Dutch, particularly if Britain's commander in the Far East was seen to have precipitated the crisis?[36] Unable to determine with certainty where the convoys were headed, Brooke-Popham decided not to launch Matador.[37] Instead, he placed Far East Command at the highest state of readiness and ordered continuous reconnaissance flights to monitor the convoys.[38] Unfortunately, poor weather, and the shooting down of one of the shadowing aircraft, meant that there were no further reports until the evening of 7 December, when Japanese warships were found seventy miles off Singora. Early that morning, Brooke-Popham had received an impassioned plea from Crosby not to breach Thailand's neutrality. "For God's sake, do not allow British forces to occupy one inch of Thai territory unless and until Japan has struck the first blow at Thailand."[39] By then, however, it was too late to launch Matador. If the Eleventh Indian Division was to arrive before the Japanese landed, they needed at least twenty-four hours' warning.[40] Brooke-Popham would have had to have acted no later than midnight 6–7 December to forestall the landings that took place in the early hours of 8 December. As he explained to the official historian:

There have been many criticisms about Matador, some fully justified. But there are a few points which generally seem to be missed.
First *indecision*. It was not a question of having to decide, in the
middle of a war, whether, say, to order an attack to commence the
next morning or to postpone for a week on account of weather conditions; but of involving the British Empire, already stretched to
the utmost, in a new war, when the information available left the
Japanese intentions still uncertain. It's hard enough to make a correct
judgement of the enemy's intentions during a war; but it's still more
difficult when it's not known whether he's going to start a war or not;
nor what the atti-tude of a neutral (Siam) is going to be.[41]

He made a similar point to Russell Grenfell. "The delay in ordering Matador
was not due *mainly* to Crosby's telegrams. These certainly had some effect
but the main factor was that same policy of avoiding war with Japan."[42] On
the other hand, he had pressed London for the necessary authority: "I know
that I asked for it and don't blame the War Cabinet in the least. I ought to
have thought out more thoroughly all its possible implications; it was just
unfortunate that the event followed so quickly in the granting of my request
and before I'd had time to acclimatise myself to the new conditions. I remember General Playfair saying when I showed him the signal, 'So they've now
made you responsible for declaring war.'"[43]

The fear that he might start a war through recklessness was not imagi-
nary. The Japanese were alert to the possibility of blaming the British for their
intervention in Thailand. On 7 December 1941, the Foreign Office in Tokyo
had cabled their embassy in Bangkok with a range of statements for use in
the event of Japanese landings. If force was involved, the ambassador should
explain that for some time Britain had been massing troops on the Malayan
and Burmese borders on the pretense of defense. "Since these British troops
had attacked Thailand, the Imperial government had begun to occupy Thailand as a defensive measure."[44] Concerns about the possibility of a Japanese
trap led Brooke-Popham to complain about newspaper reports speculating
on the threat posed by the Japanese convoys (reported by Reuters), personally contacting one editor to say that he thought they had been irresponsible.[45] There were two other aspects that may have created uncertainty in
his mind, his belief that the Japanese thought "differently" than Westerners

(hence their motives were obscure and actions unpredictable) and Japan's apparent preference for acquiring territory on a step-by-step basis, rather than an "all or nothing" approach.[46] In this gigantic game of "Grandma's Footsteps," he may have assumed that the Allies would have both the time and the opportunity to respond to any Japanese intervention in Thailand, little realizing that Matador represented the last opportunity for the Allies to take the initiative in the Far East before 1943.

In Brooke-Popham's opinion, the real error he made over Matador was in thinking that the Eleventh Indian Division could be switched at an hour's notice from an offensive to a defensive role. The change created confusion and delay, as units previously poised to advance now attempted to reposition and reorganize themselves for defensive operations.[47] Percival might have alerted the CinC to these implications had they been working from the same headquarters, but a face-to-face meeting committed one or the other to a roundtrip of at least an hour and a half.[48] Poor communication between Brooke-Popham and Percival may also account for continuing uncertainty about whether Matador could still be launched. The operation was not formally cancelled until the morning of 8 December, even though it was clear from the previous evening that it was no longer practicable. To make matters worse, the confusion extended to Krohcol, the supporting operation aimed at securing the Ledge against any Japanese advance from Patani (this would have a serious impact on the subsequent efforts to hold the Japanese at the border).[49] Brooke-Popham had realized earlier in the year that the decision to collocate GHQ with the Naval Headquarters was a mistake. Proximity to the FECB and CinC China was no compensation for being unable to talk directly to his senior commanders. He was loath to move without the FECB but concerned about the disruption this might cause in splitting their resources at a critical juncture.[50] These uncertainties disappeared the moment the war started. Within a matter of days, he had moved GHQ to the army/air operations headquarters at Sime Road. This did not resolve every problem, since the "Battlebox" at Fort Canning (previously Headquarters Malaya Command) continued to receive important operational calls and signals (as well as hosting the Singapore Garrison and the Royal Navy extended defenses offices), but it was a distinct improvement over the previous arrangements and allowed Brooke-Popham to work closely with Percival and Pulford, while sparing them the daily journey to and from the naval base to attend briefings and routine meetings.[51]

The news that Japanese convoys had been spotted entering the Gulf of Siam reached Phillips in Manila on the afternoon of 6 December, just as a joint dispatch was being prepared summarizing his discussions with Hart and MacArthur. That morning, he had advised the Americans that four more battleships would be arriving at Singapore by Christmas, although he was still short of destroyers and aircraft carriers.[52] He had also announced plans for closer cooperation with the Asiatic Fleet. Cutting short the discussion, Phillips flew back to Singapore, where he arrived on the morning of 7 December. Before leaving Manila, he told Hart that, had he been at Singapore, "he would go to sea with such ships as he could collect," but this was wishful thinking—the *Repulse* would not get back until midday and the *Prince of Wales* was still under repair.[53] It was not until the evening that Phillips met with Brooke-Popham and Percival to discuss Matador and the question of how best to employ Force Z. Since Matador had never included a naval component, there were no existing plans to guide their deliberations. Shortly afterward, in response to an immediate signal from the Admiralty inquiring what action might be viable against a possible Japanese expedition in the South China Sea, Phillips advised that he intended to attack the Japanese should they attempt to land.[54] This was to be a naval, rather than a joint operation, although he looked to the RAF to provide fighter cover (while conducting its own attacks against any invasion forces). Phillips realized that he had probably lost the chance to stop the initial landings, but there remained the possibility of intercepting the convoys on their return journey or any follow-up landings. It has been said that the decision to sail north reflected his well-known habit of downplaying the threat posed by aircraft, but there is some evidence that he was aware of the dangers. Indeed, in discussion with MacArthur, he had stressed the importance of fighter cover for warships in defeating attacks by torpedo planes and bombers.[55]

Shortly after the meeting at the naval base broke up, just after midnight on 7–8 December, news was received that enemy transports had been seen off the beaches of Kota Bharu.[56] Further reports advised that the defenses had been shelled and troops were on the beaches. Pulford ordered all available aircraft at Kota Bharu to attack the landings and arranged for further attacks at first light by torpedo-carrying Vildebeestes, supported by a further five squadrons from other airfields.[57] All three Japanese transports off Kota Bharu suffered damage and one was set on fire, sinking the next day.[58] The heavy casualties suffered by the first wave forced the Japanese to temporarily withdraw their landing forces, until stronger air cover could be provided, but, despite serious losses, they had secured a strong foothold by dawn.[59] A local counterattack failed and, although Malaya Command dispatched reinforcements, continuing air and ground attacks made the airfield at Kota Bharu untenable by late afternoon. In the meantime, the daylight attacks ordered by Pulford found few targets since the landing force had now been withdrawn.[60]

Professor Arthur Marder claims that there was a further meeting early that morning involving Phillips, Brooke-Popham, Shenton Thomas, and Pulford to discuss the proposed operation by Force Z. There is no record of this in Brooke-Popham's papers, Shenton Thomas's diary, or Layton's confidential report.[61] It is not referred to in the Official History.[62] The list of participants is improbable, if not impossible, and the reported discussion, including cameo parts by Brooke-Popham and Thomas, is less than convincing.[63] There are no supporting documents in the public archives and only one witness (Captain James McClelland), who did not come forward until 1979.[64] There are several reasons to believe that this second meeting is an invention, created for the purpose of linking Phillips' decision to attack the Japanese to an impassioned plea by Brooke-Popham for the Navy to save the day. It is disconcerting how this unsubstantiated (but colorful) story based on a single individual's recollection of distant events has gained traction and been repeated by successive authors—even when they have expressed reservations about its credibility.[65] The risks of relying on such evidence was highlighted by Brooke-Popham in a series of letters to the Air Ministry during a long-running discussion about the Malayan commanders' dispatches. He was mistrustful of people's memories without corroborative evidence. "I feel strongly that further effort should be made to obtain documentary evidence and that where statements are only conjecture that the fact should be stated."[66]

Any doubts about Japanese intentions were dispelled by a bombing raid on Singapore at 4:00 a.m. that morning. The incoming aircraft were detected by RAF radar at more than one hundred miles, but no air raid warning was issued, as the civil air raid precaution headquarters was unmanned. Surprisingly little physical damage was caused, given the absence of defending night fighters and ineffectual antiaircraft fire, although there were more than two hundred civilian casualties.[67] At 6:30 a.m., Brooke-Popham issued an order of the day, drawn up with Layton in May 1941, and written in multiple languages. As a "call to arms," the wording was flowery and self-congratulatory, including lines such as, "We are ready. We have had plenty of warning and our preparations are made and tested." It is routinely referenced to demonstrate that the High Command was grievously out of touch with actual events and was guilty of deliberate falsehoods, although the contemporary view was more mixed.[68] Brooke-Popham, who agreed that the tone was bombastic, insisted it had helped to encourage the Indian troops forming the bulk of the ground forces and to rally the civil population. Ian Morrison felt that such pronouncements were foolish, unless the speaker had something to say, and "afterwards they tend to react on reputations."[69] Efforts to reassure the population were not improved by several inaccurate, misleading, or wildly optimistic communiqués issued by GHQ. These included news that the Japanese had been repulsed at Kota Bharu and the announcement of a (nonexistent) landing at Kuantan.[70] The confusion reflected GHQ's own uncertainties, rather than a conscious effort at misinformation, but deliberate omissions (such as any reference to the evacuation of Penang) and curious phrasing (rather than "retreat," British forces had "successfully disengaged the enemy") disturbed correspondents and bewildered civilians. Communicating bad news in wartime, without exacerbating the damage to public morale, is a difficult task but it was managed particularly badly in Singapore.[71] Responsibility must rest with Brooke-Popham, although, as we have seen, he had little control over the fragmented propaganda organization. The work of compiling the daily communiqués soon proved too much for GHQ's small staff and passed to the army/air headquarters, under Brigadier Kenneth Torrance (Percival's chief of staff).[72]

The Japanese landings in Thailand, at Singora and Patani, had been mostly unopposed, and the leading formations advanced rapidly toward the frontier, supported by aircraft operating from Indochina (and soon from bases in Thailand itself). Their initial targets were the RAF airfields in northern Malaya, which were continuously attacked from dawn on 8 December, often by large formations. The intensity of these raids grew as more airfields (including Singora) were occupied. Counterattacks were carried out, but heavy opposition and a lack of fighter cover resulted in severe losses. By the evening, only fifty aircraft remained out of the 110 that had been available that morning.[73] By 10 December, Pulford decided to evacuate all the RAF airfields in the north (including Alor Star, Sungei Patani, and Butterworth). In less than forty-eight hours, the RAF had lost the battle for air superiority. The decision to abandon the airfields in northern Malaya was sensible, in view of the losses being suffered, but it was not well executed and there were several incidents of poor discipline, causing Brooke-Popham to write to Pulford expressing his displeasure.[74] As disappointing as this was, it is worth considering what might have been achieved if the RAF front line had been closer to the 336 aircraft promised by the chiefs of staff or (ideally) the 566 requested by the local commanders.[75] The northern airfields could have been the springboard for inflicting serious damage on the invading forces, when they were most vulnerable.

Shortly after midday on 8 December, Phillips called a staff meeting on the *Prince of Wales* to discuss his plan to attack Singora and Kota Bharu at dawn on 10 December.[76] No member of GHQ or the Air Headquarters attended, but Brooke-Popham had put Phillips in direct contact with Pulford to discuss possible air support, including the need for reconnaissance and fighter cover. Shortly after Force Z left Singapore that evening, Pulford advised that he could not provide fighter cover over Singora because of the deteriorating situation (and imminent withdrawal from the northern airfields). It is claimed that Darvall visited Phillips before his departure to explain the position, although there is no record of this meeting.[77] However, Phillips had already been informed by Brooke-Popham about the large Japanese navy bomber force in southern Indochina and was aware of the risk he faced.[78] There has been speculation that the two argued about the provision of air cover at some point that afternoon. It is also claimed that Spooner challenged Pulford, while they were stranded on Chibia Island (in their joint attempt to escape Singapore), about an informal prewar agreement that fighters would be deployed north to protect capital ships operating along the coast.[79] There is no evidence for either suggestion, just as there is no basis for the allegation that Shenton Thomas demanded the RAF's fighters be held back to defend Singapore.[80] Phillips, with or without air cover, hoped that surprise and poor weather would provide adequate protection against an enemy attack. There is no need to invent RAF "promises" or government interference to explain his actions. In the event, Force Z was spotted less than a day after sailing by a Japanese submarine, although it was only when aircraft were seen on the evening of 9 December that Phillips realized he had no alternative but to abandon the operation. The return journey was slowed by his decision to investigate the false report of Japanese landings at Kuantan. On the morning of 10 December, when Force Z was some two hundred miles northeast of Singapore, the Japanese launched a series of intensive bombing and torpedo attacks, focusing on the two battleships. Although several of the attackers were shot down, both the *Prince of Wales* and the *Repulse* had been sunk by

1:20 p.m., with the loss of nearly nine hundred lives, including Phillips. It was only after the air attacks had commenced that fighters from Singapore were alerted. They arrived to find the accompanying destroyers picking up survivors from both warships. When news of the sinking was received, Brooke-Popham was in the Battlebox at Fort Canning, together with Captain George Mulock, a World War I Navy veteran and noted polar explorer, who was responsible for the area defense of the naval base. According to Mulock's secretary, Paymaster Lieutenant David Copley, Brooke-Popham said nothing, but buried his head in his hands.[81]

The sinking of the *Prince of Wales* and *Repulse* remains one of the Royal Navy's greatest disasters. It had a devastating effect on morale in Singapore, cast doubt over the Allies' ability to resist the Japanese, and damaged British prestige throughout the Far East.[82] It had a direct and far-reaching effect on the course of the campaign. Brooke-Popham's shock ran deeper than an immediate concern for the loss of life. "Englishmen have had no experience of what it means to lose command of the sea since 1667. In Malaya, therefore, it was very hard for us all to bear constantly in mind the full implications of that loss," adding that "I don't recall any peace exercise in which Great Britain started with losing command of the sea."[83] The circumstances have been subject to considerable analysis and blame has been attributed widely. Phillips invariably features for his decision to fight a greatly superior force in the absence of air cover, although capital ships were not necessarily easy prey for bombers or torpedo-carrying aircraft.[84] Only two months later, three German battleships, *Gniesenau*, *Prince Eugen*, and *Scharnhorst*, safely negotiated the Channel (the "Channel Dash") despite a vigorous response from British air and naval forces.[85] The presence of several reporters on the *Repulse* (including Cecil Brown) suggests a general confidence that Force Z would return safely.[86]

The failure of Matador and the destruction of Force Z have come to epitomize British military incompetence—the implication being that Brooke-Popham should have been more impulsive and Phillips less so. Brooke-Popham made no criticism of Phillips' decision to venture north, other than to question whether it should have been conducted as a combined operation, rather than Navy with RAF cooperation.[87] Communications between the Navy and RAF should, and could, have been better, but it was not for Brooke-Popham to endorse or oppose Phillips' plan, even if he had concerns. "I have a clear recollection of Sir Geoffrey Layton speaking to me, I think on 8 December, and although he does not mention it, expressing great anxiety over the decision to move these ships towards the Gulf of Siam owing to the danger of air attack."[88] He rejected the claim that there was "an undoubted lack of liaison between sea and air forces," but the opportunity to place an RAF officer in the Naval Base Operations Room had been turned down by Pulford when it was first suggested in July 1941.[89] Three days after the loss of the *Prince of Wales* and *Repulse*, naval liaison officers were appointed to the army/air operations room at Sime Road. Even so, there were too few air staff to cope with the workload, including naval cooperation.[90]

The loss of air superiority in Malaya was not simply due to the overwhelming strength of the enemy. The Japanese conducted a comprehensive campaign to eliminate British airpower as quickly as possible; indeed, the landing at Kota Bharu had this sole aim in mind.[91] For the first few days, the Japanese Army Air Force provided little direct support for ground operations, all their efforts were focused on destroying the RAF's aircraft, in the air and on the ground, through "aerial exterminating action."[92] To support this strategy, aviation ground units were included in the initial landings at Singora, tasked with making captured airfields operational as quickly as possible. Inexperience and a degree of overconfidence undoubtedly played their part in facilitating Japanese success, but the lack of an integrated defense system meant that the RAF's airfields could be attacked with little or no warning, catching aircraft in the open or being bombed up. These problems were compounded by inadequate numbers of antiaircraft guns and the difficulties experienced in directing airborne fighters. The radios installed in the Buffalo were unreliable and of limited range. More powerful VHF sets were due to be fitted, but not before 1942.[93] As a result, the Buffalo squadrons were often out of communication once they took off.[94] Conversely, the RAF's counter-air efforts achieved very little. Unescorted bombing raids on Japanese airfields suffered severe losses. Unable to guide their air defense fighters to achieve combat on favorable terms, or to strike against the enemy's bombers, the RAF was constantly on the back foot, with rapidly tiring pilots, faltering leadership, and a diminishing number of serviceable aircraft.[95] The RAF's failure and the destruction of Force Z led to considerable public criticism.[96] The Channel Dash and events in Burma and North Africa encouraged accusations that the RAF had shown a lack of courage, as well as a lack of cooperation, and that military aviation should once again be subordinated to land and sea commanders. Trenchard wrote to Churchill about what he saw as a deliberate campaign on the part of the popular press and some speakers in Parliament.[97] A small number of postwar writers have repeated these arguments, asserting that the RAF (notably Brooke-Popham and Pulford) abandoned Phillips to his fate or were, at the very least, weak and indecisive.[98] More recently, Brooke-Popham has been criticized for the way he employed airpower in the campaign, particularly the evacuation of the northern airfields, although, given the shortfall in aircraft and inadequate airfield defenses, he had little choice in the matter.[99]

The campaign on the ground started as badly as that in the air. With the decision not to implement Matador, it was vital that Eleventh Indian Division move quickly to the preplanned defensive positions at Jitra and the Ledge. Brooke-Popham knew that the Japanese had landed at Kota Bharu, but his orders did not allow him to launch Krohcol unless there were also landings in Thailand.[100] He had already highlighted this anomaly in a signal to the chiefs of staff, but their permission to launch Matador, if only Malaya was attacked, was received on the morning of 8 December, shortly before an aerial reconnaissance confirmed that the Japanese had indeed landed at Singora and Patani.[101] The official historian expresses surprise that Brooke-Popham had not immediately ordered the occupation of the Ledge, speculating that he may not have fully appreciated how quickly the Japanese would move.[102] However, once he did have confirmation, Brooke-Popham instructed Malaya Command to launch Krohcol and occupy the Jitra position. Unfortunately, Percival was away from his headquarters, attending a meeting of the Legislature Council. It is not obvious why this meeting was so important that it demanded GOC Malaya's absence during the first hours of the invasion but, as a result, it was not until 11:30 a.m. that III Corps was ordered to move.[103] Even then, there was a further delay of two hours until Heath confirmed his orders personally with Percival. When the advance finally began at 3:00 p.m., there were immediate problems in forcing a way through the local Thai constabulary. By morning, they were within five miles of the Ledge before they encountered Japanese troops, supported by light tanks. Krohcol fought to hold its position, but repeated attacks forced the column to retire at dawn on 12 December. Brooke-Popham's hesitation about moving into Thailand was understandable, but regrettable. Equally disappointing was the delay and confusion within Malaya Command. However, the resistance faced by Krohcol (taking eighteen hours to cover some twenty-five miles) does suggest that Brooke-Popham was justified in not launching Matador.[104] With almost twice as much ground to cover, it seems highly unlikely that Eleventh Indian

Division could have reached Singora in the allotted twenty-four hours.[105] When Grenfell asked directly why he did not give the word to go until about twelve hours after the Japanese attack had begun, Brooke-Popham replied that "orders to start Matador were never given," suggesting that he saw Krohcol as subordinate to Matador, rather than a major operation in its own right.[106] Reflecting on the delay and confusion in Malaya Command, Compton Mackenzie commented that it was "difficult to discover a good reason why Heath was not told sooner to occupy the Jitra position and impossible to discover a good reason for waiting to authorise Krohcol."[107]

23

THE FALL OF SINGAPORE
1941–1942

With Matador cancelled, the Eleventh Indian Division attempted to halt the Japanese advancing south from Singora. The position at Jitra was unfinished (it was not scheduled to be completed until February 1942) and waterlogged, although it should still have provided a serious obstacle, but little further work had been carried out while Murray-Lyon waited for the decision to launch Matador.[1] First contact was made on the morning of 10 December. In just thirty-six hours, the Japanese advance guard of two battalions supported by a company of tanks defeated the Eleventh Indian Division and forced it to retire after inflicting heavy losses. Major Angus Rose, a staff officer in the Joint Operations Room, regarded the Jitra position as tactically unsound but, even though the width of the position could only be secured at the disregard of depth, still felt that the Japanese should have been held for days, if not weeks.[2] The loss of the only good defensive position to the north of Kroh had serious implications for the entire defense of northern Malaya, forcing a succession of retreats and half-hearted stands that repeatedly dissolved when outflanked. Within a matter of days, the RAF lost its remaining airfields in the north. To add insult to injury, the same airfields were soon in use by the Japanese, despite frantic efforts to disable the runways and destroy stores. Even without this reverse, only limited RAF assistance would have been available to the Eleventh Indian Division. As Pulford had prophesied just three months earlier, "long stretches of beach cannot be strongly defended everywhere and fighting inland is therefore certain to occur. In these conditions our troops might expect to receive little support from the air."[3]

The same day as Force Z was lost, Churchill had appointed Duff Cooper "Resident Cabinet Minister at Singapore for Far Eastern Affairs" and authorized the creation of a war council under his chairmanship. This met daily at Sime Road, but fared little better than the war committee it replaced. There was immediate uncertainty about whether the council had executive power and differing views about its function.[4] Duff Cooper felt that Brooke-Popham was unhelpful, "his failing powers render him jealous of any encroachment on his sphere of influence," accusing him at the first meeting of being "the worst example of the old school tie."[5] Duff Cooper's criticisms, contained in a personal letter to Churchill, have been described as "a fine example of easy literary style applied to character assassination."[6] From Brooke-Popham's perspective there was little that Duff Cooper could offer that had not already been considered by the chiefs of staff.[7] Matters were not helped when the War Office asked Brooke-Popham to comment on Duff Cooper's criticism of Percival, sent directly to the prime minister (without Brooke-Popham's knowledge).[8] Shenton Thomas resented Duff Cooper's interference and blamed him for the botched evacuation of Penang, while Percival believed Duff Cooper had allowed himself to be influenced "by certain persons who were, and for years had been, critical of the Government. The result was confusion."[9] With hindsight, much of the staff effort expended during December seems particularly pointless. The frequent meetings and discussions contributed little to strengthening Malaya's defenses; the air and land reinforcements that were scraped together and rushed to Singapore did little more. Connell highlights the fruitless exchanges between the Far East and London. "It was characteristic of the nightmarish quality of the period that a great deal of bureaucratic thought and the most important grades of signaling equipment and ciphering skill were employed in the second week of the campaign in a scrupulous, yet utterly indecisive series of telegrams."[10] As the military situation deteriorated, Duff Cooper hosted an Allied conference to make recommendations for common action. The meeting sought immediate reinforcements, including eight squadrons and a further division as well as antiaircraft guns and tanks.[11] Penang "Fortress" had been evacuated two days earlier and the RAF was in a poor state. Just eighteen Buffalo fighters remained at Ipoh, the remaining squadrons (comprising ninety-four aircraft) were concentrated on Singapore Island to protect the port and dockyard.[12] In the next week, the Japanese landed in Borneo (in this instance, the planned demolitions had been successfully completed) while continuing their advance in Malaya, reaching Ipoh (captured on

26 December) and closing in on Kuantan and its important airfield. Although Allied reinforcements were now arriving, there was little hope that the enemy could be halted, in the absence of air superiority and without critical equipment such as tanks, antitank guns, and artillery.

The news was equally bleak elsewhere. The Japanese had moved against Hong Kong at the same time as their attack on Malaya. They greatly outnumbered the defending forces (notwithstanding the two recently arrived Canadian battalions) and soon forced the evacuation of the mainland. Without further reinforcements, and in the absence of air or naval support, there was little that could be done to avert defeat. Two weeks later, on 25 December 1941, the garrison surrendered. The Japanese had suffered more than 6,000 casualties against Allied losses of some 4,500, with 11,000 made captive. Under the circumstances, the defenders of Hong Kong had extracted a high price. The Japanese planned to attack Burma, but only once they had made good progress in Malaya. Nevertheless, the importance of the staging post at Victoria Point meant that a small force crossed the Kra Isthmus to seize the airfield on 14 December—effectively cutting the air route from India and forcing all reinforcements to be brought in by sea. Two days earlier, on 12 December 1941, responsibility for the defense of Burma had transferred to Wavell, on the personal authority of Churchill. The main Japanese attack against Burma did not begin until 15 January 1942, but Wavell had already decided to replace McLeod by someone with "real organisational ability." After consultation with Dorman-Smith, Thomas Hutton (Wavell's chief of staff in India) was appointed in McLeod's place, and arrived in Rangoon on 27 December.[13] He immediately assumed command, leaving McLeod to pack up his house and return to England.[14] McLeod believed that this was the correct decision, given that he had lost the governor's confidence, but still felt that neither Dorman-Smith nor Wavell understood the problems he had faced. It is difficult to avoid the impression that McLeod's replacement was a case of moving the military deckchairs on a sinking ship. When the Japanese continued to make progress in Burma, Wavell decided on 17–18 February 1942 to replace Hutton with Alexander, to provide "the required drive and inspiration" to stimulate the troops, but not before he had publicly berated him.[15] There is a certain irony in Wavell's determination to sack two otherwise competent generals in a manner that echoed his own treatment by Churchill.

Brooke-Popham struggled during the three weeks that followed the outbreak of war. The relentless Japanese advance, and depressing news from Hong

Kong, weighed heavily on his shoulders. There was mounting public criticism of the authorities, exacerbated by the events at Penang and failures in the scorched-earth policy. His surviving notebooks and letters say little, but he was under immense strain.[16] One of the CinC's bodyguards recalled that "he was a very quiet type of person. A very studious man. We didn't actually speak to him apart from when it was necessary to allow people to see him. He was a man who was very confused and a person who was obviously in great difficulties."[17] There is no evidence that Brooke-Popham was on the verge of a nervous collapse, as Duff Cooper claimed (his comments were far from disinterested), but the pressure was beginning to tell.[18] A meeting with civic leaders and the press, held at the Legislative Council on 22 December, did not go well and was widely regarded as a failure.[19] "Sir Robert stood up before the group and spoke in an abashed, unconfident, uninspiring way."[20] He attempted to explain the reasons for the Japanese advance and to instill confidence in Malaya's defenses, but struggled with hecklers and questions that he could not answer on the grounds of security. It was a thankless task and, as Duff Cooper and Shenton Thomas had already attempted to answer these issues over the radio without success, it might have been better not to have called the meeting at all.[21] This was a difficult period for everyone on the War Council. None of its members emerge with much credit. According to Vivian Bowden, Brooke-Popham showed "an extraordinary diffidence of manner for a man in his position" and was "definitely too old for such a post in wartime." He was hardly more positive about Percival ("able but not a particularly strong personality") and Pulford ("very worried, but greatly overworked"). Duff Cooper could not give the War Council the leadership it required ("not a dominant personality") while Shenton Thomas was "more ready to produce reasons for not doing things than for doing them."[22] For his part, Duff Cooper thought that Bowden was of no account.[23] If relations with Shenton Thomas were not already bad, Duff Cooper complained directly to Lord Moyne (secretary of state for the colonies) that the Malayan government "had failed lamentably in making adequate preparations for war." He attempted to have Shenton Thomas replaced but, frustrated in this aim, secured the dismissal of Stanley Jones, the colonial secretary (whom he heartily disliked).[24] The governor appealed, claiming that Moyne and the prime minister had been misled and that Jones was "widely respected for his honesty of purpose and ability."[25] Moyne (who had doubts about much of Duff Cooper's detailed criticism) turned to Wavell, who advised that Shenton Thomas must stay, but that Jones should be replaced. Duff Cooper's subsequent decision, agreed by the War Council in Shenton Thomas's absence, to appoint Brigadier Ivan Simson (chief engineer, Malaya Command) to oversee civil defense may have been justified, but it had the added benefit (from Duff Cooper's perspective) of further weakening Shenton Thomas and isolating Percival, over whom he felt the governor had an excessive influence.[26] There is evidence that Duff Cooper regularly briefed against the Malayan government (Shenton Thomas gives several examples where the *Straits Times* was privy to inside information).[27] One observer has suggested that Duff Cooper argued with Brooke-Popham (and took a dislike to others in authority at the War Council) because he found it irksome and frustrating to be sitting round with no special powers to do anything.[28] It is little wonder that the atmosphere in the High Command has been described as "Wagnerian without grandeur."[29]

Pownall reached Singapore on 23 December and four days later took over command in the Far East. Brooke-Popham had allowed Pulford and Percival to get on with fighting the war and restricted his direct involvement to matters of coordination and cooperation, while focusing on the wider aspects of the campaign, including the provision of reinforcements and interaction with the Allies (notably the Dutch).[30] Pownall's arrival had little impact on these arrangements or the subsequent conduct of the campaign. Had he reached Singapore earlier, events would not necessarily have taken a different course. Implementation of Matador could have slowed the Japanese (although it might easily have had the opposite effect by spreading weak forces over a larger area) but would not have stopped their advance given the relative quality of the opposing forces.[31] Matador has been described as "an irresponsible fantasy" that endeavored to fit the military situation to the plan. In the absence of adequate warning or suitable forces there was little hope that it would succeed.[32] However, abandoning Matador, and focusing on improving Malaya's physical defenses, would have conceded the initiative to the Japanese who, no doubt, would have adjusted their plans accordingly. Moreover, there were very few fixed sites in the north that could be defended without the possibility of the flanks being turned.[33] Within a few days of his arrival, Brooke-Popham had advised Ismay that the jungle was not impenetrable and "it was dangerous to rest one's flank on it thinking that nothing will get through."[34] The strongest defensive line lay across Johore, from Malacca to Mersing, but would mean abandoning the north and middle of the country, including Penang and Kuala Lumpur. This would have been politically difficult, if not impossible. The casualties suffered by the Japanese during the landings at Kota Bharu (their heaviest losses in the entire campaign) suggest that Brooke-Popham's forward strategy was valid, if more forces had been available.[35] On the other hand, Slessor's statement that "many of us who knew him [Brooke-Popham] best were disappointed and angry when he was relieved as Supreme Commander Far East shortly after the Japanese declaration of war and felt that the sad history of Singapore might have been different but for that unhappy decision,"[36] must be taken with a large pinch of salt. Only more aircraft, tanks, antiaircraft guns, and trained troops would have made a difference in the face of a formidable enemy, well equipped and brilliantly led. The official historian, having detailed in nearly five hundred pages the events leading to the fall of Singapore, concluded that the commanders entrusted with its defense had an impossible task and "the Naval Base at the western gateway to the Pacific, the keystone of British strategy in the Far East, was doomed before the war started."[37] Pownall, confronted by the greatest professional challenge of his or any general's career (taking command of an army in retreat) was not critical of his predecessor. "He has done a lot of admirable work here and the newspaper criticisms of him in the local rags are most unfair. With the resources at his disposal he could have done no more."[38]

As it turned out, Pownall had little chance to make a difference. Within a matter of days, Far East Command had been dissolved and he was appointed chief staff officer to Wavell, who became supreme commander ABDACOM, responsible for all Allied land, air, and sea forces in the southwest Pacific.[39] With the military situation in Malaya continuing to weaken, Wavell moved his new headquarters to Java, but by 22 February it was clear that ABDACOM was no longer viable and it was dissolved. Hong Kong, Malaya, Singapore, and Thailand had fallen to the enemy. Borneo, Burma, Java, Sumatra, and the Philippines would soon follow. Faced by a catastrophe of immense proportions, it became popular to blame Japanese success on a lack of an "offensive spirit" by the defending forces, who were victim to a "retreat mentality." Linked to this was the chimera of the "fighting general," the charismatic, aggressive field commander, embodying the nation's martial spirit, who would transform Britain's battlefield performance. Brooke-Popham's age, rhetorical skills, and character ill-suited him to this role, but the repeated changes in senior military leadership generated little obvious improvement—only time and effort could achieve the necessary changes in training, tactics, equipment, and logistics needed to defeat an enemy imbued with high morale, exemplary discipline, remorseless efficiency, and a relentless determination to maintain the offensive.[40] In some ways, the detailed and interminable analysis of the British defeat has served to obscure the outstanding quality of the Japanese army and its ability to maintain a consistently high operational tempo. Time and again, the speed and vigor of the Japanese advance caught the defenders by surprise.[41] By acting faster than GHQ's decision cycle, Yamashita's "driving charge" forced Brooke-Popham and Percival into a reactive mode that lost them the initiative and sapped morale.[42] None of this was accidental. From the moment that the first convoys sailed from Hainan, the Japanese had set out to confuse and distract, while moving quickly to blunt any countermove into Thailand and eliminate the striking power of the Air Force and Navy. This outcome was undoubtedly helped by the fragmented and overlapping responsibilities, multiple headquarters, and significant capability gaps that characterized Far East Command but, without the persistent pressure exerted by the Japanese army and air services, these weaknesses could possibly have been resolved, or at least their effects ameliorated.

The Japanese victory at Singapore was a defeat for Brooke-Popham. He never viewed it as anything other than his failure. It has been suggested that he tried to avoid blame, yet his official dispatch and extensive correspondence reveals a man willing to admit what he had got wrong and identify the lessons learned. While his tenure as CinC Far East ended badly, he had achieved a great deal in the previous twelve months. Churchill's congratulations and the offer of a baronetcy were well deserved, even if intended to sweeten a bitter pill. He had created an effective alliance across the Far East, where previously there had been only separate interests. Admittedly, Japanese actions helped focus minds on the need for collaboration, but it was his achievement all the same.[43] He had equal success in improving defense cooperation within Malaya, notably between the Air Force and Army. More could have been done, but only if Whitehall had been willing to give him authority over the Navy and the civil government. His assessment of Malaya's defense needs was sound, as was the disposition of the limited forces available to meet an attack.[44] The efforts to sustain China, and the support provided to the AVG, showed both strategic judgment and pragmatism.[45] Confident that the Japanese would strike in the north, he nevertheless accepted intelligence showing that they planned a southern advance and brought Malaya to the highest alert state in the days before the onslaught. It is difficult to see what more he might have done in the weeks prior to the outbreak of war. To paraphrase his much-maligned order of the day, "Malaya was ready." There was no Pearl Harbor or Clark Field at Singapore.

On the debit side, Brooke-Popham grievously underestimated the Japanese. This colored his public comments and certainly influenced his decision-making, although GHQ was not alone in believing that the Allies were militarily superior.[46] His media efforts were, at best, mediocre, and damaged his personal reputation more than they deterred the Japanese. He readily admitted deficiencies in this respect, noting that he was not comfortable with interviews and would have benefitted from professional support. The lack of a communications strategy, coherent plan or single authority to oversee a fragmented propaganda organization guaranteed failure. As much as Matador was a bold and forward-thinking plan that offered the prospect of inflicting heavy casualties on an invasion force, it was naïve to assume that the Japanese would signal their intentions in sufficient time to allow it to be implemented.[47] He had not properly thought through what was involved nor appreciated how little time there was to exercise a decision. More damaging, however, was the delay in ordering Krohcol. As Compton Mackenzie observed, Brooke-Popham showed "a caution that even the Foreign Office might have found excessive."[48] It was here that the Japanese demonstrated their superior decision-making and ability to operate at a higher tempo than GHQ. Thereafter, neither Brooke-Popham nor Percival could regain the initiative. However, even if they had made no mistakes, there was ultimately nothing they could have done to save the naval base and island.[49]

The strongest criticism of Brooke-Popham's performance has come from Australia. Within a week of the landings there were vehement attacks in the press, driven by allegations that the commanders in Malaya had lied about the strength of the defenses. Some of this anger was aimed at the heavy-handed censorship that had constrained reporting since the start of the war.[50] An editorial in the *Sydney Daily Telegraph* ("We Can Put Better Men at the Top") castigated Brooke-Popham and accused Bennett, Burnett, Duff Cooper, Layton, Percival, and Sturdee of making grossly overconfident statements.[51] The mood worsened following allegations of British betrayal (stemming from a letter written by Curtin to Churchill about the possible evacuation of Singapore).[52] The idea that Australian needs were arbitrarily disregarded by Churchill, and Australian lives (some 18,000 casualties) needlessly sacrificed to British interests, gained popularity after the war, fed by a widespread belief that the invasion of Australia had only narrowly been averted.[53] In this resentful and sometimes bitter narrative, Brooke-Popham is depicted as both incompetent and an enthusiastic cheerleader for Churchill's deceitful efforts to keep Australian forces in the Middle East. There are dissenting views, offering a more balanced account of the campaign in Malaya, that point to the absence of any Japanese plans to move against Australia, but they have struggled to demolish a myth that has deep political and cultural roots.[54] In 1992, Paul Keeting, the Australian prime minister, felt moved to highlight Britain's betrayal over Singapore as the reason for his country to forge its own place in the world.[55] By contrast, there has been little direct criticism in India, notwithstanding the considerably higher number of Indian Army casualties (more than 67,000) and the very real threat of invasion that followed the fall of Burma.[56]

Robert and Opal Brooke-Popham sailed from Singapore on New Year's Day 1942, bound for South Africa, via Tanjong Priok (Batavia).[57] Not all the local press was hostile. "Already some English and Australian newspapers have demanded that his head should be delivered on a charger, on the contrary, Malaya owes a great deal to Sir Robert Brooke-Popham."[58] Pownall was also sorry to see him leave: "It is, of course, time that Brooke-Popham left; he is pretty tired and is quite out of business from dinnertime onwards. However, both he and Lady Brooke-Popham are very kind and bear no malice at being replaced. He himself wants to stay on here in some capacity. Because he doesn't want to look as if he had cleared out just when the war started."[59] Also on board was Lady Layton and numerous service wives and families, including Brooke-Popham's sister-in-law, Joan Hugonin (with daughter) and his nephew Fred's wife Philippa Pooley (with their son). Lieutenant Colonel Francis Hugonin, commanding 3rd Heavy Anti-Aircraft Battery, remained in Singapore where he became a prisoner of war (POW).[60] Fred Pooley, one of the many Straits Volunteers, also remained behind and was captured. Although the Japanese conquest of Malaya was not yet assured, none of the passengers could have left in an optimistic mood; indeed, Singapore would fall before any of them reached the UK. Foster Cox, who stayed on in Singapore to work for Pownall, wrote a private letter to his "Master:" "I don't know why the British find it as hard to tell someone to his face they think he is wonderful as they do to administer a rebuke. In my case, it is lack of moral courage, hence a letter rather than a spoken word."[61] Cox was not the only member of the

GHQ staff to record their admiration for Brooke-Popham. Darvall, Dewing, and Grey all expressed similar sentiments. Major Ian Graham, who described himself as one of Brooke-Popham's "much maligned staff in Malaya" and was later captured by the Japanese (spending the remainder of the war as a POW), was always at pains to uphold Brooke-Popham's work while CinC.[62] Other members of the headquarters were equally supportive:

> A stout defense of Air Chief Marshal Sir Robert Brooke-Popham, formerly British Commander-in-Chief in the Far East, and his work in Singapore, is maintained by a West Australian girl who was his secretary for some months, and who recently returned to Australia after many adventures. "Contrary to a lot of criticism I have heard about Sir Robert," Miss Hetherington said, "I know that he was a very hard-working man. His time was short for all that had to be done, but he worked incessantly. He had good cooperation from his staff and they all worked well together."[63]

Even after the disasters in the north, RAF personnel never wavered in their confidence and respect for Brooke-Popham, while a Far East prisoner of war (FEPOW) insisted that Brooke-Popham had done his best and did not deserve to be the center of controversy: "I can recall his slender figure atop of a control tower at a Singapore air base watching the first Bristol Beauforts fly in from Australia. Nobody ever seems to have told the story of the improvising and fruitless experiments which were made to stave off disaster, but it might well be that when the whole sorry chapter is written then the ill-timed criticism will be silenced."[64] Brooke-Popham's final Singapore notebook is full of details about the passengers, their personal circumstances and future needs. Landing at Durban, he arranged to see Smuts and used the opportunity to update himself on progress with the flying training scheme. By now, Churchill had recalled Duff Cooper to London. The prospective capture of a member of the British Cabinet may have weighed in the decision, but Shenton Thomas, who remained in Singapore and spent three years as a POW, was delighted to see the back of Duff Cooper. "A rotten judge of men, arrogant, obstinate, vain; how he could have crept into Office is beyond me."[65] The Duff Coopers reached London on 16 February 1942 and his report (as resident Cabinet minister) was published just three days later.[66] It contained few insights or criticisms and largely comprised a record of his four weeks as chairman of the War Council. The speed of the report did nothing to save Duff Cooper from being linked with events in Singapore, even though he was careful to point out that "it was primarily a naval and military disaster and I had had no connection whatever with naval or military affairs."[67] He did, however, circulate a private "diary" that provided a more intimate record of the struggles he had faced, levelling blame at both Brooke-Popham and Shenton Thomas.[68]

The Brooke-Pophams left Durban bound for Liverpool on 23 January 1942, but engine delays at Cape Town meant that they did not reach England (via Freetown) until 25 February, ten days after Singapore had fallen.[69] Unlike her husband, Opal was willing to give an interview to the waiting press, in which she criticized the "deadly inertia" she had found in the colony. "I suppose long years of that climate, with luxury living in a land where everything was done for them by native boys galore, was largely responsible. Most of them never had to lift a hand for themselves." She robustly defended her husband, who "did all he could, but it was like making bricks with straw. He had to help everywhere—with nothing to do it with."[70]

24

THE VERDICT OF HISTORY
1942–1953

Brooke-Popham's first week back in England was taken up by a series of meetings. Lunch with Alan Brooke and "Pug" Ismay on 3 March was followed by an audience with the king. He also met with Portal and agreed to provide an immediate report on lessons learned from the Malayan campaign. Other than Opal's unscripted comments about the behavior of the civilian population in Singapore, widely reported at home and abroad, there were no statements to the press and no interviews. This purdah, both official and self-imposed, would prove lifelong. He sought an interview with Churchill, but the prime minister declined: "I see no reason at present. His wife has told us all about it."[1] Three days after his arrival at Liverpool, Brooke-Popham had been notified by the Air Ministry that, as there was no further appointment available appropriate to his rank, he would revert to the retired list with effect from 31 March 1942.[2] Although this was normal procedure, rather than a sign of official displeasure, it provided little time to prepare the report requested by CAS, let alone write his official dispatch as CinC Far East. The Air Ministry was sympathetic, and his retirement date was deferred until 15 May 1942.[3]

In his first few months at home, Brooke-Popham faced continuing public criticism. This had emerged initially in Australia (the Packer-owned *Sydney Telegraph* and *Mirror* were particularly hostile) and was then picked up by the mainstream British newspapers.[4] Only the *Economist* criticized the "shameful treatment" of Sir Robert Brooke-Popham, "who has been allowed to slip into the role of scapegoat because nobody in London had the moral courage to reveal that he had been protesting for months to the inadequacy of the

forces that were sent to him."[5] The endemic hostility meant that the baronetcy, offered by Churchill in November, was held back from the New Year's
Honours List—in case the announcement attracted further press criticism or
exacerbated Australian sensitivities.[6] Efforts were made during the first few
months of 1942 to get the prime minister to make a decision on the matter,
but without success.[7] Although Trenchard and others had defended Brooke-
Popham's actions in Parliament, it was a difficult time and led to some (rare)
cross words between husband and wife. The occasion was Polly's suicide and
Opal's comment that the events at Singapore had added to his sister's depression: "I suppose my nerves were a bit on edge when you said that Polly had
been worrying about me and Singapore more than anything else, it made me
feel in some way responsible for her death."[8] Opal was also feeling the strain.
Neither the quiet solitude of Cottisford (notwithstanding the war babies) nor
the opportunity to see their own children overcame her sense of despair and
physical tiredness.[9] The couple suffered from a range of ailments over the next
six months, including boils and insomnia, while Opal spent several weeks in
hospital because of a stomach ulcer and associated problems. Her husband's
dignified silence in the face of public attacks did little to help her peace of
mind: "Everything seems to have got on my nerves and I know really that I've
bottled up for weeks and weeks the awful gnawing pain in my heart for the
way you have been treated, never being able to speak to anyone about it."[10]

There was still no news of those left behind in Singapore (including his
two nephews and her brother). To make matters worse, Opal's father, Edgar
Hugonin, who was in a nursing home at Bournemouth, was increasingly frail
and desperate for company. In early May, his health started to deteriorate, and
she spent more and more time in Bournemouth until his death on 17 May
1942. The succession of family tragedies would have tested any marriage.
Robert and Opal's answer was to throw themselves into a range of official and
voluntary work. He joined the local Home Guard and became increasingly
active in the Air Training Corps (ATC),[11] while Opal reengaged with the RAF
Comforts Committee and the Girl Guides. Brooke-Popham and Arthur
Longmore (who had been replaced in Egypt by Tedder in May 1941 and
placed on the retired list) agreed to help the Training Directorate by inspecting ATC squadrons and camps across the country. Longmore took northeast
England and Scotland while Brooke-Popham took the south and west.[12]

Brooke-Popham had started work on his official dispatch in early April.
The writing progressed rapidly, building on notes made on the journey home,

and the final proofs were ready at the printers by June. He had been provided with a young historian, Denis Richards, to help in the drafting but he did most of the writing—much to the surprise of Richards, who had little to do other than correct poor punctuation. Notwithstanding the hurry, publication would be delayed until well after the war (although an abbreviated copy was circulated to the War Cabinet by the chiefs of staff),[13] to allow those in captivity (notably Percival and Thomas) to be consulted. Singapore was never far from Brooke-Popham's mind and he was determined to do all he could for the families of those killed, missing, or captured. Information was scarce, particularly about the fate of those who tried to escape shortly before the fall. It was only in January 1944 that he could write to Elinore Pulford with definite news that her husband and Jack Spooner had reached the island of Tiebe (Chibia).[14] Similar uncertainty surrounded the fate of his nephew and brother-in-law. It was not until 1943 that the family discovered they were prisoners of war. In the meantime, Brooke-Popham continued to press the authorities to improve the conditions faced by all those in captivity and to increase the help available to their families.[15] His morale was lifted by the support he received from friends, colleagues, and the occasional unexpected quarter, such as a personal letter from Private Alfred Carter (ex-Oxfordshire Light Infantry), who fondly remembered his old company commander. The indignant veteran offered to take Lord Addison to task for his despicable words of criticism directed at "a Thorough Gentleman, a Soldier, a True and Right Leader of Men."[16] Trenchard had already defended Brooke-Popham in Parliament: "I am surprised that Lord Addison, whom I always thought fair in his criticism, should have thought fit to criticise Sir Robert Brooke-Popham so severely."[17] In response, Addison insisted that "there was no reason for an officer to say soft things to the public." According to Victor Goddard, Brooke-Popham was an example of how to take misrepresentation and adversity.[18] An unwelcome development, but one that still gave some comfort, came in the form of an anonymous cable from Kenya, "Request going to [Secretary of State for the Colonies] Cranborne for your return. We all await you."[19] Brooke-Popham was duly skeptical: "[T]he criterion for selecting a new governor will not be what a few hundred British settlers would like but what the Colonial Office consider best for the three million Africans."[20] As Opal pointed out, this was not a realistic prospect unless the current governor (Sir Henry Moore) intended to resign; however, the mere possibility that they might travel to Kenya prompted a nervous Colonial Office to advise the Air Ministry that the ex-governor's return would break existing convention and should be avoided.[21]

In February 1943, Air Marshal Guy Garrod, Air Member for Training (AMT), asked him to write a history of the Battle of Britain. This was not a case of finding gainful employment for an old friend at a loose end. Brooke-Popham was already heavily involved in a busy program of ATC visits and "Wings for Victory" fundraising. In his favor, however, he had considerable air defense experience, knew the key personalities, and had toured Fighter Command stations during September 1940 when the air fighting was at its most intense. Just as importantly, he was a capable, conscientious, and (from the Air Ministry's perspective) reliable author.[22] "I have been asked to write a new pamphlet on the Battle of Britain with the object of showing that the whole of the Air Force contributed to that battle and that it was not entirely an affair of the single-seater fighter."[23] Allocated an office in the Air Ministry, he spent a lot of time on the road, researching and interviewing, including meetings with Frederick Bowhill, John Bradley, Hugh Dowding, and Bert Harris.[24] He also corresponded with other participants, such as Cecil Bouchier, Hazleton Nicholl, and Trafford Leigh-Mallory, but was careful to look beyond Fighter Command and consider the wider employment of the RAF.[25] This more inclusive approach (in marked contrast to the account published by the MOI in March 1941 that focused almost exclusively on Fighter Command) sat well with Brooke-Popham's training and logistic background, although he reassured Nicholl that this would not detract from the achievements of "The Few."[26] The project had the energetic support of Air Marshal Richard Peck (assistant chief, Air Staff), responsible for the Air Ministry's public relations. The latter had already discussed with Trenchard the need for the Air Ministry to follow the lead of the military and naval authorities and employ retired officers to contribute articles to the daily papers and reputable magazines.[27] Brooke-Popham was one of a small number of Air Force officers, serving or retired, both capable of and inclined to undertake such work.

The meeting with Dowding touched on a range of subjects, including the effectiveness of antiaircraft guns in airfield defense, the number of phases in the battle, and the object of the German attack on London. Discussions at Coastal Command addressed the transfer of squadrons and pilots, air sea rescue, and the allocation of convoy protection duties. At Bomber Command, he focused on the bombing of ports and invasion barges, while at Maintenance

Command he searched for stories about the work of motor transport, salvage and repair personnel, and examples of extemporization in maintenance activities, including the lessons learned from the Battle of France. The completed typescript was ready by 19 July 1943 and was published (as Air Ministry Pamphlet 156) a month later, by which time Brooke-Popham had already started work on a series of RAF campaign histories to be used at training establishments.[28] Air Ministry Pamphlet 156 was a considerably more substantial document than the narrative issued by the MOI in 1941. It was longer (ninety-four compared to thirty-two pages) and more measured, avoiding much of the eulogistic language while encouraging the reader to reflect on the reasons for the German defeat. Most importantly, however, it established a structure and breadth to the story that has provided the foundation for all subsequent histories of the Battle of Britain. Churchill was keen to use the "admirable" Air Ministry Pamphlet 156 when constructing his own account of the Battle of Britain.[29] In response, Ismay advised Churchill that, while Brooke-Popham was nominally the author, "the man who did most of the work was Flight Lieutenant [Albert] Goodwin, who is now a Professor of History at Jesus College, Oxford."[30] Goodwin had certainly contributed to the Ministry of Information's 1941 history (authored by Hilary Saunders),[31] but there is no evidence, other than Ismay's statement, that he was involved in the 1943 version. Indeed, the published text conforms almost exactly with Brooke-Popham's preliminary drafts that he circulated for corrections and comment.[32] The confusion may have arisen because Goodwin was assigned by the Air Historical Branch to help Brooke-Popham, who was otherwise busy writing the Battle of Britain narrative, with research for the separate campaign histories commissioned by AMT.[33] A personal letter from Portal to Brooke-Popham in August 1943 offered congratulations on his recently published Battle of Britain pamphlet.[34] Either Ismay was confused about which publication Churchill was referring to or he felt that Brooke-Popham might harbor resentment about Churchill's failure to honor the promised baronetcy.

Brooke-Popham relinquished his Home Guard commission in October 1943, not long before the organization stood down. Aside from his writing for AMT, he remained heavily involved in the ATC, visiting annual camps, lecturing and helping to train ATC officers. This involved considerable travelling. In February 1943, for example, he toured units in Leeds, Barnsley, and Sheffield, speaking to numerous individuals and groups.[35] Many of the instructors and staff were World War I veterans, such as Air Commodore

Sydney Smith (commandant, North East Region), who had served with him in France. Toward the end of 1943 he was asked to chair a working group to advise on the postwar organization for the ATC.[36] His recommendations, encompassing the size, role, funding, and accommodation of the organization were largely accepted and still underpin today's ATC. Brook-Popham's involvement continued until September 1945; thereafter he undertook the occasional inspection until, following a reorganization, these duties were transferred to AOCinC Reserve Command (Air Marshal Sir Alan Lees) and his staff in 1947.[37] From 1943 until 1948, Brooke-Popham was one of the RAF's representatives on the Council of the Navy, Army, and Air Force Institutes (NAAFI).[38] He served as president for most of this time. This was an extremely busy period for the organization, not only because of the immense size of the armed forces (and their welfare needs) but also because of the special arrangements needed to support the Allied forces involved in the liberation of Europe and occupation of Germany and Austria. As ever, Brooke-Popham was not content to remain in London and visited NAAFI establishments in the Middle East, the Mediterranean, and Iceland. At the end of the war, he led the work to reorganize the NAAFI for peacetime needs and to create permanent clubs across the UK.

Brooke-Popham's last five years were spent in peaceful retirement at Cottisford. He no longer rode, but still enjoyed country life and the company of his family and friends. Following his sister's death, he was also the central figure in the Pooley family, providing advice and guidance to the younger generation. The publication of his official dispatch in 1948 generated fresh interest in Singapore. The official history on the war in Malaya, *The War against Japan*, vol. 1, was not published until 1957 but the author, Major-General Woodburn Kirby, conducted extensive correspondence with him until August 1953, when he was taken ill and admitted to the RAF hospital at Halton. Advanced bowel cancer was diagnosed and, with a matter of months to live, he spent the time left tidying his affairs and commenting on the initial drafts of the official history.[39]

Henry Robert Moore Brooke-Popham died peacefully in his sleep in the early hours of Tuesday, 20 October 1953, aged seventy-five years. His funeral was held at St. Edburg's parish church, Bicester, close to the family home at Cottisford. A field marshal, two marshals of the RAF, and three air chief marshals were pallbearers.[40] He was buried at East Bagborough in Somerset, next to Bagborough House. He did not leave a large estate (£17,000),[41] but

Opal was able to repurchase Bagborough House in 1955 when it came on the market, living there until her death in 1981. She is buried alongside her husband, on the slopes of the Quantock Hills where they had both hunted before the war and where generations of Pophams had owned estates. A memorial service for Brooke-Popham was held at St. Mark's, North Audley Street, London, on Tuesday, 17 November 1953. Philip "Tubby" Clayton, founder padre of the Toc H movement, spoke movingly about his friend's humility and dedication to the RAF. Other colleagues testified to Brooke-Popham's qualities of heart and mind, his unerring rectitude, and his loyalty. The most commonly used words in the many letters of condolence were "humility" and "selflessness." Foster Cox, who had known Brooke-Popham as well as anyone, in good times and bad, described his moral courage as second to none.[42] Even allowing for the natural emotion that can cloud such reminiscences, there is little doubt that Brooke-Popham was loved and respected by a great many people. Praise for his qualities came from the highest and the lowest. Jack Salmond knew no one who "during his life, gathered round him more affection and respect."[43] Anne Phillips, a secretary in GHQ Far East who helped Foster Cox maintain the headquarters war diary, recalled that "he was a kind, thoughtful and inspiring boss," who was a pleasure and privilege to work for.[44]

Throughout Brooke-Popham's long career he never fell prey to the temptation to engage in public (or private) arguments with his colleagues, unlike many of his contemporaries. Douglas, Dowding, Joubert de la Ferté, Leigh-Mallory, Park, and Slessor, all had long-running, sometimes bitter, disagreements with their fellow air marshals. This was not in Brooke-Popham's nature. According to John Baldwin, "Some great brains cannot suffer fools gladly but 'Brookham' had the knack of getting the best out of fools and never showed it, even if he was bored with them."[45] The *Kenya Weekly News* reported that he would be remembered in Kenya "as a Governor who restored a happy atmosphere to the public life of the Colony after long and dreary years of bitter and acrimonious strife."[46] The same article went on to describe the deep respect that "Brookham" had won, the schemes he had initiated for economic and social advance, and the contribution of Lady Brooke-Popham. Miles Lampson wrote that he was a truly lovely man who "radiated something, an undefinable something, to all whose good fortune it was to come into contact with him."[47] Brooke-Popham's "niceness" and his genuine interest in others did not stop him from making difficult decisions. There is always a danger that, in endeavoring to please, a commander can lack ruthlessness, particularly in dealing with underperforming subordinates. Brooke-Popham was undoubtedly a well-liked and a popular leader who generated great loyalty and affection. "He did not drive, but he definitely led."[48] However, this did not stop him from acting decisively when he thought it was required—witness the resignation of Vlieland and the concurrent replacement of Babington and Bond.

It is not easy to sum up a life so full as Robert Brooke-Popham's, or one so dominated by a single, traumatic event. The fall of Singapore was an unmitigated disaster and the catalyst for the momentous changes that would see the British Empire rapidly dismantled over the following twenty years. There can be no escaping his role as Britain's senior military commander in the Far East at the outbreak of war. According to J. F. C. Fuller, contemporary and regimental colleague, it was "the most disastrous campaign fought by Great Britain since Cornwallis' capitulation at Yorktown in 1781."[49] Brooke-Popham never shied away from acknowledging that he had been defeated—although he had been relieved of command well before Singapore surrendered. Thereafter, his twin aims were to help the families of those captured as best he could, and to ensure that the military lessons were not forgotten—even if this excited individual sensibilities or departmental politics. He was heartbroken over Singapore and felt deeply for his colleagues who had been killed or captured, but he never allowed this pain (and the death of his sister) to cloud his thinking or to provide an excuse to castigate others. There was no public criticism of Gordon Bennett, Duff Cooper, Arthur Percival, Tom Phillips, or Shenton Thomas. He had the opportunity to do so, especially when the first volume of the official history was under way, but even in private correspondence he consistently expressed sympathy and understanding with those most closely associated with the campaign. At his funeral service, the RAF's chaplain-in-chief highlighted Brooke-Popham's stoicism in the face of public criticism about the Far East. "His inheritance lacked much; he was bidden to make bricks with little straw and less clay, and with no hope of further supplies. Never once did we hear any querulous railing against fate."[50] It was only with his death that there was public recognition that he had been unfairly criticized: "Thank heaven *The Times* gave us the truth—so long delayed—and said what ought to have been said in the house when Singapore fell. I don't think I have ever admired 'Brookham' more than I did when I met him in the closing stages of the war and worked under him. He showed one how to put Country first and last."[51]

Brooke-Popham married late but, although twenty years separated them, found his ideal partner in Opal. The couple shared a passion for the countryside and a lifelong love of horses. Their marriage was close, built around family, friends, and riding. Whenever they were parted, they exchanged letters almost every day. Her husband's death in 1953 was a huge blow to Opal, but the determination and resilience that had enabled her to support him in difficult times sustained her for the next thirty years. It was a role that she had willingly taken on, knowing what would be involved: "When you marry me it's not just only myself you join up with, it's something bigger, you become part of the spirit of the Air Force, something that began way back in 1911, that developed during the war, that is still growing. It's a wonderful thing to come into, but you must take your share of responsibilities as well as of its benefits."[52] Although their relationship was not without its tensions (as he readily admitted), the bond between them remained strong.[53] After ten years of marriage, he was just as likely to quote poetry to her as he had when courting. "Do you remember Rupert Brooke? 'And turn and toss your brown delightful head, Amusedly amongst the ancient Dead.' Only it's more red than brown."[54] We should also applaud Opal's determination not to destroy their private correspondence and her foresight and generosity in placing her husband's papers with King's College and the Bodleian—well before such archives became fashionable. There are no words that can fully encapsulate any life, let alone one so rich in achievement and controversy. It seemed appropriate, in selecting an epigraph for this book, to draw on the verse of Rudyard Kipling, a man of the empire who lived through the same turbulent times. As this manuscript neared completion, I discovered the same poem cited by Evelyn Garrod in describing the misfortunes and cruel misjudgments she felt that Brooke-Popham had suffered.[55] To his mind, however, what mattered most was your impact on others: "I'll own to many faults, to many blemishes, to much unsoundness and I'll merely claim to be faithful to my friends."[56]

Writing on the twenty-fifth anniversary of the Royal Air Force, Brooke-Popham explained what he felt were the continuing principles that flowed through the organization and its people. "High hearted gallantry, loyalty to the Service, determination to see the job through at whatever cost to oneself, being content with the simple knowledge that the work has been well done without seeking for reward or the applause of men."[57] He could just as well have been talking about himself. A contemporary, recalling the story of how

Brooke-Popham went to sleep on the stairs of a hotel during World War I, rather than turn out two headquarters drivers who had occupied his room, added that he "was one of those few—the selfless few—who believed that horses should have first consideration, as they could not help themselves, that men came next and the officers last of all."[58] His generous nature was attested to by Edward Ellington, writing in the *Journal of the Royal Central Asiatic Society*: "Throughout his service with his enviable personality he inspired the respect and affection of all those with whom he worked and among the many officers I have known he was one of the three who most noticeably placed the interest of their service before personal advancement and carried out the tasks that fell to their lot with equal devotion and good grace, whether they were congenial or otherwise."[59] Brooke-Popham had few airs or graces. "A silly young gunner subaltern in my carriage from Waterloo, we were travelling first as we get cheap vouchers ... at the last moment three young troopers of the XII Lancers tumbled in being unable to find room elsewhere. And he began to complain and wanted to turf them out, so I growled at him from my opposite corner and he collapsed. But it is so silly to be snobbish like that, and the men were quite nice."[60] He was notably successful in guiding and developing the careers of his personal staff including Taaffe, Carter, and Fressanges. All spoke to his kindness, encouragement, and support. It is a rare commander who can generate such affection.

In his heart, Robert Brooke-Popham was a Victorian—as were his values and concept of service. By temperament he was an Edwardian—with an enquiring mind and a passion for what science could offer society and the advance of civilization. His enthusiasm for aeronautics and his willingness to deploy modern business practices spoke to the latter. His studied silence in the face of unwarranted criticism and cynical politics spoke to the former.[61] He was god-fearing with a strong sense of his responsibilities and the importance of moral values, but his impulses were more country squire than evangelist. He was not a troubled man, and while he thought deeply about spiritual issues, he had a lightness of heart and a sense of his good fortune. He welcomed modernity but subscribed wholeheartedly to the empire; he was, after all, the product of an educational system designed to provide the empire's servants and leaders. Pioneer airman, innovative logistician, airpower strategist, amateur diplomat, and family man, Brooke-Popham achieved many things in a long and distinguished career but, above all, he was an honorable man. He was not without faults. He lacked self-interest—so often the mark of a successful commander. He was a natural optimist and, although he was not naïve about individual motives, was liable to see the best in others. He seems to have had no inkling of Layton's jealousy or Hart's hostility and was unaware (at least initially) that he had lost Dorman-Smith's confidence or earned Duff Cooper's derision. A more ruthless commander might have had greater success in forcing action on the chiefs of staff in 1941, but enjoyed less success in working with the Australians, Chinese, and Dutch. His instinct was for action, but it was sometimes overshadowed by an exaggerated concern for the human costs. A more selfish and less sensitive man would not have worried about the tiredness of his pilots in 1918, the risks of interning German nationals in 1939, or the danger of starting a war in 1941. He could never entirely manage the emotional detachment needed in wartime. George Bulman drove back to St-Omer in Brooke-Popham's company in 1917 "with gun flashes lightening the sky in the not far distance of the front and their muttering rumble as a background. Then, heaven knows why, he opened his heart to me on the hideousness and futility of war and the strain under which he lived."[62]

Brooke-Popham took immense pride in the RAF but was liable to exaggerate the moral over the physical. At the height of the Battle of Britain, he prophesied that "when historians had had time to catch up with events, and write a history of the present war, they would find that not least of the causes of Hitler's defeat was our airmen's faith in the cause for which they fought."[63] He was not a racist, and genuinely cared for those he governed in Africa and the Middle East, but his language occasionally revealed the prejudices of his class and time.[64] Above all, he benefitted from his friendship with Trenchard. Would he have risen so far and so fast, without the latter's influence and support? Trenchard's patronage was undoubtedly critical to his career during the lean interwar years, even if it was a relationship built on professional competence as much as shared experience. There are several errors in the description of Brooke-Popham's life and achievements presented in the *Dictionary of National Biography*, but there can be little argument with its concluding sentiments: "An able and sometimes brilliant professional officer, and a talented amateur diplomat, it was tragic for him that after his active career should have ended his reputation became closely linked with the greatest calamity ever to strike British arms. This was evidently unjust, since he was allowed neither the time nor the power to solve a problem already beyond solution."[65]

278 ~ CHAPTER TWENTY-FOUR

Did the fall of Singapore precipitate the end of the British Empire?[66] World War II certainly hastened the process. Postwar Britain, exhausted and bankrupt, had little appetite and fewer resources to maintain the status quo. The impact was felt almost immediately in India, where heightened nationalism and imperial malaise undermined any hope of restoring the old order.[67] Clement Attlee's announcement in the House of Commons that British rule in India would end was made on 20 February 1947, virtually five years to the day since British and Dominion forces surrendered in Singapore (including more than 60,000 Indians). Was Brooke-Popham to blame? At a personal level, he cannot be held accountable, but then neither can any single individual. It was a collective failure, embracing military and civil personnel and extending from Malaya to Whitehall. As Connell has remarked, in describing the all-pervasive unpreparedness of the Allies: "This failure was as marked (so far as the British were concerned) in the War Cabinet and the Chiefs of Staff as in the tired, bewildered soldiers caught up in the swirl of defeat and retreat down the length of the Malayan peninsula, or in the civilian authorities in Singapore who regarded the most obvious defence precautions as likely to endanger public morale. To apportion blame is massively irrelevant. We all failed."[68]

George Sansom, the highly experienced diplomat who predicted Japan's attack and served in Singapore until shortly before its fall, coordinating intelligence and organizing covert operations, insisted that an explanation was not to be found in incompetent generals or neglectful politicians, but in a lack of airpower and sea power resulting from the difficult choices forced on a nation with limited resources fighting a world war against formidable enemies.[69] In *Singapore: The Chain of Disaster*, the official historian offered his personal perspective on how Britain came to lose Singapore (and an empire). There was another chain, however: the events that took Japan (an ally in World War I) from Manchuria via Indochina and Thailand to Singapore and a confrontation with the ABCD (American, British, Chinese, and Dutch) powers in World War II.[70] It is difficult to see how either chain could have been averted. Brooke-Popham never sought to disguise his responsibility for the loss of Singapore, nor did he engage in denigrating the performance of others. He felt strongly that a commander should accept blame as well as honors, as the representative of all his command. It was easier to bear "when it's directed against oneself than when it's laid against one's subordinates." His passivity in the face of personal criticism, and his willingness to accommodate alterations to his draft dispatch, did not prevent him from expressing his views forcefully—as he did when the Cabinet Office demanded yet more changes: "Our failure to defeat the Japanese in December 1941 led to appalling misery both mental and physical, to a very heavy death toll and serious loss of prestige. It may have been inevitable, but mistakes were made; we can at least learn our lessons and ensure that they are not repeated where conditions may be more equal and similar mistakes make the difference between success and failure."[71]

Churchill, in soliciting the support of the Australian government over Brooke-Popham's treatment, referred to the need to "do justice to an officer who has been the victim of most violent and unjustifiable attacks."[72] Fine words and estimable sentiments, but no defense was forthcoming, except in the most general terms—even though the chiefs of staff asked for action in response to the negative press reports.[73] Speaking in the House of Commons, the prime minister refused to "throw the blame on any generals or air marshals or admirals," but directed his most vigorous comments at rebutting any criticism of the chancellor of the Duchy of Lancaster (Duff Cooper).[74] He made passing mention of CinC Far East, but only to say that even half of the munitions supplied to Russia "would have dazzled the eyes of Sir Robert Brooke-Popham."[75] Brooke-Popham's name is not mentioned anywhere in Churchill's *History of the Second World War*. He is simply referred to as "the Commander-in-Chief," whereas Percival, Pownall, Cooper, Layton, and Dorman-Smith are at least identified. Churchill was a great wartime leader and a man of vision, but he was also a consummate politician. Having promised Brooke-Popham a baronetcy, he quietly shelved the idea for fear of exciting public opinion, particularly in Australia. The potential recipient of one of the nation's highest honors raised no complaint. We can only speculate why Brooke-Popham did not provide his own account about the fall of Singapore. An accomplished author, he produced a wide and varied output for nearly forty years, yet none of his writings offer a personal perspective or explanation. It is only in his letters to Opal that we glimpse his private thoughts and opinions. When asked about his philosophy in life, Brooke-Popham would invariably reference the "Soldier's Faith."[76] He felt that it perfectly captured his own feelings—perhaps no more so than the penultimate line:

> It is right. It is, as the colonel would have had it. This also is part of the soldier's faith: Having known great things, to be content with silence.[77]

NOTES

INTRODUCTION

1. For example: P. Brendon, *The Decline and Fall of the British Empire* (London: Jonathan Cape, 2007); J. Darwin, *Britain and Decolonisation: The Retreat from Empire in the Post-War World* (London: Macmillan, 1988), *The End of the British Empire: The Historical Debate* (Oxford: Blackwell, 1991), and *The Empire Project: The Rise and Fall of the British World System 1830–1970* (Cambridge: Cambridge University Press, 2009); N. Ferguson, *Empire: How Britain Made the Modern World* (London: Allen Lane, 2003); R. Hyam, Britain's *Declining Empire: The Road to Decolonisation, 1918–1968* (Cambridge: Cambridge University Press, 2007); and L. James, *The Rise and Fall of the British Empire* (London: St. Martin's Press, 1994).

2. James, *Rise and Fall*, 415–16.

3. Darwin, *The Empire Project*, 512–13.

4. The National University of Singapore's select bibliography, published in 2002, lists nearly one hundred books on the military campaign alone. Relevant works that have appeared in the last two decades include: H. Frei, *Guns of February* (Singapore: Singapore University Press, 2004); B. Bond and K. Tachikawa, eds., *British and Japanese Military Leadership in the Far Eastern War* (London: Frank Cass, 2004); B. Farrell, *The Defence and Fall of Singapore 1940–1942* (Stroud, UK: Tempus, 2005); A. Nicholson, *Hostages to Fortune: Winston Churchill and the Loss of the* Prince of Wales *and* Repulse (Stroud, UK: Sutton, 2005); P. Thompson, *The Battle for Singapore* (London: Portrait, 2005); C. Smith, *Singapore Burning* (London: Penguin, 2006); K. Kotani, *Japanese Intelligence in World War II* (Botley, UK: Osprey, 2009); B. Farrell and S. Hunter, eds., *A Great Betrayal? The Fall of Singapore Revisited* (Singapore: Marshall Cavendish, 2010); M. Arnold, *The Sacrifice of Singapore* (Singapore: Marshall Cavendish, 2011); E. Mawdsley, *December 1941: Twelve Days That Began a World War* (New Haven, CT: Yale

University Press, 2011); J. R. Cox, *Rising Sun, Falling Skies* (Oxford: Osprey, 2014); F. Pike, *Hirohito's War: The Pacific War 1941–1945* (London: Bloomsbury, 2015); and R. McCrum, *The Men Who Lost Singapore, 1938–1942* (Singapore: NUS Press, 2017).

5. Based on the figures calculated by Alan Warren, *Singapore, 1942: Britain's Greatest Defeat* (London: Hambledon and London, 2002), 301–6.

6. One writer has compared the fall of Singapore to the fall of Constantinople in 1453. R. Callahan, "Seventy Days to Singapore—Review Article," *American Historical Review* 82, no. 3 (June 1977): 645–46.

7. C. Bose, *Chalo Delhi: Netaji Subhas Chandra Bose, Collected Works*, edited by S. Bose (Delhi: Permanent Black, 2007), 12:45–48.

8. Lee Kuan Yew, *The Singapore Story: Memories of Lee Kuan Yew* (Singapore: Times, 1998), 100.

9. *Times* (London), 18 February 1942. Ian Morrison, who had served as secretary to Sir Robert Craigie, the British ambassador in Tokyo, covered the Pacific for the *Times* throughout World War II. He was killed in 1950 while reporting from Korea.

10. *The Economist*, 21 February 1942, p. 242.

11. W. S. Churchill, *The Hinge of Fate* (London: Cassell, 1951), 88.

12. *Sydney Daily Telegraph*, 16 December 1941; *Daily Mail*, 18 December 1941; Lord Addison, House of Lords, *Hansard*, 8 January 1942, col. 381.

13. R. Davenport-Hines, ed., *Hugh Trevor-Roper: The Wartime Journals* (London: I. B. Tauris, 2012), 55.

14. "Purge of Pansies Suggested by British MP," *Argus*, 6 January 1942.

15. N. Dixon, *The Psychology of Military Incompetence* (London: Jonathan Cape, 1976), 133–34.

16. Ibid., 137.

17. M. Torre, "Did Singapore Have to Fall? Hope Is Not a Strategy," *Finest Hour*, no. 138 (Spring 2008): 35–41.

18. R. Callahan, "Did Singapore Have to Fall? Responsible but Not Unrepentant," *Finest Hour*, no. 138 (Spring 2008): 35–41.

19. H. R. M. Brooke-Popham, "Operations in The Far East, from 17 October 1940 to 27 December 1941," *Supplement to The London Gazette*, 22 January 1948, pp. 535–76.

20. A. E. Percival, "Operations of Malaya Command from 8 December 1941 to 15 February 1942," *Supplement to The London Gazette*, 26 February 1948, pp. 1245–346; A. E. Percival, *The War in Malaya* (London: Eyre & Spottiswoode, 1949).

21. Churchill, *The Hinge of Fate*; D. Cooper, *Old Men Forget* (New York: Dutton, 1954); and G. Bennett, *Why Singapore Fell* (Sydney: Angus and Robertson, 1944). For a robust defense of Phillips, see: B. Ash, *Someone Had Blundered* (London: Michael Joseph, 1960) and M. Stephen, *Scapegoat: The Death of* Prince

of Wales *and* Repulse (Barnsley, UK: Pen and Sword, 2014). For an equally robust defense of Thomas, see: B. Montgomery, *Shenton of Singapore* (London: Leo Cooper, 1984). For Duff Cooper's side of the story, in response to the criticisms contained in Montgomery's book, see: J. Charmley, *Duff Cooper: The Authorised Biography* (London: Weidenfeld and Nicolson, 1986). Finally, for an eloquent defense of Percival, see: C. Kinvig, *Scapegoat: General Percival of Singapore* (London: Brassey's, 1996).

22. S. Woodburn Kirby, *The War against Japan*, vol. 1 (London: Her Majesty's Stationery Office, 1957); S. Woodburn Kirby, *Singapore: The Chain of Disaster* (New York: Macmillan, 1971).

23. A. Marder, *Old Friends, New Enemies: The Royal Navy and the Imperial Japanese Navy* (Oxford: Clarendon Press, 1981), xi.

24. Brooke-Popham was a lifelong collector of military maxims and worthy aphorisms, written in a series of notebooks or on loose slips of paper.

25. Conversation with Philip Brooke-Popham, Bagborough House, 2014.

26. N. Barber, *Sinister Twilight* (London: Collins, 1968), 44. Mawdsley, in an otherwise admirable book, describes Brooke-Popham as "something of a combination of Biggles and Colonel Blimp," although he notes Louis Allen's view that Brooke-Popham was by no means incompetent. Mawdsley, *December 1941*, 140; L. Allen, *Singapore 1941–1942* (Newark: University of Delaware Press, 1979), 54.

27. P. Wykeham, "Sir (Henry) Robert Moore Brooke- (1878–1953)," rev. T. P. Ofcansky, *Oxford Dictionary of National Biography* (Oxford: Oxford University Press, 2004), online edition, January 2008, 144–46. For Brooke-Popham's achievements in World War I, see: P. Dye, *The Bridge to Airpower* (Annapolis, MD: Naval Institute Press, 2015); for his role in the development of RAF doctrine see: N. Parton, "The Development of Early RAF Doctrine," *Journal of Military History* 72 (October 2008): 1155–77; and for his contribution as CinC Air Defence of Great Britain see: T. C. G. James, *The Growth of Fighter Command* (London: Frank Cass, 2002).

28. T. Jun, "The Navy's Role in the Southern Strategy," in *The Fateful Choice: Japan's Advance into Southeast Asia, 1939–1941*, edited by J. W. Morley (New York: Columbia University Press, 1980), 241–95.

29. Robert Brooke-Popham's letters, often separated from their envelopes, were scattered through several trunks, but he had carefully assembled those written by his wife and tied them into bundles organized by date. Robert to Opal, 26 July 1931, BPFP.

30. The title of an appreciation provided by an anonymous Far East prisoner of war (FEPOW) on Brooke-Popham's death in 1953.

CHAPTER 1. EARLY LIFE AND MILITARY SERVICE

1. Polly was an accomplished artist and a member of the Ipswich Art Club (1890–91). She exhibited several paintings at Wetheringsett in 1890.

2. *London Gazette*, 5 August 1859, p. 3005, and 11 December 1862, p. 6269. The Black Watch had been heavily involved in suppressing the revolt.
3. On 11 February 1863 at Hartismere, Suffolk.
4. Dulcibella Brooke was recorded as insane and resident at Torquay in 1901. On her daughter and son-in-law's return from Africa, she went to live with them in Sheffield, accompanied by two resident nurses. She died in 1915, aged seventy-five.
5. Robert Brooke Personal Album, BPFP.
6. L. Milford, *Haileybury Register 1862–1900* (London: Richard Clay & Sons, 1900), 391.
7. Haileybury Housemaster's Report, July 1896, Robert Brooke Personal Album, BPFP.
8. Milford, *Haileybury Register*, 358–65.
9. Civil Service Commissioners to Robert Brooke, 18 December 1895, BPFP.
10. One of the "juniors" joining Haileybury that year (when Brooke-Popham was in the "senior" school) was the future Labour prime minister, Clement Attlee. Other eminent OHs included Marshal of the Royal Air Force Sir John Slessor and Air Chief Marshal Sir Trafford Leigh-Mallory.
11. He also gained a junior cap for rugby. Milford, *Haileybury Register*, 359.
12. D. S. Russell, *Winston Churchill, Soldier* (London: Brassey's, 2005), 34.
13. J. F. C. Fuller, *Memoirs of an Unconventional Soldier* (London: Ivor, Nicholson and Watson, 1936), 5–6.
14. G. Philips, *Text-Book on Fortifications* (Sandhurst, UK: Royal Military Academy, 1884).
15. Robert Brooke Personal Album, BPFP. (Emphasis in original.)
16. Telegram, War Office to Brooke, 6 May 1898, Robert Brooke Personal Album, BPFP. The Oxfordshire Light Infantry had been created in 1881 by the amalgamation of the Forty-Third and Fifty-Second Regiments. *London Gazette*, 6 May 1898, p. 2822.
17. A. F. Mockler-Ferryman, *The Oxfordshire Light Infantry Chronicle*, vol. 7 (London: Eyre & Spottiswoode, 1898), 34.
18. Ibid., 7:36.
19. B. H. Reid, *J. F. C. Fuller: Military Thinker* (London: Macmillan, 1987).
20. Mockler-Ferryman, *Light Infantry Chronicle*, 7:36.
21. Reid, *J. F. C. Fuller*, 8–9.
22. There must have been a degree of interaction between the pair—if only when Brooke-Popham was at Andover and Fuller was the senior lecturer at Camberley (1923–26).
23. Mockler-Ferryman, *Light Infantry Chronicle*, 7:81–106. The Second Battalion had formed part of the Tirah Expeditionary Force sent to punish the Afridi and Orakzai tribes. H. D. Hutchinson, *The Campaign in Tirah, 1897–1898* (London: Macmillan, 1898).
24. A. F. Mockler-Ferryman, *The Oxfordshire Light Infantry Chronicle*, vol. 8 (London: Eyre & Spottiswoode, 1899), 55.

25. Ibid., 8:100. His "bag" included blackbuck, chiakara, houbara, kullum, and panther. The heads of several blackbucks can still be found at Bagborough House.
26. *London Gazette*, 29 December 1899, p. 8657.
27. Frith served throughout World War I and retired from the Army in 1924. Brooke-Popham was best man at his marriage in November 1925.
28. A. F. Mockler-Ferryman, *The Oxfordshire Light Infantry Chronicle*, vol. 10 (London: Eyre & Spottiswoode, 1901), 219–21.
29. Proceedings of Medical Board, 18 November 1901, BPFP.
30. Mockler-Ferryman, *Light Infantry Chronicle*, 10:112. *Times* (London), 4 November 1901 and 17 December 1902.
31. These include: P. Bishop, *Singapore Burning* (London: Penguin Books, 2006), 50, and Thompson, *The Battle for Singapore*, 40.
32. *London Gazette*, 25 April 1902, p. 2793, and 6 May 1902, p. 3014.
33. When the Second Battalion hosted a regimental dinner at the Cecil Hotel in October 1902 for the officers of both battalions who had served in the South African War, Robert Brooke was one of the hosts.
34. Robert Brooke-Popham to Opal Brooke-Popham, 12 September 1925, BPFP. The Pashtuns proved to be formidable fighters, skilled marksmen, enterprising, bold, and worthy of respect. Hutchinson, *The Campaign in Tirah*, 225–34.
35. *London Gazette*, 25 April 1902, p. 2793.
36. He had agreed to give Polly away, but a serious riding accident meant that he was in the hospital recovering from head injuries on the day of the wedding.
37. Brooke-Popham to Opal, 18 June 1942, BPFP.
38. Polly died at Hampstead on 23 June 1942.
39. Brooke-Popham to Opal, 1 July 1942, BPFP.
40. The king granted the necessary royal license, and authority to take and use the surname of Popham, on 6 May 1904. *London Gazette*, 14 June 1904, p. 3788.
41. Brooke-Popham to Opal, 10 November 1925, BPFP.
42. "Notes on RAF Personalities," LH/11/1935/122, LHCMA.
43. *London Gazette*, 24 January 1905, p. 580.
44. A. F. Mockler-Ferryman, *The Oxfordshire Light Infantry Chronicle*, vol. 14 (London: Eyre & Spottiswoode, 1905), 51.
45. Adjutant 2 Oxf & Bucks LI to Captain Brooke-Popham, 14 July 1906, BPFP.
46. Soldiers of Oxfordshire Museum, Manuscript History of Fifty-Second Regiment, 190–91.
47. The Chronicle Editorial Committee, *The Oxfordshire and Buckinghamshire Light Infantry Chronicle*, vol. 39, *1931* (Oxford: Slatter and Rose, 1932), 272–76.
48. General Sir Neville Lyttelton.
49. Some thirty places were selected through competitive examination. The remainder were filled by nomination.
50. P. Harris, "The Men Who Planned the War: A Study of the Staff of the British Army on the Western Front, 1914–1918," PhD thesis, King's College, London, 2013, p. 53.

51. Harington to Brooke-Popham, 2 October 1909, BPFP. Brooke-Popham scored a total of 4,422 marks out of a possible 5,500. His nearest rival scored 4,354 marks. By way of comparison, Sir James Edmonds, who came top of the entrance exam in 1895, scored 4,700 marks.

CHAPTER 2. ARMY STAFF COLLEGE AND AIR BATTALION

1. C. G. Higgins, *Oxfordshire & Buckinghamshire Light Infantry Chronicle*, vol. 55, *January–December 1953* (Oxford: Slatter & Rose, 1954), 242–47.
2. B. Bond, *The Victorian Army and the Staff College, 1854–1914* (London: Eyre Methuen, 1972), 196–98.
3. K. Jeffery, *Field Marshal Sir Henry Wilson: A Political Soldier* (Oxford: Oxford University Press, 2006), 68.
4. Ibid., 69.
5. Brooke-Popham was seconded to the Staff College on 22 January 1910. *London Gazette*, 8 February 1910, p. 951.
6. Robertson was appointed to Camberley on 1 August 1910.
7. "Cloudland at the Staff College," *Times* (London), 28 September 1910.
8. Jeffery, *Henry Wilson*, 68.
9. RAF College Opening Address, BP/1/5/1, LHCMA.
10. Richard Pope-Hennessy married Una Birch (author and biographer) in June 1910.
11. The two men would remain close until Pope-Hennessy's death in 1942. Other subjects studied by the Junior Division included the Waterloo campaign, the American Civil War, and law (military, international, and martial).
12. A. Whitmarsh, "Far from a Useless and Expensive Fad, Aircraft at British Army Manoeuvres, 1910–1913," *Cross & Cockade International Journal* 39, no. 2 (2008): 98–99.
13. R. Dallas Brett, *History of British Aviation 1908–1914* (Surbiton, UK: Air Research, 1988), 129.
14. Anonymous newspaper cutting, 1911, BPFP.
15. G. S. Jones, "70 Years of Brooke-Popham," *The Hawk*, 1992, 84–85.
16. S. Pixton, *Howard Pixton: Test Pilot and Pioneer Aviator* (Barnsley, UK: Pen & Sword, 2014), 95.
17. C. G. Grey, "On Making a Note of It," *The Aeroplane* 18, no. 21 (26 May 1920): 972–73.
18. P. Joubert de la Ferté, *Fun and Games* (London: Hutchinson, 1964), 36. Joubert joined No. 3 Squadron on 15 June 1913.
19. Brooke-Popham to Opal, 14 September 1925, BPFP.
20. Notes by General Brooke-Popham, p. 3, AIR 1/1/4/1, TNA. During the summer of their first year, students were attached to different arms from their own.
21. P. W. L. Broke-Smith, *History of Early British Military Aeronautics* (Bath, UK: Cedric Chilvers, 1968), 46.

22. The other officers were: Captain P. W. L. Broke-Smith; Capt. C. J. Burke; Capt. A. D. Carden; Capt. J. D. B. Fulton; Capt. E. M. Maitland; Lt. B. H. Barrington-Kennett; Lt. R. A. Cammell; Lt. D. G. Connor; Lt. A. G. Fox; Lt. G. B. Hynes; Lt. F. H. Kirby; Lt. R. P. Reynolds; Lt. C. M. Waterlow; and 2/Lt. J. N. Fletcher.

23. Broke-Smith, *Military Aeronautics*, 52.

24. W. Raleigh, *The War in the Air* (Oxford: Clarendon Press, 1922), 1:189.

25. Cammell was killed in a flying accident on 17 September 1911 (the Air Battalion's first casualty).

26. Raleigh, *The War in the Air*, 1:193–94. The pair became lifelong friends (Brooke-Popham was godfather to Burke's son). When in command of No. 2 Squadron, Burke was affectionately known as "Pregnant Percy," owing to his substantial girth. P. Playfair and J. Jarvis, *'Pip' Playfair: A Founding Father of the RAF* (Ilfracombe, UK: Arthur Stockwell, 1979), 32.

27. Notes by General Brooke-Popham, p. 4, AIR 1/1/4/1, TNA.

28. Broke-Smith, *Military Aeronautics*, 53.

29. The lecture was delivered at Camberley on 3 November 1911. H. R. M. Brooke-Popham, "Military Aviation," *The Army Review* (January 1912): 87–102.

30. *Flight*, 13 January 1912, p. 26. (Emphasis in original.)

31. Brooke-Popham, "Military Aviation," p. 96. (Emphasis in original.)

32. Roberts to Brooke-Popham, 21 November 1911, BPFP. "Unreadiness for War—Lord Roberts and National Defence," *Times* (London), 16 December 1911, p. 15.

33. Brooke-Popham to Guy Garrod, 6 December 1949, BP/9/9/37, LHCMA.

34. Ibid. Brooke-Popham attributed these comments to the summer of 1910, but he may have been mistaken as the Air Battalion was not formed until April 1911. Bannerman's interest lay in airships and he did not obtain an airplane certificate until 30 April 1912.

35. Notes by General Brooke-Popham, p. 1, AIR 1/1/4/1, TNA.

36. C. Burke, "The Aeroplane as an Aid to the Solution of Existing Strategical Problems," *RUSI Journal* 55 (July–December 1911): 1625–42.

37. Burke participated in two further discussions, organized by the Aeronautical Society at RUSI, on 6 and 16 December respectively, when the potential of aeroplanes in future wars was explored by several distinguished speakers including Colonel (later Major-General Sir) John Capper, who had previously commanded the Balloon School.

38. "I see that in the December issue of *Aeronautics* I am credited with speaking at a lecture delivered at the Royal United Service Institute on November 15th. I was not present at that lecture, and the views, which I am made to express, are diametrically opposed to those I hold. I therefore venture to ask you for this opportunity of disclaiming them, and also the fact that I delivered an oration at all. The practical business of flying leaves me no time to get up lecture subjects, even were I able or inclined to do so." Captain John Fulton, letter, *Flight*, 23 December 1911, p. 1448.

39. Raleigh, *The War in the Air*, 1:137.
40. Ibid., 1:173. Both officers were to die relatively young, Dickson in 1913 (because of injuries received in a flying accident in 1910) and Fulton in 1915.
41. Notes by General Brooke-Popham, p. 25, AIR 1/1/4/1, TNA.
42. N. Macmillan, *Sir Sefton Brancker* (London: William Heinemann, 1935), 26. Brancker joined the RFC in June 1913, after learning to fly, and worked for David Henderson in the War Office. He ended World War I as a major general and became the controller-general of Civil Aviation in 1922 but died in the R101 accident on 5 October 1930.
43. Raleigh, *The War in the Air*, 1:252–53; Papers Received from General Brooke-Popham, Some Maxims by Colonel C. J. Burke, AIR 1/6A/4/30, TNA.
44. Brooke-Popham's article in *The Army Review* is referenced in: J. N. Pugh, "The Conceptual Origins of the Control of the Air: British Military and Naval Aviation, 1911–1918," PhD thesis, University of Birmingham, UK, 2012, p. 69.
45. Lieutenant Jean Fournie to Brooke-Popham, 23 February 1912, BPFP.
46. J. Bruce, *The Aeroplanes of the Royal Flying Corps, Military Wing* (London: Putnam, 1982), xiii. Capper had written nearly two years earlier about the military potential of airplanes but had described their likely contribution as modest and failed to mention the potential for air fighting. "Military Aspects of Dirigible Balloons and Aeroplanes," *Flight*, 29 January 1910.
47. Under-Secretary of State for War (Colonel Seely), House of Commons Debate, 30 October 1911, *Hansard*, cols. 663–67.
48. *Flight*, 23 December 1911, p. 1109.
49. Raleigh, *The War in the Air*, 1:198.
50. The Naval Wing returned to Admiralty control in July 1914 as the Royal Naval Air Service (RNAS).
51. Raleigh, *The War in the Air*, 1:199–200.
52. *Flight*, 27 January 1912, p. 84.
53. *Flight*, 18 May 1912, p. 449. The formal handover of the Salisbury Plain Aeroplane Station between Fulton and Brooke-Popham was completed on 10 May 1912. Air Battalion Work Diary, May 1911–August 1912, AIR 1/737/204/2/6, TNA.
54. Brooke-Popham had been offered the post of GSO3 at Northern Command (York) but chose to reject this in favor of the Air Battalion. Brooke-Popham to Hilary St. George Saunders, 16 August 1951, V/1/6, Trenchard Archive.
55. Brooke-Popham to Charles Grey, 28 May 1936, BP/4/10/4, LHCMA.
56. This was one of eight Boxkites allocated to the Air Battalion. F7 was Bristol No. 20, fitted with a 50 hp Gnome engine.
57. Barrington-Kennett was killed in 1915. His two brothers also died during the war. The Brooke-Popham family maintained a close friendship with his widow, Violet (Vi), until her death in 1977.

58. R. Pigot, "Some Memories of the Earliest Days of Military Aviation in England," *Royal Air Force Quarterly*, Spring 1973, pp. 51–57. Edward Ellington to Opal, 22 October 1953, BPFP.

CHAPTER 3. ROYAL FLYING CORPS

1. Broke-Smith, *Military Aeronautics*, 56.
2. Raleigh, *The War in the Air*, 1:239.
3. "An Interview with Mr W. J. Smyrk," *The 1914–1918 Journal*, Australian Society of WWI Aviation Historians, 1970, pp. 55–68.
4. J. T. B. McCudden, *Flying Fury* (London: Hamilton, 1930), 8–10. Brooke-Popham remained close to the squadron throughout his career and was delighted at McCudden's success. "I'm always so glad to find people from my old squadron distinguishing themselves." AC 74/8/47, RAFM.
5. "Report on Experiments in Observation of Artillery Fire from Aeroplanes," AIR 1/742/204/2/43, TNA.
6. S. Bidwell and D. Graham, *Fire Power—The British Army Weapons and Theories of War 1904–1945* (London: George Allen & Unwin, 1982), 101.
7. Robert Brooke-Popham Flying Logbook, 1912–13, BPFP.
8. Ibid.
9. Raleigh, *The War in the Air*, 1:235.
10. "British Army Airmen Killed," *Times* (London), 6 July 1912, p. 8.
11. Brooke-Popham to Opal, 6 September 1925, BPFP.
12. "Notes by General Brooke-Popham on Early History of the RFC," p. 9, AIR 1/1 /4/1, TNA.
13. Flying Log Book, July 1912, BPFP. Ridd was the RFC's first noncommissioned pilot.
14. "Portal: Britain's Chief of Air Staff," *Life*, 6 October 1941, p. 122; D. Richards, *Portal of Hungerford* (London: Heinemann, 1978), 29–30.
15. Bettington had joined No. 3 Squadron at the end of May. Hotchkiss was on loan from the Bristol Company, where he was their chief test pilot.
16. Hamilton to Brooke-Popham, September 1912, BPFP.
17. Raleigh, *The War in the Air*, 1:236.
18. Macmillan, *Brancker*, 29; Whitmarsh, "Far from a Useless and Expensive Fad," pp. 98–99.
19. Notes by General Brooke-Popham, pp. 14–15, AIR 1/1/4/1, TNA.
20. Dallas Brett, *History of British Aviation*, 14. The other members were Brigadier-General David Henderson, Major Frederick Sykes, and Lieutenant Spencer Grey.
21. Macmillan, *Brancker*, 29.
22. The lecture took place on 26 October 1912 and was subsequently printed in the *Army Quarterly*.
23. L. E. O. Charlton, *Charlton* (London: Penguin Books, 1938), 211–14.

24. "Army Aerial Display at Farnborough," *Times* (London), 10 May 1913, p. 6.

25. "Ceremonial Parade on Salisbury Plain," *Times* (London), 23 May 1913, p. 10.

26. Smith-Dorrien served as a corps commander in France but was sacked by Sir John French in 1915. He later served on the Committee on the Administration and Command of the RFC, chaired by Mr. Justice Bailhache.

27. A. Boyle, *Trenchard: Man of Vision* (London: Collins, 1965), 95.

28. Goddard to Brooke-Popham, 8 October 1947, BPFP.

29. *London Gazette*, 3 June 1913, p. 3908.

30. No. 3 Squadron Orders, AIR 1/737/204/2/1, TNA.

31. H. R. M. Brooke-Popham, "Some Reminiscences of the RFC in 1914," *The Hinaidian*, July 1930, pp. 1–5. The date is likely to have been some time after October 1913 (when Brooke-Popham first flew in a Farman).

32. Macmillan, *Brancker*, 34.

33. Ibid., 29.

34. Charlton, *Charlton*, 219.

35. Macmillan, *Brancker*, 44.

36. Notes by General Brooke-Popham, p. 20, AIR 1/1/4/1, TNA.

37. RFC Training Manual, Part II, Correspondence and Proofs, AIR 1/785/204/4/558, TNA.

38. Ibid.

39. Pugh, "The Conceptual Origins," pp. 97–99.

40. Royal Engineers Library, Chatham, Extracts from "Diary of Major H. Musgrave," 13 and 19 April 1913; RFC Training Manual, Part II, AIR 1/785/204/4/558, TNA. Part I of the RFC Training Manual was issued (in provisional form) in May 1914, Training Manual Royal Flying Corps Part I Provisional, AIR 10/1/179.

41. Brooke-Popham to Garrod, 6 December 1949, BP/9/9/37, LHCMA.

42. Brooke-Popham to Barrington-Kennett, 14 July 1913, AIR 1/785/204/4/565, TNA.

43. Brooke-Popham to Garrod, 6 December 1949, BP/9/9/37, LHCMA.

44. Pugh, "The Conceptual Origins," pp. 260–61.

45. The RFC benefitted enormously during the war from the experience of the French Aviation Service. Brooke-Popham made several trips to France (including a visit in May 1914) to assess their progress.

46. *Flight*, 26 June 1914, pp. 670–77.

47. Ibid., p. 675.

48. Notes by General Brooke-Popham, p. 23, AIR 1/1/4/1, TNA.

49. P. Joubert de la Ferté, *The Fated Sky* (London: Hutchinson, 1952), 40.

CHAPTER 4. THE WESTERN FRONT

1. Journal of the War, 27 July–23 August 1914, BPFP.

2. Macmillan, *Brancker*, 59.

3. On 5 August 1914.

4. The ten were: Brancker; Brooke-Popham; Ellington; Thomas Frankland; Henderson; Dowding; Musgrave; Geoffrey Salmond; Sykes; and Charlton. Musgrave and Frankland chose to return to army duties shortly after the outbreak of war. As a proportion, this was possibly no worse than the Regular Army, but this small cadre would have to provide the RFC's staff and senior leadership for the first few years of the war, denuding the squadrons of good commanders. Harris, "The Men Who Planned the War," pp. 200–201.

5. Philip Game to Gwendolen Game, 28 March 1916, Private Papers of Air Vice-Marshal Sir Philip Game, IWM Documents 10986.

6. E. Ash, *Sir Frederick Sykes and the Air Revolution, 1912–1918* (London: Frank Cass, 1999), 50–52.

7. Journal of the War, 4–5 August 1914, BPFP.

8. Playfair and Jarvis, *'Pip' Playfair*, 39.

9. Percy Threadkell later joined the RFC and worked for Brooke-Popham for much of World War I.

10. Journal of the War, 7 August 1914, BPFP.

11. Boyle, *Trenchard*, 115–17.

12. Ash, *Sir Frederick Sykes*, 51.

13. Brooke-Popham suffered from seasickness all his life and missed an impressive RAF torpedo attack on the fleet in April 1922 because he was incapacitated below decks. E. Ironside, *High Road to Command: The Diaries of Major-General Sir Edmund Ironside, 1920–1922* (London: Leo Cooper, 1972).

14. In future years, when passing through Boulogne, Brooke-Popham would always make a point of shaking hands with the buffet manager and talking of the people that he had had with him that day—most of whom were killed during the war. Brooke-Popham to Opal, 8 August 1929, BPFP.

15. M. Baring, *Flying Corps Headquarters 1914–1918* (Edinburgh: G. Bell & Sons, 1920), 18.

16. Ibid., p. 19.

17. Raleigh, *The War in the Air*, 1:294.

18. The importance of the information supplied by the RFC has been questioned, but at the very least it proved extremely helpful in confirming other intelligence sources at a time of considerable strategic uncertainty. Ash, *Sir Frederick Sykes*, 54–55.

19. Macmillan, *Brancker*, 84; "Notes on Administrative Matters," AIR 1/6A/4/55, TNA.

20. Brooke-Popham, "Some Reminiscences of the RFC in 1914," pp. 1–5.

21. W. R. Read, "Cavalryman in the Flying Machines," in *People at War*, edited by M. Moynihan (Newton Abbott, UK: David & Charles, 1973), 23. Read arrived in France with No. 3 Squadron on 13 August 1914.

22. "Sir John Salmond (Draft) Autobiography," B2621/4, RAFM. Baring, *Flying Corps Headquarters*, 27–28. According to Baring, Brooke-Popham purchased

292 ⌒ NOTES TO PAGES 35–40

supplies using a stash of three hundred gold coins carried in his portmanteau—
much to the surprise of the French.

23. McCudden, *Flying Fury*, 32.
24. Brooke-Popham to Opal, December 1926, BPFP.
25. Baring, *Flying Corps Headquarters*, 54–55.
26. Brooke-Popham to Opal, December 1926, BPFP.
27. Macmillan, *Brancker*, 64 and 106–8.
28. Pope-Hennessy, who was serving as a brigade major in Home Forces, had no aviation experience, but he was Staff College–trained. Brooke-Popham to Saunders, 16 August 1951, V/1/6, Trenchard Archive.
29. Diary, 9 April 1915, Private Papers of Major-General L. H. R. Pope-Hennessy, IWM Documents 12641.
30. Pope-Hennessy also spent time with the First Wing and had been promoted to GSO2 before he left the RFC for the Forty-First Division in October 1915.
31. H. A. Jones, *The War in the Air* (Oxford: Clarendon Press, 1928), 2:87.
32. On 20 February 1915. Jones, *The War in the Air*, 2:94.
33. Macmillan, *Brancker*, 108.
34. Brooke-Popham to Saunders, 16 August 1951, V/1/6, Trenchard Archive.
35. J. Pugh, "David Henderson and Command of the Royal Flying Corps," in *Stemming the Tide: Officers and Leadership in The British Expeditionary Force, 1914*, ed. S. Jones (Solihull, UK: Helion, 2013), 263–90.
36. Macmillan, *Brancker*, 62. Boyle, *Trenchard*, 137.
37. Grey, "On Making a Note of It," pp. 1023–24.
38. Field Marshal Sir John French, 31 May 1915.
39. BP/5/7/2, LHCMA.
40. Brooke-Popham to Guy Garrod, 6 December 1949, BP/9/9/37, LHCMA.
41. Henderson to Opal, 21 October 1953, BPFP.
42. The respective seniorities (as a major) were: Trenchard, August 1902; Edward Ashmore, June 1909; Brancker, January 1913: Sykes, June 1913; and Brooke-Popham, June 1913. At one point, Henderson considered sending Trenchard back to London as DMA while retaining control of the RFC in the field.
43. S. Hoare, *Empire of the Air* (London: Collins, 1957), 44.

CHAPTER 5. WORKING FOR TRENCHARD

1. Boyle, *Trenchard*, 143.
2. Ibid., 145.
3. Diary, 13 May 1916, Private Papers of Major-General L. H. R. Pope-Hennessy, IWM Documents 12641.
4. Brooke-Popham greatly admired Pope-Hennessy, believing that "he had a brain that was almost brilliant," however, he was also "unbalanced and would pursue a line of thought beyond any logical conclusion." Brooke-Popham to Saunders, 16 August 1951, V/1/6, Trenchard Archive.
5. Trenchard to Brancker, 9 March 1916 and 15 May 1916, MFC76/1/6 (1), RAFM.

6. Boyle, *Trenchard*, 145–46.

7. Trenchard to Brancker, 19 August 1916, MFC76/1/7 (4), RAFM.

8. Diary, 22 June 1915, Private Papers of Major-General L. H. R. Pope-Hennessy, IWM Documents 12641.

9. RFC Training Manual, Part II, June 1915, AIR 1/785/204/558, TNA. A more comprehensive document (*Fighting in the Air*), summarizing the lessons learned since the start of the war and especially the experience gained during the Battle of the Somme, was produced in March 1917 by Brooke-Popham's colleague, Philip Game.

10. Baring, *Flying Corps Headquarters*, 106–33.

11. Trenchard Autobiographical Narrative, p. 75, MFC76/1/61, RAFM.

12. Brooke-Popham to Saunders, 6 July 1951, V/1/6, Trenchard Archive.

13. War Office, *Statistics of The Military Effort of the British Empire* (London: HMSO, 1922), 495–504.

14. Jones, *The War in the Air*, 2:143.

15. Ibid., 2:147–48.

16. From 12 March 1916. Brooke-Popham received his second mention in dispatches on 31 May 1915.

17. Philip Game to Gwendolen Game, 20 March 1916, Private Papers of Air Vice-Marshal Sir Philip Game, IWM Documents 10986.

18. "Organisation and Establishment of RFC Headquarters," AIR 1/529/16/12/70, TNA. Brooke-Popham's responsibilities ranged from the posting of officers and the handling of casualties to the supply of matériel and the allotment of airplanes.

19. Diary, 16 May 1916, Private Papers of Major-General L. H. R. Pope-Hennessy, IWM Documents 12641. Part of the problem was Trenchard's insistence on creating both brigades and wings, to match the Army's organization, even though HQ RFC generally issued orders direct to the wings. Private Papers of Wing Commander Sir Archibald James, IWM Documents 11963.

20. Brooke-Popham to Saunders, 16 August 1951, V/1/6, Trenchard Archive.

21. R. Miller, *Boom* (London: Weidenfeld & Nicolson, 2016), 121.

22. Hugh Trenchard to Philip Game, 7 May 1943, BPFP. The other members were: Charles Longcroft and William Mitchell.

23. Trenchard to Brancker, 4 December 1916, MFC76/1/8, RAFM; Trenchard to Brancker, 18 January 1917, MFC76/1/9, RAFM.

24. Philip Game to Gwendolen Game, 12 November 1916, Private Papers of Air Vice-Marshal Sir Philip Game, IWM Documents 10986.

25. Philip Game to Gwendolen Game, 18 April 1916, Private Papers of Air Vice-Marshal Sir Philip Game, IWM Documents 10986.

26. Trenchard to Brooke-Popham 10 May 1919, MFC76/1/140/1, RAFM.

27. L. A. Strange, *Recollections of an Airman* (London: John Hamilton, 1933), 92–93.

28. The six were: Brigadier-General H. R. M. Brooke-Popham; Brigadier-General P. W. Game; Lieutenant-Colonel F. Festing; Major E. B. Gordon; Major A. Christie; and Lieutenant G. Garrod.

29. Baring, *Flying Corps Headquarters*, 66.
30. Trenchard Autobiographical Narrative, p. 79, MFC76/6/61, RAFM.
31. Baring, *Flying Corps Headquarters*, 53.
32. Tizard had been working at CFS on the calibration of bombsights. R. W. Clark, *Tizard* (London: Methuen, 1965), 32–33. Brooke-Popham sent Tizard for a week to a bombing squadron on the Somme to give him an opportunity to fly as an observer on a raid. Draft Autobiography, Tizard Papers, 713, IWM.
33. When Brooke-Popham was CinC of Air Defence Great Britain (ADGB) and Tizard was chairman of the Aeronautical Research Committee.
34. Baring, *Flying Corps Headquarters*, 136–37.
35. E. Pollard and H. Strouts, eds., *Wings over the Western Front: The First World War Diaries of Collingwood Ingram* (Charlbury, UK: Day Books, 2014), 38.
36. Baring, *Flying Corps Headquarters*, 152.
37. Brooke-Popham received his third mention in dispatches on 13 November 1916.
38. Dye, *The Bridge to Airpower*, 91.
39. Brooke-Popham, "The Air Force," *RUSI Journal* 65 (February 1920): 70.
40. Staff College Andover Papers, AIR 69/1, TNA.
41. Burke to Brooke-Popham, 7 January and 15 March 1917, BPFP.
42. Brooke-Popham to Saunders, 2 August 1951, V/1/6, Trenchard Archive.
43. Festing was first appointed DAA & QMG at HQ RFC in March 1915, on transfer from the Northumberland Fusiliers. He chose not to serve in the post-war RAF, instead joining Sefton Brancker at the Department of Civil Aviation.
44. Trenchard to Brancker, 7 July 1917, MFC76/1/7, RAFM.
45. T. B. Marson, *Scarlet and Khaki* (London: Jonathan Cape, 1930), 158.
46. "Sir John Salmond (Draft) Autobiography," B2621/4, RAFM.
47. "Distribution of Duties Chart: HQ RAF Equipment Branch," AIR 1/1159/204 /5/2459, TNA.
48. Salmond was willing to release Philip Game, but not Brooke-Popham. The former returned to the UK in the summer of 1918, to take up the post of GOC South Western Area.
49. Philip Game to Gwendolen Game, 31 March 1918, Private Papers of Air Vice-Marshal Sir Philip Game, IWM Documents 10986.
50. Brooke-Popham to Huggins, 13 April 1918, AIR 1/1/4/11, TNA.
51. Baring, *Flying Corps Headquarters*, 127. Desclos, a graduate of Westminster City School, joined HQ RFC in January 1916 and was awarded the Military Cross (MC) and Legion d'Honneur for his work. He later became director of the College Franco-Britannique in Paris. During World War II, he helped organize an escape route for Allied airmen. His daughter, Anne Desclos (Dominique Aury), was the author of the controversial novel, *Story of O*.
52. Desclos to Brooke-Popham, 20 December 1925, BPFP.
53. H. A. Jones, *The War in the Air*, vol. 4 (Oxford: Clarendon Press, 1934), 356–57.

54. Huggins to Brooke-Popham, 6 January 1917, Hynes to Brooke-Popham, 5 June 1919, BPFP.

55. Lord Brabazon of Tara, *The Brabazon Story* (London: William Heinemann, 1956), 101–2.

56. The other member of Brooke-Popham's personal staff in France was Percy Threadkell, his prewar groom and batman. Threadkell continued working for Brooke-Popham until well after World War II. When he retired, he was provided with a cottage and an annuity.

57. *The Aeroplane*, 30 October 1953, p. 591.

58. Dye, *The Bridge to Airpower*, 116–26.

59. Pollard and Strouts, *Wings over the Western Front*, 236–37.

60. "War Experiences," pp. 9–10, AIR 1/2390/228/11/124, TNA.

61. Havers to Brooke-Popham, 14 June 1944, BPFP.

62. Bowler to Opal, 22 October 1953, BPFP. Air Vice-Marshal Geoffrey Bowler was AOC 40 & 42 Groups during World War II.

63. L. F. R. Fell, "The Engine Repair Shops Pont de L'Arche," *Royal Aeronautical Society Journal*, 1966, p. 168.

64. G. P. Bulman, "Early Days," *Royal Aeronautical Society Journal*, 1966, pp. 176–77.

65. Game to Opal, 25 October 1953, BPFP.

66. Grey, "On Making a Note of It," 1023.

67. Trenchard to Brooke-Popham, 4 June 1919, BPFP.

68. Captain Thomas Bertrand Marson, London Yeomanry, served as private secretary to Trenchard for seven years (1919–27). Marson, who lost a leg at Gallipoli, was seconded to the RFC in November 1916 and served as the recording officer of No. 56 Squadron (February–December 1917). After a period with the RFC Mission in the U.S.A., he served with the 8th Brigade (later the Independent Force), returning to the UK in February 1919. He was mentioned in dispatches and awarded the MBE (Member of the British Empire) in 1919 for services in France.

69. Marson wanted Brooke-Popham's assessment of Robert Clark-Hall, who had been the deputy commandant at Andover. Marson to Brooke-Popham, 7 March 1925, MFC76/1/189/1, RAFM.

70. In the event, Steel stayed in post for a further year until being replaced by Cyril Newall.

71. Bruce, *The Aeroplanes of the Royal Flying Corps*, xiii.

CHAPTER 6. DIRECTOR OF RESEARCH

1. R. Brooke-Popham, foreword to *The First War in the Air*, by R. H. Kiernan (London: Peter Davies, 1934), 13.

2. *London Gazette*, 1 August 1919, p. 9864, and 22 August 1919, p. 10655.

3. Defence Statement, Mayhew vs. Brooke-Popham, 12 July 1918, BPFP.

4. Robert Brooke-Popham Record of Service, DC76/74/130, RAFM.
5. Fell would later join Rolls Royce, where he would become a key figure in the development of the Merlin aero-engine. Major Harry Wimperis, later director of scientific research at the Air Ministry, was responsible for navigational duties. "Directorate of Research Staff Duties," 4 July 1919, BPFP. George Bulman headed the Air Ministry's engine team from 1928 to 1944 and was a key figure in the development of the Rolls Royce Merlin. Sergeant (later Group Captain) Frederick Victor Charles Laws, a prewar Coldstream Guardsman, transferred to the RFC on its formation in 1912, where his expertise in the field of photography made a crucial contribution, then and later, to the development of aerial reconnaissance techniques.
6. Warrington-Morris to Opal, 20 October 1953, BPFP. Air Commodore Alfred Warrington-Morris commanded the Observer Corps during the Battle of Britain.
7. With effect from 13 July 1919.
8. Secretary of State for Air, *Permanent Organization of the Royal Air Force* (London: HMSO, 1919).
9. Brooke-Popham to Woodburn Kirby, October 1953, BPFP.
10. *Flight*, 20 March 1919, p. 378; *Flight*, 18 March 1921, p. 309; *Flight*, 3 March 1921, p. 149.
11. H. R. M. Brooke-Popham, "The Air Force," *RUSI Journal* 65 (February 1920): 43–70.
12. Notes on Policy of Directorate of Research, BP/1/3/23, LHCMA.
13. M. C. Neale, *The Memoirs of George Purvis Bulman* (Derby, UK: Rolls Royce Heritage Trust, 2002), 96.
14. Dunn had learned to fly at Hendon in 1913, aged nineteen, and volunteered for the RFC on the outbreak of war. He joined No. 3 Squadron as a Sergeant Pilot in October 1914 and was commissioned the following April. He spent much of the war flight-testing aircraft and was awarded the Air Force Cross for his work in November 1918.
15. D. Mountjoy, *The Melody of God and Other Papers* (New York: Dutton, 1922), 51.
16. Ibid., 47–49.
17. Advisory Committee for Aeronautics, *Technical Report of the Advisory Committee for Aeronautics: 1919–1920* (London: HMSO, 1923); Advisory Committee for Aeronautics, *Technical Report of the Aeronautical Research Committee: 1920–1921* (London: HMSO, 1924).
18. T. Hashimoto, "The Wind Tunnel and the Emergence of Aeronautical Research in Britain," in *Atmospheric Flight in the Twentieth Century*, edited by P. Galison and A. Roland (London: Kluwer Academic, 2000), 229.
19. Ibid., 237.
20. J. Erskine-Murray, "Wireless in the Royal Air Force," *Journal of the Institution of Electrical Engineers* 59, no. 302 (June 1921): 693–700.

21. Goldschmidt had worked with Westinghouse before the war.

22. BP/1/3/10, LHCMA.

23. BP/1/3/14, LHCMA.

24. P. Dye, "The Cairo-Baghdad Air Route," in *Lawrence of Arabia & Middle East Airpower*, edited by P. Dye (Warwick, UK: Cross & Cockade International, 2016), 41–48.

25. Report by Air Commodore Brooke-Popham on the Flight from Amman to Baghdad, BP1/3/15, LHCMA.

26. He joined the society in 1929, later becoming vice-president. A fellow member was Edward Ellington.

27. BP/1/3/20, LHCMA.

28. H. R. M. Brooke-Popham, "Aeroplanes in Tropical Countries," *Royal Aeronautical Society Journal* 25 (1921): 563–80; H. R. M. Brooke-Popham, "Some Notes on Aeroplanes with Special Reference to the Air Route from Cairo to Baghdad," *Journal of the Royal Central Asian Society* 9, no. 3 (1922): 218–19.

29. Brooke-Popham, "Tropical Countries," p. 577; Report on Junkers Monoplane, AIR 10/494, TNA.

30. P. Kelly, "Biplane to Monoplane: Twenty Years of Technological Development in British Fighter Aircraft, 1919–1939," PhD thesis, University of Edinburgh, 2013.

31. AIR 2/1208, TNA.

32. "Draft specification F.7/30," produced by Air Commodore Holt, Director Technical Development, AIR 2/2815, TNA.

33. BP/1/3/24, LHCMA.

34. Brooke-Popham to Marson, 11 October 1921, MFC76/1/189/1, RAFM.

35. C. G. Grey, *A History of the Air Ministry* (London: George Allen & Unwin, 1940), 187–88.

CHAPTER 7. ROYAL AIR FORCE STAFF COLLEGE

1. R. A. Mason, *History of the Royal Air Force Staff College 1922–1972* (Bracknell, UK: RAF Staff College, 1972), 2–3; "The Formation of the RAF Staff College," BP/9/12/52, LHCMA.

2. "The Formation of the RAF Staff College," BP/9/12/52, LHCMA.

3. "The Formation of the RAF Staff College—Air Chief Marshal Sir R. Brooke-Popham," BP/9/12/52, LHCMA. Henry Edward Bethell (No. 348) joined the RFC in September 1912. He served with HQ RFC from August 1914 until the armistice. He was later commissioned into the Equipment Branch, retiring as a wing commander. Brooke-Popham was godfather to his son.

4. The senior instructor was Air Commodore Robert Clark-Hall. The four supporting instructors were: Wilfrid Freeman, Bertine "Bertie" Sutton, Charles Edmonds, and Philip Joubert de la Ferté.

5. Report on Ecole Supérieure, 3 December 1921, BP/1/3/25, LHCMA.
6. Ibid.; Report on the Preliminary Education of Candidates for RAF Commissions, March 1919, BP/1/8/3, LHCMA.
7. Joubert de la Ferté, *The Fated Sky*, 86–87.
8. *The Alpine Journal*, November 1989, p. 305; Beauman to Brooke-Popham, 7 June 1931, BPFP. Beauman was the RAF liaison officer with the BBC during World War II.
9. The Work of the RAF Staff College, 5 May 1925, BP/1/5/10, LHCMA.
10. Baldwin had been commissioned into the 8th Hussars before transferring to the RFC in 1915. He attended IDC in 1928.
11. John Baldwin to Opal, 21 October 1953, BPFP.
12. Andre Walser to Opal, 28 October 1953, BPFP.
13. Betty Leslie to Opal, 24 October 1953, BPFP; Bottomley to Opal, 21 October 1953, BPFP. Wing Commander Sir Norman Leslie later served in the Secretariat of the Committee for Imperial Defence.
14. Guy Garrod to Opal, 22 October 1953, BPFP.
15. Chris Courtney to Opal, 20 October 1953, BPFP.
16. P. Wykeham, "Popham, Sir (Henry) Robert Moore Brooke- (1878–1953)."
17. Brooke-Popham to Opal, 13 September 1925, BPFP.
18. Brooke-Popham to Opal, 17 August 1925, BPFP.
19. V. Orange, *Churchill and His Airmen* (London: Grub Street, 2013), 87; R. A. Mason, "British Air Power," in *Global Airpower*, edited by J. Olsen (Washington, D.C.: Potomac Books, 2011), 26–27; V. Orange, *Park: The Biography of Air Chief Marshal Sir Keith Park* (London: Grub Street, 2001), 44–45. Orange appears to have changed his mind about both Andover and Brooke-Popham in the years since his biography of Keith Park was published.
20. R. Mahoney, "The Forgotten Career of Air Chief Marshal Sir Trafford Leigh-Mallory," PhD thesis, University of Birmingham, 2015, pp. 215–34.
21. J. Birley, "A Lecture on the Psychology of Courage Delivered at the Royal Air Force Staff College," *The Lancet*, 21 April 1923, pp. 779–785. He would return to Andover in 1925 to lecture on "The Science of Psychology; Its Past and Present."
22. Summary of Remarks by Air Commodore Brooke-Popham, BP/1/5/3, LHCMA.
23. P. Meilinger, "Trenchard and 'Morale Bombing': The Evolution of Royal Air Force Doctrine before World War II," *The Journal of Military History* 60 (April 1996): 263.
24. BP/1/5/3, LHCMA.
25. Ibid.
26. A. English, "The RAF Staff College and the Evolution of RAF Strategic Bombing Policy 1922–1929," MA thesis, Royal Military College of Canada, April 1987, pp. 45–65.

27. Parton, "RAF Doctrine," pp. 1155–77.
28. Final Address to the First Course, 1923, BP/1/5/7, LHCMA.
29. Parton, "RAF Doctrine," p. 1160.
30. Brooke-Popham to Marson, 26 March 1923, MFC76/1, RAFM.
31. J. Haslam, "Archaeology from the Air: A Note," *Antiquity* 58, no. 240 (July 1979): 140; BP/4/10/4, LHCMA. Brooke-Popham would maintain a long correspondence during the 1930s with O. G. S. Crawford, editor of *Antiquity*, on aerial photography of historic sites in the Middle East.
32. Joubert de la Ferté, *The Fated Sky*, 87–89.
33. R. V. Dodds and R. Collishaw, *Air Command—A Fighter Pilot's Story* (London: Kimber, 1973), 224–26. Collishaw commanded Egypt Group (Desert Air Force) from April 1939 to June 1942. He retired as an air vice-marshal in 1943.
34. English, "The RAF Staff College," pp. 74–78.
35. W. Ralph, *William Barker V.C.—The Life, Death and Legend of Canada's Most Decorated War Hero* (Mississauga, Ontario: John Wiley, 2007), 215–16.
36. A. Furse, *Wilfrid Freeman, The Genius behind Allied Survival and Air Supremacy 1939–1945* (Staplehurst, UK: Spellmount, 1999), 47–48.
37. Portal to Brooke-Popham, 6 October 1946, BPFP.
38. Ismay to Brooke-Popham, January 1947, BPFP; Report by Commandant at Conclusion of Third Course, Ismay/1/1/23, LHCMA. In his end-of-course report, Brooke-Popham recorded that Ismay "by his knowledge and ability, has contributed in no small degree to the value of the course and he has been most helpful to the Directing Staff."
39. Powell to Brooke-Popham, 21 October 1953, BPFP.
40. Brooke-Popham to Opal, 27 September 1925, BPFP.
41. Air Ministry: Royal Air Force Staff College, Andover, Reports and Papers, AIR 69, TNA. Brooke-Popham's handwritten annotations, refining and developing points, appear throughout these papers.
42. H. R. M. Brooke-Popham, "Air Warfare," in *The Study of War for Statesmen and Citizens: Lectures Delivered in the University of London during the Years 1925–26*, edited by G. Aston (London: Longmans, Green, 1927), 149–94.
43. A. Searle, "Inter-service Debate and the Origins of Strategic Culture: The 'Principles of War' in the British Armed Forces 1919–1939," *War in History* 21, no. 1 (2014): 15.
44. B. Liddell Hart, *Paris or The Future of War* (New York: Dutton, 1926); Brooke-Popham to Liddell Hart, 17 July 1925, LH/1/111/1, LHCMA.
45. Brooke-Popham to Marson, 17 July 1925, MFC76/1/189/1, RAFM.
46. D. Reynolds, *In Command of History: Churchill Fighting and Writing the Second World War* (London: Allen Lane, 2005), 396–98. The Air League had been formed in 1909, as the Aerial League of the British Empire, to argue the case for British aviation. Garrod provided material on the strategic bomber offensive for Churchill's *History of the Second World War*.

47. Brooke-Popham to Garrod, 6 December 1949, BP/9/9/37, LHCMA.

48. Brooke-Popham to Saunders, 25 July 1951, V/1/6, Trenchard Archive.

49. Brooke-Popham to Garrod, 6 December 1949, BP/9/9/37, LHCMA.

50. The commandant at Camberley also served for four years.

51. Report at the end of the Fourth Course, RAF Staff College, 30 March 1926, BP/1/5/13, LHCMA.

52. Mason, *Staff College*, 5, 13.

53. Trenchard to Brooke-Popham, 1 January 1924, MFC76/1/189/1, RAFM.

54. English, "The RAF Staff College," p. 102.

55. Carey to Brooke-Popham, 8 December 1943, BPFP.

56. *Cheltenham Chronicle*, 17 January 1925. He also attended successive balls at Gloucester and Cricklade in the next two days.

57. Major Sir John Dearman Birchall had been elected for Leeds North East in 1918. His brother, Edward, was killed on the Western Front in 1916, while serving with the Oxf & Bucks LI.

58. Sir Granville Wheler had served as the MP for Faversham since 1910. The family owned large estates at Ledston Hall in Yorkshire and Otterden Place in Kent.

59. Opal to Brooke-Popham, 28 January 1925, BPFP.

60. Opal to Brooke-Popham, 28 February 1925, BPFP.

61. Brooke-Popham to Opal, 24 October 1925, BPFP.

62. Her mother, Ethel Hugonin (née Clarke) died in 1913 when Opal was just thirteen. Her aunt, Faith Wheler (née Clarke), helped looked after the three children (Francis, Marjorie, and Opal). Opal, being the youngest, was particularly close to her aunt.

63. Brooke-Popham to Opal, 17 August 1925, BPFP.

64. Brooke-Popham to Opal, 19 August 1925, BPFP.

65. Brooke-Popham to Opal, 21 September 1925, BPFP.

66. Trenchard to Brooke-Popham, 26 August 1925, BPFP.

67. Brooke-Popham to Opal, 25 September 1925, BPFP.

68. Brooke-Popham to Opal, 21 September 1925, BPFP.

69. Brooke-Popham to Opal, 23 September 1925, BPFP.

70. Brooke-Popham to Opal, 13 October 1925, BPFP.

71. "RAF Home Defence Force," *Times* (London), 27 November 1925, p. 11.

72. Brooke-Popham to Opal, 10 September 1925, BPFP.

CHAPTER 8. THE FIGHTING AREA

1. The Fifth Course started on 4 May 1926.

2. P. Addison, *Churchill on the Home Front, 1900–1955* (London: Faber & Faber, 2013), 258–65.

3. *The British Gazette* was published in eight editions from 5 to 13 May 1926.

4. Brooke-Popham to Opal, 9 May 1926, BPFP.

5. C. Wrigley, "Churchill and the Trade Unions," *Transactions of the Royal Historical Society* 6, Series 11 (March 2003): 289.

6. Brooke-Popham to Opal, 6 May 1926, BPFP.

7. Brooke-Popham to Opal, 9 May 1926, BPFP.

8. Brooke-Popham to Opal, 10 May 1926, BPFP.

9. Sassoon was undersecretary of state for Air from 1924 to 1929 and again from 1931 to 1937.

10. Brooke-Popham to Opal, 11 May 1926, BPFP.

11. Hoare to Trenchard, 13 May 1926, BPFP.

12. M. Howard, "The Armed Forces and the Community," *RUSI Journal* 141, no. 4 (August 1996): 9–12.

13. *Flight*, 3 June 1926, p. 325.

14. Air Historical Branch, *A Short History of the Royal Air Force* (London: Air Ministry, 1929), 431–32.

15. House of Lords Debate, 26 June 1923, *Hansard*, cols. 570–2.

16. James, *The Growth of Fighter Command*, 1–6.

17. P. Wykeham, *Fighter Command: A Study of Air Defence 1914–1960* (London: Putnam, 1960), 26–27.

18. The origins of the raid intelligence system can be traced to the Romer Committee of 1924, which recommended a network of observation posts organized into Observer Groups, each with an Observer Centre. James, *The Growth of Fighter Command*, 3.

19. Ibid., 27.

20. Wykeham, *Fighter Command*, 28.

21. *Flight*, 6 May 1926, p. 272; James, *The Growth of Fighter Command*, 128.

22. Ibid., 20.

23. Herbert was one of the original RFC officers who flew to France in August 1914. He later commanded No. 13 Squadron but spent much of the war in training appointments.

24. Hillingdon House had been previously occupied by Headquarters Inland Area but this had moved to Bentley Priory.

25. Brooke-Popham to Opal, 16 September 1925, BPFP.

26. Group Captain (later Air Chief Marshal) Wilfrid Freeman was commandant of the Central Flying School based at Upavon.

27. Brooke-Popham to Opal, 2 June 1926, BPFP. Wing Commander Charles Gould was the senior technical officer at Headquarters Fighting Area. He had been one of Brooke-Popham's depot commanders in France.

28. For a comprehensive overview of the development of acoustic detection in Britain during the interwar years see: C. Dobinson, *Building Radar: Forging Britain's Early-Warning Chain, 1935–1945* (London: Methuen, 2010), 1–52.

29. Ibid., 50.

30. Orange, *Park*, 50.
31. Wykeham, *Fighter Command*, 28.
32. Trenchard to Brooke-Popham, 4 July 1927, BPFP.
33. Stanley Baldwin, House of Commons Debate, 10 November 1932, *Hansard*, vol. 270, col. 632.
34. *Flight*, 4 August 1927, p. 536; *Flight*, 23 August 1928, pp. 721–28.
35. *Flight*, 16 August 1928, p. 715.
36. *Flight*, 28 July 1927, p. 526.
37. Brooke-Popham to Opal, 16 June 1926, BPFP. Flying Officer Anthony Clifford Addams, No. 41 Squadron, was killed at Northolt on 16 June 1926 when he stalled in a Siskin. The accident was attributed to pilot error.
38. Brooke-Popham to Opal, 26 September 1925, BPFP.
39. Trenchard to Brooke-Popham, 7 August 1928, MFC76/1/5, RAFM. This included structural failure, as in the case of Flight Lieutenant Lance Browning, killed on 2 August 1928, while flying a Woodcock over Holbeach Ranges.
40. Brooke-Popham to Opal, 20 June 1926, BPFP; Brooke-Popham to Opal, 1 September 1927, BPFP. Flying Officer Alexander Montgomery crashed at Locks Heath School, Warsash, on 4 March 1925 while low flying. Dora Bell (age thirteen) was killed and her teacher badly injured, although Montgomery survived unhurt. The next year, yet another pilot was court-martialed for low flying (while trying to impress a young woman).
41. G. Ellis, *Toolbox on the Wing* (Shrewsbury, UK: Airlife, 1983), 41–42.
42. Joubert de la Ferté, *Fun and Games*, 149.
43. M. Francis, *The Flyer: British Culture and the Royal Air Force 1939–1945* (Oxford: Oxford University Press, 2008), 99.
44. S. Jervis, "Moving Experiences: Responses to Relocation among British Military Wives," in *Gender and Family among Transnational Professionals*, edited by A. Coles and A. Fechter (London: Routledge, 2006), 159.
45. M. Tristrum, *Women of the Regiment* (Cambridge: Cambridge University Press, 1984), 10–11.
46. J. James, *The Paladins* (London: Macdonald, 1990), 168–79.
47. K. Carroll, *Compass Course: The Log of an Air Force Officer's Wife* (London: Hutchinson, 1941).
48. Joubert de la Ferté, *Fun and Games*, 149.
49. Brooke-Popham to Opal, 15 February 1929, BPFP.
50. Francis, *The Flyer*, 95.
51. Brooke-Popham to Opal, 11 October 1932, BPFP.
52. Brooke-Popham to Opal, 9 June 1926, BPFP.
53. Brooke-Popham to Opal, 11 June 1926, BPFP.
54. "Why Queen Mary Turns the Cold Shoulder to Divorcees," *Detroit Free Press*, 23 November 1930, p. 64.

55. "Personal Assistant" equated to ADC. Taaffe was appointed on 5 July 1926. He served with No. 55 Squadron in Iraq and by 1938 was in command of No. 223 Squadron, Eastleigh, Nairobi. He was awarded the OBE in 1940 and mentioned in dispatches in 1944, retiring as a group captain in 1951.

56. J. Laffin, *Swifter than Eagles* (London: William Blackwood, 1964), 204–7.

57. Scarlett to Brooke-Popham, 15 October 1928, BPFP.

58. Vi Barrington-Kennett was godmother to Diana, and Hugh Trenchard was godfather to Philip.

59. *Supplement to The London Gazette*, 3 June 1927, p. 3605. Brooke-Popham was made a Knight Commander of the Order of the Bath (KCB).

60. Much to Brooke-Popham's surprise, and genuine disappointment, Scarlett was never knighted, although he took over the Fighting Area in January 1929 and then commanded RAF Middle East, before retiring in 1932.

61. Opal to Robert, 13 February 1927, BPFP.

62. Robert to Opal, 15 February 1927, BPFP. The reference is to Isabella Linton, a fictional character in *Wuthering Heights*, who fled her unhappy marriage.

63. Draft Poem, June 1927, BPFP.

64. *Times* (London), 15 December 1927, p. 18. Sir Granville Wheler died at Otterden Place on 14 December 1927.

65. Aunt Faith survived her husband by nearly twenty years, dying at Folkestone in March 1945.

66. All three of Herbert's sons were killed on RAF operations during World War II.

67. *Flight*, 7 March 1930, p. 284.

68. Bouchier to Brooke-Popham, 10 March 1953, BPFP. Bouchier was a flight commander with No. 41 Squadron at Northolt.

69. LH/15/3/123, LHCMA.

70. *Flight*, 10 March 1927, p. 4.

71. *Flight*, 23 August 1928, p. 722.

72. A practice famously followed by Keith Park, when he commanded No. 11 Group in 1940.

73. Including the Sir Philip Sassoon Cup competed for by pilots in the Fighting Area, and the Brooke-Popham Cup, for the best performance at armament practice camp.

74. Orange, *Park*, 50.

75. *Flight*, 12 July 1928, p. 603.

CHAPTER 9. IRAQ COMMAND

1. K. C. Ulrichsen, "The British Occupation of Mesopotamia, 1918–1922," *Journal of Strategic Studies* 30, no. 2 (April 2007): 349–77.

2. A. A. Allawi, *Faisal I of Iraq* (London: Yale University Press, 2014), 278–79.

3. Ibid., 359.

4. W. Dockter, *Churchill and the Islamic World* (London: I. B. Taurus, 2015), 103–20.

5. Air Historical Branch, *A Short History*, 438.

6. M. Paris, "Air Power and Imperial Defence (1880–1919)," *Journal of Contemporary History* 24 (1989): 209–25. The potential for airpower in imperial defense had been recognized as early as 1880. The concept was tested before World War I, although the capabilities involved were modest. Air control in Iraq drew on these longstanding ideas.

7. One issue that was not resolved was the proposed creation of an independent Kurdish state.

8. D. Silverfarb, "Great Britain, Iraq and Saudi Arabia: The Revolt of the Ikhwan, 1927–1930," *International History Review* 4, no. 2 (May 1982): 222–48.

9. J. B. Glubb, *War in the Desert* (London: Hodder & Stoughton, 1960), 247.

10. Brooke-Popham also met with the king at Buckingham Palace on 31 October and with the secretary of state later the same day.

11. Trenchard to Brooke-Popham, 1 November 1928, BPFP.

12. T. Paris, *In Defence of Britain's Middle East Empire: A Life of Sir Gilbert Clayton* (Brighton, UK: Sussex Academic Press, 2015). Clayton had served as chief secretary of Palestine, 1922–25, and had recently negotiated with Ibn Saud on behalf of the British government.

13. The RAF also operated a fortnightly airmail service using the same route. The total journey time for mail between the UK and Iraq was approximately five days.

14. Brooke-Popham, "Tropical Countries," p. 574.

15. Brooke-Popham to Opal, 25 November 1928, BPFP.

16. Ibid.

17. Brooke-Popham to Opal, 8 January 1929, BPFP. Buss had converted to Islam and had a Turkish wife. He spoke Arabic fluently and was regarded by Brooke-Popham as "most valuable." Buss retired as an air commodore in 1943 but continued to be employed on intelligence duties until the end of the war.

18. Guy Carter had served as a fighter pilot in World War I, before being shot down and captured in 1918. He died (as an air commodore) in a flying accident in 1944.

19. Brooke-Popham to Opal, 28 September 1929, BPFP. The officer concerned was Squadron Leader David Stodart, DSO, DFC, a World War I veteran. He was not entirely honest with Brooke-Popham about the circumstances. He had shot his victim five times, after returning to his office to retrieve his pistol.

20. Silverfarb, "The Revolt of the Ikhwan," pp. 223–25.

21. Allawi, *Faisal*, 465–66.

22. CID Paper 149-C, 26 July 1921, CAB 5/4, TNA.

23. Diary entry, 9 December 1921, cited in *Field Marshal Sir Henry Wilson, His Life and Diaries*, edited by C. E. Callwell (London: Cassell, 1927), 316.

24. Boyle, *Trenchard*, 383.

25. *Daily Telegraph*, 21 November 1921.
26. E. L. Howard-Williams and S. Hay, *Air over Eden* (London: Hutchinson, 1937); E. L. Howard-Williams, "Air Control," *Popular Flying*, January 1939, pp. 493–95 and 524–25.
27. J. Slessor, *The Central Blue* (London: Cassell, 1956), 63.
28. P. Satia, *Spies in Arabia* (Oxford: Oxford University Press, 2008), 250; W. Reid, *Empire of Sand: How Britain Made the Middle East* (Edinburgh: Birlinn, 2013), 318–19.
29. February to September 1923.
30. D. Omissi, *Air Power and Colonial Control: The Royal Air Force 1919–1939* (Manchester, UK: Manchester University Press, 1990), 175; Charlton, *Charlton*, 271–86.
31. Omissi, *Air Power and Colonial Control*, 176.
32. R. Graves, *T. E. Lawrence to His Biographer* (London: Jonathan Cape, 1938), 111.
33. *Times* (London), 8 May 1930, p. 12.
34. P. Satia, "The Defence of Inhumanity: Air Control and the British Idea of Arabia," *American Historical Review* 111 (February 2006): 18.
35. R. M. Douglas, "Did Britain Use Chemical Weapons in Mandatory Iraq?," *Journal of Modern History* 81.4 (December 2009): 859–87; R. Fisk, "Iraq 1917," *Independent*, 16 June 2004; Omissi, *Air Power and Colonial Control*, 212. David Omissi, who is otherwise critical about air control, makes it clear that British strategic bombing doctrine owed little to the RAF's experiences in Iraq.
36. Brooke-Popham to Opal, 8 January 1928, BPFP. A description of this same action can be found in Glubb, *War in the Desert*, 239–42.
37. Much to his chagrin, Brooke-Popham discovered that Murdhi Ar Rufidi, whose life he had helped save in July 1921, was one of the Ikhwan rebels.
38. *Report on the Operations Carried Out in the Southern Desert in Connection with the Iraq-Najd Borders June 1928–May 1929, CD 76* (London: Air Ministry, 1930), p. 13; Silverfarb, "The Revolt of the Ikhwan," p. 230.
39. Silverfarb, "The Revolt of the Ikhwan," pp. 235–36.
40. Brooke-Popham to Trenchard, 19 July 1929, MFC76/1/142, RAFM.
41. Brooke-Popham to Trenchard, 30 July 1921, MFC76/1/5, RAFM.
42. Brooke-Popham to Opal, 3 January 1929, BPFP.
43. C. Bowyer, *RAF Operations, 1918–1938* (London: William Kimber, 1988), 95. He routinely flew in a D.H. 9A biplane, painted blood red with white inter-plane struts, a tradition started by Ellington.
44. Satia, "The Defence of Inhumanity," p. 27; Brooke-Popham, "Tropical Countries," p. 573.
45. Brooke-Popham to Opal, 25 November 1928, BPFP.
46. Bowyer, *RAF Operations*, 188–97; A. Baker and R. Ivelaw-Chapman, *Wings over Kabul* (London: William Kimber, 1975). The RAF mounted a series of evacuation flights between 23 December 1928 and 25 February 1929, with the loss of one Victoria due to engine failure.

47. A further five Victorias were sent to India in February. One aircraft, flown by Squadron Leader Rice, was written off in a landing accident on the return journey.

48. I. M. Philpott, *The Royal Air Force: An Encyclopedia of the Inter-War Years*, vol. 1, *1918–1929* (Barnsley, UK: Pen and Sword, 2005), 81.

49. Brooke-Popham to Opal, 28 December 1928, BPFP.

50. Trenchard to Clayton, 29 January 1929, MFC76/1/66, RAFM.

51. Clayton to Trenchard, 28 July 1929, MFC76/1/66, RAFM.

52. Clayton to Trenchard, 8 April 1929, MFC76/1/66, RAFM.

53. Brooke-Popham to Trenchard, 16 September 1929, MFC76/1/142, RAFM.

54. Brooke-Popham to Lord Passfield (Secretary of State for the Colonies), 16 September 1929, BP/2/3/10, LHCMA.

55. Control of the Levies (largely recruited from Assyrian Christians) passed from the Colonial Office to the RAF in 1928.

56. C. Morris, "RAF Armoured Car Companies in Iraq (Mostly) 1921–1946," *RAF Historical Society Journal*, no. 48 (2010): 20–38. Eight sections were originally deployed, from Kirkuk in the north to Basra in the south. By April 1930 there were just four sections, each comprising three to four armored cars, plus support vehicles and tenders.

57. Brooke-Popham to Trenchard, 10 June 1929, MFC76/1/142, RAFM.

58. Trenchard to Brooke-Popham, 15 July 1929, MFC76/1/142, RAFM.

59. Glubb, *War in the Desert*, 226.

60. John Glubb to Brooke-Popham, 20 April 1936, BPFP. Glubb commanded the Arab Legion from 1939 to 1956.

61. Glubb, *War in the Desert*, 235.

62. Ibid., 261.

63. Brooke-Popham to Opal, 7 March 1929, BPFP.

64. Brooke-Popham to Opal, 27 March 1929, BPFP.

65. Clayton to Trenchard, 28 July 1929, MFC76/1/66, RAFM.

66. Brooke-Popham to Air Ministry, October 1930, BP/2/1/49, LHCMA.

67. Brooke-Popham to Opal, 9 August 1929, BPFP.

68. Brooke-Popham, "Tropical Countries," p. 574.

69. Satia, "The Defence of Inhumanity," p. 40.

70. Brooke-Popham to Opal, 25 January 1929, BPFP.

71. "The Cape Ragging Case," *Times* (London), 11 June 1903, p. 4; "A Shocking Offence," *Adelaide Advertiser*, 13 June 1903, p. 5.

72. Brooke-Popham to Opal, 10 August 1929, BPFP.

73. Brooke-Popham to Opal, 13 September 1929, BPFP.

74. Young, who arrived on 30 September 1929, had already been selected to take over as counsellor from Bernard Bourdillon. He served in Iraq until 1932.

75. Allawi, *Faisal*, 464.

76. Ibid., 509–10.

77. Brooke-Popham to Opal, 18 September 1929, BPFP.

78. Brooke-Popham to Trenchard, 18 November 1929, MFC76/1/142, RAFM.

79. Brooke-Popham would also act as high commissioner in September 1930, during Humphrys' temporary absence.

80. Brooke-Popham to Opal, 4 October 1930, BPFP.

81. C. H. Keith, *Flying Years* (London: John Hamilton, 1938), 282.

82. Silverfarb, "The Revolt of the Ikhwan," p. 246.

83. Notes on the Conference Held at Ibn Saud's Camp, BP/2/1/43, LHCMA.

84. Allawi, *Faisal*, 526–28.

85. Air Headquarters Iraq, 26 February 1930, MFC76/1/142, RAFM.

86. Handwritten Notes of a Meeting of King Faisal and King Ibn Saud, February 1930, BPFP.

87. Ibid.

88. Brooke-Popham to Opal, 20 May 1930, BPFP; "Relations with Other Services," *Times* (London), 2 May 1930, p. 15.

89. S. Roskill, *Naval Policy between the Wars*, vol. 1, *The Period of Anglo-American Antagonism 1919–1929* (London: Collins, 1968), 523–24.

90. H. Montgomery Hyde, *British Air Policy between the Wars 1918–1939* (London: Heinemann, 1976), 101–2.

91. Bowyer, *RAF Operations*, 101–3. Coincident with Brooke-Popham's arrival, new aircraft types had begun to replace the World War I–era D.H. 9As and Bristol Fighters that had previously equipped the RAF squadrons in Iraq. This changeover was completed by early 1931.

92. Satia, *Spies in Arabia*, 240.

93. Telegrams, 5 April 1924 and 7 August 1924, AIR 23/547, TNA.

94. Brooke-Popham to Marson, 11 October 1921, MFC76/1/189/1, RAFM.

95. Lecture to Army Staff College, 16 June 1931, BP/2/3/10, LHCMA. The resources available to Brooke-Popham comprised: five squadrons (forty-nine aircraft); four sections of armored cars (sixteen vehicles); 2,126 RAF personnel; 1,772 Levies; and 8,750 Iraqi Army personnel.

96. Allawi, *Faisal*, 536.

97. Omissi, *Air Power and Colonial Control*, 212.

98. Brooke-Popham to Opal, 15 July 1930, BPFP.

99. Brooke-Popham to Opal, 24 August 1930, BPFP.

100. Brooke-Popham to Opal, 22 May 30, BPFP.

101. D. Silverfarb, *Britain's Informal Empire in the Middle East: A Case Study of Iraq, 1929–1941* (Oxford: Oxford University Press, 1986), 30.

102. BP/2/1/48, LHCMA.

103. Silverfarb, *Britain's Informal Empire*, 31.

104. Brooke-Popham to Opal, 3 September 1930, BPFP.

105. Humphrys to Brooke-Popham, 15 December 1930, BPFP.

106. Humphrys to Brooke-Popham, 5 July 1930, BPFP.

107. Brooke-Popham to Opal, 14 November 1928, BPFP.

108. D. Omissi, "Britain, the Assyrians and the Iraq Levies 1919–1932," *Journal of Imperial and Commonwealth History* 17, no. 3 (1989): 301–22.

109. Jack Salmond to Brooke-Popham, 18 September 1930, MFC76/1/142, RAFM.

110. J. Corum, "The Myth of Air Control: Reassessing the History," *Air Power Journal*, Winter 2000, pp. 61–77. This was aimed at discrediting the use of similar methods by the U.S. Air Force.

111. Air Headquarters Memorandum, 29 November 1923, MFC76/1/38/54, RAFM.

112. Brooke-Popham to Jack Salmond, 28 May 1930, MFC76/1/104, RAFM.

113. Brooke-Popham to Liddell Hart, 26 July 1932, LH/1/111/5, LHCMA.

114. "Aspects of Air Operations in the Present War," Notes for South African Broadcast, BP/9/9/8, LHCMA.

115. J. Slessor, *The Great Deterrent* (London: Cassell, 1957), 139–40.

CHAPTER 10. IMPERIAL DEFENCE COLLEGE

1. Brooke-Popham to Trenchard, 10 December 1929, MFC76/1/104, RAFM.

2. T. Gray, ed., *The Imperial Defence College and the Royal College of Defence Studies 1927–1977* (Edinburgh: HMSO, 1977), 1.

3. Ibid., 3.

4. Among the forty-nine students from the UK, Australia, India, and Canada that attended the IDC between 1931 and 1932 were: Lieutenant-Colonel (later General Sir) Arthur Grasett; Captain (later Admiral Sir) Henry Harwood; Wing Commander (later Air Marshal Sir) Paul Maltby; Lieutenant-Colonel (later General) Donald McLeod; Lieutenant-Colonel (later General Sir) Henry Pownall; and Lieutenant-Colonel (later Lieutenant-General Sir) Vernon Sturdee.

5. During Brooke-Popham's tenure as commandant, the directing staff included: Captain (later Admiral Sir) Bertram Ramsay; Captain (later Admiral of the Fleet Sir) James Somerville; Group Captain (later Air Marshal Sir) Bertie Sutton; and Brigadier (later General Sir) Guy Williams.

6. Gray, *Imperial Defence College*, 27. The IDC closed on the outbreak of war but, when it reopened in 1945, the opportunity was taken to relocate to Seaford House in Belgravia, where there was more space and better facilities. It was restyled the Royal College of Defence Studies in 1971.

7. R. Higham, *The Military Intellectuals in Britain* (New Brunswick, NJ: Rutgers University Press, 1966), 51–61; Roskill, *Naval Policy between the Wars*, 1:429.

8. M. E. Chatfield, *It Might Happen Again*, vol. 2, *The Navy and Defence* (London: Heinemann, 1947), 60–61; S. Roskill, *Naval Policy between the Wars*, vol. 2, *The Period of Reluctant Rearmament 1930–1939* (London: Collins, 1976), 56. The First Sea Lord (Ernle Chatfield) regarded Richmond as an unwelcome influence on the prime minister and an irresponsible (albeit able) writer.

9. Chatfield, *It Might Happen Again*, 70. Chatfield claimed that Richmond's lectures and articles disadvantaged the Admiralty in their battle with the air protagonists.

10. B. D. Hunt, *Sailor-Scholar, Admiral Sir Herbert Richmond* (Waterloo, Canada: Wilfrid Laurier University Press, 1982), 163.

11. Boyle, *Trenchard*, 576–77.

12. Private Papers of Wing Commander Sir Archibald James, IWM Documents 11963.

13. A. Wells, "Staff Training and the Royal Navy, 1918–1939," in *War and Society*, Vol. 2, edited by B. Bond and I. Roy (London: Croom Helm, 1977), 86–106.

14. Hunt, *Sailor-Scholar*, 160; Joubert de la Ferté, *The Fated Sky*, 101, and *Fun and Games*, 82–83.

15. Brooke-Popham to Ellington, 13 February 1936, BP/4/3/22, LHCMA.

16. Hunt, *Sailor-Scholar*, 163.

17. Portal to Opal Brooke-Popham, 22 October 1953, BPFP.

18. Jack Salmond to Brooke-Popham, 29 April 1930, MFC76/1/142, RAFM.

19. Brooke-Popham to Opal, 13 September 1931, BPFP.

20. Brooke-Popham to Opal, 14 July 1931, BPFP.

21. Brooke-Popham to Opal, 28 June 1931, BPFP.

22. Brooke-Popham to Opal, 10 July 1931, BPFP.

23. The Chronicle Editorial Committee, *Oxfordshire and Buckinghamshire Light Infantry Journal*, 39:272–76. Eight years younger, Holt had joined Brooke-Popham's company at Chatham, from where he had followed in his mentor's footsteps, learning to fly in 1912 and serving with distinction in the RFC during World War I.

24. Orange, *Churchill and His Airmen*, 128–29.

25. He felt that Brigadier-General John Charteris, *Field Marshal Earl Haig* (London: Cassell, 1929), had given too much credit to Haig for the events of 1918, and not enough to Foch.

26. Foch, commanding 13 Division, had attended the 1912 maneuvers at the invitation of the secretary of state for War. Brooke-Popham joined Trenchard at Foch's funeral in 1929.

27. Brooke-Popham to Liddell Hart, 28 July 1932, LH/1/111/5, LHCMA.

28. Brooke-Popham to Opal, 7 July 1932, BPFP.

29. Brooke-Popham to Opal, 19 September 1932, BPFP; A. Longmore, *From Sea to Sky* (London: Geoffrey Bles, 1946), 179.

30. Brooke-Popham to Opal, 22 October 1931, BPFP.

31. George Ambrose Lloyd, politician and diplomat. He had advocated rearmament as early as 1930. Lloyd was appointed secretary of state for the colonies by Churchill in 1940 but died suddenly a year later.

32. Brooke-Popham to Opal, 7 July 1931, BPFP.

33. Brooke-Popham to Ellington, 13 February 1936, BP/4/3/22, LHCMA.
34. Gray, *The Imperial Defence College*, 6.
35. R. J. Gowen, "British Legerdemain at the 1911 Imperial Conference: The Dominions, Defence Planning and the Renewal of the Anglo-Japanese Alliance," *Journal of Modern History* 52, no. 3 (September 1980): 385–413.
36. Woodburn Kirby, *The War against Japan*, 1:4–5. The alliance was technically in effect until 1923 when the parties failed to ratify it.
37. Ibid., 1:2.
38. Roskill, *Naval Policy between the Wars*, 1:278–79.
39. Woodburn Kirby, *The War against Japan*, 1:7.
40. Ibid., 1:11.
41. Ibid., 1:12.
42. "Z" being the day that the Japanese fleet moved south of the Pescadores Islands. Brooke-Popham later recorded that CID 1084B (Imperial Defence Policy), issued in 1932, calculated that, allowing ten days for the tankers to start, it would take thirty days for the main fleet to reach Singapore.
43. The British commercial counsellor in Shanghai.
44. The British consul-general in Hankow.
45. The British military attaché in Tokyo, 1931–32.
46. Buckingham Gate Notebook No. 1, 1933 BPFP.
47. C. C. Ong, *Operation Matador: Britain's War Plans against the Japanese 1918–1941* (Singapore: Marshall Cavendish, 2011), 35–37.
48. Ibid., 39–42.
49. H. Richmond, "Singapore," *Fortnightly Review*, March 1942, pp. 240–43.
50. Roskill, *Naval Policy between the Wars*, 2:221.
51. "Commandant's Final Remarks, IDC Exercise No 3, 1933," RMSY/5/8, Churchill Archives Centre.
52. Furse, *Wilfrid Freeman*, 48. The defense of Singapore was also the subject of joint sessions with the Royal Navy when Brooke-Popham was commandant at Andover.
53. Hunt, *Sailor-Scholar*, 163.
54. Joubert de la Ferté, *The Fated Sky*, 100.
55. LH/11/935/122, p. 235, LHCMA.
56. Hyde, *British Air Policy between the Wars*, 98–104.
57. Notes on Policy for the Directorate of Research, BP/1/3/23, LHCMA.
58. Lecture to RN War College on "Cooperation," 29 March 1932, BP/9/4/5, LHCMA.
59. Fayle to Brooke-Popham, 26 December 1932, BPFP. Fayle, who was appointed as adviser and lecturer on economics in 1931, was the author of the British official history, *Seaborne Trade*, published in three volumes between 1920 and 1924. He was awarded an OBE in 1937 for his services at the IDC.
60. AOCinC's Notes on the Emergency in the Far East 1935/36, BP/4/12/1, LHCMA.

61. H. Probert, *High Commanders of the Royal Air Force* (London: HMSO, 1991), xxi.

62. *Times* (London), 20 December 1928, p. 14; *Flight*, 16 August 1928, p. 714, and 27 December 1928, p. 1080. *Flight* magazine confidently predicted that Jack Salmond would replace Trenchard as CAS in January 1930.

63. *Flight*, 29 July 1932, p. 704. It was stated that Jack Salmond's retirement would "accelerate the promotion in the junior ranks."

64. Boyle, *Trenchard*, 678–79. Jack Salmond's marriage was under considerable strain at this point and his decision to retire appears to have been driven by family considerations. R. Davenport-Hines, *Ettie: The Intimate Life and Dauntless Spirit of Lady Desborough* (London: Weidenfeld & Nicolson, 2008).

65. Marquess of Londonderry, *Wings of Destiny* (London: Macmillan, 1943), 162.

66. "Notes on RAF Personalities," pp. 234–39, LH/11/1935/122, LHCMA. According to Peck, Geoffrey Salmond was appointed partly because he was favored by the Army and partly because he did not share Trenchard's views.

67. Trenchard to Freeman, 23 February 1948, and Freeman to Trenchard, 24 February 1948, MFC76/1/486, RAFM.

68. *Flight*, 16 August 1928, p. 714.

69. LH/11/1935/122, LHCMA, p. 235. Peck worked closely with Brooke-Popham in 1934–35 when they were both members of the Reorientation Sub-Committee.

70. Ibid.

71. Air Ministry to Brooke-Popham, 26 September 1932, BPFP.

72. Brooke-Popham to Opal, September 1932, BPFP.

CHAPTER 11. AIR DEFENSE OF GREAT BRITAIN

1. Sir Robert Brooke-Popham's Report on War Organisation of the Air Ministry, AIR 2/673, TNA.

2. C. S. Sinnott, "RAF Operational Requirements 1923–39," PhD thesis, Kings College, London, 1998, p. 72.

3. Air Ministry to Brooke-Popham, 26 September 1932, BPFP.

4. In October 1933.

5. Fressanges to Brooke-Popham, 4 January 1950, BPFP. Fressanges was one of the earliest cadets to graduate from the RAF Cadet College at Cranwell. After a distinguished wartime career, he attended the IDC and later served as the RAF's director of intelligence. His last appointment was as CinC Far East Air Force.

6. Although the ten-year rule was regularly reviewed, it dominated defense planning during the interwar period.

7. James, *The Growth of Fighter Command*, 7–8.

8. Ibid., 8.

9. "Defence Requirements," 31 July 1934, CAB 205 (34), TNA.

10. "The Defence of London," *Times* (London), 30 July 1927, p. 11; X005–6545 /004/013, RAFM. From 1932 onward, there was also an annual staff exercise

to develop common methods and more effective cooperation across functional areas within ADGB Headquarters.

11. *Times* (London), 17 July 1933, p. 9.
12. P. R. Burchall, "The Air Attacks on London," *The Spectator*, 2 August 1934, pp. 157–58.
13. Brooke-Popham to Opal, 26 July 1934, BPFP.
14. *Times* (London), 27 July 1934, p. 11.
15. *Flight*, 26 July 1934, pp. 772–73; Joubert de la Ferté, *The Fated Sky*, 106–8.
16. "Co-operation 1934 Acoustical Mirror," AIR 16/318, TNA; "Air Defence of Great Britain: Air Exercises, 1934," AIR 20/186, TNA.
17. "Air Defence of Great Britain: Air Exercises, 1934," AIR 20/186, TNA.
18. J. Ferris, "Fighter Defence before Fighter Command: The Rise of Strategic Air Defence in Great Britain, 1917–1934," *Journal of Military History* 63, no. 4 (1999): 845–84. Unlike the London Air Defence Area of 1918, all the air defense elements (including aircraft) were in communication.
19. Ibid., 850. Air Commodore Charles Higgins commanded the Home Defence Brigade in 1917 and later served as director of staff duties.
20. Orange, *Park*, 50.
21. Brooke-Popham to Opal, 23 September 1925, BPFP.
22. Sefton Brancker to Hugh Trenchard, 19 January 1917, MFC76/1/9, RAFM.
23. James, *The Growth of Fighter Command*, 5.
24. Orange, *Churchill and His Airmen*, 128–29.
25. Other committee members were: Major-General Harold Salt (Commander, Territorial Army Air Defence Formations), Air Vice-Marshal Philip Joubert de la Ferté (AOC Fighting Area), Colonel Thomas Hutton (Directorate of Military Operations in the War Office), and Group Captain Hallam Peck (Deputy Director of Operations and Intelligence in the Air Ministry).
26. "Committee for Imperial Defence, Ad Hoc Sub-Committees, 1935–1936," CAB 16/133, TNA.
27. James, *The Growth of Fighter Command*, 13. This "shopping list" included twenty-five fighter squadrons, antiaircraft guns, balloon aprons, and a comprehensive system of telephone communications.
28. "Air Defence Research: Committee of Imperial Defence," CAB 21/146, TNA; K. Middlemas and J. Barnes, *Baldwin* (London: Weidenfeld & Nicolson, 1969), 844. Although the Cabinet accepted the committee's recommendations, because of Treasury objections approval was only given for Phase 1.
29. James, *The Growth of Fighter Command*, 15.
30. "Aspects of Air Operations in the Present War," Notes for South African Broadcast, 11 May 1940, BP/9/9/8, LHCMA.
31. "Air Defence Systems of Great Britain Meeting Reports," CAB 13/18, TNA.
32. P. Judkins, "Making Vision into Power: Britain's Acquisition of the World's First Radar-based Integrated Air Defence System, 1935–1941," PhD thesis, Cranfield University, UK, 2007, p. 93.

33. "Science and Air Bombing," *Times* (London), 8 August 1934, p. 11.
34. AIR 2/4481, TNA.
35. F. Furneaux-Smith, *The Prof in Two Worlds: The Official Life of Professor F. A. Lindemann, Viscount Cherwell* (London: Collins, 1961), 175–76. Lindemann regarded the Tizard Committee as "somewhat unimportant."
36. Middlemas and Barnes, *Baldwin*, 782–83.
37. CAB 21/426, TNA.
38. Air Ministry to Tizard, 12 December 1934, Tizard Papers, 111, IWM. Tizard was invited to "chair a small committee for the scientific survey of air defence." The other members were: Professor Patrick Blackett, Professor Archibald Hill, and A. P. "Jimmy" Rowe, Wimperis' deputy.
39. Joubert, *Fun and Games*, 87–89; Joubert de la Ferté, *The Fated Sky*, 109–10.
40. Judkins, "Making Vision into Power," p. 106. Brooke-Popham's 1934 diary contains Tizard's contact details (but not his 1933 or 1935 diaries).
41. Joubert, *Fun and Games*, 88.
42. Judkins, "Making Vision into Power," pp. 105–17.
43. Ibid., 107.
44. W. S. Churchill, *The Gathering Storm* (London: Cassell, 1948), 136; P. Bishop, *Battle of Britain* (London: Quercus, 2009), 60–61; J. Holland, *The Battle of Britain* (London: Transworld, 2010), 447–50.
45. R. Watson-Watt, *Three Steps to Victory* (London: Odhams, 1957), 163.
46. Notes on Policy of the Directorate of Research, BP/1/3/23, LHCMA.
47. Judkins, "Making Vision into Power," p. 40.
48. M. Kirby and R. Capey, "The Air Defence of Great Britain 1920–1940: An Operational Research Perspective," *Journal of the Operational Research Society* 48, no. 6 (1977): 555–68.
49. R. W. Clark, *Rise of the Boffins* (London: Phoenix House, 1962), 10–11.
50. "The Royal Air Force Staff College," *Flight*, 7 December 1922, pp. 720–21.
51. Brooke-Popham, Functions of a Staff College, 5 May 1925, BP 1/5/11, LHCMA.
52. D. Edgerton, *Warfare State: Britain 1920–1970* (Cambridge: Cambridge University Press, 2005), 129; A. P. Rowe, *One Story of Radar* (Cambridge: Cambridge University Press, 1948), 1.
53. Tizard to Brooke-Popham, 7 August 1940, BP/8/16/4, LHCMA.
54. Dobinson, *Building Radar*, 54–55.
55. B. Bond, "Outsiders' Influence on Defence Policy," *RUSI Journal* 127 (1982): 11.
56. D. Dempster and D. Wood, *The Narrow Margin* (London: Hutchinson, 1961), 81–88; P. Wykeham, *Fighter Command: A Study of Air Defence 1914–1960* (London: Putnam, 1960), 62.
57. Sinnott, "RAF Operational Requirements," pp. 194–95.
58. Ibid., p. 246.
59. Ibid., p. 196.

60. G. Wallace, "Royal Air Force Guns in the Second World War," *Aerospace*, May 1979, pp. 22–29. The RAF did employ cannon in later marks of the Spitfire, but initially without success. The Luftwaffe also fitted cannon to some models of the Bf 109.

61. Ibid., p. 22.

62. Ibid., p. 23; J. Ferris, "Achieving Air Ascendancy: Challenge and Response in British Strategic Air Defence, 1915–1940," in *Air Power History Turning Points from Kitty Hawk to Kosovo*, edited by S. Cox and P. Gray (London: Frank Cass, 2002), 21–51. This more positive view is echoed by John Ferris in his survey of British air defenses during the interwar period.

63. Notes on Policy of the Directorate of Research, BP 1/3/23, LHCMA.

64. Notes on a Visit to Germany, September 1924, BP 1/3/26, LHCMA. He was airsick for the very first time when flying in an enclosed aircraft in 1924.

65. Evans to Brooke-Popham, 3 January 1935, BPFP.

66. Air Ministry to Brooke-Popham, 30 April 1935, BPFP.

67. *Flight*, 11 July 1935, pp. 40–45.

68. *Times* (London), 7 July 1935.

69. Report on Royal Review, BP/3/1/12, LHCMA.

70. *Times* (London), 29 June 1935, p. 10. The post had originally been held by Air Vice-Marshal Sir Godfrey Paine but had lapsed in 1920.

71. Ellington to Dowding and Steel, 16 November 1936, BP/1/7/7, LHCMA.

72. Air Ministry to Brooke-Popham, 20 June 1935, BPFP.

73. Ferris, "Fighter Defence before Fighter Command," 863; R. Higham, "British Air Exercises of the 1930s," *1998 National Aerospace Conference Proceedings* (Dayton, OH: Wright State University, 1999), 311.

74. Orange, *Park*, 50.

CHAPTER 12. INSPECTOR GENERAL

1. S. Morewood, *The British Defence of Egypt 1935–1940: Conflict and Crisis in the Eastern Mediterranean* (London: Frank Cass, 2005), 86–97; S. Morewood, "'This Silly African Business': The Military Dimension of Britain's Response to the Abyssinian Crisis," in *Collision of Empires: Italy's Invasion of Ethiopia and Its International Impact*, edited by G. B. Strang (Farnham, UK: Ashgate, 2013), 73–108.

2. Morewood, "'This Silly African Business,'" 81.

3. Bowyer, *RAF Operations*, 238–39. The RAF reinforcements were sent in secrecy to the Middle East between September and October 1935.

4. P. Harris, "Egypt: Defence Plans," in *Britain and the Middle East in the 1930s: Security Problems 1935–1939*, edited by M. J. Cohen and M. Kolinsky (New York: Palgrave Macmillan, 1992), 61–62.

5. Ellington to Brooke-Popham, 26 September 1935, AIR 20/5489, TNA.

6. Viscount Swinton (Philip Cunliffe-Lister) served as secretary of state for air from June 1935 to May 1938.

7. *Times* (London), 11 October 1935, p. 13; *Flight*, 26 December 1935, p. 674.

8. Brooke-Popham to MacLean, 21 September 1935, BP/4/1/1, LHCMA.

9. Ellington to Brooke-Popham, 26 May 1936, BP/4/6/3, LHCMA.

10. Brooke-Popham to Ellington, 21 May 1936, BP/4/3/37, LHCMA. He knew Collishaw from Staff College and their time at ADGB.

11. Brooke-Popham to Opal, 25 October 1935, BPFP.

12. Brooke-Popham to Ellington, 23 December 1935, BP/4/3/18, LHCMA.

13. Brooke-Popham to Ellington, 3 December 1935, BP/4/3/14, LHCMA; Brooke-Popham to Opal, 30 November 1935, BPFP. Writing to Opal, he added that Clark Kerr "would be clever if he were not so conceited."

14. Brooke-Popham to Ellington, 3 December 1935, BP/4/3/14, LHCMA.

15. Brooke-Popham to Opal, 30 November 1935, BPFP.

16. Brooke-Popham to Opal, 10 January 1936, BPFP.

17. Wing Commander F. C. Richardson, Interview 4623, IWM; F. C. Richardson, *Man Is Not Lost* (Shrewsbury, UK: Airlife, 1997), 81–82. In just six weeks, five aircraft had been written off.

18. Brooke-Popham to Ellington, 27 May 1936, BP/4/3/39, LHCMA.

19. Brooke-Popham to Ellington, 24 January 1936, BP/4/3/21, LHCMA.

20. Brooke-Popham to Opal, 17 November 1935, BPFP; Richardson, *Man Is Not Lost*, 88–89. The rumor in Kenya was that he had been injured in a plane crash while being flown by a drunken pilot.

21. Ellington to Brooke-Popham, 21 February 1936, BP/4/4/29, LHCMA.

22. Brooke-Popham to Opal, 16 October 1935, BPFP.

23. Brooke-Popham to Ellington, 20 December 1935, BP/4/3/17, LHCMA.

24. FO Telegrams 94 and 95, 21 February 1936, TNA.

25. "British Delegation in Cairo," *Times* (London), 14 February 1936, p. 14.

26. Morewood, *The British Defence of Egypt*, 92.

27. L. Morsy, "The Military Clauses of the Anglo-Egyptian Treaty of Friendship and Alliance, 1936," *International Journal of Middle East Studies* 16 (1984): 85–86.

28. Morewood, *The British Defence of Egypt*, 91.

29. Brooke-Popham to Ellington, 22 April 1936, BP/4/3/33, LHCMA.

30. T. Evans, ed., *The Killearn Diaries 1934–1946* (London: Sidgwick & Jackson, 1972), 73.

31. Morewood, *The British Defence of Egypt*, 92.

32. Evans, *The Killearn Diaries 1934–1946*, 74.

33. Brooke-Popham to Opal, 24 July 1936, BPFP.

34. Morewood, *The British Defence of Egypt*, p. 95.

35. That same month, the *Times* celebrated the twenty-fifth anniversary of his pilot's license (granted on 18 July 1911), noting that Brooke-Popham was one of just four surviving members of the Air Battalion still on active service.

36. Morsy, "The Military Clauses of the Anglo-Egyptian Treaty of Friendship and Alliance 1936," 67–97.

37. Brooke-Popham to Opal, 12 August 1936, BPFP.

38. Lampson to Brooke-Popham, 24 July 1936, BPFP; Brooke-Popham to Opal, 28 July 1936, BPFP.

39. Cypher Telegram, War Office to CinC Middle East, 3 September 1936, BP/4/6/53, LHCMA; Brooke-Popham to Ellington, 7 September 1936, BP/4/3/50, LHCMA.

40. Brooke-Popham to Opal, 5 September 1936, BPFP.

41. Air Ministry to Brooke-Popham, 16 February 1937, BPFP.

42. Brooke-Popham to Opal, 13 July 1936, BPFP.

43. Brooke-Popham to Opal, 19 July 1936, BPFP.

44. Ormsby Gore to Brooke-Popham, 21 October 1936, Brooke-Popham Papers, III/2/1, Bodleian Library.

45. *Times* (London), 14 November 1936, p. 12.

46. Newall was appointed CAS on 1 September 1937. Born in 1886, he was four years younger than Dowding and five years his junior in seniority.

47. Draft Letter, Brooke-Popham to Ellington, undated, BP/1/7/8, LHCMA.

48. Sir Donald Banks [Permanent Secretary at the Air Ministry] to Brooke-Popham, 4 March 1937, BPFP.

49. *Times* (London), 19 February 1937, p. 9; Brooke-Popham to Opal, 23 October 1939, BPFP.

CHAPTER 13. GOVERNOR OF KENYA

1. A. Kirk-Greene, "On Governorship and Governors in British Africa," in *African Proconsuls: European Governors in Africa*, edited by L. H. Gann and P. Duignan (New York: Free Press, 1978), 209–64.

2. Draft Submission to His Majesty, November 1936, CO 850/70/10, TNA.

3. Ormsby-Gore to Brooke-Popham, 21 October 1936, Brooke-Popham Papers, Bodleian Library.

4. Brooke-Popham to Ellington, 24 January 1936, BP/4/3/21, LHCMA.

5. Brooke-Popham to Opal, 10 November 1939, BPFP. Ailsa Turner was president of the EAWL for more than fifteen years (1925–40). The EAWL was active in influencing government policy on the welfare of the African population, including health, hospitals, maternity facilities, the training of African nurses and midwives, and the education of both boys and girls. It lobbied for new legislation and was directly involved in the creation of rural circulating lending libraries as well as film censorship.

6. Kirk-Greene, "On Governorship and Governors in British Africa," 244–50.

7. Ibid., 229–30.

8. "Air Chief Marshal Sir Robert Brooke-Popham, Former Governor of Kenya," *Empire News*, 29 October 1953, p. 227.

9. Ibid., p. 165.

10. *Colonial Report No. 1858*—Annual Report on the Social and Economic Progress of the People of the Kenya Colony and Protectorate, 1937 (London: HMSO, 1937), p. 5.

11. Ibid., pp. 8–10.

12. A. Clayton and D. Savage, *Government and Labour in Kenya: 1895–1963* (Abingdon, UK: Frank Cass, 1974), 176.

13. Ibid., 215.

14. D. Anderson, "Depression, Dust Bowl, Demography and Drought," *African Affairs* 83, no. 332 (1984): 321–43.

15. R. L. Tignor, "Kamba Political Protest: The Destocking Controversy of 1938," *The International Journal of African Historical Studies* 4, no. 2 (1971): 237–51.

16. M. Osborne, *Ethnicity and Empire in Kenya* (Cambridge: Cambridge University Press, 2014), 102.

17. Brooke-Popham to Ormsby-Gore, 17 July 1937, Brooke-Popham Papers, III/3/8, Bodleian Library.

18. Gurney to Brooke-Popham, 9 August 1942, Brooke-Popham Papers, III/10/1, Bodleian Library.

19. Tignor, "Kamba Political Protest," 246.

20. Brooke-Popham to Wade, 18 October 1938, Brooke-Popham Papers, III/4/12, Bodleian Library; Montgomery to Brooke-Popham, 9 August 1942, Brooke-Popham Papers, III/10/1, Bodleian Library.

21. Brooke-Popham to MacDonald, 17 December 1938, Brooke-Popham Papers, III/4/27, Bodleian Library.

22. Tignor, "Kamba Political Protest," 250.

23. L. Spencer, "Notes on the Kamba Destocking Controversy of 1938," *International Journal of African Historical Studies* 5, no. 4 (1972): 629–36.

24. Ibid., 631.

25. F. Gadsden, "Further Notes on the Kamba Destocking Controversy of 1938," *International Journal of African Historical Studies* 7, no. 4 (1974): 681–87.

26. R. E. K. Ward, F. J. Khamisi, and L. J. Beecher, "The East African Political Scene," *African Affairs* 45, no. 180 (July 1946): 152.

27. *Kenya National Assembly Official Record* (*Hansard*), Legislative Council Debates, Third Session, 29 October 1937; L. A. Gardner, *Taxing Colonial Africa: The Political Economy of British Imperialism* (Oxford: Oxford University Press, 2012), 142–43.

28. *Times* (London), 6 August 1938, p. 9.

29. E. S. Atieno-Odhiambo, "The Colonial Government, the Settlers, and the Trust Principle in Kenya to 1939," *Transafrican Journal of History*, July 1972, pp. 94–113.
30. Brooke-Popham to Colonial Secretary, 28 December 1937, BPFP.
31. "European Settlement in Kenya Colony," East Africa and Rhodesia, 18 November 1943, pp. 211–13, Brooke-Popham Papers, III/10/8, Bodleian Library.
32. "Air Chief Marshal Urges Greater War Effort," *Singapore Free Press*, 21 April 1941.
33. Atieno-Odhiambo, "The Trust Principle," pp. 109–10.
34. *Kenya National Assembly Official Record* (*Hansard*), Legislative Council Debates, Third Session, 29 October 1937.
35. D. Wilkin, "Refugees and British Administrative Policy in Northern Kenya, 1936–1938," *African Affairs* 79, no. 317 (1980): 510–30.
36. E. Steinhart, *Black Poachers, White Hunters: A Social History of Hunting in Colonial Kenya* (Oxford: James Currey, 2005), 181–84.
37. M. Cowie, *Fly Vulture* (London: Harrap, 1961), 98.
38. Ibid., 100.
39. G. Campbell, *The Charging Buffalo: A History of the Kenya Regiment 1937–1963* (London: Leo Cooper, 1986), 15.
40. Ibid., 19.
41. C. S. Nicholls, *Red Strangers: The White Tribe of Kenya* (London: Timewell Press, 2005), 212–13.
42. D. Miller, "Raising the Tribes: British Policy in Italian East Africa, 1938–1941," *Journal of Strategic Studies* 22, no. 1 (1999): 96–123.
43. Ibid., 104; "Italian Rule in Ethiopia, Italian Rule in 1938," FO 371/23377, TNA.
44. J. Aldrick, "An Ethiopian Escapade," *Africa: Rivista Trimestale di Studi & Documentaziano*, Anno 50, no. 3 (1995): 387–98; "Mrs. C. Fannin's Journey through Italian East Africa," FO 371/23382, TNA.
45. Brooke-Popham to Ironside, 7 October 1939, Brooke-Popham Papers, III/9/1, Bodleian Library.
46. M. R. D. Foot, *SOE—The Special Operations Executive 1940–46* (London: BBC, 1984), 190.
47. T. H. Parsons, "The Evolution of the Girl Guide Movement in Kenya," in *Scouting Frontiers, Youth and the Scout Movement's First Century*, edited by N. R. Block and T. M. Proctor (Newcastle-Upon-Tyne: Cambridge Scholars, 2009), 143–56.
48. T. Jeal, *Baden-Powell, Founder of the Boy Scout Movement* (New Haven, CT: Yale University Press, 2007), 554–66.
49. Both men had considerably younger wives. Robert Baden-Powell married Olave in 1912, when he was fifty-five and she was twenty-three.
50. Brooke-Popham to Olave Baden-Powell, 21 January 1941, and Olave Baden-Powell to Brooke-Popham, 8 February 1941, BPFP.

51. J. Fox, *White Mischief* (London: Jonathan Cape, 1982), 1–5. Joss Erroll was shot dead near Nairobi on 24 January 1941. There were no eyewitnesses and no one was ever convicted of his murder. The Happy Valley set were a group of colonial expatriates who became notorious for drinking, drug use, and promiscuity.

52. Brooke-Popham won the Nairobi Polo Club's Captain's Pot in 1938 with a team that included Erroll and the Duke of Gloucester.

53. Brooke-Popham to Hay, 5 December 1939, Brooke-Popham Papers, III/9/20, Bodleian Library.

54. Opal to Brooke-Popham, 26 January 1941, and Brooke-Popham to Opal, 2 February 1941, BPFP.

55. Italian nationals were excluded because Mussolini did not declare war on Great Britain until June 1940.

56. C. S. Nicholls, "Kenya and the Outbreak of the Second World War," *Old Africa Magazine*, 20 June 2015.

57. I. M. Philpott, *The Royal Air Force: An Encyclopedia of the Inter-War Years*, vol. 2, *1930–39* (Barnsley, UK: Pen and Sword, 2008), 345; Kirk-Greene, "On Governorship and Governors in British Africa," 244–50.

58. Brooke-Popham to Opal, 21 December 1940, BPFP.

59. Brooke-Popham to Young, 22 September 1939, CO 967/165, TNA.

60. *Times* (London), 25 September 1939, p. 5.

61. Air Ministry to Brooke-Popham, 2 November 1939, BPFP.

62. In 1942, Harrigan would prosecute Jock Delves Broughton for the murder of Joss Erroll.

63. R. M. Maxon and T. P. Ofcansky, *Historical Dictionary of Kenya*, 3rd ed. (Lanham, MD: Rowman & Littlefield, 2014), 231–32.

64. Ibid., 41.

65. S. Coldham, "Colonial Policy and the Highlands of Kenya, 1933–1944," *Journal of African Law* 23, no. 1 (March 1979): 65–83. For example, the lack of African membership on the LegCo and the whites-only policy of land ownership in the Highlands.

66. Brooke-Popham to Moore, 25 October 1939, Brooke-Popham Papers, III/9/9, Bodleian Library.

67. R. Palmer, "The Nyasaland Tea Industry in the Era of International Tea Restrictions, 1933–1950," *Journal of African History* 26 (1985): 231.

68. D. A. Mungazi, *The Last British Liberals in Africa: Michael Blundell and Garfield Todd* (Westport, CT: Greenwood, 1999), 44.

69. Brooke-Popham to Moore, 25 October 1939, Brooke-Popham Papers, III/9/9, Bodleian Library.

70. "The Governor to Relinquish His Post," *East African Standard*, 26 September 1939.

CHAPTER 14. WORLD WAR II

1. Cottisford had been rented out when they moved to Kenya, but the family was able to return there in October, once the tenants had left.
2. Brooke-Popham to Opal, 3 October 1939, BPFP.
3. W. A. B. Douglas, *The Creation of a National Air Force* (Toronto: University of Toronto Press, 1986), 191–92.
4. R. Higham, "Selected Aspects of RAF Concepts of and Planning for War, 1934–1941," in *Actas del XVII Congresso Internacional de Ciencias Historicas* (Madrid: International Commission of Military History), 141–57.
5. Douglas, *The Creation of a National Air Force*, 195.
6. Ibid., 195–96.
7. Dempster and Wood, *The Narrow Margin*, 27.
8. A. D. Stewart, "Managing the Dominions: The Dominions Office and the Second World War, 1939–42," PhD thesis, Kings College, London, 2001, pp. 64–98.
9. Brooke-Popham to Opal, 15 October 1939, BPFP.
10. Brooke-Popham to Opal, 23 October 1939, BPFP; Brooke-Popham to Newall, 1 November 1939, BP/8/10/4, LHCMA. Burnett would later serve as CAS of the Royal Australian Air Force from February 1940 to May 1942.
11. Brooke-Popham to Opal, 23 October 1939, BPFP.
12. Brooke-Popham to Opal, 11 October 1939, BPFP.
13. Brooke-Popham to Opal, 18 October 1939, BPFP.
14. Air Ministry Notice, 11 October 1939, BP/5/3/1, LHCMA.
15. Brooke-Popham to Opal, 15 November 1939, BPFP.
16. Diaries of William Lyon Mackenzie King, 16 November 1939, Item 20972, Library and Archives Canada.
17. Brooke-Popham to Opal, 4 December 1939, BPFP.
18. I. E. Johnston, "The British Commonwealth Air Training Plan and the Shaping of National Identities in the Second World War," *Journal of Imperial and Commonwealth History* 43, no. 5 (2015): 903–26; Stewart, "Managing the Dominions" pp. 91–98; A. Stewart, "The 1939 British and Canadian Empire Air Training Scheme Negotiations," *The Round Table* 93, no. 377 (October 2004): 739–54. Stewart provides an excellent overview of the considerable difficulties faced during the negotiations.
19. Tweedsmuir (John Buchan) had been appointed governor-general in 1935. He was popular and greatly admired.
20. Brooke-Popham to Opal, 4 December 1939, BPFP.
21. Brooke-Popham to Opal, 27 November 1939, BPFP.
22. Ibid.
23. Brooke-Popham to Opal, 17 December 1939, BPFP; Diaries of William Lyon Mackenzie King, 15 December 1939, Item 21047, Library and Archives

Canada. Mackenzie King overheard a remark made by Brooke-Popham about the size of squadron groundcrews and decided that the RAF's main concern was not about finance but giving Canadians command over "Englishmen."

24. Brooke-Popham to Opal, 17 December 1939, BPFP.

25. Douglas, *The Creation of a National Air Force*, 218.

26. C. Meredith, "The Rhodesian Air Training Group, 1940–1945," *Rhodesiana*, no. 28, July 1973.

27. Diaries of William Lyon Mackenzie King, 16 December 1939, Item 21055, Library and Archives Canada.

28. Campbell to Stephenson, 20 December 1939, DO 35/539/2, TNA.

29. Brooke-Popham to Opal, 17 December 1939, BPFP.

30. Ibid.

31. Diaries of William Lyon Mackenzie King, 17 December 1940, Item 21059, Library and Archives Canada.

32. Brooke-Popham to Kingsley Wood, 17 December 1939, BP/5/2/15, LHCMA.

33. Campbell to Stephenson, 20 December 1939, DO 35/539/2, TNA.

34. Brooke-Popham to Opal, 14 February 1940, BPFP.

35. Brooke-Popham to Kingsley Wood, 17 December 1939, BP/5/2/15, LHCMA.

36. D. Gillison, *Royal Australian Air Force 1939–1942* (Canberra: Australian War Memorial, 1962), 106–7.

37. Brooke-Popham to Opal, 31 March 1940, BPFP.

38. "Leader of British Air Mission Recalls Old Days of Aviation," *Vancouver Daily Province*, 18 January 1940.

39. Douglas, *The Creation of a National Air Force*, 293.

40. "The Empire and Commonwealth Air Training Scheme," BP/5/6/8, LHCMA.

41. K. Fedorowich, "Caught in the Crossfire: Sir Gerald Campbell, Lord Beaver-brook and the Near Demise of the British Commonwealth Air Training Plan, May-October 1940," *Journal of Military History* 79 (January 2015): 37–68.

42. D. Richards and H. St. G. Saunders, *Royal Air Force 1939–1945*, vol. 1, *The Fight at Odds* (London: HMSO, 1953), 73.

43. Loose Minute, 8 December 1941, AIR 19/561, TNA.

44. Brooke-Popham to Street, 20 February 1940, BP/5/2/22, LHCMA.

45. Secretary of State to Brooke-Popham, 26 February 1939, BP/5/4/1, LHCMA. In September 1939, the South African Air Force (SAAF) had fewer than two thousand personnel and boasted just three squadrons with largely obsolete air-craft.

46. Longmore, *From Sea to Sky*, 214. Brooke-Popham had encountered McKean when he toured Training Command, where McKean was the senior Air Staff officer, the previous October.

47. Diaries of William Lyon Mackenzie King, 19 March 1940, Item 21397, Library and Archives Canada.

48. "Notes for Sir Henry Tizard to Take to USA," 8 August 1940, BP/8/16/8, LHCMA. Brooke-Popham provided a briefing note for Tizard describing the latest operational, technical, and training developments.

49. Brooke-Popham to Street, 9 March 1940, BP/5/4/3, LHCMA.

50. Opal joined the mission at Brooke-Popham's request, and at his personal cost.

51. AIR 2/5084, TNA.

52. Brooke-Popham to Dill, 7 May 1940, Dill/3/3/2, LHCMA.

53. J. A. Brown, *A Gathering of Eagles: The Campaigns of the South African Air Force in Italian East Africa, June 1940–November 1941, with an Introduction 1912–1939* (Cape Town: Purnell, 1970), 36–37.

54. Notes for South African Broadcast, 11 May 1940, BP/9/9/8, LHCMA. A recording of his broadcast, provided by the South African Broadcasting Corporation, still survives.

55. Opal sailed for England on 17 May 1940.

56. Meredith, "The Rhodesian Air Training Group, 1940–1945." No. 25 Elementary Flying Training School, at Belvedere, Salisbury, on 24 May 1940. Eventually there would be ten flying schools in Southern Rhodesia.

57. Brooke-Popham to Opal, 22 May 1940, BPFP.

58. H. Moolman, "South Africa's Part in the War," *Journal of the Royal Society of Arts* 89, no. 4578 (10 January 1941): 103.

59. Brown, *A Gathering of Eagles*, 29; A. Wessels, "The First Two Years of War," *Military History Journal* 11, no. 5 (June 2000): 2–4.

60. BP/8/11, LHCMA. Such as investigating the deployment of Blenheims and Hurricanes from Tangmere to the Middle East on 18 June 1940 that resulted in the loss of seven aircraft.

61. A. Byford, "What Lessons about Strategy and Its Relationship to National and Military Doctrine Are Illustrated by the Royal Air Force's Experience in France and Flanders, May–June 1940," Seaford House Papers, Royal College of Defense Studies, 2011.

62. "RAF Establishments, 1940," AIR 2/4679, TNA.

63. Learoyd was being rested from operations after a raid on the Ems Canal for which he was awarded the Victoria Cross. He brought his Hampden down to 150 feet during the target run and, although the aircraft was badly damaged, managed to bring his crew back safely to Scampton.

64. Sir Robert Brooke-Popham Air Ministry Notebook No. 2, September–October 1940, BPFP.

65. "Hand in Hand They Find New Courage," *Daily Mirror*, 18 October 1940, p. 7.

66. "Lady Brooke-Popham's Work for Blitzed Children," *Morning Tribune*, 27 November 1941, p. 6. When Opal left for the Far East in the summer of 1941, her sister-in-law, Polly, assisted with the accounts.

67. "Register of War Nurseries," Children's Society Archive, AR 81.0466.

68. 1940 Diary, 14 October, BPFP.

69. Woodburn Kirby, *The War against Japan*, 1:50; A. Roberts, *Masters and Commanders* (London: Allen Lane, 2008), 107–8. The chiefs of staff met daily throughout the war (other than Sundays) and sometimes twice a day. The three chiefs also attended the War Cabinet meeting on Mondays and the Joint Intelligence Committee on Tuesdays.

70. *BPFP*, Robert Brooke-Popham Personal Diary 1940.

71. "Mr. Churchill's Eyes on Singapore & Far East," *Singapore Free Press*, 5 December 1940.

CHAPTER 15. COMMANDER-IN-CHIEF FAR EAST

1. N. Tarling, *Britain, Southeast Asia and the Onset of the Pacific War* (Cambridge: Cambridge University Press, 1996), 6–20.

2. G. Sansom, "Japan's Fatal Blunder," *International Affairs* 24, no. 4 (October 1948): 543–54.

3. A. Best, *Britain, Japan and Pearl Harbour: Avoiding War in East Asia, 1936–41* (London: Routledge, 1995), 8–15.

4. Woodburn Kirby, *The War against Japan*, 1:3.

5. "Far Eastern Policy," 27 July 1940, CAB 66/10, WP (40) 289, and COS (40)568 Revise, TNA.

6. "The Situation in the Far East in the Event of Japanese Intervention against Us," 31 July 1940, CAB 66/10, WP (40)302, and COS (40)592, TNA.

7. S. Roskill, *Naval Policy between the Wars*, 2: 436–37; Ong, *Operation Matador*, 94–95.

8. Ong, *Matador*, 67–75.

9. "Far Eastern Policy," CAB 66/10, TNA. The First Sea Lord, Sir Dudley Pound, was of the view that Britain should not fight—even if the Dutch resisted. The other chiefs disagreed.

10. W.M. (40) 222, War Cabinet Conclusions, 8 August 1940, CAB/65/8/34, TNA.

11. W.M. (40) 222, War Cabinet Conclusions, Confidential Annex, 8 August 1940, CAB/65/14/20, TNA.

12. Prime Minister to Prime Ministers of Australia and New Zealand, 11 August 1940, CAB/65/14/20, TNA.

13. Telegrams to and from the Far East, WO 106/5402B, TNA.

14. Woodburn Kirby, *The War against Japan*, 1:49. The conference report contained an appendix identifying issues to be discussed with the Dutch and Americans when this became politically possible.

15. P. Hasluck, *Australia in the War of 1939–1945*, Series Four (Civil), vol. 1, *The Gov-ernment and the People 1939–1941* (Canberra: Australian War Memorial, 1952), 294–96.

16. Gillison, Royal Australian Air Force 1939–1942, 143.

17. The actual strength in November 1940 was eighty-eight frontline aircraft and seventeen infantry battalions.

18. COS Response to Tactical Appreciation, 10 January 1941, BP/6/1/6, LHCMA; Woodburn Kirby, *The War against Japan*, 1:48–49.

19. Hasluck, *The Government and the People*, 297–99.

20. "Co-ordination of Defence: Burma and Far East," COS (40) 703 (JPS), TNA.

21. COS (40) 298th Meeting, 6 September 1940, CAB/79/6/48, TNA.

22. COS (40) 347th Meeting, 12 October 1940, CAB 79/7, TNA.

23. Dewing Diaries, 12 October 1941, LHCMA.

24. Brooke-Popham to Dill, 27 May 1940, Dill/3/3/2, LHCMA.

25. P. Thompson and R. Macklin, *The Battle of Brisbane: Australians and the Yanks at War* (Sydney: ABC Books, 2000), 65.

26. "Air Chief Marshal Sir Robert Brooke-Popham," *Times* (London), 21 October 1953, p. 11.

27. W. A. B. Douglas, *The Creation of a National Air Force* (Toronto: University of Toronto Press, 1986), 216–19; R. Callahan, *The Worst Disaster: The Fall of Singapore* (Newark: University of Delaware Press, 1977), 67.

28. Senior commanders who passed through the IDC during Brooke-Popham's tenure included: General Arthur Grasett, commander of British troops in China; Air Vice-Marshal Paul Maltby, assistant AOC Far East Command and AOC RAF in Java (the brother of Major-General Christopher Maltby who took over command of the Hong Kong Garrison from Grasett—both brothers became prisoners of the Japanese); Lieutenant-General Henry Pownall, who replaced Brooke-Popham as CinC Far East (and later served as chief of staff to General Wavell); and Lieutenant-General Vernon Sturdee, chief of the Australian General Staff.

29. COS Committee Meeting, 18 October 1940, CAB 79/7, TNA.

30. A. Marder, *Old Friends, New Enemies: The Royal Navy and the Imperial Japanese Navy* (Oxford: Clarendon Press, 1981), 35.

31. Brooke-Popham, "Operations in the Far East," p. 536; Ong, *Matador*, 132–33.

32. Brooke-Popham to Ismay, 26 October 1940, BP/6/2/1, LHCMA.

33. Brooke-Popham, "Operations in the Far East," p. 536.

34. Brooke-Popham to Opal, 22 June 1941, BPFP. "He seems a good type, cheerful and musical."

35. Fawcett was replaced by Colonel Scott in August 1941. He was later captured by the Japanese and died in captivity. Grey, who had been awarded the DSO when in command of HMS *Fleetwood* for his rescue of troops from Aandalsnes during the Norwegian Campaign, avoided capture and retired in 1948. Darvall also survived the war and retired as an air marshal in 1956, having served as AOC 46 Group during the Arnhem operation. His final posting was commandant of the NATO Defence College in Paris where he met Kurt Hahn—together

they founded the Atlantic College movement. Back, who had commanded the cruiser *Capetown* before joining the staff of CinC Far East, returned to the UK in March 1942. He was appointed to HMS *Bermuda* in July 1942 but suffered a stroke in February 1944 while on convoy cover duties in the Arctic Circle, retiring on medical grounds in 1946. Back was the complainant in the 1908 Archer-Shee case (dramatized by Terence Rattigan in 1946 as *The Winslow Boy*). Other staff included Wing Commander (later Air Vice-Marshal) Brian Yarde and Major Robert Dobbin, who was later awarded the OBE for his work in Java.

36. Brooke-Popham to Opal, 15 October 1939, BPFP.
37. Squadron Leader Foster Cox, Interview 12675/3/1–3, IWM. Foster Cox was interviewed by the Imperial War Museum in 1995 (when he was ninety-five). Although slightly rambling, the recording provides some interesting details on Singapore and Brooke-Popham's time as CinC. Cox was one of the two executors of Brooke-Popham's will—the other being his brother-in-law, Francis Hugonin.
38. Brooke-Popham to Woodburn Kirby, 16 April 1953, BPFP.
39. Singapore Notebook No. 1, BPFP.
40. Brooke-Popham to Woodburn Kirby, 16 April 1953, BPFP.
41. Singapore Notebook No. 1, BPFP; Brooke-Popham, "Operations in the Far East," p. 536.
42. F. McLynn, *The Burma Campaign: Disaster into Triumph 1942–1945* (New Haven, CT: Yale University Press, 2011), 23.
43. Monteith to Amery, 3 September 1941, MSS Eur E 215/1–2, India Office, British Library; Woodburn Kirby, *The War against Japan*, 2:14.
44. M. Hickey, *The Unforgettable Army* (Staplehurst, UK: Spellmount, 1992), 53; "Thunder in the East," p. 41, Private Papers of Major-General G. E. Grimsdale, IWM.
45. O. S. Greenlaw, *The Lady and the Tigers* (New York: E. P. Dutton, 1943), 53.
46. B. Montgomery, *Shenton of Singapore* (London: Leo Cooper, 1984), 64. Shenton Thomas had completed the full term of his appointment, but it was agreed to extend this for the duration of the war.
47. Brooke-Popham to Ismay, 15 November 1940, CAB 21/1044, TNA.
48. AOCinC's Notes on the Emergency in the Near East 1935/36, BP/4/12/1, LHCMA.
49. P. Elphick, *Far Eastern File* (London: Hodder and Stoughton, 1997), 259.
50. "*Automedon* Movement Card," 1939–1941, BT 389/2/235, TNA. The *Automedon* had been under repair in Liverpool since arriving from Sydney the previous month.
51. Elphick, *Far Eastern File*, 255–67; J. Rusbridger and E. Nave, *Betrayal at Pearl Harbor* (New York: Summit Books, 1991), 99. The interception was facilitated by the Germans' ability to read the British Allied Merchant Shipping Code.
52. B. Rogge and W. Frank, *The German Raider* Atlantis (New York: Ballantine Books, 1956), 114–18.

53. J. Chapman, *The Price of Admiralty—The War Diary of the German Naval Attaché in Japan*, vols. 2 and 3, *23 August 1940–9 September 1941* (Lewes, UK: Saltire Press, 1982), 327.

54. Ibid., 337.

55. Opal to Brooke-Popham, 2 February 1941, BPFP.

56. Elphick, *Far Eastern File*, 32.

57. L. Allen, *Singapore 1941–1942*, rev. ed. (London: Franck Cass, 1993), 3–4; E. Seki, *Mrs. Ferguson's Tea-Set: Japan and the Second World War* (Folkestone, UK: Global Oriental, 2007), 92–93; Kotani, *Japanese Intelligence in World War II*, 48–49. However, Drea is less convinced: E. Drea, "Reading Each Other's Mail: Japanese Communication Intelligence, 1920–1941," *Journal of Military History* 55 (April 1991): 185–205.

58. Jun, "The Navy's Role in the Southern Strategy," 248.

59. Allen, *Singapore 1941–1942*, 4.

CHAPTER 16. IMPROVING DEFENSE COOPERATION

1. Labuan Island was seven hundred miles from Singapore, off the northeast coast of Borneo.

2. For example: Woodburn Kirby, *The War against Japan*, 1:457; and Percival, *The War in Malaya*, 181.

3. Brooke-Popham to Woodburn Kirby, 16 April 1953, p. 2, BPFP.

4. Woodburn Kirby, *The War against Japan*, 1:24–25.

5. Charles Vlieland, who had served in the MCS since 1915, was appointed military secretary of Malaya in 1938, largely on the recommendation of Air Commodore (later Marshal of the Royal Air Force Lord) Arthur Tedder when he was AOC RAF Far East Command. V. Orange, *Tedder: Quietly in Command* (London: Frank Cass, 2006), 101.

6. "Malaya Defence Organisation," 23 October 1940, BP/6/1/2, LHCMA.

7. Brooke-Popham to Woodburn Kirby, 16 April 1953, p. 2, BPFP; Dickinson to Bryson, F.48, RCS/RCMS 103/15/2, Cambridge University Library. Arthur Dickinson, the inspector general of police, believed that Jones was a major obstacle in progressing defense measures, but Percival found him helpful, if rather colorless.

8. Vlieland, "Memoirs of a Nonentity," p. 79, LHCMA.

9. Montgomery, *Shenton of Singapore*, 69–73.

10. Brooke-Popham to Opal, 8 December 1940, and 15 December 1940, BPFP.

11. Shenton Thomas to Parkinson, 11 March 1941, CO 967/76, TNA.

12. Allen, *Singapore 1941–1942*, 228–31; Singapore Notebook No. 1, BPFP.

13. Vlieland, "Memoirs of a Nonentity," p. 107, LHCMA.

14. Singapore Notebook No. 2, BPFP.

15. "Comments on Draft Despatch," 25 June 1942, BP/6/11/17, LHCMA. The work of the committee was further weakened by the absence of a formal agenda and the lack of minutes detailing actions.
16. Notes on the Far East, 12 March 1942, BP/6/9/5, LHCMA.
17. Dewing Diaries, 3 March 1941, LHCMA.
18. A. Martin and P. Hardy, eds., *Dark and Hurrying Days: Menzies' 1941 Diary* (Canberra: National Library of Australia, 1993), 23–24. Liddell Hart was skeptical about Bond's professional abilities (although this may have been influenced by Bond's description of Hart's tactical theories as "flapdoodle"). Basil Liddell Hart, *The Memoirs of Captain Liddell Hart*, vol. 1 (London: Cassell, 1965), 58–59.
19. Percival would have arrived earlier, but his aircraft broke down, delaying him by several weeks.
20. Brooke-Popham to Opal, 14 April 1941, BPFP; Brooke-Popham to Ismay, 16 May 1941, BP/6/2/12, LHCMA. Brooke-Popham believed that Bond had behaved "admirably over the whole affair."
21. Brooke-Popham to Ismay, 5 December 1940, BP/5/1/3, LHCMA.
22. Singapore Notebook No. 1, BPFP.
23. Shenton Thomas to Parkinson, 16 March 1941, CO 967/76, TNA.
24. "Malaya Defence Organisation—Most Confidential Note," 23 October 1940, BP/6/1/2, LHCMA.
25. Allen, *Singapore 1941–1942*, 236–38; Vlieland, "Memoirs of a Nonentity," LHCMA.
26. Ong, *Matador*, 110 and 115.
27. Montgomery, *Shenton of Singapore*, 75. Brooke-Popham had already spoken to Shenton Thomas about Vlieland's performance.
28. Brooke-Popham to Ismay, 6 January 1941, BP/5/1/4, LHCMA.
29. C. A. Vlieland, "Singapore: The Legend and the Facts," *Daily Telegraph*, 13 February 1967.
30. Vlieland uses the term "nincompoop," indicating that he drew on subsequent press reports. Layton and Brooke-Popham both supported the policy of defending Malaya rather than just Singapore but, by claiming the opposite, Vlieland attempts to present their criticism as motivated by a disagreement over strategy, rather than his performance. He also claims that Babington was so fearful of Brooke-Popham that he was forced to remain silent. In reality, the two were very close.
31. S. Roskill, *Churchill and the Admirals* (London: Collins, 1977), 202.
32. Martin and Hardy, *Dark and Hurrying Days*; *Time*, 25 November 1940. Several reports refer to Brooke-Popham's "falsetto" voice, but a recording of a talk he gave for the South African Broadcasting Corporation in May 1940 suggests otherwise.

33. *Morning Bulletin Rockhampton*, 21 January 1942.

34. C. Brown, *Suez to Singapore* (New York: Random House, 1942), 148. Brown resigned from CBS in 1943 following a reprimand over breaching editorial guidelines.

35. O. D. Gallagher, *Retreat in the East* (London: George Harrap, 1942), 30–31; L. A. Mills, "Suez to Singapore," *Far Eastern Quarterly* 2, no, 3 (1943): 301; A. Kennaway, *Journey by Candlelight* (Bishop Auckland, UK: Pentland Press, 1999), 58. Anne Kennaway describes Brown as bad-tempered, even if subsequent events proved him right.

36. Singapore Diary, DUFC 3/7, Churchill Archives.

37. Spooner Diaries, 3 December 1941, LHCMA.

38. "The Empire's New B-P," *Australasian*, 8 March 1941, p. 14.

39. Brooke-Popham to Ismay, 8 May 1942, CAB 21/1044, TNA.

40. A. B. Tinsley, *One Rissole on My Plate* (Braunton, UK: Merlin Books, 1984), 83–84.

41. R. Braddon, *The Naked Island* (London: Werner Laurie, 1952), 42–43; CinC Far East Tour of AIF Units, 7–9 October 1941, BP/6/4/23, LHCMA. The date is likely to have been 9 October 1941 when CinC Far East, on a two-day tour of the AIF, inspected 2/15 Field Regiment (Braddon's unit) and 2/29 Battalion at Tampin.

42. Foster Cox, Interview 16275/3/1–3, IWM; A. Gil-christ, *Malaya 1941* (London: Robert Hale, 1992), 169.

43. "Biographical File," Radio Broadcast, 15 November 1940, DC 76/74/130, RAFM.

44. Helmuth von Moltke the Elder.

45. Brooke-Popham to Opal, 29 January 1941, BPFP.

46. I. Morrison, *Malayan Postscript* (London: Faber & Faber, 1942), 151–52.

47. R. Aldrich, *Intelligence and the War against Japan* (Cambridge, UK: Cambridge University Press, 2000), 23.

48. "Thunder in the East," pp. 19–20, Private Papers of Major-General G. E. Grimsdale, IWM. The move was carried out over the course of just two days. Interestingly, given Brooke-Popham's subsequent concerns, there was a debate about whether the FECB should be in the city, close to the military and civil authorities (including the censors and the police), but this was forestalled by Layton, who directed that it should be accommodated in the naval base, within the same block as his own headquarters.

49. K. Beesly, *Very Special Admiral: The Life of Admiral J. H. Godfrey* (London: Hamish Hamilton, 1980), 202.

50. Roskill, *Churchill and the Admirals*, 269; Vlieland, "Memoirs of a Nonentity," p. 85, LHCMA. Vlieland, who was not well disposed to Layton, described him as blunt and forthright (albeit energetic).

51. Brown, *Suez to Singapore*, 192–93.

52. Ibid., 190.

53. Brooke-Popham, "Operations in the Far East," p. 538.

54. A. Michie, *Retreat to Victory* (London: George Allen & Unwin, 1942), 290. He went on to assert that these inter-service rivalries impeded the military response to the Japanese invasion.

55. C. Thorne, *Allies of a Kind* (Oxford: Oxford University Press, 1968), 55; Claire Chennault Papers, Box 4, Hoover Institution. The journalists were Ed Mowrer and Vincent Sheean. Mowrer was, in fact, an agent for the OSS.

56. "Final Report of Edward Ansel Mowrer to Colonel William J. Donovan, Coordinator of Information, Concerning a Mission to the Far East in the Autumn of 1941, 3 December 1941," CIA-RDP13X00001R000100420003-5, CIA CREST, pp. 9–10.

57. Supplementary Report on Events in the Far East, 25 April 1947, ADM 199 /1472B, TNA.

58. Dewing Diaries, 3–22 February 1941, LHCMA.

59. J. Connell, *Wavell, Supreme Commander 1941–1943* (London: Collins, 1969), 40.

60. Marder, *Old Friends, New Enemies*, 394.

61. P. Maltby, "Report on the Air Operations during the Campaigns in Malaya and the Netherland East Indies from 8 December 1941 to 12 March 1942," *London Gazette*, 26 February 1948, pp. 1347–1415. Air Vice-Marshal Paul Maltby arrived in Singapore in November 1941 and, although senior to Pulford, offered to serve as his assistant to relieve him of his heavy workload. With Pulford's death in February 1942 (along with Admiral Jack Spooner) on a deserted island south of Singapore, while attempting to escape the Japanese following the fall of Singapore, it fell to Maltby to write the air officer commanding's official dispatch. Norman Macmillan, who also knew Pulford, described him as an able, painstaking officer of steadfast character. N. Macmillan, *The Royal Air Force in the World War*, vol. 4, *1940–1945* (II) (London: Harrap, 1950), 261.

62. Percival, *The War in Malaya*, 30.

63. J. McEwan, *The Remorseless Road* (Shrewsbury, UK: Airlife, 1997), 57.

64. "Final Report of Edward Ansel Mowrer," CIA CREST, p. 6.

65. Lieutenant Commander J. S. Mosher, Report on Malaya, Java and Australia: 2 March 1941–10 March 1942, 4697018, National Archives, Washington, D.C.; Bennett, *Why Singapore Fell*, 220–29. Bennett's subsequent escape from Singapore, where many of his troops were captured, was controversial. On the flight, from Java to Australia, he expressed great bitterness at the way he felt the British had let him down. Bennett immediately wrote a report and later published his own account of the campaign.

66. *Time*, 9 March 1942; Farrell, *The Defence and Fall of Singapore*, 118.

67. Bennett to Brooke-Popham, 26 January 1944, BP/6/9/29, LHCMA.

68. Admiral Thomas C. Hart, "Narrative of Events, Asiatic Fleet Leading Up to War and from 8 December 1941 to 15 February 1942," p. 70, 4697018, National Archives, Washington, D.C.; J. Leutze, *A Different Kind of Victory: A Biography of Admiral Thomas C. Hart* (Annapolis, MD: Naval Institute Press, 1981), 196. Darvall was well regarded by Brooke-Popham and would later impress Hart. Hart's initial opinion (based on secondhand information) had been less favorable.

69. Elphick, *Far Eastern File*, 168–69; R. Aldrich, *Intelligence and the War against Japan* (Cambridge, UK: Cambridge University Press, 2000), 63; A. N. Grey, "Fall of Singapore and the Dutch East Indies," p. 11, Spooner Papers, LHCMA; A. J. C. Boyd, "Worthy of Better Memory: The Royal Navy and the Defence of the Eastern Empire 1935–1942," PhD thesis, University of Buckingham, 2015, p. 262.

70. "Thunder in the East," p. 43, Private Papers of Major-General G. E Grimsdale, IWM. Under these circumstances, it is difficult not to feel some sympathy for Darvall.

71. Ibid., p. 42 and p. 48.

72. ADM 199/1472B, Events in Far East: Official and Personnel Records of Admiral Sir Geoffrey Layton, TNA; Group Captain Frank Brockman, Directorate of Staff Duties Air Ministry, to Brooke-Popham, 9 May 1947, BP/6/8/40, LHCMA.

73. Boyd, "Worthy of Better Memory," pp. 250–60.

74. W. H. Bartsch, *December 8, 1941: MacArthur's Pearl Harbor* (College Station: Texas A&M Press, 2003), 82–83.

75. Ibid., 399–410.

76. A. D. Harvey, "Army Air Force and Navy Air Force: Japanese Aviation and the Opening Phase of the War in the Far East," *War in History* 6, no. 2 (1999): 174–204; Boyd, "Worthy of Better Memory," pp. 261–63. There were genuine reasons for doubting the effectiveness of the Japanese air services.

77. J. Ferris, "Double-Edged Estimates: Japan in the Eyes of the British Army and the Royal Air Force, 1900–1939," in *The History of Anglo-Japanese Relations, 1600–2000*, vol. 3, *The Military Dimension*, edited by I. Gow, Y. Hirama, and J. Chapman (Basingstoke, UK: Palgrave Macmillan, 2003), 91–108; G. Kennedy, "Anglo-American Strategic Relations and Intelligence Assessments of Japanese Air Power, 1934–1941," *Journal of Military History* 74 (July 2010): 744–45.

78. D. Ford, *Flying Tigers: Claire Chennault and the American Volunteer Group* (Washington, D.C.: Smithsonian Institution Press, 1991), 72.

79. J. Ferris, "'Worthy of Some Better Enemy? The British Estimate of the Imperial Japanese Army, 1919–41, and the Fall of Singapore," *Canadian Journal of History*, August 1993, p. 250.

80. Kennedy, "Anglo-American Strategic Relations," 737–73.

81. Spooner Diaries, 29 November 1941, LHCMA.
82. "Thunder in the East," p. 43, Private Papers of Major-General G. E. Grimsdale, IWM.
83. Lieutenant-Colonel B. H. Ashmore, "Some Personal Observations of the Malayan Campaign," 27 July 1942, Percival Papers, F49, IWM.
84. Major-General Ian Playfair, "Some Personal Reflections on the Malayan Campaign," BP/6/9/27, LHCMA.
85. Captain A. N. Grey Collection, 2005–05–26, IWM; Brooke-Popham to Pound, 27 October 1941, BP/6/7/11, LHCMA. Scott was captured by the Japanese but survived the war, serving as Britain's commissioner-general in Singapore and commandant of the Imperial Defence College. Brooke-Popham wrote to the Admiralty recommending Grey for promotion.
86. Connell, *Wavell, Supreme Commander*, 164–66.
87. Brown, *Suez to Singapore*, 163. Major-General Keith Simmons commanded the Singapore Garrison. Simmons ("urbane, affable, intelligent and vigorous") impressed Cecil Brown, who had little time for most of the British officers he encountered.
88. Spooner Diaries, 29 November 1941, LHCMA.
89. "Hiatus at Singapore," *The Economist*, 17 January 1942, p. 61.
90. P. Elphick, *Singapore: The Pregnable Fortress* (London: Hodder & Stoughton, 1995), 180. Elphick documents the bad relationships between the senior British leaders in Malaya but exaggerates when he claims that "there was never another military theatre where so many wrong leaders were in the wrong place at the wrong time."
91. Woodburn Kirby, *The War against Japan*, 1:51. The description of Brooke-Popham's post as "another cog" appears to have originated with Layton.
92. Brooke-Popham to Woodburn Kirby, 26 September 1953, p. 2, BPFP. The wing commander in question was Brian Yarde (later an air vice-marshal).
93. BP/6/7/17, LHCMA.
94. Chiefs of Staff to Brooke-Popham, 24 April 1941, BP/6/1/14, LHCMA.
95. Callahan, *The Worst Disaster*, 107–8.

CHAPTER 17. "TOO GREAT TO BE CHALLENGED"

1. There was initial suspicion in Tokyo that the information contained in the documents provided by the Germans was so good that it was simply a ploy to get them to enter the war.
2. "Final Report of Edward Ansel Mowrer," CIA CREST, p. 4; *Times* (London), 28 January 1942.
3. Brooke-Popham, "Operations in the Far East," p. 567.
4. Brooke-Popham to Woodburn Kirby, January 1953, BPFP.
5. Information warfare includes psychological operations, propaganda, and offensive operations to deny the enemy battlefield information.

6. Brooke-Popham to Woodburn Kirby, January 1953, p. 10, BPFP.

7. Woodburn Kirby, *The War against Japan*, 1:155–56.

8. P. Woods, *Reporting the Retreat: War Correspondents in Burma* (London: Hurst, 2016), 53–56. It little helps that the government propaganda service in Burma seems to have been even less effective.

9. V. Thompson, *Postmortem on Malaya* (New York: Macmillan, 1943), 299. The MBC was established in 1940 and received substantial government investment.

10. Joan Hugonin to Opal, 15 November 1940, BPFP.

11. Brooke-Popham to Opal, 22 November 1940, BPFP.

12. Brooke-Popham to Opal, 16 November 1940, BPFP.

13. Brooke-Popham to Woodburn Kirby, 16 April 1953, BPFP.

14. "Final Report of Edward Ansel Mowrer," CIA CREST, pp. 10–11.

15. "Frank Clune's Stirring Story of Singapore," *Smith's Weekly*, 28 December 1940.

16. *Hong Kong Sunday Herald*, 29 December 1940.

17. "CinC Far East and Essentials of Hong Kong Defence," *China Mail*, 9 April 1941.

18. "Far East Commander-in-Chief's Broadcast, Sir Robert Brooke-Popham On Need for Sacrifices," *Straits Times*, 21 April 1941.

19. "Importance of Volunteers in Defence of Malaya," *Straits Echo & Times of Malaya*, 20 March 1941.

20. "Singapore Defences," *Times* (London), 11 June 1941, p. 5.

21. Connell, *Wavell, Supreme Commander*, 45.

22. "RAF Girds for Japanese Attack," *Detroit Free Press*, Times Foreign Service, 9 November 1941, p. 54.

23. "Singapore, Britain's Far Eastern Fortress," *Life* 11, no. 3 (21 July 1941): 61–73. Carl Mydans was one of *Life*'s earliest staff photographers. He and his wife were captured in the invasion of the Philippines but released by the Japanese in 1943 as part of a prisoner exchange.

24. "Singapore—Class A Naval Base Guards the White Man's Stake in East Asia," *Life* 9, no. 15 (7 October 1940): 30–32.

25. Brooke-Popham to Opal 15 August 1941, BPFP.

26. Brown, *Suez to Singapore*, 187.

27. M. Gellhorn, "Singapore Scenario," *Collier's Weekly*, 9 August 1941.

28. Darwin, *The Empire Project*, 515. This was also the view of the U.S. Navy observer in Singapore. Mosher, Report on Malaya, Java and Australia, 4697018, National Archives. These concerns did not disappear with the outbreak of war. J. Davies, "Anglo-American Cooperation in East Asia, 15 November 1943," 1–2, CIA-RDP13X00001R000100030012–8, CIA CREST.

29. Brooke-Popham to Ismay, 16 May 1941, BP/6/2/12, LHCMA.

30. Percival, *The War in Malaya*, 87–90. Percival also felt that there was a "Press Problem."

31. Brown, *Suez to Singapore*, 165.

32. F. Gervasi, "Around a World at War," *Collier's Weekly*, 22 November 1941, p. 63.

33. Kennaway, *Journey by Candlelight*, 55–56. Frustrated journalists would refer to the department as "ASPRO for headaches."

34. H. Guard and J. Tring, *The Pacific War Uncensored* (Havertown, PA: Casemate, 2011), 47–52. Complaints about censorship were confined largely to foreign journalists. The English-language newspapers in Malaya were generally happy with the regime. Thompson, *Postmortem on Malaya*, 293. Strict censorship did not prevent Mosher from assembling an accurate estimate of British strength in Malaya from reports of regimental sports events. Mosher, Report on Malaya, Java and Australia, 4697018, National Archives.

35. Brooke-Popham, "Operations in the Far East," p. 547.

36. Cooper, *Old Men Forget*, 294. This view is supported by Grimsdale who noted that heavy-handed censorship also played its part. Matters only improved following Clark Kerr's personal intervention. Grimsdale, "Thunder in the East," p. 47, IWM. American correspondents who reported from Singapore over this period included: Martha Gellhorn (*Collier's Weekly*); Frank Gervasi (*Collier's Weekly*); Yates McDaniel (Associated Press); Tillman Durdin (*New York Times*); Cecil Brown (CBS); Howard Guard (United Press); Leland Stowe (*Chicago Daily News*); Martin Agronsky (NBC); John Young (NBC); Ed Mowrer (*Chicago Daily News*); and Vincent Sheean (*New York Herald Tribune*).

37. Prime Minister to Duff Cooper, 12 December 1941, CHAR 20/46/94, Churchill Archives. Sir George Sansom, a highly respected and hugely knowledgeable diplomat, had served in the British embassy at Tokyo for more than thirty years.

38. Percival, *The War in Malaya*, 87–90; P. Knightley, *The First Casualty: The War Correspondent as Hero and Myth-maker from the Crimea to Iraq* (Baltimore: Johns Hopkins University Press, 2004), 272–88.

39. Lecture to Staff College, 2 March 1942, BP/6/7/17, LHCMA.

40. F. Gervasi, *War Has Seven Faces* (Garden City, NY: Doubleday, Doran, 1942), 246–53. The nearest Lysanders were two thousand miles away.

41. Walter Davenport, "Impregnable Pearl Harbor," *Collier's Weekly*, June 1941, p. 11–12.

42. Gervasi, "Around a World at War," p. 64.

43. Woods, *Reporting the Retreat*, 1–8.

44. Brooke-Popham to Grenfell, 22 November 1950, GREN 2/6, Churchill Archives.

45. Notes for Discussion, Maymyo, 6 June 1941, BP/6/7/8, LHCMA; A. Best, "'This Probably Over-Valued Military Power': British Intelligence and Whitehall's Perception of Japan, 1939–41," *Intelligence and National Security* 12, no. 3 (1997): 83.

46. Brooke-Popham to Ismay, 29 October 1941, BP/6/2/19, LHCMA.

47. Brooke-Popham, "Operations in the Far East," p. 547; M. Tsuji, *Singapore* (London: Constable, 1962), 8.

48. Tarling, *Onset of the Pacific War*, 278–79. In Brown's opinion, British propaganda did not fool the Japanese, but it did make it much harder to mobilize American public opinion. Brown, *Suez to Singapore*, 234–36.

49. C. Cruickshank, *SOE in the Far East* (Oxford: Oxford University Press, 1983), 224–26.

50. The Joint Intelligence Committee Singapore enabled the varied intelligence agencies to share information and coordinate activities. I. Nish, "Sir George Sansom: Diplomat and Historian," in *Collected Writings of Ian Nish, Part 2* (Abingdon, UK: Routledge, 2013), 186–87; Cooper, *Old Men Forget*, 293–94.

51. P. Kratoska, *The Japanese Occupation of Malaya: A Social and Economic History* (London: Hurst, 1997), 27–28. It had been intended that all propaganda activities would be transferred to the FEB if war broke out. In the event, these responsibilities were taken over by the Orient Mission Propaganda (OM/P).

52. G. Kennedy, "British Propaganda and the Protection of Empire in the Far East 1933–1942," in *British Propaganda and Wars of Empire: Influencing Friend and Foe 1900–2010*, edited by G. Kennedy and C. Truck (London: Routledge, 2014), 13–32.

53. U.S. Department of Defense, *The "Magic" Background of Pearl Harbor* (Washington, D.C.: U.S. Government Printing Office, 1977), 2:199.

54. Brooke-Popham to Opal, 8 August 1941, BPFP.

55. *Reports of General MacArthur: Japanese Operations in the Southwest Pacific Area*, vol. 2, Part 1 (Washington, D.C.: Center for Military History, 1966), 32.

56. Magic was a joint U.S. Army/Navy organization tasked with intercepting and deciphering Japanese communications. The Japanese Foreign Office cipher machine (Purple), used to encrypt its diplomatic messages, had been broken before the outbreak of war, but the process was lengthy and the information gained often out of date.

57. U.S. Department of Defense, *The "Magic" Background*, 3:219.

58. "From Our Hong Kong Correspondent: Hong Kong's Trade Prospects," *The Economist*, 25 January 1941, Issue 5083, p. 106.

59. Brooke-Popham to Opal, 2 March 1941, BPFP.

60. Brooke-Popham to Opal, 29 June 1941, BPFP.

61. Scott to Grey, 24 February 1960, Captain A. N. Grey Collection, 2005–05–26, IWM.

62. Commandant, IDC, Final Address, 15 December 1932, BP/1/6/4, LHCMA.

63. J. Record, *A War It Was Always Going to Lose: Why Japan Attacked America in 1941* (Washington, D.C.: Potomac Books, 2011), 98–102.

64. Trenchard, "Defence of Aerodromes," House of Lords Debate, 20 January 1942, *Hansard*, vol. 121, cols. 417–18; "Vigorous Defence of Sir R. Brooke-Popham," *Daily Telegraph*, 21 January 1942.

65. Lord Strabolgi, *Singapore and After* (London: Hutchinson, 1943), 60.

66. Bennett, *Why Singapore Fell*, 43.

67. M. Smith, *The Emperor's Codes* (London: Bantam Press, 2000), 9–10; J. R. Cox, *Rising Sun, Falling Skies* (Oxford, UK: Osprey, 2014), 45–46; F. Pike, *Hirohito's War: The Pacific War 1941–1945* (London: Bloomsbury, 2015), 222; and P. Brune, *Descent into Hell* (Sydney: Allen & Unwin, 2014), 95–96. These include ignoring signs of an imminent Japanese invasion, predicting that amphibious landings were impossible as the jungle was impenetrable, asserting that the Japanese would never set foot in Malaya (comments made by Shenton Thomas to his cipher clerk, Muriel Reilly), and consciously lying to the Australian government about the strength of Malaya's defenses.

CHAPTER 18. STRENGTHENING MALAYA'S DEFENSES

1. Brooke-Popham to Ismay, 6 January 1941, BP/6/2/4, LHCMA. A staff officer in Malaya Command felt that "the exercise was of tremendous value and exposed numerous defects in the system." Ashmore, "Some Personal Observations of the Malayan Campaign," Percival Papers, F49, IWM.

2. Brooke-Popham to Opal, 16 March 1941, BPFP. At that time, the petrol ration in the UK was the equivalent of just three gallons per week.

3. Brooke-Popham to Opal, 9 March 1941, BPFP.

4. Sayre to Roosevelt, 30 November 1941, 4697018, National Archives, UK.

5. "Mr Duff Cooper on Singapore," *Times* (London), 18 March 1942.

6. Connell, *Wavell, Supreme Commander*, 28, 41.

7. Percival, *The War in Malaya*, 185. The joint operations room became functional at the beginning of December, just before the Japanese attack.

8. Woodburn Kirby, *The War against Japan*, 1:48.

9. Ong, *Matador*, 128–29.

10. The name Siam had been changed to Thailand in 1939, under military dictatorship. The Allies refused to recognize this after the war, but the name was formally adopted in 1948.

11. Brooke-Popham to Opal, 9 June 1941, BPFP.

12. Brooke-Popham to Ismay, 3 February 1941, BP/6/2/5, LHCMA; R. Aldrich, "A Question of Expediency: Britain, the United States and Thailand, 1941–42," *Journal of Southeast Asian Studies* 19, no. 2 (1988): 209–44.

13. N. Tarling, "Atonement before Absolution: British Policy Towards Thailand During WW2," *Journal of the Siam Society (Bangkok)* 66, Pt. 1 (January 1978): 22–65; J. Crosby, *Siam: The Crossroads* (London: Hollis and Carter, 1945), 2–5.

14. Tarling, *Onset of the Pacific War*, 266–68.

15. Allen, *Singapore 1941–1942*, 87; Tarling, *Onset of the Pacific War*, 343–52; Singapore Notebook No. 4, BPFP.

16. GHQFE 838/JP, dated 24 January 1941, AIR 23/1970, TNA.

17. Singapore Notebook No. 1, BPFP. Brooke-Popham wrote on the very first page of his Singapore notebook, "What forms a casus belli?" immediately above the line, "Are conversations with Dutch and Americans to take place or not?

18. Percival, *The War in Malaya*, 54. It might be better to say that the operation matched the forces available. The Eleventh Indian Division was not strong enough to advance to the Kra Isthmus (and so protect the airfield at Point Victoria) or to occupy *both* Singora and Patani.

19. Ong, *Matador*, 143–44. It has been suggested that Brooke-Popham crossed into Thailand in civilian clothes to inspect the border area. This may be so, but his private papers don't mention such a visit. He did, however, visit Bangkok several times, including 3–4 June and 18–19 September 1941.

20. Percival, *The War in Malaya*, 227.

21. Percival to Brooke-Popham, 4 August 1946, BP/6/8/36, LHCMA.

22. Elphick, *Far Eastern File*, 168. Over time, the figure claimed by Percival would rise to 60 percent and eventually 70 percent.

23. R. Callahan, *Burma 1942–1945* (London: Davis-Poynter, 1978), 25.

24. He spent several days in Rangoon at the end of October 1941 (visiting the AVG at Toungoo) before flying on to Malaya.

25. Connell, *Wavell, Supreme Commander*, 30.

26. I. Grant and K. Tamayama, *Burma 1942: The Japanese Invasion* (Chichester, UK: Zampi Press, 1999), 37; Connell, *Wavell, Supreme Commander*, 29. Lewin goes as far as describing the situation as one of the least rational misconceptions in the history of British defense arrangements. R. Lewin, *The Chief: Field Marshal Lord Wavell, Commander-in-Chief and Viceroy, 1939–1947* (London: Hutchinson, 1980), 153.

27. CinC Far East to Chiefs of Staff, 15 September 1941, BP/6/7/11, LHCMA. Callahan argues that the War Office did not want India distracted from focusing on its military support to the Middle East. Callahan, *Burma 1942–1945*, 22–23.

28. A. Wavell, "Operations in Burma from 15 December 1941 to 20 May 1942," *Supplement to The London Gazette, 11 March 1948*, pp. 1667–68.

29. H. Probert, *The Forgotten Air Force: The Royal Air Force in the War against Japan 1941–1945* (London: Brassey's, 1995), 83. The siting of airfields and the early warning system would likely have been different.

30. Wavell to Brooke-Popham, 13 November 1941, BP/6/5/13, LHCMA.

31. Connell, *Wavell, Supreme Commander*, 61–63, 147–48.

32. R. Mitter, *China's War with Japan* (London: Allen Lane, 2013), 252–53; Woodburn Kirby, *The War against Japan*, 2:16–19. The possibility of Chinese assistance in the defense of Burma had been raised as early as July 1941. Brooke-Popham to Ismay, 3 July 1941, CAB 21/1044, TNA.

33. Wavell, "Operations in Burma," p. 1670.

34. Thorne, *Allies of a Kind*, 180.

35. Connell, *Wavell, Supreme Commander*, 74–75.

36. Wavell, "Operations in Burma," pp. 1667–68.

37. Connell, *Wavell, Supreme Commander*, 41.

38. McLeod to Brooke-Popham, 4 March 1942, BP/6/5/67, LHCMA.

39. B. Bond, *Chief of Staff: The Diaries of Lieutenant-General Sir Henry Pownall*, vol. 2, *1940–1944* (London: Leo Cooper, 1974), 66.

40. Connell, *Wavell, Supreme Commander*, 29–30.

41. Woodburn Kirby, *The War against Japan*, 1:34–36.

42. "Far Eastern Policy," Report by the Chiefs of Staff, 27 July 1940, CAB 66/10, TNA.

43. Ong, *Matador*, 135–36.

44. Notes on Signal X776 of 10 January 1941 BP6/1/7, LHCMA.

45. Percival to Chiefs of Staff, 2 August 1941, BP/6/1/18, LHCMA.

46. D. Richards and H. St. G. Saunders, *Royal Air Force 1939–1945*, vol. 2, *The Fight Avails* (London: HMSO, 1954), 15.

47. COS Response to Tactical Appreciation, 10 January 1941, BP/6/1/6, LHCMA.

48. Percival to Brooke-Popham, 4 August 1946, BP/6/8/36, LHCMA.

49. Orange, *Tedder*, 93–97.

50. It was Tedder who initially argued for the move of Air Headquarters from Seletar to Sime Road where it would be closer to Headquarters Malaya Command based at Fort Canning. Construction commenced in 1937 and was completed by 1940. Orange, *Tedder*, 93. Brian Farrell argues that, in adopting this strategy, Darvall and Tedder were also driven by their belief in independent air action. Farrell, *The Defence and Fall of Singapore*, 60–61.

51. Brooke-Popham to Ismay, 26 March 1941, BP/6/2/8, LHCMA.

52. Percival, *The War in Malaya*, 101.

53. G. Till, "Competing Visions: The Admiralty, the Air Ministry and the Role of Air Power," in *British Naval Aviation: The First 100 Years*, edited by T. Benbow (Farnham, UK: Ashgate, 2011), 57–78.

54. Woodburn Kirby, *Singapore: The Chain of Disaster*, 113–15; R. Holmes and A. Kemp, *The Bitter End* (Strettington, UK: Antony Bird Publications, 1982), 73.

55. Singapore Notebook No. 1, BPFP.

56. Brooke-Popham felt that Group Captain Edward Rice should receive much of the credit for this remarkable achievement. Rice was captured after the fall of Singapore and died in a POW camp on Formosa in 1943. Brooke-Popham to Philip Babington, 28 February 1942, BP/6/9/3, LHCMA. Air Marshal Sir Philip Balington (John Babington's brother) was Air Member for Personnel.

57. Private Papers of Wing Commander T. C. Carter, Documents 10847, IWM; Montgomery, *Shenton of Singapore*, 79.

58. Private Papers of Wing Commander T. C. Carter, Documents 10847, IWM; Brooke-Popham to Woodburn Kirby, 16 April 1953, BPFP.

59. "Popham East," *Time*, 25 November 1940.

60. Woodburn Kirby, *The War against Japan*, 1:57.

61. This includes: Rusbridger and Nave, *Betrayal at Pearl Harbor*, 135; K. Caffrey, *Out in the Midday Sun* (London: Andre Deutsch, 1974), 38; A. Stewart, *The Underrated Enemy* (London: William Kimber, 1987), 12.

62. Gallagher, *Retreat in the East*, 66–67. Since the RAF at that time did not possess a frontline aircraft named "Tornado" (although there was a single Hawker prototype of this name), it is likely that Brooke-Popham said "hyper-Hurricanes." The veracity of some of Gallagher's reporting in the Far East has been questioned elsewhere. Woods, *Reporting the Retreat*, 130–31.

63. Brown, *Suez to Singapore*, 281–82. These comments were made in an "off the record" briefing and were not reported at the time. Elphick, *Singapore: The Pregnable Fortress*, 157. Elphick has been used by several historians—without referencing Brown's account, including Dixon, *The Psychology of Military Incompetence*, 134, and Bishop, *Singapore Burning*, 110.

64. Dixon, *The Psychology of Military Incompetence*, 134. Dixon makes great play of these remarks, using them to accuse Brooke-Popham of stupidity, arrogance, and dishonesty.

65. COS Meeting, 25 April 1941, CAB 79/11, TNA. The possibility of other fighter types was considered, but dismissed, at a chiefs-of-staff meeting on 25 April 1941. It was stated that the Buffalo was eminently satisfactory and would probably prove more than a match for any Japanese aircraft.

66. During the Continuation War, June 1941–September 1944.

67. During the summer of 1939, the Japanese and Soviet armies clashed on the Manchurian–Mongolian border. Known as the Nomonhan Incident (by the Japanese) and the Battle of Khalkhin Gol (by the Russians), the Japanese were heavily defeated, but only after high casualties on both sides.

68. Brune, *Descent into Hell*, 95–96.

69. Aldrich, *Intelligence and the War against Japan*, 36; Singapore Notebook No. 1, BPFP. Chappell was appointed head of the FECB's air intelligence section in March 1941 (following Brooke-Popham's request to the chiefs of staff for stronger RAF representation), although he had to double as the travelling air attaché for Southeast Asia.

70. J. W. Toland, *The Rising Sun: The Decline and Fall of the Japanese Empire, 1936–1945* (New York: Random House, 1970), 231.

71. E. M. Cox, "Memorandum on the Royal Air Force in Malaya," 11 April 1942, Ludlow-Hewitt Papers, Box 4/File 14, RAF Historical Branch.

72. C. Shores and B. Cull, *Bloody Shambles*, vol. 1, *The Drift to War to the Fall of Singapore* (London: Grub Street, 1992), 65.

73. There remains some controversy over the results of the air fighting. The Japanese claimed to have destroyed 1,349 Russian aircraft between May and September

1939 for the loss of 120 of their own. The Russians claimed to have destroyed 215 Japanese aircraft by the end of August for the loss of 130 of their own. S. D. Goldman, *Nomonhan, 1939* (Annapolis, MD: Naval Institute Press, 2012), 101–53. The actual losses are likely to have been around 250 Soviet and 164 Japanese aircraft (from all causes). D. Nedialkov, *In the Skies of Nomonhan* (Manchester, UK: Crecy, 2011), 138.

74. Nedialkov, *Nomonhan*, 140–41.

75. Brooke-Popham, "Operations in the Far East," Annex J.

76. Shores and Cull, *Bloody Shambles*, 1:52–54. Reserves were of the order of 153 aircraft. Percival Papers, F42, IWM.

77. SD98 provided predicted attrition rates for aircraft and aircrew, to be used in operational planning and to assess training and production/repair needs under wartime conditions. Higham, "Selected Aspects of RAF Concepts of and Planning for War, 1934–1941," 141–57.

78. W. Green, and G. Swanborough, "Brewster's Benighted Buffalo," *Air Enthusiast Quarterly*, no. 1 (1975): 66–83.

79. In the event, the first aircraft reinforcements arrived some six weeks after the Japanese attack, but only by diverting a Hurricane squadron already at sea. Without adequate spares or repair facilities, serviceability rapidly fell and the Hurricanes were ineffective within a few weeks.

80. Chiefs of Staff to Prime Minister, 24 January 1942, CAB 120/517, TNA.

81. Notes on the Far East, Brooke-Popham to Portal, 12 March 1942, BP/6/9/5, LHCMA.

82. Brooke-Popham, "Operations in the Far East," Annex J. Of the original 167 Buffaloes, more than 20 had been lost in training accidents.

83. Ibid., 151.

84. A single Repair and Salvage Unit (RSU) arrived at Seletar in September 1941. A second RSU was on its way from England but was diverted to India after the Japanese attack. R. S. Sansome, *The Bamboo Workshop* (Braunton, UK: Merlin Books, 1995), 35.

85. Playfair to Air Ministry, 20 August 1941, BP/6/1/25, LHCMA.

86. Brooke-Popham, "Operations in the Far East," p. 552.

87. R. J. Brownell, *From Khaki to Blue* (Lyneham, ACT: Military History Society of Aus-tralia, 1978), 202. Group Captain Raymond Brownell commanded the RAAF Malaya 1940–1941.

88. Notes on the Far East, Brooke-Popham to Portal, 12 March 1942, BP/6/9/5, LHCMA. Brooke-Popham judged that the comparative failure of the Buffalo was owed to a combination of poor performance and inexperienced pilots.

89. *War diary and logbooks of a WW2 fighter pilot* (blog), "Leigh Bowes RAAF Flying Log Book & Service Diary," by P. Bowes, posted 28 August 2013, https://leighbowes76.files.wordpress.com/2014/08/leigh-bowes-flying-log-book-service-diary_small_file_size-2.pdf.

90. Singapore Notebook No. 1, BPFP. Of the seventy Beauforts scheduled to be delivered by the end of 1941, just six had arrived by the start of the war and five of these had to be returned to Australia for operational training and the installation of further equipment.

91. "Air Operations in Malaya," Report by Wing Commander A. W. D. Miller, 25 February 1946, AIR 20/5572, TNA.

92. Boyd, "Worthy of Better Memory," p. 293.

93. Richards and Saunders, *Royal Air Force,* 2:11; Playfair to Air Ministry, 20 August 1941, BP/6/1/25, LHCMA.

94. P. C. Smith, *Mitsubishi Zero* (Barnsley, UK: Pen & Sword, 2014), 52.

95. For example: Probert, *The Forgotten Air Force*, 28–29; Brune, *Descent into Hell*, 182; and P. Preston-Hough, *Commanding Far Eastern Skies* (Solihull, UK: Helion, 2015), 140–147.

96. Shores and Cull, *Bloody Shambles*, 1:52–53.

97. Woodburn Kirby, *The War against Japan*, 1:240.

98. Green and Swanborough, "Brewster's Benighted Buffalo," 66; "Comments on Maltby Draft Despatch," Brooke-Popham to McEvoy, 17 November 1946, BP/6/8/8, LHCMA. UK Flight testing of the Buffalo commenced in April 1941 and the initial handling report, issued on 3 July (which never reached Malaya), highlighted its advanced control reactions—compared to the Spitfire and Hurricane.

99. N. Millman, *Ki-27 "Nate" Aces* (Oxford, UK: Osprey, 2013), 59; B. Cull, *Buffaloes over Singapore* (London: Grub Street, 2003), 223. The Buffalo was at least 1,000 kilograms heavier than either the Nate or the Oscar.

100. Brooke-Popham complained as early as February 1941 that Singapore was not receiving regular information from the Air Ministry on operational lessons. Brooke-Popham to Ismay 6 January 1941, BP/6/2/4, LHCMA; Harvey, "Army Air Force and Navy Air Force," 182; Preston-Hough, *Commanding Far Eastern Skies*, 108–31.

101. Kennedy, "Anglo-American Strategic Relations," 772–73.

102. O. Tagaya, "The Imperial Japanese Air Forces," in *Why Air Forces Fail*, edited by R. Higham and S. J. Harris (Lexington: University Press of Kentucky, 2006), 177–202.

103. Portal to Brooke-Popham, 7 November 1941, AIR 19/561, TNA.

104. *Times* (London), 28 January 1942, p. 8.

105. L. Freedman, *The Official History of the Falklands Campaign* (Abingdon, UK: Routledge, 2007), 218–22. Although not mentioned in Freedman's book, this analysis was taken from a secret report prepared by Deputy-Director GCHQ Douglas Nicholl, shortly before the Argentinian invasion. *Times* (London), 20 November 2015.

106. His views changed during November 1941 with increasing evidence that Japan would move in the south.

107. E. Hemingway, "China's Air Needs," *PM* (New York), 17 June 1941.

108. *Times* (London), 28 January 1942, p. 8.

109. Ismay to Lord Privy Seal (Clement Atlee), 29 December 1941, CAB 120/517, TNA.

110. Woodburn Kirby, *The War against Japan*, 1:51. The FECB was initially known as the Combined Intelligence Bureau.

111. Brooke-Popham to Ismay, 15 November 1940, BP/6/2/2, LHCMA; CinC Far East to Air Ministry, Secret Cypher Telegram, WO 193/920, TNA.

112. M. S. Goodman, *The Official History of the Joint Intelligence Committee*, vol. 1 (London: Routledge, 2014), 103.

113. Woodburn Kirby, *The War against Japan*, 1:240; R. J. Aldrich, "Britain's Secret Intelligence Service in Asia during the Second World War," *Modern Asia Studies* 32, Issue 1 (February 1998): 187.

114. Aldrich, *Intelligence and the War against Japan*, 23.

115. K. Jeffery, *MI6: The History of the Secret Intelligence Service* (London: Blooms-bury, 2010), 468–69.

116. "SIS in the Far East," 15 July 1940, ADM 223/496, TNA.

117. "Final Report of Edward Ansel Mowrer," CIA CREST, p. 4. "Organisation X" was the propaganda arm of the Orient Mission (OM/P). Sansom had arrived in Singapore in May 1941 as an adviser to the Far East Mission, and was instrumental in improving coordination between GHQ, the FECB, and the MOI. Sansom's primary responsibility was organizing a comprehensive propaganda campaign across the Far East, involving the *Sydney Morning Herald* and the MBC, to dissuade the Japanese from attacking the Allies. "Establishment of Killery Mission in Singapore," HS 1/110, TNA; J. Murray, *Watching the Sun Rise: Australian Reporting of Japan, 1931 to the Fall of Singapore* (New York: Lexington Books, 2004), 233–38.

118. Jeffery, *MI6*, 472. A contemporary review, conducted by the FECB in August 1941, was extremely critical of SIS.

119. Brooke-Popham, "Operations in the Far East," pp. 537, 564–565; Notes on the Far East, Brooke-Popham to Portal, 12 March 1942, BP/6/9/5, LHCMA; "Comments on Maltby Draft Despatch," BP/6/8/8, LHCMA.

120. Comments on Draft Despatch, 25 June 1942, BP/6/11/17, LHCMA. These comments were removed from the final document at the request of the director of military intelligence.

121. The FECB, Malaya Command, Naval Command, Air Command, Defence Security Officer (MI5), Foreign Office, MEW, and the Malayan Security Service. Note by Inspector General Police, Straits Settlement, 12 January 1946, Percival Papers, F43, IWM.

122. Elphick, *Far Eastern File*, 168–71; Aldrich, *Intelligence and the War against Japan*, 51.

123. Ferris, "Worthy of Some Better Enemy?," 223–56. Aldrich fatally misunderstands the complaints about the SIS. Brooke-Popham's concern was not whether the Japanese were about to attack, but where they were going to attack. During November 1941, the FECB and other sources were increasingly persuaded that the Japanese were intent on a southern advance, but remained uncertain about the target, until the outbreak of war. Aldrich, "Britain's Secret Intelligence Service in Asia," 188–90.

124. J. Ferris, "'Consistent with an Intention': The Far East Combined Bureau and the Outbreak of the Pacific War, 1940–41," *Intelligence and National Security* 27, no. 1 (2012): 5–26. There is absolutely no evidence to support claims that Brooke-Popham knew from "Secret Intelligence" the exact time, place, and composition of the Japanese landings, but could not reveal the fact for fear of compromising his sources. Elphick, *Far Eastern File*, 316–17; Thompson, *The Battle for Singapore*, 129.

125. Mawdsley, *December 1941*, 56–63; Goodman, *The Official History of the Joint Intelligence Committee*, 1:105–6.

126. Ashmore, "Some Personal Observations of the Malayan Campaign," Percival Papers, F49, IWM.

127. "Comments on Maltby Draft Despatch," BP6/8/8, LHCMA.

128. Cox, "Memorandum on the Royal Air Force in Malaya," p. 20, Ludlow-Hewitt Papers, Box 4/File 14, RAF Historical Branch.

129. A. Best, *British Intelligence and the Japanese Challenge in Asia 1914–1941* (Basingstoke, UK: Palgrave Macmillan, 2002), 177.

130. Boyd, "Worthy of Better Memory," pp. 246, 254.

131. Brooke-Popham to McEvoy, 17 November 1946, BP/6/8/8, LHCMA.

132. Crosby to Brooke-Popham, 12 August 1941, BP/6/6/21, LHCMA; Clark Kerr to Brooke-Popham, 28 April 1942, BP/6/5/69, LHCMA. The feeling appears to have been mutual. Crosby regarded Brooke-Popham as "a tower of strength to us all in the Far East," while Clark Kerr believed that the attacks on Brooke-Popham were "beneath contempt."

CHAPTER 19. "STIFFENING THE CHINESE"

1. The Kuomintang (the Nationalist Party of China) had been founded in 1911. By 1928, led by Chiang Kai-shek, it had become the ruling party of mainland China.

2. Mitter, *China's War with Japan*, 73.

3. Including the cities of Beijing, Canton, Nanking, Shanghai, and Wuhan.

4. Brooke-Popham to Opal, 19 December 1940, BPFP.

5. "Australian War Minister in Singapore," *Singapore Free Press*, 24 December 1940, p. 3.

6. "Far Eastern Policy," 27 July 1940, CAB 66/10, TNA.

7. Brooke-Popham to Ismay, 6 January 1941, BP/6/2/4, LHCMA.

8. J. W. Dower, *War without Mercy: Race and Power in the Pacific War* (New York: Pantheon Books, 1986), 99; Ferris, "Worthy of Some Better Enemy?," 225–26; G. Home, *Race War: White Supremacy and the Japanese Attack on the British Empire* (New York: New York University Press, 2005), 139. Home attributes to Brooke-Popham the disparaging remarks made by Gordon Bennett about the martial qualities of Indian troops.

9. Brooke-Popham to Ismay, 6 January 1941, BP/6/2/4, LHCMA.

10. Brooke-Popham to Street, 15 January 1941, BP/6/3/3, LHCMA; D. Ford, "British Intelligence on Japanese Army Morale during the Pacific War: Logical Analysis or Racial Stereotyping?," *Journal of Military History* 69 (2005): 447; K. C. Man and T. Y. Lun, *Eastern Fortress: A Military History of Hong Kong, 1840–1970* (Hong Kong: Hong Kong University Press, 2014), 128.

11. Foster Cox, Interview 16275/3/1–3, IWM.

12. Brooke-Popham to Opal, 9 April 1941, BPFP.

13. Brooke-Popham to Opal, 9 March & 29 March 1941, BPFP.

14. "Final Report of Edward Ansel Mowrer," CIA CREST, p. 26.

15. Brooke-Popham to Opal, 30 August 1941, BPFP. He was more impressed by Northcote's successor, Sir Mark Young (whom he knew from their time together in East Africa), when he passed through Singapore in August 1941.

16. Brooke-Popham to Opal, 9 April 1941, BPFP.

17. Foster Cox, Interview 16275/3/1–3, IWM.

18. A. Hewitt, *Bridge with Three Men* (London: Jonathan Cape, 1986), 2.

19. "Notes for Talk," 8 April 1941, BP/6/7/4, LHCMA. The notes used by Brooke-Popham in preparing for his talk on the afternoon of 8 April do not indicate that he used this language, but there is no way of knowing exactly what he said to his audience.

20. Sergeant H. S. G. Hale, Royal Scots, Interview 6125/1982, IWM.

21. Talk with Lord Trenchard, 27 June 1935, LH/9/13/22, LHCMA. Liddell Hart had a meeting with Lord Trenchard in 1935 at which "he thought, and I agree, that the Japanese were not nearly so formidable as many people believed. Their military qualities were over-rated and they were internally shaken."

22. Wavell to Brooke-Popham, 13 November 1941, BP/6/5/13, LHCMA. It has been said that Wavell never relinquished his contempt for the Japanese soldier. A. K. Lathrop, "The Employment of Chinese Nationalist Troops in the First Burma Campaign," *Journal of Southeast Asia Studies* 12, no. 2 (1981): 405.

23. Dorman-Smith, Draft of Unfinished Memoirs, pp. 76–77, MSS Eur 215/320, India Office, British Library.

24. *Times* (London), 24 November 1941.

25. Ford, "British Intelligence on Japanese Army Morale," pp. 444–45. Chappell, the head of the FECB air intelligence section, may have been the source for Brooke-Popham's negative views on Japanese airmanship. Best, *British Intelligence and the Japanese Challenge*, 118; J. R. Ferris, "Student and Master: The United Kingdom,

Japan, Airpower, and the Fall of Singapore, 1920–1941," in *A Great Betrayal? The Fall of Singapore Revisited*, edited by B. Farrell and S. Hunter (Singapore: Marshall Cavendish, 2010), 74–97; Kennedy, "Anglo-American Strategic Relations," 744–45.

26. Comments on Maltby Despatch, Brooke-Popham to McEvoy, 17 November 1946, BP/6/8/8, LHCMA.

27. C. Ciocirlan, E. Chung, and C. McLarney, "Against All Odds: A Strategic Analysis of the Fall of Hong Kong, 1941," *Management Decision* 49, no. 6 (2011): 984–1000.

28. Liddell Hart, *The Memoirs of Captain Liddell Hart*, 1:292.

29. K. Fedorowich, "Cocked Hats and Swords and Small Little Garrisons: Britain, Canada and the Fall of Hong Kong, 1941," *Modern Asia Studies* 37, no. 1 (2003): 111–37. Grasett had been replaced by Maltby in July 1941 but used his influence to persuade the Canadian government to offer troops for Hong Kong.

30. Singapore Notebook No. 2, p. 66, BPFP.

31. J. L. Granatstein, *The Generals: The Canadian Army's Senior Commanders in the Second World War* (Toronto: Stoddart, 1993), 98.

32. Brooke-Popham to Woodburn Kirby, 16 April 1953, BPFP. By the time of the Japanese attack, the Canadian government was considering bringing the Canadian presence up to a brigade group. Although British strategy had not formally changed since 1940, there was a perception that the war situation had improved, and that Japan could be successfully deterred with American support. C. M. Bell, "Our Most Exposed Outpost: Hong Kong and British Far Eastern Strategy," *Journal of Military History* 60, no. 1 (1996): 61–88.

33. Mitter, *China's War with Japan*, 220.

34. F. D. Macri, "C Force to Hong Kong: The Price of Collective Security in China, 1941," *Journal of Military History* 77 (January 2013): 141–71; Fedorowich, "Cocked Hats," 155; Lecture to Staff College, 2 March 1942, BP/6/7/17, LHCMA.

35. F. D. Macri, *Clash of Empires in South China* (Lawrence: University Press of Kansas, 2012), 341. Playfair's view was that the two battalions would have been much more effective (from a military rather than a political perspective) if they had been sent to Malaya. Playfair, "Some Personal Reflections," p. 3.

36. Brooke-Popham to Woodburn Kirby, 16 April 1953, p. 1, BPFP.

37. "Final Report of Edward Ansel Mowrer," CIA CREST, p. 40.

38. U.S. Department of Defense, *The "Magic" Background*, 2:55.

39. Best, *Britain, Japan and Pearl Harbour*, 111–18.

40. Strictly speaking, the "American Volunteer Group of the International Air Force."

41. E. Buchan, *A Few Planes for China, the Birth of the Flying Tigers* (Lebanon, NH: University Press of New England, 2017), 189–90.

42. Brooke-Popham had already been alerted by Clark Kerr. William Pawley (president of the China National Aviation Corporation), who was closely associated

with the creation and support of the AVG. With his brother Edward, they organized an assembly plant at Mingaladon (Rangoon) through the family holding company, Intercontinent.

43. C. P. Romanus and R. Sunderland, *Stillwell's Mission to China* (Washington, D.C.: Center of Military History, 1952), 18.

44. Singapore Notebook No. 3, BPFP.

45. Greenlaw, *The Lady and the Tigers*, 65. During the flypast, he advised her on how to photograph the formation.

46. The War Department's failure to send any ammunition meant that operational training could not have started before September 1941, by which date the veto had already been lifted. Buchan, *A Few Planes for China*, 147–48.

47. Brooke-Popham to Ismay, 20 August 1941, BP/6/2/16, LHCMA; "Notes on Burma," 18 March 1942, BP/6/7/18, LHCMA.

48. Playfair, "Some Personal Reflections," p. 11; Thorne, *Allies of a Kind*, 79.

49. Chennault to Brooke-Popham, 5 May 1950, BPFP.

50. Brooke-Popham, "Operations in the Far East," p. 540.

51. Woodburn Kirby, *The War against Japan*, 1:53.

52. Dennys was killed in an air crash in March 1942.

53. Brooke-Popham to Opal, 10 May 1941, BPFP.

54. H. J. Van der Ven, *China, War and Nationalism* (London: Routledge, 2003), 23; M. Yu, "'In God We Trusted, In China We Busted': The China Commando Group of the Special Operations Executive, *Intelligence and National Security* 16, no. 4 (2001): 41–42.

55. Brooke-Popham to Opal, 15 June 1941, BPFP.

56. Cruickshank, *SOE in the Far East*, 4.

57. Dewing to War Office, 19 November 1940, WO 193/605, TNA.

58. "Notes on General Gordon Bennett's Report," 8 April 1942, BP/6/9/11, LHCMA.

59. Brooke-Popham to Opal, 14 April 1941, BPFP.

60. Yu, "In God We Trusted," 37–60.

61. "Failure of the British Commando Effort, April 1942," CIA-RDP13X00001 R000100310003–7, CIA CREST; Grimsdale, "Thunder in the East," p.15, IWM.

62. "History of the Oriental Mission," HS 1/207, TNA.

63. F. Spencer Chapman, *The Jungle Is Neutral* (London: Chatto & Windus, 1949), 6.

64. Ibid., 12; I. Trenowden, *Operations Most Secret, SOE: The Malayan Theatre* (London: William Kimber, 1978), 76–77; R. Gough, *Special Operations Singapore 1941–42* (Singapore: Heinemann, 1985), 21.

65. Cruickshank, *SOE in the Far East*, 61–62; Smith, *Singapore Burning*, 80–82.

66. Cruickshank, *SOE in the Far East*, 68–69.

67. "History of the Oriental Mission," HS 1/207, TNA.

68. Grimsdale to Ismay, 8 March 1942, Ismay/4/14/1a, LHCMA.

69. Chapman, *The Jungle Is Neutral*, 11; Gough, *Special Operations Singapore*, 156.

70. Woodburn Kirby, *The War against Japan* 1:467–68.

CHAPTER 20. BUILDING ALLIANCES

1. Brooke-Popham, "Operations in the Far East," p. 538.

2. Callahan, *The Worst Disaster*, 126.

3. The first international air service to Singapore was provided by the Dutch, who operated flights between Batavia and Singapore from 1930 and between Batavia and Australia from 1938. Regular commercial flights from London to Singapore commenced in 1934. From 1938, the service used Short C-class flying boats with up to three flights every week. The route between Australia and Singapore continued after the outbreak of war in Europe, but on a reduced frequency. The first international service to the United States began in May 1941 with a semi-monthly service from San Francisco via Guam, Honolulu, and Manila.

4. Playfair, "Some Personal Reflections," p. 13.

5. Brooke-Popham to Playfair, 3 July 1943, BP/6/9/28, LHCMA.

6. Gillison, *Royal Australian Air Force*, 143.

7. Menzies arrived on 28 January from Java and departed the next day for Bangkok (via Penang). Martin and Hardy, *Dark and Hurrying Days*, 23–24.

8. Ibid. The situation would not have come as a total surprise to the Australian Cabinet since Percy Spender (minister for the army) and Lieutenant-General Vernon Sturdee (chief of the General Staff) had reported back on Singapore's weaknesses following their visit in December to discuss arrangements for receiving the Australian brigade group.

9. Charles Burnett (chief of the Air Staff), Sturdee (chief of the General Staff), and Admiral Ragnar Colvin (chief of the Naval Staff). It had been hoped that the NEI chief of staff (Major-General Hein ter Poorten) would join Brooke-Popham in Australia.

10. Hasluck, *The Government and the People*, 319–26. In October 1941, two independent members of the House of Representatives crossed the floor, allowing Curtin, the Labour leader, to form a government.

11. Ibid., 329; Gillison, *Royal Australian Air Force*, 151.

12. Gillison, *Royal Australian Air Force*, 151; Hasluck, *The Government and the People*, 327–29; and L. Wigmore, *The Japanese Thrust* (Canberra: Australian War Memorial, 1957), 58. It is difficult to reconcile Woodburn Kirby's comments with the Australian official histories; moreover, Brooke-Popham worked with the Australian chiefs of staff in preparing the strategic appreciation discussed at the meeting.

13. Singapore Notebook No. 2, BPFP. Brooke-Popham met with Charles Gauss, the American minister to Australia, who had more than twenty years' experience in China. Among the advice offered (based on secondhand knowledge) was that the Japanese air force had been "laughable three years ago, but much improved now."

14. Brooke-Popham to Opal, 16 February 1941, BPFP.

15. Brooke-Popham to Ismay, 26 March 1941, CAB 21/1044, TNA.

16. Woodburn Kirby, *Singapore: The Chain of Disaster*, 73–74; Hasluck, *The Government and the People*, 323–24; Callahan, *The Worst Disaster*, 130; "The Empire's New 'B-P,'" *Australasian*, 8 March 1941, p. 14. Brooke-Popham's appreciation of the risk presented by Japan was shared by the Australian chiefs of staff. Callahan also calls Brooke-Popham's performance "weak" but only references Woodburn Kirby.

17. Hasluck, *The Government and the People*, 329.

18. H. T. Bussemaker, "Paradise in Peril: The Netherlands, Great Britain and the Defence of the Netherlands East Indies, 1940–41," *Journal of Southeast Asian Studies* 31, no. 1 (March 2000): 132. These instructions were further refined by an Allied Planning Committee (based in Singapore) between July and December 1941.

19. He left Singapore on 13 October, travelling by Qantas flying boat as far as Darwin, where he transferred to an RAAF Hudson for the final leg to Melbourne, arriving on 15 October 1941. He caught the return Qantas flight at Darwin on 25 October, reaching Singapore on 26 October.

20. "Defences of the Pacific," *Melbourne Age*, 17 October 1941.

21. Advisory War Council Minute 533, 16 October 1941, Department of Foreign Affairs, National Archives of Australia. Brooke-Popham has been accused of using spin and untruths to deceive the Australian government. Brune, *Descent into Hell*, 95–96.

22. "Pacific Defences Now Stronger," *Melbourne Argus*, 17 October 1941, p. 1.

23. Brooke-Popham to Opal, 20 March 1941, BPFP.

24. Brooke-Popham, "Operations in the Far East," p. 566.

25. Commonwealth of Australia to Dominions Office, 22 November 1941, CAB 120/517, TNA.

26. Cipher Telegram No. 750, Commonwealth of Australia to Dominions Office, 22 November 1941, CAB 120/517, TNA.

27. Woodburn Kirby, *The War against Japan*, 1:14.

28. Bussemaker, "Paradise in Peril," 115–36.

29. Ibid., 125–26.

30. Bussemaker, "Australian-Dutch Defence Cooperation, 1940–1941," *Journal of the Australian War Memorial* 29 (November 1996): 1–15.

31. Martin and Hardy, *Dark and Hurrying Days*, 22.

32. Brooke-Popham travelled by scheduled airlines. While in Java he stayed with the British consul.

33. Note by Mr S. M. Bruce, High Commissioner in London, of conversation with Jonkheer E. Michiels van Verduynen, Netherlands Minister to the United Kingdom, 18 February 1941, Historical Documents 307, Department of Foreign Affairs and Trade, National Archives of Australia.

34. Woodburn Kirby, *The War against Japan*, 1:55.

35. Brooke-Popham to Ismay, 28 February 1941, BP/6/2/7, LHCMA; "Anglo-Dutch Cooperation," FO 371/27786, TNA.

36. Tarling, *Onset of the Pacific War*, 230.

37. Berenschot died in a flying accident when returning from the conference. His Lockheed Lodestar suffered engine problems shortly after takeoff from Kemajoran and crashed, killing all on board including the RAF liaison officer, Wing Commander Trevor Watkins.

38. Brooke-Popham, "Operations in the Far East," p. 567.

39. Hein ter Poorten to Brooke-Popham, 28 December 1941, BP/6/5/57, LHCMA.

40. W. T. Johnsen, *The Origins of the Grand Alliance—Anglo-American Military Collaboration from the Panay Incident to Pearl Harbor* (Lexington: University Press of Kentucky, 2016), 34–48.

41. Ibid., 54.

42. "AASAC (Joint) Third Meeting, 31 August 1940," WO 193/311, TNA.

43. Johnsen, *The Origins of the Grand Alliance*, 178.

44. *Time*, 24 November 1941. The growing importance of Hart's command was reflected in a major article published by *Time* magazine shortly before the outbreak of war.

45. Leutze, *A Different Kind of Victory*, 395. Hart was a year older than Brooke-Popham.

46. *Tribune* (Manila), 4 April 1941.

47. Brooke-Popham to Opal, 10 April 1941, BPFP; Brooke-Popham to Ismay, 19 April 1941, BP/6/2/10, LHCMA.

48. Brooke-Popham to Ismay, 29 October 1941, CAB 21/1044, TNA.

49. "Singapore's Chief Confers In Manila," The *New York Times*, 3 April 1941; "Sir R. Brooke-Popham and U.S. Army Leaders," *Sydney Morning Herald*, 4 April 1941; "The Manila Talks," *Singapore Free Press*, 7 April 1941, p. 4; "U.S. Part in Defense Parley Hints at Far East Trends," *Brooklyn Eagle*, 6 April 1941, p. 12A; "Far East Defence Talks—Parley in Manila," *South China Morning Post*, 7 April 1941.

50. "Van Kleffens Arrives, Will Leave Friday," *Manila Daily Bulletin*, 9 April 1941.

51. Matsuoka signed the Soviet-Japanese Neutrality Pact in Moscow on 13 April 1941.

52. "Japan Scents a Plot," *Detroit Free Press*, 22 April 1941, p. 6.

53. Hart, "Narrative of Events," p. 3, 4697018, National Archives. He argued that threatening the Japanese achieved nothing, and likely affected their good judgment as well as putting them on guard.

54. E. S. Miller, *War Plan Orange: The U.S. Strategy to Defeat Japan, 1897–1945* (Annapolis, MD: Naval Institute Press, 1991), 262.

55. K. Tolley, *Cruise of the* Lanikai: *Incitement to War* (Annapolis, MD: Naval Institute Press, 2014), 52; "British Far East Commander Here," *Herald*, 3 April 1941; "Sir Robert Here for Unofficial Confabs, Chief of British Forces in Far East Making Informal Calls on U.S. Army, Navy Officials; Feted by Hart Today," *Manila Daily Bulletin*, 7 April 1941.

56. "Final Report of Edward Ansel Mowrer," CIA CREST, p. 45.

57. Johnsen, *The Origins of the Grand Alliance*, 229; Hart, "Narrative of Events," p. 8 and p. 26, 4697018, National Archives.

58. "Final Report of Edward Ansel Mowrer," CIA CREST, p. 45.

59. ADM 199/1472B, Events in Far East, TNA. "Under him, the initial operations of the Asiatic Fleet certainly appeared to myself, and to Admiral Helfrich, the Dutch Naval Commander-in-Chief, to be quite ineffective."

60. Leutze, *A Different Kind of Victory*, 272–78; T. Womack, *The Allied Defence of the Malay Barrier* (Jefferson, NC: McFarland, 2016), 152.

61. Brooke-Popham to Ismay, 16 May 1941, BP/6/2/12, LHCMA. Brooke-Popham was disappointed that neither Grunert nor Hart could be there in person.

62. Johnsen, *The Origins of the Grand Alliance*, 178–83.

63. Ibid., 187.

64. These talks did not take place until the beginning of December 1941.

65. Brooke-Popham to Opal, 12 October 1941, BPFP. While at Clark Field, Brooke-Popham seized the opportunity to fly in one of the recently delivered Boeing B-17 bombers, before he returned to Singapore. Brooke-Popham to Ismay, 10 October 1941, BP/6/2/18, LHCMA.

66. R. Collier, *1941* (London: Hamish Hamilton, 1981), 213; Singapore Notebook No. 4, BPFP.

67. Bartsch, *MacArthur's Pearl Harbor*, 101, 145–46.

68. Captain A. N. Grey Collection, 2005–05–26A, IWM; Bartsch, *MacArthur's Pearl Harbor*, 101; Brooke-Popham to Dill, 7 May 1940, Dill/3/3/2, LHCMA. Brooke-Popham reportedly shared his "Most Secret Memo," outlining plans for the defeat of Japan.

69. Brooke-Popham to Dill, 7 May 1940, Dill/3/3/2, LHCMA.

70. Hart, "Narrative of Events," p. 23, 4697018, National Archives.

71. Leutze, *A Different Kind of Victory*, 210. Brook-Popham mentioned the potential demise of fox-hunting in one of his personal letters to Ismay (who also hunted), but not in the context suggested. Brooke-Popham to Ismay, 6 January 1941, CAB 21/1044, TNA.

72. Leutze, *A Different Kind of Victory*, 212–18; H. W. Baldwin, *Great Mistakes of the War* (New York: Harper & Brothers, 1949), 62.

73. Hart, "Narrative of Events," pp. 2–3, 4697018, National Archives.

74. Johnsen, *The Origins of the Grand Alliance*, 247. The problem was compounded by the existence of three different plans for the defense of the Philippines. Baldwin, *Great Mistakes of the War*, 68.
75. Brooke-Popham, "Operations in the Far East," p. 567.
76. Major-General Lewis Heath, "Lecture on Malayan Campaign," 21 June 1942, Percival Papers, F42, IWM.
77. Captain Archer Allen, 7 August 1941, quoted in Brown, *Suez to Singapore*, 139–40.

CHAPTER 21. "AN ARMY OFFICER WITH MORE RECENT EXPERIENCE"

1. A. Roberts, *Eminent Churchillians* (London: Weidenfeld & Nicolson, 1994), 201. Dorman-Smith replaced Cochrane as governor of Burma in May 1941.
2. Cato [pseud.], *Guilty Men* (London: Victor Gollancz, 1940). "Cato" was a pseudonym for the journalists Michael Foot, Frank Owen, and Peter Howard.
3. Dorman-Smith's "crime," as minister for agriculture, was inadequate food production, although there was little evidence to support this allegation.
4. A. Draper, *Dawn Like Thunder: The Retreat from Burma* (London: Leo Cooper, 1987), 10.
5. J. L. Hodson, *War in the Sun* (London: Victor Gollancz, 1942), 331–32.
6. Dorman-Smith to Amery, 14 August 1941, CAB 120/517, TNA; "Far East," PREM 3/52/4, TNA; and MSS Eur E 215/1–2, India Office, British Library.
7. The advocacy of Paget is curious (two months later he would be the chiefs of staff candidate for the post of CinC Far East), but it seems that they had known each other when Dorman-Smith was attached to CinC Home Forces (June–December 1940), where Paget was chief of staff.
8. Brooke-Popham to Ismay, 3 July 1941, CAB 21/1044, TNA; Brooke-Popham to Ismay, 20 August 1941, BP/6/2/16, LHCMA.
9. Amery to Dorman-Smith, 20 August 1941, AMEL/2/3/20, Churchill Archives; Amery to Dorman Smith, 21 August 1941, MSS Eur E 215/1–2, India Office, British Library.
10. Dorman-Smith to Amery, 27 August 1941, MSS Eur E 215/1–2, India Office, British Library.
11. C. Bayley and T. Harper, *Forgotten Armies: The Fall of British Asia 1941–1945* (London: Allen Lane, 2005), 353. Richmond was appointed by Dorman-Smith as his military liaison officer on 1 August 1941, working alongside the military secretary, Lieutenant-Colonel G. T. Miller, who had joined Dorman-Smith three months earlier. Richmond, who was small and short-sighted, spoke both Burmese and Kachin.
12. Air Ministry: Department of the Master-General of the Personnel: Officer's Service Records, AIR 76/426, TNA. Richmond served with No. 20 Squadron. R. Dunlop, *Behind Japanese Lines: With the OSS in Burma* (New York: Skyhorse Publishing, 2014), 48–49. The Burma Civil List for September 1942 records Richmond as the governor's military assistant.

13. McLeod to Brooke-Popham, 4 March 1942, BP/6/5/67, LHCMA.
14. T. J. Sacquety, "The Organizational Evolution of OSS Detachment 101 in Burma, 1942–1945," PhD dissertation, Texas A&M University, 2008, p. 46.
15. Brooke-Popham, "Operations in the Far East," p. 8; Singapore Notebook No. 4, BPFP.
16. J. M. A. Gwyer and J. R. M. Butler, *Grand Strategy* (June 1941–August 1942), Part 1 (London: HMSO, 1964), 284; Clark Kerr to Foreign Office, 25 June 1941, PREM 3/155, TNA.
17. War Cabinet Loose Minute, 18 July 1941, PREM 3/155, TNA; Amery to Dorman-Smith, 31 July 1941, AMEL 2/3/20, Churchill Archives. Amery was skeptical about Duff Cooper's mission, believing that someone of the under-secretary class attached to Brooke-Popham would have been enough.
18. Roberts, *Eminent Churchillians*, 208.
19. Evans, *The Killearn Diaries 1934–1946*, 74. Brooke-Popham had first encoun-tered Duff Cooper at the Anglo-Egyptian Conversations Committee in June 1936.
20. Dorman-Smith to Amery, 18 February 1942, MSS Eur E 215/1–2, India Office, British Library; McLeod to Brooke-Popham, 4 March 1942, BP/6/5/67, LHCMA. Dorman-Smith would develop something of a track record for undermining military commanders. Having encouraged Wavell to sack McLeod and replace him with Hutton, he then informed Amery that Hutton was not really a fighting soldier. Woods, *Reporting the Retreat*, 28–30. Woods argues that Dorman-Smith did not interfere in the military campaign. The removal of Brooke-Popham, McLeod, and Hutton suggests otherwise.
21. Monteith to Amery, 16 August 1941, MSS Eur E 215/1–2, India Office, British Library.
22. Chiefs of Staff to Prime Minister, 3 September 1941, CAB 120/517, TNA.
23. Ibid.
24. Babington to Brooke-Popham, 15 September 1941, BP/6/11/2, LHCMA.
25. Brooke-Popham to Ismay, 10 October 1941, BP/6/2/18, LHCMA.
26. Cooper's private diaries have been published, but they do not include the period he was in Singapore. J. J. Norwich, *The Duff Cooper Diaries* (London: Weidenfeld & Nicolson, 2005). There is, however, a daily record of his activities and events, titled "Singapore Diary," in the Churchill Archives, DUFC 3/7. Duff Cooper passed this document, which is highly critical of Shenton Thomas and other officials in Malaya, to friends and colleagues on his return to London.
27. "Final Report of Edward Ansel Mowrer," CIA CREST, p. 10.
28. Spooner Diaries, 13 September 1941, LHCMA.
29. Ibid., 3 December 1941.
30. Lady Dorman-Smith Diary, 5 October 1941, MSS Eur E 215/40, India Office, British Library.

31. Montgomery, *Shenton of Singapore*, 77. Charmley denies the story, but when Duff Cooper sought compensation for the loss of his baggage that was left on the dockside in Singapore, he claimed the not inconsiderable sum of five hundred pounds, which Diana Cooper argued underestimated its actual value. Colonial Office to Duff Cooper, 10 June 1942, CHAR 20/57A/40–61, Churchill Archives; Charmley, *Duff Cooper*, 159.

32. U.S. Department of Defense, *The "Magic" Background*, 3:218.

33. Montgomery, *Shenton of Singapore*, 77; D. Cooper, *Trumpets from the Steep* (London: Rupert Hart-Davis, 1960), 107.

34. Duff Cooper returned to Singapore on 17 October but departed for Australia and New Zealand immediately his report was completed, only returning to Singapore at the end of November.

35. Cooper, *Trumpets from the Steep*, 114–16.

36. Cooper to Amery, 5 October 1941, CAB 10/517, TNA.

37. Cooper to Margesson, 1 October 1941, MRGN 1/6, Churchill Archives; Cooper to Amery, 13 October 1941, AMEL 2/3/20, Churchill Archives.

38. Amery to Prime Minster, 14 October 1941, CAB 120/517, TNA.

39. Chiefs of Staff to Prime Minister, 22 October 1941, CAB 120/517, TNA. This presumably alludes to Admiral Hart's complaint from Manila.

40. Prime Minister to Chiefs of Staff, 24 November 1941, CAB 120/517, TNA.

41. Prime Minister to Ismay, 28 October 1941, CAB 120/517, TNA.

42. A. Danchev and D. Todman, eds., *Field Marshal Lord Alanbrooke, War Diaries 1939–1945* (London: Weidenfeld & Nicholson, 2001), 196–97.

43. Foster Cox, Interview 16275/3/1–3, IWM.

44. G. St. John Barclay, "Singapore Strategy: The Role of the United States in Imperial Defence," *Military Affairs* 39, no. 2 (April 1975): 54–59.

45. Churchill to Brooke-Popham 5 November 1941, AIR 19/561, TNA.

46. Air Ministry to Brooke-Popham, 6 November 1941, AIR 19/561, TNA.

47. Brooke-Popham to Prime Minister, 7 November 1941, AIR 19/561, TNA.

48. Amery to Dorman-Smith, 10 November 1941, AMEL 2/3/20, Churchill Archives.

49. Prime Minister to Duff Cooper, 26 November 1941, CHAR 20/45/109, Churchill Archives.

50. Brooke-Popham to Portal, 7 November 1941, AIR 19/561, TNA.

51. Brooke-Popham to Air Ministry, 8 November 1941, AIR 19/561, TNA.

52. Duff Cooper to Brooke-Popham, 3 December 1941, BP/6/5/23, LHCMA.

53. P. Ziegler, foreword to *Old Men Forget*, by Duff Cooper (London: Century Publishing, 1986), 9.

54. Private Papers of Wing Commander Sir Archibald James, IWM Documents 11963. James served in France as a squadron commander and later as a staff officer at Headquarters RFC. He entered Parliament as a Conservative MP in 1931 but lost his seat in 1945.

55. Woodburn Kirby, *The War against Japan*, vol. 1.

56. Woodburn Kirby, *Singapore: The Chain of Disaster*, 55–56.

57. M. Baring, *Flying Corps Headquarters 1914–1918* (Edinburgh: G. Bell & Sons, 1920), 84–85.

58. *The Aeroplane*, 10 May 1933, p. 798.

59. Higgins, *The Oxfordshire and Buckinghamshire Light Infantry Chronicle*, 55:242.

60. J. D. Potter, *A Soldier Must Hang* (London: Frederick Muller, 1963),16; A. Yoji, "General Tomoyuki Yamashita: Commander of the Twenty-Fifth Army," in *A Great Betrayal? The Fall of Singapore Revisited*, edited by B. Farrell and S. Hunter (Singapore: Marshall Cavendish, 2010), 149.

61. GHQ Far East staff that have left diaries or reminiscences covering this period include: Cox, Dewing, Grey, and Playfair. A. Gilchrist, *Malaya 1941* (London: Robert Hale, 1992), 169–72.

62. Diana Cooper to John Julius Norwich, 31 October 1941, in *Darling Monster: The Letters of Lady Diana Cooper to Her Son John Julius Norwich*, by D. Cooper (London: Chatto & Windus, 2013), 141.

63. Hodson, *War in the Sun*, 243 (Hodson was a war correspondent for the *Daily Mail*); *Time*, 5 January 1942.

64. This includes: Auchinleck (born 1884), Hutton (born 1890), Layton (born 1884), McLeod (born 1885), Phillips (born 1888), and Wavell (born 1883).

65. Dewing to Brooke-Popham, 30 November 1941, BP/6/5/20, LHCMA.

66. D. Richards, *It Might Have Been Worse* (London: Smithson Albright, 1998), 31–34.

67. RAF Historical Society, "The RAF and the Far East War: A Symposium on the Far East War," *Bracknell Paper No. 6*, 24 March 1995, p. 75.

68. Gilchrist, *Malaya 1941*, 169.

69. Brooke-Popham to Opal, 6 May 1941, BPFP.

70. Brooke-Popham to Opal, 8 May 1941, BPFP.

71. Brooke-Popham to Opal, 8 August 1941, BPFP.

72. Brooke-Popham to Opal, 12 October 1941, BPFP.

73. Brown, *Suez to Singapore*, 277.

74. Brooke-Popham, "Operations in the Far East," p. 564.

75. Danchev and Todman, *War Diaries*, 199. Mamoru Shigemitsu, Japan's deputy foreign minister and previously their ambassador in London, saw Pownall's removal (and Dill's retirement) as part of a program to purge all those people who might have leanings toward Japan. U.S. Department of Defense, *The "Magic" Background*, 4:186.

76. Loose Minute, Freeman to Sinclair, 11 December 1941, AIR 19/561, TNA.

77. Duff Cooper to Prime Minister, 13 December 1941, FO 954/6, TNA. This sense of urgency was not reflected in Pownall's progress. He eventually arrived in Singapore on 22 December 1941.

78. Joan Hugonin to Opal, 15 November 1940, BPFP.
79. Brooke-Popham to Opal, 20 March 1941, BPFP. In December 1940, the Australian government had agreed to allow Lady Blamey, wife of Lieutenant-General Thomas Blamey, commander of the AIF, to join him in Egypt. This caused a great furor in the press and accusations that senior officers had been allowed a privilege denied to other ranks. Hasluck, *The Government and the People*, 285–86.
80. *South China Morning Post*, July 1940.
81. Brooke-Popham to Opal, 4 August 1941, BPFP.
82. Brooke-Popham to Opal, 30 August 1941, BPFP.
83. It had been intended that Opal would fly via Bangkok, where she was to meet Grimsdale (sent there by Brooke-Popham to persuade Crosby to install a wireless station in the Legation Compound) and relay the outcome of his discussions with the minister. In the event, Opal travelled directly to Singapore. According to Grimsdale, Crosby vehemently rejected the wireless idea, claiming that "we must keep British Diplomacy clean." Grimsdale, "Thunder in the East," p. 52, IWM.
84. Brooke-Popham to Taylor, July 1942, BPFP.
85. The RAF Comforts Committee was formed by the Air Council in October 1939 to determine the type and quantities of "knitted comforts" required for the RAF.
86. Foster Cox, Interview 16275/3/1–3, IWM.
87. "Duff Cooper's Mission to the Far East," FO 371/27856, TNA. The report, completed on 29 October 1941, made several recommendations, including the creation of a commissioner general for the Far East; however, none had been implemented before the Japanese attacked.
88. Brooke-Popham to Dulcie Pooley, 6 October 1941, BPFP.
89. H. Chihiro, "The Japanese-Soviet Neutrality Pact," in *The Fateful Choice, Japan's Advance into Southeast Asia, 1939–1941*, edited by J. W. Morley (New York: Columbia University Press, 1980), 94–114.
90. CinC Far East to Chiefs of Staff, 1 October 1941, HS 1/332, TNA.
91. Duff Cooper to Margesson, 1 October 1941, MRGN 1/6, Churchill Archives; Woodburn Kirby, *Singapore: The Chain of Disaster*, 119; Playfair, "Some Personal Reflections," p. 10; "Comments on Maltby Draft Despatch," p. 5, BP/6/8/8, LHCMA.
92. Roskill, *Churchill and the Admirals*, 196–98.
93. Marder, *Old Friends, New Enemies*, 388–89.
94. It had been intended that the aircraft carrier HMS *Indomitable* would join the task force, but it ran aground in the West Indies and needed repairs. In any event, it would not have reached Singapore in time to accompany Force Z.
95. Boyd, "Worthy of Better Memory," pp. 306–7.
96. Eden to Prime Minister, 21 September 1941, CAB 120/517, TNA.
97. Boyd, "Worthy of Better Memory," pp. 309–11.

98. I. Cowman, "Defence of the Malay Barrier? The Place of the Philippines in Admiralty War Planning, 1925–1941," *War in History*, 1996, pp. 398–417.

99. R. Grenfell, *Main Fleet to Singapore* (London: Faber & Faber, 1951), 97.

100. Spooner Diaries, 2 December 1941, LHCMA. Diana Cooper was not quite so impressed, describing the two warships as "camouflaged to kill, a lovely sight but on the petty side." Cooper, *Trumpets from the Steep*, 127.

101. Marder, *Old Friends, New Enemies*, 392–94.

102. Nicholson, *Hostages to Fortune*, 26–28.

103. D. Macintyre, *Fighting Admiral: The Life and Battles of Admiral of the Fleet Sir James Somerville* (London: Evans Brothers, 1961), 121, 169; Roskill, *Churchill and the Admirals*, 198–99.

CHAPTER 22. MATADOR

1. Chihiro, "The Japanese-Soviet Neutrality Pact," 95–98.

2. Ibid., 110–14.

3. Kotani, *Japanese Intelligence in World War II*, 126–58.

4. Jun, "The Navy's Role in the Southern Strategy," 248.

5. *Reports of General MacArthur*, vol. 2, Part 1, p. 79.

6. Ibid., p. 3.

7. Ibid., 60. The Japanese rated British and Dutch fighting power as no greater than that of French Indochina, based on the mixed composition of their armies and the intellectual weakness of their leaders. U.S. Department of Defense, "Detailed Report of the Landing on the Eastern Shore (Patani) of Southern Thailand," *MISLS Document No. 471*, 15 February 1945.

8. *Reports of General MacArthur*, vol. 2, Part 1, p. 81.

9. Ibid., p. 22.

10. A document recovered in 1942 from a crashed Japanese aircraft in China gave the British air strength in the Far East as 336 aircraft, indicating that the intelligence gained from the *Automedon* was widely disseminated. Woodburn Kirby, *The War against Japan*, 1:54.

11. Dorman-Smith, Draft of Unfinished Memoirs, 76–77, MSS Eur 215/320, British Library.

12. *The Economist*, 11 October 1941, Issue 5120, p. 442.

13. Singapore Notebook No. 4. BPFP.

14. Brooke-Popham, "Operations in the Far East," p. 554.

15. As the JIC believed during the "war scare" of February 1941. Goodman, *The Official History of the Joint Intelligence Committee*, 1:106.

16. T. Womack, *The Dutch Naval Air Force against Japan* (Jefferson, NC: McFarland, 2006), 43.

17. Ong, *Matador*, 185–87.

18. Ibid., 200–5.
19. The president's assurances emerged during a lunchtime meeting with Lord Halifax, the British ambassador to the United States, on 1 December 1941. Chiefs of Staff to Brooke-Popham, 5 December 1941, BP/6/1/41, LHCMA; R. Esthus, "President Roosevelt's Commitment to Britain to Intervene in a Pacific War," *Mississippi Historical Review* 50, no. 1 (June 1963): 28–38; Ong, *Matador*, 203.
20. Creighton had arrived in Singapore in July 1941 to relieve Captain Archer Allen as Naval Observer on the staff of CinC China. He worked closely with the war plans section and had an office within the naval headquarters building. Creighton's military counterpart, Lieutenant-Colonel Francis Brink, was based with CinC Far East.
21. The "Brooke-Popham affair" became notorious because of postwar investigations into the events at Pearl Harbor and the belief that Roosevelt had committed the United States to a Pacific war prior to the Japanese attack.
22. COS to GHQ Far East, 5 December 1941, BP6/1/41, LHCMA.
23. J. M. Creighton, Notes on Singapore and Java, 17 July 1941 to 19 April 1942, 4697018, National Archives, UK.
24. Hart, "Narrative of Events," p. 34, 4697018, National Archives.
25. Marder, *Old Friends, New Enemies*, 403; Gilchrist, *Malaya 1941*, 176–78.
26. Brooke-Popham, "Operations in the Far East," p. 557; Singapore Notebook No. 5, BPFP. Boyd questions why Layton did not brief Phillips on the level and type of air threat he faced. A. Boyd, *The Royal Navy in Eastern Waters* (Barnsley, UK: Seaforth, 2017), 324–30.
27. Ong, *Matador*, 232–33. Callahan also makes this point. Callahan, *The Worst Disaster*, 191.
28. It is said that the convoys deliberately changed course toward Thailand when they thought they had been spotted, to deceive the British about their actual destination. For the same reason, the escorting warships did not join the troop transports until they were near Malaya. Potter, *A Soldier Must Hang*, 48.
29. Gilchrist, *Malaya 1941*, 164; Ong, *Matador*, 232.
30. Gillison, *Royal Australian Air Force*, 204.
31. Woodburn Kirby, *The War against Japan*, 1:175.
32. Farrell, *The Defence and Fall of Singapore, 1940–1942*, 169.
33. Dachev and Todman, *War Diaries 1939–1945*, 208.
34. Percival to Woodburn Kirby, 23 May 1947, Percival Papers, F43, IWM.
35. Callahan, *The Worst Disaster*, 191.
36. Record, *A War It Was Always Going to Lose*, 104–6.
37. Failure to authorize Matador also stymied the SOE's plans to disrupt communications and damage key industries in Thailand. "The organisation was ready to function. It merely required the pressing of a button." Cruickshank, *SOE in the Far East*, 73.

38. Brooke-Popham to Kirby, 16 April 1953, p. 4, BPFP.
39. Crosby to Foreign Office, 7 December 1941, FO 371/28163, TNA; Gilchrist, *Malaya 1941*, 114–18.
40. Compton Mackenzie felt that even a start of forty-eight hours would have been sanguine. C. Mackenzie, *Eastern Epic* (London: Chatto & Windus, 1951), 1:228.
41. Brooke-Popham to Woodburn Kirby, 16 April 1953, BPFP.
42. Brooke-Popham to Grenfell, 28 November 1950, GREN 2/6, Churchill Archives.
43. Brooke-Popham to Woodburn Kirby, 16 April 1953, BPFP.
44. U.S. Department of Defense, *The "Magic" Background*, 4:281.
45. This included both the *Straits Times* and the *Sunday Tribune*. E. M. Glover, *In 70 Days* (London: Frederick Muller, 1946), 71–72.
46. There was a view among many Western commentators that the Japanese thought differently than other people and that they relied on intuition and the spiritual in taking decisions. It would be misleading to describe such thinking as racist, or even ethnocentric, but it did create uncertainty about Japanese motives and intentions, encouraging the idea that they were difficult to read. Dower, *War without Mercy*, 106–7. Churchill was convinced that Japan would pursue a cautious step-by-step strategy. Mawdsley, *December 1941*, 61.
47. A. Percival, "Operations of Malaya Command from 8 December 1941 to 15 February 1942," *Supplement to The London Gazette*, 26 February 1948, para. 129.
48. Brooke-Popham, "Operations in the Far East," p. 542.
49. Farrell, *The Defence and Fall of Singapore*, 184.
50. Brooke-Popham to Street, 15 January 1941, BP/6/3/3, LHCMA.
51. R. Bose, *Singapore at War* (Singapore: Marshall Cavendish, 2012), 69–71.
52. "Report of Conference, Manila, December 1941," pp. 6–7, 4697018, National Archives.
53. Hart, "Narrative of Events," p. 36, 4697018, National Archives.
54. Marder, *Old Friends, New Enemies*, 406; M. Middlebrook and P. Mahoney, *Battleship: The Loss of the* Prince of Wales *and the* Repulse (London: Allen Lane, 1977), 100–2.
55. Roskill, *Churchill and the Admirals*, 199; "Report of Conference, Manila, December 1941," pp. 6–7, 4697018, National Archives.
56. Woodburn Kirby, *The War against Japan*, 1:182. Brooke-Popham had toured these beaches to discuss their defenses earlier in the year. Visit Programme, 23 May 1941, BP/6/4, LHCMA.
57. Seven Vildebeestes had been sent to Kota Bharu on the initial sighting of the convoys, but later moved to Gong Kedah because of overcrowding. Maltby, "Report on the Air Operations," pp. 390, 394–95.
58. There was a short delay between sighting the transports and attacking them because of the residual concerns over initiating hostilities. Maltby, "Report on the Air Operations," 395.

59. *Reports of General MacArthur*, vol. 2, Part 1, p. 75; Woodburn Kirby, *The War against Japan*, 1:188–89; H. Frei, *Guns of February* (Singapore: Singapore University Press, 2004), 44.

60. The short time taken by the Japanese to execute the landings (less than eight hours) took GHQ by surprise.

61. "Comments on Maltby Draft Despatch," p. 11, BP6/8/8, LHCMA. At the time of the "meeting," Brooke-Popham was asleep in his office at the naval base when he was woken by Group Captain Rice's phone call warning him that enemy aircraft were heading for Singapore.

62. Montgomery, *Shenton of Singapore*, 83–85; ADM 199/1472B, Events in Far East, TNA.

63. Brooke-Popham makes it clear that Pulford was not present when he met Phillips prior to the departure of Force Z. "Comments on Official History," Brooke-Popham to Woodburn Kirby, January 1953, BPFP. The words attributed to Brooke-Popham and Shenton Thomas are a crude pastiche of postwar comments by other authors.

64. Marder, *Old Friends, New Enemies*, 406–11; Montgomery, *Shenton of Singapore*, 6–9.

65. For example: Nicholson, *Hostages to Fortune*, 61–62; Gilchrist, *Malaya 1941*, 125–29; Thompson, *The Battle for Singapore*, 121–23; Cox, *Rising Sun*, 424; S. Weintraub, *Long Day's Journey into War* (London: Penguin, 1991), 280–81; Brune, *Descent into Hell*, 188–89; and R. McCrum, *The Men Who Lost Singapore, 1938–1942* (Singapore: NUS Press, 2017), 135–36. At least one author has questioned McClelland's veracity, adding that "any issue relying solely on his testimony becomes questionable." Ferris, "Consistent with an Intention," 26.

66. "Comments on Maltby Draft Despatch," p. 1, BP6/8/8, LHCMA.

67. Woodburn Kirby, *The War against Japan*, 1:183. There were three Buffalo aircraft on standby for a night attack, but they were held on the ground because there were no arrangements to deconflict with the defending antiaircraft guns.

68. Brooke-Popham, "Operations in the Far East," Appendix M; Woodburn Kirby, *The War against Japan*, 1:183–84; K. Attiwell, *The Singapore Story* (London: Frederick Muller, 1959), 24–25; Morrison, *Malayan Postscript*, 50–51; Barber, *Sinister Twilight*, 39–40; T. Hall, *The Fall of Singapore 1942* (North Ryde, NSW: Methuen Australia, 1983), 60.

69. Woodburn Kirby, *The War against Japan*, 1:183–84; Morrison, *Malayan Postscript*, 148–49.

70. Morrison, *Malayan Postscript*, 66; Brown, *Suez to Singapore*, 346.

71. Brown, *Suez to Singapore*, 350–51.

72. Singapore Notebook No. 5, BPFP. Brooke-Popham believed there was a need for more robustness in compiling GHQ's communiqués.

73. Richards and Saunders, *Royal Air Force*, 2:22.

74. Probert, *The Forgotten Air Force*, 48–49. Brooke-Popham's memorandum has been described as a rebuke, but it was written at Pulford's specific request. "Comments on Maltby Draft Despatch," BP/6/8/8, LHCMA; Cox, "Memorandum on the Royal Air Force in Malaya," pp. 17–20, Ludlow-Hewitt Papers, Box 4/File 14, RAF Historical Branch.

75. Allen, *Singapore 1941–1942*, 243–44.

76. Woodburn Kirby, *The War against Japan*, 1:193–99. Grenfell says that there was an earlier meeting that same morning, involving Brooke-Popham, Phillips, and Palliser, to discuss possible courses of action, held in Brooke-Popham's office at the naval base. Grenfell, *Main Fleet to Singapore*, 110.

77. Marder, *Old Friends, New Enemies*, 420; Middlebrook and Mahoney, *Battleship*, 107–8.

78. The range of Japanese torpedo-bombers was much greater than thought. Boyd, *The Royal Navy in Eastern Waters*, 321–22.

79. Marder, *Old Friends, New Enemies*, 428, 433–34; Middlebrook and Mahoney, *Battleship*, 107.

80. Richards and Saunders, *Royal Air Force*, 2:25.

81. R. Hughes-Mulock, "White Ribbon, White Flag," *Journal of the Naval Historical Collectors & Research Association*, 2006.

82. Roskill, *Churchill and the Admirals*, 197; Guard, *The Pacific War*, 68–69.

83. Brooke-Popham to Grenfell, 28 September 1950, GREN 2/6, Churchill Archives.

84. For example: R. Hough, *The Hunting of Force Z* (London: William Collins, 1963), 152–54; Nicholson, *Hostages to Fortune*, 179–88; Middlebrook and Mahoney, *Battleship*, 283–314; and Grenfell, *Main Fleet to Singapore*, 126–36.

85. The critical differences were poor weather, a lack of coordination on the British side, and the presence of large numbers of protective German fighters that disrupted successive air attacks.

86. Brown, *Suez to Singapore*, 295–323; Gallagher, *Retreat in the East*, 30–60.

87. Singapore Notebook No. 5, BPFP. A draft telegram, prepared for the War Council on 12 December, implies as much. Montgomery, *Shenton of Singapore*, 88.

88. "Comments on Layton's Despatch," 15 January 1947, BP/6/8/48, LHCMA.

89. Brooke-Popham to Barrington-Ward, 11 December 1942, BP/6/9/5 LHCMA; "The War in the Pacific," *Times* (London), 5 December 1942; Singapore Notebook No. 4, BPFP.

90. Notes on the Far East, Brooke-Popham to Portal, 12 March 1942, BP/6/9/5, LHCMA.

91. Tsuji, *Singapore*, 48.

92. Millman, *Ki-27 "Nate" Aces*, 55–56.

93. Private Papers of Wing Commander T. C. Carter, vol. 2, p. 112, Documents 10847, IWM.

94. Probert, *The Forgotten Air Force*, 31.

95. Air Ministry, *Wings of the Phoenix—The Official Story of the Air War in Burma* (London: HMSO, 1949), 4; C. Shores and B. Cull, *Bloody Shambles*, vol. 2, *The Defence of Sumatra to the Fall of Burma* (London: Grub Street, 1993), 463–67.

96. Sir Roger Keyes blamed the government for failing to invest in an efficient naval air service. *News Chronicle*, 18 December 1941.

97. Trenchard to Churchill, 26 March 1942, MFC76/1/4, RAFM.

98. B. Ash, *Someone Had Blundered* (London: Michael Joseph, 1960), 235–36; M. Stephen, *Scapegoat: The Death of Prince of Wales and Repulse* (Barnsley, UK: Pen & Sword, 2014), 158–59; Brune, *Descent into Hell*, 196. Gordon Bennett later argued that Brooke-Popham should have stopped Phillips from going beyond air cover. G. Bennett, "Someone Had Blundered," *Journal of Southeast Asian History* 2, no. 2 (1961): 121–22.

99. J. Burton, *Fortnight of Infamy: The Collapse of Allied Airpower West of Pearl Harbor* (Annapolis, MD: Naval Institute Press, 2006), 288–93.

100. Woodburn Kirby, *The War against Japan*, 1:175.

101. Elphick erroneously claims that this reconnaissance, by the sole Beaufort in Malaya, was carried out the day before (i.e., 7 December), based on the recollections of a single witness based in Singapore. Elphick, *Far Eastern File*, 322–24.

102. Ibid., 186.

103. Percival, *The War in Malaya*, 114. Kinvig attempts to explain the sequence of events, but it remains unclear why Malaya Command did not act sooner. What is certain, however, is that relations between Percival and Heath deteriorated rapidly from this moment. Kinvig, *Scapegoat*, 142–43.

104. K. D. Bhargava and K. N. V. Sastri, *Campaigns in South-East Asia 1941–42* (New Delhi: Combined Inter-Services Historical Section, 1960), 155.

105. Woodburn Kirby argues that they could have reached Singora by the evening of 7 December, even allowing for resistance by the frontier guards. Woodburn Kirby, *Singapore: The Chain of Disaster*, 128.

106. Grenfell to Brooke-Popham, 29 November 1950, GREN 2/6, Churchill Archives.

107. Mackenzie, *Eastern Epic*, 243. Heath blamed both Percival and Brooke-Popham for the delay. Elphick, *Singapore: The Pregnable Fortress*, 359.

CHAPTER 23. THE FALL OF SINGAPORE

1. I. Simson, *Too Little, Too Late* (London: Leo Cooper, 1970), 47. It is claimed that Murray-Lyon, the division's commander, was so obsessed with Matador that he neglected the frontier defenses. Ashmore, "Some Personal Observations of the Malayan Campaign," Percival Papers, F49, IWM.

2. A. Rose, *Who Dies Fighting* (London: Jonathan Cape, 1944), 33–34.

3. Playfair to Air Ministry, 20 August 1941, BP/6/1/25, LHCMA.

4. "The Far East: Report of the Chancellor of the Duchy of Lancaster on the Termination of His Appointment as Resident Minister," 19 February 1942, PREM 3/155, TNA.

5. Montgomery, *Shenton of Singapore*, 87–88; Duff Cooper to Prime Minister, 18 December 1941, PREM 3/161/1, TNA.

6. Callahan, *The Worst Disaster*, 249; Duff Cooper to Prime Minister, 18 December 1941, PREM 3/161/1, TNA.

7. "Criticism by Duff Cooper," CO 967/77, TNA; Holmes and Kemp, *The Bitter End*, 118; N. Barber, *Sinister Twilight* (London: Collins, 1968), 50–52.

8. Duff Cooper to Prime Minister, 17 December 1941, CHAR 20/47/32, Churchill Archives. Duff Cooper had initially expressed favorable views about Percival. Duff Cooper to Margesson, 1 October 1941, MRGN 1/6, Churchill Archives.

9. Montgomery, *Shenton of Singapore*, 87–106; Charmley, *Duff Cooper*, 159–61; "Comments on Sir Shenton Thomas' Comments," 22 November 1954, Percival Papers, IWM. The two individuals who most excited Percival's ire were: Brigadier Ivan Simson (appointed by Duff Cooper as director-general of Civil Defence), and his deputy, Frank Bisseker, a civilian on the legislative council.

10. Connell, *Wavell, Supreme Commander*, 57.

11. The meeting was held at Singapore on 18 December. Woodburn Kirby, *The War against Japan*, 1:233.

12. "Notes for Captain Tennant by Air Officer Commanding," 20 December 1941, WO 216/78, TNA.

13. McLeod was sacked on 25 December 1941. Connell, *Wavell, Supreme Commander*, 66. Amery had a high opinion of Hutton from when they served together in Salonika. Lieutenant-Colonel Thomas Hutton had attended the 1932 IDC course with McLeod.

14. Woodburn Kirby, *The War against Japan*, 2:16.

15. Connell, *Wavell, Supreme Commander*, 181–82; Lewin, *The Chief*, 181. In his relentless efforts to defend Rangoon, Wavell nearly destroyed the remaining British forces in Burma. Callahan, *Burma 1942–1945*, 35–36.

16. There are few letters to Opal after August (once she was en route to Kenya), while his final Singapore Notebook (No. 5) starts in early December (based on a reference to Marmon-Herrington armored cars) but is not dated until 21 December. It is difficult to know which entries predate the outbreak of war.

17. Corporal S. W. E. Linsley, Interview 11220/1990, IWM.

18. Holmes and Kemp, *The Bitter End*, 118; Callahan, *The Worst Disaster*, 214.

19. Glover, *In 70 Days*, 122–23. Brooke-Popham had taken over responsibility for press relations on Phillips' arrival (and Layton's planned departure).

20. Brown, *Suez to Singapore*, 358–60.

21. Glover, *In 70 Days*, 123; Barber, *Sinister Twilight*, 58.

22. Bowden attended the War Council as the Australian government's official representative from 20 December 1941. His comments were forwarded to Canberra in a personal letter. Bowden was executed by the Japanese while attempting to escape. Wigmore, *The Japanese Thrust*, 204–5.

23. Cooper to Churchill, 18 December 1941, CO 967/77, TNA.
24. Barber, *Sinister Twilight*, 64–66; Duff Cooper to Prime Minister, 11 January 1942, CHAR 20/68A/67–68, Churchill Archives. Percival regarded Shenton Thomas as "slippery," and later claimed that he would always do his best to "pass the baby." Percival Papers, F48, IWM.
25. Shenton Thomas to Moyne, 22 January 1942, CO 867/78, TNA.
26. Cooper, *Trumpets from the Steep*, 135. "Percival plays Trilby to the Governor's Svengali." In the eponymous novel by George du Maurier, Trilby falls under the hypnotic spell of Svengali.
27. Shenton Thomas to Moyne, 8 February 1942, CO 967/78, TNA.
28. Callahan, *The Worst Disaster*, 248. Up to the moment of his departure, Duff Cooper was still set on getting Wavell's support for the removal of Shenton Thomas. Cooper, *Trumpets from the Steep*, 135–37.
29. Barclay, "Singapore Strategy," p. 57.
30. Elphick, *Singapore: The Pregnable Fortress*, 285; Brooke-Popham, "Operations in the Far East," p. 545. Brooke-Popham has been criticized for not instructing Percival to build fixed defenses on Singapore Island. He agreed that more could have been done (before the war) but pointed out that it had been necessary to defend a great many areas, including those where the Japanese did not attack. He might have added that the forward defense strategy (including Matador) meant that turning Singapore into a fortress was not a high priority, given the limited resources available.
31. Simson, *Too Little, Too Late*, 47; Mawdsley, *December 1941*, 55.
32. Farrell, *The Defence and Fall of Singapore*, 128–30.
33. Simson, *Too Little, Too Late*, 43.
34. Brooke-Popham to Ismay, 5 December 1940, BP/6/2/3, LHCMA.
35. Tsuji, *Singapore*, 93–96.
36. Slessor, *The Central Blue*, 40. Slessor, a future chief of the Air Staff with a reputation for shrewdness and open-mindedness, was serving as assistant chief of the Air Staff (Policy) in 1942. M. Howard, "Sir John Slessor," *Survival* 21, no. 6 (November/December 1979): 242–43.
37. Woodburn Kirby, *The War against Japan*, 1:460.
38. Bond, *Chief of Staff*, 2:74.
39. Connell, *Wavell, Supreme Commander*, 69–75.
40. Ford, "British Intelligence on Japanese Army Morale," 439.
41. Japanese confidence was strengthened by Yamashita's belief that he faced no more than 30,000–50,000 troops. K. Tachikawa, "General Yamashita and his Style of Leadership," in *British and Japanese Leadership in the Far Eastern War 1941–1945*, by B. Bond and K. Tachikawa (London: Frank Cass, 2004), 75–87.
42. Mawdsley, *December 1941*, 268; Farrell, *The Defence and Fall of Singapore*, 193–99.
43. Playfair, "Some Personal Reflections," p. 13; Tarling, *Onset of the Pacific War*, 222.

44. M. H. Murfett, J. N. Miksic, B. P. Farrell, and C. M. Shun, eds., *Between Two Oceans: A Military History of Singapore* (Singapore: Marshall Cavendish, 2011), 185.

45. Playfair, "Some Personal Reflections," p. 11.

46. Best, "'This Probably Over-Valued Military Power'", 67–94.

47. Ong, *Matador*, 249.

48. Mackenzie, *Eastern Epic*, 236.

49. Woodburn Kirby, *Singapore: The Chain of Disaster*, 254.

50. Murray, *Watching the Sun Rise*, 238.

51. *Sydney Daily Telegraph*, 16 December 1941.

52. Curtin to Churchill, 24 January 1942, CHAR 20/69A/6–8, Churchill Archives.

53. For example: D. Day, *The Great Betrayal: Britain, Australia and the Onset of the Pacific War 1939–42* (New York: Norton, 1989); R. Connolly and B. Wilson, *Cruel Britannia: Britannia Waives the Rules 1941–42, Singapore Betrayed, Australia Abandoned* (Belmont, Australia: Kingsgrove, 1994); P. Knightley, *Australia: A Biography of a Nation* (London: Jonathan Cape, 2000); P. Ewer, *Wounded Eagle: The Bombing of Darwin and Australia's Air Defence Scandal* (Sydney: New Holland, 2009); R. Perry, *The Fight for Australia: From Changi and Darwin to Kokoda* (Sydney: Hachette Australia, 2012); and Brune, *Descent into Hell*.

54. For example: C. Baxter, "A Question of Blame? Defending Britain's Position in the South China Sea, the Pacific and South-East Asia, 1919–1941," *RUSI Journal*, (August 1997): 66–75; I. Hamill, *Strategic Illusion: The Singapore Strategy and the Defence of Australia and New Zealand 1919–1942* (Singapore: Singapore University Press, 1981); J. McCarthy, "The Great Betrayal Reconsidered: An Australian Perspective," *Australian Journal of International Affairs* 48, no. 1 (May 1994); P. Dennis, "Australia and the Singapore Strategy," in *A Great Betrayal?*, edited by Farrell and Hunter, 20–31; A. Meaher, *The Road to Singapore: The Myth of British Betrayal* (North Melbourne: Australian Scholarly Publishing, 2010); P. Stanley, "Dramatic Myth and Dull Truth: Invasion by Japan in 1942," in *Zombie Myths of Australian Military History*, edited by C. Stockings (Sydney: University of New South Wales Press, 2010), 140–60; and S. Bullard, *Japanese Army Operations in the South Pacific Area* (Canberra: Australian War Memorial, 2007).

55. Parliamentary Debate, House of Representatives, 27 February 1992, p. 373, National Archives of Australia.

56. For example: Mackenzie, *Eastern Epic*, vol. 1; Bhargava and Sastri, *Campaigns in South-East Asia 1941–42*; and A. Warren, "The Indian Army and the Fall of Singapore," in *A Great Betrayal? The Fall of Singapore Revisited*, edited by B. Farrell and S. Hunter (Singapore: Marshall Cavendish, 2010), 220–38. The desertion of large numbers of Indian prisoners, who joined the Japanese-sponsored Indian National Army, has tended to overshadow any controversy about the quality of British generalship.

57. The Brooke-Pophams sailed on the troop transport *Marnix van Sint Aldegonde* (a converted Royal Dutch mail liner). The ship had been in dry dock since arriving in Singapore on 11 November 1941. P. Plowman, *Across the Sea to War* (Sydney: Rosenberg Publishing, 2003), 248.

58. *Straits Times*, 27 December 1941.

59. Bond, *Chief of Staff*, 2:67–68.

60. Hugonin, a county-class cricketer, was awarded the OBE in September 1946 for his outstanding leadership during captivity. K. Blackburn, *The Sportsmen of Changi* (Sydney: New South Publishing, 2012), 21.

61. Cox to Brooke-Popham, 1 January 1942, BPFP.

62. Ian Graham to Opal, 21 October 1953, BPFP.

63. *West Australian*, Saturday 7 March 1942.

64. Cox, "Memorandum on the Royal Air Force in Malaya," p. 20, Ludlow-Hewitt Papers, Box 4/File 14, RAF Historical Branch; "A Man Who Took the Rap," FEPOW, *North Western Evening Mail*, 22 October 1953. The first Australian-built Beauforts arrived at Seletar on 6 December 1941.

65. Secretary of State to Viceroy and Governor of Burma, 8 January 1942, PREM 3/155, TNA; Montgomery, *Shenton of Singapore*, 109.

66. "The Far East: Report of the Chancellor of the Duchy of Lancaster on the Termination of His Appointment as Resident Minister," 19 February 1942, PREM 3/155, TNA.

67. Cooper, *Old Men Forget*, 310. The Vichy Press had already labelled Duff Cooper as *le premier bouc émissaire* (the first scapegoat). *Le Petit Parisien*, 13 January 1942. With his various travels, Duff Cooper spent no more than forty days in Singapore before the outbreak of war.

68. Singapore Diary, DUFC 3/7, Churchill Archives.

69. The Brooke-Pophams embarked on the SS *Oronsay*. "*Oronsay* Movements Card," BT 389/22, TNA.

70. "Brooke-Popham Takes Report to Ministry," *Evening Standard*, 27 February 1942; "Deadly Inertia in Singapore," *Melbourne Argus*, 28 February 1942. The obstacles Opal had encountered during her few weeks in Singapore attempting to organize war work were the cause for her unguarded comments.

CHAPTER 24. THE VERDICT OF HISTORY

1. Loose Minute, 13 March 1942, CHAR 20/28/107, Churchill Archives.

2. Air Ministry to Brooke-Popham, 1 March 1942, BPFP.

3. Air Ministry to Brooke-Popham, 14 April 1942, BPFP.

4. *Daily Mail*, 18 December 1941. The *Daily Mail* demanded "no more lame excuses" from Brooke-Popham and Shenton Thomas.

5. *The Economist*, 24 June 1942, Issue 5135, pp. 93–94.

6. Prime Minister to CinC Far East, 5 November 1941, AIR 19/561, TNA.

7. Note for File, Under Secretary of State for Air, 27 March 1942, AIR 19/561, TNA.
8. Brooke-Popham to Opal, 1 July 1942, BPFP.
9. Philip was at Dartmouth and Didie at boarding school in Oxford.
10. Opal to Brooke-Popham, May 1942, BPFP.
11. The Home Guard had been created in 1940 to provide a secondary local defense force using volunteers from personnel unfit or otherwise unavailable for regular service. It was disbanded in 1945. The ATC had been established in 1941 as a national youth organization providing air-related and adventure training, replacing the existing Air Defence Cadet Corps. By 1942, it boasted over 170,000 members and was an important source of recruits for the RAF.
12. Brooke-Popham to Opal, 2 July 1942, BPFP.
13. "Air Chief Marshal Sir Robert Brooke-Popham's Despatch on the Far East," COS (42)336, 8 July 1942, PREM 3/168/3, TNA.
14. Brooke-Popham to Elinore Pulford, 10 January 1944, BPFP. Pulford had stayed in Singapore while there were still RAF personnel to be evacuated. Wing Commander Carter, 2:22, Documents 10847, IWM.
15. Bottomley (Air Member for Personnel) to Brooke-Popham, 2 March 1942, BPFP; Brooke-Popham to Opal, 16 June 1942, BPFP.
16. Carter to Brooke-Popham, 20 September 1942, BPFP.
17. "Lord Trenchard on Lost Aerodromes, Vigorous Defence of Sir R. Brooke-Popham," *Daily Telegraph*, 21 January 1942,
18. Goddard to Brooke-Popham, 8 October 1947, BPFP.
19. Opal to Brooke-Popham, 17 June 1942, BPFP. The request likely came from the settler community, who had not warmed to Brooke-Popham's successor as governor.
20. Brooke-Popham to Opal, 18 June 1942, BPFP.
21. Colonial Office to Air Ministry, 13 May 1942, AIR 19/546, TNA.
22. He started work on 18 February, once he had completed articles promised for the *RAF Journal* and the *ATC Gazette* ("The Formation of the Royal Air Force," *Royal Air Force Journal*, no. 5 (March 1943): 5–7).
23. Brooke-Popham to Nicholl, 20 March 1943, AIR 20/3535, TNA.
24. Air Chief Marshal Frederick Bowhill, CinC Coastal Command (1937–41); Air Vice Marshal John Bradley, AOC Maintenance Command (1938–42); Air Chief Marshal Bert Harris, AOCinC Bomber Command (1942–45); and Air Chief Marshal Hugh Dowding, AOCinC Fighter Command (1936–40).
25. AIR 20/3535, TNA; Sir Robert Brooke-Popham Notebooks ATC (3) and ATC (4), 1943, BPFP. Bouchier had commanded RAF Hornchurch throughout the fighting, while Nicholl was AOA Fighter Command and Leigh-Mallory AOC 12 Group.
26. Brooke-Popham to Nicholl, 26 March 1943, AIR 20/3535, TNA. Supply and maintenance issues had featured heavily in the 1933 ADGB staff exercise.

27. Peck to Trenchard, 15 April 1943, and Trenchard to Peck, 20 April 1943, MFC76/1/525(1), RAFM. Brooke-Popham also worked closely with John Nerney, head of the Air Historical Branch (AHB).
28. *Evening Standard*, 18 September 1943.
29. Churchill to Ismay, 22 November 1946, Ismay/2/3/19, LHCMA; W. S. Churchill, *Their Finest Hour* (London: Cassell, 1949), 263–79.
30. Ismay to Churchill, 29 November 1946, Ismay/2/3/20, LHCMA; C. A. V. Wilson, "Hiding behind History: Winston S. Churchill's Portrayal of the Second World War East of Suez," PhD thesis, University of Hull, 2012, p. 29. Goodwin was later professor of modern history at Manchester. "Professor Albert Goodwin," *Independent*, 26 September 1995.
31. H. St. G. Saunders, *The Battle of Britain* (London: His Majesty's Stationery Office, 1941).
32. Battle of Britain Papers, AIR 20, 3535–3542, TNA.
33. These included: *The Role of the RAF in War and the Strategical Use of Air Power*, Part 10, *Operations 1939–1942, The Norwegian Campaign, 1940* (London: Air Member for Training, 1943) and *The Role of the RAF in War and the Strategical Use of Air Power*, Part 9, *Operations 1939–1942, Operations in France September 1939—June 1940* (London: Air Member for Training, 1944). Among the other commissions was *Notes on the Traditions of the Royal Air Force, ATCP No. 55*, April 1944. The narrative incorporates many of Brooke-Popham's personal experiences. Hill to Brooke-Popham, 19 September 1945, BPFP.
34. Portal to Brooke-Popham, 15 September 1943, BP/9/12/33, LHCMA.
35. "Air Chief Marshal's Visit to Yorkshire," *Yorkshire Post*, 13 February 1943.
36. "Committee to Consider Post-War Organisation of ATC," BP/7/3/7, LHCMA.
37. Slessor to Brooke-Popham, 22 March 1947, BPFP.
38. The NAAFI had been founded in 1921 to provide recreational facilities for service personnel at home and abroad.
39. The first volume of the Official History was published four years later.
40. Field Marshal Lord Wilson, Marshal of the RAF Viscount Portal, Marshal of the RAF Sir John Slessor, Air Chief Marshal Sir Christopher Courtney, Air Chief Marshal Sir Arthur Longmore, and Air Chief Marshal Sir Roderic Hill.
41. *Times* (London), 26 January 1954.
42. Cox to Opal, 21 October 1953, BPFP.
43. Salmond to Opal, 21 October 1953, BPFP.
44. Phillips to Brooke-Popham, 31 December 1941, and Peasley (Phillips) to Opal, 21 October 1953, BPFP.
45. Baldwin to Opal, 21 October 1953, BPFP.
46. *Kenya Weekly News*, October 1953, p. 12.
47. Miles Lampson to Opal, 21 October 1953, BPFP.
48. Baldwin to Opal, 21 October 1953, BPFP.

49. J. F. C. Fuller, *The Second World War* (London: Eyre & Spottiswoode, 1948), 143.

50. Funeral Address, Bicester Parish Church, 23 October 1953, BPFP.

51. Baldwin to Opal, 21 October 1953, BPFP.

52. Brooke-Popham to Opal, 26 September 1925, BPFP.

53. Brooke-Popham to Opal, 26 July 1931, BPFP.

54. Brooke-Popham to Opal, 6 September 1931, BPFP.

55. Garrod to Brooke-Popham, 15 June 1942, BPFP.

56. Brooke-Popham to Opal, 17 August 1925, BPFP.

57. Brooke-Popham, "The Formation of the Royal Air Force," 7.

58. P. Joubert de la Ferté, *The Forgotten Ones* (London: Hutchinson, 1961), 73.

59. *Journal of the Royal Central Asiatic Society*, 1953, pp. 61–62.

60. Brooke-Popham to Opal, 6 December 1925, BPFP.

61. Maltby to Opal, 21 October 1953, BPFP.

62. Neale, *George Purvis Bulman*, 62–63.

63. *Times* (London), 29 August 1940.

64. His language sometimes betrayed a casual prejudice, including the profiteers he encountered at the Adlon Hotel in 1924 and those he thought were behind the General Strike of 1926. Brooke-Popham to Opal, 10 May 1926, BPFP; Notes on a Visit to Germany, September 1924, BP/1/3/26, LHCMA.

65. Wykeham, "Popham, Sir (Henry) Robert Moore Brooke- (1878–1953)," 146.

66. Farrell offers a balanced analysis on the political impact (not only in India), commenting that the consequences were serious, but not always uniform and in some cases, exaggerated. Farrell, *The Defence and Fall of Singapore, 1940–1942*, 444–46.

67. W. Dalrymple, "Divide and Quit," *The Spectator*, 25 July 2015.

68. Connell, *Wavell, Supreme Commander*, 15.

69. G. Sansom, "The Story of Singapore," *Foreign Affairs* 22, no. 2 (1944): 279–97.

70. R. Scalapino, "Introduction, Part Two, Southern Advance," in *The Fateful Choice, Japan's Advance into Southeast Asia, 1939–1941*, edited by J. W. Morley (New York: Columbia University Press, 1980), 122–23.

71. BP/6/11/6, LHCMA.

72. Curtin to Churchill, 22 January 1942, PREM 3/52/4, TNA. The Australian government declined to allow their comments about Brooke-Popham's achievements (predating the Fall of Singapore) to be published on the basis that they were purely personal and valedictory in character. Curtin did confirm that he had sent a telegram to Brooke-Popham thanking him for working to provide a defensive capacity in the Far East, adding that Brooke-Popham was not to be blamed for the supply shortages in Malaya. *The Age*, 28 January 1942.

73. Ismay to Lord Privy Seal (Clement Atlee), 29 December 1941, CAB 120/517, TNA.

74. Churchill, House of Commons, 27 January 1942, *Hansard*, cols. 604–6. Louis Allen provides an excellent overview of the Parliamentary debates. Allen, *Singapore 1941–1942*, 15–22.

75. Churchill, House of Commons Debate, 29 January 1942, *Hansard*, col. 1012.

76. Oliver Wendell Holmes Jr., "The Soldier's Faith, An Address delivered on Memorial Day, 30 May 1895, to the Graduating Class of Harvard University," BPFP. Brooke-Popham cited its influence in his final address to No. 4 ASC at Andover in 1926.

77. Brooke-Popham admitted as much to Hilary Saunders. Brooke-Popham to Saunders, 28 August 1951, V/1/6, Trenchard Archive.

Bibliography

PRIMARY SOURCES
British Library, London
India Office MSS Eur 215/320. Dorman-Smith, Draft of Unfinished Memoirs.
India Office MSS Eur E 215/1–2. Leo Amery to Reginald Dorman Smith, 14 August 1941.
India Office MSS Eur E 215/1–2. David Monteith to Amery, 16 August 1941.
India Office MSS Eur E 215/1–2. Monteith to Amery, 3 September 1941.
India Office MSS Eur E 215/1–2. Dorman-Smith to Amery 18 February 1942.

Brooke-Popham Family Papers, Liddell Hart Centre
for Military Archives, King's College London
Defence Statement, Mayhew vs. Brooke-Popham, 12 July 1918.
War Diary, August 1914.
Brooke-Popham Personal Album.
1940 Diary, 14 October.
Haileybury Housemaster's Report, July 1896.
Oliver Wendell Holmes Jr., "The Soldier's Faith, An Address delivered on Memorial Day, 30 May 1895, to the Graduating Class of Harvard University."
Journal of the War, 27 July–23 August 1914.
Letters.
Brooke-Popham Flying Logbook, 1912–13.
Air Ministry Notebook No. 2, September 1940–October 1940.
Buckingham Gate Notebook No. 1, 1933.
Singapore Notebook No. 1, October 1940–November 1940.
Singapore Notebook No. 2, November 1940–February 1941.
Singapore Notebook No. 3, March 1941–June 1941.
Singapore Notebook No. 4, June 1941–October 1941.
Singapore Notebook No. 5, October 1941–February 1942.

Notes of a Meeting of King Faisal and King Ibn Saud, February 1930.
Draft Poem, Robert Brooke-Popham to Opal Brooke-Popham, June 1927.
Proceedings of Medical Board, 18 November 1901.
Telegram, War Office to Brooke, 6 May 1898.

Brooke-Popham Papers, Bodleian Library, Oxford, UK
Brooke-Popham Papers, III/2/1, William Ormsby Gore to Brooke-Popham, 21 October 1936.
Brooke-Popham Papers, III/3/8, Brooke-Popham to Ormsby Gore, 17 July 1937.
Brooke-Popham Papers, III/4/12, Brooke-Popham to Armigel Wade, 18 October 1938.
Brooke-Popham Papers, III/4/27, Brooke-Popham to Malcolm MacDonald, 17 December 1938.
Brooke-Popham Papers, III/9/1, Brooke-Popham to Edmund Ironside, 7 October 1939.
Brooke-Popham Papers, III/9/9, Brooke-Popham to Henry Moore, 25 October 1939.
Brooke-Popham Papers, III/9/20, Brooke-Popham to Josslyn Hay, 5 December 1939.
Brooke-Popham Papers, III/10/1, Harold Montgomery to Brooke-Popham, 9 August 1942.
Brooke-Popham Papers, III/10/1, Henry Gurney to Brooke-Popham, 9 August 1942.
Brooke-Popham Papers, III/10/8, "European Settlement in Kenya Colony," East Africa and Rhodesia, 18 November 1943.

Cambridge University Library, Cambridge, UK
RCS/RCMS 103/12/6, Malaya's War Effort.
RCS/RCMS 103/12/20, Hutchinson Memoir.
RCS/RCMS 103/12/24, Reilly War Diary.
RCS/RCMS 103/15/2, Dickinson Papers.
RCS/RCMS 103/15/3, Shenton Thomas Papers.

Central Intelligence Agency (CREST), U.S.A.
CIA-RDP13X00001R000100030012–8, "Anglo-American Cooperation in East Asia, 15 November 1943."
CIA-RDP13X00001R000100310003–7, "Failure of the British Commando Effort, April 1942."
CIA-RDP13X00001R000100420003–5, "Final Report of Edward Ansel Mowrer to Colonel William J. Donovan, Coordinator of Information, Concerning a Mission to the Far East in the Autumn of 1941, 3 December 1941."

Churchill Archives, Churchill College, Cambridge, UK
AMEL 2/3/20, Leo Amery Papers.
CHAR 20/28/107, Loose Minute, 13 March 1942.
CHAR 20/45/109, Prime Minister to Duff Cooper, 26 November 1941.
CHAR 20/46/94, Prime Minister to Duff Cooper, 12 December 1941.
CHAR 20/47/32, Duff Cooper to Prime Minister, 17 December 1941.

CHAR 20/47/67, Duff Cooper to Prime Minister, 21 December 1941.
CHAR 20/57A/40–61, Colonial Office to Duff Cooper, 10 June 1942.
CHAR 20/68A/67–68, Duff Cooper to Prime Minister, 11 January 1942.
CHAR 20/69A/6–8, Curtin to Prime Minister, 24 January 1942.
DUFC/3/7, Singapore Diary.
GREN/2/6, Grenfell Papers.
MRGN 1/6, Margesson Papers.

Hansard Parliamentary Debates, UK
Hansard, cols. 663–67, House of Commons, 30 October 1911.
Hansard, cols. 570–72, House of Lords, 26 June 1923.
Hansard, col. 632, House of Commons, 10 November 1932.
Hansard, col. 381, House of Lords, 8 January 1942.
Hansard, cols. 417–18, House of Lords, 20 January 1942.
Hansard, cols. 604–6, House of Commons, 27 January 1942.
Hansard, col. 1012, House of Commons, 29 January 1942.

Imperial War Museum, London
IWM 11220/1990, Interview with Corporal S. W. E. Linsley.
IWM Documents 10847, Private Papers of Wing Commander T. C. Carter.
IWM 16275/3/1–3, Interview with Squadron Leader Foster Cox.
IWM 2005–05–26, Captain A. N. Grey Collection.
IWM Documents 11963, Private Papers of Wing Commander Sir Archibald James.
IWM, Percival Papers, Comments on Sir Shenton Thomas' Comments, 22 November 1954.
IWM 4623, Interview with Wing Commander F. C. Richardson.
IWM 6125/1982, Interview with Sergeant H. S. G. Hale, Royal Scots.
IWM Documents 10986, Private Papers of Air Vice-Marshal Sir Philip Game.
IWM Documents 12641, Private Papers of Major-General L. H. R. Pope-Hennessy.
IWM, Private Papers of Major-General G. E. Grimsdale.
IWM, Tizard Papers

Library and Archives Canada, Ottawa
Item 20972, Diaries of William Lyon Mackenzie King, 16 November 1939.
Item 21047, Diaries of William Lyon Mackenzie King, 15 December 1939.
Item 21055, Diaries of William Lyon Mackenzie King, 16 December 1939.
Item 21324, Diaries of William Lyon Mackenzie King, 16 December 1939.
Item 21059, Diaries of William Lyon Mackenzie King, 17 December 1939.
Item 21397, Diaries of William Lyon Mackenzie King, 19 March 1940.

Liddell Hart Centre for Military Archives, King's College London
BP/1/3/10, Report on Visit to Berlin, 1 March 1920.
BP/1/3/14, Special Order for Flight of Handley Page and Vickers Vimy from Amman to Baghdad.

BP/1/3/15, Report by Air Commodore Brooke-Popham on the Flight from Amman to Baghdad.

BP/1/3/20, Notes by Air Commodore Robert Brooke-Popham on Visit to Egypt, Palestine and Mesopotamia, 12 July–12 August 1921.

BP/1/3/23, Notes on Policy of the Directorate of Research.

BP/1/3/24, Notes on Departure.

BP/1/3/25, Report on École Supérieure, 3 December 1921.

BP/1/3/26, Notes on a Visit to Germany, September 1924.

BP/1/5/1, RAF College Opening Address.

BP/1/5/3, Summary of Remarks by Air Commodore Brooke-Popham.

BP/1/5/7, Final Address to the First Course, 1923.

BP/1/5/10, The Work of the RAF Staff College, 5 May 1925.

BP/1/5/11, Functions of a Staff College, 5 May 1925.

BP/1/5/13, Report at the end of the Fourth Course, RAF Staff College, 30 March 1926.

BP/1/6/4, Commandant, IDC, Final Address, 15 December 1932.

BP/1/7/7, Edward Ellington to Hugh Dowding and John Steel, 16 November 1936.

BP/1/7/8, Draft Letter, Brooke-Popham to Ellington, undated.

BP/1/8/3, Report on the Preliminary Education of Candidates for RAF Commissions, March 1919.

BP/2/1/43, Notes on the Conference Held at Ibn Saud's Camp.

BP/2/1/48, Brooke-Popham to John Salmond, 28 May 1930.

BP/2/1/49, Brooke-Popham to Air Ministry, October 1930.

BP/2/3/10, Brooke-Popham to Lord Passfield, 16 September 1929.

BP/2/3/10, Lecture to Army Staff College, 16 June 1931.

BP/3/1/12, Report on Royal Review.

BP/4/1/1, Brooke-Popham to Cuthbert MacLean, 21 September 1935.

BP/4/3/14, Brooke-Popham to Ellington, 3 December 1935.

BP/4/3/17, Brooke-Popham to Ellington, 20 December 1935.

BP/4/3/18, Brooke-Popham to Ellington, 23 December 1935.

BP/4/3/21, Brooke-Popham to Ellington, 24 January 1936.

BP/4/3/22, Brooke-Popham to Ellington, 13 February 1936.

BP/4/3/33, Brooke-Popham to Ellington, 22 April 1936

BP/4/3/37, Brooke-Popham to Ellington, 21 May 1936.

BP/4/3/39, Brooke-Popham to Ellington, 27 May 1936.

BP/4/4/29, Ellington to Brooke-Popham, 21 February 1936.

BP/4/6/3, Ellington to Brooke-Popham, 26 May 1936.

BP/4/3/50, Brooke-Popham to Ellington, 7 September 1936.

BP/4/6/53, Cipher Telegram, War Office to CinC Middle East, 3 September 1936.

BP/4/10/4, Brooke-Popham to Charles Grey, 28 May 1936.

BP/4/12/1, AOCinC's Notes on the Emergency in the Near East, 1935/36.

BP/5/1/3, Brooke-Popham to Hastings Ismay, 5 December 1940.

BP/5/1/4, Brooke-Popham to Ismay, 6 January 1941.

BP/5/2/15, Brooke-Popham to Kingsley Wood, 17 December 1939.

BP/5/2/22, Brooke-Popham to Arthur Street, 20 February 1940.

BP/5/3/1, Air Ministry Notice, 11 October 1939.

BP/5/4/1, Secretary of State to Brooke-Popham, 26 February 1939.

BP/5/4/3, Brooke-Popham to Street, 9 March 1940.

BP/5/6/8, The Empire and Commonwealth Air Training Scheme.

BP/5/7/2, Final Report of the Chief of the Air Staff to the Members of the Supervisory Board, British Commonwealth Air Training Plan, 16 April 1945.

BP/6/1/2, "Malaya Defence Organisation—Most Confidential Note," 23 October 1940.

BP/6/1/6, COS Response to Tactical Appreciation, 10 January 1941.

BP/6/1/7, Notes on Signal X776 of 10 January 1941.

BP/6/1/14, Chiefs of Staff to Brooke-Popham, 24 April 1941.

BP/6/1/18, Arthur Percival to Chiefs of Staff, 2 August 1941.

BP/6/1/25, Ian Playfair to Air Ministry, 20 August 1941.

BP/6/1/41, Chiefs of Staff to Brooke-Popham, 5 December 1941.

BP/6/2/1, Brooke-Popham to Ismay, 26 October 1940.

BP/6/2/2, Brooke-Popham to Ismay, 15 November 1940.

BP/6/2/3, Brooke-Popham to Ismay, 5 December 1940.

BP/6/2/4, Brooke-Popham to Ismay, 6 January 1941.

BP/6/2/5, Brooke-Popham to Ismay, 3 February 1941.

BP/6/2/7, Brooke-Popham to Ismay, 28 February 1941.

BP/6/2/8, Brooke-Popham to Ismay, 26 March 1941.

BP/6/2/10, Brooke-Popham to Ismay, 19 April 1941.

BP/6/2/12, Brooke-Popham to Ismay, 16 May 1941.

BP/6/2/14, Brooke-Popham to Ismay, 3 July 1941.

BP/6/2/16, Brooke-Popham to Ismay, 20 August 1941.

BP/6/2/18, Brooke-Popham to Ismay, 10 October 1941.

BP/6/2/19, Brooke-Popham to Ismay, 29 October 1941.

BP/6/3/3, Brooke-Popham to Street, 15 January 1941.

BP/6/4, Visit Programme, 23 May 1941.

BP/6/4/23, CinC Far East Tour of AIF Units, 7–9 October 1941.

BP/6/5/13, Archibald Wavell to Brooke-Popham, 13 November 1941.

BP/6/5/20, R. H. Dewing to Brooke-Popham, 30 November 1941.

BP/6/5/23, Duff Cooper to Brooke-Popham, 3 December 1941.

BP/6/5/57, Hein ter Poorten to Brooke-Popham, 28 December 1941.

BP/6/5/67, Kenneth McLeod to Brooke-Popham, 4 March 1942.

BP/6/5/69, Clark Kerr to Brooke-Popham, 28 April 1942.

BP/6/6/21, Crosby to Brooke-Popham, 12 August 1941.

BP/6/7/4, Notes for Talk, 8 April 1941.

BP/6/7/8, Notes for Discussion, Maymyo, 6 June 1941.

BP/6/7/11, CinC Far East to Chiefs of Staff, 15 September 1941.

BP/6/7/11, Brooke-Popham to Dudley Pound, 27 October 1941.

BP/6/7/17, Lecture to Staff College, 2 March 1942.

BP/6/7/18, Notes on Burma, 18 March 1942.

BP/6/8/8, Comments on Maltby Despatch, Brooke-Popham to McEvoy, 17 November 1946.

BP/6/8/36, Percival to Brooke-Popham, 4 August 1946.

BP/6/8/40, Frank Brockman to Brooke-Popham, 9 May 1947.

BP/6/8/48, Comments on Layton's Despatch, 15 January 1947.

BP/6/9/3, Brooke-Popham to Philip Babington, 28 February 1942.

BP/6/9/5, Brooke-Popham to Barrington-Ward, 11 December 1942.

BP/6/9/5, Notes on the Far East, Brooke-Popham to CAS, 12 March 1942.

BP/6/9/27, "Some Personal Reflections on the Malayan Campaign," Chief of Staff [Major-General Ian Playfair], Far East, July 1941 to January 1942.

BP/6/9/28, Brooke-Popham to Ian Playfair, 3 July 1943.

BP/6/9/29, Gordon Bennett to Brooke-Popham, 26 January 1944.

BP/6/11/2, John Babington to Brooke-Popham, 15 September 1941.

BP/6/11/6, Further Remarks by ACM Sir Robert Brooke-Popham on the Comments on his Despatch, 28 July 1946.

BP/6/11/17, Comments on Draft Despatch, 25 June 1942.

BP/7/3/7, Committee to Consider Post-War Organisation of ATC.

BP/8/10/4, Brooke-Popham to Newall, 1 November 1939.

BP/8/11, Report on Reinforcement Flight of Blenheims and Hurricanes That Left Tangmere for the Middle East, 18 June 1940.

BP/8/16/4, Tizard to Brooke-Popham, 7 August 1940.

BP/8/16/8, Notes for Sir Henry Tizard to Take to USA, 8 August 1940.

BP/9/1/13, Lecture to RN War College on "Cooperation," 29 March 1932.

BP/9/9/8, "Aspects of Air Operations in the Present War," Notes for South African Broadcast, 11 May 1940.

BP/9/9/37, Brooke-Popham to Guy Garrod, 6 December 1949.

BP/9/12/33, Portal to Brooke-Popham, 15 September 1943.

BP/9/12/52, "The Formation of the RAF Staff College."

Dewing Diaries, 3–22 February 1941.

Dewing Diaries, 3 March 1941.

Dewing Diaries, 12 October 1941.

Dill/3/3/2, Brooke-Popham to John Dill, 7 May 1940.

Dill/3/3/2, Brooke-Popham to Dill, 27 May 1940.

Ismay/1/1/23, Report by Commandant at Conclusion of Third Course.

Ismay/2/3/19, Winston Churchill to Ismay, 22 November 1946.

Ismay/2/3/20, Ismay to Churchill, 29 November 1946.

LH/1/111/1, Brooke-Popham to Basil Liddell Hart, 17 July 1925.

LH/1/111/5, Brooke-Popham to Liddell Hart, 26 July 1932.

LH/1/111/5, Brooke-Popham to Liddell Hart, 28 July 1932.

LH/9/13/22, Talk with Lord Trenchard, 27 June 1935.

LH/11/1935/122, "Notes on RAF Personalities."

LH/15/3/123, Brooke-Popham to Liddell Hart, "Lecture on History of the RAF," 21 October 1929.

Spooner Diaries, 13 September 1941.

Spooner Diaries, 29 November 1941.

Spooner Diaries, 2 December 1941.

Spooner Diaries, 3 December 1941.

Spooner Papers, Grey, A. N. "Fall of Singapore and the Dutch East Indies."

Charles Vlieland Papers.

National Archives of Australia, Canberra

Advisory War Council Minute 533, 16 October 1941.

Department of Foreign Affairs and Trade, Historical Documents 307, Note by Mr.
   S. M. Bruce, High Commissioner in London, of conversation with Jonkheer
   E. Michiels van Verduynen, Netherlands Minister to the United Kingdom, 18
   February 1941.

House of Representatives, Parliamentary Debate, 27 February 1992, p. 373.

The National Archives, UK

ADM 199/1472B, Events in the Far East: Official and Personnel Records of Admiral Sir Geoffrey Layton.

ADM 223/496, "SIS in the Far East."

AIR 1/1/4/1, Notes by General Brooke-Popham.

AIR 1/1/4/11, Brooke-Popham to Huggins, 13 April 1918.

AIR 1/6A/4/30, Papers Received from General Brooke-Popham.

AIR 1/6A/4/55, Notes on Administrative Matters.

AIR 1/529/16/12/70, "Organisation and Establishment of RFC Headquarters."

AIR 1/737/204/2/1, No. 3 Squadron Orders.

AIR 1/737/204/2/6, Air Battalion Work Diary, May 1911–August 1912.

AIR 1/742/204/2/43, "Experiments in Observation of Artillery Fire from Aeroplanes."

AIR 1/746/204/3/22, "Fighting Hostile Aeroplanes in the Air."

AIR 1/785/204/4/558, RFC Training Manual, Part II, Correspondence and Proofs.

AIR 1/785/204/4/565, Brooke-Popham to Barrington-Kennett, 14 July 1913.

AIR 1/1159/204/5/2459, "Distribution of Duties Chart: HQ RAF Equipment
   Branch."

AIR 1/2390/228/11/124, "War Experiences."

AIR 2/673, Sir R. Brooke-Popham's Report on War Organisation of the Air Ministry.

AIR 2/1208, "Aircraft: Equipment."

AIR 2/2815, "Draft specification F. 7/30."

AIR 2/4481, "Committee on Air Defence."

AIR 2/5084, "Sir R. Brooke-Popham's Mission to South Africa."

AIR 10/179, Training Manual Royal Flying Corps Part I Provisional.

AIR 10/494, Report on Junkers Monoplane.

AIR 16/318, "Co-operation 1934 Acoustical Mirror."

AIR 19/546, Colonial Office to Air Ministry, 13 May 1942.

AIR 19/561, "Sir Robert Brooke-Popham, Relinquishment of Command, Retirement and Award of Baronetcy."

AIR 19/561, Churchill to Brooke-Popham, 5 November 1941.

AIR 19/561, Loose Minute, 8 December 1941.

AIR 19/561, Portal to Brooke Popham, 7 November 1941.

AIR 19/561, Air Ministry to Brooke-Popham, 6 November 1941.

AIR 19/561, Brooke-Popham to Prime Minister, 7 November 1941.

AIR 19/561, Brooke-Popham to Portal, 7 November 1941.

AIR 19/561, Brooke-Popham to Air Ministry, 8 November 1941.

AIR 19/561, Loose Minute, Freeman to Sinclair, 11 December 1941.

AIR 19/561, Prime Minister to CinC Far East, 5 November 1941.

AIR 19/561, Note for File, Under Secretary of State for Air, 27 March 1942.

AIR 20/186, "Air Defence of Great Britain: Air Exercises, 1934."

AIR 20/3535, Brooke-Popham to Nicholl, 20 March 1943.

AIR 20/3535, Brooke-Popham to Nicholl, 26 March 1943.

AIR 20/3535, Battle of Britain Papers.

AIR 20/5489, Ellington to Brooke-Popham, 26 September 1935.

AIR 20/5572, "Air Operations in Malaya."

AIR 23/547, Telegrams, Iraq Command to Air Ministry, 5 April 1924 and 7 August 1924.

AIR 23/1970, GHQFE 838/JP, 24 January 1941.

AIR 69, Air Ministry: Royal Force Staff College, Andover: Reports and Papers.

AIR 69/1, Staff College Andover Papers.

AIR 76/426, Air Ministry: Department of the Master-General of the Personnel: Officer's Service Records.

BT 389/2/235, "*Automedon* Movement Card."

BT 389/22, "Oronsay Movement Card."

CAB 5/4, CID Paper 149-C, 26 July 1921.

CAB 10/517, Cooper to Amery, 5 October 1941.

CAB 21/1044, Brooke-Popham to Ismay, 6 January 1941.

CAB 21/1044, Brooke-Popham to Ismay, 26 March 1941.

CAB 21/1044, Brooke-Popham to Ismay, 29 October 1944.

CAB 21/1044, Brooke-Popham to Ismay, 8 May 1942.

CAB 21/1044, Brooke-Popham to Ismay, 8 May 1942.

CAB 21/1044, Brooke-Popham to Ismay, 3 July 1941.

CAB 120/517, Amery to Prime Minster, 14 October 1941.

CAB 120/517, Chiefs of Staff to Prime Minister, 22 October 1941.

CAB 120/517, Prime Minister to Ismay, 28 October 1941.

CAB 120/517, Commonwealth of Australia to Dominions Office, 22 November 1941.

CAB 120/517, Prime Minister to Chiefs of Staff, 24 November 1941.

CAB 120/517, Chiefs of Staff to Prime Minister, 24 January 1942.

CAB 120/517, Ismay to Lord Privy Seal (Clement Atlee), 29 December 1941.

CAB 120/517, Ismay to Lord Privy Seal (Clement Atlee), 29 December 1941.

CAB 120/517, Eden to Prime Minister, 21 September 1941.

CAB 13/18, "Air Defence Systems of Great Britain Meeting Reports."

CAB 16/133, "Committee for Imperial Defence, Ad Hoc Sub-Committees, 1935–1936."

CAB 205 (34), "Defence Requirements, 31 July 1934."

CAB 21/1044, Brooke-Popham to Ismay, 15 November 1940.

CAB 21/1044, Brooke-Popham to Ismay, 29 October 1941.

CAB 21/146, "Air Defence Research: Committee of Imperial Defence."

CAB 21/426, "Air Defence Research."

CAB 65/14/20, Prime Minister to Prime Ministers of Australia and New Zealand, 11 August 1940.

CAB 65/14/20, W. M. (40) 222, War Cabinet Conclusions, Confidential Annex, 8 August 1940.

CAB 65/8/34, W. M. (40) 222, War Cabinet Conclusions, 8 August 1940.

CAB 66/10, WP (40) 302, "The Situation in the Far East."

CAB 66/10, "Far Eastern Policy," Reports by the Chiefs of Staff, 27 July 1940.

CAB 66/10, WP (40) 289 & COS (40)568 Revise, "Far Eastern Policy", 27 July 1940.

CAB 79/6/48, COS Meeting, 6 September 1940.

CAB 79/7, COS Meeting, 12 October 1940.

CAB 79/7, COS Meeting, 18 October 1940.

CAB 79/11, COS Meeting, 25 April 1941.

CAB 120/517, Chiefs of Staff to Prime Minister, 3 September 1941.

CO 850/70/10, Draft Submission to His Majesty, November 1936.

CO 867/78, Shenton Thomas to Moyne, 22 January 1942.

CO 967/76, Shenton Thomas to Parkinson, 11 March 1941.

CO 967/76, Shenton Thomas to Parkinson, 16 March 1941.

CO 967/77, Criticism by Duff Cooper.

CO 967/77, Cooper to Churchill, 18 December 1941.

CO 967/78, Shenton Thomas to Moyne, 8 February 1942.

CO 967/165, Brooke-Popham to Young, 22 September 1939.

COS (40) 703 (JPS), "Co-ordination of Defence: Burma and Far East."

DO 35/539/2, Campbell to Stephenson, 20 December 1939.

FO 371/23377, "Italian Rule in Ethiopia."

FO 371/23382, "Mrs. C. Fannin's Journey through Italian East Africa."

FO 371/27786, "Anglo- Dutch Cooperation."

FO 371/27856, "Duff Cooper's Mission to the Far East."

FO 371/28163, Crosby to Foreign Office, 7 December 1941.

FO 954/6, Duff Cooper to Prime Minister, 13 December 1941.

FO Telegrams 94 and 95, 21 February 1936.

HS 1/110, "Establishment of Killery Mission in Singapore."

HS 1/207, "History of the Oriental Mission."

HS 1/332, CinC Far East to Chiefs of Staff, 1 October 1941.

PREM 3/52/4, "Far East."

PREM 3/155, Clark Kerr to Foreign Office, 25 June 1941.

PREM 3/155, War Cabinet Loose Minute, 18 July 1941.

PREM 3/155, "The Far East: Report of the Chancellor of the Duchy of Lancaster on the Termination of His Appointment as Resident Minister," 19 February 1942.

PREM 3/155, Secretary of State to Viceroy and Governor of Burma, 8 January 1942.

PREM 3/161/1, Duff Cooper to Prime Minister, 18 December 1941.

PREM 3/168/3, "Air Chief Marshal Sir Robert Brooke-Popham's Despatch on the Far East," COS (42)336, 8 July 1942.

WO 106/5402B, Telegrams to and from the Far East.

WO 193/311, "AASAC (Joint) Third Meeting, 31 August 1940."

WO 193/315, Note on JP (41) 648, 10 August 1941.

WO 193/605, Cipher Telegrams from CinC Far East, Dewing to War Office, 19 November 1940.

WO 193/920, "Intelligence Organisation."

WO 193/920, CinC Far East to Air Ministry, Secret Cypher Telegram.

WO 216/78, "Notes for Captain Tennant by Air Officer Commanding," 20 December 1941.

National Archives and Records Administration, U.S.A.

National Archives 4697018, J. M. Creighton, Notes on Singapore and Java, 17 July 1941 to 19 April 1942.

National Archives 4697018, T. Hart, "Narrative of Events, Asiatic Fleet Leading Up to War and from 8 December 1941 to 15 February 1942."

National Archives 4697018, J. Mosher, Report on Malaya, Java and Australia, 2 March 1941–10 March 1942.

National Archives 4697018, "Report of Conference, Manila, December 1941."

Royal Air Force Museum, London

B2621/4, "Sir John Salmond (Draft) Autobiography."

DC76/74/130, Robert Brooke-Popham Record of Service.

MFC76/1, Brooke-Popham to Thomas Marson, 26 March 1923.

MFC76/1/4, Trenchard to Churchill, 26 March 1942.

MFC76/1/5, Brooke-Popham to Trenchard, 30 July 1921.

MFC76/1/5, Trenchard to Brooke-Popham, 7 August 1928.

MFC76/1/6, Trenchard to Sefton Brancker, 9 March 1916 and 15 May 1916.

MFC76/1/7, Trenchard to Brancker, 7 July 1917.

MFC76/1/7, Trenchard to Brancker, 19 August 1916.

MFC76/1/8, Trenchard to Brancker, 4 December 1916.

MFC76/1/9, Trenchard to Brancker, 18 January 1917.

MFC76/1/9, Brancker to Trenchard, 19 January 1917.

MFC76/1/38/54, Air Headquarters Memorandum, 29 November 1923.

MFC76/1/66, Clayton to Trenchard, 8 April 1929.

MFC76/1/66, Clayton to Trenchard, 28 July 1929.

MFC76/1/66, Trenchard to Gilbert Clayton, 29 January 1929.

MFC76/1/104, Brooke-Popham to Trenchard, 10 December 1929.

MFC76/1/104, Brooke-Popham to Salmond, 28 May 1930.

MFC76/1/140/1, Trenchard to Brooke-Popham, 10 May 1919.

MFC76/1/142, Air Headquarters Iraq, 26 February 1930.

MFC76/1/142, Brooke-Popham to Trenchard, 10 June 1929.

MFC76/1/142, Brooke-Popham to Trenchard, 19 July 1929.
MFC76/1/142, Brooke-Popham to Trenchard, 16 September 1929.
MFC76/1/142, Brooke-Popham to Trenchard, 18 November 1929.
MFC76/1/142, Salmond to Brooke-Popham, 29 April 1930.
MFC76/1/142, Salmond to Brooke-Popham, 18 September 1930.
MFC76/1/142, Trenchard to Brooke-Popham, 15 July 1929.
MFC76/1/189/1, Brooke-Popham to Marson, 11 October 1921.
MFC76/1/189/1, Brooke-Popham to Marson, 17 July 1925.
MFC76/1/189/1, Marson to Brooke-Popham, 7 March 1925.
MFC76/1/189/1, Trenchard to Brooke-Popham, 1 January 1924.
MFC76/1/486, Freeman to Trenchard, 24 February 1948.
MFC76/1/486, Trenchard to Wilfrid Freeman, 23 February 1948.
MFC76/1/525, Richard Peck to Trenchard, 15 April 1943.
MFC76/1/525, Trenchard to Peck, 20 April 1943.
MFC76/6/61, Trenchard Autobiographical Narrative.

The Trenchard Archive, RAF Museum, London
Trenchard Archive, V/1/6, Brooke-Popham to Hilary Saunders, 6 July 1951.
Trenchard Archive, V/1/6, Brooke-Popham to Saunders, 25 July 1951.
Trenchard Archive, V/1/6, Brooke-Popham to Saunders, 2 August 1951.
Trenchard Archive, V/1/6, Brooke-Popham to Saunders 16 August 1951.
Trenchard Archive, V/1/6, Brooke-Popham to Saunders, 28 August 1951.

Miscellaneous Archives
Children's Society Records and Archives Centre, London, AR 81.0466, "Register of War Nurseries."
Hoover Institution, Stanford, California, Claire Chennault Papers, Box 4.
RAF Historical Branch, Northolt, London, UK, Ludlow-Hewitt Papers, Box 4/File 14, E. M. Cox, "Memorandum on the Royal Air Force in Malaya," 11 April 1942.
Royal Engineers Library, Chatham, UK, "Diary of Major H. Musgrave," 13 and 19 April 1913.
Soldiers of Oxfordshire Museum, Woodstock, UK, Manuscript History of 52nd Regiment.

Official Histories and Government Publications
Advisory Committee for Aeronautics. *Technical Report of the Advisory Committee for Aeronautics, 1919–1920.* London: His Majesty's Stationery Office (HMSO), 1923.
Aeronautical Research Committee. *Technical Report of the Aeronautical Research Committee, 1920–1921.* London: HMSO, 1924.
Air Historical Branch. *A Short History of the Royal Air Force.* London: Air Ministry, 1929.
Air Ministry. *Wings of the Phoenix—The Official Story of the Air War in Burma.* London: HMSO, 1949.
Bhargava, K. D., and K. N. V. Sastri. *Campaigns in South-East Asia 1941–42.* New Delhi: Combined Inter-Services Historical Section, 1960.

Brown, J. A. *A Gathering of Eagles: The Campaigns of the South African Air Force in Italian East Africa, June 1940–November 1941, with an Introduction 1912–1939,* Cape Town: Purnell, 1970.

Brooke-Popham, R. "Operations in the Far East, from 17 October 1940 to 27 December 1941." *Supplement to the London Gazette,* 22 January 1948, pp. 535–76.

Colonial Report No. 1858. Annual Report on the Social and Economic Progress of the People of the Kenya Colony and Protectorate, 1937. London: HMSO, 1937.

Cruickshank, C. *SOE in the Far East.* Oxford: Oxford University Press, 1983.

Douglas, W. A. B. *The Creation of a National Air Force.* Toronto: University of Toronto Press, 1986.

Gillison, D. *Royal Australian Air Force 1939–1942.* Canberra: Australian War Memorial, 1962.

Gwyer, J. M. A., and J. R. M. Butler. *Grand Strategy* (June 1941–August 1942), Part 1. London: HMSO, 1964.

Hasluck, P. *Australia in the War of 1939–1945,* Series Four (Civil), vol. 1, *The Government and the People 1939–1941.* Canberra: Australian War Memorial, 1952.

Jones, H. A. *The War in the Air.* Vol. 2. Oxford: Clarendon Press, 1928.

———. *The War in the Air.* Vol. 4. Oxford: Clarendon Press, 1934.

Kenya National Assembly Official Record (Hansard). Legislative Council Debates, Third Session, 1937.

London Gazette, 5 August 1859, p. 3005.

———, 11 December 1862, p. 6269.

———, 6 May 1898, p. 2822.

———, 29 December 1899, p. 8657.

———, 25 April 1902, p. 2793.

———, 6 May 1902, p. 3014.

———, 14 June 1904, p. 3788.

———, 24 January 1905, p. 580.

———, 8 February 1910, p. 951.

———, 3 June 1913, p. 3908.

———, 1 August 1919, p. 9864.

———, 22 August 1919, p. 10655.

———, 3 June 1927, p. 3605.

Maltby, P. "Report on the Air Operations During the Campaigns in Malaya and the Netherland East Indies from 8 December 1941 to 12 March 1942." *Supplement to the London Gazette,* 26 February 1948 , pp.1347–1415.

Ministry of Information. *The Battle of Britain.* London: HMSO, 1941, S.O. Code No 70–9999.

Percival, A. "Operations of Malaya Command from 8 December 1941 to 15 February 1942." *Supplement to the London Gazette,* 26 February 1948, pp. 1245–1346.

Raleigh, W. *The War in the Air.* Vol. 1. Oxford: Clarendon Press, 1922.

Report on the Operations Carried out in the Southern Desert in Connection with the Iraq–Najd Borders, June 1928–May 1929, CD 76. London: Air Ministry, 1930.

Reports of General MacArthur: Japanese Operations in the Southwest Pacific Area. Vol. 2, Part 1. Washington, D.C.: Center for Military History, 1966.

Richards, D., and H. St. G. Saunders. *Royal Air Force 1939–1945*. Vol. 1, *The Fight at Odds*. London: HMSO, 1953.

———. *Royal Air Force 1939–1945*. Vol. 2, *The Fight Avails*. London: HMSO, 1954.

Saunders, H. St. G. *The Battle of Britain*. London: His Majesty's Stationery Office, 1941.

Secretary of State for Air. *Permanent Organization of the Royal Air Force* (London: HMSO, 1919).

Supplement to the London Gazette, 3 June 1927, p. 3605.

U.S. Department of Defense. "Detailed Report of the Landing on the Eastern Shore (Patani) of Southern Thailand." *MISLS Document No. 471*, 15 February 1945.

U.S. Department of Defense. *The "Magic" Background of Pearl Harbor*. Vol. 2. Washington, D.C.: U.S. Government Printing Office, 1977.

———. *The "Magic" Background of Pearl Harbor*. Vol. 3. Washington, D.C.: U.S. Government Printing Office, 1977.

———. *The "Magic" Background of Pearl Harbor*. Vol. 4. Washington, D.C.: U.S. Government Printing Office, 1977.

War Office. *Statistics of The Military Effort of the British Empire*. London: HMSO, 1922.

Wavell, A. "Operations in Burma from 15 December 1941 to 20 May 1942," *Supplement to the London Gazette*, 11 March 1948, pp.1667–68.

Wigmore, L. *The Japanese Thrust*. Canberra: Australian War Memorial, 1957.

Woodburn Kirby, S. *The War against Japan*. Vols. 1 and 2. London: Her Majesty's Stationery Office, 1957.

SECONDARY SOURCES

Books and Leaflets

Addison, P. *Churchill on the Home Front, 1900–1955*. London: Faber & Faber, 2013.

Aldrich, R. *Intelligence and the War against Japan*. Cambridge: Cambridge University Press, 2000.

Allawi, A. A. *Faisal I of Iraq*. London: Yale University Press, 2014.

Allen, L. *Singapore 1941–1942*. Rev. ed. London: Frank Cass, 1993.

Arnold, M. *The Sacrifice of Singapore*. Singapore: Marshall Cavendish, 2011.

Ash, B. *Someone Had Blundered*. London: Michael Joseph, 1960.

Ash, E. *Sir Frederick Sykes and the Air Revolution, 1912–1918*. London: Frank Cass, 1999.

Attiwell, K. *The Singapore Story*. London: Frederick Muller, 1959.

Baker, A., and R. Ivelaw-Chapman. *Wings over Kabul*. London: William Kimber, 1975.

Baldwin, H. W. *Great Mistakes of the War*. New York: Harper & Brothers, 1949.

Barber, N. *Sinister Twilight*. London: Collins, 1968.

Baring, M. *Flying Corps Headquarters 1914–1918*. Edinburgh: G. Bell & Sons, 1920.

Bartsch, W. H. *December 8, 1941: MacArthur's Pearl Harbor*. College Station: Texas A&M University Press, 2003.

Bayley, C., and T. Harper. *Forgotten Armies: The Fall of British Asia 1941–1945*. London: Allen Lane, 2005.

Beesly, K. *Very Special Admiral: The Life of Admiral J. H. Godfrey.* London: Hamish Hamilton, 1980.

Bennett, G. *Why Singapore Fell.* Sydney: Angus and Robertson, 1944.

Best, A. *Britain, Japan and Pearl Harbour: Avoiding War in East Asia, 1936–41.* London: Routledge, 1995.

———. *British Intelligence and the Japanese Challenge in Asia 1914–1941.* Basingstoke, UK: Palgrave Macmillan, 2002.

Bidwell, S., and D. Graham. *Fire Power—The British Army Weapons and Theories of War 1904–1945.* London: George Allen & Unwin, 1982.

Bishop, P. *Singapore Burning.* London: Penguin Books, 2006.

———. *Battle of Britain.* London: Quercus, 2009.

Blackburn, K. *The Sportsmen of Changi.* Sydney: New South Publishing, 2012.

Bond, B. *Chief of Staff: The Diaries of Lieutenant-General Sir Henry Pownall.* Vol. 2, *1940–1944.* London: Leo Cooper, 1974.

———. *The Victorian Army and the Staff College, 1854–1914.* London: Eyre Methuen, 1972.

———, and K. Tachikawa, eds. *British and Japanese Military Leadership in the Far Eastern War.* London: Frank Cass, 2004.

Bose, C. *Chalo Delhi: Netaji Subhas Chandra Bose, Collected Works.* Vol. 12, edited by S. Bose. Delhi: Permanent Black, 2007.

Bose, R. *Singapore At War.* Singapore: Marshall Cavendish, 2012.

Bowes, P. "Leigh Bowes RAAF Flying Log Book & Service Diary." *War diary and logbooks of a WW2 fighter pilot* (blog). Posted 28 August 2013. https://leighbowes 76.files.wordpress.com/2014/08/leigh-bowes-flying-log-book-service-diary _small_file_size-2.pdf.

Bowyer, C. *RAF Operations 1918–1938.* London: William Kimber, 1988.

Boyd, A. *The Royal Navy in Eastern Waters.* Barnsley, UK: Seaforth, 2017.

Boyle, A. *Trenchard: Man of Vision.* London: Collins, 1962.

Brabazon, Lord of Tara. *The Brabazon Story.* London: William Heinemann, 1956.

Braddon, R. *The Naked Island.* London: Werner Laurie, 1952.

Brendon, P. *The Decline and Fall of the British Empire.* London: Jonathan Cape, 2007.

Broke-Smith, P. W. L. *History of Early British Military Aeronautics.* Bath, UK: Cedric Chilvers, 1968.

Brooke-Popham, H. R. M. "Air Warfare." In *The Study of War for Statesmen and Citizens: Lectures Delivered in the University of London during the Years 1925–26,* edited by G. Aston, 150–62. London: Longmans, Green, 1927.

———. *Notes on the Traditions of the Royal Air Force, ATCP No 55.* London: Air Training Corps, 1944.

———. *The Role of the RAF in War and the Strategical Use of Air Power,* Part 9, *Operations 1939–1942, Operations in France September 1939–June 1940.* London: Air Member for Training, 1944.

———. *The Role of the RAF in War and the Strategical Use of Air Power,* Part 10, *Operations 1939–1942, The Norwegian Campaign, 1940.* London: Air Member for Training, 1943.

Brown, C. *Suez to Singapore*. New York: Random House, 1942.

Brownell, R. J. *From Khaki to Blue*. Lyneham, ACT: Military History Society of Australia, 1978.

Bruce, J. M. *The Aeroplanes of the Royal Flying Corps, Military Wing*. London: Putnam, 1982.

Brune, P. *Descent into Hell*. Sydney: Allen & Unwin, 2014.

Buchan, E. *A Few Planes for China: The Birth of the Flying Tigers*. Lebanon, NH: University Press of New England, 2017.

Bullard, S. *Japanese Army Operations in the South Pacific Area*. Canberra: Australian War Memorial, 2007.

Burton, J. *Fortnight of Infamy: The Collapse of Allied Airpower West of Pearl Harbor*. Annapolis, MD: Naval Institute Press, 2006.

Caffrey, K. *Out in the Midday Sun*. London: Andre Deutsch, 1974.

Callahan, R. *Burma 1942–1945*. London: Davis-Poynter, 1978.

———. *The Worst Disaster: The Fall of Singapore*. Newark: University of Delaware Press, 1977.

Callwell, C. E. *Field Marshal Sir Henry Wilson, His Life and Diaries*. London: Cassell, 1927.

Campbell, G. *The Charging Buffalo: A History of the Kenya Regiment 1937–1963*. London: Leo Cooper, 1986.

Carroll, K. *Compass Course: The Log of an Air Force Officer's Wife*. London: Hutchinson, 1941.

Cato [pseud.]. *Guilty Men*. London: Victor Gollancz, 1940.

Chapman, F. S. *The Jungle Is Neutral*. London: Chatto & Windus, 1949.

Chapman, J. *The Price of Admiralty—The War Diary of the German Naval Attaché in Japan*. Vols. 2 and 3, *23 August 1940–9 September 1941*. Lewes, UK: Saltire Press, 1982.

Charlton, L. E. O. *Charlton*. London: Penguin Books, 1938.

Charmley, J. *Duff Cooper: The Authorised Biography*. London: Weidenfeld and Nicolson, 1986.

Charteris, J. *Field Marshal Earl Haig*. London: Cassell, 1929.

Chatfield, M. E. *It Might Happen Again*. Vol. 2, *The Navy and Defence*. London: Heinemann, 1947.

Chihiro, H. "The Japanese-Soviet Neutrality Pact." In *The Fateful Choice, Japan's Advance into Southeast Asia, 1939–1941*, edited by J. W. Morley, 13–114. New York: Columbia University Press, 1980.

The Chronicle Editorial Committee. *The Oxfordshire and Buckinghamshire Light Infantry Chronicle*. Vol. 39, *1931*. Oxford: Slatter & Rose, 1932.

Churchill, W. S. *The Gathering Storm*. London: Cassell, 1948.

———. *The Hinge of Fate*. London: Cassell, 1951.

———. *A Roving Commission—My Early Life*. New York: Charles Scribner, 1930.

———. *Their Finest Hour*. London: Cassell, 1949.

Clark, R. W. *Rise of the Boffins*. London: Phoenix House, 1962.

———. *Tizard*. London: Methuen, 1965.

Clayton, A., and D. Savage. *Government and Labour in Kenya: 1895–1963.* Abingdon, UK: Frank Cass, 1974.

Collier, R. *1941.* London: Hamish Hamilton, 1981.

Connell, J. *Wavell, Supreme Commander 1941–1943.* London: Collins, 1969.

Connolly, R., and B. Wilson. *Cruel Britannia: Britannia Waives the Rules 1941–42, Singapore Betrayed, Australia Abandoned.* Belmont, Australia: Kingsgrove, 1994.

Cooper, D. *Darling Monster: The Letters of Lady Diana Cooper to Her Son John Julius Norwich.* London: Chatto & Windus, 2013.

———. *Old Men Forget.* New York: Dutton, 1954. Reprinted with a foreword by P. Ziegler. London: Century Publishing, 1986.

———. *Trumpets from the Steep.* London: Rupert Hart-Davis, 1960.

Cowie, M. *Fly Vulture.* London: Harrap, 1961.

Cox, J. R. *Rising Sun, Falling Skies.* Oxford, UK: Osprey, 2014.

Crosby, J. *Siam: The Crossroads.* London: Hollis and Carter, 1945.

Cull, B. *Buffaloes over Singapore.* London: Grub Street, 2003.

Dallas Brett, R. *History of British Aviation 1908–1914.* Surbiton, UK: Air Research, 1988.

Danchev, A., and D. Todman, eds. *Field Marshal Lord Alanbrooke, War Diaries 1939–1945.* London: Weidenfeld & Nicholson, 2001.

Darwin, J. *Britain and Decolonisation: The Retreat from Empire in the Post-War World.* London: Macmillan, 1988.

———. *The Empire Project: The Rise and Fall of the British World System 1830–1970.* Cambridge: Cambridge University Press, 2009.

———. *The End of the British Empire: The Historical Debate.* Oxford: Blackwell, 1991.

Davenport-Hines, R. *Ettie: The Intimate Life and Dauntless Spirit of Lady Desborough.* London: Weidenfeld & Nicolson, 2008.

———, ed. *Hugh Trevor-Roper, The Wartime Journals.* London: I. B. Tauris, 2012.

Day, D. *The Great Betrayal: Britain, Australia and the Onset of the Pacific War 1939–42.* New York: Norton, 1989.

Dempster, D., and D. Wood. *The Narrow Margin.* London: Hutchinson, 1961.

Dixon, N. *The Psychology of Military Incompetence.* London: Jonathan Cape, 1976.

Dobinson, C. *Building Radar: Forging Britain's Early-Warning Chain, 1935–1945.* London: Methuen, 2010.

Dockter, W. *Churchill and the Islamic World.* London: I. B. Tauris, 2015.

Dodds, R. V., and R. Collishaw. *Air Command—A Fighter Pilot's Story.* London: Kimber, 1973.

Dower, J. W. *War without Mercy: Race and Power in the Pacific War.* New York: Pantheon Books, 1986.

Draper, A. *Dawn Like Thunder: The Retreat from Burma.* London: Leo Cooper, 1987.

Dunlop, R. *Behind Japanese Lines: With the OSS in Burma.* New York: Skyhorse Publishing, 2014.

Dye, P. *The Bridge to Airpower: Logistics Support for Royal Flying Corps Operations on the Western Front, 1914–18.* Annapolis, MD: Naval Institute Press, 2015.

———. "The Cairo-Baghdad Air Route." In *Lawrence of Arabia & Middle East Airpower,* 41–48. Warwick, UK: Cross & Cockade International, 2016.

————, ed. *Lawrence of Arabia & Middle East Airpower*. Warwick, UK: Cross & Cockade International, 2016.

Edgerton, D. *Warfare State: Britain 1920–1970*. Cambridge: Cambridge University Press, 2005.

Ellis, G. *Toolbox on the Wing*. Shrewsbury, UK: Airlife, 1983.

Elphick, P. *Far Eastern File: The Intelligence War in the Far East 1930–1945*. London: Hodder & Stoughton, 1997.

————. *Singapore: The Pregnable Fortress*. London: Hodder & Stoughton, 1995.

Evans, T., ed. *The Killearn Diaries 1934–1946*. London: Sidgwick & Jackson, 1972.

Ewer, P. *Wounded Eagle: The Bombing of Darwin and Australia's Air Defence Scandal*. Sydney: New Holland, 2009.

Farrell, B. *The Defence and Fall of Singapore 1940–1942*. Stroud, UK: Tempus, 2005.

————, and S. Hunter, eds. *A Great Betrayal? The Fall of Singapore Revisited*. Singapore: Marshall Cavendish, 2010.

Ferguson, N. *Empire: How Britain Made the Modern World*. London: Allen Lane, 2003.

Ferris, J. "Achieving Air Ascendancy: Challenge and Response in British Strategic Air Defence, 1915–1940." In *Air Power History Turning Points from Kitty Hawk to Kosovo*, edited by S. Cox and P. Gray, 21–50. London: Frank Cass, 2002.

————. "Double-Edged Estimates: Japan in the Eyes of the British Army and the Royal Air Force, 1900–1939." In *The History of Anglo-Japanese Relations, 1600–2000*, vol. 3, *The Military Dimension*, edited by I. Gow, Y. Hirama, and J. Chapman, 91–108. Basingstoke, UK: Palgrave Macmillan, 2003.

————. "Student and Master: The United Kingdom, Japan, Airpower, and the Fall of Singapore, 1920–1941," in *A Great Betrayal? The Fall of Singapore Revisited*, edited by B. Farrell and S. Hunter. Singapore: Marshall Cavendish, 2010, 74–97.

Foot, M. R. D. *SOE—The Special Operations Executive 1940–46*. London: BBC, 1984.

Ford, D. *Flying Tigers, Claire Chennault and the American Volunteer Group*. Washington, D.C.: Smithsonian Institution Press, 1991.

Fox, J. *White Mischief*. London: Jonathan Cape, 1982.

Francis, M. *The Flyer: British Culture and the Royal Air Force 1939–1945*. Oxford: Oxford University Press, 2008.

Freedman, L. *The Official History of the Falklands Campaign*. Abingdon, UK: Routledge, 2007.

Frei, H. *Guns of February*. Singapore: Singapore University Press, 2004.

Fuller, J. F. C. *Memoirs of an Unconventional Soldier*. London: Ivor, Nicholson and Watson, 1936.

————. *The Second World War*. London: Eyre & Spottiswoode, 1948.

Furneaux-Smith, F. *The Prof in Two Worlds: The Official Life of Professor F. A. Lindemann, Viscount Cherwell*. London: Collins, 1961.

Furse, A. *Wilfrid Freeman: The Genius Behind Allied Survival and Air Supremacy 1939–1945*. Staplehurst, UK: Spellmount, 1999.

Gallagher, O. D. *Retreat in the East*. London: George Harrap, 1942.

Gardner, L. A. *Taxing Colonial Africa: The Political Economy of British Imperialism*. Oxford: Oxford University Press, 2012.

Gervasi, F. *War Has Seven Faces.* Garden City, NY: Doubleday, Doran, 1942.

Gilchrist, A. *Malaya 1941.* London: Robert Hale, 1992.

Glover, E. M. *In 70 Days.* London: Frederick Muller, 1946.

Glubb, J. B. *War in the Desert.* London: Hodder & Stoughton, 1960.

Goldman, S. D. *Nomonhan, 1939.* Annapolis, MD: Naval Institute Press, 2012.

Goodman, M. S. *The Official History of the Joint Intelligence Committee*, Vol. 1. London: Routledge, 2014.

Gough, R. *Special Operations Singapore 1941–42.* Singapore: Heinemann, 1985.

Granatstein, J. L. *The Generals: The Canadian Army's Senior Commanders in the Second World War.* Toronto: Stoddart, 1993.

Grant, I., and K. Tamayama. *Burma 1942: The Japanese Invasion.* Chichester, UK: Zampi Press, 1999.

Graves, R. *T. E. Lawrence to His Biographer.* London: Jonathan Cape, 1938.

Gray, T., ed. *The Imperial Defence College and the Royal College of Defence Studies 1927–1977.* Edinburgh: HMSO, 1977.

Greenlaw, O. S. *The Lady and the Tigers.* New York: E. P. Dutton, 1943.

Grenfell, R. *Main Fleet to Singapore.* London: Faber & Faber, 1951.

Grey, C. G. *A History of the Air Ministry.* London: George Allen & Unwin, 1940.

Guard, H., and J. Tring. *The Pacific War Uncensored.* Havertown, PA: Casemate, 2011.

Hall, T. *The Fall of Singapore 1942.* North Ryde, NSW: Methuen Australia, 1983.

Hamill, I. *Strategic Illusion: The Singapore Strategy and the Defence of Australia and New Zealand 1919–1942.* Singapore: Singapore University Press, 1981.

Harris, P. "Egypt: Defence Plans." In *Britain and the Middle East in the 1930s: Security Problems 1935–1939*, edited by M. J. Cohen and M. Kolinsky, 61–78. New York: Palgrave Macmillan, 1992.

Hashimoto, T. "The Wind Tunnel and the Emergence of Aeronautical Research in Britain." In *Atmospheric Flight in the Twentieth Century*, edited by P. Galison and A. Roland, 223–240. London: Kluwer Academic, 2000.

Hewitt, A. *Bridge with Three Men.* London: Jonathan Cape, 1986.

Hickey, M. *The Unforgettable Army.* Staplehurst: Spellmount, 1992.

Higgins, C. G. *The Oxfordshire and Buckinghamshire Light Infantry Chronicle.* Vol. 55, *January–December 1953.* Oxford: Slatter & Rose, 1954.

Higham, R. "British Air Exercises of the 1930s." *1998 National Aerospace Conference Proceedings.* Dayton, OH: Wright State University, 1999.

———. *The Military Intellectuals in Britain.* New Brunswick, NJ: Rutgers University Press, 1966.

———. "Selected Aspects of RAF Concepts of and Planning for War, 1934–1941," in *Actas del XVII Congreso Internacional de Ciencias Historicas.* Madrid: International Commission of Military History, 141–57.

Hoare, S. (Viscount Templewood). *Empire of the Air.* London: Collins, 1957.

Hodson, J. L. *War in the Sun.* London: Victor Gollancz, 1942.

Holland, J. *The Battle of Britain.* London: Transworld, 2010.

Holmes, R., and A. Kemp. *The Bitter End.* Strettington, UK: Antony Bird Publications, 1982.

Home, G. *Race War: White Supremacy and the Japanese Attack on the British Empire.* New York: New York University Press, 2005.

Hough, R. *The Hunting of Force Z.* London: William Collins, 1963.

Howard-Williams, E. L., and S. Hay. *Air over Eden.* London: Hutchinson, 1937.

Hunt, B. D. *Sailor-Scholar, Admiral Sir Herbert Richmond.* Waterloo, Canada: Wilfrid Laurier University Press, 1982.

Hutchinson, H. D. *The Campaign in Tirah, 1897–1898.* London: Macmillan, 1898.

Hyam, R. *Britain's Declining Empire: The Road to Decolonisation, 1918–1968.* Cambridge: Cambridge University Press, 2007.

Ironside, E. *High Road to Command: The Diaries of Major-General Sir Edmund Ironside, 1920–1922.* London: Leo Cooper, 1972.

Ismay, L. *The Memoirs of Lord Ismay.* London: William Heinemann, 1960.

James, J. *The Paladins.* London: Macdonald, 1990.

James, L. *The Rise and Fall of the British Empire.* London: St. Martin's Press, 1994.

James, T. C. G. *The Growth of Fighter Command.* London: Frank Cass, 2002.

Jeal, T. *Baden-Powell, Founder of the Boy Scout Movement.* New Haven, CT: Yale University Press, 2007.

Jeffery, K. *Field Marshal Sir Henry Wilson: A Political Soldier.* Oxford: Oxford University Press, 2006.

———. *MI6: The History of the Secret Intelligence Service.* London: Bloomsbury, 2010.

Jervis, S. "Moving Experiences: Responses to Relocation among British Military Wives." In *Gender and Family among Transnational Professionals*, edited by A. Coles and A. Fechter, 103–23. London: Routledge, 2006.

Johnsen, W. T. *The Origins of the Grand Alliance—Anglo-American Military Collaboration from the Panay Incident to Pearl Harbor.* Lexington: University Press of Kentucky, 2016.

Jordan, D. "The Battle for the Skies: Sir Hugh Trenchard as Commander of the Royal Flying Corps." In *Leadership in Conflict, 1914–1918*, edited by M. Hughes and M. Seligmann, 68–92. Barnsley, UK: Leo Cooper, 2000.

Joubert de la Ferté, P. *The Fated Sky.* London: Hutchinson, 1952.

———. *The Forgotten Ones.* London: Hutchinson, 1961.

———. *Fun and Games.* London: Hutchinson, 1964.

Jun, T. "The Navy's Role in the Southern Strategy." In *The Fateful Choice, Japan's Advance into Southeast Asia, 1939–1941*, edited by J. W. Morley, 241–95. New York: Columbia University Press, 1980.

Keith, C. H. *Flying Years.* London: John Hamilton, 1938.

Kennaway, A. *Journey by Candlelight.* Bishop Auckland, UK: Pentland Press, 1999.

Kennedy, G. "British Propaganda and the Protection of Empire in the Far East 1933–1942." In *British Propaganda and Wars of Empire: Influencing Friend and Foe 1900–2010*, edited by G. Kennedy and C. Tuck, 13–32. London: Routledge, 2014.

Kiernan, R. H. *The First War in the Air.* London: Peter Davies, 1934.

Kinvig, C. *Scapegoat: General Percival of Singapore.* London: Brassey's, 1996.

Kipling, Rudyard. "If—." *Rewards and Fairies.* London: Macmillan, 1910.

Kirk-Greene, A. "On Governorship and Governors in British Africa." In *African Proconsuls: European Governors in Africa*, edited by L. H. Gann and P. Duignan, 244–50. New York: Free Press, 1978.

Knightley, P. *Australia: A Biography of a Nation*. London: Jonathan Cape, 2000.

———. *The First Casualty: The War Correspondent as Hero and Myth-maker from the Crimea to Iraq*. Baltimore: John Hopkins University Press, 2004.

Kotani, K. *Japanese Intelligence in World War II*. Botley, UK: Osprey Publishing, 2009.

Kratoska, P. *The Japanese Occupation of Malaya: A Social and Economic History*. London: Hurst, 1997.

Laffin, J. *Swifter than Eagles*. London: William Blackwood, 1964.

Lee Kuan Yew. *The Singapore Story: Memories of Lee Kuan Yew*. Vol. 1. Singapore: Times, 1998.

Leutze, J. *A Different Kind of Victory: A Biography of Admiral Thomas C. Hart*. Annapolis, MD: Naval Institute Press, 1981.

Lewin, R. *The Chief: Field Marshal Lord Wavell, Commander-in-Chief and Viceroy, 1939–1947*. London: Hutchinson, 1980.

Liddell Hart, B. *The Memoirs of Captain Liddell Hart*. Vol. 1. London: Cassell, 1965.

———. *Paris or The Future of War*. New York: Dutton, 1926.

Londonderry, Marquess of. *Wings of Destiny*. London: Macmillan, 1943.

Longmore, A. *From Sea to Sky*. London: Geoffrey Bles, 1946.

Macintyre, D. *Fighting Admiral: The Life and Battles of Admiral of the Fleet Sir James Somerville*. London: Evans Brothers, 1961.

Mackenzie, C. *Eastern Epic*. Vol. 1. London: Chatto & Windus, 1951.

Macmillan, N. *The Royal Air Force in the World War*. Vol. 4, *1940–1945*. London: Harrap, 1950.

———. *Sir Sefton Brancker*. London: William Heinemann, 1935.

Macri, F. D. *Clash of Empires in South China*. Lawrence: University Press of Kansas, 2012.

Mahan, A. T. *Naval Strategy*. London: Sampson Low Marston, 1911.

Man, K. C., and T. Y. Lun. *Eastern Fortress: A Military History of Hong Kong, 1840–1970*. Hong Kong: Hong Kong University Press, 2014.

Marder, A. *Old Friends, New Enemies: The Royal Navy and the Imperial Japanese Navy*. Oxford: Clarendon Press, 1981.

Marson, T. B. *Scarlet and Khaki*. London: Jonathan Cape, 1930.

Martin, A. W., and P. Hardy, eds. *Dark and Hurrying Days: Menzies' 1941 Diary*. Canberra: National Library of Australia, 1993.

Mason, R. A. "British Air Power." In *Global Airpower*, edited by J. Olsen, 7–62. Washington, D.C.: Potomac Books, 2011.

———. *History of the Royal Air Force Staff College, 1922–1972*. Bracknell, UK: RAF Staff College, 1972.

Mawdsley, E. *December 1941: Twelve Days That Began a World War*. New Haven, CT: Yale University Press, 2011.

Maxon, R. M., and T. P. Ofcansky. *Historical Dictionary of Kenya*. 3rd ed. Lanham, MD: Rowman & Littlefield, 2014.

McCrum, R. *The Men Who Lost Singapore, 1938–1942.* Singapore: NUS Press, 2017.

McCudden, J. T. B. *Flying Fury.* London: Hamilton, 1930.

McEwan, J. *The Remorseless Road.* Shrewsbury, UK: Airlife, 1997.

McLynn, F. *The Burma Campaign: Disaster into Triumph 1942–1945.* New Haven, CT: Yale University Press, 2011.

Meaher, A. *The Road to Singapore: The Myth of British Betrayal.* North Melbourne: Australian Scholarly Publishing, 2010.

Michie, A. *Retreat to Victory.* London: George Allen & Unwin, 1942.

Middlebrook, M., and P. Mahoney. *Battleship: The Loss of the* Prince of Wales *and the* Repulse. London: Allen Lane, 1977.

Middlemas, K., and J. Barnes. *Baldwin.* London: Weidenfeld & Nicolson, 1969.

Milford, L. *Haileybury Register, 1862–1900.* London: Richard Clay & Sons, 1900.

Miller, E. S. *War Plan Orange: The U.S. Strategy to Defeat Japan, 1897–1945.* Annapolis, MD: Naval Institute Press, 1991.

Miller, R. *Boom.* London: Weidenfeld & Nicolson, 2016.

Millman, N. *Ki-27 "Nate" Aces.* Oxford, UK: Osprey, 2013.

Mitter, R. *China's War with Japan.* London: Allen Lane, 2013.

Mockler-Ferryman, A. F. *The Oxfordshire Light Infantry Chronicle.* Vol. 7. London: Eyre & Spottiswoode, 1898.

———. *The Oxfordshire Light Infantry Chronicle.* Vol. 8. London: Eyre & Spottiswoode, 1899.

———. *The Oxfordshire Light Infantry Chronicle.* Vol. 9. London: Eyre & Spottiswoode, 1900.

———. *The Oxfordshire Light Infantry Chronicle.* Vol. 10. London: Eyre & Spottiswoode, 1901.

———. *The Oxfordshire Light Infantry Chronicle.* Vol. 14. London: Eyre & Spottiswoode, 1905.

Montgomery, B. *Shenton of Singapore.* London: Leo Cooper, 1984.

Montgomery Hyde, H. *British Air Policy between the Wars 1918–1939.* London: Heinemann, 1976.

Morewood, S. *The British Defence of Egypt 1935–1940: Conflict and Crisis in the Eastern Mediterranean.* London: Frank Cass, 2005.

———. "'This Silly African Business': The Military Dimension of Britain's Response to the Abyssinian Crisis." In *Collision of Empires: Italy's Invasion of Ethiopia and Its International Impact,* edited by G. B. Strang, 70–105. Farnham, UK: Ashgate, 2013.

Morrison, I. *Malayan Postscript.* London: Faber & Faber, 1942.

Mountjoy, D. *The Melody of God and Other Papers.* New York: Dutton, 1922.

Mungazi, D. A. *The Last British Liberals in Africa: Michael Blundell and Garfield Todd.* Westport, CT: Greenwood, 1999.

Murfett, M. H., J. N. Miksic, Brian P. Farrell, and C. M. Shun, eds. *Between Two Oceans: A Military History of Singapore.* Singapore: Marshall Cavendish, 2011.

Murray, J. *Watching the Sun Rise: Australia Reporting of Japan, 1931 to the Fall of Singapore.* New York: Lexington Books, 2004.

Neale, M. C. *The Memoirs of George Purvis Bulman.* Derby, UK: Rolls Royce Heritage Trust, 2002.

Nedialkov, D. *In the Skies of Nomonhan.* Manchester, UK: Crecy, 2011.

Nicholls, C. S. *Red Strangers: The White Tribe of Kenya.* London: Timewell Press, 2005.

Nicholson, A. *Hostages to Fortune: Winston Churchill and the Loss of the* Prince of Wales *and* Repulse. Stroud, UK: Sutton, 2005.

Nish, I. *Collected Writings of Ian Nish, Part 2.* Abingdon, UK: Routledge, 2013.

Norwich, J. J. *The Duff Cooper Diaries.* London: Weidenfeld & Nicolson, 2005.

Omissi, D. *Air Power and Colonial Control: The Royal Air Force 1919–1939.* Manchester, UK: Manchester University Press, 1990.

Ong, C. C. *Operation Matador: Britain's War Plans against the Japanese 1918–1941.* Singapore: Times Academic Press, 1997.

Orange, V. *Churchill and His Airmen.* London: Grub Street, 2013.

———. *Park: The Biography of Air Chief Marshal Sir Keith Park.* London: Grub Street, 2001.

———. *Tedder: Quietly in Command.* London: Frank Cass, 2006.

Osborne, M. *Ethnicity and Empire in Kenya.* Cambridge: Cambridge University Press, 2014.

Owen, F. *The Fall of Singapore.* London: Michael Joseph, 1960.

Paris, T. *In Defence of Britain's Middle East Empire: A Life of Sir Gilbert Clayton.* Brighton, UK: Sussex Academic Press, 2015.

Parsons, T. H. "The Evolution of The Girl Guide Movement in Kenya." In *Scouting Frontiers: Youth and the Scout Movement's First Century*, edited by N. R. Block and T. M. Proctor, 143–56. Newcastle-Upon-Tyne, UK: Cambridge Scholars, 2009.

Percival, A. E. *The War in Malaya.* London: Eyre & Spottiswoode, 1949.

Perry, R. *The Fight for Australia: From Changi and Darwin to Kokoda.* Sydney: Hachette Australia, 2012.

Philips, G. *Text Book on Fortifications.* Sandhurst, UK: Royal Military Academy, 1884.

Philpott, I. M. *The Royal Air Force: An Encyclopedia of the Inter-War Years.* Vol. 1, *1918–1929.* Barnsley, UK: Pen and Sword, 2005.

———. *The Royal Air Force: An Encyclopedia of the Inter-War Years.* Vol. 2, *1930–1939.* Barnsley, UK: Pen and Sword, 2008.

Pike, F. *Hirohito's War: The Pacific War 1941–1945.* London: Bloomsbury, 2015.

Pixton, S. *Howard Pixton: Test Pilot and Pioneer Aviator.* Barnsley, UK: Pen & Sword, 2014.

Playfair, P., and J. Jarvis. *'Pip' Playfair: A Founding Father of the RAF.* Ilfracombe, UK: Arthur Stockwell, 1979.

Plowman, P. *Across the Sea to War.* Sydney: Rosenberg Publishing, 2003.

Pollard, E., and H. Strouts. *Wings over the Western Front: The First World War Diaries of Collingwood Ingram.* Charlbury, UK: Day Books, 2014.

Potter, J. D. *A Soldier Must Hang.* London: Frederick Muller, 1963.

Powers, B. D. *Strategy without Slide-Rule.* London: Croom Helm, 1976.

Preston-Hough, P. *Commanding Far Eastern Skies.* Solihull, UK: Helion, 2015.

Probert, H. *The Forgotten Air Force: The Royal Air Force in the War against Japan 1941–1945.* London: Brassey's, 1995.

———. *High Commanders of the Royal Air Force.* London: HMSO, 1991.

Pugh, J. "David Henderson and Command of the Royal Flying Corps." In *Stemming the Tide: Officers and Leadership in the British Expeditionary Force, 1914*, edited by S. Jones, 263–90. Solihull, UK: Helion, 2013.

Puleston, W. D. *Mahan*. London: Jonathan Cape, 1939.

Ralph, W. *William Barker V.C.—The Life, Death and Legend of Canada's Most Decorated War Hero*. Mississauga, Ontario: John Wiley, 2007.

Read, W. R. "Cavalryman in the Flying Machines." In *People at War*, edited by M. Moynihan, 19–41. Newton Abbott, UK: David & Charles, 1973.

Record, J. *A War It Was Always Going to Lose: Why Japan Attacked America in 1941* Washington, D.C.: Potomac Books, 2011.

Reid, B. H. *J. F. C. Fuller: Military Thinker*. London: Macmillan, 1987.

Reid, W. *Empire of Sand: How Britain Made the Middle East*. Edinburgh: Birlinn, 2013.

Reynolds, D. *In Command of History: Churchill Fighting and Writing the Second World War*. London: Allen Lane, 2005.

Richards, D. *Portal of Hungerford*. London: Heinemann, 1978.

———. *It Might Have Been Worse*. London: Smithson Albright, 1998.

Richardson, F. C. *Man Is Not Lost*. Shrewsbury, UK: Airlife, 1997.

Roberts, A. *Eminent Churchillians*. London: Weidenfeld & Nicholson, 1994.

———. *Masters and Commanders*. London: Allen Lane, 2008.

Rogge, B., and W. Frank. *The German Raider* Atlantis. New York: Ballantine Books, 1956.

Romanus, C. P., and R. Sunderland. *Stillwell's Mission to China*. Washington, D.C.: Center of Military History, 1952.

Rose, A. *Who Dies Fighting*. London: Jonathan Cape, 1944.

Roskill, S. *Churchill and the Admirals*. London: Collins, 1977.

———. *Naval Policy between the Wars*. Vol. 1, *The Period of Anglo-American Antagonism 1919–1929*. London: Collins, 1968.

———. *Naval Policy between the Wars*. Vol. 2, *The Period of Reluctant Rearmament 1930–1939*. London: Collins, 1976.

Rowe, A. P. *One Story of Radar*. Cambridge: Cambridge University Press, 1948.

Royal Air Force (RAF) Historical Society. "The RAF and the Far East War: A Symposium on the Far East War." *Bracknell Paper No. 6*, 24 March 1995.

Rusbridger, R., and E. Nave. *Betrayal at Pearl Harbor*. New York: Summit Books, 1991.

Russell, D. S. *Winston Churchill, Soldier: The Military Life of a Gentleman at War*. London: Brassey's, 2005.

Sansom, K. *Sir George Sansom and Japan*. Tallahassee, FL: Diplomatic Press, 1972.

Sansome, R. S. *The Bamboo Workshop*. Braunton, UK: Merlin Books, 1995.

Satia, P. *Spies in Arabia*. Oxford: Oxford University Press, 2008.

Scalapino, R. "Introduction, Part Two, Southern Advance." In *The Fateful Choice, Japan's Advance into Southeast Asia, 1939–1941*, edited by J. W. Morley, 117–23. New York: Columbia University Press, 1980.

Scott, R. L. *Flying Tiger: Chennault of China*. New York: Doubleday, 1959.

Seki, E. *Mrs. Ferguson's Tea-Set: Japan and the Second World War*. Folkestone, UK: Global Oriental, 2007.

Shores, C., and B. Cull. *Bloody Shambles*. Vol. 1, *The Drift to War to the Fall of Singapore*. London: Grub Street, 1992.

———. *Bloody Shambles*. Vol. 2, *The Defence of Sumatra to the Fall of Burma*. London: Grub Street, 1993.

Silverfarb, D. *Britain's Informal Empire in the Middle East: A Case Study of Iraq, 1929–1941*. Oxford: Oxford University Press, 1986.

Simson, I. *Too Little, Too Late*. London: Leo Cooper, 1970.

Slessor, J. *The Central Blue*. London: Cassell, 1956.

———. *The Great Deterrent*. London: Cassell, 1957.

Smith, C. *Singapore Burning*. London: Penguin, 2006.

Smith, M. *The Emperor's Codes*. London: Bantam Press, 2000.

Smith, P. C. *Mitsubishi Zero*. Barnsley, UK: Pen & Sword, 2014.

Steinhart, E. *Black Poachers, White Hunters: A Social History of Hunting in Colonial Kenya*. Oxford: James Currey, 2005.

Stephen, M. *Scapegoat: The Death of* Prince of Wales *and* Repulse. Barnsley, UK: Pen and Sword, 2014.

Stewart, A. *The Underrated Enemy*. London: William Kimber, 1987.

Stockings, C., ed. *Zombie Myths of Australian Military History*. Sydney: University of New South Wales Press, 2010.

Strabolgi, Lord. *Singapore and After*. London: Hutchinson, 1943.

Strange, L. A. *Recollections of an Airman*. London: John Hamilton, 1933.

Tagaya, O. "The Imperial Japanese Air Forces." In *Why Air Forces Fail*, edited by R. Higham and S. J. Harris, 177–202. Lexington: University Press of Kentucky, 2006.

Tarling, N. *Britain, Southeast Asia and the Onset of the Pacific War*. Cambridge: Cambridge University Press, 1996.

Thompson, P. *The Battle for Singapore*. London: Portrait, 2005.

Thompson, P., and R. Macklin. *The Battle of Brisbane: Australians and the Yanks at War*. Sydney: ABC Books, 2000.

Thompson, V. *Postmortem on Malaya*. New York: Macmillan, 1943.

Thorne, C. *Allies of a Kind*. Oxford: Oxford University Press, 1968.

Till, G. "Competing Visions: The Admiralty, the Air Ministry and the Role of Air Power." In *British Naval Aviation: The First 100 Years*, edited by T. Benbow, 57–78. Farnham, UK: Ashgate, 2011.

Tinsley, A. B. *One Rissole on My Plate*. Braunton, UK: Merlin Books, 1984.

Toland, J. W. *The Rising Sun: The Decline and Fall of the Japanese Empire, 1936–1945*. New York: Random House, 1970.

Tolley, K. *Cruise of the* Lanikai: *Incitement to War*. Annapolis, MD: Naval Institute Press, 2014.

Tomlinson, M. *The Most Dangerous Moment*. London: William Kimber, 1976.

Trenowden, I. *Operations Most Secret, SOE: The Malayan Theatre*. London: William Kimber, 1978.

Tristrum, M. *Women of the Regiment*. Cambridge: Cambridge University Press, 1984.

Tsuji, M. *Singapore*. London: Constable, 1962.

Van der Ven, H. J. *China, War and Nationalism.* London: Routledge, 2003.

Warren, A. "The Indian Army and the Fall of Singapore," in *A Great Betrayal? The Fall of Singapore Revisited*, edited by B. Farrell and S. Hunter. Singapore: Marshall Cavendish, 2010, 220–38.

———. *Singapore, 1942: Britain's Greatest Defeat.* London: Hambledon & London, 2002.

Watson-Watt, R. *Three Steps to Victory.* London: Odhams, 1957.

Weintraub, S. *Long Day's Journey into War.* London: Penguin, 1991.

Wells, A. R. "Staff Training and the Royal Navy, 1918–1939." In *War and Society*, vol. 2, edited by B. Bond and I. Roy, 86–106. London: Croom Helm, 1977.

Womack, T. *The Allied Defense of the Malay Barrier.* Jefferson, NC: McFarland, 2016.

———. *The Dutch Naval Air Force against Japan.* Jefferson, NC: McFarland, 2006.

Woodburn Kirby, S. *Singapore: The Chain of Disaster.* New York: Macmillan, 1971.

Woods, P. *Reporting the Retreat: War Correspondents in Burma.* London: Hurst, 2016.

Wykeham, P. *Fighter Command: A Study of Air Defence 1914–1960.* London: Putnam, 1960.

———. "Popham, Sir (Henry) Robert Moore Brooke- (1878–1953)." Revised by T. P. Ofcansky, in *Oxford Dictionary of National Biography.* Oxford: Oxford University Press, 2004; online edition, January 2008.

Yoji, A. "General Tomoyuki Yamashita: Commander of the Twenty-Fifth Army," in *A Great Betrayal? The Fall of Singapore Revisited*, edited by B. Farrell and S. Hunter. Singapore: Marshall Cavendish, 2010, 146–66.

Periodicals

Byford, A. "What Lessons about Strategy and Its Relationship to National and Military Doctrine Are Illustrated by the Royal Air Force's Experience in France and Flanders, May–June 1940." Seaford House Papers, Royal College of Defence Studies, 2011.

Jansen, M., and A. Wright. "Sir George Sansom: An Appreciation." *Journal of Asian Studies* 24, no. 4 (August 1965).

Moolman, H. "South Africa's Part in the War." *Journal of the Royal Society of Arts* 89, no. 4578 (10 January 1941): 101–13.

Dissertations and Theses

Boyd, A. J. C. "Worthy of Better Memory: The Royal Navy and the Defence of the Eastern Empire 1935–1942." PhD thesis, University of Buckingham, 2015.

English, A. "The RAF Staff College and the Evolution of RAF Strategic Bombing Policy 1922–1929." MA thesis, Royal Military College of Canada, April 1987.

Harris, P. "The Men Who Planned the War: A Study of the Staff of the British Army on the Western Front, 1914–1918." PhD thesis, King's College, London, 2013.

Judkins, P. "Making Vision into Power: Britain's Acquisition of the World's First Radar-based Integrated Air Defence System, 1935–1941." PhD thesis, Cranfield University, UK, 2007.

Kelly, P. "Biplane to Monoplane: Twenty Years of Technological Development in British Fighter Aircraft, 1919–1939." PhD thesis, University of Edinburgh, 2013.

Mahoney, R. "The Forgotten Career of Air Chief Marshal Sir Trafford Leigh-Mallory." PhD thesis, University of Birmingham, UK, 2015.

Pugh, J. N. "The Conceptual Origins of the Control of the Air: British Military and Naval Aviation, 1911–1918." PhD thesis, University of Birmingham, UK, 2012.

Sacquety, T. J. "The Organizational Evolution of OSS Detachment 101 in Burma, 1942–1945." PhD dissertation, Texas A&M University, 2008.

Sinnott, C. S. "RAF Operational Requirements 1923–39." PhD thesis, Kings College, London, 1998.

Stewart, A. D. "Managing the Dominions: The Dominions Office and the Second World War, 1939–42." PhD thesis, Kings College, London, 2001.

Wilson, C. A. V. "Hiding behind History: Winston S. Churchill's Portrayal of the Second World War East of Suez." PhD thesis, University of Hull, 2012.

INDEX

Abyssinia, 121, 123, 124, 133, 134–35, 136
acoustic detention and mirror warning system, 75–76, 112–13, 114, 301n28
Advanced Air Striking Force (AASF), 141
Advisory Committee for Aeronautics, 56
aerial photography/photography, 29, 36, 64, 290n45, 296n5, 299n31
Aeronautical Research Committee (ARC), 56, 116, 294n33
Africa, 10, 277. *See also* Kenya; South Africa
Air Battalion: accidents and casualties in, 17, 287n25; air offensive views while serving in, 17–20, 66; aircraft for, 17; aviation career choice, 21, 288n54; B-P attachment to, 16–17, 286n20; celebration of B-P pilot license and surviving members of, 316n35; creation of, 17; Larkhill to Cambridge flight, 17; No. 2 Company command by B-P, 21; officers in, 17, 287n22; organization of, 17; RFC development from, 17, 20, 22; skepticism about military aviation, 18–19, 287n34
Air Council, 38, 54, 56, 109, 119, 354n85
Air Defence of Great Britain (ADGB): accommodations at, 111; achievements and success of B-P at, 119–20; air defense exercises, 76, 112–13, 311–12n10; air defense system development, 43, 294n33; Air Ministry review during time at, 111; B-P as CinC, 110, 111, 294n33; CinC term length at, 111; expansion of home defense and commitment to rearmament, 112; extension of tour at, 118; force strength for air defense, 74; formation of, 74; HQ staff at, 111, 311n5; importance of command position in careers, 109; integrated modern air defense system development, 113–17, 119, 312n18, 312n25, 312nn27–28; as last operational appointment for B-P, 111; location of HQ,

111; No. 1 Air Defence Group, 74; plan of air defense, 74; raid intelligence system, 74, 113, 301n18; staff exercises at, 112–13, 311–12n10, 365n26; Wessex Bombing Area, 74, 76, 111. *See also* Fighting Area
air defense: acoustic detention and mirror warning system, 75–76, 112–13, 114, 301n28; early warning requirements analysis, 114–15; exercises to practice air defense and coordination of air and ground defenses, 76; force strength for, 74, 82; integrated modern air defense system development, 113–17, 119, 312n18, 312n25, 312nn27–28; operational developments and improvements under B-P as AOC, 82; processing acoustic detection information for in timely manner, 113; review of by ADGB sub-committee, 113–15, 119, 312n25, 312nn27–28; standing patrols, 76; Tizard Committee for scientific survey of, 115–17, 313n35, 313n38. *See also* radar
Air League, 66, 299n46
Air Ministry: aeronautical research, 55–57; aircraft for defense of Singapore naval base, controversy about, 105; articles for papers and magazines, support for writing of, 270, 366n27; budget for, 55; Crisis attachment of B-P, 72–73; director of research appointment, 54–58, 109, 296n7; letter of appreciation on occasion of B-P retirement, 127–28; metal use in aircraft construction research, 57–58, 118; notebooks from time at, 4; office in for B-P, 270; public relations efforts of, 270; quality of officers sent to, 67; RAF campaign histories pamphlets, 271, 366n33; recall of B-P from Kenya, 137–38, 140; review of by B-P, 111; Tarrant Tabor triplane accident, 55–56

About the Author

PETER DYE is a graduate of Imperial College and Birmingham University. He served in the Royal Air Force for more than thirty-five years and was awarded the Order of the British Empire for his work in support of the Jaguar Force during the First Gulf War, retiring as an air vice-marshal. He was appointed Director General of the Royal Air Force Museum in 2008 before retiring six years later to concentrate on lecturing, research, and writing on airpower topics. He is an Honorary Research Fellow at the University of Birmingham.

The Naval Institute Press is the book-publishing arm of the U.S. Naval Institute, a private, nonprofit, membership society for sea service professionals and others who share an interest in naval and maritime affairs. Established in 1873 at the U.S. Naval Academy in Annapolis, Maryland, where its offices remain today, the Naval Institute has members worldwide.

Members of the Naval Institute support the education programs of the society and receive the influential monthly magazine *Proceedings* or the colorful bimonthly magazine *Naval History* and discounts on fine nautical prints and on ship and aircraft photos. They also have access to the transcripts of the Institute's Oral History Program and get discounted admission to any of the Institute-sponsored seminars offered around the country.

The Naval Institute's book-publishing program, begun in 1898 with basic guides to naval practices, has broadened its scope to include books of more general interest. Now the Naval Institute Press publishes about seventy titles each year, ranging from how-to books on boating and navigation to battle histories, biographies, ship and aircraft guides, and novels. Institute members receive significant discounts on the Press's more than eight hundred books in print.

Full-time students are eligible for special half-price membership rates. Life memberships are also available.

For a free catalog describing Naval Institute Press books currently available, and for further information about joining the U.S. Naval Institute, please write to:

Member Services
U.S. NAVAL INSTITUTE
291 Wood Road
Annapolis, MD 21402-5034
Telephone: (800) 233-8764
Fax: (410) 571-1703
Web address: www.usni.org